Thomas Nugent

A New Method of Learning with Facility the Latin Tongue

Vol. II

Thomas Nugent

A New Method of Learning with Facility the Latin Tongue
Vol. II

ISBN/EAN: 9783337106744

Printed in Europe, USA, Canada, Australia, Japan

Cover: Foto ©Paul-Georg Meister /pixelio.de

More available books at **www.hansebooks.com**

NEW METHOD

Of learning with Facility the

LATIN TONGUE,

Containing the Rules of

GENDERS,   SYNTAX,
DECLENSIONS, QUANTITY, and
PRETERITES, LATIN ACCENTS.

Digested in the clearest and concisest Order.

Enlarged with variety of solid remarks, necessary not only for a perfect knowledge of the Latin tongue, but likewise for understanding the best authors: extracted from the ablest writers on this language.

With a Treatise on LATIN POETRY.

TRANSLATED *from the* FRENCH *of the Messieurs* DE PORT ROYAL, *and* IMPROVED,

By T. NUGENT, LL.D.

A NEW EDITION,
Carefully Revised and Corrected.

In TWO VOLUMES.

VOL. II.

LONDON:
Printed for F. WINGRAVE, Successor to Mr. NOURSE, in the Strand.
MDCCXCI.

BOOK V.

SYNTAX.

General distribution of the whole Syntax.

CONSTRUCTION, by the Greeks called syntax, is nothing more than a fit composition and arrangement of the parts of speech.

It is divided into simple or regular, and figurative or irregular.

The regular is that which follows the natural order, and resembles greatly the manner of speaking in vulgar languages.

The irregular or figurative is that which recedes from this common usage, in order to follow some particular turns and forms of speaking, which have been studied by authors, for the sake of conciseness and elegance.

Construction is divided into two sorts, one of concord, and the other of government.

The syntax of concord is when the parts agree among themselves in some thing, and is of four sorts.

1. That of the substantive with the adjective; *deus sanctus*.
2. That of the relative with the antecedent; *deus qui est*.
3. That of the nominative with the verb; *ego amo*.

And these concords ought to be attentively considered in discourse; for there is no adjective that hath not its substantive, nor relative that hath not its antecedent, nor verb that hath not its nominative, either expressed or understood.

4. To these three concords we add another, which is that of the accusative with the infinitive; *me amare: supplicem esse victori.* But in Greekish phrases, the nominative is frequently joined to the infinitive.

The syntax of government is when one part of speech governs another: which is done, either according to the force of some preposition expressed or understood, or according to the property and nature of each case.

1. The genitive of itself always denotes the possessor, or that one thing is said of another, as *liber Petri*, Peter's book: *vulnus Achillis*, the wound of Achilles, whether it be taken actively for the wound which he made, or passively for that which he received. Wherefore this case is always governed by another substantive, though frequently understood; which has occasioned a multitude of false or useless rules, as hereafter we shall make appear. We are only to observe

observe that in Greekish phrases, this case may be governed also by the preposition ἐκ. *Plenus vini* (subaud. ἐκ) as in French we say, *plein de vin*.

2. The dative always denotes that to which the thing or action refers. For which reason there is neither noun nor verb to which it may not be joined in this sense. *Affinis regi; communis omnibus; est mihi; peto tibi, sibi sapit.* Sometimes there are even two datives; *do tibi pignori*, &c.

3. The accusative either denotes the subject into which the action of the verb passeth, *amat patrem*; or agrees with the infinitive, as above, No. 4. or is governed by some preposition expressed or understood, as after the verbs of teaching, moving, in the questions of time and measure, and others. Neither is there ever an accusative which does not depend on one of these three things.

4. The ablative, according to Sanctius, ought rather to be called the case of the preposition, because it is always governed by a preposition expressed or understood, as we shall demonstrate in the questions UBI, QUA, and UNDE, in the comparatives, in the verbs passive and others, and also in the ablatives which are called absolute.

5. As to the vocative, it is never governed by any thing, but only signifies the person to whom we speak, or with whom we converse; for which reason it agrees sometimes with the verb in the second person, as *Domine, miserere mei*.

These fundamental rules, being short and easy, may without any difficulty be retained, and give us a general idea of the whole syntax, which may likewise serve for all languages, in which the distinction of these six cases is in some measure necessary. And this alone is almost sufficient for an introduction to those who begin with the reading of Latin books, or with a translation, provided care be taken to ground them thoroughly therein, according to the explication we propose to give in the particular rules, wherein we shall conform as much as possible to the order abovementioned.

I only beg of the reader to remember what has been often mentioned, that the smaller type is not intended for children; and therefore this syntax may be considered as very short in regard to them, since it contains only 36 rules that are easy to retain: and as very copious in regard to persons of riper age, because it points out not only the things themselves, but likewise the reasons on which each is founded.

THE RULES OF SYNTAX.

RULE I.

Of the adjective and substantive.

The adjective must always be made to agree in gender, number, and case, with its substantive.

EXAMPLES.

THE ADJECTIVE, whether noun, pronoun, or participle, hath always it's substantive expressed or understood, with which it agrees in gender, number and case, as *vir bonus*, a good man. *Ille Philósophus*, that philosopher. *Parva sæpe scintilla contêmta magnum éxcitat incéndium*, a small spark neglected oftentimes stirs up a great fire. *Amícus certus in re incérta cérnitur*, a true friend is known in adversity. *Stellæ inerrántes*, the fixed stars.

ANNOTATION.

Sometimes the substantive is understood. *Paucis te volo* (supple *verbis*) I want to speak a word to you. *Brevi veniet* (supple *tempore,*) he'll come quickly. *Triste lupus stabulis*, Virg. Ecl. 3. (supple *negotium*, thing,) the wolf is a vexatious thing to the sheepfolds. For the word *negotium* was antiently taken for *res*. See the figure of ellipsis at the end of the remarks after syntax.

When the adjective is put with two substantives, it should naturally agree with that which is the principal: as *Semiramis puer credita est*, Just. *Puteoli Dicæarchia dicti. Porcus fæmina natus.*

And yet the adjective frequently agrees with the latter. *Gens universa Veneti appellati*, Liv. *Non omnis error stultitia dicenda est*, Cic.

―― *Numquam æquè ac modò paupertas mihi onus visum est & miserum & grave*, Ter. *Ludi fuere Megalesia appellata*, Liv.

The same substantive may admit of different adjectives; *Ut neque privatam rem maritimam, neque publicam gerere possimus*, Cic. *Ad malam domesticam disciplinam accesserunt etiam poëtæ*, Id. *Sequitur ut de una reliqua parte honestatis dicendum sit*.

As for the adjectives *qualis*, *quantus*, and such like, see the annotation to the next rule.

RULE II.

Of the relative and antecedent.

The relative qui, quæ, quod, *generally agrees in gender and number with the antecedent.*

EXAMPLES.

The relative *qui, quæ, quod*, ought generally to be considered as between two cases of the same substantive expressed or understood. And then it agrees with the antecedent in gender and number, and with the word that follows also in case, as with its substantive by the preceding rule. *Bellum tantum, quo bello omnes premebántur, Pompéius confécit*, Cic. Pompey put an end to this war, which was burdensome to the several nations. *Ultra eum locum, quo in loco Germáni confēderant*, Cæsar; beyond that place where the Germans were encamped. *Non dejéci te ex loco, quem in locum prohibui ne veníres*, Cic. I did not turn you out of a place, which I hindered you from coming into. *Diem instáre, quo die fruméntum militibus metíri oportéret*, Cæs. that the day was drawing near, on which the corn was to be measured out to the soldiers.

ANNOTATION.

Cæsar seems to have particularly affected this manner of expressing himself, because he was fond of perspicuity; and we ought always to imitate him when there is any danger of ambiguity. *Leodamantem Cleophili discípulum, qui Cleophilus*, &c. Apul. If he had not repeated *qui Cleophilus*, the *qui* might have referred to Leodamas as well as to Cleophilus.

The following case understood.

Except on this account we generally leave out the following case, because it is sufficiently expressed by the relative itself, which always supplies its place and represents it, as: *cognosces ex iis litteris, quas liberto tuo dedi*, Cic. instead of *ex litteris, quas litteras*, you will know by the letters which I gave your freedman.

man. *Odi sapiéntem qui sibi non sapit*; as if it were *qui sapiens*, &c. I hate the wise man who is not wise for himself, and a great many others.

The preceding case understood.

Sometimes we understand the antecedent likewise, and this in a twofold manner.

EITHER BY PUTTING the substantive after the relative, and of course in the same case as this relative, according to what we have above observed, as *nemini credo, qui dives blanditur pauperi*, instead of *nemini diviti, qui dives*, &c.

And thus we account for these elegant turns of expression; *populo ut placerent, quas fecisset fabulas*, Ter. for *ut fabulæ quas fabulas fecisset*, &c. *Quibus de rebus ad me scripsisti, quoniam ipse venio, coram videbimus*, Cic. *Illi scripta quibus comœdia prisca viris est*, Hor. *Quas credis esse has, non sunt veræ nuptiæ.* Ter. for *hæ nuptiæ non sunt veræ*; *quas has nuptias credis esse veras*, says Sanctius. *Quam ille triplicem putavit esse rationem, in quinque partes distribui debere reperitur*, Cic. And such like forms of speaking, which become still more clear and more elegant, by adding a demonstrative pronoun to the second member; as *Quam quisque norit artem, in hac se exerceat*, Cic. *Ad Cæsarem quam misi epistolam, ejus exemplum fugit me tum tibi mittere*, Id.

OR BY PUTTING the substantive before the relative, but in such a manner as it shall supply only the place of the following word, on which account it agrees therewith in case; but this is seldom used except by poets, as *Urbem quam statuo vestra est*, Virg. for *ea urbs, quam urbem statuo*, &c. *Eunuchum quem dedisti nobis, quas turbas dedit*, Ter. for *ille eunuchus, quem eunuchum dedisti nobis*, &c. *Naucreatem quem convenire volui, in navi non erat*, Plaut. Which has puzzled a great many commentators.

And it is by this rule we are to explain a great many difficult passages, as that of the Adelphi. *Si id te mordet, sumtum filii quem faciunt.* For *id* supposeth *negotium*, and is there for *sumtus*: that is, *Si id negotium te mordet, nempe sumtus, quam sumtum filii faciunt.* Where we see likewise that there is an apposition understood of *id negotium* with *sumtus*.

The preceding and the following case both understood.

It oftentimes happens that there is no substantive put either before or after the relative; though it must always be understood, both as antecedent and subsequent. *Est qui nec spernit: sunt quos juvat collegisse*, Hor. instead of saying *homo est, qui homo non spernit: sunt homines quos homines juvat*, &c. *Sunt quibus in satyra videor nimis acer*, Id. for *sunt homines, quibus hominibus*, &c.

―――― *En dextra fidésque,*
Quem secum patrios aiunt portare penates, Æn. 4.
that is to say, *En dextra fidésque hominis, quem hominem aiunt*, &c. *Scribo ad vos cùm habeo qui ferat*, &c. Cic. *Qualis esset natura montis, qui cognoscerent misit*, Cæs. and the like.

The relative betwixt two nouns of different genders.

When we said that the relative was considered as betwixt two cases of the same noun, this is to be understood in the natural construction, for in the figurative the contrary sometimes happeneth. Thus because when the relative is followed by a substantive differing in gender or number from the antecedent, the relative may agree with either the one or the other, whether one of them be a proper name or not; if it agrees with the former, it shall follow the analogy of the Latin construction, and be placed as it were between the two cases of the same noun; as *Propius à terra Jovis stella fertur, (quæ Jovis stella) Phaëthon dicitur*, Cic. and in like manner, *Nacti portum qui appellatur Nymphæum*, Cæs. *Herculi sacrificium fecit in loco, quem Pyram appellant*, Liv. *Darius ad eum locum, quem Amanicas Pylas vocant pervenit*, Curt. *Tum etiam eloquentem constat fuisse Scipionem Nasicam, qui est Corculum appellatus*, Cic.

But if it agrees with the latter, which seems more elegant and more usual, it shall follow the Greek construction, and then it will not be placed between the two cases of the same noun; as *Animal providum & sagax quem vocamus hominem*, Cic. *Pompeius, quod imperii Romani decus & ornamentum fuit*, Id. *Quamobrem, hoc quidem constat ut opinor, bonis inter bonos quasi necessariam benevolentiam esse, qui est amicitiæ fons à naturâ constitutus*, Id. *Ad eum locum quæ appellatur Pharsalia, applicuit*, Cæs. *Globus quem in templo hoc medium vides, quæ terra dicitur*, Cic. *Concilia cœtusque hominum jure sociati, quæ civitates appellantur*, Id. *Carcer ille qui est à Dionysio factus Syracusis, quæ Latumiæ vocantur*, Id. *Gladiatores, quam sibi ille maximam manum fore putavit in potestate vestra continebuntur*, Id. Which should be considered as an hellenism, whereof we shall treat at the end of the figures.

The relative agreeing with a gender or number understood.

Sometimes we make the relative agree with a gender or a number understood, and not with the antecedent expressed. *Daret ut catenis fatale monstrum, quæ generosius perire quærens*, &c. Hor. Where the relative *quæ* is in the feminine, because it refers to Cleopatra of whom he is speaking, and not to the gender of *monstrum*, which is neuter. *Si tempus est ullum jure hominis necandi, quæ multa sunt*, Cic. where he makes the reference to *tempora*. *Soli virtute præditi, quod est proprium divitiarum, contenti sunt*, Cic.

And sometimes it agrees even with the substantive derived from the sense of the preceding period, *Inter alia prodigia etiam carne pluit, quem imbrem*, &c. Liv. See the figure Syllepsis in the remarks.

Of those nouns which are called relatives of quantity or quality.

Tantus, quantus; talis, qualis; tot, quot, have only a relation in the sense, the same as *pater* and *filius*; and therefore are mere adjectives, which belong rather to the preceding rule than to this.

Yet these nouns sometimes follow the nature of the relative, and therefore conform likewise to the construction thereof. As *In hoc autem maximo crudelissimoque bello, quale bellum nulla unquam barbaria cum sua gente gessit, quo in bello lex hæc fuit à Lentulo constituta,* Cic. Catil. 3. where *quale bellum* is the same as if he had said *quod tale bellum;* and is the same construction as if he had afterwards said *quo in bello,* repeating the antecedent in both places, according to what hath been already observed.

Except in this case, these nouns follow simply the nature of the other adjectives, agreeing with their substantive, which is generally that which followeth, as *Dixi de te quâ potui tantâ contentione, quantum est forum, tanto clamore consensuque populi ut,* &c.

Though Horace sometimes, in imitation of the Greeks, makes it agree with the antecedent.

Sed incitat me pectus, & mammæ putres
Equina quales ubera, Epod. Od. 8.

instead of *qualia sunt ubera equina.* And there is no doubt, adds Vossius, but he might have also said with propriety *Mammæ quantæ ubera equina,* However this is not to be imitated.

Rule III.

Of the case which the verb requires before it.

1. *Every verb hath a nominative case before it.*
2. *Except it be of the infinitive mood, and then it is preceded by an accusative.*

Examples.

1. Every verb of a finite mood, requireth before it a nominative of the same number as itself, either expressed or understood. *Petrus flet,* Peter weepeth. *Tu doces, nos discimus,* thou teachest, we learn. *Obsequium amicos, véritas ódium parit,* Ter. compliance begets friends, and truth enemies. *Non te hoc pudet?* are not you ashamed of this? and in all these examples the nominative is expressed.

But when we say: *legit,* he reads: *audimus,* we hear; *aiunt, ferunt,* it is said, or they say: *pluit,* it rains;

rains: the nominative is understood; namely, *ille, nos, homines,* and *pluvia,* or *cælum,* or *Deus.*

Oftentimes an infinitive or a whole period supplieth the place of the nominative. *Scire tuum nihil est,* your knowledge is nothing. *Ingenuas didicisse artes emollit mores,* Ovid. to learn the liberal arts, polishes the manners. *Deprehendi miserum est,* it is a sad thing to be caught. *Docto et erudito homini vivere est cogitare,* Cic. to think is the life of a man of learning.

ANNOTATION.

In the first and second person they do not generally express the nominative except it be to denote some difference of action or affection. *Tu ludis, ego studeo. Tu nidum servas, ego laudo ruris amœni rivos,* Hor. Or to signify some emphasis or particular force. *Tu audes ista loqui? Cantando tu illum?* supple, *vicisti,* Virg. Because it is always easy to understand it, as there can be no other than *ego* and *tu*.

OF THE INFINITIVE.

2. The infinitive requireth before it an accusative, which is resolved by *quod, ut, ne,* or *quin,* and generally rendered by the particle *that. Scio Petrum flere,* id est, *quod Petrus flet,* I know that Peter weeps. *Volo vos bene sperare et confidere,* i. e. *ut bene speretis* and *confidatis,* I am willing that you should hope and confide. *Prohibuerunt eum exire,* i. e. *ne exiret,* they hindered him from going out. *Non dubitat Christum id dixisse,* i. e. *quin dixerit:* he does not doubt that Christ said this.

ANNOTATION.

1. When a verb is in the infinitive after another verb, it is generally the same construction as this here, because we must understand its accusative, and particularly one or other of these pronouns, *me, se, illum: statui proficisci,* for *me proficisci: negat velle,* for *se velle:* which appears plainly from the antients having often used it thus. *Hic vocem loquentis me audire visus sum,* Plaut. *Quæ sese optavit parere hic divitias,* Ter. *Omnes homines qui sese præstare student cæteris animantibus,* Sal.

2. In Greek the infinitive may agree with the nominative, which the Latins have sometimes imitated, as Ovid, *Seu pius Æneas eripuisse ferunt,* for *pium Æneam.* And the like.

3. There are some who intirely reject the *quod* by which we resolve the accusative before the infinitive, insisting that it ought never

ver to be put for the Greek ὅτι. But we shall take farther notice of this, in the remarks, and in the chapter of adverbs.

4. The particle *ut* is used only after verbs of asking, fearing, commanding, or those which express desire and affection: as *jubeo, volo, curo, laboro*; or which signify some event, as *fit, evenit, contingit*, &c.

OBSERVATIONS IN REGARD TO THE NEXT RULE.

We see naturally enough that two singulars are equivalent to a plural, and therefore that two substantives in the singular require the adjective, or the noun which is joined to them by apposition, in the plural; as *Július & Octávius imperatóres fortíssimi*, Julius and Octavius, most valiant emperors. *Remus et Rómulus fratres*, Remus and Romulus, brothers. Hence the verb must be put in the plural after two nominatives singular. *Ecclésiæ duo sy'dera Augustínus & Hierónymus hǽreses debellárunt*, Saint Austin and St. Jerome, two stars of the church, overthrew heresies.

But if the two singulars are of different genders, or of different person, then you are to observe the following rule.

RULE IV.
Of the difference of genders and persons.

1. *When substantives of different genders or persons are joined, the noblest is to be preferred to that which is least so.*
2. *But the reference is often made to the latter substantive; or things without life have the adjective in the neuter.*

EXAMPLES.

1. When two substantives of different genders or different persons meet, then the adjective or the relative being in the plural, agrees with the noblest gender, and the verb (being also in the plural) agrees with the noblest person.

The first person is more noble than the second, and the second than the third. *Ego, túque sumus Christiáni*, you and I are Christians. *Tu patérque vultis*, you and your father are willing.

The

The masculine is more noble than the other two genders. *Tu, sorórque boni estis,* (speaking of a boy) you and your sister are good. *Pater & mater mórtui,* Ter. my father and mother are dead. *Decem ingénui decemque vírgines ad id sacrificium adhibiti,* Liv. they pitched upon ten free born youths, and on ten young maids to perform this sacrifice.

But if there happens to be a difference in the substantives, in regard to the number, still the adjective must be made to agree with the noblest gender, putting it always in the plural; as *Suscepisti onus grave Athenárum & Cratíppi, ad quos cùm profectus sis,* &c. Cic. you undertook great matters in going to Athens, and under the care of the philosopher Cratippus.

2. Oftentimes the reference is made to the latter substantive, either in regard to the verb, or to the adjective, or to the gender, or to the number, or even to the person; as *Ego & Cicero meus flagitábit,* Cic. my son Cicero and I will ask. *Senátus & C. Fabrícius pérfugam Pyrrho dedit,* Cic. The senate and Fabricius delivered up the traitor into the hands of Pyrrhus. *Utrùm vos an Carthaginénses príncipes orbis terrárum videántur,* Liv. whether you or the Carthaginians appear masters of the world. *Legátos, fortésque expectándas,* Liv. that it was proper to wait for the return of the ambassadors, and the answer of the oracle. *Toti sit provínciæ cógnitum, tibi ómnium quibus præsis, salútem, líberos, famam, fortúnas esse charíssimas,* Cic. let it be known over the whole province that the lives, the children, the honour, and property of those over whom you preside, are most dear to you. *Sóciis & rege recépto,* Virg. having recovered our comrades and our king.

When the substantives are things without life, the adjective is frequently put in the neuter, unless we chuse to make it agree with the latter, in the manner as above; as *Divítiæ, decus, & glória in óculis sita sunt,* Sal. riches, honour, and glory, are things exposed to public view.

Sometimes however inanimate things conform to the general rule, of referring to the noblest gender.

Agros

Agros villásque intáctos sinebat, Tac. he spared the lands and houses.

ANNOTATION.

Whether the feminine ought to be preferred to the neuter.

Here a question arises, whether the feminine, supposing it be not the last, ought to be preferred to the neuter gender, just as the masculine is generally preferred to the other two. Grammarians are divided upon this point. Linacer and Alvarez say not, and that we ought to prefer the neuter to the feminine. Vossius is of the same way of thinking in his lesser grammar, though he has established the contrary in his larger work *de Arte Grammatica*, when he treats of construction.

The surest way of proceeding in this matter, is to distinguish betwixt things animate and inanimate. For in things animate, one would think that we ought rather to follow the feminine, and to say for instance, *Uxor & mancipium salvæ: ancilla et jumenta repertæ*, according to the opinion of Vossius. Though as Linacer and Alvarez observe, it is oftentimes more proper to make use of a periphrasis, and to say for example, *Lucretia castissima fuit, quâ virtute ejus etiam mancipium floruit*, and not *Lucretia & ejus mancipium fuerunt castæ*.

In regard to things inanimate, generally speaking, the adjective ought either to agree with the latter substantive, or to be put in the neuter gender. Yet it would not be an error to do otherwise, and to prefer the feminine to the neuter, since in Lucretius we find, *Leges et plebis-scita coactæ*, as Priscian himself acknowledges. Cicero likewise at the end of his 2d book *de Nat. Quid de vitibus olivetisque dicam, quarum uberrimi fructus*, &c.

Of the reason of these governments, with some particular remarks on the construction of inanimate things.

The reason of these governments depends on the knowledge of the figures, of which we shall treat hereafter.

When the verb or the adjective is put in the plural, it is commonly a syllepsis, where the construction is regulated by the sense, and not by the words. If we refer to the latter only, it is a zeugma. But if we put it in the neuter, it is an ellipsis, because we understand NEGOTIA, *things*. Thus, *Decus & gloria in oculis sita sunt*, Sal. that is, *sunt negotia sita*, are things exposed to public view.

And this figure may also take place, when only one of the things is inanimate. *Delectabatur cereo funali & tibicine, quæ privatus sibi sumpserat*, Cic. Though we may express it otherwise, by referring it to the noblest gender. As

Jane, fac æternos pacem, pacisque ministros.

Propter summam & doctoris autoritatem & urbis, quorum alter te Scientiâ augere potest, altera exemplis, Cic.

But they used this construction also, in speaking of the passions and movements of the soul; as *Labor et voluptas dissimillima*, Liv.

Ira

Ira et avaritia imperio potentiora, Id. *Huic ab adolescentia bella intestina, cades, rapinæ, discordia civilis, grata fuere*, Sal. in Catil.

And sometimes in the construction of animate things, as in Solinus, *Polypus & chamæleon glabra sunt*. In Lucret. book 3. *Sic anima atque animus, quamvis integra, recens in corpus eunt*. And in Livy, *Gens cui natura corpora animosque magis magna quàm firma dedit*. And sometimes even in referring to a thing that includes a masculine and a neuter, they are made to agree with the neuter, as *Ibi capta armatorum duo millia quadringenti*, Liv. And what is most extraordinary, is their doing it even when the masculine is nearest, as *Tria millia quàdringenti cæsa*, Liv.

Whether we ought always to name ourselves the first in Latin, and in what manner we ought to do it in French.

In Latin we ought always to follow the order and dignity of the persons in speaking, so that we should say *ego et tu*, and not *tu & ego*. Yet there are examples of the contrary, for Livy hath, *pater & ego fratresque mei, pro vobis arma tulimus*, lib. 7. Dec. 4. Which shews that Nebrissensis had not such mighty reason for finding fault with this phrase of scripture, *Pater tuus & ego dolentes quærebamus te*, Luc. 2.

But in French it would be uncivil to do so, or to say *moi & vous*, I and you; for we ought always to say *vous & moi*, you and I; *lui & moi*, he and I; the natural modesty of this language not permitting the French to name themselves the first. Hence nobody will do it even in Latin, or say for instance, *ego túque*, for fear of appearing uncivil. And it is true that in prudence we ought to avoid it, if we foresee that persons deserving of respect are likely to be offended at it, though there is no reason.

This should be extended even to the titles and superscriptions of letters, where the custom of the Romans was, that he who spoke, always placed himself the first, though he was equal or even inferior in station. *Curius Ciceroni, S. D. Cicero Cæsari imperatori, S. D.* &c. Which Budeus, Erasmus, and other literati of the last century were not afraid to imitate, in writing even to princes, sovereigns, and crowned heads.

Rule V.

Of verbs that have the same case after as before them.

1. *Every verb that denotes the union or connexion of words, hath the same case before as after it, as* Deus est æternus.
2. Scit nos esse malos.
3. Licet esse bonis, licet esse bonos.

Examples.

Verbs that denote only the union and connexion of words,

words, or the relation of terms to each other, make no alteration in the government; for which reason they require the same case after as before them, as in the preceding rules. *Deus est etérnus*, God is eternal. *Amántium iræ amóris redintegrátio est*. The falling out of lovers is the renewal of love. *O'bvius fit ei Clódius*, Clodius went out to meet him. *Septem dicúntur fuísse uno témpore, qui sapiéntes & haberéntur & vocaréntur*, Cic. it is said that there were seven men at one time, who were entitled and esteemed as wise men. *Ut hoc latrocínium pótiùs quàm bellum nominarétur*, Cic. that this should be called rather a pyratical depredation than a war. *Cur ergo poéta salútor?* Hor. why then am I called a poet?

Verbs neuter have sometimes the same force: *Terra manet immóbilis*, the earth remains immoveable. *Petrus rédiit irátus*, Peter returned in a passion. *Vénio in Senátum frequens*, I go often to the senate house. And the like.

If after these verbs there comes a genitive, still there is the same case after as before them, but the same noun is also understood. *Hic liber est Petri*, this is Peter's book; that is, *Hic liber, est liber Petri*.

2. The infinitives of all these verbs require likewise an accusative after them, when there is one before them. *Deus scit nos esse malos*, God knows that we are wicked, because *malos* refers to *nos*. *Cúpio me esse cleméntem*, I desire to be merciful. But in this there is no manner of difficulty.

3. The difficulty is, when these infinitives, such as, *esse, dici, habéri, fieri*, and the like have not their natural accusative before them. Because if, for example, there is a dative before, either expressed or understood, we may put one also after. *Licet esse bonis*, or *licet nobis esse bonis*, it is lawful for us to be good. And if we understand an accusative before, as the analogy of the Latin tongue requireth, we may say likewise, *licet esse bonos*, that is, *nos esse bonos*; just as Cicero said, *Quibus abundántem licet esse misérrimum*, amidst the plenty of which one may be very miserable. *Médios esse jam non licébit*, it will be no longer allowed us to remain neuter. But

But if you say, *licet nobis esse bonos*; the strength of the phrase will be still, *licet nobis nos esse bonos*. In like manner, *Cupio dici doctum*, that is *me dici doctum*. And *Cupio dici doctus*, that is, *ego doctus*; I am desirous of being called a learned man.

ANNOTATION.

Hence we may here take notice of three very different forms of speaking: *Licet esse bonis, licet esse bonos*, (or else *licet nobis esse bonis*, and *licet nos esse bonos*, which are the same as the foregoing) and *licet nobis esse bonos*. In like manner *Cupio dici doctus*, and *cupio dici doctum*, where we see that in the former government the noun following the infinitive refers to the case of the first verb, and agrees with it, as here, *doctus* with *ego*. *Non tibi vacat esse quieto*: *quieto* with *tibi*, &c. which is quite a Greek phrase, because the Greek language hath this in particular, that having made a case go before, it generally draws what follows after it: hence in Horace we find, *Patiens vocari Cæsaris ultor*, instead of *patiens te vocari ultorem*, and in another place, *Uxor invicti Jovis esse nescis*, instead of *te esse uxorem*; and Lucan, *Tutumque putavit jam bonus esse Socer*. And Ovid, *Acceptum refero versibus esse nocens*; and Virgil, even without expressing the infinitive, *sensit medios delapsus in hostes*, instead of *se esse delapsum*.

Whereas in these other phrases, in which an accusative is made to follow; *Licet esse beatos. Expedit vobis esse bonos. Utor amico cupienti fieri probum. Si civi Romano licet esse Gaditanum*, Cic. *Quibus licet esse fortunatissimos*, Cæs. This accusative refers to the infinitive, and to the accusative which is understood before it (though it is not always necessary to express it, as Valla pretends) and not to the other verb. And this last expression would be more natural to the Latin tongue, if custom had not introduced the other, perhaps to avoid obscurity, as when I say, *Cupio fieri doctus*, there can be no ambiguity; but when I say *Cupio fieri doctum*, it is dubious whether I mean *me* or *alium*; unless I expressly mark the accusative before, as *Me fieri doctum*, and then this whole phrase, *me fieri doctum*, supplies the case or the government of the preceding verb: *Cupio hoc*, *nempe me fieri doctum*. And as often as there are two different meanings in a sentence, that is, two different members, the second of which is put by one of these infinitives, there can never be more than one accusative along with it. *Fuit magni animi, non esse supplicem victori*, Cic. *Quo tibi Tulle, fieri tribunum*, Hor. *Mihi videtur, ad beate vivendum satis posse virtutem*. Which ought always to be resolved by the article *hoc*, as Scaliger observeth; *Hoc* (*nempe, non esse supplicem victori*) *fuit magni animi*. And in like manner the rest.

Rule VI.

Of two substantives of the same or of different sense.

1. *When two substantives are joined, and signify the*

the same thing, they are put in the same case, *as* urbs Roma.

2. *But if they have a different meaning, as* amor virtútis, *then the second is put in the genitive.*

EXAMPLES.

When there are two substantives that refer to the same thing, they are put in the same case, *urbs Roma*, the city of Rome; as much as to say Rome the city, and this is what they call apposition.

Sometimes the gender and number are different, though the case be alike. *Tulliola deliciæ nostræ*, Tulliola my whole delight. *Urbs Athénæ*, the city of Athens. *Q. Horténsius, lumen & ornaméntum reipublicæ*, Cic. Hortensius, the glory and ornament of the republic.

ANNOTATION.

If in the apposition, the substantive, which is the first and chief in the order of nature, signifies an animate thing, the adjective or verb will agree with it. *Cùm duo fulmina nostri imperii Cn. & Pub. Scipiones extincti occidissent*, Cic. *Tullia deliciæ nostræ tuum munusculum flagitat*, Cic. *Passer deliciæ meæ puellæ, quicum ludere, quem sinu tenere solet*, Catul. *Primum signum aries Marti assignatus est.*

But if the first substantive signifies an inanimate thing, the adjective or substantive will agree with the latter. *Tungri civitas Galliæ fontem habet insignem. Flumen Rhenus, qui agrum Helvetium à Germanis dividit.*

If the verb hath two substantives, one before and another after it, generally speaking it will agree with the principal. *Omnia Cæsar erat*, Luc. *Sanguis erat lacrymæ*, Id. *Gaudia principium nostri sunt doloris*, Ovid. Yet it is not always so: *Vestes quas geritis sordida lana fuit*, Ovid. *Quæ loca, Numidia appellatur*, Sall. *Tui Consulatus fuit initium ludi Compitalitii*, Cic. There are even some passages in which it would be an error to follow this 3d rule, as *Magnæ divitiæ sunt lege naturæ composita paupertas*, Sen. We should not say *est*. *Contentum suis rebus esse, magnæ sunt certissimæque divitiæ*, Cic. For which reason we must be directed by the use of authors.

GOVERNMENT OF THE GENITIVE.

2. When there are two substantives that signify different things, that is, one of which is said of the other, the second must be put in the genitive, *Amor virtútis*, the love of virtue. *Splendor lucis*, the brightness of the light; and this case is never governed but by

by another noun substantive, though the noun that governs it is very often understood, as we shall shew hereafter.

Now this genitive may still govern another that signifies a different thing. *Magnam partem laudis hujus rei ad Libónem esse ventúram*, Cic. that a great share of the glory of this enterprise would fall to Libo. Sometimes a single noun governs two different genitives. *Quæ sit hóminum queréla frontis tuæ*, Cic. how greatly people complain of your impudence.

ANNOTATION.

Of the different senses in which the genitive is taken.

Even when the substantives belong to the same thing, the second is frequently put in the genitive; *Regnum Galliæ*, the kingdom of France. *Res cibi* for *cibus*, Phædr. meat. *Oppidum Antiochiæ*, Cic. the town of Antioch. *Arbor fici*, Cic. *Vitium iræ*, Hor. *Nomen Mercurii est mihi*, Plaut. Which is an imitation of the Greeks, and very common in the French language.

We might also mark down here the different senses in which the genitive is taken, in order to shew the great extent of this government. For beside the examples above given, where it denotes the relation of the proper name to the common, or of the individual to the species, it further denotes the relations

Of the whole to its part, as *caput hominis; vertex montis.*

Of the part to the whole, as *homo crassi capitis.*

Of the subject to the accident, or to the attribute; *facundia Ulyssis; felicitas rerum; color rosæ.*

Of the accident to the subject; *puer optimæ indolis.*

Of the efficient cause to the effect; *Venus Praxitelis; oratio Ciceronis.*

Of the effect to the cause; *Creator mundi.*

Of the final cause to the effect; *potio soporis; apparatus triumphi*, Cic.

Of the matter to the compound; *vas auri.*

Of the object to the acts of the mind; *cogitatio belli; officii deliberatio; contemtus mortis.*

Of one of the things which has a relation to the other; *mater Socratis.*

Of the possessor to the thing possessed; *pecus Melibæi: divitiæ Crassi.*

Of time; *spatium horæ; iter bidui; tempus spatii.*

Of what is done in time: *tempus belli; hora cænæ.*

Of place; *incolæ hujus urbis; vinum majoris cadi.*

Of that which is contained; *cadus vini: navis auri aut paleæ*, Cic.

In all these governments if some action be marked, the genitive may be taken, either actively or passively, or in both senses together. Actively, *providentia Dei*, the providence of God by which

which he conducts us. Passively, *timor Dei*, the fear of God, by which we fear him. *Præstantia animantium*, Cic. the advantage which we have over brute beasts. *Patris pudor*, Ter. the respect I have for my father; the shame I should have to offend him In both senses, *amor Dei*, the love of God, whether it be that by which he loves us, or that by which we love him. *Victoria Germanorum*, the German victory, whether it be that which they obtained, or that which was obtained over them.

But in all these examples we see the substantive, by which the genitive is governed. There are other occasions where it is understood, as we shall make appear, in each rule, and in the remarks when we come to the figure of ellipsis.

Further, the adjectives and pronouns, especially if they be of the neuter gender, oftentimes supply the place of the substantive, and elegantly govern a genitive. *Ad id loci. Quid rei est ? Abs te nihil literarum*, Cic. instead of *nullæ litteræ. Dedit in sumptum dimidium minæ*, Ter. *Tantum habet fidei*, Juv. &c. Though we are always to understand *negotium*, as we shall observe hereafter.

That the same noun agreeing with the possessive, governs also a genitive.

Sometimes it is an elegance for the same noun agreeing with the possessive, to govern also a genitive, either of a proper name, or of any other, whether this refers to the same person, or to another, as *Imperium tuum Apollinis* Plaut.
Herilem filium ejus duxisse audio uxorem, Ter.
Dico meâ unius operâ rempublicam esse liberatam, Cic. *Solius enim meum peccatum corrigi non potest*, Cic. *Noster duorum eventus ostendet utra gens bello fit melior*, Livy.

In like manner, *Tuum hominis simplicis pectus vidimus*, Cic. *Literis tuis primorum mensium nihil commovebar*, Id. *Quantum meum studium extiterit dignitatis tuæ*, Id. *Nostra propugnatio ac defensio dignitatis tuæ*, Id.

Et pater ipse suo superûm jam signat honore, Æn. 6.
That is, *suo superûm honore*.

Postquàm arma Dei ad Vulcania ventum est, Æn. 12.
——— *Nocturnáque orgia Bacchi* Æn. 4.
Paternum amicum me assimilabo virginis, Ter. Phorm.

And an infinite number of other examples are to be found, all contrary to the rule of L. Valla, and which shew the little foundation he had to censure the antient interpreter, in the epistle to the Corinthians, for using this Greekish expression, *Salutatio meâ manu Pauli*.

These nouns joined to possessives, may likewise govern the genitive of the participle itself, especially in poetry.

Cùm mea nemo
Scripta legat vulgo recitare timentis, Hor.

But in prose, Vossius thinks that the expression, by the relative, is better on these occasions; as in Cicero, *Sed omnia sunt meâ ulpâ commissa, qui ab iis me amari putabam, qui invidebunt. Vestrâ, qui dixiſtis, hoc maximè intereſt*. And this turn of expreſſion may be uſed even when there is no participle, as *Id meâ minimè refert, qui ſum natu maximus*, Ter. *Vehementer intereſt veſtrâ, qui patres eſtis*, Plin. lib. 4. epiſt. Which is ſometimes more clear and elegant. See the advertiſement to the 11th rule.

All verbal nouns heretofore governed the caſe of their verb.

It is further to be obſerved that the verbal noun may likewiſe govern the caſe of its verb inſtead of the genitive: for as we ſtill ſay *reditio domum*, Cæſ. like *redeo domum*. *Traditio alteri*. Cic. like *tradere alteri*: and as Cicero alſo ſaith *Scientiam quid agatur, memoriamque quid à quoque dictum ſit*: ſo heretofore they ſaid *Spectatio rem*, or *ſpectatio rei*. *Curatio rem*, or *curatio rei*. *Quid tibi hanc curatio eſt rem?* Plaut. *Quid tibi ludos ſpectatio eſt?* Id. And hence it is that the gerunds and ſupines, which are only nouns ſubſtantives, govern alſo the caſe of their verb, as we ſhall ſhew in the remarks.

RULE VII.

Of ſome particles that require a genitive.

Tunc, ubi, ſat, inſtar, eò, poſtrídie, ergo, *and* prídie, *require a genitive.*

EXAMPLES.

Several abverbs govern a genitive.

Thoſe of time. *Tunc témporis*, at that time. *Poſtrídie abſolutiónis*, the day after abſolution. *Prídie hujus diéi*, the day before. But obſerve that we ſay alſo *prídie nonas*, the day before the nones: and ſuch like, where the accuſative is governed by *antè* underſtood.

Thoſe of place. *Ubi terrárum*, in what part of the earth. *Unde géntium*, from what nation. *Nuſquam géntium*, no where. *Longè géntium*, far from hence. *Eò conſuetúdinis addúcta res eſt*, the thing became ſo cuſtomary. *Huc malórum ventum eſt*, they came to ſuch a pitch of miſery.

Thoſe of quantity. *Sat fautórum*, partiſans enough. *Affatim matériæ*, plenty of matter. *Amplius liberórum*, more children.

We ſay alſo *Inſtar montis*, like a mountain. *Illius ergo*, for his ſake. And ſuch like.

ANNOTATION.

The reaſon why the genitive is put after theſe particles, is becauſe they are taken as noun ſubſtantives: for *inſtar* is a noun which ſignifies reſemblance; as *exemplar*. *Quantum inſtar in illo eſt*, Virg.

Parvum

Parvum instar, Liv. See the heteroclites, p. 167. *Ergo* comes from the Greek ablative ἔργῳ. *Pridie* and *postridie* come from the ablative *die:* and the others are also taken as substantives. *Tunc temporis:* just as in French we should say, *lors du siege de la Rochelle.* And the like.

In regard to adverbs of quantity, it may be said that if they come from a noun adjective, they always retain its nature; and suppose *negotium* for their substantive, *multum cibi,* that is, *multum negotium cibi.* And then *negotium cibi* will be put only for *cibus:* just as Phædrus has made use of *res cibi,* merely to signify *food.* Otherwise it will be an imitation of the Greeks, by understanding their preposition, *parum vini,* that is, *ἐκ vini,* as in French we say, *un peu de vin.* But we shall examine this more particularly in the remarks, where we treat of the adverbs.

RULE VIII.

Of nouns of property, blame, or praise.

Nouns signifying property, blame, or praise, are put either in the ablative, or in the genitive.

EXAMPLES.

The noun implying property, blame or shame, as well as praise, is put in the genitive or in the ablative. *Puer ingenui vultûs,* a boy of a comely countenance. *Vir máximi ánimi,* a man of very great courage. *Homo præstánti prudéntiâ,* a man of excellent wisdom. *Eunúchus nómine Photínus,* Hir. an eunuch named Photinus. *Múlier ætáte íntegrâ,* Ter. a woman in the flower of life.

ANNOTATION.

When there is a genitive, it is no more than the construction of two substantives: for *Vir maximi animi,* is *vir* governing *animi.* When there is an ablative, it is governed by a preposition understood: for *Mulier ætate integrâ* implies *in ætate integrâ. Photinus nomine,* implies, *ex nomine.* For which reason the antients made use of the preposition also; for as in Terence we read, *Homo antiquâ virtute ac fide:* so in Plautus we find, *Amicus fidus,* and *cum antiquâ fide:* and in another place, *Microtrogus nomine ex vero vocor.* And in almost all the modern languages the preposition is added; thus in French, *Un homme de grande sagesse,* a man of great wisdom, as much as to say, *De præstanti prudentia:* where it is observable that the French prepositions inform us almost in every government where they are to be understood in Latin.

Cicero has sometimes joined these two governments of the genitive and the ablative. *Lentulum eximiâ spe, summæ virtutis adolescentem.* And we shall hereafter see, that whatever governs one of these cases, generally speaking governs also the other.

RULE

Rule IX.

Of nouns adjectives derived from verbs.

1. *The adjectives called verbal, govern a genitive, as* tenax iræ.
2. *To which we must join those which signify an affection of the mind, as* cónscius scéleris:
3. *And some others which govern a genitive in imitation of the Greek.*

Examples.

A great many adjectives require a genitive after them.

1. Those derived from verbs, as *tenax iræ*, whose anger is lasting. *Amans virtútis*, a lover of virtue. *Fugax vítii*, who shuns vice. *Pátiens labóris*, who endures labour. *A'vidus novitátis*, greedy of novelty. *A'ppetens aliéni*, covetous of what belongs to others. *Religiónum colentes*, who have a regard for religion.

2. Those which denote some care, affection, desire, knowledge, ignorance, guilt, or such like things which relate to the mind or to consciousness; as *Cónscius scéleris*, Cic. conscious of guilt. *A'nxius gloriæ*, Liv. anxious after glory. *Secúrus damni*, who fears no hurt. *Tímidus procéllæ*, afraid of a storm. *Perítus músicæ*, skilled in music. *Musicórum perstudiósus*, Cic. who is very fond of music. *Rudis ómnium rerum*, Cic. ignorant in every thing. *Mihi vero fatigatiónis hestérnæ étiam nunc saúcio da véniam*, Apul. excuse a person who is still fatigued after yesterday's labour. *I'nsolens infámiæ*, Cic. unaccustomed to receive affronts.

3. There are many others which in imitation of the Greek govern a genitive, especially in poetry. *Lassus viárum*, tired of the journey. *Felix ac libera legum*. Luc. happy and exempt from laws. *Vini somnique benígnus*, who has drunk heartily and slept soundly. *Miror te purgátum illíus morbi*, Hor. I am surprized at your being cured of that distemper. *Pauper argénti*, Hor. poor in cash, and the like, which must be learnt by the use of authors. But you should take care not to employ any of these phrases, till you have seen them in pure authors. For there are a multitude of them

them not only in Tacitus (without mentioning the poets) but likewise in Salluſt and Livy, which ought not to be imitated.

ANNOTATION.

Difference between the participle and the verbal noun.

The participle always denotes ſome time; but the noun verbal denotes no time. Thus *Amans virtutem*, a man who actually loves virtue; and *amans virtutis*, he who is a lover of virtue; that is who habitually loves it, ſo that *amans* is then the ſame as *amator*. Thus the participle generally becomes a noun by taking the genitive, when the verb hath no ſupine from whence may be formed another noun in OR, as *indigens pecuniæ*, and the like, though it may alſo become a noun without that, and even in the preter tenſe, as in Salluſt, *Alieni appetens, profuſus ſui*, for *profuſor*, &c. Hence we frequently ſay *ſtudentes* for *ſtudioſi* or *ſcholaſtici: medentes* for *medici*:

——— *Nihil artes poſſe medentum.*

And the like.

Cauſe of the government of theſe verbal nouns.

And hereby the cauſe of this government is obvious, ſince it is nothing more than the government of two ſubſtantives, for *Amans virtutis*, is put inſtead of *Amator virtutis*: which happens alſo to other adjectives; *Amicus patris. Veritatis amiciſſimus*. Cic. *Affinis regis. Domini ſimilis es.* Ter. *Catilinæ ſimiles*, Cic. *Æqualis, par, affinis, cognatus, propinquus ejus*, juſt as we ſay *Frater ejus*.

As to the others which we have here hinted at, they take the genitive rather in imitation of the Greeks, who in putting this caſe here underſtand ἐκ, *of*; ἕνεκα, *causâ*, or χάριν, *gratiâ*; for *timidus procellæ*, is as much as to ſay, *causâ procellæ*; and the reſt in the like manner.

Of the active verbals in BUNDUS.

The verbal nouns in BUNDUS govern an accuſative, as well as the verb from which they are derived; hence we ſay, *Populabundus agros, vitabundus caſtra*; juſt as we ſay *populari agros, vitare caſtra*, and the reſt in the ſame manner. For which reaſon Scioppius will have it that they are participles, though with very little foundation, ſince they do not follow the analogy of the others: and the reaſon of participles bearing that name, is not becauſe they govern the caſe of the verb, for this is common alſo to the verbal ſubſtantives; but becauſe being nouns, they include ſome time in their ſignification, as the verb does.

RULE X.
Of affective verbs.

1. *Affective verbs require a genitive after them*, as miſerére fratris; hic ánimi pendet.

2. *But* miseror *takes an accusative.*
3. *And some others have moreover an ablative.*

EXAMPLES.

We place this rule here, because of the relation which these verbs have to the nouns of the preceding rule.

1. The pathetic or affective verbs, that is, which express some passion or affection of the soul, some care or disposition of the mind, or some such thing, require after them a genitive. *Miserére fratris*, have pity on my brother. *Hic ánimi pendet*, this man is in doubt, or suspense. *Sátage rerum tuárum*, mind your own affairs. *Veréri alicújus*, Ter. to stand in awe of some person. *Lætári malórum*, Virg. to rejoice at misfortunes.

2. Nevertheless *miseror, áris*, governs an accusative. *Miserári fortúnam alicújus*, to pity a person's misery.

3. There are also some more verbs of this sort, which take after them not only a genitive, but likewise an ablative. *Discrúcior ánimi* or *ánimo*, I am troubled in mind. *A'nimi se angébat*, Ter. he tormented himself inwardly. *Angor ánimo*, I am troubled in mind, Cic. *A'nimi pendeo*, Cic. *A'nimis pendémus*, Id. we are in doubt. *Desípere mentis*, Plaut. *Desípere ánimo*, (more usual) to doat. *Falli ánimi*, Lucr. *Falli ánimo* (more usual) to be mistaken, to be deceived. Heretofore they used also to say *Fastidíre alicújus*, Plaut. to slight a person; but now it more frequently governs an accusative.

ANNOTATION.

Hereto we may refer the verbs of desire, of admiration, of repelling, taking care, neglecting, ceasing, delivering, partaking, and others which we meet with in the genitive, from an imitation of the Greeks, who use this government on a thousand occasions, because of their prepositions which govern this case, and which they frequently suppose without expressing them.

But since we have no such prepositions in Latin, to account for this government: if there be a genitive, we may understand another general noun that governs it. *Discrucior animi*, supple, *dolore,*

lore, curâ, or *cogitatióne, mente,* &c. as Plautus has expreſſed it, *Nullam mentem animi habeo.* If there be an ablative, we underſtand *in, de, ab:* as much as to ſay, *Diſcrucior in animo; pendemus ab animis,* &c.

As to the others, *Miſerére fratris,* we may underſtand *fratris causâ:* have pity and compaſſion for my brother.

Rule XI.
Of *ſum, refert,* and *intereſt.*

1. Sum, refert, *and* intereſt, *ſignifying poſſeſ-ſion, property, or duty, require a genitive.*
2. *But* refert *and* intereſt *inſtead of the genitive of the pronoun poſſeſſive, have* mea, tua, ſua, cuja, noſtra, veſtra.
3. *On the contrary* EST *takes the nominative neuter of thoſe very pronouns, as* meum eſt, tuum eſt, &c.

Examples.

1. The verb *ſum,* with theſe two *refert* and *intereſt,* ſignifying duty, poſſeſſion, or property, require a genitive, *Sum ejus opiniónis,* I am of that opinion. *Nullius ſum conſilii,* Ter. I am at a loſs what to determine. *Tu non es Chriſti,* you are not a diſciple of Chriſt. *Eſt veri Chriſtiáni contempſiſſe divítias,* it is the duty of a true Chriſtian to deſpiſe riches. *Tantæ molis erat Románam cóndere gentem,* Virg. of ſuch importance was it to lay the foundation of the Roman nation. *O'mnium refert,* it is every body's concern. *Intereſt reipúblicæ,* it concerns the commonwealth.

2. *Refert* and *intereſt,* beſides the genitive of the pronouns poſſeſſive, take theſe caſes. *Noſtrâ refert,* it behoves us. *Et tuâ & meâ máximè intereſt te rectè valére,* Cic. your health is of great conſequence both to your ſelf and to me. *Hoc illórum magis quàm ſuâ retuliſſe vidétur,* Sal. this ſeems to have concerned them more than him. *Cujâ intereſt,* Cic. who is chiefly concerned in it.

3. *Eſt* on the contrary, inſtead of the genitive, takes the nominative neuter of thoſe very pronouns. *Meum eſt hoc fácere:* it is my buſineſs to do this. *Noſtrum eſt pati,* it belongs to us to ſuffer. *Si memória fortè*

defécerit, tuum est ut súggeras, if my memory should fail me, it is your business to put me in mind. *Cujum pecus* (sup. *est*) *an Melibæi?* Virg. whose flock is this? is it *Melibæus*'s?

ANNOTATION.

The two governments of the genitive and the pronoun are sometimes elegantly used, in nouns of price. *Illud mea magni interest.* And in proper names, *non mea Cæsaris interest.* But in regard to the rest, though we may say likewise, *Interest tua oratoris, refert mea militis;* yet it is better to make use of the relative, as in Terence, *Id mea minimè refert qui sum natu maximus.* See above, p. 17.

Now when we put a genitive here, another noun is always understood. *Sum ejus opinionis,* sup. *vir, philosophus, doctor. Non est regis,* sup. *officium :* and the like.

As to *refert* and *interest,* Sanctius and Scioppius, after Scaliger and Donatus, will have it that these cases, *mea, tua, sua,* are neuter accusatives, and therefore that *mea interest,* is as much as to say, *est inter mea negotia.* And in regard to REFERT, they pretend that to say *mea refert,* is much the same as when we say, *hoc rem tuam minimè refert,* where it intirely retains the force of the verb active.

On the contrary Vossius, after L. Valla, Saturnius, and Priscian, says that these are feminine ablatives, which Priscian resolves by *in; interest* or *refert mea for in re mea :* just as we say *in re mea est* in the same sense; *that concerns me.* For Sanctius's assertion, that it is not good Latin to say, *hoc est in re mea,* has more boldness than truth, since beside the passage of Plautus, *Utrumve veniat, nec ne, nihil in re est mea.* Terence has, *Si in re est utrique ut fiant, arcessi jube,* in Andr. Act. 3. Sc. 3. It is true others read *in rem :* but thus it is quoted by Linacer, and marked in the manuscripts which Rivius and Vossius made use of.

But one would think that this question may be solved by these words, which we find in the ablative in the following verses;

Vos me indotatis modò
Patrocinari fortasse arbitramini :
Etiam dotatis soleo. C. *Quid nostra ?* Ph. *Nihil.*

Ter. in Phor.
where the verse would be good for nothing, unless *nostra* was in the ablative. Which is further illustrated by this verse of Plautus, who with *mea* understands *gratia.*

Mea istuc nihil refert, tua refert gratia.

And therefore, *mea refert, mea interest,* is properly speaking, *mea causa,* or *mea gratia,* for *mea de causa, mea de gratia.*

From whence it is easy to collect the reason of the government of the genitive; for when we say, *Refert naturæ hominum,* &c. *Interest Ciceronis, civium, reip.* &c. we have only to understand *causa* or *gratia ;* just as the Greeks frequently understand χάριν or ἕνεκα. And then it will be the same as, *Interest Ciceronis gratiâ. Refert civium causâ ;* and in like manner the rest.

As for *meum, tuum, suum*, and the others, it is obvious that these are adjectives, to which we must suppose a substantive, as *officium, negotium*, &c.

RULE XII.
Natural signification of the dative.

1. *The dative always signifies acquisition, or relation. Hence it is put after the following verbs,*
2. *Sum,*   3. *and its compounds:*
4. *Médeor, occúrro, fáveo, stúdeo, grátulor.*
5. *Also after verbs of excelling:*
6. *Of assisting, except* juvo,
7. *And of commanding, except* jubeo.

EXAMPLES.

1. The dative, as the very name sheweth, which comes from *dare* to give, always signifies something acquired or attributed, either to advantage or disadvantage; or else it implies some relation, either in the objects, or in the intention, being the end as it were to which a thing is referred. Hence there is scarce a passage in which it does not bear this sense, as well after nouns as after verbs, to express not only the person, but likewise the thing to which this relation or attribution is made.

After nouns. *Tu illi amícus*, you are his friend. *Affinis regi*, related to the king. *Contérminus Gállíæ*, bordering upon France. *Par virtúti orátio*, Cic. a speech equal to virtue. *Similia prodígiis*, Virg. like to prodigies. *Autor consíliis*, one who gives the first counsel. *Cónscius facínori*, Cic. an accomplice. *Supérstes dignitáti*, who survived his dignity. And the rest in the same manner, especially those which signify conveniency, inconveniency, favour, pleasure, trust, and the like.

After verbs: *Tibi soli amas*, you love for yourself only. *Hoc mihi non sapit*, this does not please me. *Tibi peto*, I ask for you. *Non ómnibus dórmio*, I do not sleep for all, or in regard for all. *Métuo exercítui*, I am afraid for the army. *Assuéscere labóri*, to be inured to toil. *Mihi peccat, si quid peccat*, Ter. if he commits any faults, it is for me he commits them. *Neque istic, neque álibi tibi usquam erit in me mora*. Ter.

you

you will always find me ready to obey you, both in this, and in every thing else. *Huic cervíxque comæ'que trabúntur per terram,* Virg. his neck and hair drag along the ground. *Pennas pavóni quæ decíderant sústulit,* Phædr. took up the feathers which fell from the peacock. The same with verbs of

Obeying. *Obedíre, parére, morem gérere alícui,* to obey a person. *Auscultáre parénti,* to listen to the commands of his father. *Non parébo dolóri meo, non iracúndiæ sérviam,* Cic. I will not indulge my grief, I will not be a slave to my passion.

Resisting. *Obstat, repúgnat volúptas sanitáti:* pleasure is prejudicial to health.

Profiting. *Providére rebus suis,* to take care of his affairs. *Consúlite vobis, prospícite pátriæ,* Cic. take care of yourselves, consider your country.

Hurting. *Nocet mihi cibus,* food disagrees with me. *Mentis quasi lumínibus ófficit altitúdo fortúnæ,* Cic. excess of good fortune darkens the understanding. *Invidére alícui.* Cic. to envy a person.

It is the same in regard to impersonals. *Mihi libet, placet,* it pleases me. *Tibi licet,* it is lawful for you. *Nobis decet,* Ter. it becomes us. *Quid refert intra natúræ fines vivénti,* Hor. what does it signify to a person that lives within the bounds prescribed by nature; and in like manner the rest. But all this is easily understood.

There are some other verbs which might occasion greater difficulty to beginners, for which reason I have made particular mention of them, though they might be comprehended in the general rule.

2. SUM. *Est mihi liber,* I have a book: as much as to say, a book belongs to me. *Est mihi iter in Lemnum.* I am going to Lemnos. *Causa fuit pater his,* Hor. my father was the cause of all this.

To this may be referred such expressions as these. *Radix vescéndo est decócta,* Plin. this root is good to eat, when it is boiled. *Quæ restinguéndo igni forent,* Liv. which might serve for extinguishing the fire. But then the dative seems to be governed by some adjective understood, as *aptus, idóneus, par,* or such like, since they are often expressed. 3. The

3. The compounds of SUM. *Adésse patri*, to assist his father. *Adésse sacro*, to hear mass. *Deésse officio*, to be deficient in his duty. *Praéesse exercítui*, to command an army.

4. Some particular verbs. *Medétur ánimo virtus*, virtue cures the mind. *Occúrrere alícui*, to go to meet a person. *Favére nobilitáti*, to favour the nobility. *Velle aut cúpere alícui*, Cic. to wish well to a person, to have his interest at heart. *Studére lectióni*, to study his lesson. *Studére eloquéntiæ*, to study eloquence. Though we say likewise, *Studére áliquid*, meaning *to desire*, Ter. Cic. Hor. *Grátulor tibi*, I congratulate you, I rejoice at your success.

5. Verbs of excelling, *Præstat, excéllit virtus divítiis*, virtue is preferable to riches. *Anteférre pacem bello*, to prefer peace to war. *Antecéllit sénsibus glória cæléstis*, the glory of heaven is beyond all perception of the senses. *Præsidére pópulis*, to preside over the people.

6. Those of helping. *Opitulári, auxiliári, subveníre alícui*, to help or to assist a person. *Succúrrere míseris*, to relieve the miserable.

Except JUVO, which takes an accusative by the general rule. *Juváre áliquem*, to help a person.

7. Those of commanding. *Præcípio, ímpero, præscríbo tibi*, I command you.

But JUBEO is never put with a dative in Cicero, nor in any other author of pure latinity. The natural and usual construction of this verb, is to join it with an infinitive, either single, or preceded by its accusative. *Líteræ tuæ recte speráre jubent*, Cic. your letters command us to have good hopes. *Júbeo te bene speráre*, Cic. I desire you to have good hopes. As for *juvat*. See rule 15th.

ANNOTATION.

We must therefore take notice that it would by no means be good Latin to say, *Jubeo te ut bene speres*, or *ut hoc facias*. For if *jubeo* occurs sometimes with the accusative of the person only, this accusative is constantly governed by an infinitive understood, as in Cic. *Et hercle, ut me jubet Acastus, confido te jam ut volumus valere*, where we are to understand *ut me jubet facere*. *Literæ non quæ te aliquid juberent*, Cic. sup. *facere*. *Excepere patres ne postea eosdem tribunos juberent*, Liv. sup. *esse*. *Jubeo Chremetem*, Ter. sup. *salvere*.

But

But though *jubeo* does not take the accusative of the person, yet it receives some particular accusatives of the thing, as *quid, hoc, illud, id, aliquid, nihil, pauca, multa, unum, duo, tantum, quantum;* and the like. *Lex jubet ea quæ facienda sunt,* Cic. *Renuis tu quod jubet alter,* Hor.

We are also to observe that authors of less purity have put this verb with the dative. *Ubi Britannico jussit exurgere,* Tacit. *Hispanis Gallisque jubet,* Claud.

Some extraordinary constructions with the dative.

To this rule we must refer a multitude of nouns, which of their own nature should seem rather to require a genitive, as in Plautus, *Vino modo cupidæ estis*; in Ovid, *participem studiis:* or an ablative with the preposition; as in Cic. *alienus causæ*; in Quintil. *diversus huic*; though we say rather, *alienus à causa,, diversus ab hoc,* &c.

It is likewise by this rule that *par* and *similis* govern a dative not only when they make a comparison between persons, as when Horace says, *Tydidem superis parem;* or between things, one of which may be referred to the other, as *par virtuti oratio,* Cic.: but likewise between a thing and a person, or another thing to which it cannot be referred, as in the civil law, *in pari causa cæteris servis habendus est.* And Horace hath likewise, *Quum magnis parva mineris——falce recisurum simili te,* lib. 1. Sat. 3. since you threaten to punish small faults with the same punishment as great ones; that is, with a punishment like that which great faults deserve. And this is very usual in Greek;

Οὐ γὰρ μιλίιχις τὰς ἴσας πληγὰς ἰμοί, Aristoph.
Non enim participasti pares plagas mihi.

To this we must refer a great many verbs, which seem rather to require an accusative; as *cætera quæ huic vitæ comitantur,* Cic. *Pergin' precari pessimo,* Plaut. *Curare rebus alienis,* Id. *Voluptati mæror sequitur,* Plaut. *Homini servos suos——Domitos oportet habere oculos,* Plaut. for *hominem servum habere oportet,* &c. *Si hoc fratri cedetur,* Plaut. *Ut messem hanc nobis adjuvent,* Id.

There are likewise a great many which usually require rather an accusative or an ablative with the preposition, that occur also with a dative; as in Livy, *incidere portis,* for *in portas.* *Et magno bellare parenti,* Stat. for *cum magno parente. Longè mea discrepat istis, ——et vox et ratio,* Hor. for *ab istis discrepat. Nec sæ enitar tragico differre colori,* Id. And an infinite number of others which are more common in Greek than in Latin.

It is by the same rule that we put this case likewise after verbs passive, *Neque cernitur ulli,* Virg. for *ab ullo. Cui non dictus Hylas puer,* Id. By whom has not he been praised? *Ego audita tibi putabam,* Cic. *Honesta bonis viris, non occulta quæruntur,* Cic. *Nunquam enim præstantibus in Rep. gubernanda viris laudata est in una sententia perpetua permansio,* Cic. and such like. See the annotation to the 30th rule.

To this likewise we must refer the prayer of the liturgy, *miserere nobis.* But in order to know whether in the purest language, *miseror,* or *miseresco,* have been joined with a dative, as well as *facio, allatro,*

OF SYNTAX.

allatro, interest, and some others; see lower down the list of different governments.

We must likewise take notice, that *Non esse solvendo*, is a dative in which *æri alieno* is understood; hence according to Budeus, it is a mistake of the transcriber in Livy to say, *Nec solvendo ære alieno Resp. erat*, where we should read *æri alieno*, just as this author says in another place, *Qui oneri ferendo essent*: and the like.

RULE XIII.
Of verbs which take two datives.

You must join two datives to sum, habeo, do, verto, *and some others.*

EXAMPLES.

There are some verbs, which require two datives, one of the person to whom the thing happens: and the other of the end, or the intention to which the thing refers. Such are *sum, hábeo, do, verto, tríbuo, duco, relínquo, puto*, and some others. *Est illi lucro, voluptáti, honóri, infámiæ*, &c. This is a pleasure, an advantage, an honour, a disgrace to him, and the like. *Do, relínquo tibi pígnori*, I give, or I leave this in pledge with you. *Utrùm stúdio id sibi habet, an laudi putat*, Ter. does he take a pleasure in this, or does he think it an honour that, &c.

Jam sibi tum curvis malè témperat unda carínis, Virg. The sea begins to rage against the ships.

ANNOTATION.

We frequently omit the dative of the person after those verbs, and there remains only the dative of the thing. *Exemplo est Regulus.* Cic. *Ea res quæstioni diu fuit*, Cic.

To this we may likewise refer the following examples. *Est mihi nomen Petro. Cui nunc cognomen Iülo.* Though we say also by apposition, *cui cognomen Iülus*; or with the genitive, *cognomen Iüli*, as *flumen Rheni*. And according to some, *cognomen Iülum*, taking it as an adjective, otherwise it would be a mistake to say, for example, *est mihi nomen Petrum*.

RULE XIV.
Of the accusative which the verb governs after it.

1. *Verbs active always govern an accusative of the thing after them.*
2. *And sometimes verbs neuter govern this accusative likewise.*

EXAMPLES.

1. Verbs active, and such as are of an active signification, always have after them, either expressed or understood, an accusative of the thing, or more properly speaking, of the subject to which their action passeth. *Virtus sibi glóriam parit,* virtue begets glory. *Venerári áliquem ut Deum,* to worship a person as a God. *Et me déstinat aræ,* Virg. he designs to sacrifice me upon the altar.

2. Verbs neuter have oftentimes this accusative. For in the first place they may always govern the accusative of the name of their original, as *Vivere vitam, gaudére gaúdium,* Ter. to live, to rejoice. *Lúdere ludum,* to play. *Servíre servitútem,* Cic. to be reduced to slavery. *Eádem peccáre semper,* sup. *peccáta,* always to commit the same faults.

Secondly, they may govern the accusative of nouns, whose signification borders upon their own. *Ire viam,* to walk. *Sitíre humánum sánguinem,* to thirst after human blood. *Olet unguénta,* Ter. he smells of perfumes. *Sonat horréndum,* Virg. he makes a terrible noise. *Multa cavére alicui,* sup. *mala,* to preserve a person from a great many misfortunes.

Thirdly, they may govern all sorts of accusatives, when they are taken in a metaphorical sense. *Ambuláre mária, & terras navigáre,* Cic. to walk upon the sea, and to sail upon land. *Ardébat Alexin,* he was passionately fond of Alexis. *Vinéta crepat mera,* Hor. he talks of nothing but vineyards.

ANNOTATION.

The reason why these verbs, called neuter, govern thus the accusative, is because properly speaking they are then verbs active.

Now this case of the accusative is almost the only government that belongs to the verb itself, all the rest depend on something understood: hence it ought to be generally supposed after all verbs, though it be not expressed, as it particularly happens to those whose action is confined within themselves; as *terra movit. Tum prora avertit,* Virg. *Nox cœlo præcipitat: volventibus annis,* where we are to understand *se,* which is suppressed merely because the sense is sufficiently determined by the verb only.

The like also happens to some other verbs, which in common use are understood by every body; as *nubere alicui,* sup. *se,* or *vultum;* for *nubere* properly signifies *velare,* being taken from *nubes,*

because

because the new married women used to veil themselves and to cover their faces. And it is in this same signification that Virgil says, *Arjurâsque comas obnubit amictu.* See the list of the verbs and of the ellipses.

Even the infinitive sometimes supplies the place of the accusative. *Odi tuum vociferari* for *clamorem tuum, Amat cœnare,* for *cœnam:* or even an intire period, *Cupio videri doctum,* where *videri doctum* supplies the place of the accusative. *Quod te purges, hujus non faciam,* &c.

But we must likewise take notice, that there are a great many verbs, which receive an accusative after them, which accusative is governed rather by a preposition understood, as in Ter. *Hæc dum dubitas.* And in Cic. *Illud non dubito:* that is properly *circa illud.*

In the same manner verbs of motion compounded with *In*: *Negat ullam pestem majorem, vitam hominum invasisse, quàm eorum opinionem qui ista distraxerint,* Cic. Off. 3. That is to say, *invasisse in vitam,* as he has said in another place, *in multas pecunias invasit.*

Rule XV.

Of verbs that govern the person in the accusative.

In these verbs, decet, delectat, fugit, fallit, pudet, præ'terit, *and* juvat, *the thing is governed in the nominative case, and the person in the accusative.*

Examples.

This rule is only an explication of the foregoing, which shews us that in these seven verbs the thing is put in the nominative, and the person in the accusative. *Hæc res me decet,* this thing becomes me. *Pietas pium delectat,* piety entertains the religious man. *Istud me prætériit, fugit,* that escaped me, I did not know it. *Non te fallit,* you are not ignorant. *Id me juvat,* I take pleasure in that. *Non te hæc pudet?* Ter. are not you ashamed of these things?

Annotation.

In order thoroughly to understand in what manner this rule is only an appendix to that of the verbs active, we must observe that the verb active, making its action pass into a thing, or person, as to its subject, always takes it in the accusative. Hence we may find several other verbs, which have the person also in the accusative, as *vox eum defecit,* Cic. his voice failed him.

But *latet,*-though generally joined to these, has only the dative in Cicero *Nihil moliris quod mihi latere valeat. Ubi nobis hæc autoritas tamdiu tanta latuit.* And if we read in the oration pro Sylla, *Lex populum Rom. latuit,* this must be a mistake of the transcriber, who seeing *Pop. Rom.* put the accusative for the dative. It is true that in other authors we find it with an accusative. *Sed res Annibalem non dix latuit,* Juſt. *Nec latuere doli fratrem Junonis,* Virg. Though this is rather a Greek than a Latin phraſe, owing to this that λανθάνω, as an active, governs an accuſative: whereas in Latin *lateo,* ſignifying a permanent action, it would be no more permitted to ſay *latet me,* than *patet me,* if the cuſtom had not been borrowed of the Greeks.

On the contrary *decet* ſometimes governs the dative. *Locum ditiorem quàm victoribus decebat,* Sal. *Decet principi terrarum populo,* Liv. *Imò Hercle. ita nobis decet,* Ter. It even ſeems that this manner of ſpeaking ſhould be more natural, as it is more conformable to modern languages; and that the other, though more uſual in Latin is only an ellipſis of the infinitive underſtood. For the antients, ſays Donatus, adding the infinitive *facere,* uſed to ſay *non decet facere*; but omitting the infinitive, they ſaid *nobis decet.* Yet Cicero never uſes it but with the accuſative. For in regard to the paſſage which Linacer quotes from him, in his fourth book, and Robert Stephen in his theſaurus, viz. *Quandoque id deceat prudentiæ tuæ,* de Orat. it is very probably a miſtake, becauſe we find in the third de Oratore, *Scire quid quandoque deceat, prudentiæ:* but *prudentiæ* is there a genitive, and ſignifies, *eſt prudentiæ,* or *eſt proprium prudentiæ.*

Rule XVI.

Of five verbs that take the perſon in the accuſative, and the thing in the genitive.

Theſe five verbs miſeret, pœ'nitet, pudet, piget, tædet, *govern the perſon in the accuſative, and the thing in the genitive, as* hujus me piget; tui non te pudet.

Examples.

This rule has a great relation to the foregoing, ſince theſe verbs likewiſe govern the perſon in the accuſative the ſame as the precedent. But there is this further to obſerve, that they govern the thing in the genitive; as *Miſeret me hóminis,* I have pity on the man. *Pœ'nitet me fratris,* I am ſorry for my brother. *Tui non te pudet?* are not you aſhamed of yourſelf? *Hujus facti me piget,* I am ſorry for having done this. *Piget me tálium,* I am tired of ſuch doings. *Tædet me harum ineptiárum,* I am tired of theſe follies. And in like manner their derivatives, as *miſeréſco; Arcádii quæſo miſeréſcete regis,* Virg. have pity, I pray you, on this poor Arcadian king.

Annotation.

Thoſe verbs, which are called imperſonals have nevertheleſs their

their nominative. *Non te hæc pudet?* Ter. *Quem neque pudet quicquam,* Id. and the like. Hence in the examples above given, the nominative is always understood, and ought to be taken from the verb itself. For, according to Priscian, *pœnitet me fratris,* is the same as, *pœna fratris habet me,* or *pœnitet me.* Where it appears that the genitive *fratris* is governed by *pœna,* as the French say *j'ai honte* DE *mon frere,* which is the same signification, as if we were to say word for word from the Latin, *la honte de mon frere me fait peine.*

RULE XVII.

Of verbs of remembering and forgetting.

Verbs of remembering and forgetting govern either a genitive or an accusative.

EXAMPLES.

Verbs of remembering and forgetting govern either a genitive or an accusative. *Memini malorum meorum,* or else *mala mea,* I remember my misfortunes. *Oblitus generis sui,* or *genus suum,* who has forgot his birth. *Venit enim mihi Platonis in mentem,* Cic. I remember Plato. *Memineram Paulum,* Cic. I remembered Paul. *Nec me meminisse pigebit Elisæ,* nor shall I be displeased to remember Dido.

ANNOTATION.

1. Vossius in his lesser grammar, says that verbs of memory and oblivion do indeed govern the genitive, either of things, or of persons: but as for the accusative, they take it only in regard to things, and not to persons; and therefore we cannot say *Memini Ciceronem,* but only, as he adds, *Ciceronis,* I remember Cicero. Nevertheless it is easy to prove the contrary by Cicero himself, *Memineram Paulum, videram Caium,* lib. de amicit. *Memini Cinnam, vidi Syllam, modò Cæsarem,* Phil. 5. *Quem hominem probè commeminisse aiebat,* 1. de Orat. *Balbus fuit Lanuvius, quem meminisse tu non potes;* de fin. *Antipater ille, quem tu probè meministi,* 3. de Orat. *Rupilius quem ego memini,* Off. 1. And in his book of old age speaking of Ennius, *Quem quidem probè meminisse potestis, anno enim undevigesimo post ejus mortem, hi Coss. facti sunt.*

Numeros memini, si verba tenerem, Virg. Ecl. ult.

And when we say *Memini de Cicerone,* it is in a different sense: for *Meminisse alicujus,* is to retain the remembrance of a person; whereas *Meminisse de aliquo,* is to make mention of him.

2. Nouns of remembering and forgetting govern only a genitive. They may be referred to the ninth rule, of adjectives which signify things belonging to the mind. *Immemor injuriæ. Memor accepti beneficii,* &c.

3. Now in the government of this genitive, another noun, which governs it, is still understood. *Venit in mentem illius diei,*

sup. *recordatio*. *Memini malorum*, sup. *memoriam*. But when we say *mala mea*, it is in the simple government of verbs active, and therefore belongs properly to this place. Thus when Terence says, *satagit rerum suarum*, Heaut. he thinks of his affairs, the meaning is, *agit sat rerum suarum*. Just as Plautus in his *Bacch*. says, *Nunc agitas tute sat tuarum rerum*. Where *sat* supplies the place of an accusative derived by syncope from *satis*, which is an old noun, like *magis* and *potis*, as we shall observe in the remarks on the adverbs, n. 2.

RULE XVIII.
Of two verbs coming together.

When two verbs come together, without ut *or* ne, *the second must be put in the infinitive.*

EXAMPLES.

When two verbs follow one another, without one of these conjunctions *ut* or *ne* expressed or understood, the second is always put in the infinitive. *Nescis inescáre hómines*, Ter. you don't know how to intice men. *Docémur disputáre, non vívere*, we are taught to dispute, but not to live. *Cérnere erat*, Virg. for *licébat*, one might see. *Cupit ambuláre*, he desires to walk.

If in the conjunction *ut* or *ne* is understood, the verb must be in the subjunctive. *Fac sciam*, sup. *ut*, act so that I may know. *Cave sentiant*, sup. *ne*, for *ut ne*, take care that they do not hear of it.

ANNOTATION.

1. We likewise place this rule here, because in this construction the infinitive oftentimes supplies the place of the accusative. For, *amat ludere*, for example, is the same as *amat lusum*. *Nescis inescare*, the same as *Nescis hoc*, or *illud*, as we have above observed, rule 14.

2. Nouns adjectives which retain the signification of the verbs, retain likewise this government. For as we say *Cupio discere*, we say also *Cupidus discere*. *Nescis inescare*; *nescius inescare*: and even with the infinitive passive. *Dignus amari*. *Apta regi*. But then the infinitive passive supplies the place of the dative or the ablative: so that *apta regi*, is the same as *apta regimini*: *dignus amari*, as *dignus amore*; and the infinitive active supplies the place of the genitive, as *Cupidus discere*, for *discendi* or *disciplinæ*; whereby we see likewise that the infinitive must be considered as a noun verbal and indeclinable.

Sometimes we likewise understand the former verb, by putting only the infinitive, *Mene incœpto desistere victam?* Virg. sup. *oportet* or *decet*: and sometimes we understand the infinitive itself. *Scit Latiné*, sup. *loqui*. *Discit fidibus*, sup. *canere*. And especially we

must

muſt often underſtand the ſubſtantive verb. *Spero me integritatis laudem conſecutum*, Cic. that is, *me eſſe conſecutum*.

After verbs of motion we generally put the ſupine in UM; inſtead of the infinitive, *Mea Glycerium, cur te is perditum?* Ter. *Ut cubitum diſceſſimus*, Cic. as we went to bed.

RULE XIX.
Of prepoſitions which govern the accuſative.

The following prepoſitions govern the accuſative: ad, apud, contra, adverſum, adverſus, per, circum, circa, erga, extra, juxta, cis, citra, pone, penes, inter, intra, propter, ob, poſt, ante, præter, ſupra, ſecus, ſecundum, trans, ultra, infra.

EXAMPLES.

We make mention here of the prepoſitions, becauſe moſt of the following governments are either mixed with or depend on them. Thoſe which govern an accuſative we reduce to five and twenty.

1. AD; near to, upon, towards, to, before; until, as far as, according to. *Habet hortos ad Tiberim*, he has gardens upon the river Tiber. *Ad urbem venit*, he came to town. *Ad júdicem dícere*, to ſpeak before the judge. *Ad decem annos*, ten years hence. *Ad uſum hóminum*, for the uſe of man. *Ad præſcriptum omnia gerere*, to do every thing according to orders.

2. ADVERSUM or ADVERSUS, againſt, oppoſite to, towards. *Adverſus clivum*, Plin. againſt the hill. *Adverſum patrem*, againſt my father. *Pietas adverſus Deos*, Cic. reverence of the Gods. *De illa adverſus hunc loqui*, Ter. to ſpeak to him of her.

3. ANTE, before. *Ante pedes*, before the feet. *Ante horam octávam*, before eight o'clock.

4. APUD, with, at, before, near. *Apud patrem*, at my father's. *Apud júdicem dícere*, to plead before the judge. *Apud te plúrimum valet iſta rátio*, this reaſon weighs very much with you.

5. CIRCA, near, about. *Circa forum*, near the forum. *Circa eum menſem*, about that month.

6. CIRCUM, about, near. *Circum littora*, near the ſhore.

7. Cis and Citra, on this side. *Citra flumen,* on this side the river. *Cis Euphrátem,* on this side the Euphrates.

8. Contra, against, contrary to, opposite. *Contra autoritátem,* against authority. *Contra spem,* contrary to hope. *Carthágo Itáliam contra,* Virg. Carthage over against Italy.

9. Erga, towards. *Cháritas erga próximum,* charity towards our neighbour.

10. Extra, without, besides, except. *Extra urbem,* without the city. *Extra modum,* beyond measure. *Extra fámulos,* except the servants.

11. Infra, under, below, beneath. *Infra se,* beneath himself.

12. Inter, among. *Inter cæ'teros,* among the rest. *Inter arénam,* among the sand.

13. Intra, within. *Intra párietes,* within the walls.

14. Juxta, near, over against. *Juxta viam,* near the road. *Juxta ripam,* near the bank.

15. Ob, for, before. *Ob emoluméntum,* for profit. *Ob amórem,* for love. *Ob óculos,* before his eyes.

16. Penes, in the power, in the disposal, in possession. *Isthæc penes vos psáltria est,* Ter. that singer is at your house. *Omnia adsunt bona, quem penes est virtus,* Plaut. he that is possessed of virtue, possesseth all that is good. *Penes te es?* Hor. are you in your senses?

17. Per, by, during, thro'. *Per diem,* during day time. *Per ancíllam,* by my servant. *Per campos,* through the fields.

18. Pone; behind. *Ponè ædem,* behind the temple.

19. Post; after, since, within, behind. *Post finem,* after the end. *Post legem hanc constitútam,* since this law has been enacted. *Post sexénnium,* within six years. *Post tergum,* behind the back.

20. Præter; except, besides, near, before. *Omnes præter eum,* all except him. *Præter mœ'nia fluere,* to run near the walls. *Præter óculos,* before his eyes.

21. Propter; for, because of, in consideration of, for the sake of, near. *Propter honestátem,* for honour or reputation. *Propter vos,* for your sake, on your
account.

account. *Propter patrem cubántes,* Cic. lying near their father.

22. SECUS, or SECUNDUM; near, along side. *Secus flúvios,* Plin. (or as others read *secúndum*) near the rivers. *Condúctus est cæcus secus viam stare,* Quintil. a blind man was hired to stand near the river side. *Secúndum philósophos,* according to the philosophers. *Secúndum fratrem illis plúrimum tribuébat,* next to his brother, he paid the greatest deference to them. *Secúndum ripam,* along the bank side.

23. SUPRA, above. *Supra leges,* above the laws.

24. TRANS, over, on the other side. *Trans mária,* over the seas.

15. ULTRA, beyond. *Ultrà Tíberim,* beyond the Tiber, on the other side the Tiber.

ANNOTATION.

We generally join the accusative to these prepositions, *prope, circiter, usque, versus:* yet Sanct.us sheweth that these are only adverbs.

For when we say, *Prope muros; prope seditionem ventum est,* and such like, we understand *ad,* which forms the government. Otherwise we should say that *propior* and *propius; proximus* and *proximè* are likewise prepositions, since we find *proximus te,* Plaut. *Propius urbem, propior montem,* Sal. *Rex proximè formam latrocinii,* Liv. The same must be said of *pridie* and *postridie,* since we say *pridie nonas; postridie calendas,* where we understand *post* and *ante.* The same must also be said of *procul,* since we say, *Procul urbem; procul muros,* where we understand *ad,* as *procul mari, oceano, procul dubio,* where we understand *ab,* and Cicero most frequently expresses it, *procul à nobis.* And *prope* in the like manner is joined with the ablative by putting *A* or *ab, prope à Sicilia,* Cic. *Prope à muris habemus hostem. Prope ab origine,* &c. Which shews that it is not *prope* which governs either case, so much as the preposition expressed or understood.

It is the same in regard to *circiter:* for though we say, *Circiter calendas,* Cicero also hath, *Circiter ad calendas.* In like manner we say, *Dies circiter quindecim* (sup. *per*) *iter fecerunt,* Cæs. *Decem circiter millia* (sup. *ad*) Liv. *Loca hæc circiter* (sup. *ad*) Plin. Thus we see that this adverb always supposeth a preposition, whether it be taken for place, for number, or for time. And then in this last sense it may be referred to rule 26th lower down.

USQUE is as often joined with another preposition, as without. For as we say *usque Romam; usque sudorem,* we say likewise *usque ante calendas, usque extra solitudinem. Ab ovo usque ad mala; usque in flumen; usque ad summam senectutem. Trans Alpes usque. Usque sub*

sub osculum noctis; and the like, or even with an ablative, *Siculo ab usque Pachino*, Virg. *Usque à pueritia*, Ter. *Usque ab avo, atque atavo progeniem vestram referens*, Ter. *Ex Æthiopia est usque hæc*, Id. Hence, as Silvius observeth, all these phrases include the same signification, *usque palatium, ad palatium, usque ad palatium, ad palatium usque, ad usque palatium*; and all the following include another, *à palatio, usque à palatio, ab usque palatio*.

Now *usque*, when by itself, properly signifieth no more than *still*, or *till now*. *Usque laborat*, she is still in labour. *Usquéne valuisti? Animus usque antehac attentus*, Ter. and such like.

VERSUS or VERSUM are no more than adverbs, which plainly appears even from *adversus* and *adversum:* and though we find in Cicero *Brundusium versus*, we find also *Ad Alpes versus, in forum versus; sursum versus*, and the like.

Sanctius rejects *secus* also, and says that this phrase of scripture, *Secus decursus aquarum*, is not Latin: and Charisius lib. 1. title of analogy, having mentioned that *secus* is an adverb which signifies *aliter*, from whence comes *secius ἀλλοιότερως*, he adds, *Cæterum id quod vulgus usurpat; secus illum sedi, hoc est secundùm illum; & novum & sordidum est*. Nevertheless Vossius acknowledges this preposition, and says that *secundum* and *secus* seem even to be derived from the same root, namely *secundus*; shewing that it has been not only adopted by Pliny and Quintilian, whom we have quoted, but likewise by Sempronius Asellio in his history, *Non possent stationes facere secus hoc*. But he grants that those who study the purity of the language, do not make use of it. For which reason Scioppius censures Maffei for using it so frequently in his history of the Indies, as he observes some other mistakes in this agreeable author, contrary to the purity of the language. From whence appeareth, continues the same Scioppius, the error of those, who having been accustomed to authors of the latter ages, undertake to write in Latin, without taking sufficient care to acquire an exact knowledge of the laws of grammar.

RULE XX.

Of prepositions which govern the ablative.

These prepositions, coram, a, ab, abs, cum, absque, de, ex, e, pro, præ, clam, palam, tenus, sine, *govern the ablative*.

EXAMPLES.

The prepositions governing the ablative are reduced to twelve.

1. A, AB, ABS (which are the same) since, after, by, because of, in the behalf. *A fronte*, before. *A pueritia*, from one's childhood. *A morte Cæsaris*, since the death of Cæsar. *A civibus*, in the behalf of the citizens. *A frigore*, because of the cold, against the cold. *Ab aliquo perire*, to be killed by some body.

2. ABSQUE; without. *Absque te,* without thee.

3. CLAM *Præceptóre,* unknown to the master. Formerly it governed the accusative. *Clam patrem,* Ter. unknown to my father. And in the same manner *clánculum.*

4. CORAM *ipso,* before him, in his presence.

5. CUM *cupiditáte,* with desire, with passion.

6. DE, of, for, because of, concerning. *De homínibus,* of men. *De quorum número,* of whose number. *Multis de causis,* for many reasons. *De raudúsculo Numeriáno, multùm te amo,* Cic. I am very much obliged to you for that little money. *A'dii te heri de filia,* Ter. I called on you yesterday to talk about your daughter. *De lanifício, néminem tímeo,* as to the spinning, I am afraid of nobody. *Non est bonum somnus de prándio,* Plaut. it is not good to sleep after dinner.

7. E or Ex, out of, from. *E flammâ,* out of the fire. *Ex Deo,* from God, according to God.

8. PALAM *ómnibus,* before all the world.

9. PRÆ, in comparison, because of, before. *Præ nobis,* in comparison to us. *Præ multitúdine,* because of the multitude. *Præ óculis,* before his eyes.

10. PRO, for, according, instead of, by, because of, in consideration, for the sake. *Pro cápite,* for his life. *Pro mérito,* according to his merit. *Pro illo,* instead of him, in his place. *Pro fóribus,* before the door. *Pro nostrâ amicitiâ te rogo,* I beseech you for friendship sake, out of regard or consideration to our friendship.

11. SINE *póndere,* without weight. *Sine amóre,* without affection.

12. TENUS, as far as, up to. *Cápulo tenus,* up to the hilt.

This preposition is always put after the case it governs. And if the noun be in the plural, it is generally put in the genitive. *Lumbórum tenus,* Cic. up to the loins. *Cumárum tenus illi rumóres caluérunt.* Cœl. ad Cic. these reports were spread as far as Cuma. *Aúrium tenus,* Quintil. up to the ears. Though Ovid hath also in the ablative, *pectóribus tenus,* up to the stomach.

ANNOTATION.

Between these three prepositions *a*, *ab*, or *abs*, there is only this difference, that *a* is put before words beginning with a consonant, *A Pompeio, à milite*; and *ab* or *abs* before a vowel, or before a consonant difficult to pronounce, as *ab ancilla*; *ab rege*; *ab Jove*; *ab lege*; *ab Sylla*; *abs Tullio*; *abs quolibet*.

Absque, in comic poets, is taken for *sine*. *Absque eo foret*, Ter. But in prose we do not find it in that signification. Hence it is better Latin to say *Sine dubio*, without doubt, than *Absque dubio*.

RULE XXI.
Of prepositions which govern the accusative and the ablative.

Sub, super, in, subter, govern two cases, but with different significations.

EXAMPLES.

The above four prepositions generally require
1. The ablative, when there is no motion signified from one place to another. 2. The accusative, when a motion is signified. 3. They also govern very frequently the case of the preposition for which they are put, and into which they may be resolved.

SUB.

1. *Sub nómine pacis bellum latet*, under the name of peace, war is concealed. *Quo deinde sub ipso, ecce volat calcémque terit*, Virg. upon which he runs, and treads close to his heels. Where *sub* governs the ablative, because this motion does not signify a change from one place to another.

2. *Postésque sub ipsos nitúntur grádibus*, Virg. they mount by steps up to the door. Where *sub* governs the accusative, because it signifies a change from one place to another.

3. *Sub horam pugnæ*, instead of *circa*, about the hour of battle. *Sub noctem cura recúrrit*, Virg. anxiety returns towards night.

SUPER.

1. *Super fronde víridi*, upon the green leaf.

2. *Super Garamántas & Indos, próferet impérium*, Virg. he will extend his empire beyond the inhabitants of the interior Libya and the Indians.

3. *Super hac re*, instead of *de*, concerning this matter. *Super ripas flúminis effúsus*, Liv. instead of *secúndum*,

dum, stretched along the banks of the river. *Super cœnam occísus*, instead of *inter*, killed while he was at supper.

In.

1. *Deambuláre in foro*, to walk in the market. *Fundo volvúntur in imo*, they go to the bottom. With the ablative, because the motion is not made from one place to another, but in the same place.

2. —— *Evólvere posset—In mare se Xanthus*, Virg. might discharge itself into the sea. Where the accusative is put, because it signifies a change of place.

3. *Eustáthius in Homêrum*, instead of *super*, Eustathius in his comment upon Homer. *In hanc senténtiam multa dixit*, he said many things to this purpose. *In horam*, instead of *ad*, for an hour. *Amor in pátriam*, instead of *erga*, the love of one's country. *In præsens & in futúrum*, Liv. for *ad* or *quoad*, for the present and the future.

Subter.

1. *Ferre libet subter densa testúdine casus*, Virg. they are pleased to withstand all the efforts of the enemy under a thick penthouse. *Campi qui subter mœ'nia*, Stat. the fields under the ramparts.

2. *Augústi subter fastigia tecti, Æneam duxit*, Virg. she conducted Æneas into a magnificent palace.

ANNOTATION.

We find likewise that IN hath an accusative where there is no motion, as Manutius, Sanctius, and Vossius, have observed after Gellius, Priscian, and others: *numero mihi in mentem fuit*, Plaut. *Esse in magnum honorem*, Ter. to be greatly honoured. *Esse in amicitiam ditionemque populi Romani*, Cic. *Cùm vestros portus in prædonum fuisse potestatem sciatis*, Cic. *Res esse in vadimonium cœpit*, Id. *In potestatem habere*, Cæs. and Sal. *In tabulas perscribere*, Cic. *Ligneæ soleæ in pedes indutæ*, Id.

It is also found with an ablative, where motion is signified, *Venit in senatu*, Cic. *Cùm divertissem à Cumis in Vestiano*, Cic. *In conspectu meo audet venire*, Phædr. *Venit in regione*, Manil. apud Scalig. *Quà in Cælio monte itur*, Varro.

And hence it is without doubt that we find several verbs which govern both the accusative and the ablative with *in*; *incidere in æs*, Liv. *incidere in ære*, Cic. Plin. & alii, contrary to Valla's opinion. *Abdere se in tenebris*, Cic. *in domum*, Cic. *in occultum*, Cæs. *in præsentia omittere*, Cic. *in præsens tempus & in aliud omittere*, Hor. *in equum Trojanum includere*, Cic. *in fabulâ inclusa*, Id. *in dialogos includere*, Id. *in tectorio arioli includam*, Id. *imaginem includit in clypeo*, Id.

SUBTER governs either the accusative or the ablative in the same signification; *Plato iram in pectore, cupiditatem subter præcordia locavit*, Cic. Plato placed anger in the breast, and voluptuous desires in the entrails; *Subter pineta Galesi. Et subter captos arma sedere duces*. This shews that there was hardly any certain rule for the government of those four prepositions among the antients. The reader may consult Linacer upon this article, of which he treats at large.

It is also to be observed that we meet with *super*, as well as *in* and *ex*, with the genitive in some authors, which is only an imitation of the Greeks, *super pecuniæ, tutelæque suæ*, Paul. Jurisc. *Descriptio ex duodecim cœlestium signorum*, Vitruv.

CLAM, as we have observed, heretofore governed likewise an accusative, *Clam patrem, clam uxorem*; but now it hath only an ablative. Plautus has used it also with the dative, where it serves as an adverb. *Hoc fieri quàm magni referat mihi clam est*; that is, *mihi occultum est*.

That almost every government may be resolved by the prepositions.

We may further observe in this place, that the use of prepositions is so generally diffused through all languages, that there is scarce a government, phrase, or expression, but depends upon, or may be reduced to them, as may be easily shewn in every part of syntax.

In partitives; *Pauci de nostris cadunt*, Cæs.

In verbs of accusing; *Accusare de negligentia*, Cic.

In every other government of the genitive; *Fulgor ab auro*, Lucr. for *auri*. *Crepuit à Glycerio ostium*, Ter. for *Glycerii ostium*.

In the government of the dative; *Bonus ad cætera*, Liv. *Homo ad nullam partem utilis*, Cic. Which likewise shews very plainly that the dative denotes no more than the relation of attribution, since *utilis alicui rei*, is the same as *utilis ad aliquam rem*.

In the comparative; *Immanior ante alios omnes*, Virg.

In the superlative; *Acerrimum autem ex omnibus sensibus, esse sensum videndi*, Cic. *Ante alios pulcherrimus omnes*, Virg.

In nouns of plenty or want; *Liber à dilectis*, Cic.

In several particular verbs; *Celare de aliquo. Commonefacere de aliqua re. Ad properationem meam quiddam interest*, Cic. *In id jolùm student*, Quint.

In questions of place, even in names of cities; *Navis in Caieta parata est nobis*, Cic. See lower down, rule 25.

In questions of time; *In tempore ad eum veni; de nocte vigilare: regnare per tres annos.* See rule 26.

In nouns of price; *Si mercatus esset ad eam summam quam volueram*, Cic.

With gerunds; *In judicando; pro vapulando; ab absolvendum.*

With participles; *Pro derelicto habere*, Cic. and others in the same manner.

Rule XXII.
Of verbs compounded with a preposition.

1. *A verb compounded with a preposition hath the case belonging to the preposition.*
2. *And oftentimes the preposition is repeated.*

Examples.

1. The preposition preserves its force even in composition, so that the verbs with which it is compounded, take the case which belongs to the preposition, as *Adíre óppida*, to go to the cities. *Abíre óppido*, to go out of town. *Circumequitáre mœ́nia*, to ride round the town walls. *Amovére ánimum stúdio pueríli*, to divert his mind from puerile amusements, *Expéllere péctore*, to banish from the heart. *Excédere muros*, to go out of the walls, as coming from *extra*: or *excédere terrâ*, to go out of the country, as coming from *ex*.

2. But frequently the preposition is repeated; as *Nihil non considerátum exibat ex ore*, Cic. he said not one word but what was maturely considered. *Qui ad nos intempestivè ádeunt, molésti sæpe sunt*, those who come to us at an unseasonable time, are frequently troublesome. *A sole absis,* Cic. don't keep the sun from me.

Rule XXIII.
Of verbs that govern the accusative with *ad*.

A'ttinet, spectat, *and* pértinet, *require an accusative with the preposition* ad.

Examples.

These three impersonal verbs take an accusative with the preposition *ad*; as *A'ttinet ad dignitâtem*, this concerns your dignity. *Id ad te pértinet*, this belongs to you. *Hoc ad illum spectat*, this belongs to him? *Quid ad nos áttinet?* what is this to us? *Totum ejus consílium ad bellum mihi spectáre vidétur*, it seems that his whole thought is turned towards war.

Rule XXIV.
Of verbs which take two accusatives, or that have different governments.

1. *Verbs of warning,* 2. *Asking,* 3. *And cloath-*

cloathing, 4. *With* celo, 5. *And* dóceo, oftentimes govern the thing and the perfon in the accufative; or in fome other manner depend on the prepofition.

6. Interdíco *governs the thing in the ablative.*

EXAMPLES.

We include in this rule the verbs of different governments, and particularly thofe which take two accufatives, or which in fome other manner depend on the prepofition.

1. Verbs of warning with two accufatives. *Móneo te hanc rem,* I give you notice of this affair. *Iftud me admonéntes,* Cic. giving me notice of that.

The thing in the ablative with the prepofition. *Móneo te de hac re,* I give you notice of that. *Oro te ut Teréntiam moneátis de teftaménto,* Cic. I beg you will inform Terentia of the will.

The thing in the genitive. *Commonére áliquem miferiárum fuárum,* to remind a perfon of his miferies. *Grammáticos fui officii commonémus,* Plin. we put the grammarians in mind of their duty.

2. Verbs of afking, with two accufatives. *Te hoc beneficium rogo,* I beg this favour of you. *Pacem te pófcimus omnes,* Virg. we all fue for peace. *Popófci áliquem eórum qui áderant caufam differéndi,* Cic. I begged that fome members of the company would propofe the fubject of debate.

The perfon in the ablative with the prepofition. *Hoc à me pofcit, flagitat,* he afks, or begs that of me. *Scifcitári, percontári ab áliquo,* to afk a perfon.

PETO is more ufual in the latter form, and is feldom found with two accufatives. *Peto à te véniam,* I afk your pardon. We fay alfo *peto tibi,* I afk for you. *Miffiónem militibus pétere,* to afk a difcharge for foldiers. But then it is the dative of acquiring, or of the perfon.

3. Verbs of cloathing with two accufatives. In the vulgate bible, *Induit eum ftolam glóriæ,* he clad him in a robe of glory. *Quídlibet indútus,* Hor. dreffed any how. The

The person in the accusative, and the thing in the ablative. *Índuo te véste,* I put this garment on you.

The person in the dative, and the thing in the accusative. *Índuo tibi vestem,* I put this garment on you. *Exúere vestem alicui,* to undress a person.

4. CELO with two accusatives. *Celo te hanc rem,* I conceal this thing from you. *Ea ne me celet consuefêci filium,* Ter. I have accustomed my son to conceal nothing of all this from me.

The thing in the ablative with the preposition. *Celo te de hac re,* I will not tell you that.

The person in the dative. *Celáre áliquid alicui,* to conceal a thing from a person.

5. Verbs of teaching, with two accusatives. *Dóceo te grammáticam,* I teach you grammar. *Quæ te leges præceptáque fórtia belli—Erúdiit,* Stat. who taught you the laws and generous maxims of war.

The thing in the ablative with the preposition. *Qui de suo advéntu nos dóceant,* Cic. who may let us know of their coming.

6. INTERDÍCO governs the thing in the ablative. *Interdíco tibi domo meâ,* I forbid you my house. *Interdíco tibi aquâ & igni,* I forbid you the use of fire and water.

ANNOTATION.

Sanctius maintains that no verb can of itself govern two accusatives of different things at the same time, and that what we see here is only an imitation of the Greeks, who put this case almost every where, by supposing their preposition κατὰ, or περὶ, as we should say *circa, per, ob, secundum, propter, ad* or *quod ad*. For *doceo te grammaticam,* implies *secundum,* or *quod ad grammaticam,* and in the same manner the rest. Hence the passive of these verbs always retains the accusative which depends on the preposition. *Doceor grammaticam; eruditus Græcas literas,* Cic. *Galeam induitur,* Virg. *Inutile ferrum cingitur,* Id. *Rogari sententiam,* Cic.

In like manner we must explain the following passages by the preposition. *Magnam partem in his occupati sunt,* Cic. *Nostram vicem ultus est ipse sese,* Cic. *Multa gemens ignominiam plagásque superbi victoris,* Virg. *Quod te per genitorem oro,* Id. *Qui purgor bilem,* Hor. *Nunc id prodeo,* Ter. that is to say, *ob id,* or *propter id,* according to Donatus.

To this we must also refer what the grammarians have distinguished by the name of synecdoche, and may be called the accusative governed by a preposition understood. *Omnia Mercurio sim ls vocemque,* &c. Virg. *Expleri mentem nequit,* Id. *Nodôque sinus col-*

lecta ſtuentes, Id. Which is the ſame as, *Oculos ſuffuſa nitentes*, ſays Servius. *Creſſa genus Pholoë*, Virg. *Clarigenus*, Tac. *Micat auribus & tremit artus*, Virg. *Flores inſcripti nomina regum*, Id. *Eludo te annulum*, Plaut. Which occurs much oftener among the poets, though with the word *cætera* this figure has been uſed upon all occaſions. *Cætera prudens & attentus*, Cic. *Verùm cætera egregium*, Liv. *Lætum cætera*, Hor. *Argentum quod habes condonamus te*, Ter. in Phorm. *Habeo alia multa quæ nunc condonabitur*, Id. in Eunucho, according as Donatus, Politianus, Sanctius, Voſſius, Heinſius, and others read it, and as we find it in the MSS. ſo that we muſt underſtand, *ſecundùm quæ, ille condonabitur*. This ſeems to have eſcaped Julius Scaliger, when he finds fault with Eraſmus for reading it thus, pretending that it ſhould be *condonabuntur*, contrary to the meaſure of the verſe, and the authority of all copies whatever; and alledging for reaſon that *condonare aliquem argentum* is not Latin, whereas it is the very example of the Phormio, which Donatus expreſsly produces, to authoriſe this paſſage of the Eunuch.

It is alſo to be obſerved that we are not allowed to uſe indiſcriminately the different governments abovementioned. For it would not be right to ſay, *Conſulo te hæreditatem*, for *de hæreditate*. Cicero ſays, *Amicitiæ veteris commonefacere*, but never *amicitiam*. Though with the word *res* we ſay *admoneo, commonefacio te hujus rei*, or *hanc rem*, or *de hac re*. Therefore we muſt always abide by the practice of the pureſt authors.

Rule XXV.
Of the four queſtions of place.

1. *The queſtion* UBI *takes the ablative with* in, *or without* in; *and puts the names of towns of the firſt and ſecond declenſion, in the genitive.*

2. *The queſtion* QUO *takes* in *with the accuſative, and puts the names of towns in the accuſative without* in.

3. *The queſtion* QUA *takes the accuſative with* per, *or an ablative without a prepoſition.*

3. *The queſtion* UNDE *takes an ablative, with the prepoſitions* a, *or* ex; *and puts the names of towns in the ablative without the prepoſition.*

4. Rus *and* domus *are governed in the ſame manner as the names of towns.*

Examples.

We have here four queſtions of place under our conſideration.

1. Ubi, which denotes the place where one is. *Ubi eſt?* where is he? 2. Quò,

2. Quò, which denotes the place whither one goes. *Quo vadit?* where is he going to?

3. Qua, which signifies the place through which a person passeth. *Quà trânsiit?* which way did he go?

4. Unde, which denotes the place from whence a person comes. *Unde venit?* from whence comes he?

In all these questions we must first of all consider the preposition that belongs to them, and the case it governs.

Secondly, we are to take notice that small places, that is the proper names of towns and villages, and sometimes of islands, are generally put in the case of the preposition, without expressing it, though it be always understood. And the other nouns, whether they signify large places, that is, provinces or kingdoms, or whether they be appellatives, are generally put with the preposition, though the contrary sometimes happeneth.

Thirdly, we must observe that in all questions, these two nouns *rus* and *domus*, are always governed in the same manner, as if they were the proper names of towns.

Fourthly, when we are mentioning these questions, it is not necessary that the question *ubi*, *quò*, or any other should be expressed, but only that it be understood.

This being premised it is easy to retain the rules of these four questions.

1. Ubi takes the ablative with *in*. *Ambulat in horto*, he walks in the garden. *Vivit in Gallia, in urbe*, he lives in France, in the city.

Or the ablative only, *in* being understood, especially if they be names of small places. *Philippus Neápoli est, & Lentulus Puteolis*, Philip is at Naples, and Lentulus at Pozzuolo. *Degit Carthágine, Parísiis, Athénis*, he lives at Carthage, at Paris, at Athens. *Sum ruri*, Cic. *Sum rure*, Hor. I am in the country. For heretofore they said *rure* vel *ruri* in the ablative according to Charisius.

We must except those nouns which have the genitive in Æ or in I, that is, of the first or second declension, as *Romæ natus, Siciliæ sepúltus*, born at Rome, buried in Sicily. *Manére Lugdúni*, to stay at Lyons. *Esse domi*, to be at home. *Quantas ille res domi militiæque gésserit,*

gésserit, Cic. what great matters he performed both at home and in the field.

2. Quò takes *in* with the accusative, because it signifies motion, as *Quò próperas?* where are you going so fast? *In ædem B. Virginis,* to St. Mary's church. *In Africam,* to Africa.

In small places it is more usual to put the accusative alone, *in* being understood; as *Ire Parísios,* to go to Paris. *Proficísci Romam,* to go to Rome. *Ire rus,* to go to the country.

3. Qu A likewise takes the accusative with *per*; *Quâ iter fecísti?* which way did you travel? *Per A'ngliam* through England.

Or it will have the ablative only without the preposition, especially if they be names of small places. *Româ trânsiit,* he passed through Rome.

4. UNDE, joins the prepositions *ex* or *e*, or even *è* or *ab* to this same case: as *Revérsus ex agro, è cubículo* being returned from the fields, from the chamber. *Rédeo ex Itália, ex Sicília,* I come back from Italy, from Sicily. *Vénio à júdice,* I come from the judge's.

Or it takes an ablative only, if they be names of small places, the preposition being understood; as *Venit Româ, rure, domo, Lugdúno, Athénis,* he is returned from Rome, from the fields, from home, from Lyons, from Athens.

ANNOTATION.

Most grammarians observe this difference betwixt the names of towns and those of provinces, that the names of towns are put without the preposition in all questions, and the names of provinces with the preposition. Yet this is what the learned are not agreed upon, as may be seen in Sanctius, Scioppius, Vossius, and others because, say they, the antients have not always conformed to this practice, and grammarians are indeed the depositaries, but not the supreme lords or sovereigns of language.

Hence it is not only certain that the preposition is the real cause of the government, whether it be expressed or understood; but it is even frequently expressed in the name of small places, as on the contrary it is sometimes understood in the names of provinces, in all questions, as we shall make appear under the following heads.

The question UBI.

We find the names of towns and small places with the preposition: as *Naves longas in Hispali faciendas curavit,* Cæs. *In Alexandria,* Cic. *In domo mea,* Plin. Hor. *In domo Cæsaris unus vix fuit*
Cic.

Cic. *Maetrix & mater familias in una domo,* Ter. *Navis in Caieta est parata nobis & Brundusii,* Cic. where he joins the two governments. *Furtum factum in domo ab eo qui domi fuit,* Quintil.

On the contrary, we find the names of provinces in the genitive, like those of small places. *Siciliæ cum essem,* Cic. *Duos filios suos Ægypti occisos cognovit,* Val. Max. *Romæ Numidiæque facinora ejus commemorat,* Sall. Where he makes no difference between the name of the city and that of the province.

We find likewise the ablative without a preposition, *Natus regione urbis sexta,* Suet. *Domo me contineo,* Cic. *Nec densa nascitur humo,* Col. *Sustinet invidia, tristia signa domo,* Ovid. *Hunc ubi deficit abde domo,* Virg.

The question UNDE.

We meet with provinces in the ablative without the preposition. *Ægypto remeans,* Tacit. *Judæo profecti,* Suet. *Si Pompeius Italiâ cedit,* Cic. *Non rediit Cariâ,* Plaut.

But the names of towns with the preposition, are still more common. *A Brundusio,* Cic. *Ab Alexandria,* Cic. *Ab Athenis in Bœotiam ire,* Serv. Sulp. Where he makes no distinction betwixt the name of a town and that of a province, no more than Cicero, when he said, *Ab Epheso in Syriam profectus.* Livy hardly ever puts the names of towns in any question without the preposition. *Ab Româ legiones venisse nuntiatum est. Ab Antio legiones profectæ.* And an infinite number of others, which occur in every page of this author. It appears also from Suetonius, which Linacer and Sanctius have not neglected to observe, that the emperor Augustus, in order to render his stile more perspicuous and intelligible, never mentioned a place without making use of the prepositions.

The question QUA.

In regard to this question, we are to consider that *quâ* is derived from the ablative feminine, just as *quare* is said for *qua de re,* according to Vossius; therefore when we say, *quâ transiit?* we understand *parte, urbe, regione, provinciâ,* or the like. So that no wonder if we answer indifferently by the same case in all sorts of nouns. *Ibam forte viâ sacrâ,* Hor. *Totâ ambulat Româ,* Cic. *Totâ Asiâ vagatur,* Cic. *Multæ insidiæ mihi terrâ marique factæ sunt,* Cic. and in all these ablatives *in* is understood.

But if we answer with *per,* it is no extraordinary thing, since we have shewn that there is no government which may not be resolved by the prepositions.

The question QUÒ.

It is particularly in this question that authors indifferently use or omit the prepositions with all sorts of nouns.

Without the preposition they say, *Sardiniam venit,* Cic. *Cùm se Italiam venturum promisisset,* Cæl. *Ægyptum induxit exercitum,* Liv. *Bosphorum confugere,* Cic. *Epirum portanda dedit,* Val. *Proximum civitatem deducere,* Appul. But we must not be surprized at this; for since *quò,* according to Sanctius and Scioppius, is an antient accusative plural in *o,* the same as *ambo* and *duo,* which is still continued in *quocirca, quousque,* and *quoad,* as when we say, *quò vadis,* we understand *in* or *ad*; so we may answer by the accusative only, the preposition being understood.

They likewise use the names of towns with the preposition, *Consilium in Lutetiam Parisiorum transfert,* Cæs. *In Sicyonem efferre pecuniam,* Cic. Though a little before that he had said, *Projectus Argis Sicyonem,* 2. Off. *Cursus ad Brundusium,* Id. *In Messanum venire,* Id. *In Arpinum se abdere,* Id. also, *ubi vos delapsi demos, & in rura vestra fueritis,* Liv. *Ad doctas proficisci Athenas,* Propert. &c.

Now in regard to what is said, that *ad* signifies no more than near, and *in* within; and in like manner that *a* signifies near or hard by, and *ex* from within; this is generally true; when we would signify that something is situated, or done near or in a particular place, *habet exercitum ad urbem; habet hortos ad Tiberim.* But it is not generally true, when we are speaking of the question *quò*; and we shall find that Livy, and several others have indifferently used both ways of expressing. And so has Cicero too, when he says, *Te verò nolo, nisi ipse rumor jam raucus erit factus,* ad *Baias venire; erit enim nobis honestius videri venisse* in *illa loca ploratum potiùs quàm natatum,* lib. 9. epist. 2.

The amount of what may be said in regard to this distinction of the names of towns and provinces, is this, that in all probability those who studied the exactest purity of the Latin, while it was a living language, would fain establish it as a rule. Hence it is that upon Atticus's censuring Cicero for saying, *in Piræum,* Cicero alledges in his excuse that he had spoken of it, *non ut de oppido, sed ut de loco* (lib. 7. ep. 3.) Whereby it appears that this rule began to obtain, and that Cicero himself paid a regard to it, (let Scioppius say what he will) as to a thing that might contribute to the perspicuity of the language, by this distinction of the names of towns and provinces, though he has not always conformed to it. And we see something like this in the French tongue, in which the particle A denotes the small places, and EN the provinces, as *à Rome,* and *en Italie; à Paris* and *en France,* &c. For which reason it is always better to stick to this rule, though we cannot condemn a person that would swerve from it, and Quintilian's censure, who calls this a solecism, *Veni de Susis in Alexandriam,* lib. 1. c. 5. has very little foundation:

Therefore Servius on this passage of Virgil:
*Italiam fato profugus, Laviniáque venit
Littora,* Æn. 1.

having taken notice that the rules of grammar required prepositions to be joined to the names of provinces, but none to the names of towns, he adds, *Sciendum tamen usurpatum ab autoribus ut vel addant, vel detrahant præpositiones.* Where it appears that he does not particularly mention the poets, but all authors in general.

PARTICULAR OBSERVATIONS
on the question UBI.

Of the nouns which are put in the genitive in this question.

The reason why some particular names of towns are put in the genitive

genitive in this question, is because with the proper name we always understand the general noun in the ablative with its preposition; and therefore this genitive is governed by the noun understood; as *Est Romæ*, sup. *in urbe*. *Est Lugduni*, sup. *in oppido*. *Est domi*, sup. *in loco*, or *in horto*, or *in ædibus*; for *domus* signified the whole house, whereas *ædes* was in some measure an apartment or part of the house; hence Plautus, to express the whole at length, says, *Insectatur omnes per ædes domi*. Terence has put it also in the ablative; *Si quid opus fuerit, heus, domo me*; sup. *continebo*, I shall be at home, *Phorm.* Act. 2. sc. 2.

Now *domi* was not the only word they put in the genitive; for Cicero says, *Quantas ille res domi militiæque terrâ marique gesserit. Quibuscunque rebus vel belli, vel domi poterunt*: and the like. And Virgil, *Penitus terræ defigitur arbor*, for *in terrâ*. And Ovid, *terræ procumbere*, where we must understand another noun which governs this genitive, as *In solo terræ, in tempore belli*, and therefore the latter relates rather to questions of time.

Of nouns of the first declension in E.

Here a question may arise, whether these nouns ought to be put in the genitive like the rest of this declension. *Neque enim dicitur, negotiatur Mitylenes, sed Mitylenæ*, says Vossius in his grammar, where he seems to reject the genitive in *es* in this question. And Sanctius, whom we have followed, admits of this case only for nouns that make Æ or I in the genitive; and perhaps we shall find very few authorities of those other nouns, because generally speaking the ancients change them into A, in order to decline them according to the Latin termination. Nevertheless we find in Valerius Maximus, book 1. chap. 6. where he speaks of prodigies, *Cærites aquas sanguine mistas fluxisse*, that at Cærite there was a stream of water mixed with blood. Which makes Gronovius in his notes on Livy say, that in the 22d book, chap. 1. we should read, *Cæretes aquas sanguine mistas fluxisse*, where the other editions have *Cerete* nevertheless in the ablative. From whence one would think that both expressions might be admitted. Though the best way is to put them in the ablative, or to change those nouns into A, and put them in the genitive in Æ, *Mitylenæ* rather than *Mitylenes* or *Mitylene*, &c.

Concerning apposition.

Another question is, whether we ought to say, *Antiochiæ natus sum urbis celebris* by apposition, or *Antiochiæ natus sum urbe celebri*; but the former would be a solecism, says Vossius, whereas the latter may be said, and this phrase may be varied three different ways.

The first, by joining the preposition to the appellative, and putting the proper name in the genitive, as *Albæ constiterunt in urbe opportuna*, Cic. *In oppido Antiochiæ*, Cic. *In Amstelodami celebri emporio*, Vossius.

The second, by letting the proper name and the appellative be governed in the same case by the preposition; *In Amstelodami celebri emporio*, Voss. *Neapoli in celeberrimo oppido*, Cic.

The third, by understanding the preposition; *Antiochiæ loco nobili*, Cic. *Amstelodami celebri emporio*, Voss.

And if you would know the reason why the apposition is not admitted here in the genitive, for instance, *Amstelodami celebris emporii*, it is because the genitive being never governed but by another noun substantive, when we say *Est Romæ, vivit Amstelodami*, we understand *in urbe, in emporio*, or *oppido*, as hath been already observed; but if you put *urbis*, or *emporii, oppidi* in the genitive, you having nothing else to suppose that can govern it. And hence it is that with an adjective you never put the proper name in the genitive, *Est magnæ Romæ*, but in the ablative, *in magna Roma*, sup. *urbe*, in the great city of Rome. Because a thing being called great or small only comparatively to another, we cannot refer *great* to *Rome*, but to the word city; for otherwise it would seem to imply that there were two Romes, one great, the other little.

Now that this genitive is governed by a noun understood, and that this construction is right, Scaliger sheweth, because if we can say *oppidum Tarentinum*, surely we may also say, *oppidum Tarenti*; the possessive having always the same force as the genitive from which it is taken; hence in French it is generally rendered by the genitive, *Domus paterna, la maison de mon pere*; my father's house.

Concerning nouns of the third declension.

It is arguing very wrong, as Sanctius, Scioppius, and Vossius observe, to say that nouns of the third declension, and those of the plural number are put in the dative or in the ablative. For what relation is there between the government of place, which always depends on a preposition, and the dative, which is never governed by it, and which, as we have already made appear, denotes only the end, or the person, or the thing, to which another thing is referred and attributed? and though we find *Est Carthagini, Neapoli, ruri*, and the like, these are only old ablatives which, as hath been already mentioned, were heretofore every one of them terminated in *e* or in *i* in this declension. Therefore those who are more accustomed to the ablative in *e*, ought always to put it here, as Cicero does, *Est Sicyone, sepultus Lacedæmone*; *Carthagine natus*, and the like. There is only the word *rus*, whose ablative in *i* custom has rendered familiar in this question. And if any one should doubt whether *ruri* be an ablative, he may see in Charisius, lib. 1. that *rus* makes in the ablative *rure* or *ruri*; and that *Ruri agere vitam* in Ter. is an ablative and not a dative. Plautus has used it even in the other questions; *Veniunt ruri rustici*, in Mostel. Act. 5. sc. 1. the peasants come from the country.

Observations on compound Nouns.

Compound nouns intirely conform to the rule of the other proper names, though some grammarians have made a doubt of it. Thus we say *Novum Comum ducere Colonos*, Suet. *Conventus agere Carthagine nova. Quo die Theano Sidicino est profectus*, Cic. &c. And therefore we are to say, *Ire Montempessulanum, Portum petere Calatensem*, and the like.

Rule

Rule XXVI.
Of the questions of time, measure, and distance.

Time, distance, and measure, may be put either in the accusative, or the ablative; but the precise term of time is put in the ablative only.

EXAMPLES.

We may here include five things. 1. The space of time: 2. The space of place, or distance: 3. The precise term of time: 4. The precise or exact place: 5. The noun of measure; each of which may be put either in the accusative or the ablative, which are always governed by a preposition expressed or understood, and the preposition is more usually expressed with the accusative. But the precise term of time, namely that which answers the question *quando*, is put oftener in the ablative only.

1. The space *or* the duration of time, which answers to the question *quámdiu*, or *quamdúdum*, how long. *Vixit per tres annos*, or *tres annos*, or *vixit tribus annis*, sup. *in*, he has lived three years. *Quem ego bódie toto non vidi die*, Ter. whom I have not seen to day. *Te annum jam audiéntem Cratíppum*, Cic. sup. *per*, you that have attended Cratippus's lectures a whole year. *Intra annos quatuórdecim tectum non subiérunt*, Cæs. they have been without any cover these fourteen years. *Nonagínta annos natus*, sup. *ante*, he is ninety years old; he has been ninety years in this world.

Hereto we may refer those phrases where they use *ad* or *in*, but it is in a particular sense: *Si ad centésimum annum vix vixísset*, Cic. if he had lived to be a hundred years old. *In diem vívere*, Cic. to live from hand to mouth.

2. The space or distance of place is more usual in the accusative, as *Locus ab urbe dissitus quátuor milliaria*, a place distant four miles from the town; *Hercýniæ-sylvæ latitúdo novem diérum iter expedíto patet*, Cæs. the breadth of the Hercynian forest is a nine days journey; where we must understand *ad*, or *per*, though the preposition is seldom used. But sometimes they put the ablative; as *bídui spátio abest ab eo*, he is at the distance of two days journey from him.

3. The precise term of time, that is when we answer the question *quando*, is generally put in the ablative; *Superióribus diébus veni in Cumánum*, Cic. a few days ago I came to Cuma. *Quicquid est bíduo sciémus*, Cic. sup. *in*. Whatever it is, we shall know it in two days.

And in the same manner with *ante*, or *post*; as *Fit paucis pòst annis*, Cic. it happened a few years after. *Déderám perpáucis antè diebus*, I had given to him a few days before.

Sometimes the accusative is used with *ante* or *post*; *Paucos ante menses*, Suet. a few months before. *Aliquot post annos*, Cic. some months after. Which happens even with some other prepositions. *Ad octávum caléndas in Cumánum veni*, Cic. I arrived at Cuma the eighth day before the calends.

Likewise with the adverb *círciter*. *Nos círciter caléndas* (sup. *ad*) *in Formiáno érimus*, Cic. we shall be at Formia towards the calends. But with *abhinc* we join indifferently the accusative or the ablative, *Abhinc annos quingéntos*, Cic. sup. *ante*, five hundred years ago. *Abhinc annis quíndecim*, Cic. sup. *in*, fifteen hundred years ago. And this adverb in pure authors, always denotes the time past; whereas for the future they make use of *post* or *ad*: *Post sexénnium*, or *ad sexénnium*, six years hence.

4. The precise place. *Ad tértium lápidem*, Liv. three miles off. *Ad quintum milliáre*, Cic. five miles off. Sometimes they put the ablative only, and suppose *in*. *Cécidit tértio ab urbe lápide*, he fell three miles out of town.

5. The measure. *Muri Babylónis erant alti pedes ducéntos, lati quinquagínta*, sup. *ad*: The walls of Babylon were two hundred feet high, and fifty broad. *Dic quibus in terris—Tres páteat cœli spatiúm non ámpliùs ulnas*, Virg. tell me in what part of the world it is, that the sky is not above the breadth of three yards. But measure may be referred to the distance, of which above.

ANNOTATION.

A particular measure may be put sometimes also in the genitive, but this by supposing a general noun by which the other is governed, ed, as *Areolæ longæ pedum denûm*, Col. fup. *menfura, fpatio,* or *longitudine*. *Pyramide. latæ pedum feptuaginta quinûm,* fup. *latitudine,* Plin. *Altæ centum quinquagenûm,* fup. *altitudine,* Plin.

Rule XXVII.
Of the comparative and of partitives.

1. *Comparative nouns require the ablative cafe,*
2. *And partitives the genitive:*
3. *Hence the fuperlative degree governs a genitive likewife.*

Examples.

1. The comparative ought always to have the ablative of the noun, with which it forms the comparifon, whether it be exprefled or underftood; as *Fórtior eft patre fílius,* the fon is ftronger than the father. *Virtus opíbus mélior,* virtue is better than riches.

But fometimes this cafe is not exprefled, as when we fay *tríftior* (fup. *sólito*) fomewhat forrowful, that is a little more forrowful than ufual.

2. All partitive nouns, that is, which fignify part of a greater number, govern the genitive; *Octávus fapiéntum,* the eighth of the fages. *Unus Gallórum,* one of the French. *Dexter oculórum,* the right eye. And in the fame manner *álius, áliquis, alter, nemo, nullus, quis,* and the like. *Quis ómnium?* which of them all? &c.

3. Hence the fuperlative governs a genitive likewife, becaufe it is a partitive, as *Philofophórum máximus,* the greateft of philofophers. *Virginum fapientíffima,* the wifeft of virgins, or among virgins.

In this fenfe the comparative alfo governs this fame cafe; as *Fórtior mánuum,* the ftrongeft of the two hands: and in like manner the pofitive, as *Séquimur te fancte deórum,* we follow you, who are the holieft of the Gods.

ANNOTATION.

This rule includes two parts, one of the comparative, and the other of the partitive, under which the fuperlative is comprehended.

Of the comparative.

In order to underftand the government of the comparative, we have only to confider what Sanctius hath obferved; that in all languages, the force of the comparifon is generally included in a particle. Thus

Thus we shall see that as in French the particle Qu E *than* performs this office, Plus *saint* Que, holier *than*; Plus *grand* Que, greater *than*; so the Hebrews (who have no comparative degree) make use of מן *min*. The Greeks frequently of H, the Spaniards of Mas, and the Latins of Quam, *præ* or *pro*, as we shall shew hereafter.

Thereby we see that the comparative of itself governs no case, and ought to be considered merely as a noun, which adding some force to the signification of the positive, may be resolved by the same positive and by the adverb *magis*. *Doctior*, that is *magis doctus*, &c.

And this is what has given occasion to those elegant phrases, which the grammarians are at a loss to account for; *Litteris quàm moribus instructior. Similior patri quàm matri. Fortior est quàm sapientior*: he has more courage than learning. And in Cic. *Per illam, inquam, dexteram non in bellis & in præliis : quàm in promissis & fide firmiorem*, pro Dejot.

But if there be an ablative of comparison, it is always governed by the preposition *præ* or *pro* understood. This preposition is even sometimes expressed, not only after the comparative, as when Appuleius says, *Sed unus præ cæteris & animo fortior & ætate juvenior & corpore validior exurgit alacer*: and in another place, *Unus è curia senior præ cæteris*: and Q. Curtius, *Majorem quàm pro statu sonum edebat*: And Pliny, *Me minoris factum præ illo* : but moreover after other nouns, or even after verbs, as *Præ nobis beatus*, Cic. *Hic ego illum contemsi præ me*, Ter. *Cunctáne præ campo Tiberino sordent*, Hor. *Ladum et jocum fuisse dices præut hujus rabies quæ dabit*. Ter. in Eun. and such like. Where it is obvious that the whole force of the comparison is included in those particles.

Hence as it is only the effect of custom, that they are generally suppressed after the comparative, it happens also that they are sometimes suppressed after the other nouns, where they are understood nevertheless; which evidently shews that it is not a thing quite particular to the comparative, as *Nullus est hoc meticulosus æquè*, Plaut. for *præ hoc*. *Alius Lysippo*, Hor. that is, *præ Lysippo*, for *quàm Lysippus*, according to Sanctius. And the same may be said of the rest, concerning which the reader may see what we shall say further in the remarks, chapter of conjunctions.

It is by this principle we ought also to resolve all those comparisons, which by grammarians are called oblique or improper, when they are between things of a different nature ; *Ditior opinione* ; *cogitatione citiùs*, &c. always understanding the preposition, *pro*, as Cicero, and others sometimes express it: *Plus etiam quàm pro virili parte obligatum puto*, Cic. *Major quàm pro numero hominum editur pugna*, Liv.

It is likewise by this principle that we ought to answer those, who fancy the comparative is sometimes put for the positive, as when we say, *tristior, sollicitior, audacior*, somewhat sorrowful, somewhat solicitous, somewhat bold. For even in these examples, the comparative hath its natural signification, and supposeth the ablative after it, as *tristior*. sup. *solito*. *Sollicitior*, sup. *æquo*, &c. And if then it seems rather to import diminution than augmentation, this is an effect, not of the comparative, but of the ablative under-

understood, because if it were joined to another noun, it would have quite a different force, though it continued always the same; as *tristior perditis, follicitior miseris*, &c.

Difficulties in regard to the comparative.

When the reason of these governments is once understood, it is easy to solve all the little difficulties of grammarians upon this article. As when they say, that the comparative is not put with the ablative, but with the genitive, when the comparison is between two things only. For since the comparative of itself governs neither the genitive nor the ablative, doubtless it is indifferent to either case on these occasions. Thus Cæsar says: *Ex propositis duobus consiliis, explicatius videbatur, ut,* &c.

It is also an error to say that the comparative never institutes a comparison but between two things only, when it governs the genitive. For notwithstanding that this is perhaps the most usual practice, yet there are a hundred examples to the contrary: as when Cicero says, *Cæterarum rerum præstantior erat,* as quoted by Saturnius; and Horace, *O major juvenum,* in Arte: and Pliny, *Animalium fortiora quibus crassior est sanguis.* And Q. Curtius, lib. 9. *In oculis duo majora omnium navigia submersa sunt:* and in the sixth book, *Cleander priores eorum intromitti jubet:* and Plaut. in Capt. *Non ego nunc parasitus sum, sed regum rex regalior.* And Pliny, *Adolescentiores apum.* Which is only a partition that may be made between two, or an infinite number of things, if you please.

Therefore Valla, and those who have followed him, are in the wrong to object against these expressions of scripture. *Major horum est charitas. Minor fratrum,* &c. *Eo quod esset honorabilior omnium,* which comes from St. Jerome himself in his translation of Daniel. For these phrases are not only very good Latin, but moreover have the advantage of coming nearer to the Greek, which makes use of a genitive after the comparative.

But it is a different thing, when we find in Pliny, for example; *Omnium triumphorum lauream adepte majorem:* and in an epistle of Lentulus's among those of Cicero; *Naves onerarias, quarum minor nulla erat duûm millium amphorarum.* For *laurea* can make no part with *triumphi,* no more than *navis* with *duo millia:* for which reason it cannot be resolved by *inter.* But it is an ellipsis that supposeth the same word, on which the comparison falls, repeated in the ablative; as *Lauream majorem laureâ omnium triumphorum; naves, quarum nulla minor erat* navi *duûm millium amphorarum.* And there are likewise examples hereof in the Greek, as Ἐγὼ δὲ ἔχω τὴν μαρτυρίαν μείζω τῦ Ἰωάνν. *Joan.* 5. 36. *Ego autem habeo testimonium majus Joannis*; that is, *majus testimonio Joannis.* And in like manner the rest.

It is no less a mistake in the grammarians to pretend that *quisque* is never put but with the superlative, and in L. Valla to assert that we ought to say, *Imbecillima quæque animalia,* or that Lactantius did wrong in saying, *Imbecilliora & timidiora quæque animalia*; since Cicero himself hath, *Quisque gravior homo atque honestior.* And Quintilian,

Quintilian, *Pedes quique temporibus validiores.* We likewise find *quisque* with the positive, *Invalidus quisque,* Tac. *Bonus quisque liber,* Plin.

It is also a mistaken notion that the particle *quàm,* always requireth the same case before as after it: for we should not chuse to say, *Utor Cæsare æquiore quàm Pompeio,* but *quàm est Pompeius,* as in Cic. *Dixit se apertè munitiorem ad custodiendam vitam suam fore, quàm Africanus fuisset.* True it is that when a nominative precedeth, another nominative ought to follow, *Cicero est doctior quàm Sallustius*; and that if there be an accusative before, you may put an accusative after, *Ut tibi multo majori quàm Africanus fuit, me non multo minorem quàm Lælium adjunctum esse patiare,* Cic. *Ego callidiorem hominem quàm Phormionem vidi neminem,* Ter. because then the verb is understood twice, as if it were. *Ego neminem vidi callidiorem, quàm vidi Phormionem.* But with another verb we may likewise say, *Ego callidiorem vidi neminem, quàm Phormio est.*

The Comparative also occurs sometimes with the adverb *magis*; *Magis hoc certo certius,* Plaut. *Hoc magis est dulcius,* Id. *Magis invidia quàm pecunia locupletior,* Val. Max. *Qui magis optato queat esse beatior ævo?* Virg. in Culice. Which is become a kind of pleonasmus, as will appear hereafter, when we come to speak of figures. But we do not find it with *per,* except it is derived from a verb, and taken in the same sense as its verb. Thus we shall say with Cicero, *Perquisitius, pervagatior*: with Hor. *Perlucidior,* and the like: because we say, *Perquiro, pervagor, perluceo*; but we should not say, *Perurbanior, perdifficilior, permelior,* though we say, *Perurbanus, perbonus, perdifficilis*; and even in the superlative, *Peroptimus, perdifficillimus,* &c.

Of prior *and* primus.

We must not mind what Donatus, Priscian, Diomedes, L. Valla, Agrœtius, and others assert, that *prior* is said only of two and *primus* of many. *Cunctis prior Cadmeïus Heros,* Stat. *Prior omnibus Idas prosilit,* Id. *Qui prior aliis est.* Varro apud Aul. Gel. and the like. And the true reason of this is what Julius Scaliger has observed, that on those occasions, the whole multitude is considered as in two divisions, of which the former only makes one part, and the latter another.

Of Plus.

Plus is also a comparative, as we have observed in the declensions, p. 106. and there can be no doubt of it, since it institutes a comparison between things. But in regard to its government there are some who pretend to say that it governs four cases, the nominative, the genitive, the accusative, and the ablative.

And yet if it be joined with the nominative, it is no mark of government, but of concord, because it is an adjective. As when Pliny says, *Nec plus tertia pars eximatur mellis.* And Cicero, *Ut hoc nostrum desiderium ne plus fit annuum.* And Sanctius, *Nemo uno plus præmium expectato:* which he maintains is good Latin, against the opinion of those who found fault with him for it, and pretended that he should have said *plus uno præmio.*

And

And if it be joined with the ablative, as in Cicero, *Quum plus uno verum esse non possit*: and in another place, *Alterum certe non potest, ut plus unâ vera sit (opinio.)*. In Val. Max. *Uno plus Hetrusci cadunt*. In Cicero, *hoc plus ne rogum facito*. In Livy, *Ab utraque parte sexcentis plus equitibus cecidit*, &c. Then this ablative is governed in the same manner as the other comparatives, by the preposition understood.

Every where else it has no government, no more than *minus* and *amplius*. *Intervalla fere paulo plus aut minus pedum tricenûm*, ad Heren. where the genitive is governed by the name of distance *intervalla*. *Plus virium habet alius alio*, Ter. where the genitive *virium* is governed by *negotium* understood, *Plus negotium virium habet*; and the ablative *alio*, by the comparative *plus*, *præ* being understood. *Plus quingentos colaphos infregit mihi*, Ter. where the accusative is governed by the verb *infreg't*. In the same manner in Cæsar, *Quum ipsi non ampliùs quingentos equites haberent*.

And then they are taken as adverbs, though to say the truth they are real nouns that are put in the accusative, by virtue of a preposition understood, *Secundùm plus aut minus*, or *ad plus aut minus*, &c the latter coming from the comparative *minor & hoc minus*, in the same manner as *amplius*, from *amplior et hoc amplius*. *Plus annum obtinere provinciam*, Cic. that is, *ad plus tempus quàm ad annum*, &c. Hence they are joined extremely well with the nominative and the verb in the plural. *Romani non plus sexcenti cecideant*, Liv. that is, *sexcenti, non ad plus negotium*. And thus in Cæsar, *Eo die milites sunt minus septingenti desiderati*, 7. B. Gal. *Naves amplius octingentæ uno erant visæ tempore*, Id. lib. 5. See the remarks, chap. of adverbs and conjunctions.

Of the partitive in general.

In every partition, the genitive is governed by what we commonly understand *ex numero*, or by the noun substantive a second time, whether this partition be made with the positive or the comparative, of which we have given examples above, or with the superlative. For *Virginum sapientissima* implies, *Virgo virginum sapientissima*, or *Sapientissima ex numero virginum*: you have examples of both in this passage of Pliny; *Capreæ & Coturnices, animalia ex numero animalium placidissima*.

For which reason when the substantive is of another gender than the genitive plural, we may make the adjective agree with either, *Leo est animalium fortissimum*, or *fortissimus* (though the latter is more usual) for in the former we understand *animal*, with which *fortissimum* agrees; and in the latter we understand *ex numero*, as if one was to say, *Leo fortissimus ex numero animalium*. Thus Cicero has expressed himself, *Indus qui est fluviorum maximus*. And Pliny, *Boves animalium soli et retrò ambulantes pascuntur*: and in another place, *Hordeum frugum omnium mollissimum est*. See what is said lower down about syllepsis, when we treat of figures.

Of the superlative in general.

The superlative, as Sanctius sheweth extremely well, does not properly form a comparison, this being proper only to the comparative:

parative: and therefore since they resolved to distinguish three degrees in the nouns, it would have been much better to call them degrees of signification than of comparison. As when I say, *Gratæ mihi fuerunt litteræ tuæ, et Gratissimæ mihi fuerunt*, there is no more comparison in one than the other, but only an increase of signification in the latter: which does not hinder us from putting the superlative indifferently in the first place, when the subject deserves it. As, for instance, speaking of the mouths of the Nile, it may be very well to say, *Primum ostium magnum*, or I may say, *primum maximum, secundum majus, tertium adhuc majus*, &c. Where it is obvious that the comparative sometimes signifies more than the superlative, because it establishes a comparison with the superlative itself.

In this manner Cicero has expressed himself, *Ego autem hoc sum miserior quàm tu quæ es miserrima*, ad Terent. And in another place, *Persuade tibi te mihi esse charissimum, sed multo fore chariorem, si*, &c. So that though we may say that the superlative signifies the same thing as increase or excess, yet it is a mistake to think that it always expresseth the supreme degree. Thus when Virgil saith:

Danaûm fortissime gentis─────Tydide;

he did not mean that Diomedes was more brave than Achilles, or the bravest of his countrymen, but only very brave amongst his countrymen. This is extremely well expressed by the French particle *tres* which comes from *trois*, and has the same effect as if one was to say *ter fortis*, just as Virgil says,

O térque quatérque beati. And the Greeks τρισόλβιος for ὀλβιώτατος, very happy.

And if we put *le plus*, the most, *le plus genereux des Grecs*, the most brave of all the Greeks; *le plus sçavant des Romains*, the most learned of the Romans, though this may seem to import some sort of comparison, yet it is rather a partition than a real comparison.

Difficulties in regard to the superlative.

Hereby it appears that nothing hinders the superlative from being very properly joined with a noun universal (though some grammarians affirm the contrary) either out of partition, as *Omni gradu amplissimo dignissimus*, or even in partition, as *Dii isti Segulio male faciant homini nequissimo omnium qui sunt, qui fuerunt, qui futuri sunt*, Cic. And in Catullus speaking of Cicero:

Disertissime Romuli nepotum
Quot sunt quotque fuere, Marce Tulli, &c.

The superlative may be likewise put with the exclusive particles, which seem to require a comparative; *Ægyptus aliarum regionum calidissima est*, Macrob. *Cæterorum fugacissimi*, Tac. It is put with *omnis*: as *Omnes tenuissimas particulas atque omnia minima*, Cic. *Homini nequissimo omnium*, Cic.

It is also joined with other particles, which likewise augment their signification, as we have already shewn in regard to *per, peroptimus*, &c. It is even joined with *perquam*; *Perquam maximo exercitu*, Curt. We say also, *Dolorem tam maximum*, Cic. *Rei tam maximè*

maximè necessariæ tanta injuria. Id. *Longè improbissimus,* Id. *Multo mihi jucundissimus,* Id. *Oratio satis pulcherrima quæ inscribitur pro Q. Ligario,* Pompon. J. C. *Id. apprimè rectissimè dicitur,* Cic. de fin. as Saturnius reads it, as well as Robert Stephen in his thesaurus, Malaspina, and Gruterus's edition: though others read *rectè* instead of *rectissimè.* *Maximè pessima,* Colum. *Maximè humanissimi,* A. Gel. *Ante alios pulcherrimus.* Virg. *Sive hanc aberrationem à dolore delegerim quæ maximè liberalissima, doctóque homine dignissima,* Cic. and the like.

It is used in comparisons or partitions of opposite things, as *Homo non bipedum modò, sed quadrupedum impurissimus,* Cic. Which shews with how little reason L. Valla has censured Macrobius for saying, *Age, Servi, non solum adolescentum qui tibi æquævi sunt, sed senum quoque doctissime.*

It is also made use of in speaking of two things only, *Numitori qui erat stirpe maximus regnum legat,* says Livy, though there were only two sons, he and Amulius. *Ultri potissimum consulendum,* Cic. and others of the like sort.

In short we shall find that most of Valla's and Despauter's observations on this subject are false, and owing only to their not having sufficiently considered the nature of things, nor dived into the real causes of the Latin tongue.

RULE XXVIII.

Of the verbs and nouns which govern an ablative, or a genitive, the ablative being understood.

1. *Verbs of accusing, absolving, and condemning require an ablative or a genitive.*
2. *Verbs or nouns that signify plenty or want, govern these same cases:*
3. *As do also several adjectives.*

EXAMPLES.

All these nouns and verbs take an ablative of the most general words; as *Re, actióne, pœnâ, causâ, culpâ, crimine,* and the like, which is always governed by a preposition understood: or supposing some of these ablatives, they take another noun in the genitive, which is governed thereby.

1. Those of accusing: *Accusári criminibus,* to be accused of crimes. *Arcéssere majestátis,* to impeach of high treason.

Those of absolving, or acquitting; *Absólvere crimine,* to acquit of a crime. *Absólvere improbitátis,* to acquit of dishonesty. *Liberátus culpâ,* discharged from a fault.

Those

'Thofe of condemning *Condémnat cápitis*, he condemns him to death. *Damnári eódem crímine*, to be condemned for the fame crime. *Tenéri repetundárum*, fup. *pecuniárum*, to be convicted of extortion. *Damnári amícum fcéleris*, fup. *re*, or *actióne*, to charge a friend with a crime. And the reft in the fame manner.

ANNOTATION.

Sometimes the prepofition may be expreffed ; as *Damnatus de vi, de majeftate*, Cic. *Accufare de epiftolárum negligentia*, Cic. Wherein we muft be intirely determined by cuftom ; for we fhould not fay, *Accufatus de fcelere* or *de crimine* ; but *fceleris*, or *fcelere, criminis*, or *crimine*: Neither are we indifferently to put all forts of nouns in the genitive or the ablative, with all forts of verbs, but we are to confider how the ancients fpoke.

Plenty or want.

2. Nouns of plenty take the fame cafes as the preceding verbs, *Lócuples pecúniæ*, rich in money. *Fæcúnda virtútum paupértas*, poverty is fruitful in virtue. *Cumulátus omni laude*, extolled to the fky. *Pródigus æris*, lavifh of money. *Compos voti*, who has obtained his wifh.

Likewife thofe of want or privation ; *O'mnium egénus*, deftitute of every thing. *Inánis omni re útili*, void of every thing that is good. *Ratióne deftitútus*, void of reafon. *Vácuus virtúte ánimus*, a mind devoid of virtue. *Caffus lúminis, vel lúmine*, deprived of light. *Liber religióne ánimus*, a mind free from all fcruple. *Captus óculis, mente, aúribus*, &c. Who has loft his fight, his underftanding, his hearing, &c. *Confectus ætáte*, worn out with age. *Sol defectus lúmine*, the fun being eclipfed. *Præditus fingulári virtute*, adorned with fingular virtue. Where it is to be obferved that all the latter choofe rather to have the ablative, becaufe it is their natural conftruction.

Verbs of plenty or want prefer likewife moft generally the ablative.

Thofe of plenty, as *Abundáre ingénio*, to abound in wit. *Afflúere ómnibus bonis*, to abound with all forts of bleffings. *Difflúere ótio*, to be loft in idlenefs. *Satiári pánibus*, to have his belly full of bread. *Oneráre probris*, to load with abufe.

Thofe of want, as *Vacáre pudore*, to be without fhame.

shame. *Nudáre præsídio*, to deprive of the defence of. *Viduáre urbem cívibus*, to unpeople a town. *Exhauríre aquis*, to draw off the water.

There are some however that indifferently admit or either the genitive or the ablative, as *Complére erróris*, to fill with error. *Complére luce*, to fill with light. *Indigére consílii, et consílio*, to want advice.

Some other Adjectives.

3. Some other adjectives also assume the same government, as *Aliénus, expers, immúnis, conténtus, dignus, indígnus*, &c.

Aliénum dignitátis or *dignitáte*, or even *à dignitáte*: Cic. (the two last are most usual) repugnant to dignity. *Conténtus libertátis*, Liv. satisfied with his liberty. *Parvo conténta natúra*, Cic. nature is satisfied with little. And here the ablative is most usual.

Dignus laudis, or *laude* most usual; worthy or praise. *Súscipe curam & cogitatiónem dignissimam tuæ virtútis*, Balbus ad Cic. Form a plan to yourself becoming your dignity. In like manner, *Indígnus avórum*, unworthy of those ancestors.

Expers metûs or *metu* (the former most usual) void of fear.

Immúnis belli, Virg. *Immúnis militiâ*, Liv. exempt from military service, and the like.

ANNOTATION.

Here the Latins have borrowed the genitive of the Greeks, who understand their preposition *ἐκ*, of. Hence almost all vulgar languages, which generally follow the simplest and most natural construction, use a preposition on this occasion; thus the Italians say *Plene di vino*, as the French say, *Plein de vin*, full of wine. But in order to account for this government in Latin, we may understand a general noun, *copia, negotium, res*, &c. which governs the other in the genitive, so that *Vacuus curárum*, is the same as *vacuus re curarum*, for *vacuus curis* : *dignus laudis*, is for *re laudis*, and the rest in the same manner, just as Phædrus hath *res cibi*, for *cibus* ; and Plautus, *res voluptatum*, for *voluptates*.

And then this ablative must likewise be governed by a preposition understood, for *vacuus curis*, is the same as *à curis*. *Laude dignus*, for *de laude*, worthy of praise, &c. Therefore the purest authors frequently use the preposition: *Hæc à custódibus militum vacabant loca*, Cæf. *Locus à fruménto copiósus*, Cic. *De nugis referti libri*. Cic. *Liber à delíciis*, Id. *Inops à verbis, ab amicis*, Id. Hence, *Egeo pecuniis*, is just as if you said, *Egea de pecuniis*, I have need of.

Of the noun OPUS.

By this it appears that the noun *opus*, for which so many rules and different observations have been made, may be very well reduced to this rule, if it be the same thing to say, *Egeo nummis, & opus est mihi nummis*, where we constantly suppose the *de*.

But upon a nearer enquiry into the matter, we shall find that this noun is never any thing else but the substantive *opus, operis*, work, affair, business; just as the Greeks say οὐδὲν ἔργον ἔστιν, *nihil opus est*.

So that this noun does not properly import an absolute necessity, but some sort of conveniency, or what one has business with. Even Cicero makes a distinction between *opus* and *necesse*; *legem curiatam consuli ferri opus esse, necesse non esse*, lib. 2. ep. 9. *Illud tertium etiam si opus est, tamen minus est necessarium*, 2. de Orat. Therefore this noun is no more an adjective than *usus*, which is frequently taken in the same sense, and in the same government, as when Virgil says, *Nunc viribus usus*, for *opus*. And it is just as if we were to say, *Is viribus opus est*, or *de viribus*, there is need of strength; that is, our whole business consists in strength. Cicero has made use of it in this sense and in this very government, *Pergratum mihi feceris, si eum, si qua in re opus ei fuerit, juveris*, where he might have put, *si qua re* (or *aliqua*) *ei opus fuerit*, &c.

It is in this same meaning that we join *opus* with an adjective, *Sunt quibus unum opus est celebrare urbem carmine*, Hor. Or that we put it with another substantive by apposition; *Dux nobis opus est*, which is the same sense as if it were, *Dux nobis opera est*, our whole affair, or all that we have to do, is to look out for a chief leader.

But if it be put in the genitive, then there is nothing extraordinary in it, and this is still a stronger proof of its being a real substantive, *Opus est centum nummorum*, it is a work of a hundred crowns: *Magni laboris & multæ impensæ opus fuit*, Planc. ad Sen. lib. 10. ep. 8. And in this sense Virgil says, *Famam extendere factis, hoc virtutis opus*: and Martial, *Non fuit hoc artis, sed pietatis opus*.

It is also as a substantive, that it frequently serves for a second nominative after the verb: *Si quid opus est, impera*, Plaut. *Ita opus est*; just as we say *Ita negotium est*, Plaut. *Ita res erat, faciendum fuit*, Ter. And moreover, that it serves for a second accusative after the infinitive, *Dices nummos mihi opus esse*, Cic. *Sulpicii tibi operam intelligo ex tuis literis non multum opus esse*, Cic. and if an infinitive be put after the verb, it is still the same sense, *Quid opus est affirmare?* Cic. *Nunc peropus est loqui*, Ter. Where the infinitive supplies the place of a nominative, as it will supply that of an accusative, if I say, *Negat fuisse opus affirmare, puto peropus esse loqui*.

And if we say, *Opus est consulto*, instead of *consulere*, and the like, we are to understand *in consulto*, where the government must also depend on the preposition. Thus we see that *opus*, in whatever sense it be taken, is never any other than a noun substantive, which comes within the general rules.

It is also observable that we meet with *opus habeo* in Columella, who is a very pure author, just as the Greeks say χρείαν ἔχω. Which is so uncommon in Latin, that Diomedes believed it was wrong to say it.

In regard to *usus*, we might further add, that as the verbal nouns heretofore goverued the case of their verb, this here has taken the ablative like *utor* of which it is formed: *Usus viribus*, as *utor viribus*. Which is the more probable, as heretofore it governed the accusative, because *utor* governed it. *Ad eam rem usus est hominem astutum, doctum*, Plaut.

Diomedes takes notice that the antients said likewise, *Opus est mihi hanc rem*, but he gives no authority for it. And then we must needs suppose an infinitive, as *habere, facere, dicere*, or the like.

RULE XXIX.
Of nouns of price, and verbs of valuing.

1. *The price of a thing is governed in the ablative.*
2. *Except these genitives*, minóris, tanti, quanti, pluris.
3. *Verbs of valuing also govern these same genitives.*
4. *To which we may add*, parvi, nauci, flocci, nihili, minimi, æqui, boni, magni, multi, *and* plurimi.

EXAMPLES.

1. The price of a thing is governed in the ablative. *Locavit domum suam centum nummis*, he let his house for a hundred crowns. *Licere presenti pecunia*, to be valued for ready money. *Multorum sanguine ac vulneribus ea Pænis victoria stetit*, that victory was purchased by the blood of many Carthaginians. *Pretio magno stare*, Hor. to cost very dear.

2. The following nouns are governed in the genitive, when they are put without substantives; *tanti, quanti, pluris, maximi, minoris, tantidem, quanticunque,* &c. *Tanti nulla res est*, there is nothing so dear. *Emit tanti, quanti voluit*, he bought it for what he pleased. *Non pluris vendo quàm cæteri, etiam minoris*, I do not sell dearer than others, but perhaps cheaper.

3. Verbs of valuing govern also the said genitives, *Maximi facere*, to value greatly. *Pluris habere*, to value more. *Tanti ducitur*, he is so much esteemed.

4. But they govern likewise the following; *parvi, nihili, plurimi, hujus, magni, multi, minimi, nauci, flocci, pili, assis, teruncii, æqui, boni*. *Non facere flocci*, or *flocci habere*, not to value a straw. *Nauci habere*,

the same. *Pili non dúcere*, not to value a rush. *Hujus non æstimáre*, not to value this much (pointing to some trifling thing) *Teruncii non fácere*, not to value it a farthing. *Æqui, boni fácere*, to take in good part.

ANNOTATION.

These very nouns, when joined to a substantive, are put in the ablative; *Redimere minori pretio; magno pretio æstimari; parvâ mercede docere.*

Some are likewise put in the ablative without a substantive, *parvo, vel nihilo consequi; magno æstimare*; but then we understand *ære*, or *pretio*. And when they are in the genitive, we must understand one of these nouns, by which they are governed in that case; for *Minoris emi*, is the same as, *minoris æris pretio emi. Tanti duco*, that is to say, *tanti æris pretio*, unless we chuse rather to say with Henry Stephen that it is a Greek expression, περὶ πολλῆ ποιοῦμαι, *magni facio*.

But with the ablative we understand the preposition also; for *nihilo consequi*, is the same construction as when Cicero says, *Pro nihilo putare, pro nihilo ducere*, and so of the rest, *Dum pro argenteis decem, aureus unus valebat*, Liv. *Aliquando una res pro duabus valet*, Sen. &c. But when we say, *Æqui boni facio*, or *consulo*, it means, *Æqui boni animi*, or *hominis officium duco, facio*, &c.

Vossius observes that we cannot say, *Parvi curo*, as we say, *parvi facio*; and that the passage of Terence, produced on this occasion, *Quid me fiat, parvi curas*, is corrupted, since the best copies have *parvi pendas*. Neither do we find, *Majoris æstimo* (instead of which we make use of *pluris*) though we read in Cicero, *Magni putare honores*. And in Terence, *Te semper maximi feci*. Nor can we say *Plurimi interest, minimi refert*, but *plurimum interest, minimè refert*.

RULE XXX.

Of verbs passive, and others which require the ablative with the preposition *A* or *Ab*.

1. *Verbs passive frequently require the ablative with the preposition* a, *or* ab, *as* Amor à regína.

2. *Verbs of waiting, separating, distance, asking, receiving, delivering, and nouns of difference, have also this same government.*

EXAMPLES.

All the above verbs frequently require an ablative, which is governed by the preposition *a* or *ab*.

1. The passives, as *Amor à regina*, I am beloved by the queen. *Tenéri, regi ab áliquo*, to be possessed, to be governed by a person. *Provísum est nobis óptimè à Deo*,

Deo, God has provided extremely well for us. *Oppugnári ab áliquo,* to be attacked by a person.

2. Verbs of waiting, *O'mnia à te expéctat,* he expects every thing of you. *Sperat à rege,* he hopes from the king.

Those of separating, and of distance, *Distat à Lutétiâ vicus ille,* that village is distant from Paris. *Distat argumentátio à veritáte,* your argument is wide from truth. *Disjúngere, segregáre se à bonis,* to separate from, to quit the acquaintance of virtuous people. *Distráhere & divéllere áliquem ab áliquo,* to part and to tear away one person from another.

Those of asking, *Hoc à te petit, póstulat, flágitat,* he asks this of you, he begs, he prays you.

Those of receiving, *Accípere ab áliquo,* to receive of a person. *Mutuári ab áliquo,* to borrow of somebody. *Díscere ab áliquo,* to learn of somebody.

Those of delivering, *Liberáre à perículo,* to free from danger. *Redímere à morte,* to redeem from death. *Exímere à malis,* to exempt from misfortune.

Nouns of difference, *A'liud à libertáte,* a different thing from liberty. *Res divérsæ à propósita ratióne,* things quite different from the subject proposed.

ANNOTATION.
That the verb passive properly speaking governs nothing of itself.

There are a great many other verbs, which have the ablative with the preposition, as *Ordiri à principio; mercari à mercatoribus; à se aliquid facere,* Cic. *Sæpe à majoribus natu audivi,* Id. *A me hoc illi dabis,* Id. *A me argentum sumito,* Ter. *Otium à senibus ad potandum ut habeam,* Id. And a multitude of others which may be seen in Sanctius, l. 3. c. 4.

There are likewise several, to which *a* or *ab* is understood, as *Cavere malo,* for *à malo. Cibo probibere & tecto,* Cic. *Liberare curâ, infamiâ,* Id. &c.

Hence it appears that this case is not properly governed by the verb passive, nor by the other verbs which have it after them, but only by the preposition: for as Sanctius says, the passive wants nothing but its nominative to make its construction and speech complete. *Amantur boni,* honest people are beloved. If I add *ab omnibus,* it is *ab* that governs this case, to denote from whence comes this love. For *à,* generally speaking, signifies only *à parte,* and may be put every where in this sense, and after all sorts of verbs; while the passives of themselves are indifferent to this government.

vernment. For which reason Metellus writing to Cicero has made use of *per. Non existimaram fratrem meum per te oppugnatum iri,* in the same sense as *ab*; as we see by Cicero's answer, who says to him, *Quod scribis non oportuisse fratrem tuum à me oppugnari,* &c. And in the oration *pro domo sua,* he has indifferently made use of both particles, *a* and *per: Nisi ab improbis expulsus essem, & per bonos restitutus.* In the same manner as in the 11th epist. of the 3d book, *De mercenariis, nisi jam aliquid factum est per Flaccum, fiet à me.*

Besides there are many occasions on which this *a* or *ab* can neither be put nor understood, *Animus in curas diducitur omnes,* Virg. And sometimes it is even more elegant to give it a dative, as Sylvius observes; *Pacificatio quæ neque senatui, neque populo, neque cuiquam bono probatur,* Cic. *Nulla tuarum audita mihi neque visa sororum,* Virg. *Dilecti tibi poëtæ,* Hor. *Formidatam Parthis te principe Romam.* Hor. *Cui lecta potenter erit res,* Hor. Which is still more common among the Greeks, Τῶν ἐμοὶ πεπραγμένων, Demosth. the feats performed by me. And an infinite number of others of the like sort. See the 12th rule of the datives.

Of the verbs called neuter passives, veneo, vapulo, *&c.*

We have already made mention of these verbs at the end of the preterites, vol. i. p. 305. where we have shewn that they are real actives. Hence Sanctius observes that it is bad Latin to say *Servi veneunt à mangone,* are sold by him. And the grammarians can give no other authority for it but the answer of Fabricius, who, as Quintilian saith, having publicly given his vote for raising a bad man to the consulate, made answer to those who expressed their surprise, *A cive se spoliari malle quàm ab hoste venire,* Quintil. lib. 2 cap. 1. Which hath the less weight on this occasion, as Cicero quoting this very expression of Fabricius in his second book de Orat. gives it differently, *Malo,* says he, *compilari quàm venire;* than to be carried to be sold. For *veneo* comes only from *venum* and *eo.* And therefore it is no more Latin to say *venire ab aliquo,* than *ire ab aliquo.* However, if we should take it in a different sense from the passive, we may say for instance, *Servi veneunt à Cicerone,* that is, are carried to be sold in the behalf or by the order and command of Cicero: and as Plautus saith, *Ubi sunt qui amant à Lenone?*

Neither is *Vapulare ab aliquo* Latin, according to the same Sanctius, though it has also the authority of Quintilian, who speaking of a particular witness, says, *Testis in reum rogatus, an ab reo fustibus vapulasset; et innocens inquit.* But Tullus Rufianus, an antient professor of eloquence, mentioning this same passage concerning this witness, says: *Et testis interrogatus ab reo num fustibus vapulasset? innocens inquit.* Which gives room to suspect, that those passages of Quintilian were corrupted. For *vapulo* properly signifies no more than *ploro,* as we have already observed, vol. i. p. 307. So that this would be said by an ellipsis; *num fustibus exceptus ejulasset.*

Rule XXXI.
Of the matter of which any thing is composed.

The matter of which any thing is composed, is put in the ablative with the preposition ex *or* è, *as* Vas è gemmis.

EXAMPLES.

The matter of which any thing is composed, is put in the ablative with the preposition *ex* or *è*, as *Vas è gemmis*, a vessel made of diamonds. *Imágo ex ære*, a brazen image, *Signum ex mármore*, a marble statue. *Pócula ex auro*, golden cups.

ANNOTATION.

Sometimes we meet with the matter in the genitive, as *Nummus argenti*; *crateres argenti*, Perf. Which seems to agree perfectly with the French, *une tasse d'argent*, and is only an imitation of the Greeks, who use this case, with the preposition *ix* understood. Which we might resolve in Latin by a general noun, *ex re*, or *ex materia argenti*, pursuant to what we have observed, v. 2. p. 63.

Rule XXXII.
Of those nouns that are put in the ablative with a preposition.

Nouns signifying punishment, part, cause, instrument, manner, or reason of a thing, are put in the ablative.

EXAMPLES.

All the following nouns are put in the ablative after most verbs.

1. The punishment, *plecti cápite*, Cic. to be punished with death. *Punire supplício*, Cic. to put to death. *Pœnâ affici*, Cic. to be punished. *Vitia hóminum, damnis, ignomíniis, vínculis, verbéribus, exíliis, morte multántur*, Cic. human vices are punished with fines, ignominy, imprisonment, whipping, exile, and death.

2. A part; *Ut tota mente atque ómnibus ártubus contremíscam*, Cic. that I be chilled with fear, and tremble every joint of me. *Naso plus vidére, quàm óculis*, to distinguish better by his smell than by his sight.

3. The cause, *Ardet dolóre & irâ*, he is inflamed with grief and anger; that is, grief and anger are the cause of his being inflamed. *Dubitatióne æ´stuat*, he is in a quandary. *Culpâ palléscit*, he is pale through guilt.

guilt. *Licéntiâ detérior fit*, he grows worse by being indulged.

4. The instrument, *Perfódere sagíttis*, to pierce with arrows. *Lapídibus obrúere*, to overpower with stones. *Lúdere pilâ, & duódecim scrupis*, to play at tennis and at draughts.

5. The manner or the reason, *Auctus prædâ*, loaded with booty. *Florére laude*, to be greatly praised. *Affári supérba voce*, to speak haughtily. *Lento gradu procédere*, to walk slowly. *Régio apparátu excéptus*, received with regal magnificence.

ANNOTATION.

In all these nouns we understand the preposition governing the ablative, as sufficiently appears from the vulgar languages in which it is always expressed.

This is manifest even in regard to the instrument: *Percutere baculo*, to strike with a stick. And the Greeks likewise do frequently use the preposition.

But the reason why it is not generally put in Latin, says Sanctius, is because it might occasion ambiguity. For when you say, for example, *tetigi illum cum hasta*, one might doubt your meaning, whether you touched him and his spear, or whether you only touched him with a spear. Hence the *cum* is generally omitted, and the examples which Sanctius brings to prove the contrary, are suspicious, or imply a different sense, as may be seen in Vossius, *lib. de construct.*

True it is that sometimes we use other prepositions on this occasion, as *Exercere solum sub vomere*, Virg. *Castor trajectus ab ense*, Ovid. *Sempérque de manu cibos & aquam præbére*. Colum. And in the vulgate bible we frequently find the preposition *in*, agreeably to the Hebrew phrase; *Reges eos in virga ferrea. Prævaluit David in funda & lapide. Dómine, si percutimus in gladio?* and the like.

In regard to the other nouns of the cause and the manner, they are sometimes used with a preposition also; for as Ovid says, *Felix nato & conjuge*, Cicero says, *Ab omni laude felicior*. And in like manner when we say, *Jove natus; genere Afer; domo Siculus*, we must always understand *à*, or *ab*. *Elisa mulier domo Phœnix*, in Solinus, that is, *A domo Phœnix*. Just as Cicero has expressed himself with the preposition, *Ab his rebus vacua atque nuda est; laborat ex renibus*. And Terence, *E dolore, præ dolore, præ gaudio, qua de causa*, and the like.

RULE XXXIII.

Of particular verbs that govern the ablative, some of which have likewise the accusative.

1. Pólleo, affícior, dono, sterno, dignor, *govern an ablative*.

2. Vescor, fungor, fruor, utor, *and* pótior, *govern*

govern also an ablative, and sometimes an accusative.

EXAMPLES.

1. This rule is only an appendix to the foregoing, where we have seen that several verbs govern an ablative, which might be included in the cause or the manner: *Pollére ópibus,* to have great credit, power, or wealth. *Affici gaúdio,* to rejoice. *Donáre civitáte,* to grant the freedom of the city. *Stérnere flóribus,* to strow with flowers. *Dignári áliquem amóre,* to esteem a person worthy of his affection. *Qui apud nos hoc nómine dignántur,* Cic. who amongst us are honoured with this name. *Cultu & honóre dignári,* Cic. in a passive sense; to be esteemed worthy of honour and respect.

2. The following govern also the ablative, and sometimes the accusative, being considered as verbs active: *Vesci carne,* and *carnes,* to eat flesh. *Fungi áliquo múnere,* Cæs. to discharge an office. *Functus officio,* and *officium,* Ter. who has done his duty. *Fungi vice* Hor. *vicem,* Liv. to do his duty. *Vir bonus útitur mundo, non frúitur,* a good man makes use of the things of this world, but does not set his heart upon them. *Ad agrum fruéndum alléctat senéctus,* old age invites us to enjoy the pleasures of the country. *Uti áliquo familiáriter,* Cic. to be very intimate with a person. *U'tere ut voles óperam meam,* Plaut. make what use of me you please. *Mea bona utántur sine,* Ter. let them enjoy my estate. And in like manner *abútor. O'peram abútitur.* Ter. he loses his labour. *Potíri império,* to enjoy the supreme command, *Potíri gaudio,* Ter. to be extremely merry. *Urbem potitúrus,* Cic. about to become master of Sicily. *Pátria potítur cómmoda,* he enjoys all paternal advantages.

ANNOTATION.

1. We say also *potiri rerum, voluptatum, urbis, regni,* Cic. and other genitives, which are always governed by an ablative understood, as *facultate, potentiâ,* and the like.

2. There are a great many more verbs which govern the ablative, as *Lætor, gaudeo, gestio novis rebus. Delector, oblecto,* and *oblector, tristor, nitor, fraudo, fraudare se victu; vivere lactucis victu*

victitare leguminibus; *parietem cruore linire*; *gloriari victoriâ*, Cæs. and an infinite number of others. But we may refer them to the precedent rule of the manner and the cause, or we may say in general that there is a preposition understood; as appears by Cicero's expressing it, *In hoc delector*; *de lucro vivere*; *gloriari de divitiis*; *in hujus vita nititur salus civitatis*; and the like. Thus when Lucilius, Ter. Appul. Plaut. say, *Quid me fiet?* And Cic. *Quid Tulliâ meâ fit factum?* even according to Gruterus's edition, we are to understand *de*, as he expresses it in another place, *Quid de P. Clodio fiat?* And Ter. *Sed de fratre meo quid fiet?* &c.

RULE XXXIV.
Of the ablative absolute.

The ablative absolute is put every where by itself, as me consule feci, reginâ venturâ.

EXAMPLES.

We give the name of ablative absolute to that which stands alone, and as it were independent in a sentence. And this ablative is put every where, whether in speaking of two different things or persons, or whether in speaking of one only; as *Me consule id feci*, I did that when I was consul. *Reginâ venturâ, magnum erat in urbe gaudium*, the queen being expected, there was great joy in the city. *Me duce ad hunc voti finem veni*, Ovid, I compassed this design myself, by my own conduct. *Brevitátem secútus sum te magistro*, Cic. I have been more concise after your example.

ANNOTATION.

This same ablative which they call absolute, and seems independent, is governed nevertheless by a preposition understood, for *me consule*, implies, *sub me consule*. *Reginâ venturâ*, means, *de reginâ venturâ*, and the rest in the same manner, just as Horace says, *Sub duce qui templis Parthorum signa refixit*: Pyrrhus in Cic. *De volentibus, cum magnis diis*, Offic. 1. and T. Liv. *Cum diis bene juvantibus*: which we should express by this ablative absolute.

Sometimes the preposition *in* is understood, as in Martial. *Temporibusque malis, ausus es esse bonus.*

That is, *in temporibus*. And in Cicero, *Quod me in forum vocas, eò vocas unde etiam bonis meis rebus fugiebam*, ad Att. that is, *in bonis rebus*, Ovid has even expressed it.

Mens antiqua tamen fractâ quoque mansit in urnâ.

But to denote what has happened in the course of time, we ought rather to understand *à* or *ab*, with this ablative, *Oppressâ libertate patriæ, nihil est quod speremus amplius*, Cic. that is, *ab oppressâ libertate*, in the same sense as we say *à cænâ, à prandio*, after supper, after dinner; and the like, just as Cicero has expressed himself writing to Dolabella, *Non licet tibi jam à tantis rebus gestis, non tui similem esse*, after such great exploits. Here-

Hereby it appears that it is not true, absolutely speaking, that this ablative cannot be used in a sentence, except when there are two things or two different persons. For if this depends intirely on the preposition, this difference of person has nothing to do with the subject, at least in regard to grammar. Hence it is right to say; *Me duce ad hunc voti finem, me milite veni,* Ovid. *Et lætos fecit se consule factos,* Luc. And Cicero abounds in such examples. *Non potes effugere hujus culpæ pœnam te patrono. Tenebam memoriâ, nobis consulibus. Memineram nobis privatis cætera. Quæ ornamenta in Sexto Claudio, esse voluisti te consule. Mibi quidem neque pueris nobis M. Scaurus C. Mario cedere videbatur.* And Cæsar speaks thus of himself; *Dictatore habente comitia Cæsare, consules creantur J. Cæsar & P. Servilius.*

But this way of speaking is common enough, when this ablative denotes a diversity of time and condition, though in the same person. Hereof we shall give more particular examples. *Te vidente vides,* Plaut. *Qui se vidente amicam patiatur suam,* &c. Ter. *Hibericas herbas se solo nequicquam intelligense dicebat,* Quint. lib. 8. *Te volente misisti,* Idem declam. 4. *Quibus occultatis* (Tyriis) *Sidona devecti sunt,* Curt. lib. 4. c. 4. *Iterùm censente in Trebianis legatam pecuniam transferre concederetur, obtinere non potuit,* Suet. in Tiber. *Absumique etiam se inspectante patitur,* Plin. *Prodente se autor est M. Varro,* Id. *Horum supra centum viginti millia fuisse, se prodente Ctesias scribit,* Id. *Se audiente. locuples auctor scribit Thucydides,* Cic. *Nobis vigilantibus, & multum in posterum providentibus.* Pop. *Romano consentiente, erimus profecti liberi, brevi tempore,* Id. *Moderante Tiberio ne plures quàm quatuor candidatos commendaret,* Tac. Tiberius directing affairs in such a manner, that he promised not to name more than four candidates. And others, of the like sort, which may be seen in Sanctius and elsewhere.

This shews that Despauter had no great reason to find fault with this phrase, which Priscian maintains to be good Latin, *Me legente proficio*; and as he believed that no Latin author ever expressed himself in that manner, it proves that he was less versed in the writings of the antients, than those who came after him.

RULE XXXV.

Of some particles which govern different cases.

Ecce, *and* en *govern a nominative or an accusative.*

O, heu, proh, *govern a nominative, accusative, or vocative.*

Hei, *and* væ, *have only a dative.*

EXAMPLES.

These two adverbs *ecce, en,* govern either a nominative, or an accusative; as *En Priamus,* Virg. behold Priamus. *En tectum, en tegulas,* Plaut. behold the roof, behold the tiles. *Ecce*

Ecce illa tempéstas, behold that storm. *Ecce miserum hóminem,* behold that wretched man.

The interjections, O! *heu!* *proh!* govern either the nominative, accusative, or vocative.

O qualis domus! O what a house! *O me pérditum!* wretched me! *O Dave, itáne contémnor abs te?* O Davus, dost thou despise me thus?

Heu nímium felix! O too happy! *Heu pietas, heu prisca fides!* alas, where is the religion and fidelity of former days! *Heu stirpem invísam!* Virg. O unhappy race!

Proh dolor! O lamentable! *Pró deûm, atque hóminum fidem!* Ter. Cic. ye gods! ye men! *Pró sanctè Jupiter!* Cic. O sacred Jupiter!

Hei! and *væ!* are always joined to a dative; *Hei mihi!* ah me! *Væ tibi!* wo to you!

ANNOTATION.

Ecce, and *en,* more usually govern an accusative, when they denote any kind of reproach. *En animum & mentem,* there's a bright genius for you. In sudden things, Cicero frequently useth the dative with *ecce. Epistolam cùm à te avidè expectarem, ecce tibi nuncius venit.* But considering it strictly, this *tibi* is only a relative dative; and the meaning is, *behold a messenger who is come to tell me this of you,* or concerning you.

Therefore it is observable, that properly speaking, these adverbs and interjections govern no case. For which reason we have placed this rule after the rest, as a thing that may be omitted, since the following noun constantly depends on the verb which is understood. Thus when Cicero says, *En crimen, en causa,* that is, *en est crimen, en est causa.* When we say, *Ecce illum,* we understand *vide* or *respice,* and the like. Just as in Greek, ἴδε ἰδού, though taken adverbially for *en* and *ecce,* are real imperatives of the 2. aor. of εἴδω and εἴδομαι, to see, to know.

It is the same in regard to O, when we say, *O præclarum custodem!* we understand *habemus. O me miserum!* sup. *sentio.* For that the particle O does not govern this case, appears from its being frequently omitted. *Me miserum,* Ter. as likewise from several passages, where it cannot be even understood, as *Hæccine flagitia! jocularem audaciam!* Ter. where according to Donatus, we must understand only *audio,* or *dicis.*

In regard to the interjections *hei* and *væ,* so far are they from being capable of governing any cases, that they are not so much as significative words, but serve only to express the emotions of the mind, *Hei mihi! væ tibi!* where we always understand *est,* as if *væ* were a noun. Just as in the vulgate we read, *Væ unum abiit: veniunt duo væ post hæc,* &c.

Rule XXXVI.
Of the reciprocal pronouns *sui* and *suus*.

To avoid ambiguity, let the reciprocal pronoun refer to the principal noun only.

Examples.

We have placed this rule the laſt, becauſe it appears ſomewhat more difficult, and ſuppoſeth a knowledge of the others. But there is nothing more natural, when once it is rightly conſidered.

Theſe two pronouns relative *ſui* & *ſuus*, are called reciprocals, becauſe they refer the third perſon back to itſelf. As when I ſay, *Cato ſe interfécit*, Cato has killed himſelf; this pronoun *ſe*, refers Cato to Cato himſelf. And in like manner, *Ipſe ſe diligit*, he loves himſelf. *Lóquitur ſecum*, he talks to himſelf. *Sui ſemper ſimilis*, always like himſelf, &c.

Therefore if we want to refer to the caſe immediately preceding the verb in the natural order, we make uſe of the reciprocal to avoid ambiguity; *Cæſar Ariovíſto dixit, non ſeſe Gallis, ſed Gallos ſibi bellum intuliſſe*, Cæſar told Arioviſtus, that it was not he who had declared war againſt the Gauls, but the Gauls againſt him: where it appears that *ſeſe* and *ſibi* refer to Cæſar, as to the nominative, which immediately precedes the verb in the natural order of conſtruction.

But if there is no danger of ambiguity, we may put indifferently, either a reciprocal, or one of theſe relatives, *ille, ipſe, hic, is*, in the ſame place, and in the ſame ſenſe; as *Eſt verò fortunatus ille, cujus ex ſalúte non minor penè ad omnes, quàm ad illum ventúra ſit, lætitia pervénerit*, Cic. Marcellus is happy to find that his preſervation is as dear to the whole community, as to himſelf: where it is obvious that he might have ſaid *ad ſe*. And in like manner, *Omnes boni, quantum in ipſis fuit, Cæſarem interfecérunt;* all the honeſt party, as much as in them lay, had a ſhare in Cæſar's death: where he might have ſaid, *quantum in ſe fuit*.

On the contrary, authors put the reciprocal alſo, where they might have uſed the relative, *Medéam prædicant in fuga, fratris ſui membra in iis locis quà ſe parens perſequerétur diſſipaviſſe*, Cic. Medea in her flight is

ſaid

said to have scattered her brother's limbs wherever her father was in pursuit of her: where he might have said, *quà eam persequerêtur. Orâre jussit, si se ames, hera, jam ut ad sese vénias,* Ter. she bid me tell you, that she begs if you have any love for her, you will come and see her: where he might have said, *Si eam ames, ut ad eam vénias. Hæc proptêrea, de me dixi, ut mihi Túbero cum de se éadem dícerem, ignósceret,* Cic. I have said this concerning myself, to the end that Tubero might excuse me, if I said the same of him: *Cùm de ipso éadem dicerem,* would have done as well.

ANNOTATION.

It is therefore evident that all the rule we have to observe on this occasion, is to avoid obscurity.

Now in the first and second person there can never be any ambiguity, and therefore we may say in the abovementioned example: *Ut mihi Tubero, cùm de se,* or *cum de illo, eadem dicerem, ignosceret.* We may say, *Cepi columbam in nido suo,* or *in nido ejus,* or *in nido ipsius.* Just as Terence hath, *Timet ne deseras se* for *eam,* in Andr. she is afraid lest you forsake her: and further on, *Meritam esse ut memor esses sui* for *ejus.* And Cicero, *Mihi gratias agunt quod se reges meâ sententiâ appellaverim. Suis eum certis propriisque criminibus accusabo. Non emit à te enim, sed priusquam tu suum sibi venderes, ipse possedit.* And the like.

It is the same upon other occasions, where the only rule is to avoid ambiguity. *Vix tamen sibi de mea voluntate concessum est,* Cic. Where *sibi* stands expressly for *illi,* as Manutius observeth. Thus we may say, *Supplicium sumpsit de famoso fure cum sociis suis,* or *sociis ejus,* because the sense is clear: but with the copulative conjunction we should not say, *Sumpsit supplicium de fure & sociis suis,* but only *ejus;* because as *suis* then refers to the nominative of the verb, it would look as if this were said of the companions of the person that punishes. Just as when Cicero saith, *Cererem esse sublatam à Verre ex templis suis; suis* refers to *Cererem,* as to the case which immediately precedes the verb *esse.* Which might be expressed otherwise, *Quod Ceres à Verre sublata sit ex templis suis;* because *suis* would always refer to *Ceres,* the nominative of the verb. But we should not say, *Verres sustulit Cererem ex templis suis;* because *suis* would then refer to *Verres,* as now the nominative of the verb, so that to remove all ambiguity, we should say *ex templis ejus.*

And so true is this rule, that except in this case we frequently find both the relative and the reciprocal referring to the same person. *Abisari Alexander nuntiare jussit, si gravaretur ad se venire, ipsum ad eum esse venturum,* Curt. where *se* and *ipsum* both refer to Alexander. *In provincia pacatissima ita se gessit, ut ei pacem esse expediret,* Cic. where *se* and *ei* both refer to Ligarius in favour of whom he is speaking.

What wonder then is it, if they put the reciprocal, though without any relation to the nominative of the verb, when it can occasion no ambiguity, as Virgil speaking of Dido's nurse, *Namque suam patria antiqua cinis ater habebat*, where *suam* refers to Dido, though *cinis* be the nominative of the verb. Valerius Maximus speaking of Metellus, *Tectum continuò in statum suum restituit*, where *suum* refers to *tectum*, and not to Metellus.

Cicero in his second book of offices says of Dionysius the tyrant, *Candente carbone sibi adurebat capillum*, where *sibi* refers to Dionysius, because it is the nominative of the verb *adurebat*. And in the fifth book of his Tusculan Questions, mentioning the same subject, he says, *Dionysius filias suas tondere docuit, instituitque ut candentibus juglandium putaminibus barbam sibi & capillum adurerent;* where *sibi* is no longer referred to the nominative of the verb *adurerent*, which are his daughters, but to Dionysius himself; because the sense sheweth there can be no ambiguity, since his daughters have no beard. But if it was only, *Dionysius instituit ut filiæ suæ capillum sibi adurerent*, this might be understood of his daughters hair, because he has expressed them by the reciprocal *suæ*; and to remove all ambiguity we should say, *Ut capillum ipsi (Dionysio) adurerent*.

But take notice that the ambiguity arises chiefly on these occasions, where there are two third persons, and especially where there happen to be two different verbs, as *Pater jussit filio ut iret in cubiculum suum*. *Verres rogat Dolabellam ut de sua provincia decedat*. For then we must distinguish by the sense and consider which is the principal person in the sentence, in order generally to refer the reciprocal to its nominative. Thus when Cicero saith, *Tum Pythius piscatores ad se vocavit, & ab his petivit ut ante suos hortos postera die piscarentur*, Offic. 1. He ought not to have expressed himself otherwise, because the verb *petivit* has *Pythius* before it for its nominative, to whom these gardens belong, and who is the principal nominative. But if he had meant the fishermen's gardens, he should have said *hortos ipsorum*, to prevent ambiguity: as he said of Milo, *Obviam fit Clodio ante fundum ejus*, nempe *Clodii*.

In the same manner we say, *Regis est gubernare suos*. *Hunc sui cives ejecerunt*, because though one would think that this reciprocal does not refer to the nominative of the verb, yet it certainly amounts to this sense, as appears by altering it thus; *Regis officium est ut gubernet cives suos. Hic ejectus est à suis civibus*. For the same reason we say, *Trahit sua quemque voluptas*, Virg. *Justitia reddit suum cuique. Suo gladio hunc jugulo. Negligere quid de se quisque sentiat est dissoluti*, Cic. Because the meaning is, *Dissolutus negligit quid de se à quoque dicatur. Suo gladio hic jugulatur. Quisque à voluptate sua trahitur. Quisque à justitia accipit suum.*

Therefore whenever there is a periphrasis, or a perplexed meaning with the reciprocal, it ought always to be reduced to its natural order, to see which is the nominative of the verb that it refers to, as in Cicero's offices, *Ex quo, quia suum cujusque fit quod cuique obtigit, id quisque teneat*. We must reduce this, and say, *Quia ex eo tempore prædium cujusque fit suum prædium, id quisque teneat*, &c. Where we see, that *suum* constantly refers to the nominative of the verb, which is *teneat*. And the rest in the same manner.

The reciprocal generally goes before *quisque*: as may be seen in the preceding examples, and in this: *Num ista societas talis est, ut nihil suum cujusque sit*, Cic. Though Virgil has expressed it otherwise: *Quisque suos patimur manes*. Which is rare.

With *inter* we say; *Contendunt docti inter se*, and *contentio est doctorum inter se*, or *inter ipsos*. *Damonem & Pythiam ferunt hoc animo inter se fuisse. Inter se omnes partes corporis quodam lepore consentiunt. Una spes est salutis, istorum inter istos dissensio*, Cic. and the like.

BOOK

BOOK VI.

PARTICULAR REMARKS

on all the Parts of Speech.

AFTER having exhibited a general idea of construction in the introduction to the syntax, and shewn the application thereof in the particular rules, I propose giving some other remarks on the several words of which speech is composed; and I flatter myself that even such as have made some progress in the Latin tongue, will meet here with a variety of agreeable and useful observations, as well for discovering the real foundation of the language, as for understanding the different authors, and writing with elegance and purity. I shall only advise those who are desirous of attaining the real principles of language in a higher degree of perfection, to see what has been said on this subject in the general and rational grammar*, where, if I am not mistaken, even the most curious will find abundant matter of entertainment.

Section I.

REMARKS ON THE NOUNS.

Chapter I.

Of nouns common, doubtful, and epicene.

I. *Of common nouns.*

THERE are a great many nouns, whose signification agreeth with both sexes, though they never occur in construction with an adjective feminine. Such is *homo*; for we should not say, *hominem malam*, as Charisius observes; and it is a mistake, according to Vossius, in the transcriber of Plautus; to read *Hominis miseræ misereri*, where the best manuscripts have *Hominis miserè miseri*.

* This work was translated a few years ago by the same hand as the rest of the grammatical pieces of Messrs. de Port Royal, and printed for J. Nourse in the Strand.

And if Sulpicius in his letter to Cicero, says of his daughter Tullia, *Homo nata est*, this does not prove that it is of the feminine gender, since in Terence a woman says, *Virum me natam vellem;* and it is in the same signification that Plautus likewise says, *Fures estis ambæ*, that is, *vos ambæ feminæ fures estis*. For *fur* of itself is never joined with an adjective feminine.

But we shall divide these nouns into two classes, first those which Vossius believes to be common in their signification only, and next those which are common likewise in their construction.

II. *Nouns common in their signification only.*

ADVENA always masculine in construction. And in like manner,

TRANSVENA and CONVENA (from whence cometh *Convenæ*, the inhabitants of Cominges in Gascony) for as the Æolics terminated in A the masculines of the first declension in *ης*, as ἱππότα Ζεὺς for ἱππότης, the Latins, ever fond of imitating them, have frequently given the same gender to this same termination; and hence it is that we have such a number of nouns masculine in A.

AGRICOLA, likewise CÆLICOLA and RURICOLA.

ALIENIGENA, In the same manner INDIGENA, and such like.

ASSECLA, *a follower, or attendant;* and in like manner several nouns which of their nature are adjectives.

AURIGA.

CAMELUS; though the Greeks say ἡ κάμηλος, which has led several into a mistake. See the genders, vol. I. p. 57.

CLIENS, masc. we say CLIENTA in the feminine; *Jam clientas reperi*, Plaut.

Honestæ purpuræ clientæ, Hor.

COCLES, EQUES.

EXUL; therefore we should not say *vaga exul*, but *vaga & exul*; nor *ejectam exulem reducere*, but *ejectam in exilium reducere*.

FUR. See the beginning of this chap.

HOMICIDA, and the like.

PARRICIDA, and the like.

HOMO. See the beginning of this chap. But *nemo* is sometimes feminine,

Viciniam neminem amo magis, Plaut.

because this noun is become in some measure an adjective, and frequently taken for *nullus*, as in Cicero, *Facio pluris omnium hominum neminem*. The difference is, that *nemo* is properly said only of men, whereas *nullus* is said of every thing. Where we are to observe nevertheless, that not only Virgil has said, *Divûm nemo*, but even Cicero himself, *Nemo nec homo, nec Deus*.

INDEX, though its signification is feminine, *Orationis indicem vocem*, Cic.

JUVENIS indeed is common in its signification, *Cornelia juvenis est, & adhuc parere potest*, Plin. but it is always masc. in its construction. Therefore in this verse of Catullus we should read betwixt two comma's, *Cernitis, innuptæ, juvenes*, that is, *vos innuptæ, cernitis juvenes*, as Vossius observes, contrary to the opinion of Alvarez.

HOSPES, common in its signification, *Hospite cymba*, Stat. But masc. in construction. In the feminine we say, *hospita. Servilia Dionis hospita*, Cic.

INTERPRES. *Interprete lingua*, Hor.

LANISTA. LIXA. LATRO.

OBSES. *Sententiam obsidem perpetuæ in Remp. Voluntatis*, Cic.

OPIFEX. *Apes opifices*, Varro.

PEDES. PINCERNA. PRÆSUL.

PRINCEPS. *Principes fæminæ*, Plin.

PUGIL. *Si qua est habitior paulo, pugilem esse aiunt*, Ter.

RABULA.

SENEX. *Tua amica senex*, Varro in Priscian.

And if any one should pretend to say that these nouns are common in construction, because they sometimes denote two sexes, or two kinds, and are joined to a substantive feminine; the same reason would prove that *testis* is likewise of the neuter gender, because Horace says, *Testis Metaurum flumen*; and that *pecus, pecoris*, is of the feminine, since it denotes both kinds, though it is not Latin to say of a sheep, *Lanigeræ pecoris*.

III.

III. Nouns common that are put in both genders.

There are other nouns that are put in both genders, the greatest part of which are as follow.

ADOLESCENS. *Optimæ adolescenti facere injuriam*, Ter.
AFFINIS. *Affinis tua*, Cic.
ANTISTES. *Perita antistes*, Val. Max. Though we read also *antistita*, Plaut. Cic.
AUTOR. *Autor optima*, Ovid. It is more usual in the masc. And Tertullian has made use of *auctrix*, for the fem. But Servius observeth that the nouns in TOR, form their feminine in TRIX, only when they are derived from a verb, as from *lego*, cometh *lector*, which makes *lectrix*; whereas the others under a single termination, are generally common, *senator*, *balneator*, &c. To which he adds that *autor*, coming from *autoritas*, is common, but when coming from *augeo*, we say *auctor divitiarum*, and *auctrix patrimonii*.
AUGUR. *Augur cassa futuri*, Stat. But more usually in the masc.
BOS. *Abstractæque boves*, Virg. It is even more usually in the fem. except when we intend to express particularly the males.
CANIS. *Visæque canes ululare per umbram*, Virg. as quoted by Seneca, though others read *visi canes*. But this noun is more usual in the feminine, when it denotes the rage and fury of this animal, because it more properly belongs to the female.
CIVIS. *Civis Romana*, Cic.
COMES. *Comitem suam destituit*, Ovid. But it is more usual in the masc.
CONJUX. *Antiquus conjux*, Virg *Regia conjux*, Id.
CONVIVA. *Conveni omnes convivas meas*, Pompon.
CUSTOS. *Custos vestra*, Plaut.
DUX. *Quâ fidunt duce nocturnâ Phœnices in alto*, Cic. Acad. 2.
HÆRES. *Si sua bæres abstineat se bonis*, Tryphon.
HOSTIS. *Studiorum perniciosissima hostis*, Quintil.
INFANS. *Infantem suam reportavit*, Quint.
INDEX. *Sumus tam sæva judice sontes*, Luc. But it is more usual in the masc.
MILES. *Nova miles eram*, Ovid. But more frequently in the masc.
MUNICEPS. *Municipem suam*, Plin.
PARENS. *Alma parens*, Virg. Though Charisius takes notice that antiently it was only masc. and that Medea, in Pacuvius, looking for her mother, said, *Ut mibi potestatem duis inquirendi mei parentis*,
PATRUELIS. *Si mibi patruelis nulla manet*, Pers.
SUS. *Amica luto sus*, Hor. *Immundi sues*, Virg.
TESTIS. *Inducta teste in senatum*, Sueton. But oftener in the masc.
VATES. *Tuque, ô sanctissima vates*, Virg.
VINDEX. *Tu saltem debita vindex huc ades*, Stat. But more usual in the masculine.

But we are to observe that some of the above nouns seem to be rather adjectives, as *adolescens*, *affinis*; with which, strictly speaking, *homo* and *mulier* are understood; though this makes no difference in regard to practice, since it is sufficient to know that they have been used by the antients in both genders.

We must also take notice that there are some particular words in ecclesiastic writers, in the use of which these writers are to be our guides, because in this respect we cannot build upon profane authority. Such is the word *martyr*, which is frequently fem. in the fathers, though in profane authors it is only masc.

IV. Of doubtful nouns.

We must likewise recal to mind what has been said in the introduction to genders, vol. i. p. 1. concerning the difference between the common and the doubtful; and that a doubtful noun having in one part of the sentence been put in one gender, may in another part be put in another. Thus we find in Ovid:

Est specus exesi structurâ pumicis asper,
Non homini facilis, non adeunda feræ.

Where we see that *specus* is joined with *asper* in the first verse, as masculine; and with *adeunda* in the second, as feminine. Yet this seems to be a kind of a licence, more excusable in poets than in orators.

V. *Of epicenes.*

We have already mentioned these nouns in the first rule of genders, vol. i. p. 5. and in the last, p. 55. The word EPICENE is of Greek derivation, and cannot be rendered by a single term in Latin; so that it is speaking with impropriety to call these nouns, either *communia*, or *promiscua*. For as the antients called κοινὸν, *commune*, that noun which includes within itself the two genders; so they have given the name of ἐπίκοινον, that is, *supercommune*, to that noun which had something more than the common in this respect, that it included both kinds under one gender.

And at first they made use of this term only to express the names either of such animals as were least known to them, or whose males were not so easy to distinguish from the females. Hence Varro takes notice, that antiently *columba* was epicene, and included the male as well as the female; but when pigeons were grown more tame, the male was called *columbus*, and the female *columba*. Festus observes that Numa's laws had *agnum feminam*, for *agnam*. And this confusion of genders has still continued in a great many nouns, though their kind is sufficiently distinguished, as *vulpes* and *feles*, feminine; *elephas*, masculine, &c.

But what is still more remarkable, that which the antients distinguished, as *puerus* and *puera*, has sometimes reverted to the same gender; the word *puer* a child, agreeing as well with girls as boys, and having been heretofore common, as Charisius takes notice, and likewise Priscian, book 6. and 9. *Sancta puer Saturni filia regina*, Liv. in Odys. *Prima incedit Cereris Proserpina puer*, Næv. 2. bell. Pun. So that this noun being at length become epicene, a father might call his daughters *pueros meos*, my children (if custom had so determined) as well as *liberos*, which occurs in this sense in the civil law, and of which Gellius has expressly treated in the 12th chapter of his 2d book, where he says moreover, that the antients used the word *liberos* in the plural, when speaking of a man who had only one *son*, or one *daughter*. In like manner to express a female we may very well say *egregium catulum*, a fine kitten, without there being any necessity to put *egregiam*, unless we want to express particularly its sex; the epicene noun generally following the gender of its termination, and including indeterminately both kinds under this gender, and this termination.

But when they wanted to express the particular sex, they added *masculus* or *femina*, as appears from Columella, and others. *Pavo masculus, pavo femina*, &c.; or else they understood them, as when Plautus said, *Elephas gravida*, that is, *gravidâ femina*, it being

being impossible that *gravida* should refer to *elephas* masculine, but by understanding some other word between them.

It is by this rule, according to Sanctius, and even to Quintilian, that we ought to explain these passages of Virgil, *Timidi damæ, talpæ oculis capti*, where in all probability the reason of his departing from the gender of the termination, was that he supposed the word *masculi*, to refer to the most worthy: concerning which the reader may likewise see what hath been said in the list of the epicenes, vol. i. p. 56. and 57.

Sometimes they referred to the masculine according to the termination, though speaking of females, as we read in Pliny, *Polypi pariunt ova tantâ fœcunditate, ut multitudinem ovorum occisi non recipiant cavo capitis, quo prægnantes tulere*, where *occisi* refers to *Polypi*, though it is understood of females. Which is still more extraordinary among the Greeks, who do not mind the termination, as when Aristotle saith, οἱ ὄρνιθες τίκτουσι, *hi aves pariunt*, and as he said in another place ὁ λέων to signify a lioness, and Homer τὸν αἶγα for a she-goat, τοὺς οἶας for sheep and the like. This may be referred to the figure of syllepsis, of which hereafter.

Now it is very ridiculous, says Sanctius, to imagine that the word *epicene* belongs only to birds or quadrupeds. It is applicable also to insects and fishes, and even to man, as we have shewn in the word *puer*, and is further proved by all those nouns which are common in their signification only. And this is sufficiently expressed by the explication of the word and the above given etymology of it.

Chapter. II.

Remarks on some particular cases.

I. *Of the* Vocative.

THE vocative, among the Attics, was always the same as the nominative. Hence these two cases are almost always the same in Latin, and for this same reason they are frequently joined in a sentence, as *Nate meæ vires, mea magna potentia solus*. Virg. *Salve primus omnium parens patriæ appellate, primus in toga triumphum, linguæque lauream merite*. Pliny speaking of Cicero. And hereby we see, says Sanctius, that we may express ourselves these ways, *Defende me amice mi*, or *defende me amicus meus*. See the declensions, vol. i. p. 65. and the remarks on the pronouns which are to follow, chap. 1. n. 5.

II. *Of the* Dative *and the* Ablative.

In Greek the ablative is the same as the dative, hence they have always a great affinity even in Latin. Therefore as the Greeks say, τῷ Ἀνίᾳ, and the Dorians also, τῷ Ἀγχίσᾳ, τᾷ ἐπιτομᾷ, τᾷ μούσᾳ, or ΜΟΥΣΑΙ, the Latins first made *huic Anchisai, huic epitomai, huic musai* (which is the same as *musæ*) and only dropping the *i*, *hôc Anchisâ, hâc musâ, hâc epitomâ*, &c. Just as the Æolians

Æolians say τῷ 'Αινίᾳ, τᾷ μύσα, τῷ λόγῳ, &c. without ι. Concerning which you may see what hath been said in the declensions, vol. i. p. 100. 122. 125.

But what is more remarkable, the Latins have been such imitators of the Æolics, that heretofore they dropped even this *i* or this *e* in the dative as well as in the ablative, in the first declension, and in the others they made these two cases always alike. Hence it is, says Scioppius, that we find in Propertius,

  Si placet insultet Lygdame morte mea,

for *morti mea*. Likewise, *Piláque feminea turpiter apta manu* for *manui*, Id. Hence also it is, that taking *me* for *mi*, formed by contraction from *mihi*, and likewise, *te* for *tibi*, according to the remark of Donatus and Festus, we find that Terence says, *Nimis me indulgeo. Te indulgebant*, &c. Hence it is in fine, that we meet with, *In colli tundentes pabula læta*, Lucr. *Serta procul capiti tantum delapsa jacebant*, Virg. for *tantum capite*, or *à capite*. *Scriberis vario Mæonii carminis alite*, Hor. for *aliti*. For Servius saith it is the same expression as *cernitur ulli. Cum temerè anguineo creditur ore manus*, Propert. for *ori. Cum capite hoc Stygiæ jam peterentur aquæ*, Id. for *capiti huic. Ut mihi non ullo pondere terra foret*, Id. for *ulli ponderi*: in the same sense as Lucretius says,

  Ut sua cuique homini nullo sunt pondere membra,
  Nec caput est oneri collo:

where it is obvious that *sunt pondere* and *est oneri*, are in the same construction.

  ――― *Aciésque Latinæ*
  Concurrunt, hæret pede pes, densúsque viro vir, Virg.

where *pede* stands for *pedi*, even according to Linacer. *Quod haud scio an timens suo corpore posse accidere*, Cicero. And we meet with a great many more, which shew, in my opinion, that this principle cannot easily be doubted of. But this remark extends a great deal further, as we shall make appear hereafter, when we come to speak of the pronouns.

Chapter III.

Remarks on numeral nouns.

I. *Of* Ambo *and* Duo.

*A*MBO and *duo* are used in the accusative masculine, as well as *ambos* and *duos*, according to Charisius. Which is an imitation of the Greeks, who say, τὺς δύω: τὺς ἄμφω.

  Si duo præterea tales Idæa tulisset
  Terra viros. Virg.
  Verùm ubi ductores acie revocaveris ambo. Id.

according to the reading not only of Charisius, but also of Servius, who produces several other authorities besides: and this accusative was in the antient copies of Cicero, as Vossius observeth, who attributes the change to the ignorance of the correctors.

The

The neuter is in Cicero quoted by Accius, *Video sepulchra duo duorum corporum*, in Oratore: where Scioppius, Gruterus, and others, read *dua*. And indeed Quintilian observeth, that they used to say, *dua pondo*, and *trepondo*, and that Messala maintained it was right.

We meet also with *duo* in the accusative feminine, as Scipio Gentilis quotes it, *Tritavia similiter numerata facit personas triginta duo, Pauli I. C.* And Contius cites it from Scevola in the genitive, *Duo millium aureorum*, for *duorum*. But this is rare, whereas the accusative is very common; but we shall shew hereafter, that there were a great many more plural nouns of this termination in *o*.

II. *Of the other numeral nouns.*

It is to be observed that though we say, *quindecim, sedecim*, and the like numbers lower than these, yet in the writings of the antients we meet more usually with *decem & septem, decem & octo, decem & novem*, than *septemdecim, octodecim, novemdecim*, which are almost the only ones in modern use.

Priscian tells us that we should say, *decimus & tertius*, with the conjunction, putting the greater number the first, or *tertius decimus*, without the conjunction, putting the greater number the last; *decimus & quartus*, or *quartus-decimus*, and the rest in the like manner as far as twenty, though we find also *decimus-tertius, decimus-quartus*, &c. in very good authors. But as this might have been owing to the mistakes of transcribers who expressed according to their own fancy what they found written in cyphers, it seems to be the safest way to adhere to Priscian's doctrine. *Sententia septima-decima*, is in Cicero. *Nono-decimo anno*, in Ter. and the like in others. We say likewise, *duodeviginti*, for 18. *undeviginti*, for 19. And according to Linacer we may say likewise, *duodetriginta*, for 28. *undequadraginta*, for 39. *undequinquagessimo die*, is in Cicero, and such like.

From twenty to one hundred, if you put a conjunction between the two numbers, the smallest must be placed first, *unus & viginti, duo & triginta*, &c. If you do not use the conjunction, you say, *viginti unus, viginti duo*, &c. Above a hundred, you always follow the natural order, either without or with the conjunction, *centum unus*, or *centum & unus, mille unus*, or *mille & unus*, &c.

But to reckon a thousand, you are to follow the rule of numbers under a hundred. *Sex & viginti millia*, or *viginti sex millia*.

And this rule is observed in the ordinal number; *vicesimus primus*, or *primus et vicesimus*: in the distributive, *viceni singuli*, or *singuli et viceni*: in numeral adverbs, *vicies semel*, or *semel et vicies*, &c.

Mille is indeclinable in the singular, though according to Macrobius, formerly they said *mille, millis*. In the plural it is declined, *millia, ium, ibus*. We say indifferently in the singular, *mille homines*, or *mille hominum*: but in the plural we prefer *millia hominum* with the genitive, though it is not true that the other expression was erroneous, as Valla and Linacer imagined.

Tot millia gentes —— *Arma ferunt Italæ*, Virg.

Duodecim millia pedites, Liv. *Tritici modios quinque millia*, Cic. *Trecentis millibus mulieribus*, Juſt. For *millia* is alſo an adjective, as we ſhall ſhew hereafter in the chapter of ſeſterces; which ſeems to have eſcaped thoſe grammarians.

Chapter IV.

Of the motion, or variation of adjectives.

THE motion or variation of adjectives may be conſidered two different ways, either according to the genders, or according to compariſon.

I. *Of the variation according to the genders.*

Some adjectives have only one termination for the three genders, as *par*, *concors*. And in this number we ought to include *infans*, ſince we read in Horace, *Infantes ſtatuas*; in Ovid, *Infantia guttura*; and in Valerius Maximus, *Infans puer*.

The others have two terminations, IS and E for the poſitive degree: OR and US for the comparative. But antiently the termination OR ſerved in this degree for the three genders. *Bellum Punicum poſterior*, Plaut.

We find likewiſe *potis* and *pote*, in all genders.

    Qui potis eſt? inquis: quod amantem injuria talis
      Cogit amare magis, ſed bene velle minus, Catul.

Where it is obvious that he put *potis* for *pote*, δυνατὸν; as on the contrary he has put *pote* for *potis* in this other verſe:

——*Quantum qui pote plurimum perire*.

And for want of knowing this remark, a great many paſſages of the antients have been corrupted; though we do not deny but *pote* is more uſual in the neuter. See the 3d chapter of irregular verbs, and the firſt chapter of adverbs, which are to follow.

There are likewiſe ſome that have two different terminations; as *Hic acer*, *hæc acris*, *hoc acre*; or elſe *hic et hæc acris*, *et hoc acre*: and the ſame you may ſay of *ſaluber*, *alacer*, and others: *alacris*, ſays Aſconius, *five alacer*, *utrumque enim dicimus*. From thence comes *pauper*, in the feminine in Terence, as Donatus reads it.

    Potius quàm in patria honeſtè pauper vivere, in Andr.

Though in Plautus we find, *paupera hæc res eſt*.

Celer hath for the feminine *celeris*, in Ovid, and for the neuter *celere*, in Ter. *in Phorm*. But *celeris* is alſo maſc. in Cato. Hence as from *celer* comes *celerrimus*, in the ſuperlative, ſo from *celeris* came *celeriſſimus*, in Ennius.

Under the adjectives of a ſingle termination we ought likewiſe to comprehend *Dives*, *hebes*, *ſoſpes*, *teres*, *memor*, *uber*, and ſome others, though they are not ſo uſual in the neuter. But in Ovid we find, *divitis ingenii*; in Virgil, *teres flagellum*, *memoris ævi*, *pauperis ingenii*, and the like.

The names of countries in AS heretofore were terminated in *is*, so that they said, according to Priscian, *Hic et hæc Arpinatis, et hoc Arpinate*. But because they have changed their termination, they have likewise changed their gender: the termination AS being as well for the neuter as for the other two. *Ad iter Arpinas flexus,* Cic. *Bellum Privernas,* Liv. *Bellum Capenas,* Id. and it would be a mistake, if we believe Vossius, to say, *bellum Capinate*; though Priscian was of opinion that they said, *Hic et hæc Arpinas et hoc Arpinate*; and though Donatus laid it down as a rule that we should say, *Cujate, nostrate, vestrate mancipium,* instead of *cujas nostras,* &c.

Substantives sometimes become adjectives, and then they receive the variation of the adjectives, as in Virg. *Arcadium magistrum, Laticémque Lyæum,* for *Arcadicum, Lyæium: populum late regem,* for *regnantem,* and the like. It is false reasoning, to conclude with Sanctius that it is as impossible a substantive should become an adjective, or an adjective become a substantive, as that a substance should be changed into accident. As if we did not see examples to the contrary in all languages, in French, for instance, *chagrin, colere*; the names of colours, *blanc, rouge,* and others, which are sometimes adjectives, and sometimes substantives: and as if it were not a thing merely accidental and indifferent to all sorts of nouns, their being taken to express an accident or a substance.

Even the substantives continuing substantives, have sometimes their variation, as *rex, regina; tibicen, tibicina; coluber, colubra,* &c.

II. *Of the comparison of nouns.*

We have already spoken of the comparatives in the abridgment of this new method, and in the syntax, rule 27. p. 55. and following.

As the comparative particularly expresseth the quality of the thing, it is plain it cannot agree with noun substantive. But if we say, *Neronior,* then it is to denote cruelty, and it is an adjective; just as Plautus saith, *Pœnior,* to signify great subtlety and cunning.

Therefore when we read in the aforesaid Plautus, *Meritissimo ejus quæ volet faciemus;* and in Varro, *Villæ pessimo publico ædificatæ;* and in Livy, *pessimo publico aliquid facere,* these are only adjectives, which suppose their substantive by an ellipsis, two or more adjectives agreeing extremely well with the same substantive, as we have shewn in the syntax, rule 1.

It does not agree even with every adjective that expresseth quality, and therefore much less does it agree with others which express none. Thus we see that *Opimus, claudus, canorus, egenus, balbus, almus,* and others, have no degrees of comparison, because custom has settled it otherwise.

To the superlatives in LIMUS, by us mentioned, some add; *agilimus, gracillimus*; and Valla joins also, *docillimus*. But Vossius rejects it, as not founded on authority. Charisius on the contrary in the chapter of adverbs says, that of *agilis* and *docilis,* are formed *agilissimus* and *docilissimus,* from whence come *agilissime* and *docilissime.*

As to *imbecillimus*, it is true we find it in Seneca, not in the book of confolation to Marcia, where the beft copies have *corpus imbecillum*, but in the 85th letter. *Quantulum autem fapienti damus fi imbecillimis fortior eft?* But *imbecillissimus* occurs alfo in Celfus, who is a very pure author.

III. *Of defectives, or thofe which are deprived of fome degree of comparifon.*

Of adjectives, fome are

Without the pofitive, as *prior* and *primus*. To thefe are added *deterior deterrimus*, and *potior potissimus* But one cometh from *deter*, and the other from *potis*. *Ulterior* and *ultimus*, may come from *ulter*. *Ocior* and *ocissimus*, come from the Greek, ὠκὺς, which makes ὠκίων, in the comparative; and hence it appeareth that *ocior* ought to be written with an *i* and not with a *y*.

Without the comparative, *nuper* and *nuperrimus*; *novus, novissimus*; the laſt. *Sacer* an *facerrimus*; *invitus* and *invitissimus*. And in like manner, *Diverfus, falfus, fidus, perfuafus, invifus, confultus, meritus, apricus, bellus, invictus, inclytus*, and fome others perhaps, though not fo many as people imagine.

Without the fuperlative, *adolescens, adolescentior; juvenis, ior; fenex, ior*. Likewife, *ingens, fatur, dexter, finifter*. For *dextimus* and *finiftimus*, are no more than fimple pofitives. *Supinus* forms alfo *fupinior*, in Mart. We meet with *infinitior* and *divitior*, in Cicero, Plautus, and Ovid.

Anterior, hath neither pofitive nor fuperlative, no more than *licentior*. But *habitior*, which we read in Terence hath both: *Equum ftrigofum et malè habitum; fed equitem ejus uberrimum et habitissimum viderunt*, Gell.

IV. *Superlatives that are compared.*

From the fuperlative are likewife formed other degrees of comparifon; *Cum adolefcentulis poftremissimis*, Apul. *Proximus* for *vicinus*, forms *proximior*, Seneca; and fome others in the fame manner.

V. *Adjectives that are not compared.*

Thofe of countries, as *Romanus, Spartiata*. Poffeffives, *Patrius, Evandrius*. Numerals, *primus, decimus*. Thofe of matter, *aureus*. Of time, *hefternus*. Thofe in DUS, *amandus, errabundus*. In PLEX, *duplex*; except *fimplex*, and *multiplex*. In IMUS, *legitimus*, IVUS, *fugitivus*. Thofe from *gero* and *fero*, *armiger, frugifer*. Likewife *almus, balbus, canorus, canus, cicur, claudus, degener, difpar, egenus, magnanimus, mediocris, memor, mirus, vetulus, unicus*, and perhaps a few others. But *crifpus, opimus*, and *filvefter*, which Voffius ranks in this number, have their comparative. The firft we find more than once in Pliny; *Crifpiores jubæ lemum*, lib. 8 c. 16. *Crifpioris elegantiæ materies*, l. 13. c 9. The fecond is in Gellius, *Membra opimiora*, fatter, l. 5. c. 14. And the third alfo in Pliny, *Syveftriora omnia*, lib 16. c. 27. But in regard to thofe that have none, we make ufe of *magis*, to fupply the comparative, and of *maximè* for the fuperlative.

Remarks on the Diminutives. 89

To these the grammarians add all the nouns in US, that have a vowel before US: and indeed it happens that they form neither comparative nor superlative left they should occasion too great a concurrence of vowels: yet there are several that are compared, of which take the following list.

List of nouns that are compared, though they have a vowel before US.

Arduïus *and* arduissimus, *Cato.*
Assiduïores, *Varr.* Assiduissimus, *Cic.*
Egregiissimus, *Pacuv.*
Egregius *is even put for* egregiius *in Juvenal, as Priscian observes.*
    Egregius cœnat, meliúsque miserrimus horum.
Exiguïus, *Ulpian.*
Exiguissimus, *Ovid. Plin.*
Idoneïus, *is in Tertull.* Idoneïor, *in Petrus Damianus, and in all the writers of the latter ages.*
Industrior, *Plautus.*
Injurius, *Plautus.* Nihil amore injurius est, *as Douza reads it, that is,* injurïius, *or* injuriosius.
Innoxius, *or* innoxïius, *Cato.*
Necessarius, *is also a comparative in the writers of the latter ages.* Quibus utique necessarius quâ Deus, & quidem melior, quo necessarior, latere non debuit, *Tertull. lib. 1. contra*

Marcion. *This author has used the same expression in other places. Saint Ambrose and others have also spoke thus. And in the vulgate,* Quæ videntur membra corporis infirmiora esse, necessariora sunt, *S. Paul 1 Cor. 12.*
Piissimus, *is in Seneca,* Q. Curt. *Quintilian, Livy, Pliny, Apuleius, St. Jerome, and others; though Cicero condemns it in his* 13. Phil. Tu verò, *says he,* ne pios quidem, sed piissimos quæris; & quod verbum omninò nullum in lingua Latina est, id propter tuam divinam pietatem novum inducis.
Perpetuïor *and* perpetuissimus, *Prisc. ex Catone.*
Strenuïor, *Plaut. Lucil.*
Strenuissimus, *Sallust.*
Tenuïor, *Cic.*
Tenuissimus, *Id.*
Vacuissimus, *Ovid.*

We might mention others in Plautus, but it is to be observed that this author hath frequently affected to coin a number of these words according to his fancy, which by no means are to be admitted, as *verberabilissimus*, to signify one that very richly deserves to be beaten: *Parissimus*, very equal: *spissigradissimus, exclusissimus,* &c.

He does the same with the comparatives. *Confessior, tacitius*: with the pronouns, *ipsissimus*: with the substantives, *meritissimum* for *maximum meritum*, and the like. Which is not to be imitated but with great care and judgment.

Chapter V.
Of Diminutives.

AFTER having treated of nouns which augment the signification, we must mention a word or two about those which diminish it, and are therefore called diminutives.

Diminutives are generally terminated in LUS, LA, LUM; as *filiolus, adolescentulus, pagella, oscillum,* a little mouth, or little image which the antients hung up in honour of Saturn for their sins, or a kind of play amongst them. *Sigillum, pullus, flosculus, homunculus,* &c.

There

There are moreover some that terminate in io, as *senex, senecio; pusus, pusio*. Others in EUS; *equus, equulus, equuleus*.

Greek nouns are also terminated in ISCUS, *Syrus, Syriscus; mas, mariscus*, &c.

ASTER. This termination is likewise diminutive according to Scaliger. Sanctius on the contrary maintains that it augments the signification, but in derision; *theologaster*, a great theologian, a great doctor, said ironically. And if we find in Terence, *parasitaster parvulus*, in Adelph: he says that *parvulus*, only denotes the age, and makes nothing against his assertion. Vossius says, that of these nouns some mark diminution, as *surdaster, recalvaster*, and in like manner *philosophaster, poëtaster*, &c. Others denote imitation, as *Antoniaster*; and others signify neither, as *apiaster*, or *apiastrum*, taken from *apes*, a kind of herb of which bees are fond.

The diminutives form also other diminutives of themselves; as *puer, puerulus*, or *puellus*, and from thence *puellulus*. *Cistula*, a little basket, *cistella*, and from thence *cistellula*, in Plautus.

Hence it appears how greatly Valla was mistaken in asserting that no diminution could be added to diminutives, as if we did not find in Terence, *pisciculos minutos*; in Cicero, *minutis interrogatiunculis*; and in another place, *pisciculi parvi*; in Cæsar, *naviculam parvam*; in Valerius Maximus, *cum parvulis filiolis*, and others of the same sort.

Section II.

REMARKS ON THE PRONOUNS.

Chapter. I.

Of the number of pronouns, and the signification and declension of some in particular.

I. *The nature of a pronoun.*

THE Pronouns are no more than real nouns, says Sanctius, that have nothing in particular but their manner of declining. For to say that they are substituted in the room of the nouns, there is nothing particular in that, since even one noun may be taken for another.

Be that as it may, grammarians are very much divided about the number of pronouns. Some reckon *uter, qualis, quantus*, &c. others, *alius, omnis, totus*, and the like, and others also include *ambo, duo*; and others add some more. For the sake of ease and brevity, I thought it sufficient to mark eight with the relative, in the abridgment of this new method.

II. *Difference in the signification of Pronouns.*

We have already taken notice of some difference between ILLE and ISTE in the abridgment of this book. Cornelius Fronto also teacheth,

teacheth, that HIC and ISTE, are said of a person who is near us, ILLE of one who is at a distance, but not out of sight, and IS of one who is absent. And it amounts almost to the same, when Saturnius asserts that *hic* is for the first person, *istic* for the second, and *illic* for the third. We have thought proper to mention these differences, though they have not been always observed by authors.

HIC and ILLE differ also in general, inasmuch as *hic* refers to the nearest, and *ille* to the remotest; which ought always to be observed, when there is any danger of ambiguity. But except on such occasion, authors have slighted this difference.

Quocunque aspicio, nihil est nisi pontus & æther,
Fluctibus hic tumidus, nubibus ille minax, Ovid.

And Cicero, *Quid est quod negligenter scribamus adversaria? quid est quod diligenter scribamus tabulas? qua de causa? Quia hæc sunt menstrua, illa æternæ; hæc delentur statim, illæ servantur sanctè; hæc parvi temporis memoriam, illa perpetuæ existimationis fidem & religionem amplectuntur; hæc sunt dejecta, illæ in ordinem confectæ.*

The difference they make between QUI and QUIS, is of no service. For Pierius observeth that in ancient copies we find indifferently, *Nec quis sim quæris Alexi,* or *nec qui sim,* Virg. eclog. 2.

That which they make betwixt OMNIS or QUISQUE and UTERQUE, is not always true, no more than that which they suppose between ALTER and ALIUS. For *omnis* and *quisque* are said likewise of two.

Ecce autem similia omnia, omnes congruunt;
Unum cognôris, omnes nôris, Ter. in Phorm.

where he is speaking of Antipho and Phædria. And Quintilian, *An cùm duo fures pecuniam abstulerunt, separatim quadruplum quisque in duplum debeat.*

We meet also with ALIUS, where mention is made only of two: *Duas leges promulgavit; unam quæ mercedes habitationum annuas conductoribus donavit; aliam tabularum novarum,* Cæs. 3. bel. civil. And on the contrary we find ALTER, for *alius,* in Phædrus and others.

What they say likewise of UTER and QUIS, that the former is applicable to two only, and the latter to *many*, and therefore that one is joined to the comparative, and the other to the superlative; is not general. *Quanquam præstat honestas incolumitati; tamen* UTRI POTISSIMUM *consulendum sit deliberetur,* Cic. He does not say *utri potiùs*, but *utri potissimùm*. QUIS may also be used, when speaking of two only, *Duo celeberrimi duces, quis eorum prior vicisset,* Liv.

Uter is never said but of two: but its adverb UTRUM is used interrogatively in regard to divers things: *Utrùm impudentiùs à sociis abstulit, an turpiùs meretrici dedit, an improbiùs populo Rom. ademit, an audaciùs tabulas publicas commutavit?* Cic. in Ver.

ALIQUIS and QUIDAM are frequently put for one another; though speaking with propriety, *quiddam* implies a determinate thing, whereas *aliquid* is said indeterminately, as much as to say *aliud quid.*

III. Con-

III. *Concerning the Cases, and the declension of pronouns.*

Pronouns, as we have shewn in the abridgment of this grammar, have their vocative. But since the contrary is maintained by many, we must produce on this occasion some examples.

Esto nunc sol testis, & Hæc mihi terra precanti, Virg.
Ipse meas æther, accipe summe preces, Ovid.
O nox ILLA, *quæ penè æternas huic urbi tenebras attulisti*, Cic.
There is only EGO that has none, because as this case particularly expresses the person to whom we speak, the first person cannot speak to himself: and SUI, by reason it hath no nominative, on which the vocative always dependeth.

MIS and TIS are antient genitives for *mei* and *tui*, though Alvarez would fain have it that they are datives plural. Proofs thereof may be seen in Voss. *lib.* 4. *de Anal. cap.* 4.

ILLE. Antiently they said *ollus* or *olle*, for *ille*, whence also cometh *olli* for *illi* in Virgil and others.

IPSE. They used likewise to say *ipsus* for *ipse*, though the neuter *ipsud* is condemned as a barbarous term by Diomedes. HÆ was heretofore said in the neuter as well as in the feminine, just as *quæ* is used for both genders in the plural. But of *hæ* they made *hæce*, just as we say *hicce* in the singular; and afterwards by apocope they said *hæc*, which we find even in the feminine, *Periere hæc oppido ædes*, Plaut. *Hæc illæ erant itiones*, Ter. in Phorm. as quoted by Donatus, or *hæccine*, according as Heinsius reads it.

IS formerly made *im* in the accusative (as Charisius has observed) like *sitis, sitim.*

Boni im miserantur; *illunc irrident mali*, Plaut.
They used also *ibus* instead of *iis* in the dative and ablative plural.

—— *Ibus dinumerem stipendium*, Plaut.

EA made *eæ* in the genitive for *ejus:* and *eabus* in the dative and ablative plural for *iis*.

IV. *Of the nature of the relative.*

The pronoun relative, *qui, quæ, quod*, has this in common with all the rest, that it is put in the place of a noun. But it hath this in particular to itself, that it should always be considered as betwixt two cases of the noun substantive which it represents, as we have shewn in the syntax, rule 2. And that it serves as a connexion to make an incidental proposition form part of another which may be called the principal. In regard to which we refer the reader to what hath been said in the general and rational grammar part 2. c. 9.

V. *Of* QUI *or* QUIS.

QUI we find in Plautus, even in an interrogative sense. *Qui cænâ poscit? Ecqui poscit prandio? qui me alter est audacior homo?* In Amphit. *Qua* is acknowledged in the fem. even by Donatus; and Scioppius proves it from Propertius, *Fortunata meo si qua est celebrata libello*, though it seems to be put for *aliqua*, and therefore it is rejected by Vossius. But *qua* in its natural signification, may

likewise

likewise bear this meaning; *si qua est*, if there is any, &c. The neuter *quid* occurs in Plautus, *quid tibi nomen est?* In Amph.

Quis was heretofore of all genders: *Quis illæc est mulier quæ ipsa se misereatur*, Plaut. *Quisquam illarum, nostrarum quisquam*, Plaut. *Scortum exoletum ne quis in proscænio sedeat*, Id. And it is the same as *potis, magis, satis, nimæ*, which of their nature are adjectives and of all genders, though custom has made them pass for adverbs.

The antients declined *qui* and *quis* without changing the *q*, either in the genitive or the dative. Hence in order to distinguish them the more easily, they said *quoius* and *quoi*, because *qui* would have been the same as the nominative: and we find a great many more examples of it in the antient copies of Virgil and Cicero.

Quoi non dictus Hilas puer? 3. Georg.

As Pierius observes: *Quoi tu (video enim quid sentias) me comitem putas debere esse*, ad Att. lib. 8. ep. 8. *Quoi tali in re libenter me ad pedes abjecissem*, ep. 9.

Hence it cometh that dropping the *i*, as we have already observed in the second chap. of the remarks on the nouns, they said *quo* in the dative as well as in the ablative, according to Scioppius, *si quo usui esse exercitui possit*, Liv. *Ut id agam quo missus hic sum*, Plaut. for *quoi negotio*. *Est certus locus, certa lex, certum tribunal, quo hæ reserventur*, Cic. *Quo mihi fortunas, si non conceditur uti?* Hor. for *cui usui*. And the like.

The accusative was *quem, quom*, or *quum*, of which at length they made *cum*, taking the C for Q, as well as in the genitive and dative. Which is for all genders, as coming from *quis*, of all genders.

And this has produced those elegant phrases, wherein Tully useth this *cum* as a connexion, after all nouns and words expressive of time. *Ex eo tempore cùm me pro vestra incolumitate devovi*, for *ad quom*, or *cum tempus*, instead of *ad quod tempus*. In like manner *tempus cum; hic dies sextus cum; jam multos annos est cum; jam ab illo tempore cum; paucis post diebus cum; multi anni sunt cum; nunc tempus est cum; dies nondum decem intercesserant cum; illa tempora cum; nuper cum; triginta dies erant ipsi cum*, &c. *fuit tempus cum*, or *fuit cum; prope adest cum; nunc illud est cum; nondum cum; tantum veneram cum*, &c.

Quî in the ablative is of all genders, and comes from their having heretofore been used to say in the dative *qui* (or *quoi*) for *cui*. *Patera quî rex potitare solitus*, Plaut, for *in quâ*. *Restem volo emere quî me faciam pensilem*, Id. *Quî cum partiri curas*, &c.

'*Abs quivis homine, cum est opus, beneficium accipere gaudeas*,' Terence. And in another place

  Nam in prologis scribundis operam abutitur:
  Non quî argumentum narret, sed quî malevoli
  Veteris pcëtæ maledictis respondeat.

For *qui* is not a nominative in this passage, since Donatus thought it stood for *ut:* but it would have been better to say it stood for *quo* or *quo negotio*, and that it is an ablative signifying the manner. Just as Terence has again expressed himself in another place:

Hunc

Hanc fidem sibi me obsecravit, qui se sciret non deserturum, ut darem, Id. Where *qui* stands for *quo modo.* She begged I would give her my word, whereby she might be sure that I would not forsake her.

It is likewise by this principle that we so frequently repeat, *qui igitur convenit,* Cic. *Qui fieri potest* for *quomodo,* &c. This *qui* occurs even in the ablative plural, *ut anates, aut coturnices dantur qui cum lusitent,* Plaut. cap. A. 5. sc. 4. And Duza believes it is a barbarism to say *quibuscum,* though we meet with it frequently in Cicero, and in other writers. *Quibus ortus sis, non quibuscum vivas considera,* Philip. 2. *Ad eorum approbationem quibuscum vivimus,* Off. 1.

The plural of *quis* was heretofore QUES, according to Festus and Charis. from whence also cometh the dative and ablative *quibus,* just as *puppes* makes *puppibus,* whereas of *qui* is formed *queis* or *quis,* as from *illi* cometh *illis.*

The accusative plural neuter was not only *quæ*, but likewise *qua* and *quo.* QUA has still continued in *quapropter,* that is, *propter qua,* or *quæ,* sup. *tempora vel negotia.*

QUO was therefore an accusative plural, the same as *ambo* and *duo,* of which mention hath been made in the chapter of numeral nouns; and it has continued still in *quocirca, quousque,* &c. that is, *circa quo,* or *usque quo,* for *ad quo,* or *ad quæ,* sup. *tempora vel negotia,* or the like. *Prope aream facienda umbracula, quo succedant homines in æstu, tempore meridiano,* Varr. for *ad quæ. Dolia quo vinaceas condat decem,* Cato, for *in quæ.*

They used also to say *eo* in the accusative plural. *Eo redactus sum,* that is, *ad eo* (for *ea*) *negotia. Ad eos res rediit,* Ter. for *ad ea loca,* the affair is brought to that pitch.

Illo was likewise used in the same sense; *Nam ubi illo adveni,* Plaut. that is, *ad illo,* for *ad illa loca.*

But *quo* was put for all genders, just as we have above observed of *duo*——*Dignissimi quo cruciatus confluant,* Plaut. for *ad quos. Sulcant fossas quo aqua pluvia delabatur,* Varr. for *per quas.* It even seemeth that as the ablative *qui* served for all genders and numbers, so *quo* has been used for the singular and the plural: *Providendum quo se recipiant, ne frigidus locus sit,* Varr. for *ad quem locum. Me ad eam partem esse venturum, quo te maxime velle arbitrabar,* Cic. for *in quam. Nosti hunc fundum, quo ut venimus,* Cic. *Nullum portum, quo classes decurrerent,* Hirt. *Hominem beatum, quo illæ perveniant divitiæ,* Pompon. Unless we chuse to say with Scioppius, that it cometh then from the dative, *quoi,* for *cui,* instead of *ad quem;* as *It clamor cælo,* for *ad cælum.*

VI. *Of* Meus *and* suus.

The vocative singular, *mi,* is an apocope for *mie* (the same as *Virgili* for *Virgilie*; see the declensions, vol. i. p. 65.) which came from the old nominative *mius,* according to Caper and Diomedes.

The writers of the latter ages have used *meus* also in the vocative, not only as an hellenism, when the nominative is taken for the vocative,

vocative, according to what we have already mentioned, chap. 2. as *Deus meus, ut quid dereliquisti me?* but moreover by joining it with a real vocative distinct from the nominative, as in Sidonius, Salvianus, Victor Uticensis, and others, *domine meus*, and the like: which is not to be imitated. For it is true we find that the nominative may be put for the vocative, as Livy has said in the vocative *Populus Albanus*; Horace, *Popilius sanguis*; Persius, *Patricius sanguis*; and Virgil also;

Projice tela manu, sanguis meus, Æn. 6.

But it will not be an easy matter to find, that when the adjective and the substantive have each its particular terminations for these two cases, they ever took, while the purity of the language subsisted, the termination peculiar to one case, to join it with the proper and specific termination of the other. Otherwise, how came they to invent different terminations? Thus Plautus says in the vocative in the very same verse, *meus ocellus, & anime mi*.

Da meus ocellus, da mea rosa, da anime mi, Asin. act. 3. sc. 3.

But he no where says *mi ocellus*, nor *anime meus*. And it is thus likewise that Augustus writing to his nephew, as quoted by Gellius, says, *Ave mi Cai, meus ocellus jucundissimus*. Where we find that in the second member he did not chuse to say *mi ocellus*, but *meus ocellus*, like Plautus. And when we find in Pliny, *Salve primus lauream merite*; and in Virgil, *Nate mea magna potentia solus*: it is because *primus* and *solus* have no other vocative than that in US.

Mi was frequent in all genders, *Mi sidus*, Apul. *Mi conjux*, Id. And S. Jerome, *Testor, mi Paulla*, Jesum.

Mi is sometimes also a vocative plural formed by contraction for *mei*. *Mi homines*, Plaut. *ô mi hospites*, Petron.

This contraction is likewise usual in *Suus*, as *sis* for *seis*, *sos* for *suos*, *sas* for *suas*, &c. In regard to which we are however to observe that the antient passages are sometimes corrupted, and that we should understand *sam* for *eam*, and *sos* for *eos*. And this mistake has proceeded from their having taken F for E in the capital letters, and afterwards *s* for *f* in the small ones.

VII. *Pronouns in* C, *or those compounded of* En *and* Ecce.

The pronouns ending in C are not declined but in those cases where they keep the C: as *istic, istæc,* or *istuc*. *Istunc, istanc,* &c.

Those that are compounded of *en* or *ecce*, are very usual in the accusative. *Eccum, eccam, eccos, eccas; ellum, ellam, ellos, ellas*. And in like manner, *eccillum, eccistam*, which we find in Plautus.

Their nominative also occurs sometimes, though more rarely,

—— *Hercle ab se ecca exit*, Plautus.

CHAPTER II.
Remarks on the construction of pronouns.

I. *Of the construction of* IPSE.

WE have already spoken of the construction of reciprocals in the syntax, rule 36. for which reason we shall only touch on what is most remarkable in regard to the rest.

The pronoun *ipse, ipsa, ipsum*, is of all persons, and generally joined with the primitives, *Ego ipse, tu ipse, ille ipse.*

But whereas the Latin writers of modern date generally put both these pronouns in the same case, saying, for example, *Mihi ipsi placeo; te ipsum laudas; sibi ipsi nocuit;* on the contrary, in the purity of the language, *ipse* is always the nominative of the verb let the other pronoun be in whatever case it will; *Mihi ipse placeo; te ipse laudas; sibi ipse nocuit; me ipse consolor.* Cic. *Resp. per eos regebatur quibus se ipsa commiserat,* Id.

True it is that in the 1st ep. of the 7th book we find in almost all the printed editions, *Reliquas partes diei tu consumebas iis delectationibus, quas tibi ipsi ad arbitrium tuum comparares.* Which Manutius does not altogether condemn. But in this very passage Lambinus and Gruterus read *tibi ipse*, and this last reading, as Manutius confesseth, is confirmed by the Mss.

Ipse by another peculiar elegance expresseth likewise the precise thing or time. *Triginta dies erant ipsi, cùm dabam has litteras*, Cic. *Cùm ibi decem ipsos dies fuissem*, Id. *Quin nunc ipsum non dubito rem tantam abjicere,* Id. *Nunc ipsum ea lego, ea scribo, ut ii qui mecum sunt, difficiliùs otium ferant, quàm ego laborem,* Id. And hence it is that Plautus was not afraid to make a superlative of it. *Ergo ne ipsus ne es? Ipsissimus, abi hinc ab oculis*, in Trinum.

II. *Of the construction of* IDEM.

Vossius, and Tursellin before him, have observed that this phrase, *Idem cum illo*, is not Latin, though Erasmus, Joseph Scaliger, and some other able writers have made use of it.

The antients used to say *Idem qui, idem ac, atque, et, ut. Peripatetici iidem erant qui academici.* Cic. *Animus erga te idem ac fuit*, Ter. *Unum & idem videtur esse atque id quod,* &c. Cic. *Eadem sit utilitas uniuscujusque & universorum,* Id. *In eâdem sunt injustitiâ, ut si in suam rem aliena convertant.* It is true that Gellius hath, *Ejusdem cum eo musæ vir;* of the same profession as himself; but in this he is singular, and should not be imitated; besides we may say that he speaks of two different persons. So that even if it was right to say, *Virgilius est ejusdem musæ cum Homero*, this would be no proof, continues Vossius, that we might say, *Vates Andinus*, (*Andes* was the village where Virgil was born) *idem cum Virgilio.*

Idem, in imitation of the Greeks, is put likewise with the dative. *Invitum qui servat, idem facit occidenti.* Hor.

III.

III. *Of the construction of the possessives* meus, tuus, &c. *and of the genitives* mei, tui, &c.

The possessive, generally speaking, signifies the same thing as the genitive of the noun from whence it is formed; thus *domus paterna* is the same as *domus patris*. On some occasions the genitive is more usual than the adjective, *Hominum mores*, rather than *humani*; *Hominum genus*, rather than *humanum*, &c.

Now the genitive in itself may be taken either actively or passively, pursuant to what we have already observed, p. 16. and consequently so may the possessive: therefore *meus, tuus, suus, noster, vester*, shall of their own nature have the same sense and force as the genitives *mei, tui, sui, nostri, vestri*, of which they are formed. But one thing we are to observe, that those genitives are never put with other substantives, not even understood, when there is the least danger of ambiguity: so that if you say, *Est mei præceptoris*, then *mei* is an adjective coming from *meus*, and not from *ego*; genit. *mei*. It belongs to my master, and not to me who am a master.

This does not hinder however but these genitives may be taken both actively and passively, contrary to the general rule laid down by grammarians, who pretend that *mei, tui*, &c. are always taken in the passive sense; and the possessives, *meus, tuus*, always in the active sense; for instance, they say that *amor meus*, is always taken actively, that is for the love which I bear towards another person; and *amor mei* passively, for the love which another bears towards me, and whereby I am beloved.

But not to mention that these terms *active* and *passive* are insufficient to determine these expressions, since there are several of them in which we can hardly conceive either action or passion, as we shall see in the following examples; it is beyond all doubt that Latin authors have frequently made use of these genitives or these adjectives, indifferently one for the other; as we find even in Cicero, who has put the genitive where he might have used the adjective, when he says, *Uterque pro sui dignitate & pro rerum magnitudine. Ut sui & Metrodori memoria colatur, nihil malo quàm me mei similem esse, illos sui. Quis non intelligat tuâ salute contineri suam, & ex unius tui vitam pendere omnium? Ita se ipse consumptione & senio allevat sui. Imitantes effectorem & genitorem sui. Quintus misit filium non solùm sui deprecatorem, sed etiam accusatorem mei.* And Terence, *Tetigine tui quicquam?* &c.

On the contrary we find that authors have put the possessives *meus, tuus, suus*, where they might have used the genitive *mei, tui, sui*, as *Ego quæ tuâ causâ feci*, Cic. where he might have said, *tui causâ. Pro amicitiâ tuâ jure doleo*, Phil. 10. For the friendship I have for you. *Invidiæ m æ levandæ causâ*. Cic. The envy which others bear towards me. *Utilitatibus tuis possum carere: te valere tuâ causâ primùm volo, tum meâ mi Tiro:* where he might have put, *Tui causâ & mei causâ. Nam neque negligentiâ tuâ, neque odio id fecit tuo.* Ter. he did not do it either out of any flight, or hatred towards you, where *tuâ* and *tuo* are in the active sense.

And therefore the true reason why we are not allowed to say, *Hic liber est mei*, or *mei interest*, but *liber est meus*, and *meâ interest*, (sup. *causâ*) is not because one is more passive than the other, but to avoid ambiguity, for we could not tell whether it is *mei patris*, or *filii*, or another, or whether it be *mei ipsius*. Which rock has been always avoided, by making it a rule never to put the primitive genitives, where we must understand a substantive that may occasion the least ambiguity. But when there is no such danger, it may be used indifferently. Therefore since there is another noun, there is no longer any danger of being mistaken, *Hic liber est mei solius. Tui unius*, or *tuâ unius interest. Ex tuo ipsius. animo conjecturam feceris de meo*, Cic. *Inopis te nunc miserescat mei*, Ter. *Miserere mei peccatoris*, &c. In regard to which we refer to what has been further said in the Annotation to the 11th rule, p. 24.

Section III.
REMARKS ON THE VERBS.

Chap. I.
Of the nature and signification of verbs.

SCALIGER dividing all things in general, *in permanentes & fluentes*, into that which is permanent, and that which is transient; and affirming that the nature of the noun is to signify that which is permanent, and the nature of the verb to denote that which is transient, he allows but of two sorts of verbs, active and passive, which are both reduced to the verb substantive, SUM, ES, EST; *quod est*, says he, *utriusque radix et fundamentum*. Sanctius maintains the same thing, which he proves by this argument, that between action and passion there can be no medium. *Omnis motus aut actio aut passio est*, say the philosophers.

The reasoning of these authors, as we have made appear in the general and rational grammar, c. 12. proceeds from their not having sufficiently comprehended the true nature of the verb, which consists in *denoting an affirmation*. For there are words that are not verbs, which denote actions and passions, and even things that are transient, as *cursus, fluens*: and there are verbs that signify neither actions nor passions, nor things that are transient, as *existit, quiescit, friget, albet, claret*, &c.

Therefore, pursuing a more natural and easier method, we may divide the verbs into substantives and adjectives. Verbs substantives are those which barely denote the affirmation, as *sum, fio*. Verbs adjectives are those which besides the affirmation common to all verbs include also a peculiar signification of their own; as *amo*, which is the same as *sum amans*; *curro, sum currens*, &c.

Verbs adjectives are, either active, or passive, or neuter: concerning which we refer the reader to the general and rational
grammar,

grammar, c. 17. But one thing we are particularly to obferve, that there are two forts of verbs neuter: one which fignify no fort of action, as *albet, fedet, viret, adeft, quiefcit*, &c. And the others which fignify actions, but fuch as, generally fpeaking, do not pafs from the agent to any other thing, as *prandére, cœnáre, ambuláre*: for which reafon the grammarians call them *intranfitive*. Yet the latter fometimes become *tranfitive*, and then they are not diftinguifhed from actives, and they govern the fubject or object to which their action paffeth in the accufative, as we have obferved in the 14th rule. And of thefe we fhall give feveral examples in the following lift.

I. Lift of verbs abfolute and active, or intranfitive, and tranfitive.

Memoria cladis nondum aboleverat, *Liv.* was not yet effaced.	Abolere nomina, *Suet.* to efface them.
Abftinere maledictis, *Cic.*	Abftinere manus, *Id.*
Abhorrere ab re aliquâ, *Cic.*	Abhorrere aliquem, *Id.*
Affuefcere labori, *Cic.*	Affuefcere bella animis, *Virg.*
Cachinnare rifu tremulo, *Lucr.*	Cachinnat exitium meum, *Appul.*
Celerare, *abfolutely*, *Cic.*	Celerare fugam, gradum, *Virg.*
Likewife, Accelerare, *Cic.*	Accelerare iter, *Cæfar.*
Clamare cœpit, *Cic.*	Morlentem nomine clamat, *Virg.*
Ut fi inclamaro, advoles, *Cic.*	Comitem fuum inclamare, *Cic.*
Coïre in unum, *Virg.*	Coïre focietatem, *Cic.*
Concionari de re aliqua, *Cic.*	Concionari aliquid, *Liv.*
Conftitit Romæ, *Cic.*	Confiftere vitam, *Luc.* for conftituere.
Delirare, *abfolutely*, *Cic.*	Quicquid delirant reges, *Hor.*
Defperare ab aliquo, *Cic.*	Defperare vitam, falutem, *Cic.*
Definas, *Ter.*	Definere artem, *Cic.*
Differre nominibus, *Cic.*	Differre tempus, *Cic. Hor.*
Difputare de re aliqua, *Cic.*	Difputare aliquid, *Id.*
Dubitare de fide, *Cic.*	Dubitare aliquid, *Cic. Virg.*
Durare in ædibus, *Plaut.*	Durare imperiofius æquor, *Hor.*
Ejulo, *abfolutely*, *Cic.*	Ejulabam fortunas meas, *Appul.*
Emergere regno, *Cic.*	Serpens fe emergit, *Cic.*
Eructare, *fimply*, *Colum.*	Eructare cædem bonorum, *Cic.*
Erumpebat vis, *Cic.*	Erumpere ftomachum in aliquem, *Cic.*
Exire domo, *Cic.*	Exire tela, vim, *Virg.* for *vitare.*
Exhalant vapore altaria, *Lucr.*	Exhalare crapulam, *Cic.*
Feftina lentè, *Adagium.*	Feftinare iras, *Hor.* Fugam, *Virg.*
Flere de morte alicujus, *Ovid.*	Funera alicujus flere, *Ovid.*
Garrire alicui in aurem, *Mart.*	Garrire libellos, *Hor.*
Gemit turtur, *Virg.*	Gemere plagam acceptam, *Cic.*
Hyemat mare, *Hor. rages.*	Hyemare aquas, *Plin.* to cool them.
Illucefcet illa dies, *Cic.*	Dii illuxere diem. *Plaut.*
Incipit ver, *Cic.*	Incipere facinus, *Plaut.*
Inolefcit arbor, *Virg.*	Natura inolevit nobis amorem noftri, *Gell.*
Infanire & furere, *Cic.*	Infanire errorem, *Hor.* Infaniam, *Plaut.*
Inftant operi, *Virg.*	Inftare currum, *Plaut.*
Infuefcere alicui rei, *Tac.*	Infuevit pater optimus hoc me, *Hor.*
Jurare in verba, *Cic. Cæf.*	Jurare morbum, Jovem, *Cic.* Maria, *Virg.*
Lætaris & triumphas, *Cic.*	Utrumque lætor, *Cic.*
Latrare & mordere poffunt, *Cic.*	Latrare aliquem, *Hor.*
Luna luce lucet aliena, *Cic.*	Lucere facem alicui, *Plaut.*
Manere in officio, *Cic.*	Manere aliquem, *Hor. Virg.* to wait for him.

H 2 Morari

Morari sub dio, *Hor.*
Mussitare, *absolutely*, *Liv.*
Nocet emta dolore voluptas, *Hor.*

Offendere in arrogantiam, *Cic.*
Pascentes agni, *Virg.*
Penetrat ad aures, *Ovid.*
Pergere, *simply*, *Cic. Ter.*
Perseverare in errore, *Cic.*
Plaudere sibi, *Hor. Cic.*
Pergere & properare, *Cic.*

Querebatur cum Deo quod parum longè viveret, *Cic.*
Remisit pestilentia, *Liv.*
Requiescere in sella, *Cic.*
Resultant colles, *Virg.*
Ridere intempestivè, *Quint.*

Ruit urbs, nox, dies, *Virg.*
Rutilant arma, *Virg. de shine.*
Sapit ei palatus, *Cic.*
Spirant auræ, *Virg.*
Sistere, *simply*, *Cic.*
In the same manner Subsistere,
Sonat graviter, *Virg.*
Sufficit animus malis, *Ovid.*
Superabat pecunia, *Cic.*
Supersedeas hoc labore, *Cic.*
Suppeditant ad victum, *Cic.*
Transmittere, *in an absolute sense*, *Suet.*
Tardare & commorari, *Cic.*
Tinniunt aures sonitu, *Catul.*
Trepidat corde, *Cic.*
Variat fortuna, *Liv.*
Vergebat locus ab oppido, *Cæs.* *And in like manner its compounds*, Rivulos evergunt, inverguntur vina, *Virg.* Hence *we say likewise in the passive*, Vergimur in senium, *Stat.*

Vertat bene, res, *Plaut. Virg.*
Minitari & vociferari palàm, *Cic.*
Urit calore, *Cic.*

Nihil purpuram moror, *Plaut.*
Mussitabit timorem, *Appul.*
Nocere aliquem, *Plaut.* Nihil nocere, *Cic.*

Offendere aliquid, *Cic. to hit against.*
Pascere capellas, *Virg.*
Penetrare Atlantem, *Plin.*
Pergere reliqua, *Cic.*
Perseverare aliquid, *Cic.*
Plaudere aliquem, *Stat.*
Hoc opus, hoc studium parvi properemus & ampli, *Hor.*

Queritur crudelitatem regis, *Justin.* Suum factum, *Cæs.*
Remittere animum, *Cic.*
Requiescunt suos cursus, *Virg.*
Resultant sonum, *Appul.*
Ridere risum, hominem, &c. *Cic. Hor. Virg.*

Ruerem cæteros, *Ter.*
Rutilant capillos cinere, *Val. Max.*
Si recta saperet Antonius, *Cic.*
Spirant naribus ignem, *Virg.*
Sistere gradum, *Virg.*
Romanum subsistere non poterant, *Liv.*
Nec vox hominem sonat, *Virg.*
Sufficere animos, *Virg.*
Superare aliquem, *Cic.*
Aliqua supersedenda, *Auctor ad Her.*
Suppeditare cibos, *Cic.*
Transmittere maria, *Cic.*
Tardare imperium, *Cæs.* Negotium, *Cic.*
Ecquid Dolabella tinniat, *Cic.*
Mirantur ae trepidant præsagia, *App.*
Variare vicem, *Cic.*
Venenum vergere, *Lucr. Verses.*

Vertere terram aratro, *Hor.*
Vociferans talia, *Virg.* aliquid, *Cic.*
Urere aliquem *and* aliquid, *Cic.*

II. *List of verbs active which are taken in an absolute sense.*

There are also a great many verbs active that are taken as it were intransitively, and passively, or rather which reflect their action back upon themselves, the reciprocal pronoun *se* being understood; as

AVERTO. v. Verto.
AUGEO. Auxerat potentia, *Tac.* Auxit morbus, *is increased.*
CAPERO. Quid est quod illi caperat frons severitudine? *Plaut. for* caperatur & rugis contrahitur.
CONVERTO. v. Verto.
CRUCIO. Ut miseræ sunt matres, cruciantque, *Plaut.*
DECOQUO. Quibus (Pop. Rom.) inertiâ Cæsarum quasi consenuit atque decoxit, *Florus.*

EXPEDIO. Nequiter expedivit Parasitatio, *Plaut.*
EXUDO. Exudat inutilis humor, *Virg.* for *exudat se*, says Servius.
GESTO. Aretinum Clementem in eadem vel etiam in majore gratiâ habuit, quoad novissimè simul gestanti, conspecto delatore ejus: vis, inquit, hunc, nequissimum servum cras audiamus? *Suet. in Dom. Where* simul gestanti, *imports:* Being carried in the same litter.

HABEO.

HABEO. Quis hic habet? *Plaut.* for se habet, *or* habitat. Video jam quò invidia transeat, ubi sit habitura, *Cic. Where it will fix its residence, Man.*

INGEMINO. Ingeminant curæ: clamor ingeminat, *Virg.*

INSINUO. Insinuat pavor, *Virg.* Prudentia est ut penitus insinuet in causam, ut sit curâ & cogitatione intentus, *Cic.*

LAVO. Lavanti regi nunciatum est, *Liv.* Lavamus & tondemus ex consuetudine, *Quintil.*

LENIO. Dum hæ consilescunt turbæ, atque iræ leniunt, *Ter.*

MOVEO. Terra movit, *Suet. And in like manner* PROMOVEO, *Macrob.*

MUTO. Mortis metu mutabunt, *Sal.* for mutabuntur. *Which has puzzled several, who not und-rstanding this passage, would fain alter the reading. But Tacitus has expressed himself in the same sense,* Vannius diuturnitate in superbiam mutans. *And Tertullian frequently useth the word in the same signification. It is the same in regard to* DEMUTO. Aquâ paululum demutavit liber, *Appul.*

PASCO. *We say,* Juventa pascit, & pascitur, *in the same meaning, says Consentius.*

PRÆCIPITO. Fibrenus, statim præcipitat in Lirim, *Cic.*

QUASSO. Lætum siliqua quassante legumen, *Virg.* Vox activa ac significatio passiva est, *says Ramus.* Subducunt lembum capitibus quassantibus, *Plaut.*

RUGO. Vide palliolum ut rugat, *Plaut.*

SEDO. Postquam tempestas sedavit, *Cn. Velleius, apud Gell.*

TONDEO. Candidior postquam tondenti barba cadebat, *Virg.* Incanaque menta Cyniphii tondent hirci, *Virg. i. e.* tondentur.

TURBO. Et septemgemini turbant trepida ostia Nili, *Virg.*

VARIO. Variant undæ, *Prop. for* variantur.

VEHO. Adolescentia per medias laudes quasi quadrigis vehens, *Cic.* Triton natantibus invehens belluis; *Cic. i. e.* qui invehitur.

VERTO. Libertatem aliorum in suam vertisse servitutem conquerebantur, *Liv.* Vertens annus, *Cic. in somnio, for* conversus. Quod tum in morem verterat, *Tacit.* Which was become an established custom.

And in like manner AVERTO. Tum prora avertit & undis dat latus, *Virg.* CONVERTO. Regium imperium in superbiam, dominationémque convertit, *Sall. in Catil.*

VESTIO. Sic & in proximo soror civitas vestiebat, *Tertull.* dressed herself *in the same manner.* Parcius pasco, levius vestio, *App.*

VOLVO. Olim volventibus annis, *Virg.* VOLUTO. Genibúsque volutans, *Id.*

What evinceth that we ought to understand the accusative *me, se*, or such like after these verbs, is their being sometimes expressed. *Callidus assentator ne se insinuet cavendum est*, Cic. And if any one should insist that they are then intirely passive, I desire to know of him, says Vossius, how those verbs can be called passive, which cannot admit of a passive construction, since we are not permitted to say, at least in a passive sense; *Ingeminat ab iis clamor. Terra à ventis movet*, &c.

Now this remark, as well as most of those here touched upon, is as necessary for understanding Greek as Latin, which we have sufficiently shewn in the new method of learning the Greek tongue.

III. *List of verbs passive taken actively.*

There are likewise a great many verbs passive, which are sometimes taken in an active sense, being invested with the nature of verbs common, or deponent.

AFFECTOR, *for* AFFICTO. Affectatus est regnum, *Varr.*

AVERTOR, *for* AVERTO. Quàm surda miseros avertitur aure, *Boët.*

BELLOR, *for* BELLO. Pictis bellantur Amazones armis, *Virg.*

CENSEOR, *for* CENSEO. Martia censa est hinc inter comites suas, *Ovid.* Voluisti magnum agri modum censeri, *Cic. pro Flacc.* Census est mancipia Amyntæ, *Ibid.*

COMMUNICOR, for COMMUNICO. Cum quibus spem integram communicati non sint, Liv.
COMPERIOR, for COMPERIO, Sal.
CONSILIOR, for CONSILIO, as. Consilietur amicis, Hor. Let him advise his friends.
COPULOR, for COPULO, according to Priscian and Nonius. Adeunt, consistunt, copulantur dextras, Plaut.
ERUMPOR, for ERUMPO. Cùm vis exagitata foras erumpitur, Lucr. And in like manner PERRUMPOR.
FABRICOR, for FABRICO. Capitolii fastigium necessitas fabricata est, Cic.
FLUCTUOR, for FLUCTUO. Utrius populi victoriam mallet, fluctuatus animo fuerat, Liv.
JURATUS SUM, for JURAVI, Cic.
MULTOR, for MULTO. Rebellantes multatus est pœna, Suet.
MUNEROR, for MUNERO. Alexio me opiparè muneratus est, Cic. See Gellius and Diom.
In like manner, REMUNEROR, for REMUNERO.
MURMUROR, for MURMURO, Appul.
NUTRICOR, for NUTRICO, or NU-TRIO. Mundus omnia nutricatur & continet, Cic.
PERAGROR, for PERAGRO. Peragratus est regionem, Velleius.
PERLINOR, for PERLINO. Ab imis unguibus sese totam ad usque summos capillos perlita, Appul.
PIGNEROR, for PIGNERO, Gell. Non.
PRÆVERTOR, for PRÆVERTO, Plaut. Liv. Cur. Tac. But in the præterite we say only PRÆVERTI.
PUNIOR, for PUNIO, Cic. Punitus es inimicum, pro Mil.
QUIRITOR, for QUIRITO, Varr.
RUMINOR, for RUMINO, Varr.
SACRIFICOR, for SACRIFICO, Gell. Varr. Non.
SATUROR, for SATURO. Nec dum antiquum saturata dolorem. Virg. for cùm nondum saturavisset.
SPECTOR, for SPECTO. Spectatus est suem, Varr.
SUPPEDITOR, for SUPPEDITO. Quod mihi suppeditatus es, gratissimum est, Cic.
USURPOR, for USURPO. Mulier usurpata duplex cubile, Cic.

The reader may see several others in Vossius, and still more in Nonius, but which are very little, if at all in use.

IV. *List of deponents, which are taken passively.*

On the other hand there are a great many deponents, which are taken passively, and then if they occur in a passive sense in Cicero, or in some considerable author, they may be called common, since they have both significations. But if they are not to be found except in very antient authors, they ought rather to bear the name of deponents, since in the most frequent use they have lost one of their significations.

ABOMINOR. Ante omnia abominari semimares, Liv. *speaking of monsters.* Sævitiisque eorum abominaretur ab omnibus. *Verrius Flaccus apud Prisc.*
ADIPISCOR. Amitti magis quàm adipisci, Fab. Max. Non ætate, verum ingenio adipiscitur sapientia, Plaut.
ADMIROR. Turpe est propter venustatem vestimentorum admirari, Cæcilius ad Prisc.
ADORIOR. Ab his Gallos adortos, Aurel. apud Prisc.
ADULOR. Adulaterunt ab amicis, & adhortati, Cass. apud Prisc. Ne adulari nos finamus, Cic. But we say also adulo. See the next List.

AGGREDIOR. Ut à te fictis aggrederer donis. Cic.
Aggressus labor, Terenc. Maur.
AMPLECTOR. Ego me non sinam amplectier, Lucil.
Animam nostro amplexam in pectore, Petron.
ANTESTOR. Impubes non potest antestari, Liv. teste Prisciano.
ARBITROR. Arbitrata quæstio. Gell. Ex scriptis eorum qui veri arbitrantur, Cælius apud Prisc.
ASPERNOR. Qui est pauper, aspernatur, Cic. ad Nepot.
ASSECTOR. Assectari se omnes cupiunt, Enn.

ASSEQUOR.

ASSEQUOR. Nihil horum investigari, nihil assequi poterit, *Cic.*
AUGUROR. Certæque res augurantur, L. *Cæs.*
Virgil has likewise made use of the active. Si quid veri mens augurat.
BLANDIOR. Blanditus labor, *Varrius.*
CAVILLOR. Lepido sermone cavillatus, *passively, Appul.*
COHORTOR. *See* HORTOR.
COMITOR. Uno comitatus Achate, *Virg.* Jam salutantur, jam comitantur, *Just.*
COMPLECTOR. Quo uno maledicto scelera omnia complexa esse videantur, *Cic.* Cupio eum tam invidiosâ fortunâ complecti, *Cic. for* comprehendi, *according to Priscian.*
CONSEQUOR, *and* CONSECTOR. Quæ vix ab omnibus consequi possunt, *Orbil. apud Prisc.*
A populo lapidibus consectari, *Laver. apud eundem. See* sector, *lower down.*
CONSOLOR. Cùm animum vestrum erga me video, vehementer consolor, Q. *Metell. apud Gell.*
Consolabar ob ea quæ timui, *Asin. Poll. apud Prisc.*
CONSPICOR. Paupertas hæc non ita nutricata ut nunc conspicatur, *Varr. apud Prisc.*
Patrem non vult priùs conspicari, *Plaut.*
CRIMINOR. Criminor defendere res Syllanas, *Cic. They charge me with.*
Criminatus Asinus, *Appul.*
DEMOLIOR *and* IMMOLIOR. Nusquam demolitur, nusquam exoneratur pecunia, *Cur. apud Prisc.*
Immollitum & inædificatum est in loca publica, *Liv.*
DETESTOR. Bellaque matribus detestata, *Hor.*
In honestissimo cœtu detestari, *App.*
DIGNOR. Cultu quodam & honore dignari, *Cic. Virg. to be thought worthy of.*
DOMINOR. O domus antiqua! Heu quàm dispari dominare domino! *Cic.* 1. *Offic. But it bears an active sense in this passage of Virgil.* Urbs antiqua ruit multos dominata per annos, *as Vossius observeth, though R, Stephen and Alvarez were of a contrary opinion.*
ENITOR. Enixus puer, *Sev. Sulp. just born.*
EXPERIOR. Virtus experta atque perspecta, *Cic.*
Experienda ratio, P. *Nigid.*
FARI. Fasti dies sunt in quibus jus fatur, i. e. dicitur, *Suet.*

FATEOR. Hunc excipere qui publicus esse fateatur, *Cic.*
FRUSTROR. Frustratus à spe & devictus, *Fenest.*
Frustramur, irridemur, *Laver. apud Prisc.*
GLORIOR. Beata vita glorianda & prædicanda est, *Cic.*
HORTOR. Hortatus est in convivio à scorto, *Cic. where others read* exoratus. *But in Ausonius we find,* Exhortatóque somno, ut eum mitteret soporem, *&c. And Gellius informs us that they said,* hortor te, & hortor abs te, *lib.* 15. *cap.* 13. Consulem indicunt sententiam expromere, quâ hortaretur Clodius despondere Domitio, *Tacit.*
IMITOR. Si natura non feret ut quædam imitari possint, *Cic.*
Imitata & efficta simulacra, *Cic.*
IMMOLIOR. *See* MOLIOR.
INSIDIOR. In legatis insidiandis, vel in servis follicitandis, *Cic.*
INTERPRETOR. In testamentis voluntates testantium interpretantur, *Paul. Jurisc.* S. *Austin and S. Jerome often take it in this sense.* Ita illud somnium interpretatum est, *Cic. for which reason Gell. lib.* 15. *c.* 13. *looks upon it as common.*
MACHINOR. Machinata fames, *Sall. apud Prisc.*
MEDITOR. Meditata sunt mihi omnia incommoda, *Ter.*
Et quæ meditata & præparata inferuntur, *Cic.*
Tractantur lenocinia, adulteria meditantur, *Minut. Felix.*
METIOR Orbe si sol amplior, an pedis unius latitudine metiatur, *Arnob.*
MODEROR. Omnes virtutes mediocritate esse moderatas, *Cic.*
MODULOR. Lingua modesta & modulata, *Gel.*
MOLIOR. Pompa moliebatur, *App.*
Immolitum & inædificatum est in loca publica, *Liv.*
NANCISCOR. Nactâ libertate, *App.*
OBLIVISCOR. Nunc oblita mihi tot carmina, *Virg.*
Consuetudo scribendi quæ oblivisci non potest. *Schol. Juven. in Sat.* 7.
ORDIOR. Ordita lectio, *Diom.* Cùm fuerint orsa fundamenta, *Colum.* Bonæ res à raro initio exoriæ, *Vjel. apud Prisc.* But
OSCULOR. *Which most grammarians give as an example of the verb common, is not perhaps to be found in good authors, except in the active sense, as Vossius observeth. Those who use it other-*

otherwise, may however defend themselves by the testimony of Victorinus, Priscian, Cledonius, and other antient grammarians, who would hardly have ranked it in this number, unless they had found some authority for it, though as they have not produced any, the best way is to avoid it. Yet they used to say antiently, osculo, as we shall see in the next list, from whence might come the passive osculor.

PACISCOR. Filia pacta alicui, *Tac. Plin. Liv. promised in marriage.*

PERCONTOR. Percontatum pretium, *Appul.*

PERICLITOR. Periclitari omnium jura, si similitudines accipiantur, *Cic. were in danger.*
Non est sæpius in uno homine falus periclitanda Reip. *In Catil.*

POLLICEOR. Ut aliis statuæ polliceantur, *Metell. Numid.*

POPULOR. Qui nunc populati atque vexati, *Cic. But we say likewise populo. See the next list.*

POTIOR. Ne potiretur mali, *Ter. in Phor. instead of* Ne à malo opprimeretur, *according to Guillem. lest some disaster should befall her.*
Potiri hostium, *Plaut. to be taken by the enemy.*
Potiri heroum, *Id. to be subject to them, according to Palmerius.*

PRÆDOR.

PRECOR. Deus precandus est mihi, *Auson.*

SECTOR. Qui vellet se à cane sectari, *Varr. In the same manner* CONSECTOR. *See* CONSEQUOR *above*.

STIPULOR. *According to Priscian is taken in an active and passive signification, and is even joined in both senses, with an adjective governed by the preposition. For Stipulor à te, is taken for* interrogo te, *and* interrogor à te : *just as we say,* Quæro à te, *in an active sense ;* I ask you. Minæ quas à te est stipulatus Pseudolus, *Plaut. in an active sense.* Ni dolo stipulatus sis, *Plaut. in a passive sense. Cicero hath likewise,* stipulata pecunia, *in a passive sense.*

TESTOR. Hæc quæ testata sunt & illustria, *Cic.*

TUEOR. Quod à rusticis Romani alebantur & tuebantur, *Varro.*

TUOR. Tutus ab hostibus, *Cic.*
Tutus à calore & frigore, *Cic.*
Tuendam habere ædem, *Cic.*

VENEROR. Cursusque dabit venerata secundos, *Virg.*

VEREOR. *This is among the verbs common in Gellius, lib. 15. c. 13. where he says that both* vereor te, *and* vereor abs te *are used.*

ULCISCOR. Quidquid ulcisci nequitur, *Sall.*

UTOR. Supellex quæ non utitur, *Gell.*
Illa ætas magis ad hæc utenda est idonea, *Ter.*
In like manner, ABUTOR. Abusis jam omnibus locis, *Q. Hort.*

Several other verbs of the like nature may be seen in Priscian and Vossius, whereby it appeareth, says he, that there are more verbs common than one would imagine; though we ought not to make a separate class of them distinct from the deponents, because in common practice most of them have dropped one of their significations; and even among the deponents themselves we do not make two different classes, one for those that have an active signification, as *precor*, I pray, *fateor*, I confess; the other for those which are passive, as *pascor*, I am fed, *nascor*, I am born.

But what is most remarkable in these verbs deponents or common, is their participle of the preterite tense, which generally occurs in both significations, whereas the tenses of the verb are less usual.

Examples hereof may be seen in this very chapter, and we shall give some more in the remarks on the participles.

V. *List of deponents that are terminated in* O *and in* OR.

There are likewise a great many deponents, which in the same signification, are terminated in O. But most of them occur

REMARKS ON THE VERBS DEPONENT. 105

occur only in very antient authors. There are some few indeed that have been adopted by other writers, as the following list will shew.

ADULO, *Cic.* Ex *veteri poëtâ*, *Val. Max.* ADULOR, *Cic. & alii*, more usual.

ALTERCO, for ALTERCOR. Scio cum patre altercasti dudum, *Ter.*

ASSENTIO, and ASSENTIOR, were in use, according to *Gellius*, *Nonius*, and *Diomedes*. The former occurs the oftenest in MSS. and the latter in printed editions, says *Vossius*.

AMPLECTO, for AMPLECTOR. Likewise AMPLEXO, and AMPLEXOR, according to *Priscian*. And in *Ci*. Autoritatem censorum amplexato, *Pro Clu.*

AUCUPO, for AUCUPOR. Aucupare ex insidiis quid agatur, *Plaut.* Aucupans, is in *Cic.*

AUGURO, for AUGUROR. Præsentit animus & augurat, *Cic.*

AUSPICO, for AUSPICOR, *Prisc. Non. Fest.*

CACHINNO, *Lucr.* for CACHINNOR, *Cic.*

COMITO, for COMITOR. Stygias comitavit ad undas, *Ovid.*

CUNCTO, *Plaut.* CUNCTOR, *Cic.*

DEPASCO. Si hodie roscidas herbas depaverint, *Plin.*

DEPASCOR. Belluæ depascuntur sata, *Id.* Febris depascitur artus, *Virg.* Frondes depastus amaras, *Claud.*

DIGNO, for DIGNOR, *Prisc. Diom.*

EJULO, for EJULOR, *Prisc.*

ELUCUBRO, and ELUCUBROR. Epistolæ quam eram elucubratus, *Cic.* Quicquid istud est quod elucubravimus, *Colum.*

EXPERGISCO, for EXPERGISCOR. *Philoxenus*, *Hyginus*, *Dositheus*, *Isaac Vossius*.

FABRICO, and FABRICOR, *Cic.*

FRUSTRO, for FRUSTROR. Non frustrabo vos milites. *Cæs.*

FRUTICO, *Colum. Plin.* for FRUTICOR, *which Cicero makes use of.*

IMITO, for IMITOR, *Varr. apud Non.*

IMPERTIO, and IMPERTIOR, *Cic.*

INSIDIO, for INSIDIOR, in the Civil Law.

JURGO, for JURGOR, *Cic. apud Non. ex xii. Tabul.*

LACRYMO, *Ter. Ovid.* for LACRYMOR, *Cic.*

LÆTO, for LÆTOR, *Prisc.*

LARGIO, for LARGIOR, *Prisc. ex Sal. Non.*

LUDIFICO, for LUDIFICOR, *Plaut.*

LUXURIO, *Non. ex Virg.* LUXURIOR, *Colum. Plin.*

MEDICO. Medicare semina, *Virg.* But MEDICOR is taken both actively and passively: medicatæ fruges, *Virg.*

MEREO, for MEREOR, *Cic.* Quid enim mereas, *Cic.* Merui, *Virg. Cic.*

METO, AS, *Virg.* in *Culice.*

METOR, APIS, more usual. Metari castra, *Liv. Sallust.* to set out a camp, to encamp. But we find also, castra metata, *Liv.* In a passive sense.

MISERO, and MISEROR, And in the same manner MISEREO, and MISEREOR, from whence cometh, MISERET, and MISERETUR, with MISERESCO, and COMMISERESCO. Miserescimus ultrò, *Virg.*

Per finem Myrmidonum, commiserescite, *Non. ex Enn.*

MODERO, for MODEROR, *Non.* Docet moderare animo, *Plaut.*

MOLIO, for MOLIOR, *Prisc.* and in the same manner DEMOLIO. Demolivit tectum, *Varr.*

MUNERO, for MUNEROR, *Non.*

OPINO, for OPINOR, *Prisc.* and *Non. ex Plaut. & Cæcil.*

OPITULO, for OPITULOR, *Non.*

OSCULO, for OSCULOR. Lauuor quod osculavi privignæ caput, *Titin. apud Non.*

PALPO, for PALPOR, *Juv.*

PARTIO, for PARTIOR, *Non. ex Plaut. & aliis.*

PATIO, for PATIOR, *Nav.*

POLLICEO, for POLLICEOR. Ne dares, ne polliceres, *Varr. apud Non.*

POPULO, for POPULOR. Formicæ farris acervum cum populant, *Virg.*

PRÆLIO, for PRÆLIOR, *Enn.*

RECIPROCO, *Liv.* RECIPROCOR, *Cic.*

REMINISCO, for REMINISCOR, *S. Aug.*

REVERTO, for REVERTOR, Si Rōmam revertisset, *Cic. who uses it only in the tenses of the preterite.*

RIXO, for RIXOR, *Varr.*

RUMINO. Ruminat herbas, *Virg.*

RUMINOR, *Colum.*

STIPULO is not to be found in ancient writers; but only STIPULOR, *Voss.* See the preceding list.

VAGO, for VAGOR. Lib. vagat per auras, *Prud.*

VELIFICO,

4

VELIFICO, *Plin. Hence cometh,* velificatos Athos; *but Cicero always puts* velificor *in the active sense.*
URINO, *and* OR, *Plin. to dive.*
VENERO, *for* VENEROR, *Plaut.* Ut. venerem Lucinam.

VOCIFERO. Si hoc vociferare velim quàm dignum sit, &c. *Cic. in Verr.*
VOCIFEROR. Quid vociferabare decem millia talenta Sabinio esse promissa? *Cic.*

We might collect some more from the antient grammarians; but in regard to practice, care must be taken to imitate the best authors.

CHAPTER II.
Of the difference of tense and moods.

I. *Of tenses.*

IT will be of use to observe the different force, and natural signification of each tense. For besides that considerable difficulties may sometimes arise in regard to this article, and that even the most learned among the Romans, as Gellius calls them, were heretofore divided in opinion whether *surreptum erit,* was to be understood of the time past or to come, since we find in the same author, that one of the questions proposed, was whether *scripserim, legerim, venerim,* were of the preterite or future tense, or of both; it is beyond all doubt that on many occasions, we do not sufficiently understand the force of the expression, nor can we tell why we use particular modes of speaking, nor the method of explaining them, unless we are thoroughly acquainted with the nature of these things.

But in order to do this with perspicuity, we cannot, I think, follow a more natural division of the tenses of verbs, than that which we have given in the rudiments. For in the nature of things there are only three tenses, *the present, the past, and the future;* but the inflexion of a verb may, either simply express one of these three tenses, or mark two of them together in regard to two different things; and thus the tenses of the verbs may be called, either SIMPLE or COMPOUNDED in the sense: concerning which the reader may see the general and rational grammar, ch. 14.

We are further to observe for the Latin termination, that heretofore the futures of the two last conjugations were terminated also in BO; as *expedibo,* in Plautus, *Aperibo, dormibo, reperibitur: reddibitur,* for *reddetur,* and others. But Scioppius maintains that the third terminated in *ebo,* and not in *ibo,* like the fourth, and that we ought to read, *reddebo, reddebitur;* as *fugebo* for *fugiam, fideba* for *fidam,* &c.

II. *Of moods.*

In the rudiments I reduced the moods to four, for the reasons expressed in that place, and in the advertisement to the reader; in regard to which you may see the general and rational grammar, ch. 15. and 16. I shall only add that this should not be esteemed a novelty, since Palemon, a more antient writer than Quintilian, admits of no more.

Sanctius, and after him Scioppius, go a great deal further; for they cut them off intirely, as well as Ramus, and allow of no other moods or manners of the verb than those which are derived from adverbs, whose chief office is to determine the signification of the verb, as *bene, male, multum, fortiter, parum,* &c.

This is what induced them to make another distinction of the tenses, dividing every one of them into *prima & secunda*, and saying for example, *Præsens primum* AMO; *Præsens secundum* AMEM: *Imperfectum primum* AMABAM: *Imperfectum secundum* AMAREM, &c. And as for the future they put three, making the imperative pass for the third. This is not without foundation, because, as we shall see hereafter, the tenses of the subjunctive and of the indicative are oftentimes indiscriminately taken for one another. Yet as this disposition does not make the matter at all shorter, and one way or other, we must still be acquainted with so many different tenses, I have thought proper to conform as much as possible to the ordinary method, because in regard to matters once established, we should make no alteration without great reason and necessity.

III. *Of the subjunctive.*

The subjunctive always expresseth a signification dependent on and as it were connected with something; hence in every tense it partaketh in some measure of the future.

In the present; as *Si æque in posterum me ames. De qua utinam aliquando tecum loquar,* Cic. And Quintilian has taken notice, that when Virgil saith, *Hoc Ithacus velit*, this *velit* denoted the time future. Hence it is frequently the same thing to say, *Si amem*, or *si amabo*; *si legas*, or *si leges*. And perhaps it is in consequence hereof that some ecclesiastic authors have now and then put one for the other, *taceam* for *tacebo*; *indulgeam* for *indulgebo*, Sidon. *Adimpleam* for *adimplebo*; *mandem* for *mandabo*, Greg. Tur. unless we have a mind to say that then the futures of the two first conjugations have made an exchange, and form their termination in *am*, as the others in *bo*; but we meet with no examples hereof among the antients.

But the imperfect of this mood, over and above its proper signification, sometimes denotes also the present and future, and therefore it hath three different significations. That of the time present, *Cùm Titius studia multum amaret*, since he loved. That of the time past, *Cum studia magis amaret quàm nunc facit* That of the future, *Operam dedisses quam debebas, magis te amarem posth ic.*

The perfect in RIM is also taken for the future. *Ne mora sit si innuerim quin pugnus continuò in mala hæreat,* Ter. *Jussu tuo, imperator, extra ordinem nunquam pugnaverim, non si certum victoriam videam,* Liv. *Aufugerim potius quàm redeam,* Ter. *Videor sperare posse si te viderim, & ea quæ premant & ea quæ impendeant me facilè transiturum,* Cic. if I can see you, or when I shall be able to see you, the same as *si te videro*. And therefore we may say, *Romæ si cras fuerim,* for *fuero*, the same as *Romæ si heri fuerim.* But the future

future in RO is always compounded (as we have already observed) of the past and the future; so that we cannot say, *Romæ si heri fuero*.

To these Sanctius further addeth the plu-perfect, pretending that it partaketh likewise of the future: as *Nonnulli etiam Cæsari nuntiabant, quum castra moveri, aut signa ferri jussisset, non fore dicto audientes*, 1. B. Gall. *Juravit se illum statim interfecturum, nisi jusjurandum sibi dedisset se patrem missum esse facturum*, Cic.

Verùm anceps fuerat belli fortuna; suisset, Virg.

Besides the usual terminations, the subjunctive had heretofore another in IM. *Ausim, faxim*, as we likewise meet with *Duim, perduim, creduim*, in comic writers. Others add moreover the termination in XO, as *faxo, axo*, and the like. But of these we shall take proper notice hereafter in the chapter of defective verbs.

IV. *That we may oftentimes put the indicative or the subjunctive indifferently one for the other.*

The best authors have very indifferently made use of the indicative or the subjunctive, one for the other. We shall give here the following examples taken mostly from Budeus and Scioppius, who can supply the reader with a great many more.

For the present.

Quin tu agis ut velis? *Plaut.* for ut vis.

Loquere quid tibi est? & quid nostram velis operam, *Id.*

Nunc dicam cujus jussu venio, & quamobrem venerim, *Id. he might have said,* et quamobrem veni, *or* cujus jussu veniam, *&c.*

Debetis velle quæ velimus, *Plaut.* for volumus.

Quid est quod tu scis? *Id.*

And in another place, quid est id quod scias? Video quam rem agis, *Id.*

Scio quam rem agat, *Id.*

Quid est negotii quod tu tam subito abeas? *for* abis, *Id.*

Si est bellum civile, quid nobis faciendum sit ignoro, *Cic. for* si sit.

For the imperfect.

Non dici potest quàm cupida eram huc redeundi, *Ter. for* essem.

Autoritas tanta planè me movebat, nisi tu opposuisses non minorem tuam, *Cic. for* moveret.

Num P. Decius cùm se devoveret, & equo admisso in mediam aciem irruebat; aliquid de voluptatibus cogitabat? *Id. for* irrueret.

Scævola quotidie simulatque luceret, faciebat omnibus sui conveniendi potestatem, *Cic. for* lucebat.

For the perfect.

Obsecro te ut mihi ignoscas, quod animi impos, vini vitio fecerim, *Plaut. for* feci.

Chrysalus mihi nec rectè loquitur quia tibi aurum reddidi, & quia te non defraudaverim, *Id.*

Me habere honorem ejus ingenio dicet, cùm me adiit, *Id. for* adierit.

Tu humanissimè fecisti, qui me certiorem feceris, *Cic.*

Stultè feci, qui hunc amisi, *Plaut.*

Abi, atque illa si jam laverit, mihi renuntia, *Ter. for* lavit.

Non potest dici, quàm indignum facinus fecisti, *Plaut. for* feceris.

Quem enim receptum in gratiam summo studio defenderim, hunc afflictum violare non debeo, *Cic. for* defendi.

For the plu-perfect.

Expectationem non parvam attuleras cùm scripseras, *for* scripsisses, *Id.*

Cætera quæ ad te Vibullius scripsisset, erant in his litteris quas tu ad Lentulum misisses, *Cic. for* miseras.

Qui fuisset egentissimus in re sua, erat ut sit insolens in aliena, *Cic. for* fuerat. Verùm anceps pugnæ fuerat fortuna; fuisset, *Virg. perhaps it will be said that the issue of the engagement had been doubtful? be it so. Where* fuerat *implies the same as* fuisset *which followeth.*

For the future.

Venerem veneremur, ut nos adjuverit hodie, *Plaut. for* adjuvet.

Illuc sursum ascendero, inde optime dispellam virum, *Id. for* ascendam.

Ne tu linguam comprimes posthac, e-
tiam illud quod scies nesciveris, *Id.*
for nescies.

Te rogo ut advoles, respiraro si te videro, *Cic. for* respirabo.

This seems to favour the opinion of Ramus and Sanctius, who would not admit of the diversity of moods, though with the conjunctions there are certain differences to observe, as we shall shew hereafter.

V. *Of the imperative.*

The imperative, as we have above observed, is often taken for a third future; which is undoubtedly owing to an imitation of the Hebrews, who call it the first future, and the common future they call the second. And indeed we can command only in regard to the time to come, as the grammarian Appollonius observeth, *lib. de Synt. cap.* 30. Hence it is that the author of the rules by questions attributed to S. Basil, establishes this as a principle for the right understanding of the sacred scripture, as when the vulgate says, *Fiant filii ejus orphani*, Ps. 108. for *fient*.

We find also that the future is frequently used for the imperative, not only in the case of divine precepts, *Non occides, non furaberis*, &c. but likewise in profane authors, *Tu hæc silebis*, Cic. *Ciceronem puerum curabis & amabis.* Id. for *cura & ama. Sed valebis, meaque negotia videbis, meque ante brumam expectabis*, Id. ad Trebat. for *vale; cura; expecta:* and the like.

Hence also it comes that Sanctius laughs at those who distinguish betwixt *ama* and *amato*, as if one related to the time present, and the other to the future, and as if they were not often joined in the same sense and in the same passages:

  Aut si es dura, nega: sin es non dura, venito, Propert.
  Et potum pastas age Tityre, & inter agendum
  Occursare capro (cornu ferit ille) caveto, Virg.

And in the Georgics, after saying, *Nudus ara, sere nudus*, he adds, *Primus humum fodito*, &c.

The plural persons in NTO, are scarce ever used except in the enacting of laws, *Sunto, cavento*, &c. *Ad divos adeunto castè*, Cic. 5. de Leg.

And those in MINOR which I have entirely left out, are not perhaps to be found in any good author.

But if any one should ask how can there be an imperative in the verb passive, since what comes to us from others does not seem to depend upon us, so as to be an object of our command; we answer that undoubtedly it is because the disposition and cause thereof is frequently in our power: thus we say, *Amator ab hero; docetor à præceptore;* that is, act so as to make your master love you: suffer yourself to be taught something. And in like manner the rest.

VI. *Of the infinitive.*

The infinitive, as we shall shew hereafter in the chapter of impersonals, n. 1. is properly that which ought to be called impersonal, because it hath neither number nor person. But Sanctius, after Consentius, pretends that it is also indefinite in
                regard

regard to tenses; and A. Gellius seems to be of the same way of thinking, because, said he, as we say *volo legere*, we say likewise *volui legere*. For which reason Sanctius would not even have it to be made a distinct mood, and we may say that it is not one in fact, but only virtually and in power, inasmuch as it may be resolved by all the other moods.

This may serve to explain several passages whose construction seemeth extraordinary, and is therefore referred to an *enallage*, which is not at all necessary among the figures, as hereafter we shall shew. Therefore when we read in Terence, *Cras mibi argentum dare se dixit*; Sanctius saith that *dare* is not there for *daturum*, and that it only supposeth for itself, because *dare* may be a future, being undetermined and of itself indifferent to all tenses. And it is the same as when Virgil says:

Progeniem sed enim Trojano à sanguine duci
Audierat, Tyrias olim quæ verteret arces.

Where *duci* denotes a real future, because of itself it is indifferent to all the tenses. In like manner in Cic. *Qui brevi tempore sibi succedi putarent*. Who believed that they were to be soon succeeded: where he means the future. And according to this author it is thus we ought to explain an infinite number of passages, where we see the infinitive put sometimes for one tense, sometimes for another; as *Eo die multa verba fecimus, maximéque visi sumus senatum commovere*, Cic. where *commovere* signifieth the time past. *Sed ego idem qui in illo sermone nostro, qui est expositus in Bruto, multum tribuerim Latinis, recorder longè omnibus unum anteferre Demosthenem*, Cic. where *anteferre* is the same as *antetulisse*. *Hoc me memini dicere*, Cic. that I did say. *Ego illam virginem formâ bonâ memini me videre*, Ter. for *me vidisse*, I remember to have seen.

Dictus et Amphion Thebanæ conditor arcis
Saxa movere sono testudinis, & prece blanda
Ducere quò vellet———Hor. *movere* for *movisse*.

Cætera spero prolixa esse, Cic. where *esse* signifies the future. Again, *Spero amicitiam nostram non egere testibus*, Id. I hope our friendship will not have occasion for witnesses. *Nec ille intermisit affirmare sine mora venire*, Id. *Magna me spes tenet, judices, bene mihi evenire, quod mittar ad mortem*, Id. And the like. For though we do not deny but in joining different verbs together, there may be an assemblage and comparison of different tenses, and of one action in regard to another; yet it seems to be often the case that this distinction of tenses is not sufficiently clear, and that the two verbs mark but one precisely, to which of course we ought to attribute the action expressed by the infinite. At least this is Sanctius's opinion, which seems to be authorised by the preceding examples, and those which we shall further add. For

Thereby we see likewise what error it is to believe with Agrœcius and L. Valla, that we cannot join *memini* with the preterite of the infinitive, and that we ought to say, *memini me facere*, and not *fecisse*, for this reason, they say, that as *memini* sufficiently includeth the signification of the preterite, it is superfluous to join
another

another preterite to it; because *fecisse* supposeth all the tenses, as well as *facere*; and we find that Cicero and others have frequently used the like expressions. *Meministi me ita distribuisse causam,* Cic. *Tibi me permisisse memini,* Id. *Memini me non sumpsisse quem accusarem, sed, recepisse quem defenderem,* 3. in Verr. *Memini summos fuisse in nostra civitate viros,* 1. de leg. and an infinite number of others.

But this does not happen only to *memini*; it seems on several other occasions that this tense in ISSE is put indeterminately for all the rest. As when Virgil says:

——— *Magnum si pectore possit*

Excussisse Deum. Where Servius observeth that it stands for *excutere*. And Horace:

Fratresque tendentes opaco
Pelion imposuisse Olympo.

And Val. Max. *Sed abunde erit ex iis duo exempla retulisse.* It will be sufficient to give two examples thereof; which imports the future. And Seneca, *Intra coloniam meam me continui, alioquin potuissem eum audisse in illo atriolo, in quo duos grandes prætextatos ait secum declamare solitos.* In Præf. Controv. & Gellius, *Vel unus, hercle, hic versus, Plauti esse hanc fabulam, satis potest fidei fecisse.* And in another place, *Caleni, ubi id audiverunt, edixerunt, ne quis in balneis lavisse vellet, cùm magistratus Romanus ibi esset.* And the like.

However, this is no reason why in common use we should not rather make use of *amare*, for example, for the present, and *amavisse* for the preterite, as we have given it in the rudiments.

Vossius pretends further that *amare* will not stand for the imperfect, as hath been the general opinion of grammarians, because, according to him, when I say, for instance, *Gaudeo quòd amas*, it may be explained by *gaudeo te amare*: whereas when I say, *gaudeo quòd jam tum amabas*, it is not explained by *te jam tum amare*, but *amavisse*: and therefore the latter expresseth the three differences of the preterite. But Vossius's principle is false, and the example he produces, does not prove that the thing is general. For when Cicero in his letter to Varro, said, for instance, *Vidi enim (nam tu aberas) nostros inimicos cupere bellum,* &c. it is obvious that *cupere* is there an imperfect, and that it should be resolved by *quòd tum cupiebant*, since it denotes the same difference of time as *aberas* which he has expressed. In like manner in Virgil,

——— *Sæpè ego longos*

Cantando puerum memini me condere soles.

If we should want to resolve it, we must say; *memini quòd cùm puer eram, condebam longos soles cantando.* And therefore, *quòd amabas*, may be explained by *te amare*, as in the examples taken from Cicero and Virgil; or by *te amavisse*, as in that of Vossius. Which shews still further that all the tenses of the infinitive are frequently very indeterminate.

VII. Of FORE.

Grammarians say very right that the infinitive hath no future; but they except *sum*, which they think has *fore*.

Yet

Yet *sum*, properly speaking, has no more future than the rest. For *fore* does not come from *sum*, but from *fuo*, which in the infinitive made *fore* or *fure* by syncope for *fuere*: so that it may be taken indifferently for all tenses, as well as *esse*, *amare*, *legere*, and the other infinitives, as we have been just now mentioning. *Commissum cum equitatu prælium fore videbat*; Cæf. *Ex qua conficitur ut certas animo res teneat auditor, quibus dictis peroratum fore intelligat,* Cic. *Quanto robore animi is semper extitit, qui vitam sibi integram fore difficile dictu est,* Id.

Hence we find with how little foundation Valla said, that *fore* could not be joined with another future, as *fore venturum, faciendum fore,* &c. since *fore* is no more a real future than *esse*. And indeed we very often meet with the contrary in authors. *Deinde addis, si quid secus, te ad me fore venturum,* Cic. *Deorum immortalium causâ libenter facturos fore,* Liv. *Nihil horum vos visuros fore,* Cic. *Lepidè dissimulat fore hoc futurum,* Plaut. and in the passive, *Credite universam vim juventutis, hodierno Catilinæ supplicio conficiendam fore,* Cic. *Aut sub pellibus habendos milites fore,* Liv.

We have already given instances of the preterite above; and therefore *fore* may be joined to all tenses.

But we are carefully to observe, that this verb always includes something of the future, the same as μέλλω in Greek, so that as they have not a sufficient number of tenses for the infinitive in Latin, they frequently make use of this verb to mark the future, when they are obliged to distinguish different tenses; as *Scripsit ad me Cæsar perhumaniter, nondum te sibi satis esse familiarem, sed certè fore,* Cic. *Sequitur illud, ut te existimare velim, mihi magnæ curæ fore, atque esse jam.* And therefore I did not think proper to strike it out of the rudiments designed for children, being willing to conform as much as possible to the established custom.

VIII. *Manner of expressing the future of the infinitive in the other verbs.*

The participles in RUS serve likewise to express the future of the infinitive, whether they be joined with *esse* or with *fuisse*, as *Amaturum esse,* to be about to love; *Amaturum fuisse,* to have been about to love. But the latter tense seems to partake of the preterite and future both together. And the same is done in regard to the passive, *Amandum esse,* or *amandum fuisse.*

These futures are declined, and agree like adjectives with their substantive; *Verè mihi hoc videor esse dicturus,* Cic. *Ut perspicuum sit omnibus nunquam Lampsacenos in eum locum progressuros fuisse,* Cic.

But antiently they were not declined, as may be seen in A. Gellius, lib. 1. c. 7. For they said, for instance, *Credo inimicos meos hoc dicturum,* C. Gracch. *Hanc sibi rem præsidio sperant futurum,* Cic. act. 5. in Verrem: according to the reading which A. Gellius maintaineth by the authority of Tiro, Cicero's freedman. *Hostium copias ibi occupatas futurum,* Quadrig. *Est quod speremus deos bonis benè facturum,* Id. *Si res divinæ ritè factæ essent, omnia ex sententia processurum,* Valerius Antias. *Illi polliciti sese*

facturum

facturum omnia, Cato. *Ad summam perniciem rempublicam perventurum esse*, Silla. *Non putavi hoc eam facturum*, Laber.
Etiamne habet Casina gladium ? habet, sed duos,
Quibus, altero te occisurum ait, altero villicum, Plaut.

And such like passages, which those *Qui violant bonos libros*, says A. Gellius, would fain correct, while others superficially acquainted with the grounds of the Latin tongue, have attributed to the figure of syllepsis, but without any reason. For it is owing only to the antiquity of the language, which considered these words, not as nouns, but as verbs, and as tenses of the infinitive, which has neither gender nor number; and this they did in imitation of the Greeks, with whom the infinitive hath all the different tenses, and the future among the rest, ποιήσειν, ἔσεσθαι, &c. And we must not mind whether this hath the termination of a noun or any other, since it depends intirely upon use. So that we must resolve *futurum* like *fore*, and *dicturum* like *dicere*; *Credo inimicos meos hoc dicere*, I believe that my enemies do say this; *Credo eos hoc dicturum*, I believe they will say this. *Hanc sibi rem sperant præsidio futurum*, as if it were, *sperant præsidio fore*, &c.

IX. *Another manner of supplying the future of the infinitive, especially when the verbs have no supine.*

But if the verb hath no supine from whence a participle can be formed, we may with great elegance make use of *fore*, or of the participle *futurum*, by adding *ut* to it; which happens particularly after the verbs *spero, puto, suspicor, dico, affirmo*, and such like. *Spero fore ut contingat id nobis*, Cic.

But when to *futurum* we join the preterite *fuisse*, this is likewise one of those phrases which partake of the time past and the future, and contribute not a little to embellish the sentence. *Videmur enim quieti fuisse nisi essemus lacessiti*, Cic.

And both these turns of expression are so elegant, that they are frequently used in verbs, even when the other future might be formed by the participle. *Nisi eo ipso tempore quidam nuncii de Cæsaris victoria essent allati, existimabant plerique futurum fuisse ut oppidum caperetur*, Cæs. instead of *existimabant oppidum capiendum fore*. *Valde suspicor fore ut infringatur hominum improbitas*, Cic.

X. *That the infinitive hath frequently the force of a noun substantive.*

The infinitive by the antients was called, *nomen verbi*; and whensoever it drops the affirmation peculiar to the verb, it becomes a noun, as we have observed in the General and Rational Grammar. This noun being indeclinable, is always of the neuter gender, but it stands for different cases.

For the nominative. *Vivere ipsum, turpe est nobis,* Cic.
——— *Nam ambos curare, propemodum*
Reposcere illum est quem dedisti, Ter.
That is, τὸ *curare est reposcere.*
For the vocative. *O vivere nostrum!*

For the genitive. *Tempus est nobis de illa vita agere*, for *agendi*. *Tempus jam abhinc abire*; Cic. *Consilium capit omnem à se equitatum dimittere*, or *dimittendi*, or *dimissionis*.

For the dative. *Ætas mollis & apta regi*, for *apta regimini*, or *rectioni*, taken passively.

For the accusative. *Scripsit se cupere*, for *suam cupiditatem. Da mihi bibere*, for *da potum. Habeo dicere*, for *dicendum. Amat ludere*, for *ludum*.

For the ablative. *Dignus amari, puniri*, for *amore, pœnâ*.

The infinitive is moreover frequently governed by a preposition understood, which may be resolved even by the conjunction *quod* or *quia*, as

Gratulor ingenium non latuisse tuum, Ovid.

Instead of *ob non latuisse*, that is, *quia non latuerit*. And in like manner in Terence.

Quod plerique omnes faciunt adolescentuli,
Ut animum ad aliquod studium adjungant, aut equos
Alere, aut canes ad venandum, aut ad philosophos.

That is, *ad alere*; just as he says, *ad aliquod studium, aut ad philosophos*. And Cic. *Si equites deductos molestè feret, accipiam equidem dolorem, mihi illum irasci : sed multò majorem, non esse talem qualem putassem*; that is, *Ob illum irasci, ob non esse talem*.

But this happeneth particularly when the infinitive is joined to an adjective after the manner of the Greeks, which is a common thing in Horace; either in the active or passive; *Durus componere versus*, for *ad componendum. Celer irasci*, for *ad irascendum. Indocilis pauperiem pati*, for *ad patiendum*, and the like: though the infinite happening also to come after some adjectives, supplieth the place of another government. See the annotation to rule 18. P. 34.

It is likewise to this government of the preposition that we must refer the infinitive, when it happens to come after verbs of motion, as in the vulgate; *Non veni solvere legem, sed adimplere*; that is, *non ad solvere*, or *ad solutionem*, &c. And though some have pretended to find fault with this scriptural expression, yet it is very common in Latin authors. As

Ita visere eam, Ter.
Non ego te frangere persequar, Hor.
Non nos aut ferro Libycos populare penates
Venimus, aut raptas ad littora vertere prædas, Virg.

But they who have condemned these expressions, did not know perhaps that even when the supine is put, as *eo visum*, the force of the government is in the preposition, *eo ad visum*, as we shall shew hereafter; and therefore that it is the same as *ad videre*; *videre* and *visum*, being then only nouns substantives, and synonymous terms. This shews what it is rightly to understand the real foundation and principles of construction and government.

CHAP.

Chapter III.
Of irregular verbs.

WE have already touched upon this subject in the rudiments; but here we intend to treat of it more at large, and to shew from whence this irregularity arises, and wherein it consists, by which means we shall find that it is not so great as people imagine.

I. *Of* SUM *and its compounds.*

The antients, says Varro, 8. de. L. L. used to conjugate *Esum, es, est; esumus, estis, esunt,* in the same manner as *eram, as, at; ero, is, it,* &c. Hence it is that Cicero in his third book of laws hath put *esunto* for *sunto*. *Ast quando duellum gravius, discordiæ civium, esunto ne amplius sex menses, si senatus creverit.* For thus Vossius insists upon reading this passage, which has puzzled such a number of learned men.

For according to him, *esum* comes from the Greek future ἔσομαι, from whence rejecting the diphthong, they formed at first *esom*, then *esum*, and at length *sum*. But Julius Scaliger and Caninius derive it from εἰμί. Which will not appear so extraordinary to those, who have attended to the changing of letters, of which we intend to subjoin a particular treatise; though some have attempted to ridicule the opinion of these two learned men on this subject. For it is easy to shew that I final is sometimes lost, as from μέλι, is formed *mel*. 2. That the diphthong ει frequently loseth its subjunctive, as Αἰνείας, *Æneas*. 3. That the *s* is sometimes added not only for the rough breathing, as ἕπω, *sequor*; ἥμισυ, *semi*; but likewise for the smooth; as ἵ, *si*; εἴρω, *sero*; ἱρύω, *servo*. 4. That the ε is oftentimes changed into *u*, as Βρεντήσιον, *Brundusium*, from whence we may conclude, that of εἰμί, they formed at first ἰμ, afterwards ἰμ, σιμ, and at length *sum*. Neither can it be said that this conjecture is ill founded, since we give authority for the change of these several letters; and since this analogy occurreth also in the other persons. For *es* comes from εἰς, in the second person, which we meet with above fifteen times in Homer, as *est* cometh from ἐςὶ, and *sunt* from ἰςὶ, according to the Dorians for ἰσὶ.

Be that as it will, it may be likewise formed of ἔσομαι, since it is not at all extraordinary to see the futures form other verbs of themselves, as from ἄγω, fut. ἄξω, is formed ἄξω, *I do*, from whence cometh ἄξις, ἀξίτω, *fac*. From ὄιω, fut. οἴσω, is also formed οἴσω, *fero*, whence comes the imperfect οἴσον, the imperative οἴσι, &c. For there is no more absurdity to see the present formed of this Greek future, than the imperfect *eram*, which is manifestly derived from thence as well as the future *ero*, by changing S into R, which is very common, as hereafter we shall shew.

But heretofore it was usual for them to say likewise *escit* for *erit*, from whence cometh *escunt*, in a passage of the twelve tables quoted by Cicero in his second book of laws. QUOI AURO DENTES VINCTI ESCUNT. And in Gellius who quotes it from the same place; SI MORBUS ÆVITASVE VITIUM ESCIT, lib. 20. cap. 1. as Vossius and H. Stephen read it, though others read *esit*. But *escit* occurreth also in Lucret. lib. 1.

Ergo rerum inter summam, minimámque, quid escit,

Where the verse would be faulty were we to read *esit*, which has the first short, as well as *erit*.

The preterite *fui* and the participle *futurus*, come from the old verb *fuo*, taken from the Greek φύω. Even Virgil himself has made use of it, *Tros rutulúsve fuat*, &c. From thence also cometh, *forem* for *essem*, formed of *fuerem* or *furem*, as likewise *fore* for *fure*, or *fuere*, as we have already observed, chap. 2. num. 7.

The subjunctive, Sim, *is*, *it*, is a syncope for *Siem*, *es*, *et*, which followed the analogy of the other subjunctives in EM, as *Amem, es, et*. Which Cicero confirmeth in his book *de Oratore*, Siet, says he, *plenum est: fit, imminutum*. And this old subjunctive is also very common in Terence, and in the other comic writers.

This verb hath neither gerund nor supine. The participle present ought to be *ens*, which we find in some manuscript copies of Appuleius, and which Cæsar had inserted in his books of analogy, according to Priscian. But now it is hardly ever used except by philosophers, though from thence are formed *Absens, præsens, potens*, which are rather nouns adjectives than participles, because in their signification they express no time.

These nouns come from *Adsum, præsum, possum*, which are conjugated like their simple, as are all the other compounds. But

PROSUM, takes a D, when it follows a vowel, for the conveniency of the sound. *Prodes, prodest*, &c.

And POSSUM, coming from *potis* or *pote*, and from *sum*, as appeareth in Plautus.

Animadvertite, si potis sum hoc inter vos componere, in Curcul.

Tute homo, & alteri sapienter potis es consulere & tibi, in Milite. It retaineth the T wherever it followeth a vowel; and to soften the sound it changeth this T into S, when another S followeth. For the antients used to say, *potessem, potesse*, where we say, *possem, posse*. But *potis* as well as *pote*, occur in all genders. *Ergone sine Dei voluntate quicquam potis est fieri?* Arnob. *Sed quantum fieri potest*, Id. *Qui fieri potis est ut?* Id. In regard to which the reader may see what we have already observed, chap. 4th no. 1.

Potestur, occurreth in Plautus, Lucretius, Pacuvius, Ennius, and others. But there is no grounds for attributing it to Virgil Æn. 8. where we ought to read

———— *Liquidove potest electro*.

and not *potestur*, because the first syllable is long in *electro*, as it comes from *n*; which is confirmed by Vossius and Politianus, from the authority of excellent MSS, as may be seen in Vossius, book 3. of Analogy, chap. 36.

II. *Of* Edo, Queo, *and* Fio.

What hath been said in the Rudiments, is almost sufficient for the

the other irregulars. I shall only add a word or two in regard to some of them.

Edo formeth in the infinitive *esse* or *edere*. The former is in Cicero, *Claudius mergi pullos in aquam jussit, ut biberent, quia esse nollent.* 2. de Nat. *Quid attinuit relinquere hanc urbem, quasi bona comesse Romæ non liceret?* Orat. pro Flacco.

Of *est* is formed *estur*, just as of *potest*, *potestur*. And this word we find not only in Plautus, but also in Ovid,

Estur, ut occultâ vitiata teredine navis,

Æquoreos scopulos ut cavat unda salis, 1. de Ponto El. 1. *Edim*, was heretofore said for *edam*, which Nonius proves from several passages. Just as we find also *duint* for *dent*, and *perduint* for *perdant*, in comic writers.

Hence Horace says in his 3. Epode.

Edit cicutis allium nocentius.

And Plautus in Aulul.

———— *Quid tu, multum curas,*

Utrum crudum, an coctum edim, nisi tu mihi es tutor?

QUEO, follows the fourth conjugation. *Si non* QUIBO *impetrare*, Plaut. *Licere ut* QUIRET *convenire amantibus*, Id. *Trahere, exhaurire me, quod* QUIREM *ab se domo,* Id.

It occurreth also in the passive, as *quitus* and *queuntur*, in Attius; *queatur*, in Lucr. *Quitus is* in Appul. And in Ter.

———— *Forma in tenebris nosci non* QUITA *est*, in Hecyr.

We likewise make use of *nequeor. Nequeor comprehendi; cognosci*, &c. as Festus proveth. *Ut nequitur comprimi!* Plaut. *Reddi nequitur*, Appul.

FIO, heretofore made *fii*, in the preterite, according to Priscian. And in the imperative it made *fi* and *fite*, Plaut. *in Curcul.*

PH. *Sequere hac, Palinure, me ad fores, si mi obsequens.*

PA. *Ita faciam.* PH. *Agite, bibite, festivæ fores, potate, fite mihi volentes propriæ.*

The former is also in Horace, lib. 2. Sat. 5. where we must read, according to Vossius.———*Fi cognitor ipse*, though others read, *fis cognitor.* And this perfectly sheweth, what we have already observed when speaking of the preterites, that *fio* is a substantive verb, as well as *Sum*.

The infinitive was *firi*, just as from *audio* cometh *audiri*: but because the antients marked the *i* long by *ei*, *feiri*, or *feirei*, they have transposed it to *fieri*; in like manner *fierem* for *feirem*, or *firem*, as *audirem*, &c.

III. Of FERO, *and* EO, *with their Compounds.*

FERO, is irregular only as it drops the vowel after the R in some particular tenses, as in the present *fers*, *fert*, instead of *feris*, *ferit*, &c. which Priscian believes to have been designed to distinguish it from *ferio*, *feris*, *ferit*.

In the imperative it hath also *fer* instead of *fere*. In the subjunctive *ferrem*, for *fererem*, &c. In the other tenses it is regular: the imperfect, *ferebam*, as, like *legebam*: fut. *feram, es*, like *agam*, *leges*, &c.

It borrows its preterite of *tollo*, or *tolo, tetuli*; (as *fallo, fefelli*,) from whence is formed *tuli*. But *tollo* seems to come from the old verb τλῶ *fero*, or τιλάω, from whence also cometh the supine *latum* for *telatum*, unless we chuse simply to say, that *tolo* made *tetuli, tolatum*, or *tulatum*, from whence afterwards hath been formed *latum*. Vossius.

Eo, ought to make *eis, eit*, &c. and in the infinitive *eire*. But first of all they contracted it into *eis, eit*, then dropping the prepositive *e*, they made it *is, it*; the *i* long and the diphthong *ei* having been generally put one for the other, as we have often observed.

Its compounds have most commonly IBO in the future like itself; *transibo, præteribo*; but some of them have it in IAM (like *audiam*) *transiam, præteriam : inietur ratio*, Cic. &c.

Of these compounds some have their passive, though the simple verb hath none, except it be in the third person plural. For we find *adeor, ambior, ineor, obeor, subeor*, &c. And in like manner, *Itur ad me*, Ter.

Ambio, is regularly conjugated like *audio*, but we sometimes meet also with *ambibam*, in Livy and elsewhere, just as heretofore they said *audibam* for *audiebam*, as we have elsewhere observed.

Circumeo, sometimes drops the *m* : so that we say, *circumis* or *circuis, circumire* or *circuire*, &c.

IV. Of Volo, and its compounds.

VOLO ought to make *volis, volit*, &c. like *lego, legis, it*, but first of all they have syncopated it into *vis, voit, voltis*, &c. (which we still find in antient writers) and afterwards into *vult* and *vultis*, by changing *o* into *u* which is very common.

Its subjunctive takes an E in the first syllable *velim*, instead of *volim*, as well as the infinitive *velle*; which they retain throughout all their tenses, except, such as are formed of the preterite, which retain the *o* of the indicative, *volui, voluissem, voluisse*, &c.

Nolo, comes from *ne* for *non*, and from *volo* : hence we still meet with *nevis, nevult*, for *nonvis, nonvult*. The imperative *noli*, we find in Cicero; and *nolito* in Lucilius.

Malo, comes from *magis*, and *volo*; hence they used heretofore to say *mavelim* and *mavellem*, of which hath been formed *malim* and *mallem*.

Chapter IV.

Of defective verbs.

WE have likewise made mention of these verbs in the rudiments, where we gave only those tenses which are most generally received. But as they occur likewise in other tenses besides those usually marked by grammarians, I have determined here to enter into a more particular account of them, by reason that divers passages have been corrupted, for want of observing what tenses of these verbs were current among the best writers.

I. Of

I. *Of* ODI, MEMINI, *and others which are thought to have only the preterite, and the tenses depending thereon.*

ODI. Heretofore *odio* was also used; hence we find in Appul. *Orationis variæ species sunt; imperandi, narrandi, monendi, irascendi, odiendi.* And in Petronius, according to Vossius and others, we should read *odientes*, where the usual reading is *audientes*, which is nonsense. The antient interpreter useth this verb very frequently, both in the old and in the new testament, as *odiet, odient, odivi, odivit, odite, odientes*, &c. In the vulgate, Prov. c. 1. we find, *Usquequo imprudentes odibunt scientiam?*

The passive occurreth also in some authors, as *oditur*, in Tertull. *odiaris*, in Seneca, as hath been observed by Gruterus, H. Stephen, and Vossius, *Necesse est aut imiteris, aut odiaris.*

The preterite was *odi* and *osus*, just as *soleo* made *solüi*, and *solitus sum.*

Inimicos semper osa sum obtuerier, Plaut.

Hunc non probabat, osusque eum morum causâ fuit, Gell.
Whence we have still remaining the compounds *exosus, perosus.*

COEPI, as we have observed in the preterites, vol. i. p. 210. comes from the old verb *cœpio.*

Neque ego insanio, neque pugnas, neque lites cœpio, Plaut.
From thence cometh *cœpiam*, in the same author, and in Cato, according to Festus. *Cœperet*, is in Terence.

—— *Nonne sex totis mensibus*
Prius olfecissem quam ille quicquam cœperet?

Vossius insists that it makes COEPTUS also in the preterite. But COEPTUS is passive, as may be seen in Tully, *Celeriter ad majores causas adhiberi cœptus est*, de Clar. Orat. *Minor haberi est cœptus postea*, Ibid. And there can be no manner of doubt of this, for otherwise, as we say, *hoc cœpisti*, we might also say, *hoc cœptus es, you have begun this*, which every body knows to be wrong.

MEMINI comes from *meno*, as *cœpi* from *cœpio*. And this preterite is formed by reduplication, as *fefelli* from *fallo, pepigi* from *pago*, &c.

From this *meno* cometh also *mentio*, formed of the supine *mentum*, which the antients made use of instead of *commentum*, according to Festus.

Thence also came *meniscor*, from whence we have still remaining *comminisco* and *reminiscor*. And Vossius from thence also deriveth *moneo*, changing the *o* into *e*, as in *bonus* instead of *benus; forceps* instead of *ferriceps*, and others of which we shall take notice in the treatise of letters.

Now *meno* properly signifieth to have something in one's mind, from the Greek μένος: but Vossius thinks that they likewise said *memino*, whence comes *meminens* in Priscian, Donatus, Plautus, Ausonius, and frequently in Sidonius Apollinaris.

Hereto we may add *novi*, which cometh from Nosco, and is thought to have the signification of the present for no other reason than as we often make use of the present in narrations, it is generally rendered in the signification of this tense.

II. *Of*

II. *Of* FARI, *and other defective verbs of the same signification.*

Hereto we may add four or five defective verbs of the same signification, *fari, inquam, aio, infit, cedo.*

FOR is scarcely used, saith Diomedes, though we meet with *effor*; but we say *faris* and *fatur*, in the same manner as *daris* and *datur*, though there is no such word as *dor*, and yet *addor* and *redder* are in use.

Fans occurreth in Plautus;

Cum interim tu meum ingenium fans non didicisti atque infans.

INQUIO is obsolete, according to Diomedes and other antients. But Priscian pretends it is used, though the passage he produces out of Cicero is corrupted. *Aucupari verba oportebit, inquio,* 2. de Orat. where according to Lambinus, Vossius, and others, we should read *in quo.*

It may be defended by the following passage of Catull. Epig. 10. as Muretus reads it:

——— *Velo ad Serapin*

Ferri mane: inquio puellæ.

Inquam seems to be only a preter imperfect for *inquiebam*:

Inquimus is in Horace;

Communi sensu planè caret, inquimus, lib. 1. Sat. 3.

Inquitis is in Arnobius. *Inquiebant* and *inquisti* occur frequently in Cic. as likewise *inquies* and *inquiet*. *Inque* is in Plautus and Terence; *inquito,* in Plautus.

The tenses belonging to AIO may be seen in the rudiments. The imperative, of which some have doubted, as Diomedes observeth, is proved by Nevius, *vel ai, vel nega.*

Aibant is in Attius for *aiebant,* just as we say in the second person *ais* for *aiis.*

Priscian says it hath not the first person of the preterite, and him we have followed in the 69th rule, vol. i. p. 291. Yet Probus gives us *ai, aisti, ait,* &c. Tertullian makes use of the plural. *Atque ita omnes aierunt, fiet voluntas domini,* lib. de Fuga. *Aiat* is in Cic. *Quasi ego curem, quid ille aiat aut neget,* 2. de fin. And the participle *aiens: Negantia aientibus contraria,* in Top.

INFIT cometh from *info,* which Varro made use of, according to Priscian. And therefore as from *capit* is formed *incipit,* in like manner from *fit* is derived *infit,* which signifieth the same as *incipit.* We say likewise *defit,* from whence comes *defiet, defiat, defieri.*

Infit is usually rendered by *be saith,* like *ait.* But as we have just now shewn, and as Festus also explains this word, it signifies the same as *incipit.*

Homo ad prætorem plorabundus devenit,

Infit ibi postulare, plerans, ejulans, Plaut.

——— *Ita farier infit,* Virg.

But this mistake was doubtless occasioned by the infinitive of the other verb being frequently understood; *Ibi infit, annum se tertium*

& *nonagesimum agere*, sup. *loqui* or *fari*. Which is further confirmed by the glossaries of Philoxenus, *insit, ἄρχει λέγειν*.

CEDO properly signifieth no more than to give way or to permit. But it often happeneth that by process of time words are diverted into a different sense from their original meaning, as Agricola in his notes on Seneca hath learnedly observed. This appears further in *præsto*, in *amabo*, in *liceo*, *vapulo*, and *veneo*, of which we took notice when speaking of the preterites, vol. i. p. 305. and in others. For as when a person was called, he answered *præsto*, or *sto præ*, here I am: so when they intended to signify that a thing was at hand and quite ready, they said, *præsto est*, taking this word as an adverb. Again, because when a person offered to do a thing, or asked leave of another, the answer was always, *cedo*, that is, *I give you leave, I permit you*, either to do, to say, or to give, &c. therefore they began likewise to say, *Cedo manum*, give me the hand; *Cedo canterium*, lend me your horse, or barely *cedo*, give me, tell me.

Of *cedo* they have formed by syncope *cette* for *cedite*.

Cette manus vestras, measque accipite: Enn. apud Non.

III. Of FAXO, AUSIM, FOREM, and QUÆSO.

We must also mention a word or two in regard to these four other defective verbs.

FAXO seemeth to come from *facio*. For as the Greeks said ἄγω, ἄξω: τίκτω or τίκω, τίξω: so the Latins said *facio, facto, faxo. Ago, acto, axo*. From whence comes *adaxint*, in Plautus; and *axitiosi*, that is *factiosi*, according to Festus, several met together in order to perform or undertake a thing.

They used also to say *jacio, jacto*, from whence came *jaxo*: and *injicio, injecto*, from whence was formed *injexo*.

Ubi quadruplator quempiam injexit manum,
Tantidem ille illi rursus injiciat manum, Plaut.

Others nevertheless are of opinion that *faxo, axo, injexo*, &c. are tenses of the future perfect, that is of the subjunctive, for *fecero, egero, injecero*. And this verb we find also in Virgil,

———*Ego fœdera faxo Firma manu*, Æn. 12.

FAXIM in like manner seems to have been used for *facerim* (for the preterites heretofore retained the vowel of the present tense) or *fecerim*. And indeed, the sense agrees therewith: *tibi lubens bene faxim*, Ter. so of *egerim* they made *assim*, or *axim*, which is in Attius. And in Plautus we find

Utinam me Divi adaxint ad suspendium, In Aulul.

Faximus occurreth also in Plautus, as likewise *faxem* for *fecissem*. But *faxint* is frequently met with in Cic. *Dii faxint*: and the like. And *faxit* is in his 2. book of laws, *qui servus faxit*, &c.

Now as we say *faxim* for *fecerim*, so we say AUSIM for *auserim*, that is, *ausus fuerim*.

De grege non ausim quicquam deponere tecum, Virg.
I dare not wager any part of the flock.
Ausim vel tenui vitem committere sulco, Id.

FOREM is only a syncope for *fuerem*, and *fore* for *fuere*, from the old verb *fuo*, as hath been already observed, p.

QUÆSO, according to Vossius, is only an antient word for *quæro*, just as they used to say *asa* for *ara*, the *s* being frequently put for *r*, as we shall shew in the treatise of letters. Hence it is that Ennius saith *quæsentibus*, *quæsendum*, for *quærentibus*, *quærendum*. And indeed, to ask or to beg a thing, is properly to *look for it*, both being expressive of desire: so that the præterite *quæsivi* properly cometh from this old verb, pursuant to the analogy above observed, p. 116.

CHAPTER V.
Of verbs called impersonal, and of their nature.

VERBS impersonal are ranked in the number of defectives by Phocas, Donatus, and Sergius, which obliges us to say something of them on this occasion. We shall therefore examine two points, 1. What is meant by a verb impersonal. 2. Whether these verbs have not more tenses than they are allowed by grammarians.

I. *What is meant by a verb impersonal, and that in reality there is no other but the infinitive.*

Julius Scaliger, and Sanctius, allowed of no other impersonals but the infinitive, and Consentius Romanus was long before of the same opinion. Their reason is because in all verbs whatsoever the infinitive is always without number and person; whereas the other verbs, called impersonals, are not without persons, having at least the third always, and frequently being susceptible of others. This opinion is founded on reason itself, by which we are debarred from pronouncing any sentence, or forming any kind of speech that is not compounded of a noun and a verb.

The better to understand this, and to shew more distinctly the nature of those verbs called impersonals, we are to remember what hath been said above, chap. 1. That there are three sorts of verbs adjectives, namely actives or transitives; neuters, or intransitives; and passives.

Therefore if these verbs are transitives, and signify an action which passeth into a subject, they have generally their nominative taken from without themselves, which nominative formeth this action; as *hoc me juvat*, this pleaseth me; *illud te decet*, that becometh thee.

If they are absolute and intransitives, then their nominative must be either included within themselves; for *libet mihi hoc facere, licet tibi tacere, oportet illud agere*, is the same as if you were to say, *libido est mihi hoc facere, licentia* or *licitum est tibi tacere, opus est illud agere*: or the infinitive which follows this verb, will be, as it were, its nominative; so that *licet tibi tacere*, is the same as, τὸ *tacere licet tibi*, or *est res licita tibi*: *libet mihi hoc facere*, that is,

τὰ

τὸ *facere hanc rem libet mihi*, that is, the doing of this action pleaseth me: *oportet illud agere*, that is, the doing of this action is necessary. Nor does it signify at all, though we sometimes are in want of Latin nouns to resolve these phrases, for the thing is always in the sense, and subsists of itself.

But if these verbs are passives, as *statur, curritur, concurritur, sic vivitur, regnatum est, amatum est*; they ought then to be resolved by the verb substantive, *est* or *fit*, and the verbal noun derived from themselves: *fit statio, cursus* or *concursus fit, sic vita est,* or *sic vita fit, regnum fuit, amor fuit,* &c.

Hereby, we see, properly speaking, that these verbs are no more impersonals than the others, but only defectives, and deprived (at least generally speaking) of the two first persons.

Therefore what we ought most to observe in this sort of verbs, is that when I say *amo*, I include an intire proposition in a single word, making the verb comprize the subject, the affirmation, and the attribute, so that this word *amo* is equivalent to *ego sum amans*: just as when we say, *pudet, oportet, itur, statur,* &c. we include in those words an intire proposition, the verb containing in itself the subject, the affirmation, and the attribute, which ought to be resolved, as we have shewn above. Concerning which the reader may likewise see what has been said in the general grammar, c. 18.

Thus we see that what even in French we call impersonal, is not such. For when we say, *on court, on marche, on parle,* &c.; this *on,* as Monf. de Vaugelas judiciously observeth in his remarks on the French tongue, comes from the word *homme:* which appeareth from the Italian poets, who say *huom teme*, for *huomo*, people fear; and from the Germans and other northern nations, who render the French particle *on* by the word *man*, which in their language signifies the same as *homme*. And even from the Greek language, which frequently useth τὶς in the same sense; as τῦτο δὲ τις ἀποκρίναιτ' ἂν κ᾽ μαλά γε εἰκότως. *We might make this answer very justly*. So that it is the same thing to say in French, *on dit* or *l'on dit*, as *homme dit*, or *l'homme dit*, by an indefinite term, which may indifferently agree with either.

And we may further remark in regard to these expressions, that the Latin is passive, *dicitur*, where we must understand *hoc* or *illud*; and the French active, *l'on dit*, which implies *l'homme dit*. The reason hereof, and which few have ever observed, is because as the Latin always affects to use passive expressions, the French tongue on the contrary chuseth to render them by active ones.

Now these passive impersonals are not always taken in a general and indeterminate signification, as Diomedes imagined (which is peculiar only to the infinitive) since Cicero saith: *Nunciatum est nobis à Varrone eum Romā veniſſe*, Varro has told us, &c. And Seneca, *Insanitur à patre*. And others in the same manner.

But we must observe, that though these verbs be deprived of some persons, this is not so much owing to the verb, as to the defect in the thing, which may be applied to it, according as Scaliger hath remarked. Hence if we more frequently say *decet, pudet,* &c.

it

it is because the things joined in this sense, are always put in the third person; which does not however hinder Statius from saying, *Si non dedecui tua jussa.* And Plautus, *Ita nunc pudeo, atque ita paveo.* And Ennius, *Miserete mei annis.* And Plautus again, *Adolescens loquere nisi piges,* &c. Which was heretofore more frequent than at present: for it seemeth that they said also *pœniteo,* instead of *pœnitet me,* since we find in Justin, *Primi pœnitere cœperunt,* instead of *primos pœnitere cœpit:* and in Apuleius, *Quum cœperis serò pœnitere,* instead of *cùm cœperit te serò pœnitere.*

II. *That the verbs called impersonals are not deprived of all the persons we imagine, even in the most elegant language.*

The first mistake on this head is of those, who fancy these verbs have not the third person plural, whereas it is otherwise, *Parvum parva decent,* Hor. *Quæ adsolent, quæque oportent signa,* Ter. *Non te hæc pudent?* Id. *Quàm se aliena deceant,* Cic. *Hæc facta ab illo oportebant,* Ter. *Semper metuet quem sæva pudebunt,* Luc.

The same we observe in the passives. *Quo in genere multa peccantur,* Cic. *Noctes vigilantur amaræ,* Ovid. *In cæteris gentibus quæ regnantur,* Tacit. *Sacris passibus hæ natantur undæ,* Mart.

It is moreover false that impersonals are to be found only in the indicative, as Diomedes and some other antients imagined. For not to mention that Varro gives them all the moods, we find a sufficient number of authorities: *oporteto,* was in Numa's laws, according to Scaliger: *oportuerit* is from Cæcilius in Priscian. Cicero says, *Nec velle experiri quàm se aliena deceant,* Offic. 1. And Aul. Gell. *Verbisque ejus defatigari pertæduissent.*

And in like manner in the passive. *Cùm malè pugnatum esset,* Cic. *Cùm jam horis amplius sex continenter pugnaretur;* Cæs.

Ponite jam gladios hebetes, pugnetur acutis, Ovid.

The infinitive is in Terence, in Hec. act. 3. sc. 1.

Trepidari sentio, cursari sursum prorsum.

And in Cicero, *Hic maneri diutius non potest.*

In regard to *licet, piget, placet,* and others which have a double preterite, we have made mention of them in the rules of the preterites, vol. 1. p. 306.

ANNOTATION.

We might also take occasion here to speak of derivative, and compound verbs; but as this seemed more particularly to relate to the conjugations, we placed them at the end of the rules of preterites, vol. i. p. 309. and the following.

SECTION IV.
Remarks on the GERUNDS, SUPINES, and PARTICIPLES.

CHAPTER I.
Remarks on the gerunds.

I. *What the antient and modern grammarians thought of Gerunds.*

THERE is no one article, on which the grammarians have started more questions, and been more puzzled to answer them, than the gerunds. Sanctius, Scioppius, and Vossius, will have it that they are verbal nouns adjectives, or even participles.

Certain it is that they are not verbs, and that they do not make a mood apart, as some grammarians have fancied. In the first place because they do not mark a judgment of the mind, nor an affirmation, which is the property of the verb. And in the second place, because they have cases, and verbs have not. Thus we say for example, in the nominative, *dicendum est*; in the genitive, *dicendi causâ*; in the dative, *dicendo apta*; in the accusative, *ad dicendum*; the ablative, *dicendo consequi*.

They are therefore verbal nouns, and generally retain the government of their verbs: *causâ videndi Romam*; Virg. *Utendum est ætate*; Ovid. *Canes paucos et acres habendum*; Varro. But we must inquire what sort of verbal nouns they are, and what is the cause of this government.

They who pretend that these nouns are adjectives, and consider that as such they must needs have their substantives, are obliged to say, that as we see many verbs govern their original noun, as *vivere vitam, pugnare pugnam*; so those gerunds being in the neuter, suppose for a substantive the infinitive of their verb itself, which is then taken as a noun verbal. For the infinitive was called by the antients, *Nomen verbi*. So that when we say for instance, *pugnandum est*, they would have us understand τὸ *pugnare*, and that *pugnandum est pugnare*, is the same construction as *pugnanda est pugna*. But if we say, *pugnandum est pugnam*, they still would have us understand *pugnare*, and that its construction is double, namely that of the substantive and of the adjective, *pugnandum est pugnare*: and that of the verbal noun governing the case of its verb, *pugnare* (for *pugnatio*) *pugnam*, like *tactio hanc rem.*

And it is by this means they account for these expressions which seem so extraordinary, *tempus videndi lunæ, tempus legendi librorum*, and the like. For, say they, *videndi* will always suppose τὸ *videre*, as if it were *tempus visionis*: and *videre* as substantive will govern *lunæ*, as if it were *tempus videndæ visionis lunæ*. And this is the opinion I had followed after Sanctius, Scioppius, and Vossius, in the preceding editions.

But

But all things considered, this turn of expression and this supposition do not seem to be necessary, as we have already observed in the general grammar. For in the first place what they say that the infinitive is understood as a verbal noun which governeth the genitive, or even the accusative, is without probability, since there is no foundation to say that a word is understood when we have never seen it expressed, and when we even cannot express it without an absurdity, as it would be to say, *legendum est legere, tempus est videndi videre, pugnandum est pugnare*, &c.

2. Were the gerund *legendum* a noun adjective, it would not be different from the participle *legendus, a, um*; and there would not have been sufficient reason to invent this new sort of words.

3. Since they say that this infinitive in the quality of a verbal noun, governs the case that followeth, it is as easy for us to say that *legendum* being only a noun substantive derived from the verb, shall produce this same effect, by itself, without there being occasion to understand any thing.

II. *That the gerunds are nouns substantives, and what is the real cause of their government.*

Therefore I say, that the gerund is a verbal noun substantive, derived from the adjective or participle of the same termination, but which frequently addeth to the signification of the action of the verb, a kind of necessity and duty, as if one were to say *the action that is to be done*, which the word gerund taken from *gerere*, to do, seems to have been intended to signify; hence *pugnandum est*, is the same as *pugnare oportet*, we must fight, it is time to fight. Nevertheless as words do not always preserve the full strength which they had at their first invention; so this gerund frequently loseth that of *duty*, and preserves only that of the action of its verb, as *cantando rumpitur anguis*.

Now this assertion, that the gerund is a substantive, ought not to appear strange, since nothing is more common in all languages, than to see the neuter of the adjectives changed into a substantive, when it is taken absolutely; as τὸ ἀγαθὸν, *bonum*, goodness, and the like.

This being premised, it is a very easy matter to account for all those expressions that are formed by the gerund, for when we say, for instance, *pugnandum est, legendum est*, it is as if it were *pugna est, lectio est*; with this addition of duty or necessity, or proximity of action, which we said was properly and peculiarly included in the gerund.

And if we say *legendum est libros*, it is the same government as *lectio libros*, just as Plautus saith, *tactio hanc rem*. And Cæsar *reditio domum*, &c. See above, p. 18.

And if we say *tempus est videndi lunæ*, it is the same as *tempus visionis lunæ*, nothing being more common than to see a noun governed in the genitive, and governing another, in the same case; as *Consules designatos maximâ orbitate reipublicæ virorum talium*, Cic. ad Planc. *Hujus rei magna partem laudis atque existimationis ad Libonem perventuram*, Cæs. And this is the way of accounting for all these

phrases.

phrases. *Fuit exemplorum legendi potestas,* Cic. *Antonio facultas detur agrorum suis latronibus condonandi,* Id. *Dolebis tandem Stoicos nostros Epicureis irridendi sui facultatem dedisse,* Id. *Reliquorum siderum quæ causa collocandi fuerit,* Id. *Omnium rerum una est definitio comprehendendi,* Id. *Aut eorum quæ secundùm naturam sunt adipiscendi,* Id. *Nominandi tibi istorum magis erit quàm adeundi copia,* Plaut. *Venerunt purgandi sui causâ,* Cæf. and the like.

Hereby likewise it appeareth why speaking of a woman as well as of a man, we say, *cupidus sum videndi tui,* and not *videndæ,* because as we have already mentioned in the remark on the pronouns, these genitives, *mei, tui, sui, nostri, vestri,* not admitting of adjectives, it is as if it were *cupidus sum visionis tui ipsius*; and it is the same construction as *tempus videndi lunæ.* Thus Terence speaking of a young girl, hath these words: *Ego ejus videndi cupidus, rectâ sequor.* And in another passage, *ut neque ejus sit amittendi, neque retinendi copia.*

And Ovid, *Et spem placandi dántque adimúntque tui.*

Again, *Olim placandi spem mihi tolle tui.*

So that it is a mistake, when in Acontius's letter to Cydippe, this same poet is made to say,

Sit modò placandæ copia magna tui,

whereas we should read *placandi.*

We see further why it is better Latin to say with the participle *amandi sunt boni,* and the like, than *amandum est bonos*: because the verbal nouns substantives have rarely preserved the government of their verbs in the purity of the language; though there are some instances of it.

Hence also it appeareth, why it is frequently indifferent, to put the supine or the infinitive, or even the verbal noun in *io* (notwithstanding that Valla is of a different opinion) in the place of the gerund, agreeably to what we shall observe in the next chapter, as *audiendo jucunda, auditu jucunda, audire jucunda, auditione jucunda.* Because it is very natural to put a substantive of the same signification for another derived from the same verb. And thus Cicero hath made use of it, when he says; *Si qui ineunte ætate, venandi aut pilæ studiosi fuerint,* &c. *if there should be any one that had a passion, when they were young, either for hunting, or for tennis*; where we see that *venandi,* being in the same government as *pilæ,* nothing is more natural than to take it for a noun substantive, like *pila,* and to say it is there instead of *venationis*; and in all probability Cicero would not have used it thus, unless he had this notion of it.

This is likewise the reason why interpreters frequently render into one language by the gerund, that which in the other is expressed by the verbal noun or by the infinitive, as in St. Paul εἰς ὑπακοὴν πίστεως, where the antient interpreter has put *ad obediendum fidei, for the obedience of faith,* that is, to preach obedience which comes from faith. Again, ὁ κηρύσσων μὴ κλέπτειν, *qui prædicas non furandum,* thou who preachest, that we must not steal, that it is a crime to steal.

And thus we ought to explain several turns of expression which

seem

seem very intricate in Latin authors, as when Livy faith: *Neque immemor ejus quod initio consulatus imbiberat, reconciliandi animos plebis.* Not having forgot the vigorous resolution he had taken at the beginning of his consulate, of reconciling the senate to the people: for *immemor ejus reconciliandi*, is there for *ejus reconciliationis*. And *reconciliationis animos*, is like *tactio hanc rem.*

III. *Whether the gerunds are taken actively or passively.*

But it is further easy to answer this way the question which is put, whether those gerunds are taken actively or passively. For when they supply the place of the infinitive of the verb or of another verbal substantive, if this infinitive or other verbal noun, by which they may be resolved, is active, they will be likewise actives; and if it be passive, they will be passives. Thus when Virgil saith: *Quis talia fando temperet à lacrymis: fando,* being there for *fari, in fando,* or *in fari talia,* it must be active. Whereas when he says, *Fando aliquid si fortè tuas pervenit ad aures,* there it is for *dum dicitur,* and consequently passive.

And when we read in Cicero; *Hic locus ad agendum amplissimus, ad dicendum ornatissimus. Agendum* and *dicendum,* being there for *actio,* and *dictio,* that is, *ut actio habeatur,* they seem passive. But sometimes there is so very little difference between the action and the passion, that one need only to look at them with very little obliquity, to take them in either sense. Which is of no sort of consequence, and does not deserve to be a matter of dispute.

The principle we have here established, contributes also to the easy clearing up of several difficult passages, as—*Uritque videndo femina,* Virg. that is, *in videri* or *in visu ipsius,* for *dum videtur.* Just as in Lucretius,

Annulus in digito subter tenuatur habendo,

for *dum habetur.*

Thus when we find in Sallust, where he speaks of Jugurtha; *cùm ipse ad imperandum Tisidium vocaretur,* which hath puzzled a great many learned men; that is, *ad imperari,* or, *ut ei imperaretur,* as Servius, and after him Manutius, Alciatus, Gentilis, and Sanctius explain it. And it is without foundation that some have attempted to amend the text, and to read *ad imperatorem.* Even Cicero himself has made use of this expression, and explained it in his letter to Petus, *Nunc ades ad imperandum, vel parendum potiùs,* SIC ENIM ANTIQUI LOQUEBANTUR. For this meaneth, *ad imperari,* or, *ut tibi imperetur & tu pareas.* Where Cicero adding that this is an antient phrase, sheweth plainly that the use of the gerunds was heretofore different from what it has been since, and that their nature is not what we imagine it to be.

Chapter II.
Remarks on the supines.

I. *That the supines are likewise nouns substantive.*

THE supines, as well as the gerunds, are likewise verbal nouns substantive. And Priscian himself acknowledges it; though other grammarians, of a more antient date, were so greatly puzzled about this matter, that some of them, as we find in Charisius, insisted that they were adverbs.

As we have demonstrated in the foregoing chapter, that the gerund is a noun substantive taken from the neuter of the participle in *dus*: so the supine is another substantive, which may be likewise formed from the neuter of the participle in *us*. *Veniendum est*, gerund; you must come. *Ventum fuit*, supine; they came.

The differerence is that the gerund is more regular in its declension, having a genitive, *amandi*, of loving, and constantly following the second declension: whereas the supine is more irregular, having no genitive, and being referrible to the second declension for the nominative in *um, auditum*; and to the fourth for the other cases, *auditui, auditu*, &c.

Nor ought we to be surprised at this, since it hath been shewn, when treating of the heteroclites, that the same noun happens frequently to change termination and declension: and further, that the greatest part of the nouns in *us* were likewise changed into *um*. Thus they said, *Pannum, panni*, and *pannus*, Non. *Prætextum, i*; and *prætextus, ûs*, Sen. Suet. *Portum, i*, Plin. and *portus, ûs*, Hor. *Currum, i*, Liv. and *currus, ûs*, Cic. *Effectum, i*, Plaut. and *effectus, ûs*, Cic. *Eventum, i*, Lucret. and *eventus, ûs*, Cic. who likewise makes frequent use of the plural *eventa*.

But what is more deserving, I think, of our observation, the supines have been thus called, because they are words that have waxed old, or turns of expression that have been neglected during the purity of the language. Therefore when they began to distinguish, in the elegant custom of speaking, the supines from the other verbal nouns, the termination *UM* was left in the former, and that of *US* was given to the latter. Hence it is that *auditum*, for example, is taken for the supine of the verb *audire*, and *auditus* for its verbal noun, though properly speaking, it is but the same thing. In like manner they have laid aside the antient termination of the dative in *V* in the oldest word, that is in this supine, and they have given the other more modern, and elegant, to the verbal noun; though in the main it is the same word and the same case, when we say for instance, *auditu jucunda*, agreeable to the ear; and *Auditui meo dabis gaudium & lætitiam*, &c.

Others would have it, that when the termination *UM* is in the nominative, it is not then a supine, but a neuter participle, which they derive from a verb impersonal, as *amatum est* taken from *amatur*.

amatur. But this is of very little signification, since it is not at all extraordinary that the same word should come from many different quarters; as *amare* infinitive active, *amare* imperative passive, and *amare* the second person of the present indicative passive: and the like.

Besides, Priscian and Diomedes allow that *lectum est*, for example, is a real supine: and there are a great many passages much easier to resolve by taking these words for supines, than for participles; as in Livy, *Diù non perlitatum tenuerat dictatorem, ne,* &c. as if it were, *Diù non facta perlitatio,* because it had been a long time since they offered up sacrifice. And in another place, *Tentatum domi per dictatorem ut ambo consules crearentur, rem ad interregnum perduxit;* that is, *Tentatio facta domi, rem perduxit,* &c. Where it is plain that *tentatum est* is a real noun or supine, which is the nominative of *perduxit*. And in like manner in Plautus; *Justam rem & facilem à vobis oratum volo.* Where the word *oratum* ought to be taken substantively, as if it were *orationem,* that governed *justam rem,* like *tactio hanc rem,* in the same author.

Now this last example makes me imagine that all those nouns by the antients called indifferently either gerunds, or supines, or participial words, *participalia verba,* had only one gender at first; whence it is that they said also, *Credo inimicos meos hoc dicturum,* and the like, of which we have made mention here above, sect. 3. chap. 2. n. 8. So that we may say with the same appearance of probability, that the participles were formed of these gerunds and supines, as that the latter were derived from the former: not only because this is the common idea which all grammarians, both antient and modern, give us, always to form the participle in US from the supine; but moreover because it appears that they began with putting these nouns in the neuter, and that afterwards, when the language came to be improved, they gave them all the three genders.

We see something of this kind in French, where the participles very often are not declined: for we say, for instance. *J'ai trouvé cette femme lisant l'ecriture sainte,* and not *j'ai trouvée,* nor *lisante.* We say likewise, *La peine que m'a douné cette affaire,* and not *donnée,* &c. For which reason we call these participles also gerunds. Concerning which we refer the reader to the general grammar, chap. 22. But whatever rules may have been given, still on many occasions we are at a stand, where custom has not determined the expression. Just so was it at first in the Latin tongue.

I say therefore that supines are nothing else but verbal nouns substantives, seldom used except in certain cases. Nevertheless we may give them.

The nominative. *Amatum est, ventum fuit, puditum erat.*

The dative. *Horrendum auditu,* for *auditui. Mirabile visu,* for *visui,* Virg. Just as he says elswhere, *Oculis mirabile monstrum. Quod auditu novum est,* Val. Max. *Ista lepida sunt memoratu,* where others say *memoratui,* Plaut. *collocare nuptui,* Colum. &c.

The accusative. *Amatum esse. Ventum fuisse. Eo spectatum. Venimus huc, lapsis quæsitum oracula rebus,* Virg.

The ablative. *Dictu opus est*, Ter. *Migratu difficilia*, Liv. *Senatus frequens vocatu Drusi*, Cic. *Parvum dictu, sed immensum æstimatione*, Plin. Where it is of no sort of use to Scioppius to say, after Sanctius; *Si dictu supinum est, etiam æstimatione supinum erit:* Since I have shewn that supines are old nouns; so that one might answer those authors with a great deal more reason, *Si æstimatione nomen est, etiam dictu nomen erit,* but a noun that has waxed old, and for that reason is called a supine; custom requiring that we should say rather *dictum, i, o,* than *dictus, ûs, ui ;* whereas, *expectatio* has always maintained its ground during the purity of the language. And indeed when Cato saith, *Postremus cubitum eat, primus cubitu surgat,* there is nobody but will allow that *cubitum ire* is a real supine; since the idea all grammarians give us of the supine, is its being put after the verbs of motion; consequently, if *cubitum est* be a supine in this expression, *cubitu* must be one likewise, since these are two cases of the same noun; which is a proof for all the rest.

These supines or old nouns have likewise their plurals sometimes, according to Vossius, as *Supini cubitus oculis conducunt*, Plin. *O nunquam frustrata vocatus hasta meos*, Virg. To which we may also refer the plural *eventa* in Cic. since it comes from the neuter *eventum*. But whether we call this a supine or a verbal noun, is of very little consequence, since we ought never to dispute about words.

What we think more necessary to observe, is that as the supines are substantives, they do not change gender: *Vitam ire perditum,* and not *perditam*, Liv. *Latrocinia sublatum iri,* and not *sublata*, Idem. *Nutricem accersitum iit,* Ter. *Audierat non datum iri filio uxorem suo,* Id. *Vaticinatus est madefactum iri Græciam sanguine,* Cic. and the like. And these are what Sanctius and Scioppius call properly supines, not chusing to acknowledge any other.

But it is also as substantives, that these supines admit of an adjective in the ablative case; as *Magno natu*, Liv. very old. *Ipso elsactu*, Plin. *Dictu, profatuque ipso,* A. Gell. &c.

Those in the accusative ever include some kind of motion, though it be sometimes concealed, as *Dare nuptum filiam*, to marry his daughter; which denotes a change of family. But if no motion be understood, then it will be rather the accusative of the participle, as *Inventum & adductum curabo*, Ter. For which reason, speaking of a young woman, we ought to change the gender, and say: *Inventam & adductam,* &c.

II. *Whether the supines are active or passive, and what time is expressed by their circumlocution in* ire *or* iri.

The supines in UM are generally active, though there are some of them passive, as *Mulier quæ ante diem quartum usurpatum isset,* Gell. that is, *ad usurpatum,* or *ad usurpari,* for *usurpata fuisset.*

On the contrary those in U are generally passive, though we find some of them also active, as *Forenses uvæ celeres proventu*, Plaut.

The circumlocution in *ire*, of itself expresseth no time, but may be joined with any, *Gaudes cœnatum ire; gaudebis cœnatum ire; gavisa fuit cœnatum ire.*

That which is made by the infinitive *iri*, frequently includes something of the future, *Brutum ut scribis visum iri à me puto*, Cic. *Dederam equidem Sáufeio literas, sed has tibi redditum iri putabam prius*, Cic. *Et fine opera tua illam deductum iri domum*, Ter. But we are not allowed to use the circumlocution by the infinitive *ire*, says Vossius, unless it be also allowed in the indicative. Hence we ought not to say, *Puto te eum locum intellectum ire*, because we should not say *eo intellectum*: which does not hinder us from saying in the passive, *Puto eum locum intellectum iri*, just as Cæsar saith, *Ipsi nihil nocitum iri respondit*, whereby it appears that the passive phrase may be more usual than the active.

III. *What case the accusative of the supines governeth, what this accusative itself is governed by, and of some expressions of this sort difficult to account for.*

The supines, as verbal nouns, govern the case of their verb, *Me ultro accusatum advenit*, Ter. *Scitatum oracula Phœbi mittimus*, Virg. *Gratis servitum matribus ibo*, Id. Which we have already shewn to have been heretofore common to all the nouns, even substantives, derived from verbs: *Quid tibi curatio est hanc rem?* Plaut. *Quid tibi hanc aditio est?* Plaut. *Quid tibi hanc notio est?* Id. Just as we still say, *Reditio domum*, Cæs. *Traditio alteri*, Cic. and the like.

But when these supines are also in the accusative, then they themselves are governed by a preposition understood: for as we say; *Eo Romam*, for *eo ad Romam*, in like manner we say, *Ducitur immolatum*, for *ad immolatum*, or *ad immolationem*. *Eo perditum*, for *eo ad perditum*, or *ad perditionem*. But if we add the case of the verb after *perditum*, *Vitam tuam perditum ire properat*, Liv. then it will be *perditum* that governs *vitam*; just as *perditio*, *tactio*, *curatio*, and others abovementioned, heretofore governed the accusative of their verb. And in like manner, *Justam rem à vobis oratum volo*, of which we have been just now speaking.

Yet it is observable that we meet with some expressions in authors, which seem to disagree with this principle, as that of Cato authorised by A. Gellius; *Contumelia quæ mihi factum itur*; that of Quintilian, *Reus damnatum iri videbatur*; that of Plautus, *Mihi præda videbatur perditum iri*, and the like, which Scioppius and Mariangel think to have been corrupted, contrary to the authority of all MSS. and even of Gellius himself; pretending that since the government depends on the preposition, and the supine governs the case of its verb, we ought to read, *Contumeliam quam mihi factum itur*; *Reum damnatum iri videbatur*; as if it were, say they, *itur ad factum* (or *factionem*) *contumeliam*, and in like manner the rest. To which Vossius makes answer, that then the periphrasis coincides with the meaning of the simple expression, and that *Contumelia quæ mihi factum itur*, is no more than *quæ mihi fit*, and the others in the same manner, because indeed the verb *eo* does not express a local motion in that passage.

But it is not difficult to account for these phrases, without departing from our principle. For when we say, for instance, *Reus damnatum*

damnatum iri videbatur, there is nothing easier than to express it thus; *Reus videbatur iri ad damnatum*, for *ad damnationem*. *Iri* then will make the same construction as *duci*, there being no difficulty to shew that *eo* may be active, and consequently that, on certain occasions, it may have its passive, as *itur, iri*, &c. Which is so much the stronger against Scioppius, as he himself proves that we may very well say *eor*, in the first person. Thus when we say, *Contumelia quæ mihi factum itur*, it is obvious that *contumelia* is the nominative of *itur*, and therefore that we may resolve this expression thus, *Contumelia quæ itur ad factum*, (as *ad factionem*) *se* or *sui*: since it is not more strange to say *factio se*, or *sui*, than *curatio hanc rem*, or *hujus rei*.

And it is by this very principle we are to account for an expression of Pompey writing to Domitius; *Cohortes quæ ex Piceno venerunt ad me missum facias*. That is, *facias missum* or *missionem cohortes*, in the same construction as *tactio hanc rem*. And in like manner the rest.

IV. *Of the supines in* U, *what they are governed by, and how they may be rendered by the infinitive, by the gerund, or by the verbal nouns in* io.

The supines in *U* are either in the dative, as *auditu jucunda* for *auditui*: or in the ablative, and then they are governed by a preposition; as *pulchrum visu*, for *in visu*, or *in videndo*, fine to the eye. Sometimes they are also governed by the preposition *A*, as in Cato, *Primus cubitu surgat, postremus cubitum eat*, de R. R. cap. 5. that is, *primus à cubitu surgat, postremus ad cubitum eat*.

Sometimes instead of this supine in *U*, they put the infinitive only, or the gerund with the preposition, as

———*Fessis leviora tolli*
Pergama Graiis———Hor.

That is, *sublatu*. *Cibus ad coquendum facillimus*, Cic. that is, *coctu*.

And this supine is also expressed by the verbal noun in io, contrary to the opinion of L. Valla. For as we find in Quintil. *Lyricorum Horatius ferè solus legi dignus*, for *lectu*: so in Gellius we read, *Dignus sanè Seneca videatur lectione*. And Cicero has expressed himself in the same manner, *in rebus cognitione dignis*. *Gratiunculam inopem nec scriptione magnopere dignam*.

We likewise use the gerund in *do*, instead of this supine, or of a verbal noun in io, contrary to the opinion of the same L. Valla, *iidem traducti à disputando ad dicendum inopes reperiantur*, Cic. for *à disputatu*, or *disputatione*, &c. The reason is, as we have already observed, the gerunds, the supines, and sometimes even the infinitive, being verbal nouns substantives, there can be nothing more natural than to put one noun for another derived from the same original. And hereby we see of what importance it is to understand the real nature of things, in order to prevent mistakes, into which L. Valla hath often fallen.

Chapter III.

Remarks on the participles.

I. *Difference between a participle and a noun adjective.*

ALL participles are adjectives derived from a verb, and express some time. Hence *fretus, præditus, prægnans, galeatus, pilcatus*, and the like, are not participles, because they are not derived from verbs: as on the contrary *solens*, in Plautus, cometh from *soleo*, and *iratus* from *irascor*, *mæstus* from *mæreo*; and yet they cannot be looked upon as participles, because they do not express any time. For

When the participle ceaseth to express time, it becometh a mere noun adjective, which happens, 1. When it is taken purely as a substantive, as *sapiens, serpens, sponsa*, &c.

2. When it changeth the government of its verb, as *amans pecuniæ*, and the like, as we have already observed, p. 21.

Sanctius hereto adds that the participle becometh also a noun by composition, as *doctus, indoctus*: and by comparison, as *doctus, doctior*, &c. But Vossius on the contrary maintains, that in Terence, *Inspirante Pamphilo*; in Cicero, *Inscientibus nobis*; these and the like compounds are participles, just as when I say, *Me sperante, me sciente*. It is the same in regard to the participle preterite, as when Horace saith, *Dicam indictum ore alieno*. And as for the comparison, we find in Cicero, *Habeas eos à me commendatissimos*; and in another place, *Tu sic habeto me à causis nunquam districtiorem fuisse*, and a multitude of others, which Vossius maintains to be participles, since they mark time as much as their positive.

II. *Whether every participle may express every difference of time: and first of the participle in* NS.

Though the participles seem to be particularly tied down to certain difference of time according to their termination; yet Sanctius maintaineth that they may be all taken for every difference of time. So that when I say, *Pompeius discedens erat suos adhortatus*, it means, *cùm discederet*, in the present: but when I say *venies judicans*, it is the future, for it means *venies et judicabis*: and the others in the same manner.

Hence it is that in the vulgate the Greek participles of the preterite and the aorist, are oftentimes rendered into Latin by the participle present, as in St. Luke, *Sunt aliqui hic stantes*, for εἰσί τινες τῶν ἑστηκότων: and in another place, *Postulans pugillarem scripsit*, for αἰτήσας, *cùm postulasset*. And in St. Mark, *Et crucifigentes eum, diviserunt vestimenta ejus*, for σταυρώσαντες αὐτὸν, or as we read it in St. John ὅτι ἐσταύρωσαν, *cùm crucifixissent*. This is an expression, which some have attempted to find fault with in this antient interpreter, though without foundation, since the

very

very best Latin authors have used it in the same manner; *Offendi adveniens ut volebam collocatam filiam*, Ter. for *cùm advenissem. Credo hercle adveniens, nomen commutabit mihi*, Plaut. for *cùm advenerit. Hoc ipso Pansa mihi nuntium perferente, concessos fasces laureatos tenui quoad tenendos putavi*, Cic. Pansa having brought me tidings of it. *Apri inter se dimicant, indurantes attritu arborum costas*, Plin. that is, *postquam induravêre*.

—————— *Fracti bello fatisque repulsi Ductores Danaûm tot jam labentibus annis*, Æn. 2.

After such a long space of time; during so long a space of time.

But this participle also denoteth a future just at hand, like the μέλλων of the Greeks—— *Et terruit auster euntes*, Virg. that is, *ire conantes*, being ready to go.—— *Nec nos via fallet euntes*, Id. for *ire conantes*, or *cùm ibimus*. So in Horace:

Formidare malos fures; incendia, servos,
Ne te compilent fugientes, Sat. 1.

That is, lest they rob you, and afterwards run away. And in the Greek the first future participle is oftentimes rendered by this present in Latin, as in St. Matth. 27. 49. Ἄφες ἴδωμεν εἰ ἔρχεται Ἡλίας, σώσων αὐτὸν. *Sine videamus an veniat Elias liberans eum.*

And it often happens that the Latins being without the present of the participle passive, express it by the active. Thus in Virgil, *Genibusque volutans, hærebam*, that is, κυλιόμενος, says Diomedes, *volutans me*: and in another place, *Præcipitans traxi mecum*, that is, κατακρημνιζόμενος, *præcipitans me*. Just as he has made use of *volventibus annis*; whereas Homer hath, περιπλομένων ἐνιαυτῶν.

So much for what they call the participle present, that is, which terminates in *NS*. We must now examine this principle in regard to the rest.

II. *Of the participle in* US.

No doubt but the participle in *US* is likewise expressive of every difference. For as AIMÉ in French is of every time, so that all the tenses of the passive voice are formed from thence by circumlocution, *je suis* AIMÉ, *j'étois* AIMÉ, *je serai* AIMÉ, *j'avois été* AIMÉ, &c. So in Latin we may say, AMATUS *sum, eram, fui, ero*, &c. using it thus in all times. Examples hereof are frequent. *Ego si cum Antonio locutus fuero*, Cic. *Paratos fore*, Liv. *Utinam aut hic surdus, aut hæc muta facta sit*, Ter. that is, *fiat*, in the present.

Quam quibus in patriam ventosa per æquora vectis
Pontus & ostriferi fauces tentantur Abydi, 1. Georg.

Where *vectis* is said of those who were actually at sea. *Victis bona spes partibus esto*, Luc. for *vincendis*.

Hence it is that what the Greeks express by the present of the participle passive, is oftentimes rendered into Latin by this participle in *US*, as in St. Paul, *Omnes sunt administratorii spiritus missi*, &c. for ἀποστελλόμενα πνεύματα, *qui mittuntur*, and the rest in the same manner.

To this same cause it is owing that this participle in *US* ought oftentimes to be rendered by the present or the future in *dus*. Cicero says of the duty of an orator: *Hujus est in dando consilio de*

maximis

maximis rebus explicata sententia, 2. de Orat. it is his business to give his opinion upon affairs of great importance: where it is plain, that *explicata* signifies the same thing as *explicanda*. So in Virgil, 1. Æn.

Submersas obrue puppes, that is, *submergendas*, overwhelm them in order to sink them. And Æn. 3.

*Diversa exilia & desertas quærere terras
Auguriis agimur Divum:*

that is, *deserendas*, according to Sanctius, transient retreats, which we soon must quit, without knowing as yet where we shall be able to settle. Again, Æn. 1. speaking of those swans that wanted to swim to land, *aut capere, aut captas jam despectare videntur:* that is, *capiendas*, as in Lucan.

———— *Cæsosque duces & funera regum;* for *cædendos*: and the like.

But the reason why this participle in *US* seemeth rather to mark the time past than the present, is probably because as in narratives one generally is apt to use the present to express things past, in order to represent them in a more lively manner, as when Terence saith: *Ubi te non invenio, ibi ascendo in quemdam excelsum locum, circumspicio, nusquam*, in Andr. Hence it has been imagined that as this participle is often used on those occasions, it was in the time past, as well as the thing it signified; whereas the present of the other verbs with which it is commonly joined, plainly declare that it is also in the present, as *Funus interim procedit, sequimur, ad sepulcrum venimus, in ignem imposita est, fletur*, Ter. in Andr. And therefore when this same poet says in another place, *Concessum est, tacitum est, creditum est*, in Adelph. it is also the present (whether we take it as a supine, or as a participle) though for the reason I have mentioned, this participle, even in the times of the Romans, seems to have been oftener considered as of the time past.

Hence it is that Cicero in the oration pronounced before the pontiffs for the recovery of his house, treats his enemies as ignorant fellows, who endeavouring to obtain sentence of exile against him, had put in the declaration of their request: VELITIS JUBEATIS UT M. TULLIO AQUA ET IGNI INTERDICTUM SIT, instead of *interdicatur*, in the present. Whence one would imagine that the latter was more usual. Though we may likewise infer from thence, that the other was not quite contrary to practice; since it is not at all probable that persons of their rank, and whom we cannot suppose to have been strangers to their own language, would ever have made use of it, had it been a thing as exceptionable as Cicero, hurried by his passion, which appears from a torrent of injurious language, endeavours to make it. And it is obvious that *velitis ut interdictum sit*, may as well mark the present, as this phrase of Terence, *Utinam aut hic surdus aut hæc muta facta sit*, for *flat*, and others which I have quoted. But we must take notice that Cicero's opinion ought not always to pass as an oracle with us, when he undertakes to criticise on the Roman language; no more than the frequent censures he passeth on the Greeks; as 2. Tusc. Quæst. where he pretends to shew that they

they confounded *laborem* and *dolorem*, which were very properly distinguished by the Latins. Whereas the Greeks have not only different words to answer each of those terms; but Cicero himself frequently confounds them in his works, as Budeus proveth in his commentaries, p. 750. of Robert Stephen's edition. Which makes him say, that even on those occasions Cicero does not always speak according to his mind: *Hujusmodi autem interpretationes interdum calumniosas fuisse magis quàm ex sententia animi dictas, ex eo conjicere licet, quòd Cicero eas ipse non observavit*, Id. pag. 751.

III. *Of the participle in* DUS.

As for the participle in DUS, there is no difficulty at all about it, for so seldom does it denote the future, that Alvarez and Saturnius were of opinion it was rather a simple noun than a participle, since it hardly expresseth any time. And though it were not to be excluded from this rank, it is certain nevertheless that oftentimes it only signifieth duty, or what one ought to do: *Gratiam nos quoque inire ab eo defendendâ pace arbitrabamur*. Valla seems to have been sensible of this, since he says that the gerund in DUS ought to be taken as a participle present. Linacer is of the same opinion, and Donatus saith that *Mirando tam repentino bono*, is the present for *cùm miror*.

Thus it is that authors have used it on a thousand occasions. *His enim legendis redeo in memoriam mortuorum*, Cic. in reading these things. *Excitanda est memoria ediscendis quamplurimis*, Id. *Volvenda dies en attulit ultro*, instead of *quæ volvitúr*, Virg. *Quod in opere faciundo operæ consumis tuæ*, Ter. *Neque verò superstitione tollendâ religio tollitur*, Cic. &c.

IV. *Of the participle in* RUS.

The greatest difficulty is therefore about the participle in RUS, for though Scioppius, after Sanctius, says the same of this as of the rest, it is nevertheless certain that it particularly denotes the future: which Sanctius does not deny, when it happens to be joined to a present or to a future, as *facturus sum*, or *facturus ero*. For it is a mistake to believe with Valla, that it cannot be joined with the latter, since there is nothing that agreeth better with the future, than the future itself. *Demonstraturi erimus*, Cic. *Erit acturus*, Id. *Quo die aa sicam venturus ero*, Id.

Mergite me fluctus cùm rediturus ero, Mart.
Tu procul absenti cura futurus eris, Ovid.

And the like.

But since it is true, according to Sanctius, that it also denotes the future along with the present, we must conclude that it likewise denotes the future with the preterite; and that at the most, it can be considered there only as a comparison, or an assemblage of different tenses, one of which marks a thing as future in regard to another, which is considered as past; just as in Q. Curtius, *Mazeus, si transeuntibus flumen supervenisset, haud dubie oppressurus fuit incompositos in ripa*. He would have destroyed them: for if the assemblage of different tenses changeth their nature,

ture, there will be as much reason to conclude against Sanctius, that *fuit* there denotes the future, being joined with *oppressurus*, as that *oppressurus* denotes the preterite, because it is joined with *fuit*. Add to this, we find in Gellius, that Nigidius, whom he stiles *the most learned in Rome*, whom Cicero calls *the most learned and the honestest man of his time*, and who was a thorough master of his own language, Nigidius, I say, testifieth, that the verb *sum*, rather takes the tenses of the participles to which it is joined, than the participle takes the tense of the verb *sum*.

But this is only a comparison of different tenses, by which we must explain all such like phrases. *Vos visuros fuisse*, Cic. *Eum magis communem censemus in victoria futurum fuisse, quàm incertis in rebus fuisset*, Id. *Sed id erit brevi, nec dubito quin te legente has litteras confecta jam res futura sit*, Id. &c. Otherwise we should be obliged to say, that *Venturo Cæsare Roma trepidabit*, is the same thing as *Veniente Cæsare Roma trepidabit*. Which is not absolutely true, since the latter signifies Cæsar's arrival as present whereas the other signifies it only as future.

V. *Signification of the participle in verbs common and deponents.*

The participles of the verbs common in *NS* and in *RUS*, follow the active signification, as *tuens* and *tuiturus*. Those in *DUS* follow the passive, as *tuendus*; *Cujus possessio quo major est, eo plus requirit ad se tuendam*, Cic. And those in *US* have both, as *tuitus*, who looks at, or who is looked at.

As to the deponents, properly speaking none but those in *DUS* have the passive signification; *sequendus*, who ought to be followed. *Hæc ego mercanda vitâ puto*, Cic. I think these ought to be purchased even at so dear a price as life. Their preterites, as well as their futures in *RUS*, have generally the active; *secutus*, who followeth; *secuturus*, who is about to follow.

And yet the participles in *US* have very often both significations, as coming from verbs that were heretofore common: this may be seen in the following list, which is only an appendix to that above given, when we were speaking of verbs deponents taken passively, p. 102.

Deponents whose participle in US *is sometimes taken passively.*

ADEPTUS. Senectutem ut adipiscantur omnes aptant, eandem accusant adeptam, Cic. *as we read it in Vossius and in all the antient copies, whereas the late ones have adepti. Which Henry Stephen in the preface to his book de Latinit. falsò suspecta, condemns as an ignorant mistake.*
Ne cadat, et multas palmas inhonestet adeptas, *Ovid*.

ADORTUS. Ab his Gallos adortos, *Aurel. apud Prisc.*

AGGRESSUS. Facillimis quibusque aggressis, *Just*.

ANTEGRESSUS. *We find in Cicero*, Causas antegressas, & causis antegressis, *lib. de fato*.

ARBITRATUS, arbitrata quæstio, *Gell*.

ASSENSUS. Sapiens multa sequitur probabilia, non comprehensa, non percepta, neque assensa, sed similia veri, *Cic*.
De religione Bibulo assensum est, *Cic*.

AUXI-

REMARKS ON THE PARTICIPLES.

AUXILIATUS. A me auxiliatus si est, *Lucil. apud Prisc.*
BLANDITUS. Blanditus labor, *Varr.* according to *Prisc.*
COMITATUS. Uno comitatus Achate, *Virg.*
Quod ex urbe parùm comitatus exierit, *Cic.*
COMMENTATUS. Diu & multis lucubratiunculis commentata oratione, *Qu. Cic.*
COMPLEXUS. Quo uno maledicto scelera omnia complexa esse videantur, *Cic.*
CONATUS. Ne literæ interceptæ conata palàm facerent. *Liv.*
CONFESSUS. Confessa res & manifesta, *Cic.*
CONSOLATUS. Sic consolatis militibus, &c. *Just.*
CONSECUTUS. Consecutâ anaâ, *Varr.*
CUNCTATUS. Fides cunctata est, *Stat.* They *suspended their belief.*
DEPASTUS. Depastam arborem relinquunt, *Plin.* Depasta altaria liquit, *Virg.*
DEPRECATUS. Deprecati belli promissio, *Just.*
DESPICATUS. Quæ nos nostramque adolescentiam habet despicatam, *Ter.*
DETESTATUS. Bella matribus detestata, *Hor.*
DIGNATUS. Tali honore dignati sunt, *Cic.* Conjugio dignate superbo, *Virg.*
DILARGITUS. Dilargitis proscriptorum bonis, *Sall.*
DIMENSUS. See MENSUS.
EBLANDITUS. Eblanditæ preces, *Plin.* Eblandita suffragia, *Cic.*
EFFATUS. Interpretati Vatum effata incognita, *Cic.*
Agros & templa effata habento, *Id.*
EMENTITUS. See MENTITUS.
EXECRATUS. Eamus omnia execrata civitas, *Hor. Epod.* 16.
EXECUTUS. Executo regis imperio, *Just.*
EXORSUS. Sua cuique exorsa laborem, Fortunámque ferent, *Virg.*
EXPERTUS. Multa inventa expertáque in hoc sunt bona, *Att.*
Fortunam sæpiùs clade Romanâ expertam, *Tacit.*
FABRICATUS. Manibus fabricata Cyclopum, *Ovid.*
IMITATUS. See IMITOR.
INOPINATUS. See OPINATUS.
INTERPRETATUS. Interpretatum nomen Græcum tenemus, *Cic.*
INTUTUS. Intutam urbem, *Liv.* ill *fortified.*
LAMENTATUS. Fata per orbem lamentata diu, *Sil. Ital.*
MACHINATUS. *Priscian* quotes *from Sallust.* Et Lucullum Regis curâ machinata fames fatigabat; which *shews that formerly it was passive.*
MENSUS. Spatia mensa, quia conficiunt cursus Lunæ, menses vocantur. *Cic.* Dimensus in the *same manner.* Mirari se diligentiam ejus â quo essent ista dimensa, *Cic.*
MENTITUS. Mentita & falsa plenáque erroris, *Cic. also* Ementitis auspiciis, *Id.*
MERCATUS. Trullam unam mercatam à matrefamilias, *Plin.*
MERITUS. Quæ Cannis corona merita, *Plin.*
METATUS. Metato in agello, *Hor. also* immetata jugera, *Id.*
MORATUS. Sæpè simultates ira morata facit, *Ovid.*
OBLITUS. Nunc oblita mihi tot carmina, *Virg.*
OPINATUS. Improvisa nec opinata nobis, *Cic. Likewise its compound,* INOPINATUS, *is never taken in another sense.*
PACTUS. Ex quo destituit Deos, mercede pacta Laomedon, *Hor. Thus we find* pacta conventa *without a conjunction in Cic.* 2. *de Orat.* Et pacti & conventi formula, *pro Cæcil.*
PARTITUS. Partitis copiis, *Cæs.*
POLLICITUS. Pollicitis dives quilibet esse potest, *Ovid.*
PROFESSUS. Soláque deformem culpa professa facit, *Ovid.*
STIPULATUS. Stipulata pecunia, *Cic.*
TESTATUS. Res ita notas, ita testatas, *Cic.*

It is also observable, that the simple being sometimes taken actively, the Compound followeth the passive signification: for *ultus* and *ausus* are actives; whereas *inultus* and *inausus* are passives.

We may likewise take notice on this occasion of a Latin elegance, which is by putting the participle in US oftentimes after the verbs, *curo, cupio, volo, oportet, habeo,* and the like, instead of the infinitive; *Sed est quod vos monitos voluerim,* Plaut. *Adolescenti morem gestum oportuit,* Ter. *Adversarios servatos magis cupiunt quàm perditos:* And the like.

VI.

VI. *Some particular remarks on the participle in* DUS.

We have already observed, that the participle in DUS hath always the passive signification, whether it comes from a verb common or deponent, or from a verb passive: yet some pretend to say, that the civilians use it almost in an active signification; *Diminutio ex bonis fieri debet vescendi pupilli causâ*, for *alendi*, Ulpian. But one would think it may rather be inferred from thence, that *vescor* hath changed signification, and that, upon the decline of the Latin tongue, it was taken for *alo*; just as in very old authors it is taken for *utor*, as Nonius observeth.

We have also shewn, that the participle agreeth more elegantly with a substantive expressed, than to put it as a gerund with a substantive after it. Thus we say, *Discenda est lectio*, rather than *discendum est lectionem*. *Princeps vestræ libertatis defendendæ fui*, Cic. rather than *defendendi vestram libertatem*. And the like.

But it is particularly to be observed, that this is elegant only for those verbs which generally govern an accusative after them. For in regard to the rest, as Vivez observeth, it is always better to continue in the construction of the gerund: for example, we should not say, *Veni huc tui serviendi causâ*, or *ad carendam voluptatem*; but *tui observandi*, or *tibi serviendi causâ*; *Ad carendum voluptate*, and the like. And if we do say, *Justitiæ fruendæ causâ*, Cic. *Beata vita glorianda & prædicanda est*, Id. and the like: this is because *fruor, glorior*, and the rest, used to govern an accusative. And there is no doubt but as formerly most verbs, not only deponents, but moreover neuters or absolutes, did govern this case, as we have above demonstrated; one might use these expressions oftener than we do at present, and without committing a mistake; as when Celsus saith, *Abstinendus est æger*. But we ought ever to conform to the practice of good writers, and not to make use of these uncommon expressions but with great caution and good authority.

Now it is proper to take notice, that instead of joining the ablative to the preposition *à* or *ab* after these participles, it is much more elegant to use the dative, *Non paranda nobis solùm, sed fruenda etiam sapientia est*, Cic. and not *à nobis*. *Tibi ipsi pro te erit causa dicenda*, Id. not *à te ipso*: Though we find some with the ablative, *quid tandem à Socrate & Platone faciendum putes?* Cic. *Neque enim hæc à te non ulciscenda sunt*; *etiam si non sint dolenda*, Cic.

We have still one elegance more to remark, which is frequently used by Cicero. This is putting the participle in DUS in the ablative absolute, instead of the gerund with the accusative. *His enim legendis redeo in memoriam mortuorum*, instead of *hæc legendo*. *Exercenda est etiam memoria ediscendis ad verbum quamplurimis & nostris scriptis & alienis*, 1. de Orat. *Hæc vel summa laus est verbis transferendis, ut sensum feriat id quod translatum est*, 3. de Orat. *Hoc eò sæpiùs testificor, ut autoribus laudandis ineptiarum crimen effugiam*, Ibid. In the same manner in Livy, *Prolatandis igitur comitiis, quum dictator magistratu abiisset, res ad interregnum rediit*. And the like.

VII.

VII. *Of the participle of the verbs called impersonals.*

The impersonals, as grammarians call them, have also their participles sometimes

In NS, as of *pœnitet* is formed *pœnitens* very usual. Of *pudet, pudens*, in Hor. Ter.

In RUM Cic. lib. 2. ad Att. ep. 1. *Nihilo magis ei liciturum esse plebeio quàm*, &c. Plin. l. 36. c. 15. *Cùm puderet vivos, tanquam puditurum esset extinctos.* Quintil. l. 9. c. 3. seems as if he wanted to shew that Sallust had said, *non pœniturum* for *non pœnitentiam acturum*, whereas, according to analogy, he should have said, *pœnititurum*, as Vossius thinks that Sallust and Quintilian intended to write it.

In UM, which may be often referred to the supines above-mentioned, ch. 2. and these may either come from the actives, as *misertum, pertæsum, libitum, licitum,* &c. or from the passive, as from *pugnatur, pugnatum est*, from *curritur, cursum est*, &c. and these are much more usual: or from the deponents, *Quos non est veritum in voluptate summum bonum ponere,* Cic. which is very rare.

In DUS, as *Haud pœnitendus labor. Induci ad pudendum & pigendum,* Cic. as likewise *dormiendus* from *dormitur; regnandus* from *regnatur, Regnanda Alba,* Virg. *Jurandus* from *juratur; vigilandus* from *vigilatur.* And the like.

There are even a great many participles supposed to come from verbs personal, though in reality they come only from these impersonals, that is from verbs that are not used in all persons; such as *cessatus, erratus, conspiratus,* which cannot be derived from *cessor, error, conspiror,* since these are not used; but from *cessatur, erratur, conspiratur:* for which reason the circumlocution of the preterite is always formed by the neuter, *cessatum est, erratum fuit, conspiratum fuerat,* &c.

Sometimes we form participles whose verbs are never used: thus, though we do not say *obsolescor,* nor *obsolescitur,* yet we find *obsoletus.* In like manner we meet with *occasus,* though we neither say *occidor* nor *occiditur,* taking it from *cado.*

We may subjoin a list of them, where it is to be observed, that these participles frequently become nouns, because they no longer are expressive of time: and they are sometimes taken in a signification bordering upon the active.

Nouns or participles in US, whose verbs are either rare or unusual.

ADULTUS. Apud pastores adultus, *Just.* Adulta virgo, *Cic. Hor.*
ANTECESSUS. In antecessum dabo, *Sen. before-hand.*
CESSATUS. Cessatis in arvis, *Ovid.*
CIRCUITUS. Circuitis hostium castris. *Cæs.*
COENATUS. *See the next title.*
COEPTUS. Cœptum igitur per eos, destitum est per hunc, *Cic.*
Nunc de Republ. consuli cœpti sumus, *Cic.*
Cœpta est oratio fieri, *Cic.*
Ante petitam pecuniam, quam esset cœpta deberi, *Cic.*
COMMENTATUS. Commentata oratione, *Qu. Cic.*
CONCRETUS. Cujus ex sanguine concretus homo & coalitus sit, *Gell.*

CON-

CONSPIRATUS. Affidentem conspirati specie officii circumsteterunt, *Suet.*

DECESSUS. Custodibus decessis multi interficiuntur, *Cæcil.* or rather Cælius, *in Prisc.*

DECRETUS. *In the same manner as* CONCRETUS. Nocte diéque decretum et auctum: *Livius or rather Lævius, in Prisc. Whereby it appears that he would have made no difficulty to say, adds Vossius,* Luna decreta, ostreis decretis, *but this is very rare, as we have already observed, when speaking of* Cresco, vol. 1. p. 225.

DECURSUS. Decurso spatio à calce ad carceres revocari, *Cic.* Decurso lumine vitæ, *Lucr.*
Jam Leone decurso, *Solin.*

DEFLAGRATUS. Fana flammâ deflagrata, *Ennius apud Cicer.*

DESITUS. Desitum est, *Cic.* Papirius est vocari desitus, *Cic.*

EMERITUS. Emeritus miles, *Luc.* Emeritam puppim, *Mart. an old ship that has served its time.*

EMERSUS. E cæno emersus, *Cic.*

ERRATUS. Pererratis finibus, *Virg.*

EVASUS. Exercitum cæsum, evasúmque se esse, *Liv.*

EXCRETUS. Excretos prohibent à matribus hœdos, *Virg.*
Nomen vel participium absque verbi origine, *(says Calepin)* neque enim dicitur excrescor.

EXOLETUS. Exoleta annalium vetustate exempla, *Liv.*

FESTINATUS. Mors festinata, *Tacit.* Festinatis honoribus, *Plin.*

INSERVITUS. Nihil est à me inservitum temporis causâ, *Cic. I have not omitted to serve you, notwithstanding the bad situation of affairs.*

INSESSUS. Saltus ab hoste insessus, *Liv. surrounded by enemies.*

INTERRITUS. Interritis multis, *Quadrigar. apud Prisc.*

INVETERATUS. Inveterata quærela, *Cic.* Inveterata amicitia, *Id.*

JURATUS. Quid mihi juratus est argentum dare, *Plaut.* Non sum jurata, *Turp. apud Diom.* Malo ei jurato suo, quam injurato aliorum tabellas committere, *Cic. But this here ought not to appear strange, since they also said* juror, *from whence*

cometh juratur, *in Lucan. And* jurabere, *in Statius.*

LABORATUS. Arte laboratæ vestes, *Virg.*

NUPTUS. Nova nupta, *Ter.* Novus nuptus, *Plaut.*

OBITUS. Morte obitâ virgo, *Cic. Virg. Tac.*

OBSOLETUS. Obsoletum amicum, *in Qu. Curt. that is, whose services we have long made use of: which seems to prove, that this verb, and such like, come rather from* soleo, *than from* oleo, *as we have already observed,* vol. 1. p. 194.

OCCASUS. ὁ δύσας. Ante solem occasum, *Plaut. for which reason Gellius saith,* SOLE OCCASO, non insuavi venustate est, si quis autem habeat non sordidam, nec proculcatam.

PERERRATUS. *See* ERRATUS.

PLACITUS. Ubi sunt cognitæ, placitæ sunt, *Ter.*
Placita disciplina, *Colum.*

PRANSUS, POTUS. *See the next title.*

PRÆBITUS. Ubi quoque Romæ ingens præbitus error, *Liv.*

PROPERATUS. Carmina properata, *Ovid.* But Pliny *hath also,* Delubra occulta celeritate properantur. *We likewise meet with the other participle* properandus, *Virg. Val. Flac.*

REDUNDATUS. Redundatas flumine cogit aquas, *Ovid.*

REGNATUS. Regnata per arva, *Virg.* But Tacitus *hath also,* In cæteris gentibus quæ regnantur.

REQUIETUS. Requietum volunt arvum, *Colum.*
Animi meliores requieti surgent, *Sen.*

SENECTUS. ὁ γηράσας. Senecto corpore, *Sall.*

SUCCESSUS. Cùm omnia meâ causâ mihi velles successa, tum etiam tuâ, *Cic. Fil. ad Tyr.* Lambinus *has left out* mihi successa; *hence* Vossius *complains of his often acting thus.* Bonis successis, *Plaut. in Prol. Pseud.*

TITUBATUS. Vestigia titubata solo.

TRIUMPHATUS. Triumphatis Medis, *Hor.*
Triumphata Corinthus, *Virg.*

VIGILATUS. Vigilatæ noctes, *Ovid. We meet also with* Vigilandæ noctes, *Quintil. And in like manner with*

EVIGILO. Evigilata consilia, *Cic.*

VIII. *Of* Cœnatus, Pransus, *and* Potus.

Ramus and most of the grammarians insist, that *cœnatus*, *pransus*, and *potus*, are active preterits of *cœno*, *prandeo*, and *poto*, in the

the same manner as *cœnavi, prandi,* and *potavi.* A great many use them now in this sense; Varro, in Gell. lib. 2. c. 25. seems to be of the same opinion, as well as Quintil. lib. 1. c. 4. On the contrary, Vossius pretends, that *pransus, cœnatus,* and *potus,* are only simple nouns adjectives, and that we cannot say, *pransus* or *cœnatus sum apud te,* instead of *prandi* or *cœnavi apud te*; though we may very well say, addeth he, *pransus* or *cœnatus te accedam.* Concerning which we have two things to examine: the first, whether *pransus* and *cœnatus* are active preterits of *prandeo,* &c. the second, whether they are participles and passive preterits, or merely nouns adjectives; and whether we must intirely reject this Latin expression, condemned by Vossius, *Cœnatus sum apud te.*

1. In regard to the first point, it is evident, that *pransus* and the others are not active preterits of *prandeo, cœno,* and *poto.* Priscian gives them no other preterite than *cœnavi, prandi, potavi*; and speaking of verbs which form their preterit by the participle, he reckons only *gaudeo, audeo, soleo, fido,* and *fio: sunt autem hæc* SOLA, says he.

2. As to the second, it seems that Vossius ought not to have absolutely condemned this expression, *Cœnatus sum apud te,* since we meet with it still in Livy, *Cùm cœnati apud Vitellios essent,* L. 2. c. 4. Having supped with the Vitellii. And though other editions have, *cùm cœnatum esset,* this does not hinder but *cœnatum* may still be a participle, since it marks its time, and but it may come from *cœnatus, a, um,* as well as in that passage which Vossius himself quotes from Cornelius Nepos, *Nunquam sine aliqua lectione apud eum cœnatum est*; where, according to him, along with *cœnatum est* we must necessarily understand τὸ *cœnare,* for its substantive. But what led him into a mistake, was doubtless his not having sufficiently considered, that, strictly speaking, there are no verbs impersonal. And therefore, if *cœnatum est* cometh from *cœnatur,* as he imagines, *cœnatus* must come from *cœnor,* though this present is not perhaps to be found. And Cicero has manifestly used it as a passive participle, where he saith, *Cœnato mihi et jam dormienti, reddita est illa epistola,* ad Att. lib. 2. ep. 16. where *cœnato* signifies the time past, as *dormienti* the present.

What we may therefore consider on this head, is, that *cœnatus, pransus,* and *potus,* not being active preterits, it would be a mistake to say, *cœnatus sum hanc rem*; but being passive preterits, we may say, *cœnatus sum apud te,* which does not hinder us from saying also, *cœnavi apud te,* though in different senses of active and passive, the latter being always better Latin, and more generally used. But what causeth mistakes on this occasion, is the small difference there is sometimes between an active and a passive sense, and our being accustomed to render one by the other. This made Vossius believe that *cœptus sum* was active; as when Cicero saith, *Oratio cœpta est fieri,* for *cœpit,* in the preceding list: whereas it would have been better if he had said, that *cœptus sum* is then put where *cœpi* might have been, though in a different sense, nothing being more easy than to change a passive into an active sense; which has been the foundation, perhaps, of so many verbs com-

mon

mon in both significations, as may be seen above, p. 101. and following; as it has often given occasion to take the verbs put in an absolute sense, for passives, as may be seen, p. 100.

X. *Whether* Adventus *may be sometimes also an adjective.*

This is Palmerius's opinion, which he hath endeavoured to defend by some mistaken passages, as that from Terences's Phormio;
———*Patrem extimescam ubi in mentem ejus adventi venit?*
Where every body may see that *adventi* is the substantive, *of his coming*. The reader will find this error refuted in Vossius, *lib.* 4. *de Anal.* who proves extremely well, that *adventus* is never other than a substantive.

Section V.
Remarks on the indeclinable Particles.

Chap. I.
Remarks on the Adverbs.

I. *That the Adverbs admit of comparison; but not of number.*

WE find some Adverbs that are compared; as *satis, satius; secus, secius; diu, diutius, diutissime;* and some others; though there are very few of these, as Probus hath observed. For most of them, as *melius, doctius,* and the others, are real nouns, as we shall make appear hereafter.

But adverbs never admit of number, though Priscian was of a different opinion. For, properly speaking, *age* and *agite* are real imperatives, like *lege, legite. Age porro,* Cic. *Ergo agite ô juvenes,* Virg. But what leads people into an error, as well on this as on many other occasions, is their being translated by an adverb, *Age, ista omittamus,* Cic. Well, let us lay those things aside. *Age, dicat, sino,* Ter. Well, let him tell it. And for this reason we have left them among the adverbs in the rudiments.

II. *That what is taken for an adverb is frequently another part of speech.*

But there are a great many more occasions, where grammarians insist on a word's being an adverb, when it is another part of speech; as when we say, *tanti, quanti, magni;* or when we answer to local questions, *est Romæ, abit Romam, venit Româ.* And in like manner, *domi, militiæ, belli,* which are real nouns; though they have taken them for adverbs, because in Greek these questions are answered by adverbs.

This mistake is still more common, though perhaps it is more excusable, in nouns that are used only in the ablative: for by
reason

reason that this case frequently expresseth the manner as well as the adverb, thence it proceeds that they are oftentimes taken one for the other. Such is *sponte*: for, according to Priscian, we find it is a noun because of the adjective which is often joined to it, *sponte suâ*. Such are *forte* and *fortuito*. *Forte fortuna*, Ter. Cic. *Fors* is even in the nominative in Hor. And with *fortuito* we are to understand *casu*.

The same may be said in regard to *alternis*, which Priscian ranks nevertheless among the adverbs; as,

Alternis dicetis, amant alterna camœnæ, Virg.

For *alternis* in this passage is no more an adverb than *alterna*; but it is an adjective, with which we are to understand *vicibus*.

The same we may say of *repente*, the ablative of *repens*, which Cicero has made use of; *Hostium repens adventus*. For as we say, *libens* for *libenter*; *recens* for *recenter*; so we say *repens* for *repente*, as if we were to say *repenter*, though this word be not used. *Repente* ought therefore to be taken, as if it were *repentino*, sup. *tempore*.

The same again may be said of *eò, quò, primò, secundò, postremò*; as we shall observe also hereafter in treating of the figure of Ellipsis.

The same also of *amabo*, which is never an adverb. AMABO, *quem pecus grammaticorum inter adverbia reponit, purum & putum verbum est*, says Scioppius. And there can be no doubt of this, because, even where they pretend it is an adverb, it governs an accusative. *Amabo te*, I pray you.

But when we say, *Commigravit huc viciniæ*, Ter. *Huc dementiæ pervenit*, and the like, we take *huc* for *hoc*, and we understand *genus, negotium*, or *locum*; that is to say, *Ad hoc genus dementiæ; Ad hoc locum viciniæ*, &c. For heretofore they said *hoc locum*, just as we say *hæc loca*.

ID EO are two words, though custom has made them but one, taking it as an adverb. The same may be said of *quomodo, postea, interea, siquidem*.

Magis, nimis, satis, or *sat*, are old nouns: for heretofore they used to say, *magis* & *mage, satis* & *sate*, like *potis* & *pote*, for all genders and numbers. See the remarks on the nouns, ch. 4. n. 1. p. 86. and remarks on the verbs, ch. 3. n. 1. p. 115. Hence it is that they govern likewise the genitive, *nimis insidiarum*, Cic. and the like. See the syntax, rule 7. p. 18.

But sometimes these nouns are governed by a preposition understood, as we have said of PLUS, in the syntax, p. 58. As also of *nimium, plurimum, multum*, moreover of *tantum, quantum*, which have been contracted into *tam, quam*. So that if they be in the accusative, we understand KATA, *ad, per*, &c. *Ibi plurimum est* Ter. that is, *per plurimum*, sup. *tempus. Nimium vixit*, that is, *per nimium tempus*. But if they be in the ablative, we understand *in. Vixisse nimio satius est quàm vivere*, Plaut. for *in nimio tempore*.

Hence in St. John, vulg. ed. chap. 8. *Tu quis es? Principium qui et loquor vobis*. It is the same as if it were *à principio*; τὴν ἀρχήν, says the Greek, sup. κατά. And thus it is that Afranius in Charisius saith, *Principium hoc oro, in animo ut sic statuas tuo*, &c.

VOL. II.   L   Scioppius

Scioppius hereby sheweth that we may indifferently say, *tertium consul*, and *tertio consul*; though the Romans formerly were so much in doubt about it, that A. Gell. lib. 10. c. 1. takes notice, that Pompey consulted the most learned men in the city, to know how he should put it in dedicating the temple of Victory, and that the opinions were divided; Cicero, not caring to disoblige one party more than another, advised him to leave it abridged, TERT. Varro likewise made some difference between these two modes of expression, thinking that *quarto*, for instance, signified rather order and place, and *quartum* time; of which St. Austin also takes notice in his grammar, though in practice they are frequently confounded.

But the reason of the government cannot be at all contested, since we find that some of them have even the preposition expressed. *Solutus columbarum volatus, est in multum velocior.* Plaut. where he might have said *multum* alone for *in multum*, which supposeth also *negotium*.

  Nec puer Iliaca quisquam de gente Latinos
  In tantum spe tollet avos, nec Romula quondam
  Ullo se tantum tellus jactabit alumno, Virg.

Where we see that he has indifferently made use of *tantum*, and *in tantum*, just as Juvenal hath :
  In quantum sitis atque fames & frigora poscunt.
And Livy, *in tantum suam virtutem enituisse*. And in another place, *quantum magis patres plebi se insinuabant, eo acrius Tribuni contra tendebant*. And the like.

In a word, we may say with Linacer, that all words whatever which preserve the form or appearance of a noun are not adverbs, or at least they are such only by abuse and custom: and in order thoroughly to understand their force and government, together with the different connexions and transitions wherewith they are used in discourse, we should ever consider them in their natural and original signification. Which we shall now make appear in the word *quod*, and in a list of some particular words that follow.

III. *That* QUOD *is never any thing else but a pronoun relative.*

The word *quod*, which is often taken for an adverb, or for a conjunction, is properly no more than the neuter of the relative *qui, quæ, quod*. Which we may consider here on two particular occasions ; one, where *quod* commonly includes the reason of the thing ; and the other, where it is put after the verb, instead of the infinitive.

1. The causal *quod*, or which includes the reason of the thing, is a pronoun relative, governed by a preposition understood. Thus when Horace saith, for example, *Incolumis lætor quod vivit in urbe*, that is, *lætor ob id*, or *propter id negotium, quod est* ; *vivit in urbe*, taking it in an absolute sense ; or *quod est τὸ vivere, in urbe*. In like manner in Terence, *Sanè quod tibi nunc vir videatur esse hic, nebulo magnus est*. Where *quod* is put for *ad id quod, in regard to which, as to what relates*, &c. So true is this, that sometimes we find

find *id* and *quod* together. *Lætæ exclamant ; venit, id quod me repente aspexerant*, Ter. where, according to Donatus, it means *propter id quod*, &c. And Cicero has used it in the same manner, *Teneo ab accusando vix me hercule : sed tamen teneo : vel id quod nolo cùm Pompeio pugnare, vel quod judices nullos habemus.* Ad Q Fr. lib. 3. ep. 2. where having put *id quod* in the first member, and only *quod* in the second, he plainly intimates, that when this *id* is not expressed, it ought to be understood. True it is that Lambinus has struck out this *id*, like a great many other things, which he did not rightly understand; but it is in the ancient copies, as Vossius witnesseth.

And Manutius, in his commentary on this epistle, observes the same thing, adding, that this sort of expunctions, which have been made in ancient authors, are entirely owing to the rashness of those, *quorum aures imperitæ antiquam, non tamen satis usu pervulgatam loquendi rationem, non ferrent*. Which he further corroborates by this other example from Terence, *Id quod est consimilis moribus, convincet facile ex te esse natum :* and by this from Livy, *Id quod erat vetusta conjunctio cum Macedonibus :* complaining afterwards, that the persons employed on the great Thesaurus of the Latin tongue, have inserted a multitude of things of this sort, which are often apt to puzzle us in the perusal of authors.

2. The word *quod*, which is put after a verb instead of the infinitive, is also a relative. But it is frequently deprived of its pronominal use, and scarce retains any other than that of uniting the preposition where it is, to another; as we have shewn in the general grammar, chap. 9. Though this does not hinder it even then from having its antecedent expressed or understood. For example, when Cicero saith, *Cum scripsisset quod me cuperet ad urbem venire :* And Plautus, *Scio jam filius quod amet meus*, instead of *scio filium amare meum* ; it is plain that *quod* then refers to the thing known, and to the verb *scio* ; and that it is just as if we were to say, *Hoc* or *illud scio, nempe quod*, &c. where *quod* would evidently refer to this *hoc* (sup. *negotium*) as to its antecedent: thus Martial,

Hoc scio quod scribit nulla puella tibi.

Where he might have put, *Scio quod nulla scribit tibi*, for *nullam scribere tibi*, though the word *quod* would not then have changed its nature. In regard to which we might produce an infinite number of the like examples; as when Seneca says,

Probo quod non fit pudica.

And Horace,

——— *Quod quanto plura parasti,*
Tanto plura cupis, nulline faterier audes?

And the declaimer against Sallust, *Credo quod omnes tui similes incolumes in hac urbe vixissent.* And Claudian,

Non credit quod bruma rosas innoxia servet.

And Ulpian, *Sufficit mulieri notum facere quod sit prægnans.* And Cicero, *Illud extremum est, quod rectè vivendi ratio meliores efficit ;* where *quod* is constantly a relative; though these are modes of speaking that might all be rendered by the infinitive.

IV. *Whether* QUOD *may be put like the Greek* ὅτι, *after the verbs.*

What we have been saying, is almost sufficient to decide this question, though Sanctius has pretended absolutely to deny it; and the whole reason he produces, which he attempts to prove by a vast number of examples, is that *quod* is never any thing more than a relative. But since we have made appear above, that even when it comes after the verb instead of the infinitive, where it undoubtedly stands for the ὅτι, it is then as a relative; Sanctius's argument can give us no room to doubt of this use of the word. We shall inquire more particularly elsewhere into the nature of ὅτι, and we shall demonstrate that it is oftener a pronoun than the Latin *quod*, though this does not hinder them from being easily put one for the other. Hence Linacer censures those translators, who, to avoid rendering this ὅτι by *quod*, have recourse to uncouth circumlocutions. And Vossius, in his book *de constructione*, observes, that Cicero, Pliny, Ovid, Plautus, Seneca, Horace, and the other pure authors, have not scrupled to make use of this *quod*; though in his smaller grammar he says it is not very good Latin, nor fit to be imitated. But Manutius in sundry places, and particularly on the last epistle of the ninth book to Atticus, and on the 28th of the 7th book *ad familiares*, establishes this use of *quod*, as a thing beyond all manner of doubt. And though Henry Stephen, in his Thesaurus on the particle ὡς, has called it in question, yet we find that in his book *de Latin. falso suspecta*, which he wrote afterwards, and where he treats the point expresly, he has established it by a multitude of authorities. So that it would be quite unreasonable to make any doubt of the latinity of this expression; though we may grant that it would be oftentimes more elegant to render it by the infinitive; since Cicero, translating divers passages of Plato, where ὅτι was expressed, has oftener made use of the latter than of the former.

Now the reason why these expressions of the infinitive, or of the word *quod*, are equivalent in sense, and a reason which no one that I know of hath hitherto observed, is because the infinitive is among the moods, what the relative is among the pronouns, and their proper office is to join the proposition to which they belong, to some other; as may be seen more particularly in the general grammar, part 2. chap. 9 and 11.

V. *Remarkable significations of some adverbs, where the origin of several words is pointed out.*

ABHINC, properly signifieth *ab hac die*, so that it only denotes the term; and the time is afterwards put in the accusative or the ablative. *Abhinc annis*, or *annos quindecim*, &c.

This induced Erasmus and Sciopplus to believe that it might refer to the time past and to the future, and that this depended intirely on the verb, to which it was joined. And it is true that we find in Pacuvius, (*In armor. Jud.*) *Séque ad ludos jam inde abhinc exerceant.*

But every where else we find it only for the time past. And Passerat's Calepin is mistaken in saying that Sosipater approves of it for both tenses, for he does not mention a word about it, (though he quotes the

the above-given authority of Pacuvius) but speaks only of two cases which it may govern.

True it is that HINC refers to two tenses, but not *abhinc*. *Me nihilo magis conspiciet, quàm si hinc ducentos annos fuerim mortuus*, Plaut.

Aliquid convasassem, atque hinc me conjecissem protinus in pedes. Ter.

ADAMUSSIM. See lower down, Partim.

ADHUC. See lower down, Hactenus.

ADMODUM. As the Latin word *modus* may be taken either for the quantity or the quality, so the adverb *admodum*, which is derived from thence, signifies sometimes *a great deal*, and sometimes *almost* or *about*. *Non admodum grandis natu*, Cic. not very old. *Curio nihil admodum sciebat literarum*, Id. scarce knew any thing. *Exacto admodum mense Februario*, Liv. being almost expired. *Sex millia hostium cæsa, quinque admodum Romanorum*, only five thousand Romans.

ANTEHAC. Heretofore, that is, *ante hæc tempora*: for the antients used to say *hac* for *hæc*.

COMINUS, is not only taken for the place, but also for the time. So that, as Servius observeth, it not only signifies *ex propinquo*, near; but likewise *statim*, immediately, instantly.

――――*jacto qui semine cominus arva Insequitur*, Virg. 1. Georg.

Some have questioned whether it did not govern a case, and therefore might not pass for a preposition, as when Propertius saith,

Aut celer agrestes cominus ire suos.

And in another place,

Flumináque Æmonio cominus isse viro.

But we may safely affirm it does not, because in the first example it is an ellipsis of the preposition *ad*, just as when Virgil saith,

Sitientes ibimus Afros, for *ad Afros*. And in the second, it is only a relative dative, which comes in every where, just as

It clamor cælo, and the like.

CUM or QUUM, is an old accusative of *Qui, quæ, quod*. See above, p. 92.

CUR, is an abbreviation of *Cure*; and *cure*, of *cui rei*. Plautus has put it at full length.

―――― *Viscum legioni dedi, Fundásque eo præterebant folia furfuri:*

Cui rei? Ne ad fundas viscus adhæresceret.

But as we have shewn when treating of the declensions, and here above, p. 83. that heretofore the dative being always like the ablative, they afterwards struck out the *i, musa* for *musai*. In the same manner they said *cur*, or rather *quor*, according to the ancients, for *cure* or *quare*; therefore *cur* or *quare* are originally and in their signification the same thing. Now when we say *quare*, it is generally an ablative, and we are to understand the preposition *de* or *in*, which is sometimes expressed. *Qua de re obsecro?* Plautus. *In ea re maximas Diis gratias agere*, Corn. Nepos. Which does not hinder but *cur* may be also taken for the dative *cui rei*, as we have seen in the above-quoted passage of Plautus.

Hence it appears why it is the same thing to say, for instance, *Mirabar quid esset cur mihi nihil scriberes*, or *quare nihil scriberes*, or even *quod tu nihil scriberes*, Cic. The two former modes of expression coinciding with the construction of the ablative, and the latter with that of the accusative, *quod* standing there for *propter quod*.

DEIN cometh from DEINDE. Now *inde*, as well as *hinc*, is said of time as well as place; and therefore *dein*, or *deinde*, is taken for *postea*, when it refers to time, signifying either the preterite or the future; or for *consequenter*, when it refers to place. *Accepit conditionem; dein quæstum occipit*, Ter. *Factum esse non negat, & deinde facturum autumat*, Id.

HACTENUS, is said in regard to place, being formed of *hac* (sup. *fine*) and *tenus*. *Hac Trojana tenus fuerit fortuna secuta*, Virg. hitherto. *Hactenus fuit quod à me scribi posset*, Cic. hitherto. *Sed hæc hactenus*, Id. but we have said enough of that.

ADHUC, on the contrary, signifies time, because it is taken for *ad hoc*. sup. *tempus*; or in the plural, *ad hæc*, as we find it in many editions of Cicero, sup. *tempora*. And this adverb is said as well of the time present as past. *Est adhuc non Verres, sed mutius*, Cic. *Adhuc hæc erant*. Cic. *Adhuc non feci*, Id. *Adhuc unam à te epistolam acceperam*, Id. &c.

DEINCEPS cometh from *dein* and *capio*, and signifieth the succession and series of things.

DUNTS.

DUDUM comes from *diu dum*, long since; nevertheless it sometimes expresseth a thing lately past, as *Incertior multò sum quàm dudum*, Ter. I am now more dubious than before.

EDEPOL, or EPOL. See lower down the figure of Ellipsis, list. 2.

ETIAM is a word compounded of *et jam*, and has oftentimes nearly the same signification as the two separate parts. Like QUONIAM for *quo jam*, where the *n* has been added to prevent a kind of *hiatus*, the *i* consonant having had a softer sound with the ancients than with us. So that *qua*, properly speaking, is the ablative of the manner or cause.

EXAMUSSIM. See *Partim* lower down.

EXTEMPLO, as ELOCO, signifies immediately, upon the spot. For *templum* was taken for all sorts of places uncovered. *Alii extemplò agendum: alii differendum in veris principium censebant*, Liv. But of ELOCO they have formed *ilico* or *illicò*. Though we likewise meet with it disjoined, *ex loco*, or *ex hoc loco*, in Plautus.

JAMDUDUM signifies a larger space of time than DUDUM; as JAMPRIDEM than PRIDEM; as JAMDIU than DIU, and they are used in regard to time present as well as past. *Jamdudum expectant*, Cic. *Ea, quam jamdudum tractabamus stabilitas*, Id. But Seneca has put it for *jam jam* in the present: *monstrum jamdudum avehe*, in Med. Take away this monster quickly. And Virgil, *Jamdudum sumite pœnas*, Æn. 2. Punish me this instant.

MAGNOPERE is a word compounded of two ablatives, *magno* and *opere*.

MANE is an old ablative, like *sero*, *tempori*, &c. For they used to say *manis*, kind and favourable, the contrary of which was *immanis*, cruel and wicked, which is still preserved; and so they said *Dii manes*. In this manner that time which succeeds the night they called *mane*, as being more agreeable than darkness. Hence we likewise find *multo mane*, Cic. *bene mane*, Ibid. very early. See vol. 1. p. 167.

MECASTOR, MEHERCULES, MEDIUS FIDIUS. See the figure of Ellipsis, list 2.

NIMIRUM is composed of *ne* and *mirum*; as much as to say *non mirum*.

OLIM is taken for all sorts of time. For the past indefinitely; *loquebantur olim sic*, Cic. For a long while since; *Olim non stilum sumsi*, Plin. Jun. *It is a long time since I wrote*. For a little while ago; *Alium esse censes nunc me atque olim cùm dabam*, Ter. Different from what I was lately. For the present; *Ut tandem percipias gaudium quod ego olim pro te non temerè præsumo*, Plin. Jun. that is, *now*, according to Robert Stephen. For the future; *Forsan et hæc olim meminisse juvabit*, Virg. For an undeterminate time; *Ut pueris olim dant crustula blandi doctores*, Hor. do sometimes give. For always; *Hoc tibi prævalidas olim, multóque fluentes sufficiet Bacce vites*, Virg. always.

PARTIM is an old accusative, like *navim*, *puppim*, which must be governed by κατα. Hence we say *partim eorum*, the same as *pars eorum*. Cic. *Sed eorum partim in pompa, partim in acie illustres esse voluerunt*, 2. de Orat. Speaking of the disciples of Isocrates. But some of them, says he, wanted to make a figure in the schools, (*in pompa*) and others at the bar (*in acie*).

The same must be said of *adamussim*, which we read in Varro, 1. de R. R. and of *examussim*, which is in Plautus.

PARUM is also a noun as well as PAULUM, which supposeth *ad* or κατα. They come from παῦρος, *paucus*, or παῦρον, from whence striking out the letter *v*, they made *parum*, and changing the ρ into λ *paulum*. *Parvum* comes also from thence, by transposing the letter *r*.

These nouns also are to be found in different cases. In the nomin. *Parum est quod homines fefellisti*, Cic. sup. negotium. *Parum meministi quid concesseris*, Id. for *ad parum*. Likewise, *parum multi*, to signify few. *Parum sæpe*, seldom. *Paulum humanior*, &c.

PEDETENTIM comes from *pede tendendo*, little by little, insensibly.

PEREGRE is taken for different places: where we are, *peregrè absum*; where we are going to, *peregrè abeo*; where we come from, *peregrè domum redeo*.

PERENDIE, after tomorrow, is used for *perempta die*, as Charisius observeth.

PERINDE denotes resemblance, *Omnes res perinde sunt, ut agas, ut eas magni facias*, Plaut. Things are just according to the opinion we have of them. *Mithridates corpore ingens perinde armatus*, Sal.

PESSUM

PESSUM is used for *pensum*. See the preterits, *&c.* p. 287.

PASQUAM. PRÆUT.

PROUT. PROUT.
See the chapter of conjunctions, lower down.

PROTINUS is as if it were *porro tenus*, and therefore denotes continuity of place or time. *Protinus aërii mellis cœlestia dona exequar*, Virg. immediately. *En ipse capellas protinus æger ago*, Id. I drive them far from hence. *Cùm protinùs utraque tellus una foret*, Virg. signifying that Sicily was formerly joined to Italy.

QUAM. See the chapter of conjunctions, hereafter.

QUANDOQUE is an abbreviation for *quansietunque*. *Indignor quandoque bonus dormitat Homerus*, Hor. that is, *quandocunque*. *Quandoque arabitur*, Colum. As often as they shall plow. And it generally bears this signification, as Sanctius observeth, unless it be resolved into two words, *O rus quando ego te aspiciam, quandoque licebit*, &c. Hor. for *& quando licebit*.

QUIN serves sometimes to interrogate, sometimes to increase and extend the sense, and sometimes to excite. On all these occasions it is put for *qui*, and *ne*, or *non*. And then *qui* is the ablative of the relative, for *quo* sup. *modo*.

Quin vocasti hominem ad cænam, Plaut. that is, *qui non*, or *quomodo non*. Why did not you call him? how comes it that you did not call him? *Quid stas lapis? quin accipis?* Ter. *Quin tu hoc audis?* Id. *Quin morere?* Virg. &c.

Sometimes we meet with it at full length. *Effice qui uxor detur tibi; ego id efficiam mihi qui ne detur*. Ter. where even according to Donatus, *qui* stands for *quemadmodum*, and *ne* for *non*. *Quid nunc agimus, quin redeamus*, Id. that is *immo redeamus, & quid-ni*.

——— *Hic non est locus,*
Quin tu alium quæras, cui, &c.
Plaut. and the like.

QUO is ever a relative, and may be taken either for the dative, or ablative singular, or for the accusative plural. See the chapter of pronouns, p. 94.

QUOAD. Turfellinus saith that *quoad hoc*, or *quoad illud*, is not Latin; but that we should say *quod ad hoc spectat*, or *quod ad illud pertinet*. O-

thers nevertheless admit of this word *quoad* for *quantum ad*, which they prove by a passage of the civil Law, book 41. tit. 1. §. 3. *Nec interest (quoad feras, bestias & volucres) utrum in suo quisque fundo capiat an in alieno*. The great thesaurus of the Latin tongue, printed at Lyons in 1573, which is the best edition; and all Stephen's dictionaries, even the last, that of Honorat, make particular mention of *quoad* in this sense, which they support by this law of Caius: and it is true that it occurs in some editions of the body of civil law, as in that of the widow Chevalon, in 1552.

But in all probability this is a mistake, so that we ought to read *quod ad*, as we find it in the Florentine Pandects printed from the famous original of Florence, which is perhaps the best and the oldest manuscript in Europe, where we find this law thus worded, *Quod ad feras, vestias*, &c. In like manner we read it in the edition of Christopher Plantin in 1567, and in all the best printed copies, as those of Contius or le Conte, Merlinus, Nivellus, Dionysius Godofredus, and others; except that they put *bestias*, where the former have *vestias*, with a *v*, concerning which see the treatise of letters, book 9.

However, should we be inclined to approve of the word *quoad*, which some able moderns have made use of instead of *quantum ad*, as Scioppius, Sanctius, and others; we might do it even by the authority of Cicero himself, who frequently makes use of *quoad ejus facere poteris; quoad ejus fieri possit*, &c. where *quoad* stands for *quantum ad*, and *facere* or *fieri* for a noun governed by *ad* in the accusative, which afterwards governeth *ejus* in the genitive, sup. *rei* or *negotii*. So that *quoad ejus facere potero*, for example, is as much as to say, *quantum ad factum ejus rei potero*; and in like manner the rest.

Thus in the second epistle of the third book, writing to Appius, he saith, *Video ex S. C. provinciam esse habendam: si eam, quoad ejus facere poteris, quàm expeditissimam mihi tradideris, facilior erit mihi quasi decursus mei temporis*. And in another place, *Ut quoad ejus fieri possit, præsentia tuæ desiderium meo labore mi-*

nuatur,

nuatur, Id. *Nec intermittas; quoad ejus rei facere poteris*, (so far as you are able) *scribere ad me*, Id. This expression being the same as if it were *in quantum ad:* and the same may be said of the rest. For that *quoad* of itself may have the same force as *quantum ad*, there is hardly any possibility of doubting: for as *quantum* is an accusative governed by κατὰ, or *in* understood, according to what hath been already said, n. 2. so *quo* is an old accusative plural, like *ambo*, governed also by κατὰ, as it likewise is in this passage of Cicero, *quoad potuit restitit*, Ιφοσον, to the best of his power. Which is sufficient to shew that we ought not easily to censure *quoad hoc* or *illud*, instead of *quantum ad*, though the safest way is to make use of *quod ad*.

QUOD is always a relative. See the third article, p. 146.

QUUM. See *Cum*.

SCILICET, is said for *scire licet*, in the same manner as VIDELICET for *videre licet*, and ILICET for *eas licet*.

VENUM, which is taken for an adverb, or for the supine of *veneo*, is only a noun substantive. See the preterits, vol. 1. p. 286.

Chapter II.

Remarks on the prepositions.

THE prepositions that have no case are not adverbs, says Sanctius, because they have always their case understood; as, *Longo post tempore venit*, that is, *Longo tempore post id tempus*. But we have shewn in the nineteenth rule, that there are a great many words supposed to be prepositions, which are otherwise, &c.

A preposition, as the very name implies, ought always to precede its case in the natural order of construction. If it followeth, this is by means of a figure called Anastrophe, as, *Glandem atque cubilia propter pugnabant*, Hor. Thus *quamobrem* is for *ob quam rem*; *quapropter* for *propter quæ* or *qua*; *quocirca* for *circa quod*, &c.

Prepositions of both cases may be joined in composition, not only to the other parts of speech, but moreover to themselves; as, *Inante diem quintum Cal. Novemb.* Cic. *Exante diem Non. Jun.* Cic. *Insuper his*, Virg. *Insuper alienos rogos*, Lucr. We meet even with *postante* in Varro; *circumsecus* in Appul. *incircum* in Macer. Jurisc. And these compounded prepositions may be likewise joined to a verb, as *insuperhabere* in Gellius, Appul. and Papinian, for *to despise*, or *to set flight on a thing*. Now in regard to the regimen of these prepositions, we must say either that they govern the same case as the simple, which is last in composition, as *Exante diem quintum idus Oct.* Liv. or that there are, in such case, two sentences included in one, so that this signifieth, *ex die ante diem quintum*, &c.

Prepositions are sometimes derived from a noun; as *circum* from *circus*, *secundum* from *secundus*; for whatever is next a thing, comes after it. Hence some are of opinion, that when we find *præsente testibus*, *absente nobis*, and the like, *absente* and *præsente* are become prepositions, and have the same force as *clam nobis*, *coram testibus*, &c. And Vossius seems to favour this notion; though we may also explain these phrases by a Syllepsis, as we shall further observe when we come to treat of the figures of construction.

CHAPTER III.
Remarks on the conjunctions.

I. *That the conjunctions have not always the same thing before as after them.*

IN figurative syntax the conjunctions do not connect the words so much as the sense; and therefore they have not always the same case after as before; yet if we resolve the phrase by the simple construction, we shall find they have always like cases: for *emi centum aureis & pluris*, implies *emi centum aureis, & pretio pluris æris. Est domus fratris & mea*, that is to say, *Est domus fratris & domus mea.* So when we say, *Malo esse Romæ quàm Athenis*, it means, *Malo esse in urbe Romæ quàm in Athenis.* But when Boetius saith, *Mulier reverendi admodum vultus, & oculis ardentibus;* we are to understand *cum*, that is, *Et mulier cum oculis ardentibus,* And in like manner the rest.

It is the same in regard to the interrogation: for if I answer in the same case, it is because I understand the same verb: but if I suppose another, I shall answer in another case; and even supposing the same verb, if the government be changed: *Quanti emisti? Grandi pecuniâ:* and the like.

Conjunctions have not always the same degree of comparison after as before: *Homo & mei observantissimus, & sui juris dignitatisque retinens,* Cic. nor the same tense and mood; *Nisi me lactasses amantem, & falsâ spe produceres,* Ter. *Confidebam ac mihi persuaseram fore,* &c.

II. *Which conjunctions require rather the indicative, and which the subjunctive?*

We have already seen, p. 108. that these two modes are commonly taken for one another. Nevertheless they are sometimes determined by the conjunctions.

Quanquam, etsi, tametsi, are more commonly joined with the indicative, though they are sometimes found with the subjunctive. *Quanquam Volcatio assentirentur,* Cic. *Etsi illis planè orbatus essem,* Cic. *Etsi pars aliqua ceciderit,* Cæs.

Quamvis, licet, etiamsi: Quando, or *cùm* (for *since*) *quandoquidem,* are generally joined with the subjunctive; yet we sometimes find them with the indicative; *Me quamvir pietas & cura moratur,* Hor. which occurs frequently in this poet's writings. *Nam ista veritas etiamsi jucunda non est, mihi tamen grata est,* Cic. *Quando te id video desiderare;* Cic. Since I see that, &c. *Quandoquidem tu mihi affuisti,* &c. Id.

———— *Quandoquidem est ingenio bono.*
Cumque huic veritus est optimæ adolescenti facere injuriam, Ter.
QUOD, whether it be used in giving reason, as we have already observed on the chapter of adverbs, n. 3. p. 146. or whether

it

it be put after the verb instead of the infinitive, as in the following n. is joined both with the subjunctive and the indicative, because on all those occasions it is a relative. See the places here quoted.

Ut for *that*, commonly takes the present subjunctive, if it has a a verb of the present or future tense before it: *In eo vis maxima est ut simus ii qui haberi volumus*, Cic. *Ut in perpetua pace esse possitis, providebo*, Cic.

If it be a preter tense, we put the imperfect subjunctive after *ut*: *Tantum cepi dolorem, ut consolatione egerem*, Cic.

Nevertheless if the action signified by the preter tense still continueth, we may put the present after *ut*: *Orare jussit ad se ut venias*, Ter. Because she has desired it, and desires it still.

Ut for *postquam* requires the indicative.

Ut sumus in ponto, ter frigore constitit Ister, Ovid.
Since we have been.

In like manner Donec for *quamdiu*:
Donec eris fœlix, multos numerabis amicos, Ovid.

Dum likewise denoting the present. *Dum apparatur virgo*, Ter. While they are dressing her.

But Dum, signifying, *provided*, or *until*, requires the subjunctive. *Dum prosim tibi*, Ter. *Tertia dum Latio regnantem viderit æstus*, Virg.

Jamdudum and Jampridem are more elegantly joined with the indicative, when an action is implied, which still continueth. *Jamdudum animus est in patinis*, Ter.

In like manner Jam olim. *Olim jam, imperator, inter virtutes tuas, livor locum quærit*, Quint.

Quasi and ceu vero for *quasi vero*, are put with the subjunctive, *Quasi non norimus nos inter nos*, Ter. *Ceu vero nesciam*, Plin. As if I did not know, &c.

In the same manner Tanquam for *quasi*. *Tanquam nesciamus*, Plin. Likewise *tanquam si*. *Suadeo videas tanquam si tua res agatur*, Cic. But Tanquam for *sicut* governs the indicative. *Tanquam Philosophorum habent disciplinæ ex ipsis vocabula*, Ter.

Perinde by itself frequently assumes the indicative. *Hæc ipsa omnia perinde sunt, ut aguntur*, Cic. But *perinde ac si* is ever joined to the subjunctive. *Perinde ac si virtute vicissent*, Cæs.

Ne, when used for a prohibition, is joined either to the imperative, or the subjunctive. *Ne crucia te*, Ter. Don't torment yourself. *Ne post conferas culpam in me*, Id.

If it be used in interrogating, the same as *an* and *num*, it chuses the indicative.

Quid puer Ascanius? superâtne & vescitur aurâ? Æn. 3.

If it serves only to express some doubt, it requires the subjunctive. *Honestumne factu sit an turpe dubitant*, Cic.

Hereto we might also add *ne* for *ut ne*, which always requires the subjunctive, in favour of *ut*, which is understood. We shall see examples hereof in the next chapter.

The other conjunctions generally follow the nature of the discourse, sometimes admitting one mood, sometimes another, according as the context and the several particles seem to require;
which

which is easier learnt by the use of authors, than by any instructions we are capable of giving.

III. *Of negative conjunctions.*

No body can be ignorant that where there are two negatives in the Latin language, they frequently destroy each other, and therefore are equivalent to an affirmation: yet we must here observe, that the contrary oftentimes happeneth. Hence we see that Plautus hath, *Neque nescio*, for *nescio*; and Terence, *nec nemo* for *et nemo:* And in another place, *Ne temerè facias, neque tu haud dicas tibi non prædictum.* And Virgil,

At non infelix animi Phœnissa, nec unquam
Solvitur in somnos, oculisve aut pectore noctem
Accipit———— Æn. 4.

And Cic. *Negabunt id nisi sapienti non posse concedi.* And in another place, *Neminem unquam non re, non verbo, non vultu denique offendi.* And Livy, *Ut nemo non lingua, non manu promtior in civitate haberetur.*

But this is still more usual as well as more elegant, when the negative is put for the disjunctive *vel*; *Nullam esse artem nec dicendi, nec disserendi putant*, Cic. *Non me carminibus vincet, nec Orpheus, nec Linus,* Virg. *Nulla neque turpi, neque flagitioso quæstu,* Cic. *Quanquam negent, nec virtutes, nec vitia crescere,* Cic. And this remark is still more considerable in the Greek language, where we sometimes meet with three negatives successively, which only strengthen the negation, as we have shewn in the new method of learning that tongue.

The conjunction NEC is taken for *& non*. But sometimes it joins a thing, and makes the signification thereof fall upon another in the same tense, as in Virgil speaking of an old horse, that ought to be discharged from labour, *Hunc*———*abde domo, nec turpi ignosce senectæ*; that is, *Hunc abde domo, & parce senectæ non turpi*. Which some not rightly understanding, imagined it implied a contradiction.

After *non modo*, we sometimes understand also a *non*. See the figure of Ellipsis, in the next book, n. 11.

IV. *Some other remarks concerning particular conjunctions.*

LICET is properly never any thing but a verb, as *per me licet*, sup. *tibi*, or *vobis*, &c. and it is also made use of in compliances, as if one should say, *veniam ad te?* the other would answer, *licet*, you may, I agree, I permit you. See the preterites, vol. 1. p. 306. Therefore we may make use of this verb in all these tenses, *Licet facias: Licebit repotia celebret*, Hor. *Licebit curras*, Hor. *Licuit faceres*, &c. where we see that the reason why *licet* governs the subjunctive, is because *ut* is understood. And indeed we never find any other than the subjunctive mood in classic authors; which made Sanctius and Alvarez believe, that the rule was without exception; though in civilians we read, *Licet subjecta transactio est*, Ulp. *Licet non fuit damnatio secuta*, Mod.

NISI is oftentimes taken for *sed*, as Manutius and Stevech have observed, *Eodem modo, anseres alito, nisi prius dato bibere*, Cato, for *sed prius. Nisi ut periculum fiat, visam quia velis*, Plaut. *Ei liberorum, nisi divitiæ, nihil erat*, Id. *Quamobrem? P. nescio, nisi mihi Deos satis nescio fuisse iratos, qui auscultaverim*, Ter. *Nisi Pol filium meum multis modis jam expecto, ut redeat domum*, Id. *Nihil mihi gratius facere potes, nisi tamen id erit gratissimum, si quæ tibi mandant confeceris*, Cic. *Tuas literas expectabam: nisi illud quidem mutari, si aliter est, ut oportet, non video posse*, Id. *Omnino hoc eodem modo ex hac parte fiunt, nisi illud erat infinitum*, Id. *Nec cur ille tantopere contendat video, nec cur tu repugnes : nisi tamen multominus tibi concedi potest quàm illi ; laborare sine causa*, Id. *Cohortibus armatis septus senatus, nihil aliud verè potest decernere, nisi timere*, Id. Ep. ad Octav. *Quod quæ ceteri miserias vocant, voluptati habuisset : nisi tamen Repub. bene atque decorè gesta*, Sall. And in Spanish nothing so common as to see their *sino* (which properly answers to *nisi*) put for *sed*.

Now this remark helps to explain several obscure passages not only in profane, but in ecclesiastic authors. As in this celebrated expression of Pope Stephen to S. Cyprian, *Nihil innovetur, nisi quod traditum est*, which some of the learned moderns pretend to be corrupted, and that we ought to read *in id quod traditum est*. But nothing can be clearer or better expressed, if we consider that *nisi* is there for *sed. Nihil innovetur ; sed quod traditum est* ; Let there be no innovation, but abide by tradition.

In like manner in the old testament of the vulgate edition ; when Naaman, after his cure, saith to the prophet : *Non enim faciet ultra servus tuus holocaustum aut victimam diis alienis, nisi Domino soli*, for *sed Domino soli*. And in the new testament also of the vulgate edit. *quos dedisti mihi, custodivi : & nemo ex iis periit, nisi filius perditionis*, John 17. that is, *sed filius perditionis*. For Christ is speaking of his elect, to whom this son of perdition did not belong. And in St. Paul. *Miror quod sic tam citò transferimini ab eo qui vos vocavit in gratiam Christi; in aliud evangelium, quod non est aliud : nisi sunt aliqui qui vos conturbant.* Gal. 1. that is, *sed sunt aliqui*, &c. *Scientes quod non justificatur homo ex operibus legis ; nisi per fidem* JESU-CHRISTI, Ibid. that is, *sed per fidem* J. C. Again, *Panes propositionis comedit, quos non licebat ei edere, neque iis qui cum eo erant : nisi solis sacerdotibus*, Matth. 12. *Et præceptum est illis ne læderent fænum terræ, neque omne viride, neque omnem arborem : nisi tantum homines qui non habent signum Dei in frontibus suis*, Apocal. 9. *Non intrabit in eam aliquod coinquinatum, aut abominationem faciens & mendacium ; nisi qui scripti sunt in libro vitæ agni*, Ib. 21. *Unde enim scis mulier, si virum salvum facies ; & unde scis vir, si mulierem salvam facies ? Nisi unicuique divisit Dominus, ita ambulet*, 1 Cor. 17. for *sed unusquisque ita ambulet, sicut illi divisit Dominus* : But let every man behave according to the gift he has received of the Lord.

Now these turns of expression will not surprize us, if we consider the great relation between these two particles, *sed & nisi*.

Hence

Hence it is that the Hebrews express them by the same word כִּי אִם *chi im*, or אִם לֹא *im lo*, which is sometimes rendered by ἐὰν μὴ, *nisi*; as in Gen. c. 22. v. 26. sometimes by ἀλλὰ, *sed*, as in the same book, c. 24. v. 28. and sometimes by ἀλλ' ἢ, as in the 2d book of Kings, chap. 5. v. 17. Saint Paul hath also said, Τίς οὖν ἐστι Παῦλος, τίς δὲ Ἀπολλὼς ἀλλ' ἢ διάκονοι δι' ὧν ἐπιστεύσατε: 1 Cor. 3. 5. *quis igitur est Paulus, quis verò Apollo, nisi ministri per quos credidistis?* And the rest in the same manner,

QUAMVIS, says Sanctius, cometh from *quantumvis*; whereby we may judge, continues he, on what occasion we ought to make use of this particle, because it always includes a mode of complying or granting, and it can never be used, but where you may also make use of *quantumvis*. *Quamvis multa meis exiret victima septis*, Virg. that is, *quantumvis multa*. *Quamvis parvis Italiæ latebris contentus essem*, Cic. *Se beneficium dedisse arbitrantur, cùm ipsi quamvis magnum acceperint*, Cic. *Quamvis sublimes debent humiles metuere*, Phædr. Men, though never so great, ought to be afraid of little people.

We frequently meet with these two conjunctions joined together. And thus it is very common to find two particles that have the same force, or a similar signification; as *ergo igitur, post hoc dein, Dein postea, Tandem denique, quia enim, quidem certè, Extemplo, simul, En ecce, quippe quia, Olim quondam, Tandem itaque, quia nam, Nam cur, Mox deinde*, &c. Examples hereof are common in Plautus, Terence, Lucan, and even in Cicero, and Cæsar. *Itaque ergo amantur*, Ter. and the like, which we may always refer to the figure of pleonasm, as well as when there are two negatives instead of one, as *Nemo nullus, neque nescio, nulla neque*, and others, of which we have already made mention.

But when we say, *Etsi quamvis, quamvis licet*, it is not properly a pleonasm, since these words have a different signification; as appears by putting *quantumvis* instead of *quamvis*; besides, as we have already observed, *licet* is never any thing but a verb. Thus we find it in Cicero. *Etsi quamvis non fueris suasor, approbator certè fuisti*. And in another place, *quamvis licet excellas; quamvis enumeres multos licet*. And the like, which are no more pleonasms, than when he says against Verres, *quamvis callidè, quamvis audacter, quamvis impudenter facere*.

The conjunction QUAM, comes also from *quantum:* and *quanquam*, as Sanctius observeth, is an accusative for *quantum quantum*, as likewise *tanquam*, for *tantum quantum:* Thus *tam deest avaro quod habet, quàm quod non habet*, Hor. that is, *Tantum deest, quantum non habet*, for *in tantum*, &c. pursuant to what has been already said, p. 146. Thus Livy says, *quàm non suarum virium ea dimicatio esset cernebant*, How greatly it was above their strength.

Hence it is, that *quàm* is oftentimes put in one member of a period, and *tantum* in the other. *Quam magis intendas* (vincula) *tanto adstringas arctius*, Plaut.

Quam is oftentimes understood with *plus* and *amplius*. *Hominum eo die cæsa sunt plus duo millia*, Sall. *Plus quingentos colaphos infregit mihi*, Ter. *Amplius quadraginta diebus hic mansit*, Cic. *Plus millies audivi*, Ter. *Jam calesces plus satis*, Id. But the reason of the

government

government is in the prepofition; for thefe are two nouns, *ad plus calefces quàm ad fatis*. See what hath been faid concerning the rule of comparatives, p. 58.

PER, PERQUAM, and IMPRIMIS, are oftentimes joined to the comparative, and fometimes alfo to the fuperlative, though Henry Stephen thinks otherwife in his Thefaurus, upon the particle ὡς. *Perpauciffimi agricolæ*, Colum. *Herba imprimis calidiffima*, Plin. *Perquam maximo exercitu*, Curt. See the rule of fuperlatives, n. 7. p. 60.

PERQUAM is joined alfo to verbs, *Perquam velim fcire*, Plin. ad Suran. And in like manner, *fanequam*, *admodumquam*, *valdequam*, *oppidoquam* and *oppidoperquam*, are joined alfo to verbs and to adjectives in the pofitive degree, and fometimes, though more rarely, in the fuperlative. *Sanequam refrixit*, Cic. *Sanequam graviter tuli*, Id. *Valdequam paucos*, Brut. ad eund. *Oppidoquam parva*, Liv. *Oppidoperquam pauci*, Cæf.

Quam is likewife inferted elegantly between two comparatives. *Peftilentia minacior quàm perniciofior*, Liv. *Salubrior ftudiis quàm dulcior*. See the rule of comparatives, p. 55.

Now as in every comparifon we ought to underftand *præ*, according to what has been demonftrated in the 26th rule, fo that *Doctior Cicerone*, implies, *præ Cicerone*; in the fame manner it ought to be underftood with *quàm*; fo that when we fay, *Limatior quàm Salluftius*, it means *præquam*, or *præ eo quantum*, as Plautus expreffeth himfelf. Thus when we fay, *Bona eft mulier tacens, quàm loquens*, it fignifies *præquam loquens*, according to Scioppius; or elfe we are to underftand the word *magis*, as fhall be fhewn hereafter.

Hereby it appears that PRÆQUAM always forms a comparifon. *Jam minoris omnia facio, præquam quibufmodis me ludificatus eft*, Plaut. I mind every thing elfe very little in comparifon to this. *Hoc pulchrum eft præquam ubi fumtus eft*, Plaut. This is handfomer that what cofts very dear. *Nemo fine grandi malo, præquam rei patitur, ftuduit elegantiæ*, Plaut. No man ever attempted to be elegant above his circumftances, without fuffering greatly thereby.

PROQUAM ferves to exprefs the relation of one thing to another, *Igitur parviffima corpora proquam & leviffima funt, ita mobilitate feruntur*, Lucr. in proportion to their fmallnefs and lightnefs.

PRÆUT oftentimes fignifies the fame as PRÆQUAM. *Nihil hoc quidem eft præut alia dicam*, Plaut. This is nothing to what I am going to fay. *Moleftior eft, præut dudum fuit*, Id. He is more troublefome than he has been this long time.

PROUT is likewife the fame thing almoft. *Tuas literas prout res poftulabat expecto*, Cic. *Prout facultates ejus ferebant*, Id. according as.

Copulative conjunctions are alfo ufed to form comparifon. *Amicior nullus mihi vivit atque is*, Plaut. for *quàm is*, or *præquam is*. *Non Appollinis magis verum atque hoc refponfum eft*, Ter. for *præ atque*. In like manner, *Nefcio quid tibi fum oblitus hodie ac volui dicere*, Ter. that is *præ* or *proac*, as *prout volui*, &c. Unlefs we chufe rather to fay it is an ellipfis of *æquè*, underftood. For it

REMARKS ON THE CONJUNCTIONS. 159

seems that the entire phrase ought to be *æquè ac, æquè atque*, which are oftentimes used. *Te mihi fidelem esse æquè, atque egomet sum mihi——scribam,* Ter. *Me certè habebis cui carus æque sis & perjocundus, ac fuisti patri,* Cic. Thus when Plautus says, *sicut est hic, quem esse amicum ratus sum, atque ipsus sum mihi:* it is plain that he means, *æquè, atque, ipsus sum mihi.* And therefore in the above-cited passage of Plautus, *Non Apollinis magis verum atque hoc responsum est:* the meaning is, *non magis æquè verum est, atque hoc responsum.* And in the other passage of Terence, *Nescio quid tibi sum oblitus, hodie ac volui dicere;* it signifies, *æquè dicere ac volui.* Insomuch that as their having often omitted this *æquè,* which refers to *atque,* is intirely owing to custom; so the same custom, on many occasions, understands *atque,* and puts only the word *æquè;* for instance, *Tamen erat nemo, quicum essem libentius quàm tecum, & pauci quibuscum æquè libenter,* Cic. Where it is evident we are to understand *æquè libenter atque tecum;* and the rest in the like manner.

TAMEN always requires another member, or another adversative particle, says Sanctius, which should answer, and refer to it, *Qui nondum libera civitate, tamen Pop. Romani comitiis liberatus est,* Cic. for *qui, quamvis nondum libera civitate, tamen, &c.* Wherefore when it is not expressed, we are to understand it, and to take it in the same sense, as when Cicero begins the 19th letter of the 19th book in this manner, *Tamen à malitia non discedis;* that is, in short (supposing something that the other had wrote him word about) you are still as malicious as ever.

SECTION VI.

Remarks on some particular turns of expression.

CHAPTER I.

Of VEREOR UT, *&* VEREOR NE.

THESE turns of expression, *Vereor ut,* and *Vereor ne,* are different and opposite to one another. This difference is extremely well pointed out in a passage of Terence, where a servant, speaking to two young men, one of whom was afraid of marrying a girl that he did not love; and the other, who really loved her, was afraid lest he should not marry her; he says to the former, *Tu paves, ne illam ducas,* you are afraid to marry her; and to the other, *Tu autem ut ducas,* and you are afraid lest you should not marry her.

But it is not easy to account for these modes of speaking. And the difficulty is in this, that what is expressed by an affirmative in Latin, *Paves* UT *ducas,* ought to be translated by a negative; *you are afraid lest you should not marry her.* And, on the contrary, the Latin negative, *Paves* NE *ducas* ought to be rendered by the affirmative, *you are afraid to marry her.*

This

This has made several learned men imagine, that *vereor ut* and *vereor ut non* oftentimes signified the same thing; and Sanctius seems to be of this opinion: as, on the contrary, that *metuo ne* was sometimes taken for *metuo ne non*, in the same manner as *non modo* is taken for *non modo non*; and Linacer expressly declares this to be his sentiment in his sixth book *de constr. fig.*

In order therefore to unravel this difficulty, we must consider that these phrases always include the particle *ut* expressed or understood. So that when we say, for example, *vereor ne id fiat*, or *ne non id fiat*, it is as if it were *vereor ut ne*, or *ut ne non id fiat*; for the subjunctive *fiat* cannot be governed but by an *ut* understood, because the particle *ne*, as Vossius hath very well observed, being only a negative adverb, cannot have this force of itself. And here it happens to be the same thing as when Terence saith, *Nunc per amicitiam obsecro ne ducas*, for *ut ne* or *ut non ducas*. And Cicero, *Vide ne illarum quoque rerum à temetipso imminuatur autoritas*, that is, *ut ne*, or *ut non imminuatur*. Sometimes we find those two particles expressed together; as *Peto à te ut, socrus adolescentis rea ne fiat*, Cic.

This being the case, we cannot account for these turns of expression, but by considering the force of the particle *ut*. Now this particle hath two principal uses which particularly relate to our present purpose, and by which we may explain these modes of expression. The first is to be taken for *quomodo*, in the same sense, says Sanctius, as we find it in Cicero, *Tametsi vereor quomodo*, or *Timeo quemadmodum hoc accepturi sitis.* The other is properly to mark the intention and final cause, as when Tully says, *Est igitur oratori providendum, non uti illis satisfacias, quibus necesse est, sed ut illis, quibus liberè liceat judicare.* And even with the *ne*. *Ita velim ut ne quid properes*, Id. And Terence, *Ut ne id videam misera, huc effugi foras.*

And therefore when we say, *Paves ut ducas*, if we take *ut* for *quomodo*, as Sanctius pretends we ought to take it, the meaning is, *You are afraid how you will marry her*, or *how you will do to marry her*. Which expresses the same sense as that generally contained in the negative, *You are afraid lest you should not marry her.*

On the contrary, *Paves ne ducas*, supposing as we have already observed, that the subjunctive *ducas* can be governed only by an *ut* understood, must be taken for *paves ut ne*, or *ut non ducas*, that is, *quomodo non ducas*, and may be rendered thus, *You are solicitous how you shall do not to marry her*; which is the same meaning as when we say in the affirmative, *You are afraid to marry her.* And this is the first explication that may be given.

The other depends on the second signification of the particle *ut*, which signifies, as we have already taken notice, the intention and final cause.

In order rightly to understand this explication, it is requisite to observe, that the passions lying as it were between two opposite terms, one which we pursue, the other which we would avoid, it is certain that the fear of a thing always supposeth the love and desire of its opposite. Thus we are afraid of death, because we

are

are fond of life: we are afraid to marry a woman, because we desire not to marry her; and on the contrary, we are afraid lest we should not marry her, because to marry her is what we desire.

This being premised, it seems that the difference between these turns of expression in Latin and our vulgar language, *Paves ut ducas*, You are afraid lest you should not marry her; *Paves ne* (for *ut ne*) *ducas*, you are afraid to marry her, is that in our vulgar language we barely express the object of fear; whereas in Latin, after marking fear by the verb, at the same time we signify our desire of the contrary by *ut*. And thus *Paves ut ducas* signifies, word for word, *paves*, You are solicitous, *ut ducas*, to marry her; that is, You are disturbed by fear in the midst of the desire you have to marry her: and *Paves ne ducas* (where we are always to understand *ut*) may be explained thus; *Paves*, You are solicitous, *ut ne ducas*, not to marry her; that is, you are disturbed by fear, in the midst of the desire you have to get rid of her, and you are afraid lest you should be engaged.

This reason seems more natural than the other, though I never heard of its being mentioned before. But it will soon appear that this is the real meaning, and the ground of these modes of speaking, if we consider, that the conciseness studied by the Romans, oftentimes made them use this turn of expression, when of two things, either opposite or relative, they marked one by the verb, and the other by the particle. Thus they said, *Adesse ex Gallia*, Cic. *Quem ex Hyperboreis Delphos ferunt advenisse*, Id. *Aliquem ad nequitiam abducere*, Ter. *Nunc abeo ad vulgi opinionem*, Cic. *Propius abesse*, Id. and the like. Which evidently proves, as I apprehend, that these phrases, *Paves ut ducas*, *paves ne ducas*; *vereor ne fiat*, *vereor ut fiat*, and the like, were owing entirely to this conciseness, whereby they intended to signify at the same time the fear of a thing, and the desire of its opposite. And if we consider this principle rightly, we shall easily comprehend the several turns of expression that may arise from these two, and which in other respects appear sometimes very intricate. We shall reduce them all to six, according to Manutius; 1. *vereor ut*, 2. *vereor ne*, 3. *vereor ut ne*, 4. *vereor ne non*, 5. *non vereor ut*, 6. *non vereor ne*; and we shall render them in the usual manner of speaking in our language, leaving it to the reader to refer them to the principle, and to translate them verbatim as we have done, after he has formed a clear idea of their nature and force.

I. VEREOR UT.

By what has been said it is obvious, that this form of speaking, *vereor ut*, expresseth fear in regard to things which we desire, that is, fear lest they should not succeed according to our wish. This will further appear by the following examples; *Hoc fœdus veretur Hiempsal ut satis firmum sit & ratum*, Cic. He is afraid that this alliance will not be lasting. *Sin homo amens, diripiendam urbem daturus est, vereor ut Dolabella ipse vobis satis prodesse possit*, Id. If Cæsar should give up the town to be plundered, I am afraid that even the favour of Dolabella himself will not be able to protect you.

Non dubitabam quin meas literas libenter lecturus esses, verebar ut redderentur, Id. I did not at all doubt but you would be glad to read my letters, but I was afraid left they should not be delivered to you. *Videris vereri ut epistolas tuas acceperim*, Id. You seem to be afraid that I have not received your letters. *Vereor ut placari possit*, Ter. I am afraid there will be no pacifying him. *Perii, metuo ut subsiet hospes*, Ter. I am undone, I am afraid that this young man wont be able to stand it. And an infinite number of others.

II. VEREOR NE.

This manner of expression being opposite to the precedent, it signifies fear in regard to things which we don't desire, *Vereor ne turpe sit pro viro fortissimo dicere incipientem timere*, Cic. I am afraid that it will be reckoned a disgrace to an orator, to be under apprehension in attempting to defend so brave a man. *Metuebat scilicet ne indicaretur*, Ibid. Perhaps he was afraid of being discovered. *Vereor ne desideres officium meum*, Cic. I am afraid you will think I have forgot my duty. *Timet ne deseras se*, Ter. She is afraid you will forsake her. *Nimis pavebam ne peccaret*, Plaut. I was greatly afraid he would commit some mistake. And we might give an infinite number of examples, to shew that these two phrases, *vereor ut* and *vereor ne*, are opposite to one another.

I am not ignorant of the opinion of some learned men, that this difference hath not been always observed by authors, and of their having produced several passages out of Cicero to prove the contrary. But it will be easy for us to shew presently, that all those passages are corrupted, and wrested from their natural meaning. I shall only observe here in general, after Stevech and Vossius, that it is a very usual mistake in books, even on other occasions, to put *ut* for *ne*, or *ne* for *ut*; because these two particles are so like one another in manuscript, that very often it is impossible to distinguish them but by the sense.

For which reason, in one of the principal passages which they quote from Cicero in support of their opinion, *Vereor ne satis diligenter in senatu actum sit de literis meis*, where they pretend that *ne* stands for *ne non*, Stevech is for having us read, *vereor ut satis*, &c. and Vossius is of the same opinion. And this will easily coincide with the above-mentioned sense.

III. VEREOR UT NE, or VEREOR UT NON.

This manner of speaking may have a double use; one right and natural, the other false and corrupted.

The right use would be to signify the same thing as *vereor ne*, says Manutius, because *ut ne* is oftentimes taken for *ne*; and we have seen but just now, that in *vereor ne* the particle *ut* is always understood. So that it is the same thing to say, *paves ut ne ducas*, and *paves ne ducas*; *pavebam ut ne peccaret*, and *pavebam ne peccaret*: which the explication above given ought to put beyond all manner of doubt.

Hence it follows, that the other use in which we take this mode of expression, *vereor ut ne*, or *vereor ut non*, for *vereor ut*, is false, as Vossius testifieth; and Turfellinus hath also questioned it. And if we examine minutely into the thing, we shall find, that what gave rise to this error is, that a great many people, not being able to make out the words, or to comprehend that *vereor ut id fiat*, which is an affirmative, should signify, *I am afraid it will not be done*, which is a negative, they have added a negative, contrary to the use of the Latin language, saying, *vereor ut id non fiat*, to express what is signified without a negative, *vereor ut id fiat*. And it is owing to this ignorance that various passages of Cicero are corrupted in several editions: such is that of the oration pro Marcello, where most people read, *Vereor ut hoc quod dicam perinde auditu intelligi non possit, atque ego ipse cogitans sentio*; which is an evident mistake, as Manutius hath very well observed, after correcting it by the authority of antient manuscripts. And this is further corroborated by the testimony of the learned Asconius, who, in quoting this passage in his notes on the oration *de Div. in Verrem*, gives it without *non*. So that we have reason to be surprized, that this error should have been suffered to continue in the editions of Gruterus and Elzevir, which have been so carefully revised.

The same may be said of the other passages produced by those who defend this *non*. As that of the oration pro Planco, where they read, *Sed quam tempestatem nos vobiscum non tulissemus, metuit ut eam ipse non posset opibus suis sustinere*; where the best editions have, *metuit ut eam ipse posset*, &c. and among the rest those of Frigius, Gruterus, and Elzevir. And Lambinus saw plainly it was nonsense to read it with *ut*, followed by a negative, since he put *ne non possit*, which imports the same as *ut posset*.

But it is very extraordinary that this passage of Cæsar in the fifth book of the Gallic war, where he says of Labienus, *Veritus si ex Hybernis fugæ similem profectionem fecisset, ut hostium impetum sustinere non posset*, should be read thus in all the printed copies, though Stevech hath observed that this must be owing to the mistake of the transcribers, who have put *ut* instead of *ne*; and though Aldus, and Michael Brutus in his notes on Cæsar, had already endeavoured to correct it.

In regard to the passage from Cicero *de amicitia*, which P. Monet quotes in his *Schorus digestus*, or *Delectus Latinitatis*, (which is the same book, having left out the name of its first author, Schorus, in the latter editions) *Vereor ut idem fit interitus animorum & corporum*, so little does it prove what he pretends, that it is absolute nonsense to take it thus; because at least we ought to read those words in conjunction with the precedent, and make the punctuation thus, *Sin autem illa vereor; ut idem fit interitus*, &c. as we read it in Lambinus, and others, that is, *nempe ut*. But if *I apprehend, as is generally done, that the souls die with the body*, &c. Or else we should read, with Elzevir, *Sin autem illa veriora; ut idem fit,* &c. where the sense is very clear; because Cicero says in this passage, that if Scipio is in heaven, it would be envy to lament his death; and, on the other hand, if it is more probable to believe that the soul dies with the body, as some pretended, we ought no more to grieve for the death of a person, that for one that was never born.

It is the same in regard to the other passages they quote, which I could prove to be all corrupted, did not this require too long a dissertation.

IV. VEREOR NE NON.

Since with *vereor ne* we must understand *ut*, and take it for *ut ne*, it follows of course that with *vereor ne non* we must likewise understand *ut*, and take it as if it were *vereor ut ne non*; whence it is clear that, as the two negatives destroy each other, *vereor ne non* implies the same as *vereor ut*, and is more easily understood. *Vereor ne exercitum firmum habere possit*, Cic. I am afraid lest he should have a good army. *Intellexi te vereri ne superiores literæ mihi redditæ non essent*, Cic. I understood you was afraid I had not received your last letters, that is, You was afraid they were not delivered to me. *Timeo ne non impetrem*, Cic. I am afraid I shall not carry it. And an infinite number of others, where we ought to translate *ne non* like *ut*, as bearing the same signification.

V. NON VEREOR UT, *or* NON VEREOR NE NON.

The negative having ever the force in the Latin tongue to destroy whatever follows it; when it is put before verbs of fearing, it must needs remove all manner of apprehension, either that the thing we desire will not happen, (as when there follows *ut*, or *ne non*) or that the thing we dread will happen, (as when there happens to be *ne* or *ut ne*: for which reason *non vereor ut id fiat*, or *non vereor ne non id fiat* (which is the same thing) shew that we are almost certain the thing we wish for will come to pass, and therefore that we are not afraid it will not come to pass. It is in this sense that Cicero has said of Octavius, *Ne verendum quidem est ut tenere se possit & moderari*, &c. We have no reason to be afraid but he can govern and contain himself; just as he said, *Non vereor ne tua virtus opinioni hominum non respondeat*, I am not in the least afraid but you will answer the advantageous opinion the public have conceived of your virtue. *Non vereor ne hoc officium meum Servilio non probem*, I am not afraid but I shall be able to justify my conduct to Sevilius. *Non vereor ne non scribendo te expleam*, I know how to overpower you with letters, *or* I am not afraid but I shall attain my end. *Non sum veritus ne tua beneficia sustinere non possim*, I never was afraid of not being able to bear all your favours.

But sometimes we find these two negatives, *ne*, *non*, one following the other, though they fall into different members, and have nothing to do with each other; this is very proper to be remembered, in order to take their meaning, and to distinguish them properly. Thus, in the first Catil, when Cicero saith, *Credo erit verendum mihi, ne non hoc potius omnes boni serius à me, quàm quisquam crudelius factum esse dicat*; it is as if he had said, *An est vereudum mihi ne quisquam hoc crudelius à me factum esse dicat, & non potius ne omnes boni serius factum esse dicant?* so that the particle *non* falls only upon *potius*, (*non potius*) and has no manner of relation to *ne*. And therefore

fore it must not be rendered, by *vereor ne non*, but only by *vereor ne*, thus; But perhaps I shall have more reason to be afraid of being charged with too much cruelty, than to apprehend the complaints of honest men for being too mild and dilatory.

VI. NON VEREOR NE, *or* NON VEREOR UT NE.

As *non vereor ut* signifieth that we are almost certain the thing we wish for will happen; so *non vereor ne*, on the other hand, gives to understand that we are almost sure the thing to be dreaded will not happen, and therefore that we are not afraid of its happening. It is in this sense that Cicero faith, *Non vereor ne quid timidè, ne quid stultè facias*, I am not afraid that you will act either cowardly or indiscreetly. *Non vereòr ne assentatiuncula quadam aucupari tuam gratiam videar*, Id. I am not afraid of being charged with endeavouring to gain your good will by flattery.

This is what I thought incumbent upon me to mention concerning these verbs of fearing, on which I have descanted somewhat largely, because I have never yet met with any writer that treated them thoroughly by investigating their principle, without which even those who are versed in the language, acknowledge they have been often puzzled.

There is still another phrase, where, for want of properly distinguishing the affirmation and negation, obscurity often ariseth: we shall mention something about it in the following chapter.

CHAPTER II.

Of this other phrase, HAUD SCIO AN, &c.

THIS expression hath been already taken notice of in our notes on the translation of Terence; yet we shall treat of it here in its proper place.

This mode of speaking is not properly negative, but dubious, or conditional, by reason of the force of the particle *an*; whence it often bears the sense of *fortasse*, and ought to be taken as if it were *haud scio an non* (in the same manner as *non modo* is often taken for *non modo non*.) Hence Cicero, in his book upon old age, where he finds fault with an expression of Solon's, viz. that he should not chuse to die unlamented by his friends, and sets another saying of Ennius in opposition to it, hath these words, *Sed haud scio an melius Ennius: nemo me lacrymis decoret*, &c. which Gaza translates thus, Ἀλλ' ἴσως Ἔννιος ἀμείνων. *Sed fortè Ennius melius*. And Cicero abounds in the like expressions: *Aristoteles quem, excepto Platone, haud scio an rectè dixerim principem philosophorum*, Cic. Whom next to Plato I know not whether I may not stile the prince of philosophers. *Tibi non minus, haud scio an magis etiam hoc faciendum est,* 1. Offic. You are not less, but perhaps more obliged. *Capessentibus autem remp. nihil minus quàm philosophis, haud scio an magis etiam, & magnificentia & despicientia adhibenda sit rerum humana-*

rum, Cic. Those who have the administration of the republic, are not less, but perhaps more obliged than philosophers, to shew a generous contempt of all earthly things. *Est id quidem magnum, atque haud scio an maximum,* lib. 9. ep. 15. It is a great thing, and perhaps the greatest of all: or, I question whether it is not the greatest of all.

Thus when Terence faith, *Atque haud scio an quæ dixit vera sint omnia,* this does not imply, *I know not whether all he has said be true,* as if he believed nothing; but, on the contrary, it shews that he was already half persuaded, and means that what the other said was likely to be true. And in another place, when he says, *Qui infelix haud scio an illam miserè nunc amat,* this does not signify, *I question whether he loves her*; but the reverse, *I question whether he does not love her.* Thus Cicero pro Marcello, to signify that posterity will judge more impartially of Cæsar's virtue than the present age, says, *Servi iis etiam judicibus qui multis post sæculis de te judicabunt, & quidem haud scio an incorruptius quàm nos.* Where, for want of understanding this elegant turn, and to judge only according to our idiom, one would think at first that it should be, *Atque haud scio an non incorruptius quàm nos,* &c. An infinite number of such instances are to be found in Cicero, which plainly shew that *haud scio an* ought always to be resolved by *fortasse.* True it is that there are also some passages which may render it dubious, as in his book of old age, where he says of a country life, *Atque haud scio an ulla possit esse beatior vita.* But, in all probability, this example, as well as one or two more in his book de Orat. and in the oration *de Harusp. responsis,* have been corrupted by somebody that did not understand this manner of expression, and that we ought to read, *Atque haud scio an nulla possit esse beatior vita.* Just as the same writer, in his third book of offices, endeavouring to persuade his son, that there is nothing more useful than the study of philosophy, says thus, *Quod cum omnibus est faciendum qui vitam honestam ingredi cogitant, atque haud scio an nemini potius quàm tibi;* where he does not say *an ulli,* as he ought to do if the other example was not corrupted, but *an nemini.* And in his book of friendship, after speaking against those who place the whole end of friendship in utility, he adds, *Atque haud scio an ne opus sit quidem nihil unquam omnino deesse amicis.* But perhaps it is not absolutely necessary, or it is not always best in friendship, that friends should never want any thing. Where it ought to be *an opus sit,* if the example from the book on old age was to be admitted.

BOOK VII.

OF

FIGURATIVE SYNTAX.

What is meant by figures in syntax, of their use, and that they may be all reduced to four.

WE have already divided syntax into two parts, simple and figurative; and we took notice that the figurative was that which receded from the customary and natural rules, to follow some particular turns of expression, authorised by the learned, which is what we understand here by the word FIGURE.

So necessary is the knowledge of these figures, that without it it is almost impossible to understand the ancient authors, or to write pure and elegant Latin.

We shall reduce them all to four, after the example of the learned Sanctius, who says that all the rest are chimeras. *Monstrosi partus grammaticorum, in Miner. sua, lib. 4.*

For by this word figure is meant, either a defect and omission of some part of a sentence; and this is generally called ELLIPSIS.

Or something superfluous and redundant, and this is called a PLEONASM.

Or a disproportion and disagreement in the parts, when the construction is framed rather according to the sense than the words, and this we shall call SYLLEPSIS. Though some modern grammarians give it the name of SYNTHESIS.

Or an inversion of the regular and natural order of words in a sentence, and this we called HYPERBATON.

To these figures some likewise join that of HELLENISM, or GREEK PHRASE, which is when we use such expressions in Latin in imitation of the Greeks, as cannot be defended by the rules of Latin syntax.

And as for ANTIPTOSIS, or ENALLAGE, we shall prove at the latter end that it is as unnecessary as the rest which we have omitted, and that the whole may be reduced to these four figures.

CHAPTER I.
Of the first figure called ELLIPSIS.

THE first figure is called ELLIPSIS, that is, *defect* or *omission*, and this is of two sorts. For sometimes we ought to understand what is not at all mentioned in a sentence: and sometimes we understand a noun or a verb that has been already expressed, whether we take it in the same or in a different sense; this is what we call *Zeugma*.

Now the first sort of ellipsis is built particularly on what we find in ancient authors, who expressing their thoughts more at large, and with the greatest simplicity, have thereby shewn us the natural government, and what we are to suppose in the more figurative and concise manner of writing, which was afterwards adopted. The most general rules that we ought to consider here, and which have been partly hinted at already in the preceding remarks, and in the syntax, may be reduced to nine or ten heads, and these should be looked upon as fundamental maxims, in order to take the thread of the discourse, and to understand an author thoroughly.

I. *Verb understood.*

I. GENERAL MAXIM. Every sentence is composed of a noun and a verb, and therefore where the verb is not expressed, it must be understood.

Hence what the grammarians call apposition, as *Anna soror*; *Urbs Athenæ*, is properly an ellipsis of the substantive verb, for *Anna ens*, or (because this participle is obsolete) *quæ est soror: Urbs quæ est*, or *quæ dicitur Athenæ*; just as Cæsar says, *Carmonenses quæ est firmissima civitas*, lib. 2. B. C. Hence it is that the French hardly ever make an apposition by substantives only, because this language has an aversion to the figure ellipsis. But either they put one of the nouns in the genitive, *La ville de Rome, the city of Rome*; or they add a verb, *La ville qui est appellée Rome, the city which is called Rome*; or they add an adjective to one of the two substantives, *Rome ville célebre, Rome a famous city*; *Anne ma sœur, my sister Anne*; and not *Rome ville*; *sœur Anne*. For which reason they do not translate, *Ora pro nobis peccatoribus, Priez pour nous pecheurs, pray for us sinners*; but, *priez pour nous pauvres pecheurs, pray for us poor sinners*, or *priez pour nous qui sommes pecheurs, pray for us who are sinners*. And in like manner the rest.

Now the apposition is not only formed of one word, but likewise of many, *Donarem tripodas, præmia fortium*, Her. that is, *qui sunt præmia fortium*. *Vicina coëgi ut quamvis avido parerent arva colono: gratum opus agricolis*, Virg.

But it is customary to refer to apposition, words that have more of the nature of an adjective; as *Homo servus*; *Victor exercitus*; *Nemo homo*, &c.

There are also a great many occasions on which the verb is understood, especially the substantive verb, *Sed vos qui tandem*, sup. *estis?* And some other verb likewise, as *in Pompeianum cogito*, Cic. sup. *ire*. *Dii meliora*, sup. *faciant*.

When one speaks proverbially, *Fortuna fortes*, Cic. sup. *adjuvat*. By a rhetorical figure, *Quos ego?* Virg. sup. *castigarem*; and on many other occasions which may be learnt by use, or may be seen in the 2d list hereto annexed.

II. *The nominative understood before the verb.*

II. GENERAL MAXIM. Every verb hath its nominative expressed or understood: but there are commonly three ways of suppressing the nominative.

1. In the first and second person, *Amavi te*, *quo die cognovi*, Cic. sup. *ego*. *Quid facis?* sup. *tu?* &c.
2. In verbs relating to the generality of mankind, *Aiunt, ferunt, prædicant*, sup. *homines*.
3. In verbs that are called impersonal. *Vivitur*, sup. *vita*. For since we say *Vivere vitam*, it follows that we may also say *Vivitur vita*, because the accusative of the verb active may always be rendered by the nominative of the passive. In like manner when we say, *peccatur*, we are to understand *peccatum*, and Cicero has expressed it, *Quo in genere multa peccantur*. *Vigilatur*, sup. *nox*, as Ovid has it, *Noctes vigilantur amaræ*. *Festinatur, properatur*, sup. *res*, or *fuga*; as Virgil hath expressed it, *Festinate fugam*; and the rest in the same manner. The reason of this is because these verbs are called impersonal through a mistake, as we have already shewn, p. 122. and following, and that they may have their nominative and persons like the rest.

Hereto we may refer those verbs which Sanctius calleth *Verba naturæ*, that express a natural effect, as *Pluit, tonat, fulgurat, ningit, lucescit*, where we understand, *Deus, cœlum*, or *natura*; or the noun itself whence the verb is derived, as *pluvia, nix, lux*, &c. since we find that the vulgar languages oftentimes put this nominative, at least with an adjective, as in French, *il a plû une grosse pluye*, it has rained a hearty shower: And in Latin other nouns are joined, as *saxa pluunt*, Stat. *Tantum pluit ilice glandis*, Virg.

The infinitive oftentimes supplieth the place of the nominative, and ought to be understood as such in discourse, because it is considered as a verbal noun, according to what hath been already said, p. 113.

III. *The accusative understood after the verb.*

III. GENERAL MAXIM. Every verb active hath its accusative expressed or understood. But it is oftentimes omitted, and especially before the relative *qui, quæ, quod*, as *Facilius reperias* (sup. *homines*) *qui Romam proficiscantur, quàm ego qui Athenas*, Cic. See likewise what hath been said on the 14th rule, and in the remarks on the verbs, chap. 1.

But

But it is also observable that the infinitive, as a noun verbal, may be frequently understood for the case of its own verb, as we have made appear in different places. Thus when I say *currit*, we are to understand *cursum*, or τὸ *currere*, which is the same thing. *Pergit*, we must understand *pergere*, and the rest in the same manner; which would seem odd at first, if we did not find that the antients expressed themselves in this manner, *Pergis pergere*, Plaut. *Pergam ire domum*, Ter. And thus it is the Greeks say ἔφη φάναι, *dixit dicere*, and the like.

IV. *When the infinitive is alone, the verb that governs it is understood.*

IV. GENERAL MAXIM. Whenever the infinitive is by itself in a sentence, we must understand a verb by which it is governed, as *cœpit*, *solebat*, or some other. *Ego illud sedulo negare factum*, Ter. sup. *cœpi*. *Facile omnes perferre ac pati*, Id. sup. *solebat*; which is more usual with poets and historians, though we sometimes meet with it in Cicero, *Galba autem multas similitudines afferre, multáque pro æquitate dicere:* Where we ought always to understand a verb, without pretending that the infinitive is there instead of preter-imperfect, by a figure that has no sort of foundation.

Sometimes a participle is understood, as in Cæsar. *Divitiacus complexus obsecrare cœpit, ne quid gravius in fratrem statueret; scire se illa esse vera, nec quemquam ex eo plus quam se doloris capere*, for *dicens se scire*, &c.

V. *When an adjective is alone, some substantive or other is understood.* Of the word Negotium.

V. GENERAL MAXIM. Every adjective supposeth its substantive expressed or understood. Thus, because *juvenis*, *servus*, &c. are adjectives, they suppose *homo*; because *bubula*, *suilla*, &c. are also adjectives, they suppose *caro*. There are a great many of this sort, of which we shall presently give a list.

But when the adjective is in the neuter gender, the word NEGOTIUM is generally understood for its substantive, which word by the antients was taken for RES, the same as the TO` ΠΡΑΓΜΑ of the Greeks, or the VERBUM of the Hebrews.

Cicero himself has used it in this sense, when he says of C. Antony who did not pay him: *Teucris illa, lentum negotium.* Ad Attic. *It is an affair that goes on but very slowly*, And in another place; *Ad tanti belli opinionem, quod ego negotium*, &c. And in this sense Ulpian has used it, when he says, that there are more *things* than words in nature, *Ut plura sint negotia quàm vocabula.*

We even frequently find that Cicero takes *Res* and *Negotium*, for the same thing. *Ejus* NEGOTIUM *sic velim suscipias, ut si esset* RES *mea.* Which is proper to be observed in order to understand the force of several expressions, and of many elegant particles, which this author makes use of, as *Rerum autem omnium nec aptius*

est

eſt quidquam ad opes tuendas quàm diligi; nec alienius quàm timeri; Offic. 1. Where we see that *aptius* and *alienius*, being of the neuter gender, do suppose *negotium* for their substantive, which refers however to the word *res*, mentioned by him before, as to its synonymous term. Again, *Sed ego hoc utor argumento quam-ob-rem me ex animo, veréque diligi arbitrer.* For *quamobrem*, which is taken for an adverb, is composed of three words. And *res* here refers to *argumentum*, which he mentioned before, as if it were *ob quod argumentum*, or *ob quod negotium*, *on which account*.

So in his oration against Verres, where he says, *Fecerunt ut iſtum accuſarem, à quo mea longiſſime ratio, voluntáſque abhorrebat;* that is, *à quo negotio accuſationis*, according to Asconius. And when Terence says, *Utinam hoc fit modo defunctum*, we muſt underſtand *negotium*, according to Donatus.

And therefore when we say, *Triſte lupus ſtabulis; Varium & mutabile ſemper femina*, we ought to underſtand this same *negotium*, without looking for another turn by the feminine, in order to say with the grammarians, that it is *Res triſtis, Res mutabilis:* as if *Negotium*, could not perform the same office as *Res*.

In like manner the names of arts and sciences are generally in the neuter in Cicero, because this ſubſtantive is underſtood. *Muſicorum perſtudioſus*, Cic. *Niſi in phyſicis plumbei ſumus*, Cic. *Phyſica illa ipſa & mathematica quæ poſuiſti*, Cic. ſup. *negotia*.

It ought likewise to be underſtood, when the relative is in the neuter gender, as *Non eſt quod gratias agas;* that is, *non eſt negotium*, or *nullum eſt negotium propter quod gratias agas*, or *agere debeas*.

Claſſe viriſque potens, per quæ ſera bella feruntur, Ovid.
In like manner, *Lunam & ſtellas, quæ tu fundaſti;* that is, *quæ negotia*.

Hereby we see that the grammarians had no great reason to call this a Syllepſis, or to say that the neuter gender was more noble than the other two, and therefore included them both. For herein they have committed two conſiderable miſtakes: The firſt is their not underſtanding what is properly meant by the neuter, which is only a negative gender, and conſequently cannot be more noble than the other two, nor include them both. The ſecond is their miſtaking the cauſe of this conſtruction in the neuter, which is no other than the ellipſis of the word *negotia*; for which reaſon they imagined it could be uſed only in regard to inanimate things, whereas we meet with inſtances of it in others, as hath been ſhewn in the ſyntax, rule 4. p. 11. and as we are further able to demonſtrate by authorities, as when Tacitus says; *Parentes, liberos, fratres, vilia habere;* that is, *vilia negotia*, to ſlight them. And Lucretius:

Ductores Danaum delecti prima virorum.

And this figure of NEGOTIA underſtood, is ſo familar in the Latin tongue, that Cicero makes use of it on many occaſions, where he might have done otherwiſe, as when he ſays, *Annus ſalubris & peſtilens contraria* (for *contrarii*) that is, *ſunt contraria negotia*,

are

are contrary things. And in his book on old age; *Sæpe enim interfui querelis meorum æqualium, quæ C. Salinator, quæ Sp. Albinus, deplorare solebant*; he could not say, *querelis quæ*, without understanding *negotia*; since it is plain, that *quæ* refers to those complaints, as it appears likewise by Gaza's Greek translation: πολλάκις γάρ τοι περιτυχον ΟΔΥΡΜΟΙΣ ΟΥΣ ίενται κατοδύρεσθαι; and therefore that he might have put *quas*, if he had not understood this other noun, which is of the neuter gender. In regard to which we refer to what shall be said hereafter upon the Syllepsis.

And if it should be again objected, that in Hebrew the adjective feminine is oftentimes taken absolutely, as *Unam petii à Domino*, that is, *unam rem*, though we cannot understand a substantive feminine, because those words which signify *rem*, or *negotium*, are all masculine in that language.

I answer that there is never a passage in scripture, where the adjective feminine occurs alone, but a substantive feminine is to be understood, though it is neither *res* nor *negotium*, which are masculine in this language; and therefore in the abovementioned example we are to understand שאלה *scheela, petitionem*, as appears from what is expressed in another place, *Petitionem unam ego peto abs te*, 3. Reg. 2. 16.

NEGOTIUM is likewise understood in the following elegant phrases. *Quoad ejus facere poteris. Quoad ejus fieri poterit*, and the like; of which we have made mention above, Sect. 5. ch. 1. n. 5. upon the word *Quoad*. For the infinitive *facere*, or *fieri*, ought there to be considered as a noun, which governs *ejus* in the genitive, sup. *negotii*. Thus, *Quoad ejus facere poteris*; signifies, *quantum poteris ad facere* (for *ad effectum*) *ejus negotii*. And *quoad ejus fieri poterit*, signifies, *quantum ad ejus rei*, or *negotii potestas erit*. As much as possible, as far as there will be a possibility of doing it. And the rest in the same manner. This is what very few seem to have rightly comprehended.

VI. *Antecedent with the relative understood.*

VI. GENERAL MAXIM. Every relative has a relation to the antecedent, which it represents. Therefore it is an ellipsis, when the antecedent, which ought ever to be understood both before and after the relative, is mentioned only before; as *Est pater quem amo*, for *quem patrem amo*: And the ellipsis is double, when the antecedent happens to be neither before nor after, as *Sunt quos arma delectant*, and the like. But we have said enough of both in the rule of the relative, p. 4. and following.

VII. *What is to be understood when the genitive comes after an adjective, or after a verb?*

VII. GENERAL MAXIM. Whenever there comes a genitive after a noun adjective, or after a verb, either it is a Greek phrase, depending on the preposition, or we must understand a general noun by which it is governed: And it is an unquestionable

questionable truth, that neither in Greek or Latin, there is any such thing as verb or adjective, which of itself is capable of governing the genitive. This we have shewn in each particular rule, and what hath been said upon the subject, may be reduced to five principal points.

1. When the adjective is said to be taken substantively, we must ever understand the substantive *negotium, tempus,* or some other particular noun, *Ultimum dimicationis,* Liv. sup. *tempus. Amara curarum,* Hor. sup. *negotia.* Which Lucretius, Tacitus, and Appuleius seem to have particularly affected.

2. When one of the nouns, called correlatives, is understood, *Sophia Septimi,* Cic. sup. *filia. Hectoris Andromache,* Virg. sup. *uxor. Palinurus Phædromi,* Plaut. sup. *servus.*

3. When *causâ,* or *ratione,* is understood, just as the Greeks understand ἕνεκα or χάριν. *Cum ille se custodiæ diceret in castris remansisse,* sup. *causâ.*

4. When mentioning the names of place, we put the genitive after the preposition, *Ad Castoris,* Cic. *In Veneris,* Plaut. sup. *ædem.* In like manner, *Per Varronis,* sup. *fundum. Ex Apollodori,* Cic. sup. *chronicis. Ex feminini sexus descendentes,* sup. *stirpe,* &c.

5. When the genitive is put after the verb, *Est Regis,* sup. *officium. Æstimare litis,* Cæsar. ad Cicer. sup. *causâ. Abesse bidui,* Cic. sup. *itinere. Accusare furti,* sup. *crimine. Est Romæ,* sup. *in oppido.* And others of the same sort, which we have observed in the rules.

But when the genitive plural does not happen to be in the same gender, nor in the same case with its adjective, we ought to understand the noun repeated. *Corruptus vanis rerum,* Hor. that is, *Corruptus vanis rebus rerum;* so that this is the genitive of partition. Just as we read in Livy, *Neque earum rerum esse ullam rem.* Which shews the little reason there has been to call this an Antiphrasis.

VIII. *What we are to understand, when the accusative is by itself.*

VIII. GENERAL MAXIM. Whenever there is an accusative in a sentence, it is governed either by a verb active, or by a preposition (except it agrees with the infinitive, as *me amare.*) Wherefore when we find neither of these, we must supply the deficiency, as *Me miserum,* sup. *sentio.*

But the preposition is much oftener understood, as *Eo spectatum ludos,* for *ad spectatum.* See the chapter on the supines, p. 129. *Pridie Calendas,* for *ante Calendas,* and such like, of which we shall give a list hereafter.

IX. *What we are to understand, when the ablative is by itself.*

IX. GENERAL MAXIM. The ablative is never in a sentence, but when it is governed by a preposition, though frequently this

this preposition is only understood. We have given instances hereof in all the particular rules, and we shall presently give a list of them for the greater convenience of the learner.

X. *Two other very remarkable Ellipses; one where we are to understand the nominative of the verb, and the other where we must supply the verb by the context.*

1. It often falls out that the nominative of the verb is not expressed, and then we must take it by the context; as, *Cujus belli cùm ei summa esset data, eóque cum exercitu profectus esset,* &c. Corn. Nepos, for *eóque is cum exercitu profectus esset. Id cum factum multi indignarentur magnæque esset invidiæ tyranno,* Idem, for *magnæque id factum esset invidiæ,* &c. *Ain tu, te illius invenisse filiam? Inveni, & domi est,* Plaut. for *illa domi est. Dum equites præliantur, Bocchus cum peditibus, quos filius ejus adduxerat, neque in priore pugna adfuerant, postremam Romanorum aciem invadunt,* Sallust. for *neque ii adfuerant,* or else *quique non adfuerant.* Cæsar and Livy abound in such expressions.

2. We are oftentimes obliged to supply a verb in one of the members of a period, not as it is in the other, but quite different, just as the context directs us, as in Virgil;

Disce puer virtutem ex me verúmque laborem,
Fortunam ex aliis. 12. Æn.

Where, as Servius observeth, with *fortunam* we must understand *opta, pete,* or *accipe,* and not *disce,* which goes before, because *fortuna non discitur.* Again.

Sacra manu victósque Deos, parvúmque nepotem
Ipse trahit.

Where *trahit* refers only to *nepotem*; and with *sacra* and *Deos* we must understand *portat.* In like manner, 1. Georg.

Ne tenues pluviæ, rapidíve potentia solis
Acrior, & Boreæ penetrabile frigus adurat.

For the word *adurat* refers extremely well to the sun, and to cold, as Servius takes notice; but as to *tenues pluviæ,* we must understand *noceant,* or some such thing, as Linacer and Ramus have observed. In like manner in Tully, *Fortunâ, quâ illi florentissimâ, nos duriore conflictati videmur.* Where *conflictati* agrees only with the second member, whereas in the first we must understand *usi,* says Scioppius. And in Phædrus, lib. 4. fab. 16. *Non veto dimitti, verùm cruciari fame,* where it is plain, that with the second member we must understand *jubeo, volo,* or the like, and not *veto.* Which is still the more worthy of notice, as it is more contrary to the delicacy of our (the French) language, which does not admit of our making use of a verb that refers to two words or members of a period, unless it can be said separately of either.

It is by this sort of Ellipsis that we must explain a great many passages in the vulgate edition of the scripture, as in St. James, *Glorietur autem frater humilis in exaltatione suâ, dives autem in humilitate suâ,* where, according to the most probable opinion, followed by by Eſtius, we are to underſtand *confundatur* in the ſecond member, and not *glorietur*, which is in the firſt. By this ſame figure Eſtius explaineth this paſſage of St. Paul, *Prohibentium nubere, abſtinere à cibis*, where we muſt underſtand *præcipientium*. And this other, *Per fidem ambulamus, non per ſpeciem*, where *ſtamus* muſt be underſtood, becauſe the word *ambulare* is indeed applicable to thoſe whom the divines call *viatores*, but not to the bleſſed, unleſs it be ſimply to expreſs the happineſs they will have in being every where with Chriſt. *Ambulabunt mecum in albis*, Apocal. 3. The ſame may be ſaid of this other paſſage of the pſalmiſt, *Per diem ſol non uret te, neque luna per noctem:* and of this other of Geneſis, *Die noctuque æſtu urebar*. For neither the moon nor the night have any heat or burning, to occaſion a ſenſible inconveniency. Therefore we muſt underſtand ſome other word. In like manner, *Lac vobis potum dedi, non eſcam*, γάλα ὑμᾶς ἐπότισα καὶ οὐ βρῶμα, as in Homer, οἶνον και σῖτον ἔδοντι, *Vinum & frumentum edentes*, where it is evident that ſomething muſt be underſtood, ſince St. Paul did not mean that we ſhould drink what we eat, nor Homer that we ſhould eat the wine we drink.

But we muſt likewiſe take notice, ſays Linacer, that it is ſometimes almoſt impoſſible to determine which verb ought to be underſtood in order to complete the ſenſe, as in Quintilian, *Si furem nocturnum occidere licet, quid latronem?*

XI. *Of other more remarkable particles that are underſtood.*

We are oftentimes obliged to underſtand *magis* or *potius*; as, *Tacita ſemper eſt bona mulier, quàm loquens*, that is, *magis bona*. *Oratio fuit precibus quàm jurgio ſimilis*, Liv. that is, *magis ſimilis*. Thus the Greeks frequently underſtand μᾶλλον. And thence it is that we find in the Pſalmiſt, *Bonum eſt confidere in Domino, quàm confidere in homine*. And in Terence, *Si quiſquam eſt qui placere cupiat bonis, quàm plurimis*, that is *bonis potius quàm plurimis*.

With *ſimul* we are often to underſtand *ac* or *atque*, as in Virgil, Ecl. 4.

*At ſimul heroum laudes, & facta parentis
Jam legere, & quæ ſit poteris cognoſcere virtus.*

And in Cic. *Itaque ſimul experrecti ſumus, viſa illa contemnimus.*

Si is underſtood when we ſay,

——— *Tu quoque magnam
Partem opere in tanto, ſineret dolor, Icare haberes,* Virg.

——— *Decies centena dediſſes
Huic parco paucis contento, quinque diebus
Nil erat in loculis,* Hor.

Ut is not taken for *quamvis*, as ſome people imagine, but then we underſtand *eſto* or *fac*, as in Ovid, *Protinus ut redeas, facta videbor anus*, that is, *eſto ut ſtatim redeas, tamen*, &c.

Neither is *ut* taken for *utinam*, as when Terence ſays, *Ut Syre te magnus perdat Jupiter*; for we are to underſtand *oro*, or *precor ut*, &c.

When

When we say, *cave, cadas, faxis*, &c. we are to understand *ne*, as it is in Cicero, *Nonne caveam ne scelus faciam*; likewise with the *ne* we are to understand *ut*, according to Vossius and Scioppius, for otherwise this *ne* would not govern the subjunctive. See what hath been said above, in explaining *vereor ne*, p. 162.

What they call the potential or concessive mood may be likewise resolved by this figure, as *Frangas potius quàm corrigas*, that is, *fiet potius ut frangas*, &c. *Vicerit*, that is, *esto ut vicerit*. *Obsit, prosit, nihil curant*, for *an obsit*, &c. In like manner when we say, *Bono animo sis*, it means, *fac ut sis*, &c. *Ames, legas*, that is, *moneo te ut*, or *fac ut ames, legas*, &c.

After *non modò, non solùm, non tantùm*, (provided it does not hurt the sense) we are to understand NON ; as, *Alexander non modò parcus, sed etiam liberalis*, that is *non modò non parcus*. *Ita ut non modò civitas, sed ne vicini quidem proximi sentiant*, Cic. *Non modò illi invidetur ætati, verùm etiam favetur*, Id. Offic. 2. Hence it comes that the *non* is sometimes expressed. *Quia non modò vituperatio nulla, sed etiam summa laus senectutis est*, &c. Concerning which the reader may consult Muretus in his *variæ lectiones*.

The particle NEMPE is oftentimes necessary for resolving several absolute modes of speaking; as, *Sic video philosophis placuisse*; *Nil esse sapientis præstare nisi culpam*, Cic. that is, *nempe nihil esse*, &c. *Cætera verò, quid quisque me dixisse dicat, aut quomodo ille accipiat, aut qua fide mecum vivant ii qui me assiduè colunt & observant, præstare non possum*, Id. that is, *nempe, quid quisque*, &c. *Hoc verò ex quo suspicio nata est, me quæsivisse aliquid in quo te offenderem, translatitium est*, Id. that is, *nempe me quæsivisse*, &c.

These are the most considerable things we had to observe in regard to the figure of Ellipsis, whereby every body is capable of judging of all the rest. For the most general rule that can be given upon this subject is to take notice of the natural and most simple way of speaking, according to the idea we receive from vulgar languages, which oftentimes point out to us what we ought reasonably to understand.

Yet because on those occasions we may be at a loss for words, unless we happen to be very conversant in the language, I shall therefore subjoin three lists. The first shall be of nouns; and the second of verbs, where I do not intend to include all those that may be understood (for this would be too tedious a piece of work) but only the principal ones. The third is to be of prepositions, which generally form most of the governments and connexions of speech in all languages.

XII. FIRST LIST.

Of several nouns understood in Latin authors.

ÆDES is understood, when we say, *Est domi* to the question *Ubi*. See the syntax, rule 25, p. 50. and following.

ÆS is understood, when we say, *Ratio*, or *tabula accepti & expensi*, just as we have shewn that it is also understood, when we say, *Parvi pendo, Non sum solvendo*, &c.

AMBO, when we say, *Mars & Venus capti dolis*, Ovid. *Castor & Pollux alternis orientes & occidentes*. And the

the like. For this is a kind of Ellipsis according to Scioppius; unless we chuse simply to say that then the two singulars are equivalent to a plural, and refer it to the figure of syllepsis, of which hereafter.

AMNIS, when we say, *confluens, profluens, torrens, fluvius.* See the genders, vol. 1. p. 6.

ANIMUS, when we say, *Rogo te ut boni consulas,* that is, *ut statuas hanc rem esse boni animi,* proceeds from a *good will;* though we generally translate it by the person that receives, *I beg you will take this in good part.*

ARS, or SCIENTIA, when we say, *Medicina, Musica, Dialectica, Rhetorica, Fabrica,* &c.

ARVUM, when we say, *novale. Culta novalia,* Virg. But when he says, *Tonsas novales,* we are to understand *terras,* so called *à novando,* says Varro, because they are renewed, or the seed is changed.

BONÆ, when we say, *Homo frugi;* for the antients used to say, *bonæ frugis;* afterwards they said, *bonæ frugi;* and at length *frugi,* by itself, as Sanctius observes.

CAMPUM, when we say, *per apertum ire.*

CARCER, as it was heretofore neuter, ought to be understood, in saying, *Pistrinum, Tullianum,* &c.

CAUSA, in saying, *Exercitum opprimendæ libertatis habet,* Sallust. *Successorum Minervæ indoluit,* Ovid. *Integer vitæ, sceleris purus,* Hor. See the syntax, p. 22.

CARO, when we say, *bubula, vervecina, suilla, ferina,* &c.

CASTRA, when we say, *stativa, hyberna.* See heteroc. vol. 1. p. 161.

CENTENA, when we say, *Debet decies,* or *decies sestertium.* See the chapter on Sesterces, in the particular observations, book 8.

CLITELLAS, when we say, *Imponere alicui,* to impose upon him, to deceive him. For this is properly *treating him as an ass.*

COELUM, when we say, *serenum, purum,* &c.

CONSILIUM, when we say, *Arcanum, secretum, propositum. Perstat in proposito,* &c.

COPIA, when we say, *Eget medicinæ, abundas pecuniarum.*

CORONA, when we say, *Civica donatus; Muralem, Obsidionalem adeptus,* &c. As likewise when we say,

VOL. II.

serta; just as *sertum* refers to *coronamentum,* which we find in Cato and in Pliny.

CRIMINE, or ACTIONE, when we say, *Furti damnatus. Repetundarum postulatus.* See rule 28.

DATUM, when we say, *Non est te fallere cuiquam.*

DIES, when we say, *Illuxit,* or *meus est natalis,* &c.

DII, when we say, *Superi, Inferi, Manes,* &c.

DOMUS, when we say, *Regia, Basilica.*

DOMUM, when we say, *Uxorem duxit.*

EXTA, when we say, *cæsa et porrecta,* as in Cicero, *Ne quid inter cæsa & porrecta, ut aiunt, one vis nobis addatur aut temporis.* That when I shall approach towards the expiration of my time, I may not be troubled with any new protraction of my office.

The metaphor is taken from hence, that when the entrails are cut and drawn out of the belly of the victim, which is what they called CÆSA, the priest, who offered the sacrifice, held and considered them some time before he presented them upon the altar, which is what they called *Porricere.*

FACULTAS, or POTESTAS, when we say, *Cernere erat. Non est te fallere cuiquam,* &c.

FESTA, when we say, *Bacchanalia, Saturnalia, Agonalia.*

FINIS, when we say, *hactenus, quatenus.* For it means, *huc fine tenus.*

FRUMENTA, when we say, *sata;* as *fruges,* when we say, *satæ.*

FUNERA, when we say, *Justa persolvere.*

HOMO, in *adolescens, juvenis, amicus, familiaris;* and whenever the adjective which agreeth with man, is taken absolutely, as *miser sum, salvus sum;* also in *optimates, magnates, mortales, Germani, Galli,* &c.

IDEM, as *Equo ferè qui homini morbi,* Plin. for *ferè idem qui.*

INGENIUM, or INSTITUTUM, or MOREM, when we say, *Antiquum obtines,* Plaut. *Nunc cognosco vestrum tam superbum,* Ter.

IS, for *talis* or *tantus,* is very often understood, as *Homo improbus, sed cui paucos ingenio pares invenias,* for *is cui.*

ITER, when we say, *Quò pergis, quà tendis?* Virgil has even expressed it, *Tendit iter velis portúmque relinquit.*

JUDICES,

JUDICES, when we say *Mittere in consilium*. Whence, according to Asconius, it is taken for *perorare*, when the orator having finished, the judges met in order to gather the votes. *Testibus editis ita mittam in consilium ut*, &c. Cic.

JUDICIO, or JURE, when we say, *falso, merito, immerito*, which are all of them real nouns adjective.

LAPIS, when we say, *Molaris*.

LAUDEM, when we say, *Cur mibi detrabis?*

LIBER, when we say, *annalis, diurnus*. In like manner in the plural.

LIBRI, when we say, *pugillares*. As also when we say *pandectæ*, a Greek word, which Tiro, Cicero's freedman, gave for title to books that he wrote on miscellaneous questions. *Quos Græco titulo*, says Gellius, πανδέκτας *libros inscripsit, tanquam omne rerum atque doctrinarum genus continentes*. And afterwards this very title was conferred on the body of the civil law collected by Justinian, which is otherwise called *Digesta, orum*. Several have doubted of what gender this word *Pandectæ* was, because, as Varro and Priscian have very well observed, the nouns in ης of the first declension of the Greeks, which in that language are masculine, being changed into *a* in Latin, become feminine, as ὁ χάρτης, *hæc charta*. Hence Budeus has said, *Pandectas Pisanas* in the feminine. But Vossius believes that this rule of Priscian will hold good only as to nouns that have no relation to another more general word understood, as in this case *libri*; for which reason he says, *cometa* and *planeta* are masculine, because ἀστήρ is understood. Ant. Aug. H. Stephen, Mekerchus, Andr. Schot, and several others, are of this opinion. And Cujas himself has acknowledged his error, since in his latter works he always put it in the masculine.

LIBRÆ, or LIBRARUM, (genitive singular or plural of *libra*, a pound) when we say, *Corona aurea fuit pondo viginti quinque*, Liv. and the like, that is, *pondo* or *pondere librarum* 25. For *pondo* is only an ablative like *mundo*. See the genders, rule 8, and the heteroclites, list 6.

LINEAS, when we say, *Ad incitas redactus*, reduced to extremity; for *incitæ* comes from *cieo* for *moveo*, because those who play at draughts, being driven to the last row, can stir no further. Hence it is that the men at draughts are called *inciti*, that is, *immobiles*. But where Lucilius said, *Ad incita*, we are to understand *loca*. Hence it is, says St. Isidorus, that they gave the name of *incitæ* to those who had lost all hopes of ever extricating themselves from their misery.

LITERAS, where Cicero says, *Triduo abs te nullus acceperam*. And in this passage of Plautus, *Hodie in ludum occœpi ire litterarum; ternas jam scio*, A. M. O. Where there is no sort of foundation, says Scioppius and Vossius, for taking this word *ternas* for the three conjugations of verbs, as Alvarez has done, just as if a child could learn three conjugations the first day he went to school.

LOCUS, when we say, *Hic senex de proximo: ab humili* (sup. *loco*) *ad summum* (sup. *locum*.) *In medium; convenerunt in unum*, &c. *Primo, secundo, tertio*, &c. sup. *loco*.

LOCA, in the plural, when we say, *Æstiva, hyberna, stativa, pomaria, rosaria, supera, infera*, &c.

LUDI, when we say, *Circenses, Megalesii, Sæculares, Funebres*, &c.

MALUM, when we say, *Caveo tibi, Timeo tibi; Metuo à te, de te, pro te*, &c. But when we say *cavere malo*, we are to understand *se à malo*.

MARE, when we say, *profundum, altum, tranquillum*.

MENSIS, when we say, *Januarius, Aprilis, October*, &c.

MILLE, or rather MILLIA, which supposeth also *negotia*, when we say *decem* or *centum sestertia*, or *denaria*. See the chapter on sesterces in the next book.

MODIA, when we say, *Millia frumenti*.

MODO, in *perpetuo, certo*, &c.

MORTEM, when we say, *obiit*. And it is still usual to say *occumbere mortem*, &c.

NAVIM, when we say *solvit, conscendit, appulit*.

NEGOTIUM. We have already taken notice of this, as one of the most general rules. It may also be observed on this occasion, that this same noun is understood, when we say *tanto, quanto, aliquanto, hoc, eo, quo, multo, paulo, nimio*. For *multo doctior* signifies *multo negotio doctior*; or else *mulia re, multis partibus doctior*. In like manner, when we say, *Qui fieri potest? qui* is an ablative

for

OF THE ELLIPSIS.

for *quo,* that is, *quo modo,* or *quo negotio.*

When *id, quid,* or *aliquid,* are put, *negotium* is understood, those nouns being of their nature adjectives. As we see in Terence, *Andriæ id erat illi nomen.* And in Plautus, *Quid est tibi nomen? Nisi occupo aliquid tibi consilium.*

Even when *quid* governs the genitive *negotii,* still it supposeth *negotium* repeated for its substantive, as *Videri egestas, quid negotii dat homini misero mali,* Plaut. This is as if it were, *Quid negotium mali negotii dat egestas homini misero.* Where *quid negotium negotii* is the same thing as *quæ res rei,* or *rerum,* as in the same author, *Summum Jovem detestor,* said Menechmus: *Qua de re aut cui rei rerum omnium?* answers the old man. And thus Scioppius explains it.

This noun is also understood, when we say, *mille* or *millia,* sup. *negotia;* for *mille* being an adjective, like the other numeral nouns, it must needs have its substantive, concerning which see the chapter on sesterces in the next book.

NUMUS, or NUMERUS, when we say, *denarius, quinarius,* &c.

Also when we say, *quadrans, quincunx, sestertius,* &c.

NUNTIUM, when we say, *Obviam illi misimus.*

NUX, when we say, *avellana, juglans, pinea, persica, castanea,* &c.

OFFICIUM, when we say, *Non est meum,* or *Regium est bene facere.* Also when we say, *Est regis,* &c.

OPERA, when we say, *Bucolica, Georgica, Rhetorica, orum,* &c.

OPUS, when we say, *Hoc non solùm laboris, verùm etiam ingenii fuit.*

ORATIO, when we say, *prosa,* which cometh from *prorsa* for *recta,* the contrary of which is *versa.* For *prorsus* heretofore signified *rectus,* from whence comes *prorsi limites,* in Festus; *Prorsa Dea,* that presided over women in labour.

OSTIUM, when we say, *posticum,* a back-door.

OVES, when we say *bidentes;* hence it is generally feminine in this sense. But if we join it with *verres,* it will be masculine, as in Non. *bidenti verre.*

PARS, when we say, *Antica, postica, decima, quadragesima, primas, secundas,* &c. *Non posteriores feram.* Ter. *Ei secundas defert,* Quint. sup. *partes.* In like manner, *pro rata, pro virili,* sup. *parte.*

PASSUS, when we say, *Ire duo millia,* Mart. *Latitudo septingentorum millium,* Cæf.

PRÆDIUM, when we say, *suburbanum, Tusculanum,* &c.

PUER or PUELLA, when we say *infans;* for this word is an adjective: hence it is, that in Valerius Maximus we find *puerum infantem,* that could not speak.

RASTER, when we say, *bidens, tridens,* &c.

RATIO, when we say, *expensa, impensa, summa;* just as we understand *rationes,* when we say *conturbare,* to confound one's accounts, and to use some fraud, either towards the master or towards the creditors, to make them lose their turn, and to pay the last before the first.

REM FAMILIAREM, when we say, *decoquere,* to squander away his estate, to turn bankrupt; whence also we have *decoctor,* a bankrupt.

SERMO, in these familiar phrases of Cicero's, *Brevi dicam. Complecti brevi. Brevi respondere. Circumscribi & definiri brevi,* sup. *sermone.* And when he says, *Brevibus agere, brevibus aliquid dicere,* sup. *sermonibus* or *verbis,* in short, in a few words.

SERVUS or MINISTER, when we say, *Est illi à pedibus,* or *circum pedes, à manu* or *ad manum, à secretis, à libellis,* &c.

SESTERTIUM, (for *sestertiorum*) when we say *centum millia.* And both are understood when we reckon by the adverb, as *debet mihi decies,* and the like. See the chapter on sesterces in the next book.

SIGNUM, when we say, *bellicum* or *classicum canere.*

SINGULI, when we say, *in naves, in annos, in horas,* &c.

SOLUM, when we say, *Terræ defigitur arbor,* Virg. sup. *in solo.* Hence in Sallust. *Arbores quæ humi arido atque arenoso nascuntur,* that is, *in solo humi arido,* &c.

TABELLÆ, when we say, *in eboreis, laureatis,* &c. For heretofore the tablets or table-books took their name either from the matter they were made of, or from the number of leaves. As *eboreæ, citreæ, duplices, triplices,* &c. *Laureatæ,* were those which the emperors used to send to the senate after obtaining a victory.

TABERNA, when we say, *medicina, sutrina, textrina, tonstrina, fabrica, salina, laniana*, &c. which are all adjectives. See *pistrinum* in the heter. vol. 1. p. 137.

TABULIS, when we say *in duodecim*. For the twelve tables were the fundamental laws of the Roman republic.

TEMPUS, when we say *ex'eo, ex quo, ex illo: Ex illo fluere res Danaum*, Virg. *Tertio, quarto, extremo*, &c. *Optato, brevi, sero*, &c. *Tertium consul, postremum ad me venit*, &c. *Hâc noctis, id ætatis*, &c. *Antehac, posthac,* (*hac* is here taken for *hæc.*) *Antea, postea, præterea, post illa*, sup. *tempora*. Cicero hath even expressed it, *Post illa tempora quicunque remp. agitavere*, &c. *Non licebat nisi præfinito loqui*, sup. *tempore, Prope adest cum alieno more vivendum est mibi*, Ter. sup. *tempus. Erit cùm fecisse nolles*, sup. *tempus*. And an infinite number of the like sort.

TERRA, when we say, *patria continens*. Likewise when we say, *jacet humi*, instead of *in terra humi*. For the earth is divided *in aquam & humum*, according to Varro. In like manner, when we say, *Natus est Ægypti*, sup. *in terra*. See r. 25. p. 50.

VADA, when we say, *brevia*, shallows, flats.

VASA, when we say, *fictilia, vitrea, crystallina*. Just as

VAS, when we say, *atramentarium, salinum*.

VERBA. *Docere paucis*, Virg. sup. *verbis. Responsum paucis reddere*, Id. *Pro re pauca loquar*, Id. *paucis te volo*, Ter. sup. *verbis alloqui*. As also, *Paucis est quod te volo*, for *Est negotium propter quod paucis te verbis alloqui volo. Dicere pauca*, sup. *verba. Respondere pauca*, Hor. &c.

VIA, when we say, *hac, illac, istac, qua, ea, recta*, &c. *Appia, Aurelia*, &c. As also *viam*, when we say, *ire, ingredi*. Virgil has even expressed it, *Itque reditque viam*, &c..

VINUM, when we say, *mustum, merum, Falernum, Massicum*, &c. which are nouns adjectives.

VIR, UXOR, or FEMINA, when we say, *conjux, maritus*, or *marita*. And in the plural, *optimates, magnates, primates, majores*, &c. sup. *viri* or *feminæ*.

VIRGA, when we say, *rudem accipere*, that is, to be discharged from further business. For one of the ways of discharging was by the prætor's putting a rod or wand on the head of the person whom he discharged or released, and this rod was called *rudis*, from its being rough and unwrought. It had also the name of *festuca*, as likewise of *vindicta*, because by this method, *servi vindicabantur in libertatem*. Hence cometh *rude donatus*, discharged from all exercise or business, because when a gladiator came to be excused from fighting any more, they used to give him one of those rods.

URBS, when we say, *natus Romæ* for *in urbe Romæ*. See rule 25. p. 50.

UTILE or COMMODUM, when we say *consulo tibi? prospicio mibi*, &c.

It may likewise be observed on this occasion, that it is a kind of Ellipsis, at least according to Sanctius and Scioppius, when we do not follow the gender of the termination in particular nouns, but only the gender of the signification in regard to the common and general term. As,

In names of trees, *Delphica laurus, patula fagus, tarda morus*, &c. sup. *arbor*.

In the names of herbs, *Dictamnum pota sagittas pellit*, Plin. *Centunculus trita aceto*, sup. *herba*, Idem.

In the names of provinces, islands, towns, and others, concerning which see what has been said when treating of genders, rule 3, 4, 5, and 6.

But then with the Ellipsis, there is also a Syllepsis, as we shall shew hereafter, p. 189.

XIII. SECOND LIST.
Of several verbs understood.

ASPICIO or VIDEO, when we say, *En quatuor ædes, Ecce hominem, En Priamum.* But if we put the nominative *Ecce homo, en Priamus,* we are to understand *adest* or *venit,* or the like.

AMET or ADJUVET, when we say, *Mehercule, Mecastor, Medius fidius,* (heathen forms of swearing, which Christians ought not to make use of) that is, *Me Hercules, Me Deus Fidius amet* or *adjuvet.* And Cicero himself informs us, that *me-hercule* was said for *Me Hercules.*

Thus *Edepol* is composed of three words, that is of *e* for *me, de* for *Deus,* and *pol* for *Pollux,* sup. *adjuvet.* But we likewise say *epol,* that is, *me Pollux,* sup. *adjuvet.* So that it is a mistake to write *ædepol* with an *æ,* as practised by those who pretend that it means, *quasi per ædem Pollucis,* which is not true.

CANERE, when we say, *Sci· fidibus.*

COEPIT, when we say, *Ire prior Pallas,* and the like. See the Syntax, p. 34. and the figurative Syntax, p. 170.

DICI, when we say, *Malè audit,* he has a bad character. For it signifies *malè audit de se,* or *in se,* or *sibi dici;* so that *malè* does not refer to *audit,* but to *dici,* which is understood. In like manner, when we say, *Audit bonus, audit doctus,* it implies, *audit dici esse bonus,* according to the Greek construction which we explained in the 5th rule, p. 14.

DICO, when we say, *Bona verba quæso,* sup. *dic. Nugas,* sup. *dicis. Sed hæc hactenus, de his hactenus,* sup. *dixerimus,* or *dictum sit. Quid multa?* sup. *dico verba.*

ESSE, or FUISSE, or FORE, when we say, *Factum illi volo. Ne dicas non prædictum. Promisi ultorem,* sup. *me fore,* &c.

ESTO, or FAC, DA, or PONE, when we say, *Hæc negotia, ut ego absim, confici possunt,* that is, *posito ut ego absim,* or *esto,* or *fac ut,* &c. *Bono sit animo,* or *in animo.*

FACIO, when we say, *Dii meliora,* sup. *faciant. Studet, an piscaris, an venaris, an omnia simul?* sup. *facit. Illa nocte nihil præterquam vigilatum est in urbe,* that is, *nihil factum est præterquam,* &c.

IRE, when we say, *In Pompeianum cogito. Rhodum volo, inde Athenas,* &c.

LOQUI, when we say, *Scit Latinè, Græcè,* &c. See p. 34.

MONEO, or FAC UT, when we say, *amcis, legas; amctis, legatis; Istud ne dicas; Illud cogites tecum; Nihil mihi rescribas.*

OBSECRO, IMPLORO, or NUNCUPO, when we say, *Proh D.ûm atque hominum fidem.* See the Syntax, rule 35. p. 74.

ORO UT, or PRECOR UT, when we say, *Dii meliora ferant. Ut te perdat Jupiter. Qui illi Dei irati sint,* where *qui* signifies *ut,* or rather *quo,* sup. *modo.* See the remarks on the pronouns, ch. 1. n. 5. p. 93. and remarks on the adverbs, n. 2. p. 145.

PARO, INVENIO, or the like, when we say, *Unde mihi lapidem? Martis signum, quo mihi pacis autori?* &c.

SUM, ES, EST, is frequently understood: *Quid mihi tecum?* sup. *est. Haud mora* (sup. *est*) *festinant jussi. Hei mihi, væ tibi,* sup. *est.* See r. 35. p. 74. *Quænam* (*malum*) *ista servitus voluntaria,* sup. *est.*

TIMEO, *cave, vide,* or the like, when we say, *Ab te ne frigora lædant. At ut satis contemplata sis. Verùm ne quid illa titubet,* &c.

XIV. THIRD LIST.
Of prepositions that are to be understood.

A, AB, AD, IN, ought to be understood with the names of large places or provinces, where they are not expressed, as *Ægypto remeans,* Tac. sup. *ab. Degit Carthagine,* sup. *in.* See the Syntax, rule 25, p. 48.

A, AB, are also understood with nouns signifying cause, instrument, trouble, &c. as, *Culpâ pallescere, Ense perforatus, Plectere capite,* &c. See the Syntax, rule 32, p. 70. With nouns of time, when they signify *after,* as *Rediit hoste superato,* after having overcome the enemy, which is what we call the ABLATIVE ABSOLUTE. See the 34th rule, p. 72.

With nouns signifying difference, or distance, as *Stulto intelligens quid interest; Abest virtute illius.* See the 30th rule, p. 66.

When we would signify only a part

part; *animo otiosus*, for *ab animo*, in regard to the mind. *Multis rebus melior*, for *à multis rebus*. See the 32d rule, p. 69.

AD is understood in expressing measure or space. *Latus quinque pedes*. See the 26th rule, p. 53.

In expressing the end one aims at, *Quid frustrà laboramus*; for *ad quid*. *Eamus visum* or *visere*, for *ad visum* or *ad visere*. See the remarks on the supines, n. 3. p. 132.

Also when we say *Cætera lætus*, for *quoad cætera*, and the like. See the annotation to the 24th rule, p. 45.

ANTE, with nouns signifying time, *Pridie Kalendas*, sup. *ante*. *Multos abhinc annos* sup. *ante*. See the 26th rule, p. 53, and following.

CIRCA, when speaking of time, as *Tu homo id ætatis*, that is, *circa id ætatis*.

CUM, when speaking of instruments, *Sagittâ saucius*. See the 32d rule, p. 70.

When we say, *officio, honore, odio, persequi*, and the like, &c. For it is the same signification as when Cicero saith, *Cum equis persecuti sunt*.

To express time, *cras, prima luce*. Instead of which Terence hath, *Cras cum primo lucu*. But with time we may likewise understand *in*. See the 26th rule, p. 53.

DE, E, EX, with nouns that express plenty, or want, or the subject, as *Nugis referti libri*. *Plenus vino*. *Equus ligno fabre factus*. *Sacrificare tauro vel agno*, &c. See the 28th rule, p. 62.

With the names of place that express departure, *Exire Româ, Italiâ cedere*. See the 25th rule, p. 48.

With nouns signifying time, as *noctu* or *nocte*. *Horâ primâ, Tertiâ vigiliâ*. See the 26th rule, p. 53.

With nouns that denote the cause or manner, *Flere alicujus obitu*; *victitare lolio*; *quare fit qua de re*, &c. See the 32d rule, p. 70.

In like manner, *laboro dolore*, for *à dolore*. *Amoris abundantiâ hoc feci*. *Virtute clarus*, &c.

Also, *Lege agere cum aliquo*. *Vocare aliquem nomine*, &c.

IN, with nouns signifying place, whether in the ablative or the accusative, as *Domo me contineo*, Cic. *Sardiniam venit*, Cic. See the 25th rule, p. 48.

With nouns signifying time, whether in the ablative or the accusative. See the 26th rule, p. 53.

and following.

With nouns that denote the subject or object, as *Opus est mihi libris*, for *in libris*. See the annotation to the 28th rule, p. 63.

With nouns that denote the cause, *Accusat me eo quod*, &c. for *in eo quod*.

With nouns that express the state or condition, *Sum magno timore*, for *in magno timore*. *Magna est apud omnes gloriâ*. *De pace nec nullâ, nec magnâ spe sumus*, &c.

With nouns that denote the means to attain the end, as *Libris me oblecto*. *Ludis delectari*, &c.

With nouns that denote order and arrangement, as *Ordine aliquid facere* or *collocare*.

With nouns that denote a particular thing. *Non armis præstantior quàm togâ*.

OB or PROPTER is oftentimes understood, when an infinitive supplieth the place of an accusative, that denotes the cause or end, as *Accipio dolorem mihi illum irasci*, that is, *ob irasci*, See the remarks on the verbs, chap. 2. n. 10. p. 113, 114.

Quod is frequently governed by the same prepositions, when we say, *Quod ego te per hanc dexteram oro*, Cic. that is, *propter quod*. *Quod utinam minus vitæ cupidus fuissem*, for *quam-ob-rem*. See the remarks on the adverbs, n. 3. p. 146.

PER is frequently understood with nouns signifying time or distance, *Vixit centum annos*. *Distat quinque milliaria*. See the 26th rule, p. 53.

Also with nouns signifying a part, *hirsutus brachia*, for *per brachia*, and the like, of which we have taken notice, in the annotation to the 24th rule, p. 45. and shall take further notice hereafter when we come to treat of the figure of Hellenism.

PRÆ in comparisons, *Doctior cæteris*, for *præ cæteris*, &c. See the 27th rule, p. 55. and following.

To express the cause, *Homini lacrymæ cadunt gaudio*, Ter. that is, *præ gaudio*.

PRO, with nouns signifying price, *Emi magno*, that is, *pro magno pretio*. *Aureus unus valet decem argenteis*, that is, *pro decem*. See the 29th rule, p. 66.

SUB, with the ablative called absolute, especially when it denotes some post, condition, dignity, or pre-eminence, as *Te consule, Ipso teste, Aristotele autore, sole ardente*, &c. See the 34th rule, p. 72.

CHAP.

Chapter II.

Of the second sort of ellipsis, called ZEUGMA.

HITHERTO we have treated of the first sort of ellipsis, where we are obliged to understand some word which is not at all mentioned in the sentence. The second sort is, when the word has been already mentioned, and yet is again understood once or oftener. This is called

ZEUGMA, a Greek word that signifieth *connection* or *assemblage*, because under a single word are comprized several other nouns that depend thereon; and of this there are three sorts.

I. *A word understood as it was expressed before.*

The first is, when we repeat the noun or verb, in the same manner it has been already expressed. Donatus gives the following example hereof from the 3d book of the Æneid:

Trojugena interpres Divûm, qui numina Phoebi,
Qui tripodas, Clarii lauros, qui sydera sentis,
Et volucrum linguas, & præpetis omina pennæ.

For *sentis* is expressed but once, and ought to be understood five times.

It is however to be observed, that when we do not repeat the word that has been expressed, but understand a new one, it is not merely a zeugma, but an ellipsis, as already hath been observed, p. 168.

II. *A word understood otherwise than it was expressed before.*

The second sort of *zeugma*, is when the word expressed cannot be repeated without receiving some alteration.

1. Either in gender, *Et genus, & virtus nisi cum re vilior alga est*, Hor. *Utinam aut hic surdus, aut hæc muta facta sit*, Ter.

2. Or in case, *Quid ille fecerit quem neque pudet quicquam, nec metuit quemquam, nec legem se putat tenere ullam?* Ter. for *qui nec metuit*, &c.

3. Or in number, *Sociis & rege recepto*, Virg. *Hic illius arma, hic currus fuit*, Id. *Tutatur favor Euryalum lacrymæque decoræ*, Id.

4. Or in person, *ille timore, ego risu corrui*, Cic. *Quamvis ille niger, quamvis tu candidus esses*, Virg.

III. *A word understood in the enumeration of parts.*

The third is, when after a word which includes the whole, a distribution of the parts is made without repeating the verb, as *Aquilæ volarunt, hæc ab oriente, illa ab occidente*, Cic. *Consules profecti, Valerius in Campaniam, Cornelius in Samnium*, Liv. *Bestiæ aliæ mares, aliæ feminæ*, Cic. Where we may observe how wrong it is to say, that on such occasions we are always obliged to use the genitive of partition, as *bestiarum aliæ*, &c.

IV. *Elegance to be observed in regard to the Zeugma.*

It is sometimes extremely elegant to understand the same word under a different meaning; as *Tu colis barbam, ille patrem. Nero si stuit matrem, Æneas patrem*, &c.

※——————————————————※

CHAPTER. III.
Of the second figure called PLEONASM.

A PLEONASM is when there happens to be a word more than is necessary, as *majis majores nugas agere*, Plaut. where *magis* is superfluous. *Se ab omnibus desertos potius, quàm abs te defensos esse malunt*, Cic. Where *potius* is superfluous, because of the force of the word *malo*.

In the same manner in Cicero, *Omnia quæcunque.* In Terence, *Nibil quicquam*, where *omnia* and *quicquam* are superfluous.

Likewise when a noun is joined to a pronoun, in the same period, *Sed urbana plebs, ea verò præceps erat multis de causis*, Sall. *Postbumius autem, de quo nominatim senatus decrevit ut statim in Ciliciam iret, Fusanoque succederet, is negat se iturum sine Catone*, Cic. ad Att. for *is* is altogether redundant in this passage, unless it be to render the sentence more elegant and perspicuous. For which reason those pronouns are often repeated in French.

Also when there are two particles in a period, that have the same force, as *Oportuit præscisse me ante*, Ter. *Nos metipsos*, Cic. *Nullam esse alteram*, Plaut. *Quis alter, quis quisquam*, &c. or two negatives that make but one, as *neque nescio*, and others, of which we have taken notice already, p. 155.

In a word, whatever is inserted in a sentence without any dependence on the sense or government, is called a pleonasm.

But it is to be observed that sometimes what we look upon as abundant, was inserted by the antients, for the sake of elegance, strength, or perspicuity; and therefore is not really abundant.

We must likewise take notice that some grammarians happening not to understand sufficiently the real causes of government, give us as a pleonasm what is indeed a most simple and natural expression; as when Linacer says that *Venit ad Messenam*, in Cicero, *Ab Roma abire*, in Sallust, and the like, are pleonasms; whereas the construction depends intirely on the preposition, as we have shewn in the 25th rule and following, and when it is not expressed, it is an ellipsis.

Thus *vivere vitam, gaudere gaudium, furere furorem, servire servitutem*, and the like, may indeed be called pleonasms, in regard to the use of authors and to the sense, because the verb by itself signifies as much as when joined with those others words: though with respect to the construction, it is rather an ellipsis, when they are not expressed, as we have already observed, chap. 2. n. 3. But when an adjective is added, as *longam vivere vitam, duram servire servitutem*, it is then no longer a pleonasm even according to the sense, because the verbs *vivere* and *servire* do not by themselves imply this meaning

OF THE SYLLEPSIS. 185

In like manner the pronouns, *mihi, tibi, sibi,* are oftentimes taken for a pleonasm, when they are only the real dative of relation; as *me, se, te,* the real accusative, necessary in construction, *Qui mihi, tum fiunt senes,* Ter. *Mihi,* that is, *in respect to me. Me id facere studeo,* Plaut. *me facere* is only the real construction of the infinitive; and if it were simply *studeo facere,* it would be an ellipsis, where we should be obliged to understand *me*; and in like manner the rest.

CHAPTER IV.

Of the third figure called SYLLEPSIS.

SYLLEPSIS or conception, is when we conceive the sense different from the import of the words, and thus the construction is formed according to the meaning, and not to the words. This figure is of very great use for the right understanding of authors, and may be divided into two sorts according to Scioppius, one simple or absolute, and the other relative.

I. *The simple Syllepsis.*

The simple syllepsis is when the words in a sentence differ either in gender, or number, or both.

1. In gender, as when Livy saith, *Samnitium duo millia cæsi,* and not *cæsa,* because he refers it to *homines.* There were two thousand Samnites slain. *Duo millia crucibus affixi,* Curt. *Duo millia electi qui mori juberentur,* Flor. and such like; where we may see that L. Valla had no foundation to find fault with these scriptural phrases, *Duo millia signati,* &c.

And when Horace saith, *Daret ut catenis fatale monstrum, quæ generosius perire quærens,* &c. he put *quæ,* because by *monstrum* he meaneth Cleopatra. Thus it is we find *Duco importuna prodigia, quos egestas,* &c. Cic. *Potius quàm istam à me operam impetres, quod postulas,* Plaut. *Ubi est scelus qui me perdidit?* Ter. And in one of the hymns of advent.

> *Verbum supernum prodiens,*
> *A patre olim exiens,*
> *Qui natus orbi subvenis;*
> *Cursu declivi temporis.*

Verbum qui, because *verbum* is the same as *Filius Dei;* especially, after having mentioned the father. Hence it is when Urban VIII. set about revising the hymns, he did not chuse to alter this expression, but only corrected the second verse, where the measure was not observed, and put *E patris æterni sinu.* And I remember this gave occasion to a person to find fault with that Pope for leaving a solecism in this hymn; so dangerous is it to be only a smatterer in learning, and have but a slender knowledge of the real principles of the Latin tongue.

2. In number. There is also a disagreement in number, as *turba ruunt,* Virg. because the word *turba,* though a singular, includes a multitude. And in like manner, *Alterum in alterius*
mactatos

mactatos sanguine cernam, Virg. *Ut alter alterum nec opinato viderimus*, Cic. *Missi magnis de rebus uterque legati*, Hor.

Propterea quod, for *propter id quod*. In the same manner as Plautus said, *amor amara dat tibi satis quod ægrè sit*. And Cic. *Si tempus est ullum jure hominis necandi quæ multa sunt.* QUID *enim fuit in illis literis, præter querelam temporum*, QUÆ *non animum meum magis sollicitum haberent quam tuum?* Cic. *Quæ* for *quod*, referring to *quid. Servitia repudiabat cujus initio ad eum magnæ copiæ concurrebant*, Sall. in Catil. that is *cujus servitii*, for *servitium* is taken there for slaves, as Cicero hath put it, *cœptum esse in Sicilia moveri servitium*.

In like manner Terence says, *Aperite aliquis ostium*, which agrees very well with the French language, *ouvrez la porte quelqu'un*, that is, *ouvrez la porte* (speaking to them all) *& que quelqu'un de vous l'ouvre*. It is likewise by this figure that the same poet saith, according to Ramus and Scioppius, *absente nobis*, and Plautus, *præsente nobis*.

3. In gender and number, as *Pars in carcerem acti, pars bestiis objecti*, Sall. *Pars mersi tenuere ratem*, Virg. *Alterum in alterius mactatos sanguine cernam*, Virg. *Mars & Venus capti*, Ovid.

But that which is formed with the preposition *cum*, seemeth somewhat bolder, and is tolerated rather in the writings of poets, than of orators: *Ilia cum Niso de Numitore sati*, Ovid. *Syrus cum illo vestro susurrant*, Ter. *Divellimur inde Iphitus & Pelias mecum*, Virg. *Remo cum fratre Quirinus—jura dabunt*, Id. Yet Cicero has also made use of it, *Dicæarchum verò cum Aristoxeno æquali & condiscipulo suo, doctos sanè homines relinquamus*. And Q. Curtius, *Pharnabasus cum Appollonide & Athenagora vincti traduntur*, lib. 4. In like manner an excellent anthor has wrote thus in French, *laissant sa mere avec sa femme & ses enfans prisonniers*.

II. *The relative Syllepsis.*

The relative syllepsis, is when we refer the relative to an antecedent that has not been expressed, but of which we form an idea by the meaning of the whole sentence. *Inter alia prodigia etiam carne pluit, quem imbrem aves feruntur rapuisse*, Liv. The reference is here made to *imber*, which has not been expressed, but is included in the word *pluit*, as if it were *carnis imber pluit*. In like manner, *Per literas me consolatus sum, quem librum ad te mittam*, Cic. Where *per literas* is taken for the composition or work which he promises to send. *Mithridaticum verò bellum, magnum atque difficile, & in multa varietate terra marique ver,atum, totum ab hoc expressum est, qui libri non modo L. Lucullum fortissim. & clarissim. virum, verùm populi Romani nomen illustrant*, Cic. where *qui libri* refers to his work, which is included in these terms, *bellum expressum est*.

De Prætiana hereditate, quæ quidem mihi magno dolori est (valde enim illum amavi,) hoc velim cures, Cic. here *illum* refers to Pretius his friend whom he has not mentioned, but who is included in these words, *Prætiana hæreditate*. *Sed antea conjuravere pauci contra rempublic. in quibus Catilina fuit, de qua quambrevissimè potero dicam*, Sall.

That

That is, *de qua conjuratione*, says Sanctius.
> ——— *Et laudare fortunas meas,*
> *Qui gnatum haberem tali ingenio præditum*, Ter.

That is, *meas hominis qui*, &c.
> *Nam Sextianus dum volo esse conviva,*
> *Orationem in Attium petitorem*
> *Plenam veneni & pestilentiæ legit*, Catul. Carm. 45.

Where we must understand *ille*, that is *Sextius*, for the nominative of *legit*. For this nominative is included in the adjective *Sextianus*; and it is just as if it were, *Nam Sextii ipse dum volo esse conviva*, &c. Deinde *Philenorum aræ, quem locum habuere Carthaginenses*, Sall. where we must understand *locus* by apposition, as if it were *Aræ locus, quem locum*, &c. Likewise in Virgil,
> *Interea socios, inhumatáque corpora terræ*
> *Mandemus, qui solus honos Acheronte sub imo est.*

Where *honos* is the apposition of *mandare corpora terræ*. Again,
> ——— *Hortamur fari quo sanguine cretus,*
> *Quidve ferat memret, quæ sit fiduciq capto*, Æn. 2.

That is, *quæ hortatio sit fiducia capto*, in order to encourage him to speak. And in Cicero, *Atque in hoc genere illa quoque est infinita silva, quod oratori plerique duo genera ad dicendum dederunt*, 2. de Orat. where *quod* supposeth *negotium*. For the meaning is, *Quod negotium*, nempe *silvam* illam *infinitam, plerique dederunt oratori, tanquam duo genera ad dicendum*.

To this relative syllepsis we must likewise refer these modes of speaking by short parentheses, which are so graceful in the Latin language, and include a relative that has no other antecedent but the very thing expressed before; as *quare quoniam hæc à me sic petis, ut (quæ tua potestas est) id neges me invito usurum*, Cic. ad Attic. *Tamen (quæ tua suavitas est; quique in me amor) nolles à me hoc tempore æstimationem accipere*, Id. ad Rufum: that is, τὸ *nolle accipere quæ tua suavitas est*, &c. Where we see that the relative being between two nouns of different genders, agrees here with the latter, according to what was observed in the rule of the relative, p. 6.

To this figure also we must refer a great many obscure passages of the vulgate, where the pronoun relatives do not refer to the nearest noun, but to some other more distant, or which is understood; as *Præcipiens* Jesus *duodecim apostolis suis, transiit inde ut doceret & prædicaret in civitatibus eorum*, Matt. 11. where *eorum* refers to *Judæorum*, and not to the apostles who are mentioned immediately before. *Cum loquitur mendacium* (Diabolus) *ex propriis loquitur, quia mendax est, & pater ejus,* (sup. *mendacii*) Joan. 8. *Et erant pharisæi & legis doctores*, &c. *& virtus Domini erat ad sanandum eos*, Luc. 5. that is, the great multitudes mentioned before, and not the pharisees. You may likewise see S. Matt. c. 12. v. 9. S. Luke c. 4. v. 15. and the 98th psalm v. 8.

The relative adverb is sometimes resolved by the same figure, as in this passage of Job in the vulgate, *Nudus egressus sum de utero matris meæ, & nudus revertar illuc*. Where *illuc* does not refer to the preceding word, which is *uterus*, but to another understood, which is the earth, or the dust.

Chapter V.

That the Syllepsis is frequently joined with another figure, and of some difficult passages which ought to be referred thereto.

WE are also to observe that the syllepsis is frequently joined with other figures, as with the zeugma, the ellipsis, and the hyperbaton; and this is what renders it more strange and difficult. Hereto we might refer some of the passages cited in the precedent chapter; but we must illustrate the matter further by more particular examples.

I. *Syllepsis with a Zeugma.*

It is joined with a zeugma, when the adjective or relative does not refer to the gender of the nearest substantive, but to some other that precedeth; as *Amor tuus ac judicium de me, utrùm mihi plus dignitatis in perpetuum, an voluptatis quotidie sit allaturus, non facilè dixerim,* Plancus Ciceroni, where *allaturus* refers only to *amor tuus*, so that we must understand *allaturum* once more, along with *judicium.* In like manner, *Gens cui natura corpora animósque magis magna quàm firma dedit,* Liv. *Pedes ejus præcisos & caput & manus in cistam chlamyde opertos pro munere natalitio matri misit,* Valer. Max. *Ne fando quidem auditum est crocodilum aut ibim aut felem violatum ab Ægyptio,* Cic. 1. de natur. where he makes the construction in the masculine, though *feles*, which is the latter word, be of the feminine, as we have already shewn when treating of the heteroclites, vol. 1. p. 142. col. 2. *Quin etiam vites à caulibus brassicísque si prope sati sint, ut à pestiferis & nocentibus refugere dicuntur, nec eos ulla ex parte contingere,* 2. de natur. where he likewise makes the construction in the masculine, because of *caulis,* masc. though *brassica,* the latter, be feminine. *Cœlum ac terra ardere visum,* Jul. Obsequens. *Philippi vim atque arma toti Græciæ cavendam metuendámque esse,* Gell. as H. Stephen reads it, and as it is quoted by Saturnius and Sanctius. And in Virgil,

Me puer Ascanius, capitísque injuria cari,
Quem regno Hesperiæ fraudo.

Where he puts *quem,* though *caput,* the latter word, be of the neuter gender.

Thus in the second *de Natur. Deor.* by the same figure Cicero saith, *Ex æthere igitur innumerabiles* FLAMMÆ *siderum existunt, quorum est princeps sol,* &c. *Deinde reliqua* SIDERA *magnitudinibus immensis. Atque hi tanti* IGNES *tamque multi, non modò nihil nocent terris, rebúsque terrestribus; sed ita prosunt, ut si* MOTA *loco sint, conflagrare terras necesse sit à tantis ardoribus.* Where *mota,* which we find in the best copies, refers to *sidera* and not to *ignes*, which is the latter word. But if we read *motæ* in the feminine, according to Lambinus, we must needs refer it to *flammæ,* which is only in the beginning of the precedent period, and then this figure will be still more extraordinary.

And

And it may further be observed that this same figure is also practised in regard to the verb, when after two different nouns, it is not put in the plural so as to follow the noblest person, nor made to agree with the latter person, though it be put in the singular, as *Ego & populus Rom. bellum indico facióque*, Liv. not *indicit* nor *indicimus*, &c.

II. *With an entire Ellipsis.*

And though these constructions seem very extraordinary, yet there are others still more surprizing, when this figure is joined with an intire ellipsis, that is, when we must understand a word that has not been at all expressed, which happens particularly on two occasions.

1. When we make the construction and the reference in the worthiest gender, pursuant to what hath been explained, in the 4th rule, p. 9. though departing intirely from the gender of the noun expressed, as when Virgil saith, *Timidi Damæ*, *Talpæ oculis capti*, which he could not say without understanding *masculi*, with those epicenes of the feminine.

Thus Cicero saith, *Quod si hæc apparent in bestiis volucribus, agrestibus, natantibus, suibus, cicuribus, feris, primum ut se ipsi diligant*, &c. Where it is remarkable that he put *ipsi* in the masculine, though there is nothing before it to which it can be referred but to *bestiæ*, since all the other nouns refer to it, either as adjectives, or as substantives of the common gender, put by apposition. And Virgil:

Hinc pecudes, armenta, viros, genus omne ferarum,
QUEMQUE *sibi tenues nascentem arcessere vitas.*

We might mention a great many other examples of the same sort: and it may likewise be observed, that when we take the common and general noun, to refer to, rather than to the particular noun which has been expressed, this is also a syllepsis joined with an ellipsis; as *in suam Eunuchum*, sup. *fabulam*. *Centauro invehitur magna*, sup. *navi*, &c. Which is sufficient to shew that the Latin tongue hath its irregularities, or rather its figures in gender and construction, as well as the Greek; and that no expression is used in either without some grounds, or reason.

2. The second case where the syllepsis is joined with an ellipsis, is, says Scioppius, when understanding the attribute or subject of a preposition, we take the gender of the word expressed, for that of the other understood, to which it refers notwithstanding; as if holding a diamond in my hand, I were to say, *Hæc est gemma*, where *hæc* without doubt would refer to *adamas*, though masculine. And this construction occurs quite at length in Virgil, where he says:

——— *Facilis descensus Averni,*
Sed revocare gradum, superasque evadere ad auras,
Hoc opus, hic labor est.

Where *hic labor*, as well as *hoc opus*, refers to τὸ *revocare* and τὸ *evadere*. And Cicero has used it in the same manner, where he says, *Solum igitur quod se movet* . . . . . . *hic fons, hoc principium est movendi,*

movendi, in Somn. Where *quod se movet*, (what is self-moved) is the subject to which *hic fons*, and *hoc principium* refers. Thus it is elegant to say, *Hic error est, non scelus*, that is, *hoc negotium est error, & non est scelus*. We say, *Hic est panis qui de cœlo descendit*, that is, *hæc res est panis qui*, &c. And in like manner addeth Scioppius, *Hic est sanguis meus; hoc est corpus meum*, for *hæc res est sanguis meus; hæc res est corpus meum*, &c.

But this relative syllepsis occurreth also in regard to the attribute, when it is evidently understood, and yet without being referred to, as when we say, *Leo est animalium fortissimus; homo animalium divinissimus*, it seems that we ought necessarily to understand *animal: leo*, or *homo est animal*, &c. So that we conceive the neuter gender, which would require us to put *fortissimum, divinissimum*, &c. though we oftener use the masculine, that is, the gender of the substantive expressed, according to what has been observed in the rule of the partitive, p. 59.

III. *With an Hyperbaton.*

The syllepsis is joined with an hyperbaton (of which we shall treat presently) when in a sense bordering on that above explained, there is likewise an inversion of the order of words. As in the passage of Tertullian, of which the protestants have attempted to avail themselves, where he says, *Acceptum panem & distributum discipulis corpus suum illum fecit, hoc est corpus meum, dicendo, id est figura corporis mei: figura autem*. &c. where it is plain that *figura corporis mei*, is only the explication of the subject of the proposition, as Cardinal du Perron proveth admirably well in his book on the eucharist. For it means, *hoc* or *hæc res, id est figura corporis mei*, this thing which is the legal figure of my body, *est corpus meum*, is my body. For it is certain that otherwise there would be no sense or meaning in what follows.

Chapter VI.
Of the fourth figure called Hyperbaton.

AN hyperbaton is the mixture or inversion of the order of words, which order ought to be common to all languages, according to the natural idea we have of construction. But the Romans were so fond of figurative discourse, that they hardly ever used any other, and Horace is the most obscure of all in this way of writing.

This figure hath five species.

1. Anastrophe, which is the inversion of words, as *mecum* for *cum me*. *Quamobrem*, for *ob quam rem*. *Qua de re*, for *de qua re*. *His accensa super*, Virg. *Ore pedes tetigique crura*, Hor. and in like manner *Quam potius* for *potius quam; quamprius* for *priusquam*.

Illum sæpe suis decedens fovit in ulnis,
  Quam prius abjunctos sedula lavit equos, Prop.

Which is borrowed from the Attics, according to Scaliger, who say ἢ περὶ, instead of περὶ ἢ.

2. Tmesis, when a word is cut in two, as *Septem subjecta trioni*. Virg.

Virg. for *septentrioni. Garrulus hunc quando confumet cunque*, Hor. for *quandocunque*, &c. *Quo me cunque rapit tempeftas:* and the like.

3. PARENTHESIS, when the fenfe is interrupted by parenthefes; as *Tytire dum redeo (brevis eft via) pafce capellas*, Virg.

4. SYNCHISIS, when the whole order of natural conftruction is confounded, as

Saxa vocant Itali mediis quæ in fluctibus, aras, Virg.

That is, *Itali vocant aras faxa illa, quæ funt in mediis fluctibus.*

——— *Donec regina facerdos*
Marte gravis geminam partu dabit Ilia prolem, Id.

That is, *Donec Ilia facerdos regina, gravis Marte, dabit partu prolem geminam.*

Si mala condiderit, in quem quis carmina, jus eft
Judiciumque. Efto, fi quis mala: fed bona fi quis
Judice condiderit laudatur Cæfare, Hor.

That is, *Si quis bona carmina condiderit, laudatur judice Cæfare.*

Æftates peraget qui nigris prandia moris
Ille falubres finiet, &c.

That is, *Ille qui finiet prandia nigris moris, peraget æftates falubres.* He who will finifh the meal called *prandium*, with mulberries, fhall enjoy good health all the fummer.

Et malè laxus——— *In pede calceus hæret*, Id. for *malè hæret.*
Contra Lævinum Valeri genus under Superbus
Tarquinius regno pulfus fuit, unius affis
Non unquam pretio pluris licuiffe, notante
Judice, quem nofti, populo, &c. Id.

That is, *Lævinum qui eft genus Valeri, & à quo Tarquinius Superbus pulfus fuit regno fuo, aliquando licuiffe non pluris pretio unius affis, judice populo notante, quem tu nofti.*

Habet gladium; fed duos quibus altero te occifurum, ait altero villicum, Plaut. in Caffin. that is *quibus ait fe occifurum altero, quidem te, altero verò villicum.*

To this fame figure Linacer would have us refer thefe modes of fpeaking, where a conftruction is ufed in a fenfe that feems quite inverted, as in Virgil, *Ibant obfcuri fola fub nocte*, Æn. 6. for *foli fub obfcura nocte. Sceleratam intorferit haftam*, Ibid. for *ipfe fceleratus. Dare claffibus auftros*, Æn. 2. for *dare auftris, or committere auftris claffes.* To expofe them to the winds, which is generally called an HYPALLAGE. Neverthelefs, to be ingenuous, thefe modes of fpeaking are not a figure of grammar. For either they fubfift in a plain and natural conftruction as the latter example, *dare claffibus auftros*; it being indifferent in regard to conftruction to fay, *dare claffibus auftros*, or *auftris claffes*, to expofe them to the wind, or to make them receive the wind: or elfe it is a trope, or a figure of rhetoric, as *fola fub nocte*, where the night is called *fola*, juft as death is called *pallida*, becaufe it makes us pale.

But to this figure of hyperbaton we may very well refer the following elegant and ufual phrafes of Cicero's, where the relative is always before the demonftrative, which ferves for its antecedent, as, *Sed hoc non concedo, ut quibus rebus gloriemini in vobis, eafdem easdem in aliis reprehendatis,* Cic. *Quarum enim tu rerum cogitatione nos levare ægritudine voluisti, earum etiam commemoratione lenimur,* Id. for *earum rerum quarum,* &c.

Hereto we must also refer these other phrases, where the relative being placed first, it is followed by an intire period which serves for its antecedent: as in Livy, *Quod bonum, faustum, felixque sit, Quirites, regem create.* And the like.

5. ANACOLUTHON, when there is hardly any connexion or construction in the sentence, as in Terence, *Nam omnes nos quibus est alicunde aliquis objectus labor, omne quod est interea tempus priusquam id rescitum est, lucro est.* And in Varro, *Me in Arcadia scio spectatum suem* for *spectasse.* Likewise in Cicero, *Prætor interea, ne pulchrum se ac beatum putaret, atque aliquid sua sponte loqueretur, ei quoque carmen compositum est.* Cic. pro Muræna. *Et enim si orationes, quas nos multitudinis judicio probari volebamus (popularis est enim illa facultas, & effectus eloquentiæ est audientium approbatio) sed si reperiantur nonnulli, qui nihil laudarent, nisi quod se imitari posse confiderent,* Cic. 2. Tusc. *Quæ qui in utramque partem excelso animo magnoque despiciunt, cumque aliqua his ampla & honesta res objecta est, totos ad se convertit & rapit: tum quis non admiretur splendorem pulchritudinemque virtutis?* Off. 1. Where we see there is no sort of connexion in those periods. But this figure is oftentimes only a specious term to make us overlook several things in antient authors, which seem rather to have dropped from them inadvertently, than to be rationally accounted for.

CHAPTER VII.

Of HELLENISM *or Greek phrase.*

BESIDES the figures abovementioned, it is proper also to observe, that there are several phrases whose construction is borrowed from the Greeks, which way of speaking is included under the general term of hellenism.

Linacer extends this figure to an infinite variety of expressions, merely because they are more common among the Greeks than among the Latins. But we shall be satisfied with referring to this figure whatever particularly belongs to the Greek tongue, having treated of the other things by principles, which are applicable to both languages.

I. *Hellenism by* ATTRACTION.

Now in order rightly to understand the expressions borrowed from the Greek, and even to comprehend the Greek authors, we must always distinguish in the Greek phrase between attraction and government; that is to say, when one case is rather attracted by another preceding case, than governed by the verb to which it refers. This is what Budeus transiently has observed in several parts of his commentaries, and what Sanctius has made a very considerable point of; *Græci,* says he, *è duobus casibus (si se mutuò respiciant) alterum tantum regunt, alterum illi adjungunt, ita ut alter*

ab

ab altero trahatur, ut περὶ λόγων ὧν ἥλιξα, de verbis quibus dixi, for *quæ dixi.*

Thus we find in St. Paul, τὸ σῶμα ὑμῶν ναὸς τῶ ἐν ὑμῖν ἁγίω πνεύματός ἐστιν, ὃ ἔχετε ἀπὸ Θεῶ, 1 Cor. 6. 19. *Corpus vestrum templum est spiritus sancti, in vobis existentis, cujus* (for *quem*) *habetis à Deo.* And in Demosthenes, ἐκ τῶν ἐπιστολῶν τῶν ἐκείνω μαθήσεσθε ὧν εἰς Πελοπόννησον ἔπεμψι. *Ex epistolis ejus cognoscetis, quibus* (for *quas*) *in Peloponnesum misit.* And this the Latins have often imitated, as when we find, *Quum scribis & aliquid agas quorum consuevisti,* Lucceius Ciceroni, for *quæ consuevisti. Sed istum, quem quæris, ego sum,* Plaut. for *ego sum quem quæris. Occurrunt animæ, quales nec candidiores terra tulit,* for *qualibus,* which Lambinus seems not to have rightly understood.

It is by this same figure they say, *Non licet mihi esse securo; cupio esse clemens. Uxor invicti Jovis esse nescis,* Hor. *Sensit medios delapsus in hostes,* Virg. and the like. Which very few have comprehended; see what has been said already in regard to this matter in the 5th rule, p. 14.

By this also it is, that a case being betwixt two verbs, shall be sometimes attracted by the verb that it does not refer to, *Illum, ut vivat,* optant, Ter. *Hæc me, ut confidam, faciunt,* Cic. Where the accusative seems to be put for the nominative, *Optant ut ille vivat.* In like manner, *Metuo lenonem ne quid suo suat capiti,* for *metuo ne leno,* &c. in Phorm. *Atque istud quidquid est fac me ut sciam,* in Heaut. for *fac ut ego sciam.*

Hence it is that one gender is sometimes attracted by another, as
 Saxum antiquum, ingens, campo qui fortè jacebat
 Limes agro positus, Virg.
Whereto we must refer what hath been said concerning the relative betwixt two nouns of different gender, p. 6.

II. *Hellenism of the preposition* KATA.

But the Latins have imitated the Greeks in no one article so much as in those phrases, where understanding their preposition κατὰ or περὶ they put what Budeus calls an accusative absolute, as in Theognides,
 Οὐδεὶς ἀνθρώπων ἐστὶν ἅπαντα σοφός.
 Mortalis sapiens omnia nemo datur.
that is κατὰ πάντα, *secundum omnia.* And in Isocr. πέρι τὸ μὲν σῶμα εἶναι φιλόπονος, τὴν δὲ ψυχὴν φιλόσοφος. *Stude corpus quidem esse amans laboris, animum autem amans sapientiæ,* that is, *secundum corpus, secundùm animum,* κατὰ σῶμα, as it is in the antient epigram.
 Ὃς κατὰ σῶμα καλός, κατὰ νοῦν δ᾽ αὖ ἐστιν ἄμορφος,
  Αἰσχρὸς δὴ πλεῖόν μοι δοκεῖ ἢ καλός.
Qui quod ad corpus pulcher est, he says, *quod ad mentem deformis, deformis magis mihi videtur quàm pulcher.*

Thus Aristophanes says γνώμην ἐμὴν, where Plato often useth κατὰ τὴν ἐμὴν, *juxta meam,* sup. *sententiam.* Thus they say τὴν πρώτην, *primò;* τὴν ἀρχὴν, *principio;* τὸ τέλος, *tandem.* And thus in imitation of them the Latins say, *Expleri mentem nequit. Fractus membra.*

membra. Os humerosque deo similis. Pacem te poscimus. Doceo te artes, and other such phrases, which may be seen in the annotation to the 24th rule, p. 45. Thus it is that they say indifferently *primum* for *primo, tertium* for *tertio*: that they say *tantum, quantum, nimium, principium*: in regard to which see the chapter on the adverbs, p. 145.

III. *Hellenism of the preposition* EK.

It is so usual likewise with the Greeks to understand this preposition, which with them governs the genitive, or some other word of the same government, that for this very reason grammarians imagined there were a great many verbs which governed a genitive. Whereas, according to what hath been above observed, the whole government is included in the preposition understood. And hence the Latins have taken, *Abstine irarum, desine lacrymarum, regnavit populorum,* and others; concerning which see the 9th and 10th rules.

They said likewise, *Imperti me divitiarum, arripuit illum pedis, gustavit mellis, audivit musicæ,* and an infinite number of others. Hence it is that Vitruvius hath even joined the Latin preposition *ex* in this government, *Descriptio ex duodecim signorum cœlestium,* &c. which deserves more to be remarked, than imitated.

IV. *Other more particular expressions, which depend on the figure of hellenism.*

It is likewise to the figure of hellenism that we are to refer these phrases, where the nominative is put for the vocative, as hath been observed already, p. 83. *Da meus ocellus, da anime mi,* Plaut. which is an imitation of the Attics, or even of the Æolians, whom the Latins have always endeavoured to follow.

Thus it is in imitation of the Greeks that Ovid says,

Seu genus Adrasti, seu furtis aptus Ulysses,
Seu pius Æneas eripuisse ferunt.

Because they may indifferenly put either the nominative or the accusative before the infinitive, as we have made appear in the new method of learning the Greek tongue; whereas the Latin construction admits only of the accusative on this occasion.

It is likewise by this figure that an infinitive is put after a noun, understanding some particle by which it is governed, and which answers to their ὅτι, as in Persius,

―――*Et pectore lævo*
Excutias guttas, lætari prætrepidum cor:

for *usque ad lætari.* And in Virgil,

Pestis acerba boum pecorique aspergere virus,

that is, *acerba usque ad aspergere.*

Hence it is that the Latins on this occasion have sometimes put an *ut,* as Horace, lib. 1. od. 11.

―――*Neu Babylonios*
Tentaris numeros, ut melius quicquid erit pati.

That is, ὅτι φέρεις, *ut melius patiaris,* according as Sursin and Vossius explain it. And the same expression occurreth likewise in Ulpian, l. 62. as Scipio Gentilis obferveth, *In lege facienda, Julianus ait*: UT, *fi duo rei promittendi fuerint, vel fi duo ftipulandi, fiquidem focii fint, in eâ re* DIVIDI *inter eos* DEBERE *obligationem,* where according to this author, whom Voffius hath followed, *ut ought* to refer to *dividi debere,* as if it were *ut dividi debeat,* &c.

Chapter VII.
Of Antiptofis and Enallage.

I. *Whether we ought to join Antiptofis and Enallage to the foregoing figures, and what the grammarians underftand by thefe two words.*

BESIDE the above given figures of conftruction, there are who pretend that we ought at leaft to admit of antiptofis and enallage.

They give the name of enallage to every change which they fancy in fpeech, and for which, as they think, there is no foundation or reafon, as of one mood for another, one tenfe for another, one gender for another, &c. And in particular they diftinguifh by the name of antiptofis the change of one cafe for another, which may happen, fays Defpauter, as many ways as there are particular cafes, becaufe according to him, there are none but what may be interchanged for another, by virtue of this beautiful figure.

But who does not fee that if thofe changes were fo arbitrary and unaccountable, the rules of grammar would be of no fort of ufe, or at leaft we fhould have no right to cenfure a perfon for any tranfgreffion whatfoever againft them? Hence this figure is indeed the moft idle thing that can be imagined, fays Sanctius, *Antiptofi grammaticorum nihil imperitius, quod figmentum fi effet verum, fruftra quæreretur, quem cafum verba regerent,* lib. 4.

And only to touch lightly on the principal examples which Defpauter hath given of this figure, it is an eafy matter to fhew that they have other foundations than he imagined, and that the rules of grammar prefent nothing to us but what is fupported by reafon; though in fuch a multitude, we are ever to make a judicious choice, and to pick out only what is moft pure and elegant, that is, what is moft received and eftablifhed by the ufe of good authors. For though we may fometimes make ufe of particular turns of expreffion without being guilty of error, yet it is true what Quintilian fays, that ALIUD EST GRAMMATICE, ALIUD LATINE LOQUI.

II. *Examples of the Antiptofis taken particularly from Defpauter.*

Thus when Defpauter faith that in this example from Livy, *Quando duo confules ejus anni, alter morbo, alter ferro periiffet,* &c. the nominative is there for the genitive, *duo confules* for *duorum confulum;* it is evident that this is only an ellipfis or rather a zeugma, ma, where the verb which is expressed but once, ought to be understood three times, *duo consules periissent, alter morbo periisset, & alter ferro periisset.*

When he says that *fortiora horum* is a genitive for an ablative, *horum* for *his*, this is only a partition, by virtue of which the genitive may be put after the comparitive or even after the positive, as we have observed, p. 59.

When he says that *Saltui & velocitati certare*, in Sisen. according to Nonius, is a dative instead of an ablative; I say, either it is an ablative, because formerly the dative was every where like the ablative, pursuant to what hath been already demonstrated: or even that the construction by the dative may be defended, this being only the case of *relation*, which may be put every where, as hath been observed, p. 25. The same may be said of the other examples which he produces, *Vino modo cupidæ estis*, Plaut. *Moderari orationi*, Cic. *Alienis rebus curas*, Plaut. where it is only a simple government of the dative. See the 12th rule, p. 25.

When he says that *ferax oleo* in Virgil is for *olei*, this may be an ablative of the manner, abounding *in olive trees*. Just as Ovid says,

Terra ferax Cerere, multóque feracior uvis.

But we may farther observe that most editions, as those of Holland, Robert Stephen, Ascensius, Erithreus, Farnaby, and others, have *ferax oleæ*; though Pierius owns he found *oleo* in some manuscripts.

When he says that in the example from Pomponius, quoted by Nonius, ch. 9. *Quot lætitias insperatas modo mihi irrepsere in sinum*, it is an accusative for a nominative: I say, either that the passage is corrupted, having shewn elsewhere, that this author hath frequently made use of bad editions, in the examples he produces; or that in the above passage Pomponius hath taken *irrepsere* for a verb active; which hath its nominative understood, and which really governeth *lætitias*: for it is very common, as we have seen already in the list of the verbs absolute and active, p. 99. and we shall further demonstrate in the following list by various examples of verbs of different governments; that those which are called neuters, do govern the accusative as real verbs active. Were it not for this, I should have no scruple to say that *lætitias irrepsere*, for *lætitiæ*, is a downright solecism, and that neither an antiptosis, nor Nonius, nor Despauter, can justify this mode of expression. And it is evident that Nonius did not understand this example when he quoted it, since he refers to the same figure, *Urbem quam statuo vestra est*, which is quite a different expression, and a construction authorized by the use of poets, as we have already shewn in the annotation to the second rule, p. 5.

When he says that in Nevius, *Quot res hunc vis privari pulchras, quas uti solet*, this *quas* is an accusative for an ablative: it is only the natural government, and the accusative to which the action of the verb passeth. For *utor* governeth also sometimes the accusative, though it be more usual with the ablative. But *privari res pulchras*, is an hellenism, which supposeth κατὰ, just as *lætor hanc rem*, and the like, of which we have made mention already, p. 203. and in the 24th rule, p. 44. When

When he says that in Virgil——*Hæret pede pes, densusque viro vir*, Æn. 10. it is an ablative for a dative: it is only a real dative; but this is because the dative heretofore was always like the ablative, as we have made appear in the 2d chapter of the remarks on the nouns, n. 2. p. 83. and elsewhere.

And in regard to what Despauter addeth further, that in the same poet,

Forte ratis celsi conjuncta crepidine saxi
Expositis stabat scalis, & ponte parato.

Crepidine is likewise an ablative for the dative *crepidini*: I say, that the construction of the ablative in this passage with the verb *conjungo*, is as natural as that of the dative, let Servius say what he will, who insists on the same antiptosis. This we might demonstrate by an infinite number of passages even out of Cicero, *Declarat enim summam benevolentiam conjunctam pari prudentia*, lib. 5. ep. 13. *Ea summa miseria est summo dolore conjuncta*, contra Verr. *Fannii ætate conjunctus Antipater*, 1. de Leg. And the reason hereof is, this word being compounded of the preposition *cum*, it preserveth its government also; so that it is just as if we were to say *cum summo dolore conjuncta*; *cum ætate conjunctus*, &c. This is so true, that sometimes they repeated the preposition, *Varro cum Sicinio ætate conjunctus*, lib. de claris Orat. This much may be also sufficient to prove that the antient as well as modern grammarians, have oftentimes committed blunders, for want of having rightly comprehended the real causes of construction and government.

III. *Other examples taken from those who wrote upon Despauter.*

Behourt and others who wrote upon Despauter, have even given a further extent to the use of this figure. For they say that

Uxor invicti Jovis esse nescis, Hor.

is a nominative for an accusative, *uxor* for *uxorem*. Whereas it is only an hellenism, as hath been shewn in the preceding chapter.

They say that in Virgil,

Projice tela manu, sanguis meus,

is a nominative for a vocative. Whereas it is only an hellenism, as we have above demonstrated.

They say that in Pliny, *Canum degeneres*, is a genitive for the nominative *canes*. Whereas it is only a partition; for every noun in the quality of a partitive may govern the genitive, as we have shewn in the 27th rule, p. 55.

They say that *abstineo irarum* is a genitive for an ablative; whereas it is only a Greek phrase, as may be seen in the preceding chapter.

They say *Quod mihi lateat*, in Cic. is for *me lateat*, a dative instead of an accusative; which is without any manner of reason, since the verb *latet* can govern only a dative in the Latin construction, and is never used otherwise in Cicero, as hath been shewn in the 15th rule, p. 31.

They say that in Plautus, *Curatio hanc rem*, is an accusative for a genitive, *hujus rei*. But we have demonstrated that this phrase was very common in Plautus's time, and that it is only a natural construction, because as the noun verbal generally denotes the action of the verb, it may likewise preserve the government thereof, since it is only by virtue of this action that the verb governeth an accusative.

IV. *Examples of the Enallage.*

But these authors go further. For whereas Despauter speaks only of the antiptosis, or interchanging of cases, as appears in the edition of Robert Stephen, which I have made use of; they have added four verses to this rule, to mark the same change in gender, person, tense, mood, and number.

1. In gender, they say that this happeneth both to nouns and verbs. To nouns, as

Tamen vel virtus tua me, vel vicinitas,
Quod ego in propinqua parte amicitiæ puto,
Facit—————'l er.

Where *quod*, say they, is for *quæ*. Whereas *quod* supposeth *negotium* for its substantive, *which thing*. And is a mode of speaking, that ought to be referred to the figure of syllepsis, which hath been explained already, p. 185.

To verbs, as *bellantur* for *bellant*.

—————*Et pictis bellantur Amazones armis,* Virg.

But you may see other examples abovequoted, in the list of verbs deponents, p. 101. Which is owing intirely to this, that heretofore there were more verbs common than at present.

2. In person, as in Terence *in Phorm. act.* 1. *sc.* 2.

GET. *Si quis me quæret rufus.* DAV. *Præsto est, define.*

Where *præsto est*, say they, is for *præsto sum*, because Davus speaks of himself. But if there be any figure in this, it is rather of rhetoric than of grammar, because he answers to what the other had said of him in the third person, *Si quis me quæret rufus.* And it is the same figure, as when in the 4th scene Geta says of himself in the second person,

Nulius est Geta, nisi jam aliquod tibi consilium celere repperis, &c. Which is only a turn of expression where one person is introduced for another; a thing common to all languages.

3. In tense, *vicimus* for *vincemus*; as *Huic si esse in orbe tuto liceat, vicimus,* Cic. Attic. But again if this be a figure, it belongs to rhetoric, and not to grammar; as it is very common in narratives to make use of the present in recounting past transactions. For the anticipating or combining of tenses is very common in rhetoric; but this does not relate to grammar, which one way or other finds its government.

4. In mood, as *valebis* for *vale*, Cic. But we have made appear above, p. 109. that the imperative was only a real future; and therefore we ought not to be surprized if they were frequently put one for the other.

Romani festinare, parare, &c. for *festinabant, parabant,* say they. But this is only an ellipsis of a verb understood, as *cœperunt*, or some other which governs this infinitive, according to what we have shewn, p. 170.

5. In

5. *In number.* But here it can only be a figure of rhetoric, as when they give for instance, *dedimus operam*, Cic. for *dedi*, which is very common; or they must be things referrable to the precedent figures; as *Nominandi istorum tibi erit magis quàm edendi copia*, Cic. Where they will have it that *edendi* is the singular for the plural *edendorum*; whereas it is but an ellipsis of τὸ *edere* understood, as we have shewn in the chapter of gerunds, p. 125. *Si tempus est ullum jure hominis necandi, quæ multa sunt*, Cic. This is only a syllepsis, of which we have made mention above, p. 186. and the like may be said of the rest. Whence we conclude that all that can be said of the figures of grammar, may be reduced to the four above laid down, or to hellenism.

Therefore I am of opinion that upon a careful perusal of what hath been said in the syntax, and in these remarks, very few difficulties will arise in regard to government that may not easily be solved, and that hardly any passage will occur in ancient authors, but what may be accounted for. But as the chief foundation of all languages depends on practice, I have endeavoured to collect here a multitude of verbs of different governments, which perhaps will be the more useful, as some of them are not to be found even in the most copious dictionaries. They are comprised in the following list, which is only an abridgment of a more extensive work, wherein we intended to include every remark that could be made on the elegance of this language, for the service of those who endeavour to write pure Latin; and perhaps some day or other we may publish a separate work on this subject for the use of learners, if ever we find that they have derived any benefit from this abridgment.

LIST OF VERBS

OF

DIFFERENT GOVERNMENTS.

A

ABALIENARE aliquid, *or* aliquid alicujus, *Cic. to alienate.* Aliquem ab altero, se ab alio, alium à se, voluntatem alicujus ab aliquo, *id.*

ABDERE se litteris & in litteras : se in tenebris, *id. to hide or bury one's self.*

ABDICARE, *simply, or* magistratum, *or* se magistratu, *id. to abdicate, or to resign.*

ABDICARE aliquem, *Tac. to renounce him.*

ABDUCERE à consuetudine, *Cic. to break off, or wean from a custom.* Ab omni reip. cura, *id. to retire, to resign.* Vi & per vim, *id. to carry off by main force.* In aliquem locum, *id.* Ex acie, *id.* A fide, *id.* Ad nequitiam, *Ter.*

Me convivam abducebat sibi, *Cic.*

Equitatum ad se abducere, *id. to draw the cavalry to himself.*

ABERRARE proposito, & à proposito, *id. to wander from his subject.*

Nihil equidem levor, sed tamen aberro, *id. but at least I divert myself.*

Aberratio à dolore, *id. any diversion that gives an allay to grief.*

Aberrat ad alia oratio, *id. digresses.*

Aberrant inter se orationes, *Liv. do not agree.*

Artificem ne in melius quidem sinas aberrare, *Plin. do not suffer him to depart from his model, even though he were to mend it.*

ABESSE urbe, domo, &. ab urbe, ab domo, *Cic. to be absent.* Alicui abesse, *id. to be wanting towards him, to forsake him.* In altercationibus abesse, *id. not to be there.*

ABHORRET facinus ab illo, *id. he is far from committing such a wicked action.*

Parum abhorrens famam, *Liv. not at all afraid of defamation.*

Illud abhorret à fide, *Cic. that is altogether incredible.*

Ab ducenda uxore abhorret, *id. he has an aversion to matrimony.*

ABJICERE se alicui ad pedes, & ad pedes alicujus, *Cic. to throw himself at his feet.*

Abjicere se & prosternere, *id.* Consilium aedificandi abjicere, *id. to lay aside all thoughts of building.*

Abjicere ad terram, *id.* in herbam, *id.* humi, *Plin. to throw upon the ground.*

Cogitationes in rem humilem abjicere, *Cic. to apply his thoughts to it.*

Abjicere animum, *id. to despond.*

ABIRE magistratu, *id. to finish his office.*

Ab emptione, *id. to depart from his bargain.* Ad vulgi opinionem, *id. to be led away by vulgar opinion.*

Abire, à, ab, de, e, ex, loco, *id. to be gone, to go out, to retire.*

Non hoc sic tibi abibit, *Ter. you shall not escape thus.*

Abi in malam crucem, *Ter. go and hang yourself.*

ABJUDICARE sibi libertatem, *Cic. to shew himself unworthy of liberty.* Se vita, *Plaut. to part with life.*

ABNUERE aliquid alicui, *Cic.* Alicui de re aliqua, *Sal. to refuse him something.*

ARROGARE legem *or* legi, *Liv.* the former more usual, *to demand the repeal of a law.*

ABSTINERE sese dedecore, animum à scelere, *Cic. to abstain.* Ignem ab aede, *Liv. not to set fire to it.* Aegrum à cibo, *Cels.*

Abstinere jus belli ab aliquo, *Liv. not to treat him with the full severity of the rights of war.*

Abstinere maledictis & à maledictis, *Cic.*

Abstinere irarum, *Hor.* Placidis bonis, *Ovid.*

Abstine isti hanc tu manum, *Plaut.*

ABSTRUDERE in fundo, in silvam, *Cic. to hide.*

ABUTI studiis, *id. to make a wrong use of his studies.* Operam abutitur, *Ter. he loseth his labour.*

ACCEDERE alicui proximè, *Cic.* Virg. Deo ad similitudinem, *Cic. to resemble.* Ad aliquem, *Cic. to draw near*

near him. Alicui ad aurem, *id.*

Quos accedam? *Sall. sup. ad. to whom shall I apply?* Quas vento accesserit oras, *Virg. sup.* in. *to what coast the winds will drive him.*

Accedit quod, *Cic. there is this besides;* or simply, *besides, moreover.*

ACCIDERE. Omnia enim secundissima nobis, adversissima illis accidisse, *id. to have happened.* Where we see that this verb is taken either for good or bad fortune.

ACCIPERE ab aliquo, *Ter.* De aliquo, *Cic.* Ex aliquo, *Plaut. to receive or to learn from a person.*

Accipere in contumeliam, *Ter. to take in bad part.*

Acceptum plebi, *Cæs.* Apud plebem, *Plaut.* In plebem, *Tac. agreeable to the people.*

Acceptum, or in acceptum referre, *Cic. to be obliged;* properly, *it is to place to your account.*

ACQUIESCERE lecto, *Catul. to rest upon the bed.* Alicui rei, *Sen. to set one's heart upon a thing, to fix upon it.*

In tuo vultu acquiesco, *Cic. your presence gives me comfort.*

ADÆQUARE cum virtute fortunam, *id. to be no less successful than brave.* Aliquem sibi, *id. to render him equal to one's self.*

Judices adæquarunt, *id. the judges were divided.*

ADDICERE morti, *id.* In servitutem, *Liv. to condemn to.*

Addicere liberum, *Cic. to declare one free.*

Ni aves addixissent, *id. If the augural birds had not approved it by their signs.* The contrary is ABDICERE.

ADESSE omnibus pugnis, *id. to be present at every battle.* Ad exercitum, *Plaut.* Ad portam, *Cic.* In causa, in aliquo loco, ad tempus, *id.*

Adesse alicui, *id. to favour him, to assist him with one's credit, or presence.*

ADHÆRERE castris, *Appul.* In re aliqua, *Ovid.* Ad rem aliquam, *Plaut.* In rem aliquam, *Cic. to stick to, to adhere, or keep close to.*

ADHIBERE severitatem in aliquo, or in aliquem, *id. to use severity.* Reverentiam adversus, or erga aliquem, *id.*

Adhibere vinum ægrotis, *id. to give them wine.*

ADIGERE jusjurandum, or aliquem jurejurando, or aliquem ad jusjurandum, *Liv.* Per jusjurandum, *Cæs. to oblige by oath.*

ADIRE aliquem, ad aliquem, in jus, *Cic. to go to see, to go, &c.* Illa pericula adeuntur in præliis, *id. they run those risks in battle.*

ADJUNGERE aliquem alteri & ad amicitiam alterius, *id. to make him his friend.* In societatem adjungere, *Liv.*

ADMISCERE aliquid in aliud, *Plin.* Alicui, or cum aliquo, *Cic. to mingle with.*

Admisceri ad aliquod concilium, *id. to be admitted to it.*

ADMONERE, See Monere.

ADOLESCIT ætas, ratio, cupiditas, *id. Virg. grows, waxes strong.*

Adolescere ad aliquam ætatem, *Plin.* Annos ter senos, *Ovid.* In partum *Colum.*

Adolescunt ignibus aræ, *Virg. are covered with the fire of the sacrifices.*

Flammis adolere penates, *id.*

ADOPTARE sibi filium, *Cic.* Aliquem pro filio, *Plaut. to adopt him.* Aliquem in divitias, *Plin. to make him his heir.* Aliquem ab aliquo, *Cic.* Se alicui ordini, *Plin.*

ADSCRIBERE civitati, in civitatem, or in civitate, *Cic. to make him free of the city.*

ADVERSARI alicui, *id.* Aliquem, *Liv.* Contra & adversus aliquem, *Plaut. to resist, to contradict.*

Ambitionem scriptoris adversari, *Tac.* Adversari quominus aliquid fiat, *Cic. to hinder.*

ADVERTERE, simply, *Ter.* Animum, *Liv.* Animo, *Plin. to give attention.*

Advertere urbi agmen, *Virg. to make it draw near, to make it take the road towards the city.*

Scythias adverteret oras, *Ovid, was arrived.*

Advertere in aliquem, *Tacit. to punish him.*

ADULARE. Pinnatâ caudâ nostrum adulat sanguinem, *Cic. Ex veteri poetâ.*

Si Dionysium non adulares, *Val. Max. from thence cometh* ADULOR, *passive.* Cavendum est ne assentatoribus patefaciamus aures, ne adulari nos sinamus, *Cic.* Tribunus militum adulatus erat, *Val. Max.*

ADULARI deponent. Adulari aliquem, *Cic.* Alicui, *Qu. to flatter a person.* The former is preferable even according to Quintillian.

ÆMULARI alicui, *Cic. to bear envy to a person.* Aliquem, *id. to endeavour to surpass him.*

Æmulari instituta alicujus, *id. to equal, to surpass.*

Æmulari cum aliquo, *Liv. to rival a person.*

Invicem æmulari, *Quint. to rival one another.*

ÆSTIMARE aliquem, *Plaut.* De aliquo, *Cic. to esteem him.*

Æstimare magni, or magno, *id.*

Æstimare litem capitis, *id. to judge a per-*

a person deserving of death, or of banishment.

AGGREDI aliquem dictis, *Virg.* aliquem de re aliqua, *Plaut. to speak to him about something.* Aliquid, *Cic. to begin.* Ad injuriam faciendam, *id.*

AGERE rem, *or* de re, *id.* aliquem, *or* partes alicujus, *id.* Cum populo, *id.* Lege *or* ex lege, *id. to treat, to act, to do.*

Agere se pro equite, *Suet. to act as a knight.* Agere gratias de re, in re, pro re, in res singulas, *Cic. to thank.*

AGITARE animo, *Liv.* Cum animo, *Sall.* Mente, *Sall.* In mente, *Cic.* Secum, *Ter. to revolve a thing in one's mind.*

ALLATRARE magnitudinem alicujus, *Liv. to exclaim against.*

Allatrant maria oram maritimam, *Plin. to beat against.*

Allatrare alicui has not the authority of pure writers. It is true that the following passage is quoted from the book *de Viris illust.* attributed to Pliny: *In capitolium intempesta nocte eunti, canes allatraverant.* But besides that one might perhaps read *nocte eunte,* Vossius also observeth that the author of this book was not Pliny, but Sextus Aurelius Victor, who lived above two hundred years later, when the language was greatly corrupted.

ALLEGARE alicui, *or* ad aliquem, *Cic. to send towards a person.* Hominem alicui rei, *Plaut. to send him to treat about something.*

Allegare senem, *Ter. to depute an old man.*

AMBULARE pedibus, *Cic. to walk.* Foro transverso, *id. to walk across the market.* In jus, *id.* In littore, *id.*

Ambulat hoc caput per omnes leges, *Plin. to occur every where.*

Ambulare maria, *Cic.*

Ambulantur stadia bina, *Plin.*

From the last two examples it appeareth that this verb may be active, and that Quintilian, lib. 1. c. 5. had no reason to say that *ambulare viam* was a solecism, since at the most it is only a pleonasm, and every verb, as we have demonstrated in the syntax, rule 14. p. 29. and in the remarks, p. 98. may govern the accusative of a noun derived from itself, or of nearly the same signification.

ANGERE sese animi, *Plaut.* aliquem incommodis, *id.* Angit animum quotidiana cura, *Ter.*

ANGI animo, *Cic.* Re aliqua, *or* de re, *id. to be vexed.*

ANHELARE scelus, *id. to think of nothing but villainy.*

Amnis anhelat vapore, *Plin. throws out vapours.*

Verba inflata et anhelata, *Cic. pronounced with great exertion of voice, and that put us out of breath.*

ANIMADVERTO aliquid, *Ter. I look at it and consider it.* In aliquem, *Cic. I punish.*

ANNUERE cœptis, *Virg. to favour.* Victoriam, *Virg. to promise.* Aliquos, *Cic. to shew.*

ANQUIRERE aliquid, *id. to inform.* Capitis, *or* de capite, *Liv.*

ANTECEDERE alteri, *or* alterum ætate, *Cic. to surpass him in years.*

ANTECELLO tibi hac re, *id.* Illum hac re, *id.* aliis in re aliqua, *id?* Qui cæteris omnibus rebus his antecelluntur, *Ad Heren.*

ANTEIRE alicui, *Plaut.* Aliquem, *Sall.*

ANTESTARE alicui, *or* aliquem, *Gell. to excel or surpass a person in some thing.*

ANTEVENIRE alicui, *Plaut. to go to meet him.* Aliquem, *id. to prevent him.* Omnibus rebus, *id. to surpass him in every thing.* Nobilitatem, *Sall. to surpass the nobility.*

ANTEVERTERE alicui, *Ter. to outstrip, to be beforehand with, to prevent.*

Fannius id ipsum antevertit, *Cic.* Fannius *was beforehand with me in that.*

APPELLARE aliquem sapientem, *id. to call him wise.* Suo nomine, *id. to call him by his name.*

Appellare tribunos, *id.* Ad tribunos, *id. to appeal to the tribunes.*

Appellari pecuniâ, *Quint. de* pecunia, *Cic. to be dunned.*

Cæsar appellatus ab Æduis, *Cæs.* that is, *the Ædui being come to beg his assistance.* And this verb is very remarkable in this signification.

APPELLERE ad aliquem, *Cic. to bring to land.* Aliquem alicui loco, *id.* Animum ad philosophiam, *id. Ter. to apply.*

APPELLERE classe in Italiam, *Virg.* appellere classem, *Cic.* ad villam nostram navis appellitur, *id. is brought to land.*

We say therefore *navis,* or *classis appellitur,* just as we say *navem,* or *classem appellere,* but not *navis* or *classis appulit,* says Schotus. Yet *navis appulit,* occurs in Suetonius, life of Galba; which should not be imitated without great caution.

APPROPINQUARE portas, *or* ad portas, *Hirt.* Britanniæ, *Cæs. to approach.*

ARDERE,

ARDERE, or FLAGRARE ODIO, are said actively for the hatred we bear to others, and passively for the hatred others bear to us. Examples hereof are very common.

Ardebat Sirius Indos, *Virg.* for Adurebat. Ardebat Alexim, *Virg.* was *passionately fond of him.*

Ardeo te videre, *Plin. Jun. I am impatient to see you.*

Ardere in arma, *Virg.* Avaritia, *Cic.* Amore, *id.*

ARRIDERE alicui, *Cic. to smile at him, and to please him.*

Arrident ædes, *Plaut. do please me, do suit me.* Flavius id arrisit, *Gell. seemed to approve of that.*

Arrideri, *Passive, the contrary of* Derideri, *Cic.*

ASPERGERE labem alicui, or dignitati alicujus, *id. to blacken him, to speak ill of him.*

Maculis vitam aspergere, *id.*

ASPIRARE in curiam, *id. ad aliquem, id. to endeavour to reach to, or to obtain.*

Aspirat primo fortuna labori, *Virg. favoureth.*

Vento aspirat eunti, *Virg. Æn. 5.*

Et modicis fenestellis Aquilonibus aspirentur, *Colum. for inspirentur.*

ASSENTIRE or IRI alicui, *simply, or else alicui aliquid, or de re aliqua, or in re aliqua, to grant something to a person.* Instances hereof occur frequently.

But this verb ought not to be confounded with CONSENTIO, which signifieth *rather the agreement of the will,* whereas ASSENTIO is *to submit or to agree to another's judgment.*

ASSERVARE in carcerem, *Liv.* Domi suæ, *Cic. to keep.*

ASSUEFACERE and ASSUESCERE, ad aliquid, or in aliquo, *are not Latin, says Schotus.* I own they occur but seldom; yet the latter is in Quintilian.

But Schotus was still more mistaken, when he fancied that this verb could be joined with the ablative only, *Assuescere aliqua re.* Whereas its proper construction is to put a dative, as Robert Stephen observeth. For which reason Muretus and the best writers of *variæ lectiones,* have restored the dative wherever the ablative was put before, as in the 2. Catil. Assuefactus frigori & fami & siti & vigiliis perferendis, *inured to.*

There are even some passages where this government cannot be at all doubted of, *Caritas soli, cui longo tempore assuescito, Liv.* So that if there be sometimes an ablative used on this occasion, it cannot be any other than the ablative of the manner.

ASSERERE aliquid, *Cic. to affirm it.* Aliquem manu, *Liv. to set him at liberty.* In libertatem, *Id.* Asserere se, *Ovid, to assert or recover his liberty.* Aliquem cœlo, *Ovid, to canonize.* A mortalitate, *Plin. Jun.* Sibi aliquid, *Plin.* Se studiis, *Plin.*

ASTARE in conspectu, *Cic. to present himself.* In tumulum, *id. to be near.*

Astitit mihi contra, *Plaut. be opposed me strongly.*

ASSURGERE ex morbo, *Liv. to recover from sickness.* Alicui, *Cic. to rise up to one, to do him reverence.* In arborem, *Plin. to grow up to a tree.*

Assurgi, *Passive, Cic. to be done reverence to.*

ATTENDERE aliquem, *id. to listen to him.* Primum versum legis, *id. to consider it.* Animum, or animum ad aliquid, *id. to apply one's self.* Alicui rei, *id. to take notice of it.*

ATTINERE aliquem, *Tac. to retain one.* Ad aliquid, or ad aliquem, *Cic. to concern him, to belong to him.* Nunc jam cultros attinet, *Plaut. he has them already.*

Attineri studiis, *Tac. to be fond of study.*

AUSCULTARE alicui, *Plaut. Cic. to obey him.* Aliquem, *Plaut. to listen to him.*

B

BELLARE alicui, *Stat.* Cum aliquo, *Cic. to fight against him.*

Take notice that all verbs of fighting, quarrelling, resisting, contesting, and the like, are more elegantly joined with the preposition *cum* and its ablative, than with the dative.

C

CADERE alte, or ab alto, *Cic.* In plano, *Ovid.* In terram, *Lucr.* In unius potestatem, *Cic. to fall.*

Cadere formula, *Quint. to be cast in law, to lose the suit.*

Non cadit in virum bonum mentiri, *Cic. an honest man is incapable of telling a lye.*

Nihil est quod in ejusmodi mulierem non cadere videatur, *id. there is nothing but what suits her very well.*

Honesta et jucunda ceciderunt mihi à te, *id. happened to me on your part.*

CÆLARE argentum argento, & in argento, *Cic. to chase or emboss.*

Cælare flumina et bestias in vasis, *Ovid.*

Ovid. Opus cælatum novem musis, *Hor.* *where the whole force of human art and industry hath been exerted.*

CALERE. Thure calent aræ, *Virg.* Aures nostræ calent illius criminibus, *Cic.* *our ears ring with.*

Cum caletur maxime. *Plaut.* sup. *Calor.* For then it is passive, whence we may infer that it has also its active. For which reason Sanctius maintaineth that we may say, Calere rem aliquam, *or* re aliqua, *to have a passion for a thing.* And it is in this sense, according to him, that we say, Illius sensum pulchrè calleo, *Ter.* *I know him well.* Calere jura, *Cic.* *to know.*

I am not ignorant that all the dictionaries make a distinction between these two verbs, *caleo* and *calleo*, and that Cicero seems to derive the latter from *callum*. But one would think that *callum* rather comes from *caleo*, since a callosity proceeds from action often repeated, which first engenders heat, and afterwards the hardness of skin. And indeed, *callere ad suum quæstum*, in Plautus, seems rather to imply a particular attention and warmth of the mind, than an inveterate habit or custom.

CANERE aliquem, *Cic.* Super aliquo, *id.* *to sing the praises of a person.* Sibi intus canere, *id.* *to care for no body but himself, to praise himself.*

CARERE commodis, *id.* *not to have the conveniencies.*

Præterquam tui carendum quod erat, *Ter.*

Id quod amo, careo, *Plaut.*

Caruit te febris, *Plaut.* *the fever did not seize you.*

CAVERE aliquid, *Cic. Hor.* *to avoid, to take care of.* Alicui, *Cic.* *to watch over his preservation.* Ab aliquo, *id.* *to guard against him.* Malo, for à malo, *Petron.* De verbis alicujus, *Plaut.* Cavere obsidibus de pecunia, *Cæs.* *to give security by hostages.* Sibi obsidibus ab aliquo, *id.* *to take security by hostages.*

Quod nihil de iis Augustus testamento cavisset, *Suet.*

We say Cavere aliquo, *or* per aliquem, *Cic.* *to take bail or security of a person.*

Cætera quæ quidem provideri poterunt, cavebuntur, *id.*

CEDERE locum, *Stat.* Loco, *Cic. Cæs.* *to quit.* Ad locum, *Liv.* *to go thither.* E vita, *Cic.* *to die.* Exitio, *Ovid.* *to turn out to one's destruction.* In proverbium, *to become a proverb.* Intra finem juris, *Liv.* *to abide within the limits of his right.*

Cedere alicui, *Virg.* *to comply with a person.*

Cessit mihi, *id.* *it has happened to me.*

Honori non cedere, *Virg.* *to deserve no less honour than is done us.*

Hæreditas alicui cedit, *Virg.* *remains to him.*

Pro pulmentario cedit, *Colum.* *is taken for nourishment.*

Cedit dies, *Ulp.* *when the day of payment begins to draw near.*

CELARE. See the Syntax, rule 24, p. 43.

CERTARE laudibus alicujus, *Virg.* *to oppose his greatness.* Cum aliquo, *Cic.* *to fight.* Bello de re aliqua, *Liv.* Secum, *Cic.* *to endeavour to surpass him.*

Certat vincere, *Virg.* *he strives to overcome.*

Certare aliquid, *Hor.* *to strive to do a thing.*

Si res certabitur, *Hor.* *if the thing comes to be disputed.*

The latter examples shew that this is really an active verb, and therefore Regius had no reason to find fault with Ovid for saying

Certatam lite Deorum Ambraciam.

CIRCUNDARE oppidum castris, *Cæs.* Oppido mœnia, *to surround or invest.*

COGITARE animo, *id.* In animo, *Ter.* Cum animo, *Plaut.* Secum, *Ter.* *to think.*

Aliquid, *or* de re aliqua, *Cic.*

COIRE in unum, *Virg.* *to assemble together.* Societatem cum aliquo, *Cic.* *to make an alliance.*

Societas coitur, *id.*

Immitia placidis coeunt, *Hor.* *are mixed with.*

Milites coeunt inter se, *Cæs.* *to join battle, to rally.*

COLLOQUI alicui & aliquem, *Plaut.* Cum aliquo, *Cic.* *to speak.*

Inter se colloqui, *Cic. Cæs.* *to converse with one another.*

COMMITTERE se alicui, *Cic.* Se in fidem alicujus, *Ter.* *to put one's self under his protection.* Aliquem cum alio, *Mart.* Inter se omnes, *Suet.* *to set them all together by the ears.* Lacum mari, *Plin.* *to join it.*

COMMODARE aurum, *Cic.* *to lend gold.* Alicui, *simply, or* se alicui, *id.* *to assist him.* In rebus alicui, *id.* De loco alicui, *id.*

COMPLERE armato milite, *Virg.* Completus mercatorum carcer, *Cic.*

COM-

COMPONERE aliquid alicui, *or cum aliquo*, *Virg*. *to compare, to confront, to join together*.

Componere se ad exemplum, *Quint*. *to conform to example*.

CONCEDERE, *Plaut*. *to die*. Petitioni alicujus, *Cic*. *to condescend, to grant*. De jure suo, *id*. *Injurias reipub*. *id*.

Concedere in aliquem locum, &c. *See* Cedere.

CONCILIARE aliquem, *Cic*. Ad alterum, *Plaut*. Homines inter se, *Cic*. Animos aliquorum ad benevolentiam erga alios, *id*. Conjunctionem cum aliquo, *id*. Pacem ab aliquo, *Plaut*. *for* cum aliquo.

CONCLUDERE se in cellam, *Ter*. In cavea, *Plaut*. *to shut one's self up*. Res multas in unum, *Ter*. *to put them together*.

CONCURRERE cum aliquo, *Sil*. Alicui, *Virg*. *to fight*. See *Bellare* here above.

CONDEMNARE crimine, criminis, *or* de crimine, *Cic*. *to condemn for*. Omnes de consilii sententia, *id*. *with the opinion of the whole council*.

Condemnare alicui, *Ulp*.

CONDERE in sepulchro, *Cic*. Humo et in humo, *Ovid*. *to bury*. In furnum, *Plaut*. *to put in the oven*. Mœnia, *Virg*. *to build*.

CONDICERE cœnam alicui. *Suet*. Ad cœnam aliquem, *Plaut*. *to invite to supper*.

Condicere alicui, *simply*, *Cic*. *to promise to sup with him*.

CONDUCERE virgines in unum locum, *id. to bring them together*. Aliquem, *Plaut*. *to hire him to do something*. De censoribus, *Cic*. *to take a lease of the censors*.

Conducit hoc tuæ laudi, *id. is conducive to*. In rem, *Plaut*. Ad rem aliquam, *Cic*.

CONFERRE tributa, *id. to pay*. Novissima primis, *id. to compare*. Se in *or* ad urbem, *id. to go to town*. Omne studium ad rem aliquam, *id. to apply one's self intirely to it*. Crimen in aliquem, *id. to throw the blame upon him*. Seria cum aliquo, *Ovid*. *to confer*. Capita, *Cic. to have a private meeting, to speak tete to tete*.

Pestem hominibus conferunt, *Colum. do give them the plague*.

Neminem cum illo conferendum pietate puto. *Cic*. Conferunt ad temperandos calores, *Colum. contribute to*. Hæc oratori futuro conferunt, *Quint. are of service*.

CONFIDERE virtuti, *Cæs. to confide in his strength*. Animo et spe, *id*. In aliquo, *Hir^t*. Aliquâ re. Multum naturâ loci confidebant, *Cæs*.

Confiteri crimen, *Cæs. to confess*. De maleficio, *id. to acknowledge it*. Ut de me confitear, *id. to speak ingenuously of what regards me*.

CONFLICTARE & RI. Conflictati tempestatibus & sentinæ vitiis, *Cæs. incommoded to the highest degree*, &c.

Qui cum ingeniis conflictatur ejusmodi, *Ter. who haunts, who converses*.

Rempublicam conflictare, *Tac. to afflict*.

CONGERERE titulos alicui, *Sen. to load him with titles*. Crimen in aliquem, *Cic*.

CONGREDI alicui, *Cæs*. Aliquem, *Plaut. to draw near him*. Cum hoste & contra hostem, *Cic. to attack him*.

CONGRUERE. Congruunt literæ literis aliorum, *id. do agree*.

Congruunt inter se, *Ter. agree together*. Congruit sermo tibi cum illa, *Plaut*.

CONJUNGERE. Conjuncta virtuti fortuna, *Cic. joined*.

Conjuncta & sociata cum altera, *id*.

Conjuncta mihi cura de rep. cum illo, *id*.

Conjungi hospitio & amicitia, *id. to be joined by the ties of hospitality and friendship*.

CONQUERI rem aliquam, *or* de re aliqua, *id*. Ob rem aliquam, *Suet. to complain*. Cum aliquo, *Cic*. Pro aliquo, *id*.

CONQUIESCERE à re aliquâ, *id. to leave off, to be respited*. In re aliqua, *id. to take a delight in it*.

Hieme bella conquiescunt, *id. do cease*. Nisi perfecta re, de me non conquiesti, *id*.

CONSCENDERE navem, *id*. in navem, *Lent. Cic. to embark*.

CONSENTIRE sibi *or* secum, *id. to be consistent with one's self*. Alicui, *or* cum aliquo, *id. to agree with him*. Aliquid *or* de aliquo, *or* ad aliquid, *id. to agree about something*. In aliquem, *Ulp. to agree to take him for an arbitrator*.

In eum omnes illud consentiunt elogium, *Cic. they agree with one voice to bestow this encomium on him*.

Astrûm nostrum consentit incredibili modo, *Hor*.

CONSEQUI aliquem itinere, *vel* in itinere, *Cic. to overtake him*.

Aliquid consequi, *id. to obtain it, to gain his end*.

CONSERERE manum *or* manu cum hoste,

hoste, *id.* *the former more usual, to fight hand to hand, to come to bandy strokes.* Diem nocti, *Ovid. to join night with day upon an affair.* Artes belli inter se, *Liv.* Baccho aliquem locum, *Virg. to plant vines.*

CONSIDERE aliquo loco, vel in aliquo loco, *Cic. to stop there.*

CONSTARE per ipsum, *id. to depend only upon himself.* Sibi, *Cic. Hor. to be consistent with himself.* Ex multis, *Cic. to be compounded of.*

Agri constant campis & vineis, *Plin. consist of fields and vineyards.*

Constat gratis tibi navis, *Cic. costs you nothing.* Auri ratio, *id. the sum is intire.*

Non constat ei color neque vultus, *Liv. his colour and countenance changes.*

Mente vix constat, *Cic. he is hardly in his senses.*

Hoc constat, or constat inter omnes, *id. it is beyond all doubt.*

Constat hac de re, *Quint. Plin.*
Constat hoc mihi tecum, *Ad Heren.*

CONSUESCERE alicui, *Ter.* Cum aliquo, *Plaut. to frequent his company.*

Consuescere pronuntiare, *Cic. to accustom one's self to.* Adeo in teneris consuescere multum est, *Virg.* Plaustro & aratro juvencum consuescere, *Colum.* Omnia pericula pueritia consueta habeo, *Sall.*

CONSULERE boni, *Quint. Plaut. to take in good part.* Alicui, *Cic. to do him service.* Aliquem, *id. to ask counsel.* Consuli quidem te à Cæsare scribis, sed ego tibi ab illo consuli mallem, *id. but to signify, I give you counsel or advice, we say rather,* Autor tibi sum.

Consulo te hanc rem, *or de hac re, id.*

Consulo in te, *Ter. I am contriving something for you, or against you.*

Consulere in commune, *Ter. to consult the publick good.*

CONTENDERE alicui, *Hor.* Cum aliquo, *Cic.* Contra aliquem, *id. to dispute, to maintain a thing against another.*

Contendere aliquid ab aliquo, *id.*

Contendere animum, *Ovid.* Animo, *Cic. to bend one's mind.* Cursum, *Virg. Plaut. to run swiftly.* In aliquem locum, *Cic. to make all expedition to a place.*

Contendere rem cum alia re, *id.* Alicui rei, *Hor. to compare it.*

CONTINGERE se inter se, or inter sese, *Plaut. Colum. to touch one another, to be allied.*

Atque in magnis ingeniis id plerumque contigit, *Cic. hath often happened.*

Contigit mihi, *id. it has happened to me.*

Contigit mihi, *id. it relates to me, it belongs to me.*

Contingere funem, *Virg. to touch.*

CONVENIRE cum aliquo, *Cic. to agree very well with a person.* Sibi, *id. to preserve always an evenness of temper.* Ad aliquem, *id. to go to meet one.* Aliquem, *Plaut. to talk with him.* In jus, *Plaut. to sue him.*

Convenit inter utrumque, *Cic. they are both agreed.* Mihi cum illo, *id. I am of his opinion.* Ad eum hæc contumelia, *id. concerns him.*

Aliam ætatem aliud factum, *Plaut. becomes better.*

Hæc fratri mecum non conveniunt, *Ter. does not agree with me in this.*

De hoc parum convenit, *Quint. they are not well agreed about this.*

Hoc maledictum in illam ætatem non convenit, *Cic. does not suit or become.*

CUPERE alicui, *Cic. Cæs.* Alicujus causâ, *Cic. to favour him.*

Aliquem, *Ter. Cic. to seek and desire his company.*

Cupit te videre, *Plaut.* Te conventum, *id.*

D

DAMNARE sceleris, or nomine sceleris aliquem, *Cic.* De vi, de majestate, *id. to condemn.* Ad pœnam, in opus, in metallum, *Plin. Jun.*

DARE literas alicui, *Cic. to give or to put them into his hands.*

Litteras ad aliquem, *id. to send or direct letters to him.* Se fugæ & in fugam, *id. to run away.* Sed ad lenitatem, *id. to be extremely mild.* Gemitum & se gemitui, *Cic. Virg. to moan.* Operam, et operam alicui rei, in rem aliquam, ad rem aliquam faciendam, *Cic. to be employed about a thing.* Mandata alicui, *id.* Aliquid in mandatis, *Plaut. to give in charge.* Se in viam, *Cic.* In manum & in manu, *Ter. Cic.*

Dederat comas diffundere ventis, *Virg. loose was her hair, and wantoned in the wind.* Dare manum alicui, *Plaut. to shake hands.*

Dare manus, *Cic. to give up, to yield.* Cibo dare, *Plin. to give to eat.* Dare vitio, *Cic. to blame.*

Da Tityre nobis, *Virg. tell us.*

Dare oblivioni, *Liv. to forget.* The contrary is MANDARE MEMORIÆ, *Cic. to transmit to posterity, to commit to memory, to retain, to learn by heart.* But OBLIVIONI MANDARE; which several moderns make use of, is not Latin, for it cannot be found in any good writer.

OF VERBS OF DIFFERENT GOVERNMENTS. 207

DEBERE amorem et omnia in aliquem, *id.* tibi debemus, *id. we are indebted to you.*
Tibi video hoc non posse deberi, *id.*
DECEDERE alicui, *to give way to him*, Plaut. *to shun one's company,* Cæs.
Decedere, Cic. (*sup.* è vita) *to die.*
De suo jure, *or* jure suo, *id. to relinquish his right.*
De summa nihil decedet, *Ter. the sum shall be untouched.*
DECERNERE aliquid, *or* de re aliqua, *Cic. to ordain, to decree.* Armis, *id. to fight.* Pugnam, *Liv.* Pugna, *Val. Max.* Suo capite, *Cic. to expose one's self to danger.*
DECERE, see the syntax, rule 15.
DECIDERE (*from* cado) à spe, *or* de spe, *Liv.* Spe, *Ter. to fall from.*
In laqueos, *Ovid, to fall into.*
DECIDERE (*from* cædo) caput, *Vellei. to behead.* Quæstionem, *Papin. to decide.* Damnum, *Ulp. to determine.* Cum aliquo, *Cic. to transact.* De aliquo negotio, *id.* Prælio cum aliquo, *id. to decide a dispute by the sword.*
Pro se, *id.* Pro libertate, *Sen. to compound for his liberty.*
Decidere jugera singula ternis medimnis, *Cic. to tax them at three minæ.*
Decisa negotia, *Hor. finished, put an end to.*
DECLINARE loco, à loco, *or* de loco, *Cic. to turn from.* Se extra viam, *Plaut.* Ictum, *Liv. to avoid the blow.* Agmen aliquo, *Liv. to remove his camp.* Nomina & verba, *Quint. to decline and conjugate.*
DEDERE se hostibus, *Cæs.* In ditionem & arbitrium hostium, *Plaut. to surrender himself.* Aliquem in pistrinum, *Ter. to condemn him to hard labour.*
Ad scribendum se dedere, *Cic. to apply himself entirely.* Dedità operà, *id. on purpose.*
DEFERRE studium suum & laborem ad aliquem, *id. to offer one's service to him.* Opes ad aliquod negotium deferre alicui, *id.* Deferre aliquid in beneficii loco, *id. to present a thing to a person in order to oblige him.* In beneficiis delatus, *id. one that has a pension from the state.*
Deferre aliquem, *id. to inform against him.*
DEFENDERE aliquem contra iniquos, *id.* Aliquem ab injuria, *id.* Injuriam alicujus, *id. to avenge the wrong done to him.* Injuriam alicui, *Plaut. to take care that no harm is done to him.*
Defendere & obsistere injuriæ, *Cic.*
Defendere ac propulsare injuriam, *id.*

Defendere civem à periculo, *id.* Myrtos à frigore, *Virg. to preserve them.* Æstatem capellis, *Hor.* Solstitium pecori, *Virg. to shelter them from the heat.*
DEFICERE ab aliquo, *Cic. Liv. to desert his party.* Animo vel animis, *Cic.* Animum, *Varr. to lose courage.*
Dies & latera & vox me deficiunt, *Cic. begin to fail me.*
Deficiunt mihi tela, *Cæs. do fail me.*
Animus si te non deficit æquus, *Hor. has not left you.*
Si memoria deficitur, *Col. if it comes to fail you.*
Deficio à te ad hunc, *Suet. I leave you to go to him.*
Mulier abundat audaciâ; consilio et ratione deficitur, *Cic.*
Deficiórque prudens artis, ab arte mea, *Ovid.*
DEFIGERE oculos in rem aliquam, *Cic.* Mentem in aliquo, *id. to fix one's mind on a thing.*
Defigere furta alicujus in oculis populi, *id. to expose them.*
DEFINIRE aliquid alicui, *id. to shew him*, or *to lay down to him*. Imperium terminis, *id. to limit.* Magnitudinem alicujus rei, *id. to define*, or *mention precisely.*
Certus & definitus locus, *id. a particular and determined place.*
DEFLECTERE iter, *Lucan.* Ex itinere, *Plin. Cic. to turn out of one's road.*
Declinare proposito & deflectere sententiam, *id.*
Amnes in alium cursum deflectere, *id. to turn or divert their bed.*
DEGENERARE à gravitate paternâ, *id. to degenerate.*
A familia superbissima, *Liv. to degenerate, to be unlike.*
In feritatem, *Plin.*
Hoc animos degenerat, *Colum. enervates, weakens.*
DELINQUERE aliquid & in aliqua re, *Cic.* In aliquum, *Ovid, to fail, to do wrong.*
DEPELLERE loco, *Cæs.* De loco, *Cic. to drive away.*
Suspicionem à se, *id. to remove.*
DEPERIRE aliquem, *or* aliquem amore, *Plaut.* Amore alicujus, *Liv. to be passionately in love with.*
Naves deperierunt, *Cæs. are lost.*
DEPLORARE vitam, *Cic. to deplore*, or *bewail.*
De suis miseriis, *id. to lament.*
DEPONERE in gremio, *Plin. Cic.* Stratis, *Ovid.* Sub ramis, *Virg.* In terram, *Colum.* In silvas, *Cæs. to put in, upon, or under something.*

Deponere

Deponere ædificationem, *Cic. to lay aside the design of building.*

Ægrum, *id. to despair of a sick person.*

Aliquid, *Virg. to pledge or pawn, to stake.*

Deponere aliquid in alicujus fide, *Cic.* In fidem, *Liv.* Apud fidem, *Trajan. Plin. to entrust him with.*

DEPRECARI aliquid ab altero, *Cic. to ask him for a thing.* Aliquem pro re aliqua, *id.* Alicui ne vapulet, *Plaut. to intercede for him.*

Calamitatem abs se, *Cic. to avert and keep off by prayer.*

DEROGARE fidem alicui, *or* de fide alicujus, *id.*

Sibi derogare, *id. to derogate from himself.*

DESINERE artem, *id. to quit a profession.*

DESISTERE à sententia, *or* de sententia, *id. to cease, to desist.*

DESPERARE salutem, saluti, *or* de salute, *id. to despair of.* Ab aliquo, *id. to have no further expectation from him.* Sibi, *Cæs.* De se, *Plaut. Cic. to abandon one's self to despair.*

Non despero ista esse vera, *Cic.* Sive restituimur, sive desperamur, *in the passive, id.*

DESPONDERE filiam alicui, *id. to promise in marriage.* Sibi domum alicujus, *id. to promise it to one's self, to be sure of it.*

Despondere animis, *Liv. to think one's self secure of.* Animum, *id. to fall into despair.*

DETRAHERE alicui, *Ovid.* De aliquo. *Cic. to backbite.* Aliquid alteri, *id. to lessen or abate.* Laudem, *or* de laudibus, *id. to diminish his reputation.* In judicium, *id. to sue one at law.*

DETURBARI spe, de spe, vel ex spe, *Cic. to fall from his hopes.*

DIFFERRE famam aliquam alicui, *Plaut. to spread a report.* Rumorem, *Ter.* Aliquid rumoribus, *Tac.*

Differre aliquem, *to put him off, and make him wait,* Mart. *to teaze and vex him,* Ter. Rationem sperat invenisse se qui differat te, *Ter.*

Differri doloribus, *Tac. to feel violent pains.* Amore, cupiditate, lætitia, &c. *Plaut. to be transported with.*

Differre vestitu ab aliquo, *Cic.* In candore, *Plin.* Differt ab hoc, *Cic.* Huic, *Hor.*

Different inter se, *Cic.*

Ad aliquod tempus aliquid differre, *id.* In annum, *Hor. to defer, to put off.*

DIMICARE de re, *Cic.* Pro re, *Plin. to fight, to dispute about or for a thing.*

Dimicant inter se, *Plin.*

Dimicandum omni ratione, ut, &c. *Cic. we must use all our endeavours to obtain it.*

DISCEPTARE aliquid justè, *Cic. to judge, to decide, to dispute.* Damni, *Callistr.* Eodem foro, *Plaut. to come and plead in the same court.*

Disceptant inter se de negotiis, *Sall.*

DISCREPARE rei alicui, *Hor.* A re aliquâ, *Cic. the latter more usual, to vary, to disagree.* Sibi, *id. not to be always one's self.* In re aliqua, *id. in something.*

Discrepant inter se, *id.*

DISCRUCIOR animi, *Plaut.* animo & animum, *from Diomedes, who gives no authority for it.*

DISPUTARE aliquid & de aliquo, *Plaut. Cic.* Circa aliquid, *Quint. to treat about something.* Multa disputat quamobrem is qui torqueatur, beatus esse non possit, *Cic.*

DISSENTIRE de veritate ab aliquo, *id.* In re aliqua ab altero, *id.* Cum aliquo de re aliqua, *id.* Alicui opinioni, *Quint.* Colum. *to disagree about.*

Ne orationi vita dissentiat, *Sen.*

Dissentiunt inter se, *Cic.*

DISSIDERE capitali odio ab aliquo, *id. to hate him mortally.* Diffidere à se ipso, secúmque discordare, *id.*

Inter se diffident & discordant, *id.*

Si toga diffidet impar, *Hor. if it be of different length, or uneven.*

DIVIDERE nummos viris, *Cic.* In viros, *Plaut. to distribute, to divide.* Factum cum aliquo, *Plaut.*

Dividere sententiam, *Cic. to ask to divide the judge's opinion, in order to follow one part, without being obliged to follow the other.*

DOCERE de re aliqua, *Cic. to give advice of it.* Rem aliquam aliquem, *Ter. to teach it him.*

DOLERE ab animo, ex animo, *Plaut.* Successu alicujus, *Ovid.* Dolore alicujus, *Virg. to be deeply afflicted.*

Dolet mihi cor. *Plaut.* Hoc cordi meo, *id.* Caput à sole, *id.*

Doleo me, *Plaut.* Vicem alterius, *Cic.* Casum aliorum, *Cic.* Propter aliquem, *Quint.* De aliquo, *Ovid.*

DONARE aliquem re, vel rem alicui, *Cic. to make him a present of a thing.*

DUBITARE de fide alicujus, *Ad Herenn. to doubt of his fidelity.*

Hæc dum dubitas, *Ter. while you are considering.*

DOMINARI alicui, *Cic.* in aliquem, *Ovid.* In re aliqua, *Sall. Cic.* Inter aliquos, *Cæs. to domineer.*

Omne

OF VERBS OF DIFFERENT GOVERNMENTS. 209

Omne pecus indomitum curari ac dominari poteft, *Nigid.* *may be tamed.*

O domus antiqua heu quàm difpari dominare domino, *Cic.* 1. *Off. ex veteri poëta.*

DUCERE agmen, *id. to lead.* Sibi alapam gravem, *Phæd. to give one's self a box on the ear.* Ilia, *Hor. to be broken winded, to be out of breath.* Æra, *Hor. to caft in brafs.* Aliquem ex ære, *Plin.* Rationem falutis, *Cic. to have a regard.* Verfum, *Ovid. to write verfes.* Uxorem, *Cic. to marry.* Ufuras, *id. to continue the payment of ufury.*

Ducere laudi, *Ter. to efteem it an honour.* In gloria, *Plin.* In hoftium numero, *Cic.* Infra fe, *id. to efteem beneath one.* Pro nihilo, *id.*

Duci defpicatui, *id. to be defpifed.*

E

EFFERRE pedem domo vel porta, *Cic. to go abroad.* Pedem aliquo, *id. to go fome where.* De nave in terram, *id. to unload.*

Efferre laudibus, *id. to extol greatly.*
Efferre fruges, *id. to bear fruit.*
Efferri funere & cum funere, *id.* Pedibus, *Plin. to be interred.*
Efferri ftudio in re aliqua, *Cic. to have a ftrong paffion for.*
Efferri in amorem, *Plin. to be beloved.*

EGERE confilii et confilio, *Cic. to have need.*
Egere multa, -tive, *Cenforinus apud Gellium.* Hence Plautus ufeth *egetur* in the paffive. And hereby Sanctius fheweth that one may elegantly fay, *Turpem egere egeftatem.*

Nihil indigere, *Varr. See* INDIGEO.
EGREDI ab aliquo, *Ter. to go out of a perfon's houfe.* Ex provincia, *Cic.* Extra fines & terminos, *id.* Urbe, *id.* Officio, *id.* A propofito, *id.*

Elabi de, è, ex manibus, *id. to flip away.* Inter tela et gladios, *Liv. to efcape.* Pugnam aut vincula, *Tac.*

Paulatim elapfus Bacchidi, *Ter. weaning himfelf of her by degrees.*

ELABORARE in literis, *Cic.* In aliquid, *Quint.* Aliquid, *Plin.* Orationem eamque inftruere, *Cic.* Ad judicium alterius, *id. to endeavour to pleafe him, and to meris his approbation.*

EMERGERE ex malis, *Cic. Ter.* Incommodâ valetudine, *Cic.* Extra terram, *Plin.* Super terram, *Colum. to rife out of.*

Se vel fefe emergere, *Colum.*
VOL. II.

Unde emergi non poteft, *Ter.*
EMINERE inter omnes, *Cic.* In novo populo, *Liv. to appear on high, to be confpicuous.*

Eminebat ex ore crudelitas, *Cic.* In voce fceleris atrocitas, *Curt.*
Moles aquam eminebat, *Curt. appeared above the water.*

EMUNGERE aliquem argento, *Ter. to cheat one of his money.* Alicui oculos, *Plaut. to pluck out his eyes.*

ENUNTIARE confilia amicorum adverfariis, *Cic.* Apud homines quod tacitum erat, *id. to divulge.*

ERIPERE à morte aliquem, *id. to fave him from dying.* Morti aliquem, *Virg.* Mortem alicui, *Sen.* Ex periculo aliquem, *Cic.*

ERUBESCERE in re aliqua, *id.* Ore alicujus, *id. to blufh to be in his prefence.* Preces, *Claud.* Loqui, *Cic.* Fortunæ, *Q. Curt. to be afhamed of his condition of life.*

Epiftola non erubefcit, *Cic. does not blufh.*

Genis erubuit, *Ovid.*
Malis alterius erubefcere, *Ovid, to blufh at another's misfortunes.*

ERUMPERE ex cenebris, *Cic.* In aliquam regionem, *id.* In hoc tempus, *id.* In actum, *id.* In effectum, *Quint.* Portis, *Virg.* Per Caftra, *Plin.*
Loco aliquo, *Cæf.* Subito clamore, *Virg.*

Erumpunt fefe radii, *Virg.* Sefe portis foras, *Cæf.* Stomachum in aliquem, *Cic.* Gaudium, *Ter.*

Vereor ne ifthæc fortitudo in nervum erumpat denique, *Ter. left you bend the bow fo as to endanger the ftring.*

EVADERE manus alicujus, *Virg.* E manibus, *Liv.* Pugna, *Virg. to make his efcape.* Omnem viam, *Virg.* Ante oculos, *Virg. to come before one.* Ad fummi faftigia tecti, *Virg. to climb.*

In aliquod magnum malum, *Ter. to become very deftructive.*

EXARDERE & -ESCERE irâ, indignatione, *Liv.* In iras, *Mart. to be inflamed.*

Dolor exarfit imis offibus, *Virg.*
Exarfit in id quod nunquam viderat, *Cic.* Exarfere ignes animo, *Virg.*

EXCELLERE fuper alios, *Liv.* Longè aliis, *Cic.* Inter alios, *id.*
Præter ceteros, *id. to excel, to furpafs.*

EXCUSARE fe alicui & apud aliquem, *id. to excufe himfelf.* Valetudinem alicui, *to alledge his indifpofition as an excufe.*

P ——— Ille

——— Ille Philippo
Excusare laborem & mercenaria vincula, *Hor.*
Excusare se de re aliqua, *Cæs.*
Exigere aliquem è civitate, *Cic. to drive him out.* Honoribus, *Plin. to deprive him of honours.* Aliquid acerbius, *Cic. to demand it with menaces.* Columnas ad perpendiculum, *id. to try with the plummet whether they be straight.* Ævum in sylvis, *Virg.* vitam cum aliquo, *id. to pass his life.* Ensem per medium juvenem, *Virg. to run him through the body.*
Sues pastum, *Varr. to drive.*
Exigere de re aliqua, *Plin. Jun. to dispute about a thing, to discuss it.*
Eximere è vinclis, *Cic.* Vinclis, *Plaut.* Metu, *Plaut. to deliver.* In libertatem, *Liv. to set at liberty.* Aliquid de dolio, *Cic. to draw out.*
Eximere diem, *id. to waste the time.*
Eximi noxæ, *Liv. to be discharged or forgiven.*
Exorare, expetere et exposcere aliquid Deos et à Diis, *Cic. & alii, to ask.* See the 24th rule, p. 43.
Expectare alicujus adventum in aliquem locum & in aliquo loco, *Cæs. to wait for a person's arrival at a place.*
Expellere, expedire, ejicere, exterminare, extrudere, extubare, urbe, vel ex urbe, *Cic. to drive out, to put out.*
Explere aliquem, *Cic. Ter.* Animum alicujus, *Liv.* Animum alicui, *Ter. to content, to satisfy him.*
Explicare rem aliquam, vel de re aliqua, *Cic. to explain something.*
Expostulare cum altero injuriam, *id.* De injuria, *Ter. to expostulate.*
Exprimere vocem alicujus, *Cæs. to make him speak.* Risum alicui, *Plin. Jun.* Pecuniam ab aliquo, *Cic.*
Exprimere effigiem, *id. to draw to the life.* Verbum verbo, de verbo, è verbo, exprimere, *id. to translate word for word.*
Exprimere ad verbum de Græcis, *id.* Vim Græcorum poetarum, *id.*
Exprobrare vitia adversariis vel in adversarios, *id. to reproach.*
Exuere jugum & se jugo, *Liv. to shake off the yoke.* Vestem alicui, *Sen. to strip him.* Hominem ex homine, *Cic. to divest one's self of all humanity.*
Exulare Romæ, *id. to live in exile at Rome.* Domo, *Ter. to be banished from home.*
A patria, *Plaut.*
Per externas profugus pater exulat oras, *Ovid.*

Respubl. discessu alicujus exulat, *Cic.*
Exulatum abiit res patris, *Plaut.*

F

Facere ab aliquo, *Cic.* Cum aliquo, *id. to be on his side.* Bona alicui et in aliquem, *Plaut. to do good.*
Consilio alicujus, or de consilio, *Plin. Cic. with his advice.*
Cùm pro populo fieret, *id. as they were offering sacrifice for the people.*
Flocci non facere, *id.* Floccum facere, *Plaut. not to value a rush.*
Facis ex tua dignitate, *Cic. you act up to your dignity.*
Hoc facit ad difficultatem urinæ, *Plin. is a remedy against the strangury.* Non facere ad Corensem pulverem, *Quintil.*
But *facere alicui rei*, signifying to serve for that use, or to be profitable, is not good Latin. Some however have attempted to defend it by this passage of Pliny, book 23. chap. 1. *Mustum capitis doloribus facit.* Which is repugnant not only to the rules of physic, but to the purity of the Latin tongue. Therefore the manuscript copies, and all the best editions, have *Capitis dolores facit*, causeth head achs, and not, is good against head achs.
Facite hoc meum consilium, legiones novas non improbare, *Cic. suppose that.* Non faciam ut enumerem miserias omnes in quas incidi, *id.*
Facere is likewise put with the accusative an infinite number of ways, as
Nos magnum fecissem, *id. we should have struck a great blow.*
Facere gratiam alicui, *Liv. shew him favour.* Facere potam, *Plaut.*
Facere stipendium, *Liv. to serve a campaign, or to follow the army.*
Facere nomina, *Cic. to borrow money.*
Facere rebellionem, *Cæs. to raise a rebellion.* And the like.
Fastidire aliquem, *Cic. Virg. Hor.*
Alicujus, *Plaut. to despise him.*
A me fastidit amari, *Ovid.*
Fateri scelus & de scelere, *Cic. Hor. to confess, to acknowledge.*
Foenerari aliquid alicui, *Cic. to lend out at usury.*
Foenerare (and *not* foenerari) ab aliquo, *Appul. & Jurisconf. to borrow at interest.*
Hæc sapit, hæc omnes foenerat una Deos, *Mart.*
Fidere nocti, *Virg.* terrâ, *id.*

Molin

OF VERBS OF DIFFERENT GOVERNMENTS. 211

Moliri jam tecta videt, jam fidere terrâ, Æn. 3.

FORMIDARE alicui, *Plaut*. *to be afraid lest some harm befal him*. Ab aliquo, or aliquem, *Cicero*, *to fear and to dread him*.

FRAUDARE aliquem pecuniâ, *Cic*. *to cheat him*. Militum stipendium, *Cæs*. *to keep back their pay*. Genium suum, *Plaut*. *to pinch his belly*.

FUGERE conspectum alicujus, *Cic*. E conspectu, *Ter*. Oppido, *Cæs*. De civitate, *Quintil*. *to run away*. De illo fugit me ad te scribere, *Cic*. *I forgot*.

FUNGI officio, *Cic. Ter*. Officium, *Ter*. *to discharge his office*. Vice, *Hor*. Vicem alterius, *Liv. Suet*. *to perform the office of another*. Fungi munere, *to exercise an employment*, *Cic. Cæs. Hor*. *and sometimes to make a present*, *Cic*.

G

GAUDERE gaudio, *Plaut*. Gaudium, *Ter*. *to rejoice*. De aliquo propter aliquem, *Cic*.

Furit homines gavisos suum dolorem, *id*. Mihi gaudeo, *id*.

GIGNI capite vel in caput, *Plin*.

GLACIARE. Positas ut glaciet nives Jupiter, *Hor*. *to congeal*.

Humor glaciatur in gemmas, *Plin*.

GLORIARI aliquid, de re aliqua, in re aliqua, ob rem aliquam, *Cic*. *to boast*.

GRATULARI adventu, *or* de adventu, *id*. *to congratulate him upon his arrival*.

Gratulari victoriam alicui, *id*. *to congratulate him upon his victory*.

Gratulor tibi in hoc, *or* de hac re, *or* pro hac re, *id*.

GRAVARE & RI, *Ovid*, *to burden, or weigh down*.

Gravari dominos, *Lucan*, *to bear no subjection*.

Cætera tanquam supervacua gravari solet, *Quint*. *he is loth to see them*.

Ne gravere exædificare id opus quod instituisti, *Cic*.

Gravatus somno, *Ovid*.

Pluviâ cum forte gravantur, *Virg*.

H

HABERE rem certam, vel pro certo, *Cic*. *to know for certain*. Aliquid certi, *id*.

Habere quædam dubia, *id*. In dubiis, *Quint*. Pro dubio, *Liv*. *to doubt*.

Habere aliquem despicatui, vel despicatum, *Ter*. *to despise*.

Habere aliquem præcipuo honore, *Cæs*. In honore, *Cic*. Honores alicui, *id*. De aliquo, *Tac*. *to praise, to honour*.

Habere aliquem loco patris, *Brutus*. In loco patris, *Cic*. Pro patre, *Liv*. *to esteem him as a father*.

Pro stercore habere, *Plaut*. *to look upon as dirt*.

Habere aliquid odio, *Plaut*. In odium, *Cic*. *to hate it*.

Habere in numero & in numerum sapientum, *id*.

Habere orationem apud aliquem, *Quint*. Ad aliquem, *Cic*. Cum aliquo, *Cæs*. *to speak to, or before a person*.

Habere in potestate & in potestatem, *Cæs*. *to have in one's power*.

Bellè habere & bellè se habere, *Cic*.

Habere usum alicujus rei, *Cic. Cæs*. Ex re aliqua, *Cic*. In re aliqua, *Cæs*. *to have experience, to be practised*.

Habet se erga ædem, *Plato*, *she dwells*.

HABITARE in platea, *Ter*. Vallibus imis, *Virg*. sylvas, *id*.

HÆRERE. Hæret peccatum illi & in illo, *Cic*. *sticks to him, falls upon him*.

Obtutu hæret defixus in uno, *Virg*. *continues fixed*.

In multis nominibus hærebitis, *Cic*.

Si hic terminus hæret, *Virg*. *if this remains fixed and settled*.

HORRERE divinum numen, *Cic*. *to fear and to respect*. Omnium conspectum, *id*. *to dread*.

Frigoribus hyemis intolerabiliter horrent, *Colum*. *to shiver*.

Horruerunt comæ, *Ovid*, *his hair stood an end*.

Horrebant densis aspera crura pilis, *Ovid*.

I

JACTARE se in re aliqua, & de re aliqua, *Cic*. Ob rem aliquam, *to boast*.

Jactare rem aliquam, *Virg*.

ILLABI. Illabitur urbi, *Virg*. *to slip into the town*.

Animis illabere nostris, *Virg*.

Pernicies illapsa civium animos, *Cic*.

Medios illapsus in hostes, *or* delapsus, *Virg*.

Ad eos cum suavitate illabitur, *Cic*.

ILLUDERE alicui, aliquem, in aliquem, in aliquo, *Virg. Ter. Cic*. *to mock to deride*.

Vestes auro illusæ, *Virg*. *embroidered*.

IMMINERE in occasionem opprimendi ducis, *Liv*. *to seek the occasion*.

Imminent duo reges toti Asiæ, *Cic*.

Homo ad cædem imminens, *id.*
Imminenti avaritia esse, *id. to be extremely avaricious.*
Gestus imminens, *id.*
IMPENDERE. Impendebat mons altissimus, *Cæs. bung over, commanded.*
Contentio impendet inter illos, *Cic.*
Impendet nobis malum, *id.* Nos mala, *Ter. threaten us.*
IMPERTIRE & RI. Impertire alicui salutem, *Cic.* Aliquem salute, *Ter. to salute.*
Fortunas aliis impertiri, *Cic. to impart.*
Alteri de re aliqua impertire, *id.*
Collegæ meo laus impertitur, *id.*
IMPLERE veteris Bacchi, *Virg.* Mero pateram, *id.* De re aliqua, *Mart. to fill.*
IMPLICARE ossibus ignem, *Virg. to throw into.*
Implicari morbo et in morbum, *Liv. to be taken ill.*
Vim suam cum naturis hominum implicant Dii, *Cic.* Implicat ad speculum caput, *Plaut. to trim or dress.*
IMPONERE arces montibus, *Virg. to build.* In collum, in manum, in navim, *Plaut. to put upon, or in.*
Summam manum alicui operi, *Virg.* In aliqua re, *Quint.*
Imponere alicui, *Cic. to impose upon him, to deceive him.* See CLITELLAS in the first list of ellipses, p. 177.
Imponere vim alicui, *id. to constrain him.* Vulnera, *id. to wound him.* Nomen alicui, *id. to name him.* Regem regioni, *id. to appoint.* Partes alicui, *id. to give a charge.* Improbam personam alicui, *id. to make him pass for a villain.* Leges alicui, *id. to enjoin him.* Exercitum Brundusii, *id. to garrison.* Ita Stephan.
Imponere onus alicui, *id.* In aliquem, *Plaut.*
Frumentum imponere, *Cic. to tax at a certain quantity of corn.*
Imponere servitutem fundo, *id. to subject to certain duties.*
Hujus amicitia me in hanc perditam causam imposuit, *id. has thrown me into this unfortunate party.*
IMPRIMERE aliquid animo, *Plin. Jun.* In animo, & in animum, *Cic.*
INCESSERE hostes jaculis et saxis aut pilis, *Liv. to assault or set upon.* Incessere aliquem dolis, *Plaut.* Incessit eum cupido, *Liv. Curt.* Illi, *Sall. Liv. Curt. Val. Max.* In te religio nova, *Ter. Virg.* Morbus in castra, *Liv. has crept into.*
INCIDERE (*taken from* cædere) saxis,

Plin. Jun. to cut, or engrave. In æs, *Liv.* In ære, *Cic. Plin. in Panegyr.* Ludum incidere, *Hor. to break off play.*
INCLINARE omnem culpam in aliquem, *Liv. to throw the whole blame upon him.*
Huc ut sequar inclinat animus, *Liv. my mind inclines to.*
Inclinat acies vel inclinatur, *Liv. the army gives way.*
Se fortuna inclinaverat ut, *Cæs. fortune had taken such a turn that.*
INCLUDERE in carcerem et in carcere, *Cic.* Orationi suæ, *id. to shut up, to include.*
Vocem includit dolor, *id.*
Smaragdi auro includuntur, *Luc.*
INCUBARE ova et ovis, *Colum. to brood upon.*
Quod si una natura omnes incubaret, *Plin.*
INCUMBERE gladio, *Ad Heren.* Lecto, aratro, toro, *Virg. Ovid.* In gladium, *Cic. to lean upon.* In aliquem, *id. to fall upon him.*
In or ad aliquid, *Cic. Cæs.* Alicui rei, *Sil. Plin. to apply one's self to something.*
Venti incubuere mari, *Virg.* In mare, *Quint.* Incumbit in ejus perniciem, *Cic. to endeavour to ruin him.*
Verbo incumbit illam rem, *Sall.*
Incumbit illi spes successionis, *Suet. he is considered as next heir.*
INCURSARE aliquem pugnis, calcibus, &c. *Plaut. to assault with blows, &c.*
Incursare in aliquem, *Liv. to run upon him.*
Lana cui nullus color incursaverit, *Plin. that has not been dyed.*
INDICARE conjurationem, *Cic. de conjuratione, Sall. to discover or give information of a conspiracy.*
Indicare in vulgus, *Cic. to divulge.*
Se alicui, *id. to discover one's self to a person.*
Postulabat ut sibi fundus indicaretur, *id. that they would tell him the price.*
INDUCERE animum ad aliquid, or aliquid in animum, *Ter. to apply one's self to something.*
Inducere aliquid, *Cic. to introduce,* and likewise *to rase or strike out.* Aliquem, *id. to deceive him, to cajole, or draw him in.*
Inducere animum, *simply, or* animum ut, *or* ne, *or* ut ne, *Ter. to persuade himself.*
Inducere scuta pellibus, *Cæs. to cover with skins.* Inducere colorem picturæ, *Plin. to varnish.*

INDU-

OF VERBS OF DIFFERENT GOVERNMENTS. 213

INDUERE se veste, *Ter.* Sibi vestem, *Plaut.* to dress himself.

Cùm in nubem se induerint anhelitus terræ, *Cic.* will be converted into clouds.

Induere se in laqueos, *id.* to entangle himself. Induit se in florem, *Virg.* blossoms.

INDULGERE alicui, *Cæs.* In aliquem, *Liv.* to treat him gently.

Nimis me indulgeo, *Ter.* Indulgent patientiam flagello, *Mart.*

Qui malis moribus nomen oratoris indulgent, *Quint.* who grant the name of orator to a person of a bad life.

Jus trium liberorum mihi princeps indulfit, *Plin. Jun.* has granted me.

Quando animus eorum laxari, indulgerique potuisset, *Gell.*

INFERRE litem capitis in aliquem, *Cic.* Periculum capitis alicui, *id.* to draw up an indictment against him.

In periculum capitis se inferre, *id.* to bring himself into danger of his life.

Inferre rationibus, *id.* to charge to account.

INFUNDERE in naribus & per nares, *Colum.* In nares, *Cic.* Cribro, *Sen.* to pour.

Infundere venenum alicui, *Cic.*

Ceris opus infundite, *Phæd.* do your work in wax.

INGERERE convicia alicui, *Hor.* In aliquem, *Plaut.* to load a person with abusive language.

Pugnos in ventrem ingerere, *Ter.*

INGREDI orationem & in orationem, to begin to speak.

Vestigiis patris ingredi, *Cic.* to follow his father's footsteps.

INGURGITARE se cibis, *id.* to cram one's self with victuals. Se in flagitia, *id.* to plunge into debauchery.

INHIARE hæreditatem, *Plaut.* to gape after. Uberibus, *Suet.* the dative is most usual.

INIRE gratiam ab aliquo & cum aliquo, *Cic.* to curry favour.

INSANIRE amore, *Plin.* Amoribus, *Hor.*

Hilarem infaniam, *Plaut. Sen.*

INSCENDERE currum, *Plaut.* In arborem, *id.* Supra pilam, *Cato,* to mount, to climb up.

INSERVIRE suis commodis, *Cic.* to study his own interest. Honoribus, *id.* to study to obtain.

Matronæ est, unum inservire amantem, *Plaut.* Nihil est à me inservitum temporis causâ, *Cic.*

INSILIRE defossos, *Suet.* to leap in, or upon. In equum, *Liv.* In scapham, *Plaut.*

INSISTERE viis, *Cic.* Viam, iter, *Virg.* to proceed and hold on. Hastæ, *Plin. Jun.* to lean upon. Ignibus, *Cic.* to stop, or stand still. In rem aliquam, *Plaut. Cæs.* In re aliqua, *Quint.*

Alicui rei, *Plin. Tibull.* to apply himself.

Insistebat in manu dextra. Cereris simulachrum victoriæ, *Cic.* there was in the right hand.

INSTITIO. Stellarum cursus, progressus, institiones, *id.* their course, and their resting.

INSPUTARE aliquem, & alicui, *Plaut.* to spit upon.

INSTARE aliquem, *Plaut.* to urge, to press him. Currum for in currum, *Virg.* to run upon. Operi, *Virg.* to make haste with.

INSTERNERE. Pelle leonis insternor, *Virg.* to cover one's self.

Tabulasque super instravit, *Virg.*

Terræ insterni, *Stat.*

Tori instrati super pelle leonis, *Silius.*

INSULTARE, simply. *Virg.* Solo, *Virg.* to rebound. Alicui & in aliquem, *Virg. Cic.* to insult, to deride. Multos, *Sall.* apud *Serv.*

Insultare fores calceis, *Ter.* to bounce at the door with his heels.

INTENDERE arcum, *Plin.* to bend, or stretch.

Animum studiis, *Hor.* to apply one's self.

Animum in or ad rem aliquam, *Liv.* Intendere alicui rei, or curam alicui rei, *Plin.* to employ his care about it.

Intendi animo in rem aliquam, *Liv.*

Pergin' sceleste intendere? *Plaut.*

Repudio consilium quod primum intenderam, *Ter.* I alter my resolution.

INTERCLUDERE aditus ad aliquem *Cic.* to stop up the passage. Commeatum inimicis, *Plaut.* Inimicos comeatibus, *Plaut. & Cæs.*

INTERDICERE histrionibus scenam, *Suet.* Feminis usum purpuræ, *Liv.* to prohibit, to hinder.

Omni Galliâ Romanis interdixit, *Cæs.* forbad them to set foot in France.

Malè rem gerentibus bonis paternis interdici solet, *Cic.*

Interdico tibi domo meâ, *Liv.*

We may therefore say, *interdico tibi hanc rem* (which is more rare), or *tibi hac re* (which is usual), but we do not meet with *interdico tibi hac re*, says Vossius. Yet we may use it, since we find in the passive, Interdicor aquâ & igni, *as well as* ignis & aqua mihi interdicuntur, *Cic. Suet. I am forbid, I am deprived.*

Cui nemo interdicere possit, *Cic. whom none could withstand.*

Interdicere vestigiis, *Plin.*

Interdico ne hoc facias, *Ter. sup.* tibi.

Prætor interdixit de vi hominibus armatis, *Cic. decreed that those who had forcibly ejected their antagonists out of their share of the estate, should be obliged to make a reparation.*

INTERESSE conviviis & in convivio, *id.* In cædem, *id. to be present.*

Inter belluam & hominem hoc maxime interest, quod, *id. the greatest difference betwixt man and beast is that, &c.*

Nihil interest hoc & illa, nisi divisim legas, *Senec.* Hoc morari victoriam, quod interesset amnis, *Liv.*

Hoc pater ac dominus interest, *Ter. this is the difference between a father and a master.*

Stulto intelligens quid interest? *Ter.*

Quoniam ἡμέτερ' interest τοῦ φθονεῖν, *Cic.*

Seri radices illitas fimo interest, *Colum.*

Interest regis, *Liv. it behoves.*

Interest omnium recte agere, *Cic.*

Magni mea interesse putavi, *id.*

Ad nostram laudem non multum interesse video, *id.*

INTERJACERE. Planicies Capuam Tipharámque interjacet, *Liv. lies between.*

Spatium quod sulcis interjacet, *Colum.*

Interji t hæc inter eam, *Plin.*

INTUERI aliquem & in aliquem, *Cic. to look at.*

INVADERE aliquem & in aliquem, urbem & in urbem, *Cic. Virg. to invade, to seize.*

In pecunias alienissimorum hominum invadere, *Cic.*

Invasit cupiditas plerisque & plerósque, *Varro. Sall.* Furor invaserat improbis, *Cic. ad Tiron.*

Lassitudine invaserunt huic in genua fœmina, *Plaut. he was troubled with the falling down of blood to the ancles, by reason of overmuch walking.*

INVEHERE per mare, *Plin. to transport.*

Invehi ex alto in portum, *Cic.*

Portum, urbem, *Plin. to be imported.* In aliquem, *to inveigh or speak bitterly against.*

INVIDERE laudes alicui, *Liv. Hor.*

Cic. Laudibus alicujus, *Cic. to envy a person's praise.*

Invidere alicui, *Ter.* Aliquem, *Ovid, to bear him envy.* Alicujus, *Plaut.* Id hac re tibi invideo, *Cic.*

Invident Hermogenes quod ego canto, *Hor.*

The accusative only, without the dative of relation, after this verb, is more rare. Yet Cicero, in the third book of his Tusculan questions, observeth, that as we say *videre florem*, so *invidere florem* would be better than *flori*, if the custom was not against it. Hence Quin. lib. 9. c. 3. enumerates among the incorrect phrases of his time, HUIC REI INVIDERE, pro quo, adds he, *omnes veteres, & Cicero ipse* HANC REM. Whereby we see that the custom has varied.

But the accusative with the dative is common enough.

Ut nobis optimam naturam invidisse videantur qui, &c. *Cic.*

Jampridem nobis cœli te regia, Cæsar, invidet, *Virg.*

INVITARE hospitio & in hospitium, *Liv. Cic.* Ad legendum, *Cic.* Domum, *Liv.* Tecto ac domo, *Cic. to invite, to desire to come.*

INVOCARE subsidium, *id. to ask for succours.* In auxilium aliquem, *Quint.*

IRE viam, *Virg. to go.* Itineribus alicujus, *Cic. to keep the same road.* Subsidio, *Cæs.* In subsidium, *Cic.*

Accersitum, *Ter. to go to fetch.*

Si porrò ire pergant, *Liv. if they have a mind to go further.*

Eamus visere, *Ter.*

JUBERE. See the annotation to the 12th rule.

JUNGERE prudentiam cum eloquentia, *Cic.* Dextram dextræ, *Virg.* Leones ad currum, *Virg. to put to.*

Rhedam equis, *Cic.* Res inter se, *id.*

JURARE alicui, *Plin. Jun.* per sidera, *Virg.*

In leges, *Cic.* In verba aliqua, *Cæs.* Maria aspera, *Virg.* Pulcherrimum jusjurandum, *Cic.*

Qui denegat & juravit morbum, *id.* Bellum ingens juratur, *Stat.*

Jurandásque tuum per nomen ponimus aras, *Hor.*

The latter examples shew plainly that this verb may govern the accusative of itself, and that Vossius had very little ground to affirm that it never did govern this case but by virtue of the preposition *per*. For besides its being hard to say that *jurare jusjurandum*, or *morbum*, is *jurare per jusjurandum*, *gandum*, or *per morbum*; it is moreover ev'dent that since we say *jurandas aras* in a passive sense, we might likewise say *jurare aras* in a real active sense. And adding *per tuum nomen*, he plainly intimates that the force of the verb and the preposition are two different things, which ought therefore to be distinguished. So that when we say *per sidera juro*, we are to understand *juramentum per sidera*, just as *jurandas aras per tuum nomen*, &c.

L

LABORARE invidia vel ex invidia, *Cic. to be envied and hated.* Ex pedibus, *id.*

De verbo, non de re, *id. to trouble himself about terms.* A veritate, *Liv. to be examined for not telling the truth.*

Laborare arma, *Stat. to work*, or *make.* Ad rem aliquam, *Cic.*

Ambitiosè circa aliquid, *Quint. to take great care.*

Ad quid laboramus res Romanas, *Cic.* Laboratur vehementer, *id. they are in great pain, or concern.*

LATERE alicui, *id.* Aliquem, *Virg.* See the Syntax, rule 15, p. 31.

LEGARE ad aliquem, *Cic. to send an ambassador to.* Alicui, *id. to bequeath.* Ab aliquo, *id.*

Sibi aliquem legare, *id. to make him his deputy.*

LEVARE metum alicui, vel aliquem metu, *id. to ease him of*, or *to remove his fear.*

LIBERARE aliquem metu, *Ter.* Aliquem culpæ, *Liv. to acquit.* Fidem suam, *Cic. to fulfil his word.* Aliquem à creditoribus, *Sen. to set him free.*

LOQUI alicui, *Ter.* De aliquo, *Cic.* Apud aliquem, *id.* Cum aliquo, *id. to speak.*

LUDERE pilâ, *id.* Ludum, *Ter.* Aleâ & aleam, *Suet.* In numerum, *Virg.*

LUERE æs alienum, *Curt. to pay his debts.* Pœnas, *Cic. to be punished.* Se, *Ulp. to pay a ransom.*

Oblatum stuprum voluntariâ morte luit Lucretia, *Cic. expiated.*

M

MALEDICERE alicui, *Cic. & alii.* Aliquem, *Tertul. Petron.*

MANARE. Mella manant ex ilice, *Hor. flow.*

Manat picem hæc arbor, *Plin.*

Manat cruore cultor, *Liv.*

MANERE ad urbem, ad exercitum, *Liv.*

In urbe, in exercitu, *Cic. to stay or abide there.* Aliquem, *Plaut. Hor. Virg. to wait for him.*

In proposito, *Cic.* Statu suo, *id.*

Sententia manet, *vel* in sententia maneo, *Cic.* Manere promissis, *Virg. to keep his word.*

Manent ingenia senibus, *Cic.*

Ad te pœna manet, *Tibul.*

Maneat ergo istud, *Cic. let this stand good.*

Maneat ea cura nepotes, *Virg. let our posterity take care for that.*

MEDERI alicui rei, *Cic. to remedy.* Quas minus mederi possit, *Ter.*

Contra serpentium ictus medentur, *Plin.*

Hæc mederi voluerunt, *Cic.*

MEDICARE capillos, *Ovid.* Semina, *Virg. to give an artificial preparation or tincture to a thing.* Alicui, *Ter.* Cuspidis ictum, *Virg. to dress a wound.*

MEDITARI rem aliquam, aut de re aliqua, *Cic. to meditate or think on a thing.*

MEMINI me videre & vidisse, *id.* Rem aliquam & rei alicujus, *id.* De alicujus periculo, *id. to recollect.* Ciceronis & Ciceronem. *See the annotation to the 17th rule.*

MEMOROR, which Valla denies to be ever found with the genitive in classic authors, occurreth in Cicero, *Sui oblitus, alii memoretur*, for *alius*, in 4 *Catil.* which shews the little foundation this author had to censure the following passage of the Vulgate, *Memorari testamenti sui sancti.*

MERERE & RI bene vel malè de aliquo, *Cic. to deserve well or ill of a person.* Apud aliquem, *Liv. to serve or to bear arms under him.* Sub aliquo, *id.*

Stipendium in aliquo bello, *Cic.* E quo, pedibus. *Liv. to serve on foot, or on horseback.* Alicui, *Stat. Lucan. to serve to the profit of any one.*

Mereri laudem, *Cæs.* Offensam, *Quint.*

Scio hanc meritam esse ut memor esses sui, *Ter. she deserved a place in your memory.*

Sæpe quod vellem meritam scio, *Ter. that she often did whatever I would have her.*

MERGERE aliquem Æquore, *or* sub Æquore, *Virg.* Unda vel in undis, *Ovid. to put under water, to sink.*

METUERE alicui, *Plaut.* Pro aliquibus, *Cels.* Propter aliquos, *Plaut.* Aliquem, *Cic.* Ab aliquo, *id.* De vitâ, *id. to fear.* Metuo ut & metuo ne. *See* p. 159.

MINISTRARE vires alicui, *id. to furnish*,

furnish, to afford. Furor arma ministrat, *Virg.*

MIRARI aliquem, *Cic.* De aliquo, *id.* In aliquo, *id.* Justitiæ ne prius mirer, bellique laborum, *Virg. to be surprized.* Mirari se, *Mart. to value or esteem himself.*

MISCERE vinum aquâ & aquam vino, *Plin. to mix.*

Miscere in aciem, *Liv.* Miftos in fanguine dentes, *Virg.*

Miscere ad, *Colum.* Cum, *Cic. Colum.*

Miscere sacra profanis, *Hor.*

MISERERE & RI, or MISERESCERE. Laborum misereri, *Virg. to have compassion, or pity.* Mei miseret nemo, *Plin. no body pities me.* Miseret me tui, *Ter.* Atque inopis nunc te miserefcat mei, *Ter.*

Sanctius pretends that these verbs govern also the dative. And it must be allowed that examples hereof are to be found in authors of the latter ages, as in Boetius,

Dilige jure bonos & miserefce malis.

But there is no authority for this from writers of pure Latinty, if we believe Voffius. Hence in Seneca, lib. 1. contr. 4. where some read, *Ego misereor tibi puella,* the best editions have *tui*. And in regard to that passage which Linacer quotes from the 2d Tusc. it is to be observed that those are verses translated from Socrates, and they are to be pointed thus;

Perge aude nate, illacryma patris pestibus :

Miserere, gentes nostras flebunt miserias.

For we find likewise in another place that Cicero has joined the dative with *illacrymo. Quid dicam de Socrate? Cujus morti illacrymari foleo,* Platonem *legens,* 3. de nat. And Livy also, *Meo infelici errori unus illacrymafti,* lib. 10.

MODERARI animo, orationi, *Cic.*

Cantus numerosque, *id. to regulate.*

MOERERE mortem filii, *id.* Incommodo fuo, *to grieve.*

MONERE aliquem rem, *Cic. Ter.* Alicui rem, *Plaut.* Terentiam de testamento, *Cic.* Aliquem alicujus rei, *Sall.* See the 24th rule, p. 43.

MORARI in re confessa, *Plin.* Circa aliquid, *Hor.* Apud aliquem, *Cæf.* Cum aliquo, Pompon. In urbe, *Ovid.* Sub dio, *Hor. to stay, to dwell.*

Iter alicujus morari, *Cic. to delay him.* Quid moror?. *Virg. What do I stay for?*

Purpuram nihil moror, *Plaut. I do not value.*

MOVERE se loco vel ex loco, *Cæf.* De convivio, *Cic.* Ab urbe, *Liv. to be gone, to move.*

Movere aliquem senatu, vel è senatu, *Cic. ta depose him, to degrade him.* A se morum, *Plaut. to make no delay.* Risum & jocum movere alicui, *Hor. to make him laugh.*

Ego isthæc moveo aut curo? *Ter. Is it I that am the cause of this bustle ?*

MUTARE rem aliâ re, *Hor.* Bellum pro pace, *Sall.* Aliquid cum aliquo, *Ter. to change with him.*

Mutare locum, *Cic. to change place.* Mutari civitate, *id. to be removed from one town to another.*

MUTUARI auxilia ad rem aliquam, *Cæf.* In fumptum, *Cic. to afk, to borrow.*

A viris virtus nomen est mutuata, *id. has borrowed its name.*

N

NARRARE aliquid, *or* de re aliquâ, *Cic. to tell,* or *to relate.*

NATARE aquas, *Virg.* Unda natatur piscibus, *Ovid.* Pars multa natat, *Hor. the generality of mankind are inconstant and wavering.* Natabant pavimenta vino, *Cic. swam with wine.*

NITI sub pondere, *Virg.* In adversum, *Ovid.* Ad sidera, *Virg. to tend towards.* Gradibus, *Virg. to mount.* Hastâ, *Virg. to lean upon.* Humi, *Virg. to walk upon the ground.* Contra honorem alicujus, *Cic. to oppose.* Pro aliquo, *Liv.* De æquitate, *id. to defend and maintain.*

Cujus in vita nitebatur falus civitatis, *id. was supported, depended.*

Alternos longa nitentem cuspide greffus, *Virg.*

Tantum quantum quisque poteft nitatur, *Cic. let him do what he can.*

NOCERE alicui, *id.* Aliquem, *Plaut. Sen. to hurt.* Qui Deorum quemquam nocuerit, *Liv.*

NUBERE alicui *or* eum aliquo, *Cic.* the former more usual. The second occurs in *the 3d epistle of the 15th book.* Quocum nupta regis Armeniorum foror. *And against Verres.* Virorum quibuscum illæ nuptæ erant.

Now *nubere,* as we have observed p. 30, signifieth properly *velare,* to cover or to veil. *Mulier nubit,* says Caper in his orthography, *quia pallio obnubit caput fuum & genas.* Hence *nubere alicui,* is to hide and to reserve herself for him. And *nubere cum aliquo,* is *tegere & operire se uno cubiculo cum illo,* according to Donatus, on Terence's Hecyra. So that the accusative is always understood.

This

This verb is never said but of the woman, for which reason we use only *nupta sum in* the participle. It is true Plautus said, *Novum nuptum*, but it was only through theatrical buffoonery, when a man appeared upon the stage in woman's apparel.

But it is observable that in Pliny *nubere* is applicable also to trees and vines, when they are joined together.

O

OBAMBULARE muris, *Liv. to walk round the walls.* Ante portas, *Liv.*

OBEQUITARE stationibus hostium, *Liv.* Agmen, *Curt. to ride round about.*

OBJICERE feris, *Cic. to expose to wild beasts.* Ad omnes casus, *id.* Se in impetus hominum, *id.* Aliquid criminis, *Plin.* Loco criminis, *id. & Cic.*

OBLIVISCI aliquem, *Virg.* Suæ dignitatis, *Cic. to forget.*

Artificium obliviscatur licebit, *id.*

OBREPERE ad magistratum, *id. to steal by degrees, to creep in privately.* Adolescentiæ senectus obrepit, *id. succeeds immediately.* Nullæ imagines obrepunt in animos dormientium extrinsecus, *id.*

Statim te obrepet fames, *id.*

OBRUERE telis, *id. to oppress with darts.* Terrâ, *Cato.* In terra, *Ovid. to bury.* Se vino, *Cic. to get drunk.*

Nox terram obruit umbris, *Luc. covers it.*

OBSTREPERE portis, *Liv. to make a noise.* Litteris alicui, *Cic. to importune him by letters.* Hinc illi geminas vox avium obstrepit aures, *Virg.* Clamore obstrepi, *Cic. to be stunned with noise.*

OBTRECTARE laudibus & laudes alicujus, *Liv. to backbite.*

Obtrectare legi, *Cic. to oppose it.*

OBVERSARI oculis, *Liv.* Ante oculos, *Cic.* In somnis, *Liv. to present itself before us.*

OBVERTERE signa in hostem, *Liv. to turn against the enemy.* Terga alicui, *Virg. to run away.*

OBUMBRARE. Oleaster obumbrat vestibulum, *Virg. overshadows.*

Sibi ipsa non obumbrat, *Plin.*

OCCUMBERE morti, *Virg.* Morte, *Cic.* Mortem, *Liv. Suet. to die.*

Ferro occumbere, *Ovid. to be killed.*

OCCUPARE aliquem, *Cic. Curt. to be beforehand with him, to surprize him.* Se in aliquo negotio, *Cic. Ter.* Ad aliquod negotium, *Plaut. to busy or to employ one's self.* Occupare pecuniam alicui, *vel* apud aliquem, *Cic. to put money out to use.*

Quorum magnæ res aguntur in vestris vectigalibus occupatæ, *id.*

OFFENDERE aliquem, *id.* Apud aliquem, *id.* Aliquo, *id. to offend a person, to be upon bad terms with him.*

At credo si Cæsarem laudatis, in me offenditis, *Cæs. but very likely if you commend Cæsar, you offend me.* Offendere in arrogantiam, *Cicer. to give into pride or arrogance.*

Sin quid offenderit, tibi totum, tibi nihil offenderit, *id. but if he takes any wrong step, it will be all to himself.*

Cecidisse ex equo & latus offendisse, *id. that he fell from his horse and hurt his side.* Si in me aliquid offendistis, *id. if you have found any fault with me; if in aught I have offended you.*

Cum offendisset populum Atheniensium prope jam desipientem senectute, *id. having found.*

Offendere in scopulis, *Ovid.* Ad stipitem, *Colum. to run, or hit against.*

Naves in redeundo offenderunt, *Cæs. were unfortunate, fell into the enemy's hands.*

Offendere alicujus existimationem, *Cic. to hurt his reputation.* Alicui animum, *id. to shock, or to vex him.*

OLERE. Olet unguenta, *Ter. he smells of perfume.* Olet huic aurum meum, *Plaut. he hath got some inkling of my gold.*

Olent illa supercilia malitia, *Cicer.*

Olentia sulphure, *Ovid, that smells of sulphur.*

Redolentque thymo, *Virg.*

OPPONERE periculis, *Cic. to expose to danger.* Ad omne periculum, *id.*

Opponere pignori, *Plaut. Ter. to pawn, or to pledge.*

Opponere manum fronti, *or* ante oculos, *Ovid, to put before.*

OPPUGNARE aliquem clandestinis consiliis, *Cic. to endeavour to ruin him by underhand doings.* Oppugnare consilia alicujus, *Plaut.*

P

PALLERE argenti amore, *Hor. to grow pale.* Pindarici fontis haustus non expalluit, *Hor. he was not afraid of.*

PALPARE & RI. Palpare aliquem, munere, *Juv. to caress, to flatter.*

Cui male si palpêre, recalcitrat, *Hor.* Pectora palpanda manu, *Ovid.*

PARCERE labori, *Ter. to spare,* Aliquid alicui, *Ter. to forgive him.* Parcite oves nimium procedere, *Virg. do not suffer them to go too far.*

Precantes ut à cædibus & incendio parceretur, *Liv. that they would abstain from.*

PARTICIPARE fervum confiliis, *Plaut. to impart your secrets to him.* Suas laudes cum aliquo, *Liv.* Rem aliquam, *Cic. to partake*, or *have his share.*

PASCERE pratum & in prato, *Ovid. to feed.* Animum pictura pafcit ioani, *Virg.* Hic pafcor bibliotheca Faufti, *Cic. id.* Delector.

PASCI, *deponent.* Apes pafcuntur arbuta, *Virg.* Armenta pafcuntur per herbas, *Virg.* and *Ovid.*

PELLERE tectis, *Ovid.* A foribus, *Plin.* E foro, *Cic.* Ex aliqua regione, *Plin.* Domo, regno, civitate, agro, fedibus, &c. *Cic. to drive from.*

PENDERE promiffis, *id. to depend on pr mifes.* Animi et animis, *id. to be in doubt.* Pendet animus, vel animus tibi pendet, *Ter. you are in fufpenfe.* Cui fpes omnis ex fortuna pendet; *Cic.* De te pendentis, te refpicientis amici, *Hor.* Pendent opera interrupta, *Virg. remain imperfect.* Cafu pendemus ab uno, *Lucan, we depend on.* Ad fua vota pendentes, *Sen.* In fententiis civium fortunam noftram pendere, *Cic.* Dumofa pendere de rupe, *Cic. to be at the top of a rock.* Hi fummo in fluctu pendent, *Virg. are toffed to the top of the waves.* Illisáque prora perpendit, *Virg. ftuck there.* Scopuli pendentes, *Virg. hanging as it were in the middle of the air, and leaning over us.* Nubila pendentia, *Virg.*

PENDERE poenas temeritatis, *Cic.* Poenas pro fcelere, *Lucr. to pay.* Pater fe nihili pendit, *Ter. gives himfelf no fort of trouble.* Magni pendi, *Lucr. to be greatly efteemed.*

PENETRARE in coelum, *Cic. to enter into heaven.* Atlantem, *Plin. to pafs beyond.* Sub terras, *Cic.* Se in fugam, *Plaut. to run away.* Pedem intra ædes, *Plaut. to enter.* Ad Romanos, *Plin. to go towards.*

PENSARE una laude crimina, *Plin. to recompenfe.* Laudem cum crimine, *Claud.* Penfari eadem trutina, *Hor. to be weighed in the fame balance.*

PERCUNCTARI aliquem, *Quint. Hor.* Ab aliquo, *Cic.* Aliquid, aliquem, *Plaut.* Aliquid ex alio, *id. & Cic.* Aliquem de re aliqua, *id. to inform one's felf, to inquire; to ask.*

PERGO præterita, *id. to wave, or pafs over in filence.* Perge facere, *Ter. go on.*

PERMITTERE fe in fidem vel fidei alicujus, *Cæf. to put one's felf under his protection.* Equum in hoftem, *Liv. to put on, to ride full fpeed againft.* Vela ventis, *Plin. to fet fail.*

PERSEQUI veftigia alicujus, *Cic.* Aliquem veftigiis. ipfius, *id. to follow his footfteps.* Artem aliquam, *id.*

PERSONARE æquora conchâ, *Virg. to make the fea refound.* Eft mihi purgatem crebro qui perfonet aurem, *Hor.* Perfonabat domus cantu tibiarum, *Cic. echoed.* Ululatus perfonant tota urbe, *Liv. nothing elfe is heard.*

PERTÆDERE thalami, *Virg.* Igna viam fuam, *Cæf.* Morum perverfitatem, *Suet.*

PERVADERE. Pervafit murmur totam concionem, *Liv. was fpread every where.* Incendium per agros, *Cic.* Pars belli in Italiam, *id.* Conful ad caftra, *Liv.*

PETERE ab aliquo, *Cic. to afk.* Aliquem, *Virg. to fupplicate.* Auxilium fibi ab aliquo, per aliquem, *Cic.* Poenas ab aliquo, *id. to have him punifhed.* Veniam errati & errato, *id.* Aliquem gladio, lapide, &c. *to ftrive to hit him.* Locum, *id. to go to a place, and make to it.*

PIGNERARE & RI. Ex aure matris detractum unionem pigneravit ad itineris impenfas, *Suet. to pawn.* Mars ipfe ex acie fortiffimum quemque pignerari folet, *Cic. is ufed to take them as a pledge.*

PLAUDERE aliquem, *Stat. to applaud him.* Sibi, *Hor. to applaud himfelf.* Pedem fupplaudere, *Cic. to ftamp on the ground, to knock with the foot.*

Propter vicinum malum nec victoria quidem plauditur, *Cic. Attico.*

POLLERE moderatione & conftantiâ, *Cic. to be famed for moderation and conftancy.* Pollet ejus autoritas, *Sall. is very ftrong, has a great weight.*

PONERE coronam in caput vel in capite, *Gell.* Curam in re aliqua, *Cic.* Dies multos in rem aliquam, *id.* Fidem pignori, *Plaut. to pawn his word.* Cuftodias portis, *Hirt.* Infidias alicui vel contra aliquem, *Cic. to lay ambufh.* Officium apud aliquem, *id. to oblige a perfon.* Sibi aliquid in fpe optima, *id.* Spem in armis, *id.*

Ponere in beneficii loco, *id. to look upon it as a great favour.*

Ponere

Ponere de manibus, *id. to quit.*
Ponúntque ferocia Pœni———Corda volente Deo, *Virg.*
POSCERE munus ab aliquo, *Cic.* Aliquem causam differendi, *id.* Filiam alicujus sibi uxorem, *Plaut. to ask.*
Poscere majoribus poculis, *Cic. to require that one should pledge him in larger glasses.*
POSTULARE aliquem de ambitu, *id. to accuse one,* or *to sue at law.* Servos in quæstionem, *id. to insist that the plaintiff be obliged to expose his slaves to the torture, in order to come at the truth.*
Postulabatur injuriam, *Suet. he was accused of.*
POTIRI præsentibus, *Cic.* Gaudia, *Ter.* Voluptatum, *Cic. to enjoy.*
Potiri hostium, *to have the enemy in his power:* and sometimes (as in Plautus) *to fall into the hands of the enemy.* The reason hereof is, that the antients, to avoid a bad omen, frequently made use of a favourable expression to denote a bad thing; whence cometh *sacer* for execrable, and *benedicere* in the scripture for *to curse,* and the like. Hence it is that they have an infinite number of phrases and turns to signify death, without hardly ever naming it.
PRÆBERE strenuum hominem, *Ter. to shew himself brave.* Se æquum, *Cic. to shew himself just or impartial.*
PRÆCAVERE ab insidiis, *Liv.* Peccata, *Cic. to avoid.*
PRÆCEDERE, ut vestræ fortunæ meis præcedunt, *Plaut.* Vinum aliud aliud amœnitate præcedit, *Colum.*
Præcedere in re aliqua, *Plin.*
PRÆCURRERE aliquem & alicui, *Cic. to run or make speed before, to outrun.*
PRÆIRE verbis, *Plaut.* Verba, *Liv. to speak before.* De scripto, *Plin. to dictate.*
Præeunt discipulis præceptores, *Qu. to teach them.* But *præire alicui,* to signify *excelling,* is not used. See *præstare.*
PRÆSTARE, PRÆCELLERE, PRÆCEDERE, PRÆVERTERE, alicui, vel aliquem (but præire alicui only, says Vossius), *to surpass, to excel.*
Homo ceteris animantibus præstat, *Cic.* Virtus præstat ceteris rebus, *id.*
Quantum Galli virtute alios præstarent, *Liv.* Præstat tamen ingenio alius alium, *Quint.*
Vel magnum præstet Achillem, *Virg. even if he were more valiant than Achilles,* or *were he another Achilles.*
Præstare alicui scientia, ætate, &c. *Cic.*

Inter suos æquales longè præstare, *id. to excel, to be foremost.*
Præstare benevolentiam alicui, *id. to shew him affection.*
Sapientis non est præstare nisi culpam, *id. a wise man ought to answer for* (or *be sure of*) *nothing but his own faults.* Sed motos præstat componere fluctus, *Virg. it is better.*
Præstare rempublicam, *Cic. to support the republic.* Se & ministros sociis reipub. *id. to answer for himself and his officers to the allies of the republic.* Factum alicujus, *id. to approve of it.*
Aliquem ante ædes, *Plaut. to bring him out.* Hoc finibus his præstabis, *Cic.*
Se incolumem præstare, *id. to preserve his health.*
Principem præstare, *Suet. to act the part of a prince.*
Præsto hæc, *Cæcil. I give this, I bring this.*
Præstare vitium, *Cic. to take it upon himself.*
PRÆSTOLARI aliquem, *Ter.* alicui, *Cic. to wait for a person.*
PRÆVERTERE aliquem præ repub. *Plaut. to prefer, to set before.* Aliquid alicui rei, *Cic. Plaut. to prefer it,* or *to say it before.*
Huic rei prævertendum existimavit, *Cæs. that is must be prevented.*
Illuc prævertamur, *Hor. let us set this first.*
PROCEDERE in virtute, ad virtutem, ad virtutis aditum, *Cic. to advance in virtue.*
¶ Ætate processit, *id. he is advanced in age.*
Omnia ut spero prosperè procedent, *id. all will go very well.*
PROCUMBERE genibus, *Ovid.* Ad genua, *Liv.* Ante pedes alicujus, *Ovid. to prostrate one's self at his feet.* Ad arborem, *Mart. to lean against.*
Procumbit humi bos, *Virg. falls down.*
Procumbere in armos, *Mart.* In caput, *Ovid, to fall upon.*
PRODERE memoriæ, *Cic.* Memoriâ, *Cæs.* Monumentis, *Cic. to commit to posterity.*
Prodere memoriam alicujus festi, *id.*
Prodit memoria, *Colum. we find in writing.*
PROHIBERE vim hostium ab oppidis, *Cæs. to repel, to keep away, to stay.* Aditum alicui vel aliquem aditu, *Cic. to debar or hinder him from coming.*

Dolorem

Dolorem dentium, *Plin. to give ease, to* &c. Aliquem ab injuria, *Sall. to defeat him.*

Uxorem prohibent mihi, *Plaut. they keep her away from me.*

PROPERARE in campum, *Cic. Ad exitum, Brutus.*

Properare proficisci, *Cæs. to make haste to be gone.*

Pecuniam indigno hæredi properare, *Hor. to hoard in a hurry.*

Hoc opus hoc studium parvi properemus & ampli, *Hor.*

Lanæ properabantur, *Hor.*

PROPUGNARE commoda patriæ, *Cic. to defend them against the enemy.* Pro salute alicujus, *id. to fight for.*

Propugnat nugis armatus, *Hor.* that is, Pro nugis.

PROSPICERE sibi, saluti suæ, &c. *Ter. Cic. to take care of.* In posterum, *Cic.* Futura, *id. to foresee.* Senectutem, *Sen. to be near.*

Ni parum prospiciunt oculi, *Ter. if my eyes do not deceive me.*

Nec oculis prospicio satis, *Plaut.*

Villa quæ prospicit Tuscum mare, *Phæd. that has a prospect over the sea.*

PROVIDERE in posterum, *Cic.* Alicui contra aliquem, *id. to protect him.* Rei frumentariæ, vel rem frumentariam, vel de re frumentaria, *Cæs. to make provision, to look after.*

Hæc si non astu providentur, me aut herum pessumdabunt, *Ter. if they are not looked after, or prevented.*

Provisum est rationibus multis ne, &c. *Cic.* A diis immortalibus, &c. *id.*

PUGNARE pugnam, *Plaut.* Prælia, *Hor. to fight battles.* Cum hoste, *Cic.* Contra pedites, *Plin.*

Adversus latrones, *Plin. to fight against.*

Illud video pugnare te ut, &c. *Cic. I plainly see that you pretend.*

Pugnare de re aliqua, *Cic. Ter.* Pro aliquo, *Cic.*

In aliquo loco, *id.*

Pugnata pugna cum rege, *Liv.*

Pugnata bella sub Ilio, *Hor.*

Quod à vobis hoc pugnari video, *Cic.*

PURGARE se apud aliquem vel alicui de re aliqua, *Ter. to clear or to justify himself.*

Purgare crimen, *Cic.*

Mores tuos mihi purgatos voluisti, *id.*

PUTARE nihil, *Ter.* Pro nihilo, *Cic.* Aliquid minimi, *id. to make no account of.*

Rem ipsam putemus, *Ter. let us consider the affair itself.*

Putare rationem cum aliquo, *Cic. to adjust, or cast up accounts.*

Putatur prudens, *id. he is esteemed prudent.*

Q.

QUADRARE acervum, *Hor. to make square.*

Omnia in istam quadrare apte videntur, *Cic.* speaking of Clodia, *do suit her very well.*

Visum est mihi hoc ad multa quadrare, *id. may serve for many purposes.*

Quare quoniam tibi ita quadrat, *id. since you judge fit.*

QUÆRERE aliquid ab aliquo, *Cic. Cæs.* De aliquo, *Liv. Cic.* Ex aliquo, *id. to ask or enquire of him.* In aliquem, *Cic. to make inquisition,* or *to inform against him.*

Quærere omnes ad unum exemplum, *id. to want to reduce them all to one model.*

Quærere rem tormentis & per tormenta, *id. to put to the rack.*

Quærere rem mercaturis faciendis, *id. to endeavour to make a fortune by commerce.*

QUERI. Multa de mea sententia questus est Cæsari, *id. he complained.*

Acceperam Milonem meum queri per litteras injuriam meam, *id.*

Is mihi queritur quod, *id.*

Quereris super hoc quod, *Hor.*

Apud populum questus est, *Plin. Jun.*

QUIESCERE tota nocte, *Cic.* Viginti dies, *id.* Somnum humanum, *Appul. to sleep, to repose.*

Quibus quidem quamfacile poterat quiesci, si, &c. *Ter. how easy it would have been to have done without them!*

Nunquam per M. Antonium quietus fui, *Cic.*

Quiescat rem adduci ad integrum, *id. let him suffer.*

R.

RECIPERE alicui, *id. to promise.* Aliquem, *id. to receive him.* Urbem, *id. to take or to recover it.* In se omnia, *id. to take upon him.* Se ad or in locum, *id. to betake himself to.* Se ex loco, *id. to return.* Se ad aliquem, *Cæs. to retire to.* Se ad frugem, *Cic. to grow better.* Se proximo castello, *Hirtius, to shut himself up, to retire to.*

Recipere tectis, *Cic. to entertain,* or *harbour.* In navem, *id. on board.*

Recipitur in cibum hæc herba, *Plin. is good to eat.*

RECORDARI alicujus rei, aliquam rem, de re aliqua, *Cic.* Cum animo
sus

suo vitam alicujus, *id. to call to mind, to remember.*

REDDERE colori aliquid, vel colorem alicui, *Plin.*

Vitam pro republ. *Cic. to die in the service of the republic.* Spiritum alicui, *Liv. to expose his life for another's service.*

REFERRE alicui, *Ovid, to relate, to tell.* Ad aliquem, *Cic. to ask his opinion, to refer to him.* Omnia ad aliquem finem, *id.*

Aliquem ore referre, *Cic. to resemble him.*

In acceptum referre, *Cic. to acknowledge the receipt of.*

Referre mandata ad aliquem, *Cæs. Alicui, Virg.*

In vel inter reos referre, *Cic.*

Referre alicui salutem, *id.*

Acceptam salutem alicujus benevolentiæ referre, *id. to think you owe your life to his goodness.*

Referre ensem vaginæ, *Sil. to put it up in the scabbard.* Aliquid in commentarium, *Cic. to write or set down.* Se in gregem suum, *id.*

Retulit ad me pedem, *Plaut. is come back to me.*

Me referunt pedes in Tusculanum, *Cic. I return on foot to Tusculanum.*

Referunt hæc ad rem, *Plaut. This relates to the matter.*

Par pari referre, *Cic. to return like for like.*

Hæc ego illorum defensioni retuli, *id. This I said to obviate what they might allege in their defence.*

Referre cum aliquo, *id. to confer with a person.*

RENUNTIARE alicui vel ad aliquem, *id. to advertise, or acquaint.*

Renuntiare aliquid, *id.* De re aliqua, *Plaut. to speak of an affair.*

Renuntiare consulem, *Cic. to proclaim the consul.*

Renuntiare alicui amicitiam, *Suet.* Hospitium, *Cic. to renounce his friendship and alliance.* Repudium, *Ter.*

Renuntiare vitæ, *Suet.* Societati, *Paul. Jurisc.* Matrimonio, *Licin. Jurisc.* Muneri officio, *Quint. to renounce.*

Prætor renuntiatus est, *Cic. was declared prætor.*

REPONERE in numero & in numerum, *id. to place among the number.* Omnia suo loco, *id. to put in their proper place.*

REPOSCERE aliquid alterum & ab altero, *id. to ask again, to claim.*

Ad pœnas aliquem reposcere, *Virg. to insist on his being brought to justice.*

REPUGNARE alicui rei, *Cic.* Contra veritatem, *id.* Circa aliqua, *Quint. to oppose, to resist.*

REQUIESCERE lecto, *Tibull.* Humo, *Ovid.* In sella, *Cic. to rest, to repose.* In miseriis, *id.* A malis, *id. to have some respite.*

Et mutata suos requiescunt flumina cursus, *Virg. do stop.*

RESCRIBERE litteris, *Cic.* Ad litteras, *Brutus ad. Cic. to answer.* Argentum alicui, *Ter. to pay money by bill.* Legionem ad equum, *Cæs. to make horse of foot.*

RESIDERE humo, *Ovid. to sit upon the ground.*

Si quid resident amoris in te mei, *Cic. if you have any love for me still left.*

Culpa resident in te, *Brutus ad Cic.* Penes te, *Alphen.*

Pecunia publica apud eum resedit, *Martian.*

Resident spes reliquis, *Cic. the rest have hopes still.*

Quum tumor animi resedisset, *id. being abated.*

Venter gutturque resident esuriales ferias, *Plaut. cap. act. 1. that is, Sedendo agunt,* says Sanctius.

Residentur mortui, *Cic. 2. de leg. when the corpse is watched or attended.*

RESPICERE aliquem & ad aliquem, *Ter. to look, or to respect.*

Summa imperii ad nos respicit, *Cæs. belongs to us, regards us.*

RESPONDERE alicui, *Cic. Virg.* Ad aliquem, *Pliny, to answer, or to correspond.*

Contra elata mari respondet Gnosia tellus, *Virg. presents itself, shews itself.*

RESTITUERE sanitatem alicui & aliquem sanitati, *Plin. to heal, to restore to health.*

In possessionem restituere, *Cic.*

Retinere memoriam alicujus rei, & memoriâ retinere aliquid, *id. to remember.*

Pudore & liberalitate retinere pueros, *Ter. to restrain or govern.*

RIDERE aliquem, *Cic. Ter. to laugh at one.*

De re aliqua, *Cic.*

Ridere risum, *id.*

Domus ridet argento, *Hor. shines.*

RORARE. Rorat, *simply. Colum. to fall down like dew, to bedew.*

Si roraverit quantulumcunque imbrem, *Pliny, if it drops never so little rain.*

Rorare

Rorare aliquem cruore, *Sill. to besprinkle him with blood.*

Lacrimis oculi rorentur obortis, *Ovid.*

Roratæ rofæ, *Ovid, bedewed.*

RUERE ad interitum voluntarium, *Cic.* In ferrum pro libertate, *Virg. te ruſh upon.*

Ruere illa non poſſunt, *Cic. cannot fall to the ground.*

Vide ne quid imprudens ruas, *Ter.*

Spumas falis ære ruebant, *Virg.*

Cæteros ruerem, agerem, proſternerem, *Ter.*

S

SALTARE laudes alicujus, *Plin. Jun. to dance ſinging his praiſes.*

Paſtorem ſaltaret uti Cyclopa rogabat, *Hor. that he would act the part of Polyphemus in dancing.*

Nemo ferè ſaltat ſobrius, *Cic.*

SAPERE. Palatus ei fapit, *id. he has a ſmack of.*

Mare fapit, *it has the taſte of ſea-water.*

Si recta faperet, *Cic. if he were wiſe.*

Ego meam rem fapio, *Plaut. I know my own affairs.*

SATISFACERE alicui de viſceribus, *Cic. to pay him with his own money.* Alicui de re aliqua, *Cæſ. concerning ſomething.* Alicui in pecunia, *Cæl. ad Cic.*

Donicum pecuniam ſatisfecerit, *Cato de RR. till he has paid the money.*

Satisfactum eſt promiſſo noſtro, *Cic.*

SATURARE. Hæ res me vitæ ſaturant, *Plaut. give me a ſurfeit of life.*

Pabulo ſe ſaturare, *Varro.*

SCATERE moleſtiarum, *Gell.* Ferarum, *Lucr. to be full of, to overflow.*

Pontus ſcatens belluis, *Hor.*

SEDERE in equo, *Cic.* Equo, *Liv. Mart. to ride.* Poſt equitem, *Hor. to ride behind.* Supra leonem, *Plin.* Ad latus alicujus, *Cic.*

Dum apud hoſtes ſedimus, *Plaut. ſo long as we were near.*

Si ſedet hoc animo, *Virg. if it be your pleaſure.*

Memor illius eſcæ, quæ tibi ſederit, *Hor. which agreed with you beſt.*

Veſtis ſedet, *Quint. ſits well.*

Omnes conſurrexiſſe, & ſenem illum ſeſſum recepiſſe, *Cic. roſe up, and made room for the old man.*

SEQUI veſtigiis aliquem, *Liv. to follow his track.* Sententiam alicujus, *Cic. to be of his opinion.*

SERPERE humi, *Hor.* Per humum, *Plin. to creep along the ground.*

Serpit draco ſubter ſupraque revolvens ſeſe, *Cic.*

SERVIRE tempori, valetudini, rei familiari, &c. *id.* Servitutem, *id. Plaut. Liv.*

Æternum ſervire, *Hor.* Apud aliquem, *Plaut. Servius.*

Liber ſervibo tibi, *Plaut.* Martia ſervibo commodis, *Ter.* Ut communi utilitati ſerviatur, *Cic.*

Non bene crede mihi ſervo ſervituꝛ amico, *Mart.*

SITIRE ſanguinem, *Cic. to thirſt after blood.*

Sitiunt agri, *id.* Sitientes loci, *Plin. dry places.*

Quo plus ſunt potæ plus ſitiuntur aquæ, *Ovid.*

SOLVERE crimine, *Stat. to abſolve, to diſcharge.* Fidem, *to break his word.* *Ter. to fulfil his vow, Ovid.* Argumentum, *Quint. to ſolve.* Pecuniam, *Cic. to pay.* Vitam alicui vel aliquem vita, *Plaut. to put him to death.* Obſidionem urbis, & urbem obſidione, *Liv. to raiſe a ſiege.* Fœdera, *Virg. to break.*

Solvere ſimply, or ſolvere navem, or ſolvere è portu, *Cic. Cæſ. to weigh anchor, to put to ſea.*

Solvere ab Alexandria, *Cic. to ſet ſail from Alexandria.*

Solvere ab aliquo, *id. to take money from a perſon in order to pay his debts.*

Nec ſolvitur in ſomnos, *Virg. cannot ſleep.*

Solvendo non eſſe, *Cic. to have not wherewithal to pay.*

Soluturus ne ſit eos pro bonis, *id. whether he will pay them away as good money.*

SPECTARE orientem, *Plin.* Ad orientem, *Cæſ.* In meridiem, *Cato, to look towards.*

Spectare animum alicujus ex ſuo, *Tertul. to judge of another perſon from one's ſelf.*

Spectare aliquem ex cenſu, *Cic. to reſpect him according to his income.*

In unum exitum ſpectantibus, *id. tending to the ſame end.*

Stare ad curiam, *id. not to ſtir from the court.* In æquo alicui, *Jup. loco, Sen. to be upon a level with him.* Autore certo, *Liv. to abide by a particular author.* Ab aliquo, *Cic.* Cum aliquo, *id. & Liv. to be of his ſide or party.* Contra aliquem, *Cic. Virg. to be againſt him.* Pro judicio erroris ſui, *Phæd. to maintain obſtinately.* Animis *Cic. to take courage.* Fide, *Liv.* In fide,

fide, *Cic. to stand to his word.* Multorum sanguine ac vulneribus, *Liv. to cost the blood of many.*
Quorum statuæ in rostris steterunt, *Cic. were fastened to.*
Cum in senatu pulcherrimè staremus, *id. being in a very good posture, when our affairs went very well.*
Stant lumina flammâ, *Virg. are full of fire.*
Ubi jus sparso croco steterit, *Hor. will begin to grow thick.*
Qui si steterit idem, *Cic. if he continues resolute.*
Modo stet nobis illud, *id. provided we continue resolute.*
Omnis in Ascanio cari stat cura parentis, *Virg. is fixed on him.*
Per me stat, *Quint. Plin. it depends on me.*
Standum est epistolis Domitiani, *Plin. we must abide by.*
Quid agitur? Statur. *Plaut.*
STATUERE exemplum in hominem & in homine, *Cic. to inflict an exemplary punishment.* Capite aliquem in terram, *Ter. to fling headlong against the ground.*
Statuere in aliquem, *Cæs. to give sentence against him.* Apud animos vel in animum, *Liv. to determine within himself.* Statuam alicui, *Cic. to erect a statue to him.*
Statutum est, *it is decreed.*
STRUERE calamitatem alicui, *id. to contrive some mischief against him.* Odium in aliquem, *id. to endeavour to render him odious.* Mendacium, *Liv. to forge a lye.*
STUDERE alicui, *Cic. to favour, or to bear good will and affection to one.* Laudi & dignitati, *id. to aspire to.* Aliquid, *id. Ter. Hor. to have a strong desire for a thing.* In aliqua re, *Gell. to study or apply the mind to it.* In aliquid, *Quint. to aim only at that.*
Non tui studet, *Cic. he does not trouble his head about you.*
Studet rem ad arma deduci, *Cæs. he endeavours to push things to extremity.*
STUPERE in aliquo, *Val. Max.* Re aliquâ, *Hor.* Ad rem aliquam, *Ovid, to be surprized or amazed at a thing.* Rem aliquam, *Virg. to look on with amazement.*
Hæc cum loqueris nos Varrones stupemus, tu videlicet tecum ipse rides, *C.*
SUADERE legem, *id. to persuade the people to....... of a law.*
Pacem & de ......, *Cic. Quint.*
SUBIRE tectis & ad tecta, *Virg.*
In cœlum, *Plin.* Limina, *Virg. to go, to draw near.* Onus, *Liv. to undergo, to sustain.*
Mihi cunctarum subeunt fastidia, *Ovid, they displease me.*
Humeris subire aliquem, *Virg. to carry on the shoulders.*
Subire animos, *Liv.*
SUBJICERE aliquid oculis, *Plin. Jun. Liv.* Sub oculos, *id. & Quint. to put before one's eyes.* Sensibus, *Cic.*
Subjicere testamenta, *id. to forge.*
SUCCEDERE Penatibus, Muro, *Virg. to come within.* Murum, *Sallust. to draw near.* Sub primam aciem, *Cæs. to move towards the van-guard.* Alicui, *Cic. to succeed him.* Oneri, *Virg. to take it upon his back.* In locum, *Cic.*
SUCCENSERE alicui, *id.* Injuriam alicui, *Gell.*
Si id succenseat nunc, *Ter. if he is vexed at this.*
SUDARE sine causa, *Cic.* Pro communibus commodis, *id. to work.*
Sanguine multo sudare, *Liv. to sweat blood.*
Et duræ quercus sudabunt roscida mella, *Virg.*
Et vigilandæ noctes & in sudata veste durandum, *Quint.*
Sudatáque ligno ——— Thura ferat, *Cic.*
SUFFICERE omnibus, *Lucan. Cic. to be sufficient for all.*
Nec obniti contra nec tendere tantum sufficimus, *Virg. we are not able.*
Ad quas nec mens, nec corpus, nec dies ipsa sufficiat, *Quint.*
Ipse Danais animos virésque sufficit, *Virg. furnishes them.* Aliam sufficere prolem, *id. to substitute.* Ardentésque oculos suffecti sanguine & igni, *id. whose eyes were red and inflamed.*
SUPERESSE alicui, *Plaut. to survive.* Suet. *to defend as a patron his clients in law.* Labori, *Virg. to overcome and surmount the trouble.* Superest mihi, *Cic. it remains for me.* Populi superfunt auxilio, *Virg. there are more than we want for our assistance.* Tu plane superes nec ades, *Gell. you are one too many, you are not wanted.* Modò vita superfit, *Virg. if I do but live.*
SUSPENDERE arbori, in arbore, & de arbore, *Cic. to hang upon a tree.* In furcas, *Ulp.*
Suspendit picta vultum mentémque tabella, *Hor.*

T

TACERE aliquid, *Ter. Cic. Plaut.* De re aliqua, *Quint. to keep it secret.*

Potest

Potest taceri hoc, *Ter.*
Dicenda, tacenda locutus, *Hor.*
TEMPERARE iras, *Virg.* to moderate.
Cædibus, *Liv.* to refrain from.
A lacrymis, *Virg.* Alicui, *Cic.*

Ætati juvenum temperare, *Plaut.* to govern them.
Sibi temperare, *Cic.* to command himself.
TENDERE ad littora, *Liv.* In Latium, *Virg.* to go towards.
Tendit iter velis, *Virg.* begins to make sail.
Rete tenditur accipitri, *Ter.*
Manibus tendit divellere nodos, *Virg.* endeavours.
Tendere adversus autoritatem senatus, *Liv.* to resist, or withstand.
Tendere alicui metum aut spem, *Cic.* to shew or hold out to him.
Hic sævus tendebat Achilles, *sup.* pelles, *or* tentoria, *Virg.* pitched his tent.
TIMERE aliquem, *Ovid.* to fear him. Alicui, *Ter.* to fear lest some misfortune happen to him. Ab aliquo, *Cic.* to be afraid of him, to mistrust him. De republica, *id.* to be afraid for the republic. De vita, *Cælius Ciceroni,* I am afraid of my life.
Timeo ut, & timeo ne, See p. 159.
TRADERE in custodiam, *Cic.* Custodiæ, *Colum.* to deliver up, or send to prison. Se totum alicui, *Cic.* to give one's self up entirely to him.
TRANSFIGERE gladio aliquem per pectus, *Liv.* Cum armis corpus alicujus, *Liv.* to run through, to stab.

V

VACARE morbo vel à morbo, *Cels.* to be free from illness. Sibi, *Mart.* to work for himself. Philosophiæ, *Cic.* to study philosophy. In aliquod opus, *Ovid.*
Vacare culpâ, *Cic.* à culpa, *Senec.* to be free from fault. Ab omni administratione, *Cic.* to be exempt from. Animo, *id.* to be at leisure, to have nothing to do.
Vacat locus, *Cæs.* the place is empty.
Vacat mihi, *Quint.* I am at leisure.
Vacat annales audire, *Virg.*
Tantum huic studii relinquendum, quantum vacat a publicis officiis, *Cic.*
Eorum animus ponendi pecuniam nunquam vacavit, *Vul. l. 4. c. 3. sup.* vacationem, *ut vult Sanctius, lib. 3.* never gave their minds to the amassing of money.

VAGARI passim toto foro, *Cic.* In agris, *id.* to wander about.
Vagatur errore animus, *id.*
VALERE. Valet oculis, *Gell.* Valent ejus oculi, *Plaut.* his eye-sight is good.
Autoritate valet, *Cic.* Valet ejus autoritas, *id.*
Valet tanti, valet nimio, *among the civilians.* Denos æris valebant, *Varro.*
Quid igitur? Valetur, *Plaut.* we are very well.
VAPULARE. See the preterits, vol. 1. p. 305. and the Syntax, vol. 2. p. 68.
VEHERE amne, *Ovid.* Per maria, *Plin.* to convey by water, by sea.
Vehi curru, *Cic.* In curru, *Ovid.* Equo, *Ovid.* In equo, *Cic.* to travel, or ride in a coach, or on horseback.
VELLE aliquem, *Plaut.* to want to speak to him. Alicui, *Cic.* to wish him well. Alicujus causâ, *id.* Rem volo defensam, *id.* I will have it defended, Quid sibi vult istud? *Cic.* What's the meaning of this?
VENIRE alicui auxilio, *Liv.* Subsidio, *Cic.* Suppetias, *Hirt.* to come to the assistance of.
Venire alicui adversum, *Plaut.* to go to meet him. In certamen cum aliquo, *Cic.* to fight him. In consilium alicujus, *id.* to come to give him counsel. Sub jactum telorum, *Liv.* to come within shot of.
Inimicus alicui venire, *Cic.* to be his enemy.
Ad inimicitias res venit, *id.*
Venire viam, *id.* to go his own way.
Ad me ventum est, *id.*
Mihi venit in dubium fides tua, *id.* I begin to doubt of.
De sorte venio in dubium, *Ter.* I am in danger of losing the principal.
Venit mihi in mentem Platonis, *Cic.* I call Plato to mind.
In mentem venit de speculo, *Plaut.*
Venit in mentem P. Romani dignitas, *Cic.*
VERTERE aliquid in laudem, *Tac.* to turn to praise. Stultitiæ aliquid alicui, *Plaut.* to impute it to his folly. In rem suam, *Ulp.* to turn to his profit. In privatum, *Liv.* to his private use. Ad se partem alicujus rei, *Cic.* to appropriate to himself.
Vertere Platonem, *Cic.* to translate Plato. Græca in Latinum, *Quint.* Græcis, *Cic.* Ex Græcis, *Ter.*
Tribus in rebus fere vertitur omnis virtus, *Cic.* consists in, is included.

Intra

Of Verbs of different Governments. 225

Intra fines hos vertuntur omnia, *Cæl. ad Cic.*

In priorem partem funt verfa & mutata omnia, *id. are changed.*

Jam verterat fortuna, *Liv. was now changed.*

Quæ te genitor fententia vertit? *Virg. has made you change opinion.*

VIGILARE ad multam noctem, & de multa nocte, *Cic. to fit up very late.*

Noctes vigilare ad ipfum mane, *Hor.*

Vigilare ftudiis, *Proper.* In fcelus, *Stat.*

Noctes vigilantur amaræ, *Ovid.*

VINDICARE fe ab aliquo, *Sen.* De aliquo, *Cic. to be revenged of a perfon.*

Te valdè vindicavi, *Cic. Attico. I have got my full revenge of you.* Ita Man.

Peccatum in altero vindicare, *Cic. to punifh.*

In aliquem fcelera alterius vindicare, *id.*

Vindicare à labore, *id. to exempt.*

Graiis bis vindicat armis, *Virg.*

Vindicare in libertatem, *Cic. to fet at liberty, to reftore.* Libertatem, *Cæf. to defend the liberty.* Se ad fuos, *Cic. to return fafe and found to them.* Se exiftimationi hominum, *id. to maintain his reputation.*

* Some write the following examples with an *e*, VENDICARE. But we fhall make it appear in the ninth book, of Letters and Orthography, that we ought always to write VINDICARE.

Aliquid pro fuo vindicare, *Cic. to claim.*

Sibi affumere & vindicare, *id.*

Dicere fuum & vindicare, *id.*

ULULARE. Ululant canes, *Virg. to howl.*

Ædes ululant plangoribus femineis, *Virg. do ring with.*

Triftia ulularunt Galli, *Lucan.*

Centum ululata per urbes, *Lucàn.*

UTOR. See the Syntax, rule 33. p. 70.

BOOK VIII.

PARTICULAR OBSERVATIONS.

On the Roman names. On their figures or arithmetical characters. On their manner of counting the sesterces. And on the division of time.

Useful for the understanding of authors.

CHAPTER I.

Of the names of the antient Romans. Taken from VAL. MAXIMUS, SIGONIUS, LIPSIUS, *and other authors.*

THE Greeks had only one name, but the Romans had sometimes three or four, which they called PRÆNO-MEN, NOMEN, COGNOMEN, and sometimes also AG-NOMEN.

The *prænomen* is that which agreeth to each individual; the *nomen* that which denotes the family from which he is descended; and the *cognomen*, that which agreeth to a particular branch of this family.

I. *Of the proper name*, PRÆNOMEN.

The *prænomen* was therefore, as the very word expresseth, what was prefixed to the general name, and amounts to the same thing as our *proper name*, by which we distinguish brothers of the same family, as when we call them, *Peter, John, James*, &c.

The *prænomen* was not introduced till a long time after the *nomen*. Hence it was customary among the Romans to give the family name to children, of the male sex, the ninth day after their nativity; and of the female the eighth, according to Festus and Plutarch. And those days were called *dies lustrici*, because it was a ceremony whereby they were acknowledged as legitimate, and of such or such a family, whose name was given them. Whereas they did not receive the *prænomen*, till they took the *toga virilis*, that is, about the age of seventeen, as appeareth by the epitome of the 10th book attributed to Valerius Maximus. *Pueris*, says he, *non priusquam togam virilem sumerent, puellis non antequam nuberent, prænomina imponi moris fuisse Q. Scævola autor est.* This is farther confirmed by Tully's epistles, where the children are called *Cicerones pueri*, till that age, after which they are stiled *Marcus filius, Quintus filius*.

And though Cicero in the last epistle of the 6th book to Atticus calleth his nephew, *Quintum Ciceronem puerum*; yet it is very probable

Of the Roman Names.

bable that Cicero wresteth the sense of the word *puer*, to distinguish him from his father, who was also called *Quintus*; or perhaps because he had but very lately taken the *toga virilis*. And in regard to what Sigonius mentions from Plutarch and Festus, who, according to him, are of a different opinion from Valerius Maximus, we are to take notice that those authors do not speak of the *prænomen*, but of the *nomen*, which, as hath been above mentioned, was given to children the 8th or 9th day after their nativity. And there is no manner of doubt but this is what led Sigonius into a mistake.

In conferring this *prænomen*, they took care generally to give that of the father to the eldest son, and that of the grandfather and the ancestors of the family to the second, and to all the rest.

Varro observeth that there were thirty of those *prænomina*, in his time, or thereabouts, whereof the most usual may be reduced to eighteen, some of which were marked by a single letter, others by two, and others by three, as we shall here exhibit them, together with their etymology.

1. With a single letter we find eleven.

A. stands for AULUS, so called from the verb *alo*, as being born *Diis alentibus*.

C. stands for CAIUS, so called *à gaudio parentum*.

D. stands for DECYMUS, that is, the tenth born.

K. stands for KÆSO, taken from *cædo*, because they were obliged to open his mother's womb to bring him into the world.

L. stands for LUCIUS, from *lux*, *lucis*, because the first who bore this name, was born at break of day.

M. stands for MARCUS, as much as to say, born in the month of March.

But M′ with an acute accent on the top, or M' with a comma, signifieth MANIUS, that is, *born in the morning*, or rather *quite good*, because *manis* heretofore, as we have already observed, p. 150. signified *good*.

N. stands for NUMERIUS, which cometh from *numerus*, number.

P. makes PUBLIUS either from the word *pubes*, or from *populus*, as much as to say *popular and agreeable to the people*.

Q. stands for QUINTUS, that is, the fifth child of his family.

T. stands for TITUS from the word *tueri*, as if the *defender* or preserver of his country.

2. With two letters we find four.

AP. stands for APPIUS, which cometh from the Sabine word *Attius*. For *Attius Clausus* was the first, who having been expelled his country, came to Rome and changed his name into that of *Appius Claudius*.

CN. stands for CNEUS, as much as to say *nævus*, from some mark on his body.

SP. stands for SPURIUS, which denotes something ignominious in birth. For this word in the Latin tongue signifies also *spurious* or *illegitimate*. *Spurii, quasi extra puritatem, & immundi*, says St. Isidore.

TI. stands for TIBERIUS, that is, born near the Tiber.

3. With three letters, we find three.

MAM.

MAM. that is, MAMERCUS, which in the Tufcan language fignified *Mars*, according to Feftus.

SER. that is, SERVIUS, from the word *servus*, a flave, becaufe the perfon who firft took this name, was not free born.

SEX. that is, SEXTUS, as much as to fay *the fixth born*.

Thefe are the eighteen proper names moft ufual among the Romans. To which we might likewife add fome that are very well known in antient ftory; as *Ancus, Aruns, Hoftilius, Tullus,* and fome others.

II. *Of the general name,* NOMEN GENTIS.

The *nomen* or name was what agreed to the whole race or family with all its branches, and anfwered to the Greek patronymics, according to Prifcian, lib. 2. For as the defcendants of Æacus were called *Æacides*, fo the defcendants of Iulus fon of Æneas, had the name of *Julii*; thofe of the Antonian family, *Antonii*, and the reft in the like manner. Hence we may obferve that all thofe general names which they called *Gentilitia*, are properly adjectives, and that they all terminate in *ius*, except two or three, namely, *Peducæus, Poppæus,* and perhaps *Norbanus*; though Lipfius queftions whether the latter be one of thofe names.

III. *Of the particular furname,* COGNOMEN *and* AGNOMEN.

The particular furname called *cognomen*, was properly the name by which the different branches of the fame ftock or houfe, *in eadem gente*, were diftinguifhed; as when Livy fays that the houfe of the Potitians was divided into twelve families. For *gens & familia* were like the whole and its parts. Thofe of the fame ftock or houfe were called *Gentiles*; and thofe of the fame branch or family, *Agnati*. As we fee in France that the royal houfe hath been frequently divided into different branches, as thofe of Valois, Bourbon, Orleans, Montpenfier, &c. Thus when we fay that the family of the Cæfars were of the race of Julius; Julius is the general name of the race, or *nomen gentis*; and *Cæfar* that of the family, *cognomen familiæ*. But if you add *Caius* for his proper name, this will give us the *prænomen*. Therefore all three will be *C. Julius Cæsar*.

There are fome who hereto add the *agnomen*, which fignifieth as it were an increafe of the furname, and was conferred on fome particular occafion, as when one of the Scipios was entitled *Africanus*, and the other *Afiaticus*, becaufe of their great exploits in thofe parts of the world. And no doubt but a man might in this manner have fometimes a particular furname, and as it were a fourth name. Hence the author *ad Herennium* makes mention of this *agnomen*, when he fays, *Nomen autem cùm dicimus, cognomen quoque & agnomen intelligatur oportet*.

Yet it is certain that the word *cognomen* comprehendeth likewife this fort of nouns, witnefs Salluft, when he fays of Scipio himfelf, *Mafiniffa in amicitiam receptus à P. Scipione, cui poftea Africano cognomen fuit ex virtute*: and Cicero writing to *Pomponius*, who was furnamed *Atticus*, for having performed his ftudies at Athens, fays, says, *Téque non cognomen Athenis solùm deportasse, sed humanitatem & prudentiam intelligo.*

And indeed if we examine closely into the thing, we shall find that there are no surnames, I mean of those which are called *cognomina*, and distinguish families, but what are thus derived from some particular occasions; since even the proper names (*prænomina*) are originally owing to such occasions, as we have above demonstrated in pointing out their etymology.

IV. OBSERVATIONS on the names of slaves, freedmen, women, and adoptive children.

And first of slaves and freedmen.

Slaves formerly had no other name than that of their master, as *Lucipor, Marcipor*, for *Lucii puer, Marci puer*. Yet in process of time they had a name given them, which was generally that of their country, as *Syrus, Davus, Geta*, &c. Just as in France the lackeys are sometimes called *Champagne, Basque, Picard*, &c.

When they were enfranchised, they took the *prænomen* and the *nomen* of their masters, but not the *cognomen*, instead of which they retained their own *prænomen*. Thus Cicero's learned freedman was called *M. Tullius Tyro*, and others in the same manner. The like was observed in regard to allies and foreigners, who assumed the name of the person, by whose interest they had obtained the freedom of the city of Rome.

2. Of women.

Varro takes notice that the women had heretofore their proper and particular name, as *Caia, Cæcilia, Lucia, Volumnia*. And Festus says that Cæcilia and Tarratia were both called *Caia*. We likewise meet with *Titia, Marca*, &c. in Sigonius and others. And those names, as Quintilian observeth, were marked by inverted letters thus, Ↄ, Ʇ, W, &c. In process of time they were discontinued: if there was only one, it was customary to give her the name of her race or stock; or sometimes it was softened by a diminutive, as *Tullia* or *Tulliola*. But if there were many, they were called after the order of their birth, *Prima, Secunda, Tertia, Quarta, Quinta*, &c. or these were formed into diminutives, *Secundilla, Quartilla, Quintilla*, &c.

But as several are mistaken in affirming that the women had no *prænomen*; so they are also in an error in pretending that they had no *cognomen*. For it is certain that Sylla's daughter, who was married to Milo, had the surname of Cornelia; and Cælius writing to Cicero, speaks of Paula, who had the surname of Valeria.

3. Of adoptive children.

It was customary for those who were adopted, to take the names and surnames of those who adopted them. And in order to mark their birth and descent, they only added at the end the name of the house or stock from which they were descended, or the surname of their own particular branch; with this difference however,

that

that if they made use of this surname, they wrote it simply; whereas if they used the name, they formed it into an adjective; *Si cognomen, integrum servabant; si nomen, mutatum & inflexum,* says Lipsius.

For example, *M. Junius Brutus* having been adopted by *Q. Servilius Cæpio Agalo*; he took all his names, and preserved only the name of his own branch, calling himself *Q. Servilius Cæpio Agalo Brutus.* On the contrary, Octavius having been adopted by his grand uncle, *Julius Cæsar,* he preserved the name of his house, changing it into an adjective, and was called *C. Julius Cæsar Octavianus*; which did not hinder them from preserving also any surname they might have acquired, as *Atticus,* who having been adopted by *Q. Cæcilius,* had the surname of *Q. Cæcilius Pomponianus Atticus*; or from acquiring any new one by their merit, as Octavius, who had afterwards the surname of Augustus given him.

To this rule of adoption we must refer what Suetonius saith, that Tiberius having been adopted by M. Gallius, a senator, he took possession of his estate, but would not go by his name, because he had followed the party that opposed Augustus; and what Tacitus says, that Crispus Sallustius adopting his sister's nephew, made him take his name. And such like expressions.

V. Other observations on changing the order of those names.

Though the usual custom of the Romans was that above observed, of putting the *prænomen, nomen,* and *cognomen,* one after the other; yet we must take notice that this order hath not been always carefully adhered to, as Valerius Maximus testifieth: *Animadverto enim,* says he, lib. 10. *in consulum fastis perplexum usum prænominum & cognominum fuisse.* Concerning which there are several changes to be observed.

1. The *cognomen* before the *nomen.*

Manutius sheweth that they sometimes put the surname of the particular branch before the general name of the stock, *cognomen ante nomen gentis,* as in Cicero we find *Gallo Fabio, Balbi Cornelii, Papum Æmilium;* and in Livy, *Paullus Æmilius Coss.* and the like, though *Gallus, Balbus, Papus* and *Paullus,* were *cognomina non prænomina.*

2. The *cognomen* become *nomen.*

Sometimes the *cognomen* became a *nomen. Quin etiam cognomina in nomen versa sunt,* says Valerius Maximus.

3. The *prænomen* become *nomen.*

Sometimes the *prænomen* became a *nomen,* says Priscian, as *Tullus Servilius, M. Tullius.*

4. The *prænomen* put in the second place.

And sometimes the *prænomen* used to be put only in the second place, as Sigonius observeth. Thus we find in Livy, *Attius Tullus Manlius Cnæus, Octavius Metius.* In Cicero, *Maluginensis M. Scipio.* In Suetonius, *ad Pompeium.*

5. The

5. The *prænomen* or proper name put last under the emperors.

But those changes were still more considerable under the emperors. For whereas during the time of the republic, the *prænomen* was the proper name which distinguished brothers and individuals from one another, as *M. Tullius Cicero*, and *Q. Tullius Cicero*, brothers; on the contrary in the monarchical state of Rome, the proper name which distinguished individuals, was generally the last, whence it came that the brothers, commonly speaking, had nothing in particular but that; as *Flavius Vespasianus*, and *Flavius Sabinus*, brothers in Suetonius.

This new custom appeareth plainly in the case of the Senecas. For Seneca the father, a rhetor, was called *M. Annæus Seneca*; and he had three children, *M. Annæus Novatus*, *L. Annæus Seneca*, the philosopher; and *L. Annæus Mela*, father of Lucan the poet. Yet the latter of each of those names was so far the proper and particular appellation, by which they were distinguished from one another, that the other two are common to them all; and that Seneca the rhetor, father of those celebrated sons, sometimes gives both to himself and them only the latter of those three names, as appeareth by the title of his first book of controversies, *Seneca, Novato Senecæ, Melæ filiis salutem*. And his eldest son *Novatus*, having been adopted by *Junius Gallio*, he is called by Eusebius in his chronicle, *Julius Gallio frater Senecæ*; though his brother, Seneca the philosopher, generally calls him by the last of those three, which was his proper name, as in the title of his book on a happy life, and in his epistles; likewise St. Luke in the acts of the Apostles, c. 18. calls him by no other name than *Gallio*. Whence it is clear that in those days it was the last name that distinguished the brothers from each other, as might be demonstrated by several other examples.

Hence also it comes that only this last name was generally given to the principal persons of the empire in the first ages of the church, as sufficiently distinguishing them from every body else. This is the reason that though St. Jerome in the preface to his commentaries on the epistle of St. Paul to the Galatians, speaking of Victorinus, that famous professor of eloquence at Rome, observes that he was called *C. Marius Victorinus*; yet *Victorinus* was in such a manner his proper name, that this very St. Jerome in his treatise of ecclesiastic writers, chap. 101. and St. Austin in his confessions, book 8. chap. 2. call him only *Victorinus*.

It appeareth likewise that St. Paulinus, bishop of Nola, was called *Pontius Meropius Paulinus*; and yet St. Austin and other authors generally give him the latter of those three names only, as that by which his person was particularly distinguished. Thus Rufinus is called only by this name in the writings of S. Jerom, S. Austin, and S. Paulinus, though his name was *Tyrannius Rufinus*: nor has S. Prosper any other appellation in the ancient writers of the church, tho' his name was *Tyro Prosper*. Nor is Volusian, governor of Rome, mentioned by any other name in the 1st and 2d epistle of S. Austin, though we find by an antient inscription that he was called *Caius Cæionius*

Cæionius Rufius Volufianus; nor Boetius by any other than this name, though he was called *Anicius Boetius*; this name of *Anicius*, which is here put first, being nevertheleſs the name of the noble family from which he was deſcended.

6. *Exception to this rule of taking the laſt name under the emperors.*

Contrary to this general rule of the Roman names under the emperors, it is to be obſerved however, (as Father Sirmond hath obſerved in his notes on St. Sidonius) that we call *Palladius* the perſon who wrote on agriculture, though his name being *Paladius Rutilius Taurus Æmilianus*, we ſhould call him *Æmilianus*, as he is ſtiled by St. Iſidorus. In like manner we give the name of *Macrobius* to the perſon whom Avien and Boetius call *Theodoſius*, becauſe his real name was *Macrobius Ambroſius Aurelius Theodoſius*: and we give the name of *Caſſiodorus* to that great man, who was called *Caſſiodorus Senator*, the word *Senator*, which was his real name, having been taken by many rather as the name of his dignity than of his perſon.

But though a few ſuch particular caſes may occur, they muſt be conſidered notwithſtanding, either as exceptions to the general rule, or as errors that have crept into the title of the works of thoſe authors, through the negligence of thoſe, who chuſing only to put one of their names, did not reflect that the cuſtom of the antients was changed, and that the laſt name was become the proper name of individuals.

7. *Other names changed as well as the latter.*

It is alſo obſervable, as Father Sirmondus ſheweth extremely well in the ſame place, that whereas the antients always retained the name of their family together with their proper name, this cuſtom was ſo far altered in the latter ages, that not only the proper name, but likewiſe all the others were changed in regard almoſt to every individual, not attending ſo much to the general name of the family, as to thoſe which had been particular to the illuſtrious men of that ſame family, or to their relations and friends. Thus the ſon of the orator Symmachus was called *Q. Flavius Memmius Symmachus*, having taken the name of *Flavius* from his uncle by the father's ſide, and of *Memmius* from his uncle by the mother's ſide. Thus St. Fulgentius was called *Fabius Claudius Gordianus Fulgentius*, having taken the name of Claudius from his father, and that of *Gordianus* from his grandfather, which is oftentimes the cauſe of our not being able to trace the antiquity of families.

CHAPTER II.

Of figures, or arithmetical characters among the Romans.

I. *In what manner the Romans marked their numbers.*

THE Romans marked their numbers by letters, which they ranged thus:

1	I	One.
5	V	Five.
10	X	Ten.
50	L	Fifty.
100	C	One hundred.
500	Iɔ	Five hundred.
1000	cIɔ	One thousand.
5000	Iɔɔ	Five thousand.
10000	ccIɔɔ	Ten thousand.
50000	Iɔɔɔ	Fifty thousand.
100000	cccIɔɔɔ	One hundred thousand.

These are the figures of the Roman numbers, with their signification and value: for, as Pliny observeth, the antients had no number above a hundred thousand; but to reckon higher, they put this number twice or thrice. Whence comes the manner of computing by *bis, ter, quater, quinquies, decies centenam millia*, and others, of which we shall have occasion to speak in the chapter on sesterces.

II. *Proper observations in order to understand these figures thoroughly.*

In order properly to understand these figures, we must consider:

1. That there are only five different figures, which are the first five, and that all the rest are compounded of I and C; so that the C is always turned towards the I, whether it comes before or after, as may be seen above.

2. That as often as there is a figure of less value before a higher, it signifies that we are to deduct so much from the latter, as IV. four: XL. forty; XC. ninety, &c. Whereby we see that there is no number but what may be expressed by the first five figures.

3. That in all those numbers, the figures go on increasing by a fivefold and afterwards a double proportion, so that the second is five times the value of the first, and the third twice the value of the second; the fourth five times the value of the third; the fifth twice the value of the fourth, and the rest in the same manner.

4. That the figures always begin to be multiplied on the right side, so that all the ɔ which are put on that side, are reckoned by
five

five, as those on the other side are reckoned by ten; and thus we may easily find out all sorts of numbers how great soever: as when an author in the 16th century giving a list of the number of citizens in the Roman empire, puts contrary to the custom of the antients, ccccccIↃↃↃↃↃↃ. IↃↃↃↃↃↃ. cccIↃↃↃ. ccIↃↃ. taking the first c after the I for one thousand, or the first c on the right hand for five hundred, and proceeding through the whole with a tenfold progression, in each figure on either side, I see immediately that the whole comes to one billion, five hundred millions, a hundred and ten thousand citizens; which we should express thus by Arabic cyphers, 1500,110,000. But as we have already observed, the antients did not pass cccIↃↃↃ. one hundred thousand in those figures.

III. *What this manner of reckoning has been owing to, and whence these figures have been taken.*

Now if I may be permitted to reflect a little on this manner of counting, it is easy to judge that it is owing to this, that mankind having begun at first to count by their fingers, they told as far as five with one hand, then adding the other hand, they made ten, which is double; and hence it is that their progression in these numbers is always from one to five, and then from five to ten.

To this same cause the very formation of these figures is owing. For what is more natural than to say, that I is the same as if an unit was shewn by raising one finger only; and that the V is as if depressing the middle fingers no more was shewn than the little finger and the thumb, to include the whole hand; and adding the other to this, they formed as it were two V, one of which was inverted under the other, that is an X, which is equivalent to ten.

Manutius shews further that all the other figures are derived from the first, because as the V is only two I joined at the bottom, so the L is only two I, one upright and the other couchant; and adding thereto a third on the top, they expressed by this figure a hundred, instead of which the transcribers, for greater currency in writing, have borrowed the C. And if we join a fourth I to shut up the square thus ◻, this makes five hundred, instead of which they afterwards took the IↃ, and at length the D. Doubling this square ⬜ they formed their thousand, instead of which the transcribers, either for the sake of ornament, or for greater conveniency, began likewise to round this figure, and with a dash of the pen to frame it thus ∞, afterwards thus ⱷ, for which reason we frequently meet with the couchant cypher ∞, or a Greek ⱷ to mark a thousand. But afterwards they marked it thus cIↃ, and after that cD, and at length because this has a great relation to the Gothic l' ᛗ, they took a simple M to denote a thousand, as likewise C for a hundred, and D for five hundred. And hence it comes that there are but just seven letters which serve for this sort of numbers, namely, C. D. I. L. M. V. X. except we have a mind to add also the Q, which some have taken for five hundred, according to Vossius.

IV. *Whether there are other methods to mark the Roman cypher than the preceding.*

We muſt alſo take notice of the opinion of ſome, that when there is a ——— bar over the cyphers, this gives them the value of a thouſand, as V̄, X̄, five thouſand, ten thouſand. But Priſcian's manner of computing, namely, that to expreſs a thouſand, the X muſt be put between the Cs, thus CXↃ, and to expreſs ten thouſand we ſhould put the M there, thus CMↃ, is abſolutely falſe and contrary to antiquity; and it is owing to this only, that not knowing the real foundation of this manner of computing, which I have here explained, they thought to adjuſt it to ours, which proceeds by a tenfold progreſſion. And though we ſometimes find the L between the Cs, thus CLↃ, or the like, this is only a miſtake of the tranſcribers, who perceiving that on thoſe occaſions the I is generally bigger than the Cs, they took it for an L. So that even then the L ought to be reckoned only as an I, and to mark no more than one thouſand.

✤✤✤✤✤✤✤✤✤✤✤✤✤✤✤✤✤✤✤✤✤✤✤✤

Chapter III.
Of the Roman ſeſterces.

AS I have ſome notion of publiſhing a ſeparate eſſay on the antient coins, with their reſpective value reduced to the ſtandard of the preſent currency in France, I ſhall therefore ſpeak here of ſeſterces, only in regard to grammar.

The ſeſterce was a little ſilver coin in value the fourth part of a Roman denarius, or two *aſſes* and a half, which *as* was alſo called *libra*, becauſe at firſt it was of copper and weighed a pound. Hence the word *as* (*quaſi æs*, ſays Varro) came from the matter; and the word *libra*, from the weight that was given it. And when they added the ablative *pondo*, it was to determine the word *pound* or weight, which of itſelf was alſo by meaſure.

Hence it is that heretofore they marked the ſeſterce thus L. L. S. the two Ls making two pounds, and the S ſignifying *ſemi*, two pounds and a half. Whereas the tranſcribers have ſince given us an H with the S, thus H. S. And this ſeſterce, purſuant to the valuation which we have elſewhere obſerved, was equivalent to a ſou and two deniers, French money, or ſomething more.

In order to count the ſeſterces, the Romans proceed three ways.

From one to a thouſand they reckon them ſimply by the order of the numbers, without underſtanding any thing; *Seſtertii decem, viginti, centum mille*, &c.

From a thouſand to a million they reckon three ways, either by the numeral nouns, which they make agree with *ſeſtertii*, as *mille ſeſtertii*; or by putting the neuter *ſeſtertia* with *millia* expreſſed or underſtood, as *decem ſeſtertia*, or *decem millia ſeſtertia*; or in ſhort by putting *ſeſtertium* in the genitive plural formed by ſyncope for *ſeſtertiorum*, as *octo millia ſeſtertium, centena millia ſeſtertium.*. Which they likewiſe mark ſometimes by putting a bar over the capital letters, thus C̄. M. S. which

which bar sheweth that the number is taken for a thousand; so that the C which makes a hundred, stands here for a hundred thousand, though they frequently put this bar, where it is impossible to judge of the sum but by the sense.

From a million upwards they reckon by adverbs, as *decies, vicies, centies, sestertiûm,* &c. where we must always understand *centena millia, sestertii* or *sestertiûm,* or else *millia* only, when *centena* has been already expressed, as when Juvenal saith:

———— *Et ritu decies centena dabuntur*

Antiquo: that is, *decies centena millia.*

But if the adverb alone is expressed, then we are to understand all these three words *centena millia sestertiûm.* Thus *bis millies,* for example, is the same as *bis millies centena millia sestertiûm.*

We are to observe however that *sestertius* and *numus* frequently signify the same thing: thus *mille numûm, mille sestertiûm,* or *mille numûm sestertiûm,* may be indifferently said one for the other.

II. *Reason of these expressions, and that* mille *strictly speaking is always an adjective.*

Various are the opinions concerning the reason for this construction and these expressions: for not to mention those of Varro, Nonius, and some antients, who without any probability imagined that these genitives, *nummûm* and *sestertiûm* (formed by syncope, instead of *numorum* and *sestertiorum*) were accusatives; *mille* is generally taken as a noun substantive that governeth the genitive *nummûm* or *sestertiûm.*

Scioppius on the contrary pretends that *mille* is always an adjective, in the same manner as other numeral nouns; and therefore that we must suppose another noun on which the government of this genitive depends. And therefore he endeavours to shew in his fourteenth letter, that then we must understand *res* or *negotium,* just as when Juvenal says:

Quantum quisque suâ nummorum possidet arcâ:

Where *quantum* being an adjective ought necessarily to suppose *negotium.* So that if we were to say, *res* or *negotium mille nummorum est in arcâ,* the construction would be quite simple and intire: but if we say *Mille nummorum est in arcâ,* it is figurative, and then we must understand *res,* which governs *mille nummorum* (which are the adjective and substantive) in the genitive. Now *Res mille nummorum,* is the same thing as *mille nunmi,* just as Phædrus saith, *res cibi* for *cibus.* Which we have shewn elsewhere more at large.

Perhaps we might make use of this principle to solve some difficult passages, which coincide with this same construction, as when Terence saith, *Omnium quantum est qui vivunt ornatissime,* the most vain fellow in the whole world. For it meaneth, *Quantum est negotium omnium hominum qui vivunt,* for *quanti sunt homines qui vivunt.* Just as the Greeks say χρῆμα θαυμαστὸν γυναικὸς, for θαυμαστὸς γυνή, an admirable woman. And as Paul the learned Civilian said, *Si juraverit se filio meo decem operarum daturum, liber esto.* And in another place, *Cùm decem operarum jussus est dare,* for

decem

decem operas. And it is certain that he might likewise have said, *Cùm decem talentûm jussus est dare,* where there cannot be the least doubt but he must have understood *rem,* since Terence hath even expressed it, *Si cognatus talentûm rem reliquisset decem,* &c. Where it is also obvious, that *rem decem talentûm* and *decem talenta,* are the same thing, and therefore that *decem* is the adjective of *talentum,* let it be in whatever case it will. Therefore if I say, *Reliquit mihi decem talentûm* (omitting *rem,* as this Civilian has done) there is no manner of doubt but they are both in the genitive, and but that this word *res,* is understood upon the occasion.

For which reason when we say *mille hominum, mille nummûm,* it is the same construction as *decem operarum, decem talentum*; and we may further affirm that it is a construction of the adjective and substantive in the genitive governed by *res,* or *negotium,* which is understood. At least this is the opinion of Scioppius.

This seems even to be the principle, by which we ought to account for these expressions framed in the plural, as when St. Jerom saith, *Si Origenes sex millia scripsisset libros.* And Livy, *Philippei nummi quatuor millia viginti quatuor.* And Cicero, *Tritici medimnos duo millia.* For if this principle of Scioppius be just, we must resolve these phrases, and say, *Scripsit libros ad sex millia negotia illorum librorum: tritici medimnos ad sex millia negotia illorum medimnorum.* And in like manner the rest. Which will not peradventure appear so extraordinary, when we once conceive, that the word *res* or *negotium* with the genitive of a noun, always supposeth this very noun in the nominative, *res cibi* for *cibus. Millia negotiæ medimnorum,* for *mille medimni,* &c. For that *millia* in the plural is an adjective, is beyond all doubt, notwithstanding what Linacer, L. Valla, and Scaliger pretend; since we find in Pliny, *Millia tempestatum præsagia:* in Tully, *Decem millia talenta Gabinio esse promissa,* and the like.

Such is the principle laid down by Scioppius, and in the main it seems to be undeniable. This however does not hinder but in practice, which is the master of speech, *magister & dictator loquendi,* as Scaliger expresseth himself, one may say that *mille* is frequently taken as a substantive, being then rather for χιλιὰ than for χίλιοι, according to A. Gellius, as when we say *unum mille, duo millia,* &c. one thousand, two thousand, &c. And thus we are furnished with an easy method of resolving those expressions. For it is not to be imagined that the custom of language should be so confined to general rules, but it may sometimes make a substantive of an adjective, and sometimes an adjective of a substantive; nor that the human mind will take a perplexed and dark winding in order to apprehend things, when it can find a shorter and clearer method. Hence there are a great many nouns taken substantively, though in the main they are adjectives, as *vivens, mortalis, patria, Judæa, molaris,* &c. which strictly speaking, do refer to *homo, terra, deus*; and the same may be said of the rest.

And therefore when we say *mille denarium est in arca, mille equitum est in exercitu,* I see nothing that can hinder us from looking upon *mille* as a substantive; or at least as a noun taken substantive-

ly.

ly, which shall govern the genitive *denarium*, *equitum*, &c. And thus it is that Lucilius says,

Tu milli nummûm potes uno quærere centum:

With a thousand sesterces you can gain a hundred thousand.

Therefore when we say *Sex millia scripsit libros*, *tritici medimnos recipit duo millia*, we may take it, either as an apposition, *libros sex millia*; or resolve it by *ad, libros ad sex millia:* which does not hinder but in the main we may also resolve it by *negotium*, according to Scioppius's principle: just as, strictly speaking, *mortalis* ought to be resolved by *homo*, *judæa* by *terra*, and the rest in the like manner.

Be that as it may, we must observe that when a verb or an adjective is joined to this word *mille*, it is generally made to agree in the singular, whether we are to understand *negotium*, as Scioppius pretends, or whether we take it, not for χίλιοι, but for χιλιὰς, a thousand, as A. Gellius will have it *Qui L. Antonio mille nummûm ferret expensum*, Cic. *Quo in fundo mille hominum facilè versabatur*, Cic. *Ad Romuli initium plus mille & centum annorum est*, Varro. *Ibi occiditur mille hominum* and not *occiduntur*, says Quadrigar, in A. Gellius, lib. 1. c. 16 *.

III. *Other remarkable expressions in regard to the same subject.*

When we meet with *Sestertiûm decies numeratum esse*, Cic. act. 4. in Verr. it is a syllepsis of number, or *numeratum* which refers to *negotium*, understood, instead of *numerata*, which it should have been; as indeed it is in some editions, because we are to suppose *centena millia*. In like manner, *An accepto centies sestertiûm fecerit*, Velleius, lib. 2. de Curione, for *acceptis centies centenis millibus sestertiûm*, and the like.

Now as the antients said, *decies sestertiûm*, or *decies centena millia sestertiûm*; so they said likewise *decies æris*, or *decies centena millia æris*; *decies æris numeratum esse*, &c. where the word *æs* is generally taken for the *asses*, which at first were of brass, as already hath been observed.

* And this is so much the more to be observed, as in French it is quite the reverse, the construction being always in the plural with this numeral noun as well as with the rest, since we say for instance, *Les cent* or *les mille soldats venus d'Italie furent tués en ce combat*, *the hundred*, or *thousand soldiers who came from Italy*, *were killed in this battle*. Again, *il y en a eu mille tués*, or rather *mille de tués* and not *tué*, nor *de tué*, there were a thousand killed. Where it appears likewise that the above noun hath this in particular, that it does not take an *s* at the latter end, except it be to mark the miles on the highway; for every where else we write in French *un mille*, *dix mille*, *trente mille*, &c. *one thousand*, *ten thousand*, *thirty thousand*, &c. though we say *deux cens*, *two hundred*, *quatre-vingts*, *fourscore*, and the like with an *s*. But when we say *mille de tués*, it is a partition, as if it were *mille occisorum* or *ex numero occisorum*.

Chapter IV.

Of the division of time according to the antients.

THE antients had a particular manner of reckoning and expressing time, which is necessary to be known for the right understanding of authors.

I. *Of Days.*

We shall begin with a day, as the part of time most known and most natural.

The antients divided a day into natural and artificial. The natural day they called that which is measured by the space of time the sun takes in making his circuit round the earth, which includes the intire duration of day and night. Artificial day they called that space of time which the sun stays above the horizon.

The natural day is also called the civil, inasmuch as it is differently computed by different nations, some beginning it one way, and others another.

Thus the Babylonians began their day with the sun rise.

The Jews and the Athenians began it with sun set, and in this they are imitated by the modern Italians, who reckon their first hour from the setting of the sun.

The Egyptians began it at midnight, as we do.

The Umbrians at noon.

The day which commences at the setting or rising of the sun, is not altogether equal. For from the winter solstice to the summer solstice, that which begins from sunset, has a little more than 24 hours: and quite the contrary from the summer solstice to the winter solstice. But the natural day which begins at midnight, or at noon, is always equal.

On the contrary the artificial day is unequal in all parts of the earth, except under the equinoctial line. And this inequality is greater or lesser according to different climates. Now from thence ariseth the difference of hours, of which we are going to speak.

II. *Of Hours.*

There are two sorts of hours, one called equal, and the other unequal.

Equal hours are those which are always in the same state, such as those which we make use of, each of which constitutes the four and twentieth part of the natural day.

Unequal hours are those which are longer in summer, and shorter in winter for the day; or the reverse for the night; being only the twelfth part of the day or of the night.

Therefore dividing the artificial day into twelve equal parts, we shall find that the sixth hour will be at noon, and the third will be half the time, which precedes from sun rise till noon; as the ninth hour is half the time which follows from noon till sun set; and the rest in the same manner.

This

This is what gave occasion to the naming of the canonical hours of prime, tierce, sexte, none, and vespers, in honour of the sacred mysteries that were accomplished in those hours, in which the church hath therefore been used to say those prayers.

III. *Of the watches of the night.*

The twelve hours of the night were divided into four watches, and each watch contained three hours. Hence we frequently find in Cicero and other writers, *Prima vigilia, secunda vigilia*, &c.

IV. *Of Weeks.*

Weeks were composed of seven days, as the scripture sheweth. And almost all the oriental nations have made use of this method to compute their days. Whereas the western world did not adopt it till the Christian religion was established, the Romans generally reckoning their days by nines, and the Greeks by decads or tens.

But the Pagans called their days by the names of the seven planets; thus the first was *dies Solis*, the second *dies Lunæ*, the third *dies Martis*, the fourth *dies Mercurii*, the fifth *dies Jovis*, the sixth *dies Veneris*, the seventh *dies Saturni*: and these names are still in use, except that instead of *dies Saturni*, we say *dies Sabbati*, that is, the day of rest; and instead of *dies Solis*, we call the first day of the week *dies Domini*, in memory of the resurrection of the son of God: the other days from the custom of the church are called *Feriæ* according to their order; thus Monday, *Feria secunda*, Tuesday, *Feria tertia*, and so on.

V. *Of Months.*

Months are composed of weeks, as weeks of days. But months properly speaking are no more than the space which the moon takes either in her course through the Zodiac, and is what astrologers call the periodical month, or in returning from one conjunction with the sun to the next conjunction following, and is what they call the synodical month.

Yet this name hath been also given to the time which the sun takes in its course through the twelfth part of the Zodiac, whereby two sorts of months are distinguished; lunar and solar.

The lunar synodical month, the only one considered by the antients, is little more than twenty-nine days and a half.

The solar month is generally computed at thirty days, ten hours and a half.

But the month is further divided into astronomical and civil. Astronomical is properly the solar month; and the civil is that which has been adapted to the custom and fancy of particular nations, some making use of lunar, and others of solar months.

The Jews, the Greeks, and the Romans heretofore made use of lunar months; but to avoid the different fractions of numbers, they made them alternately of nine and twenty and thirty days, calling the former *cavi*, and the latter *pleni*.

The Egyptians preferred the solar months, each of which they made of thirty days only, adding to the end of the year the five days that

that arose from the rest of the hours, and neglecting the six hours or thereabouts that arose from the half hours, which was the reason that every fourth year their seasons fell back a day.

We may be said likewise to make use of those months, though we render them unequal, reserving moreover the six hours to make a day thereof every fourth year, as hereafter shall be explained.

VI. *The antient manner of reckoning the days of the month.*

The Romans made use of three terms to denote the several days of the month; these were the calends, the nones, and the ides, which they marked thus, *Cal.* or *Kal. Non. Id.*

The calends they call the first day of every month, from the verb καλίω, *voco*, because as the antients computed their months by the revolution of the moon, there was a priest employed to observe the new moon, and upon his first perceiving it, to give notice thereof to the person who presided over the sacrifices; then the people were called to the Capitol, and information was given them how many days were to be reckoned till the nones, and upon the day of the nones all those employed in husbandry were obliged to be in town, that they might receive the direction for the festivals and other ceremonies to be observed that month. Hence some are of opinion that the nones were called *nonæ,* quasi *novæ,* as much as to say new observations; though it is more likely the reason of this denomination, was because from that time to the ides there were always nine days.

The word ides, according to Varro, was owing to this, that in the Etruscan language, *iduare* signified *dividere*, because they divided the month into two almost equal parts.

After the first day, which went by the name of calends, the six following in the month of March, July, and October; and the four in the other months belonged to the nones: and after the nones there were eight days belonging to the ides; and the remainder after the ides was reckoned by the calends of the next month. These particulars may be easily retained by these two Latin verses.

Sex Maius, nonas, October, Julius & Mars;
Quatuor at reliqui : dabit idus quilibet octo.

So that in the months above-mentioned, each of which had six days for the nones after the calends, the day of the nones was properly the seventh; and of course the ides were the fifteenth. But in the other months that had only four days betwixt the calends and the nones, the nones were the fifth, and of course the ides the thirteenth. And the proper day of the calends, nones, and ides was always put in the ablative, *calendis, nonis, idibus, Januarii, Februarii,* &c. But the other days were reckoned by the following term, expressing the number of days till then, and including both terms, whether nones, ides, or calends, as *quarto nonas,* sup. ante: *sexto idus*: *quinto calend.* &c.

Now they never said *primo nonas*; but *nonis,* &c. nor *secundo nonas,* because *secundus* cometh from *sequor,* and the business here is to mark the preceding day. For which reason they made use of *pridie*; just as to signify the following day they made use of *postridie*, as *pridie nonas*, or *nonarum*. *Postridie calendas* or *calendarum*, where we are to understand the preposition *ante* or *post*, when there is an accusative; whereas the genitive *nonarum*, or the like, is governed like the ablative *die*.

VII. *Of the Year.*

A year is properly the time which the sun takes in performing its revolution through the twelve signs of the Zodiack. It is divided into astronomical and civil.

The astronomical or tropic year, is that which includes the exact time the sun is in returning to the same point of the Zodiack from which he set out; this the astronomers have not yet been able exactly to determine, though by the nicest observations it is found to consist of 365 days, 5 hours, and 49 minutes.

The civil year is that which hath been adapted to the custom and fancy of different nations.

This year appears to have been of three sorts among the Romans. That of Romulus, who made the year only of ten months, beginning it in the month of March, for which reason the last month was called *December*.

That of Numa, who corrected this gross error of Romulus, adding two months to the year, January and February, and composing it of 355 days only, which are twelve lunar months.

That of Julius Cæsar, who finding this calculation also erroneous, added ten days and something more, whereby he made the year to consist of 365 days and six hours exactly, reserving the six hours to the end of four years in order to form an intire day, which they inserted before the sixth of the calends of March, and therefore that year they reckoned twice the sixth of the calends, saying the second time *bis sexto calendas*, whence came the word *bissextus*, and then the year had 366 days, and was called bissextile. This manner of computing has continued down to our times, and because of its author is still called the Julian year. Now the ten days which Cæsar gave the year above what it had before, were thus distributed: to January, August, and December, each two: to April, June, September, and November, each one.

But as in these latter times this calculation hath been likewise found imperfect, and the equinoxes had insensibly retrograded, instead of remaining where Julius Cæsar had fixed them, thence it clearly appeared that the year did not contain exactly 365 days and six hours, but that it wanted eleven minutes: this in 131 years made the equinoxes fall back almost a day, because an hour containing sixty of those minutes, a day must contain 1440 of them, which being divided by 11. give 130.$\frac{10}{11}$, so that the equinoxes were fallen back to the tenth of March. For which reason in the year 1582, Pope Gregory XIII, in order to correct this error, left out ten days of that year, by which means he restored those equinoxes to the 21st of March, and to the 22d or 23d of September: and that the like inconveniency might be

avoided

avoided for the future, he ordained that as 131 multiplied by three make 393, that is near 400 years, the computation fhould be regulated by hundreds, in order to make a round number; and therefore that in 400 years, the firſt three terminating three centuries fhould be common without reckoning the biſſextile. And this is properly what is called the Gregorian account.

So that in this calculation, there is never a hundredth year a biſſextile, except thoſe that can be meaſured by four. Thus 1700. 1800. 1900. 2100. 2200. are not biſſextile. But the years 1600. 2000. 2400. &c. are biſſextile.

VIII. *Of the ſpaces of time compoſed of ſeveral years.*

And firſt of Olympiads and Luſtres.

I fhall but juſt touch upon theſe matters, becauſe to treat of them fully, requires too copious a diſſertation, and properly belongs to another ſubject.

The Greeks reckoned by Olympiads, each of which contained the ſpace of four intire years. And thoſe Olympiads took their name from the Olympic games, which were celebrated in the neighbourhood of *Piſa*, heretofore called *Olympia*, in Peloponneſus, whence they had the name of Olympic. Thoſe years were likewiſe denominated *Iphiti*, from Iphitus, who inſtituted, or at leaſt revived the ſolemnity of thoſe games.

The Romans reckoned by luſtres, that is, by a ſpace of four or five years: for the word *luſtrum*, according to Varro, cometh from *luo* to pay; becauſe at the beginning of every fifth year, the people uſed to pay the tax impoſed upon them by the cenſors, whoſe offices had been eſtabliſhed at firſt for that ſpace of time, though afterwards they became annual.

2. *Of the indiction and the golden number.*

The INDICTION is a revolution of 15 years, which according to Hotoman was eſtabliſhed by the emperor Conſtantine, who publiſhed an edict ordaining that the ſubjects of the Roman empire ſhould no longer reckon by Olympiads but by indictions. Their name perhaps was borrowed from ſome tax that was paid to the emperors every fifteenth year; for *indictio* ſignifieth a tribute or tax.

The GOLDEN NUMBER is a revolution of 19 years, which was invented by Meto the Athenian, in order to reconcile the lunar to the ſolar year; at the expiration of which term of 19 years it was found that the moons returned to the ſame days, and that the moon recommenced her courſe with the ſun, within an hour and ſome minutes. And this was called the golden number, either for its excellence and great utility, or becauſe, according to ſome, the inhabitants of Alexandria ſent it to the Romans in a ſilver calendar, on which thoſe numbers from 1 to 19 were in gold letters. This number was likewiſe called THE GREAT LUNAR CYCLE, or *decennovennalis*, and ἐννεαδεκαἐτηρὶς of 19 years, or *Metonicus*, from the name of its author; and has been of great uſe in the eccleſiaſtic calendar, to ſhew the epacts and the new moons, since the council of Nice had ordained that the feast of Easter shou'd be celebrated the first Sunday after the full moon in March.

3. *Of the solar cycle, and the dominical letters.*

THE SOLAR CYCLE, or the dominical letters, is a revolution of 28 years, at the end of which the same dominical letters revert again in the same order.

To understand this properly we are to observe, that as the year is composed of months and weeks, every day of the month is marked out in the calendar by its cypher, or by one of the following seven letters, A, B, C, D, E, F, G, the first beginning the first day of the year, and the others continuing in a constant round to the end.

Hence those letters would invariably distinguish each feria or day of the week, as they are invariable in regard to the days of the month, if the year had exactly but a certain number of weeks; so that as A always signifies the 1st of January, B the 2d, C the 3d; in like manner A would always stand for Sunday; B, for Monday, &c. But by reason the year has at least 365 days, which make 52 weeks, and a day over, it happens to end with the same day of the week as it began; and therefore the next year begins not with the same, but with the following day. That is, as the next year 1651 begins with a Sunday, it will finish also with a Sunday; consequently the following year 1652 will begin with a Monday. And thence it comes of course that the letter A, which always answers to the first of January, having stood for Sunday one year (which is being the DOMINICAL LETTER) it will stand only for Monday the next year, in which of course the G will be the dominical letter or characteristic of Sunday: and so for the rest.

Hereby it appears that if the year had only 365 days, this circle of dominical letters would terminate in seven years, by retrogression, G, F, E, D, C, B, A. But because from four to four years there is a bissextile, which has one day extraordinary, two things ensue from thence.

The first, that this bissextile year hath two dominical letters, whereof one serves from the 1st of January to the 25th of February, and the other from thence to the end of the year. The reason of which is extremely clear, for reckoning the sixth of the calends twice, it follows, that the letter F, which answers to that day, is also reckoned twice, and therefore it fills two days of the week, the consequence of which is, that the letter which had hitherto fallen on the Sunday, falls now on the Monday, and the precedent by retrogression takes its place in order to be the characteristic of Sunday.

The second thing that follows from thence is, that as there are thus two dominical letters every fourth year, the circle of these letters does not terminate in seven years, as it otherwise would; but in four times seven years, which make twenty-eight. And this is exactly what they call the solar cycle, which before the reformation of the calendar, began with a bissextile year, the dominical letters of which were G, F.

4. *The*

4. *The Julian period, the sabbatic years, a jubilee, an age.*

The JULIAN PERIOD is formed of those three cycles or revolutions multiplied into one another, that is of 15 for the indiction, of 19 for the golden number, and of 28 for the dominical letters; which makes 7980 years. The use of this period is very common among chronologers, and of vast advantage for marking the time with certainty; because in all that great number of years, it is impossible to find one that has all the same cycles as another: for instance 1. the cycle of the Sun, 2. the cycle of the moon, and 3. the cycle of indiction. This period was invented by Joseph Scaliger, and is called Julian, from its being adapted to the Julian year, and composed of three cycles which are proper to that year.

The Jews reckoned their years by weeks, of which the seventh was called SABATIC, during which they were not allowed to till the land, and their slaves were to be set at liberty. They had likewise their years of JUBILEE or remission, which was every 50th, or according to some every 49th year; so that every jubilee year was likewise sabbatic, but more solemn than the rest; and the years of both terms, that is, of the preceding and following jubilee, were likewise included in the number 50. And then each estate, and whatever had been alienated, was to revert to its former master.

The word AGE which is frequently used, includes the space of one hundred intire years, according to Festus. Servius observeth that *sæculum*, which we render *age*, was also taken sometimes for the space of thirty years, sometimes for a hundred and ten years, and sometimes for a thousand.

5. *Of Epochas, and the word ÆRÆ.*

We may likewise take notice of the different EPOCHAS, which are certain principles, as it were, and fixed points, that chronologers make use of for the computation of years; these they likewise call ÆRÆ, from a corrupt word taken in the feminine for the neuter *æra*, a name they gave to the little nails of brass, with which they distinguished the accounts and number of years.

The most remarkable of all is that of the birth of Christ, as settled by Dionysius Exiguus, which commences in the month of January of the 4714th year of the Julian period, and is that which we make use of.

That of the Olympiads begins 776 years before the birth of our Saviour.

That of the foundation of Rome of the year 752 before Christ, according to the most probable opinion.

And several others, which may be seen in those who treat more diffusely of these matters.

BOOK IX.

Of LETTERS,
And the Orthography and Pronunciation of the Antients.

Wherein is shewn the antient manner of pronouncing the Latin tongue, and occasion is taken to point out also the right manner of pronouncing the Greek.

Extracted from the best treatises both of ancient and modern writers on this subject.

THE Reader may consult what hath been said in regard to Letters in the GENERAL AND RATIONAL GRAMMAR*. But here we follow a different order in favour of beginners. For whereas, one would imagine, that we ought to set out with a treatise of letters, as the least constituent part of words, and consequently of speech; and afterwards proceed to quantity and pronunciation, before we entered upon the analogy of the parts of speech, and the syntax or construction which includes their arrangement; we have reserved the two former parts for the present treatise, after having previously discoursed of the other two; not only for this reason, that there can be nothing more serviceable to those who begin to learn a language, than to introduce them immediately into the practical part, but likewise because there are several things in those two latter parts which suppose some progress, and knowledge of the former.

And indeed if the point be only to know how to assemble the letters, children ought to be well acquainted with this, when they enter upon the study of languages, and therefore they have no occasion here for any instructions about it; which made Quintilian say that this is beneath the office of a grammarian. But if we would examine this point with any degree of accuracy, and develop the several difficulties that entangle the subject, we shall find the truth of the following remark of an antient writer;

> *Fronte, exile negotium*
> *Et dignum pueris putes,*
> *Aggressis labor arduus.* Terentian. Maurus.

But I hope this labor will not be unprofitable, since it may contribute, as Quintilian saith, *not only to sharpen the wits of young people, but likewise to try the abilities of those who are more advanced.* And I persuade myself that it will help to demonstrate the

---

* A translation of this work was lately published by F. Wingrave, Successor to J. Nourse in the Strand.

nature and mutual relation of letters; which is indeed the groundwork of pronunciation and orthography; the reason of the quantity of syllables and dialects; the surest way of arguing from the analogy and etymology of words; and frequently serves as a clue to find our way through the most corrupt passages of the antients, while it shews us the manner of restoring them to their genuine sense and purity.

Chapter I.

Of the number, order, and division of letters.

THEY generally reckon three and twenty letters in the Latin alphabet. But, on the one hand, K being hardly any longer of use, and the I and U being not only vowels, but also consonants, and thus forming two new letters, as consonants, which the most skilful printers distinguish even from I and U vowel, by writing J consonant with a tail, and the V consonant with a sharp point, even in the middle of words; it would be better to reckon twenty-four letters in the alphabet, giving the Hebrew names *Jod* and *Vau* to the J and V consonant.

Thus of these twenty-four letters there are six vowels, that is which have need of a vowel to form an articulate sound and compose a syllable.

The six vowels are A, E, I, O, U, and Y.

Of the eighteen consonants X and Z, as pronounced by the antients, are properly no more than abbreviations; X being only a *c* and an *s*; and Z a *d* and an *s*, as we shall demonstrate presently. For which reason they are called *double letters*.

Of the sixteen remaining there are four called liquids or gliding letters, L, R, M, N; though, properly speaking, none but L and R deserve that name, the other two, especially M, being hardly gliding.

There are ten which may be called mutes, and divided into three classes, according to the relation they have to one another, and as they may more easily be changed one for the other, thus,

Mutes, { B, P, F, V.
C, Q, G, J.
D, T.

Of the two remaining S makes a class by itself, only that we may join it to X and Z, as it constitutes the principal part of the double letters. And those three may be called *hissing letters*, though it is a fault in some to give them too hissing a sound.

In regard to H, it is only an aspiration, though it ought not to be struck out of the order of letters, as hereafter we shall more particularly observe.

This is, in my opinion, the clearest and most useful division of letters. As to the distinction of consonants into semi-vowels and mutes,

mutes, whosoever will take pains to examine into the matter, must find that this half sound which he gives to the semi-vowels, L, M, N, R, S, X, does not proceeed from their nature, but only from the vowel which he prefixes to them in telling over the alphabet, *el, em, er, es, ex*; for if it had been customary to prefix the vowel to all the others which they call mutes, and say *eb, ec, ed*, &c. they would have an half sound as well as the precedent. And it is easy to shew that it was merely through caprice, and without any solid reason, that the Latins prefixed the vowel to some letters rather than others.

1. Because the Hebrews and the Greeks, of whom the Romans borrowed their alphabet, have always begun with a consonant in naming those letters in general.

2. Because *x* being composed of *c* and *s*, it is evident that according to reason it ought rather to be pronounced after the manner of the Greeks *csi*, than *ecs*, as it is generally sounded, which is difficult and disagreeable, not only to young people, but to grown up persons.

3. The F has so great an affinity with the Greek φ, that, the φ being a mute, there is no reason to think but F was a mute likewise, and yet they put a vowel before *ef*.

Upon the whole there is room to believe that this distinction ought not to be minded, though we retain the name of mutes in opposition to that of liquids, and not of semi-vowels. Therefore letters may be divided into

Vowels	{ open,	A, E, I.	6
	shut,	O, U, Y.	
Consonants.	{ Liquids,	L, R.	4
		M, N.	
	Mutes,	B, P, F, V.	10
		C, Q, G, J.	
		D, T.	
	Hissing,	S.	3
		X, Z.	
	Aspiration,	H.	1
			24

Chapter II.

Of vowels in general, as long or short.

THERE is no one article in which the moderns have varied more from the pronunciation of the antients than in this. For the distinction of the vowels, long or short, on which depends the whole quantity of syllables, save only those which are long by position, is now no more observed, except on the penultima of words of more than two syllables.   Thus

Thus in pronouncing *amábam* and *circumdábam*, it is plain that *ma* is long in the first word, and *da* short in the second. But in pronouncing *dabam* and *stabam*, it is impossible to tell whether the first syllable of either be short or long. In sounding *legimus* in the present, and *legimus* in the preterite, we give no mark that the *e* in the first syllable of the present is short, and in the preterite is long. Reciting *mensa* in the nominative, and *mensa* in the ablative, one cannot judge whether the last be short in one, and long in the other.

Now the antients, in uttering those vowels, distinguished exactly the long and short ones, wheresoever they occurred. Hence St. Austin takes notice, that when we find this passage in writing, *Non est absconditum à te os meum*, it is impossible to tell at first whether the *o* of this word *os* be long or short; but if it be pronounced short, it comes from *os, ossis*; and if it be pronounced long, it comes from *os, oris*. And this, without doubt, added greatly to the beauty of versification. For which reason the same father says likewise, that in this verse of Virgil,

Arma virumque cano, Trojæ qui primus ab oris.

if we were to put *primis*, the last of which is long, instead of *primus*, where it is short, the ear would be offended, and cease to find the same harmony. And yet there is no ear, however so delicate, that, without knowing the rules of Latin quantity, and hearing this verse recited with *primus ab oris*, or *primis ab oris*, would be able to distinguish any thing that gave offence more in one than the other.

The antients also observed this distinction of long or short vowels in their writing, in which they frequently doubled the vowel, to denote a long syllable; which Quintilian acknowledged to have been practised till the time of Attius.

Sometimes they inserted an *h* between these two vowels, in order to strengthen the pronunciation, as *Ahala* for *Ala* or *Aala*; and, after dropping the first *A*, they likewise made *Hala*; for this is still the same noun, though some learned men have been dubious about it.

And it is for this same reason that we find in the antients *mehe* for *mee* or *me* long, *mehecum* for *mecum*, and the like; just as we say *vehemens* for *veemens*; *prehendo* for *preendo*; and *mihi* for the antient *mi* or *mii*.

But afterwards, for the sake of brevity, they were satisfied with drawing only a small stroke over the vowel, to shew it was long, thus Ā, Ē, Ō, Ū. Though for the vowel I they never used this mark, as we shall shew hereafter. And hence it is that we still meet with *totiens* for *totiēs*, *quotiens*, *vicensimus*, *formonsus*, *aquonsus*, and such like; which is owing intirely, as Lipsius observes, to the ignorance of transcribers, who took this small stroke for a tittle, that stood for an *n* or an *m*, as is still practised, not knowing that among the antients it served only as a mark of quantity.

CHAPTER

Chapter III.

Of vowels in particular. And particularly of those that are called open.

THE three first vowels, A, E, I, are called open, because in pronouncing them the mouth ought to be opened wider than in pronouncing the rest.

I. *Of* A.

Nothing more remains to be said of the A, after what hath been mentioned in the preceding chapter, except that this vowel hath a relation and affinity with a great many others, as we shall see in the sequel. We may further observe that it is the most open of them all, as the most simple and the easiest to pronounce; for which reason it is with this that children begin their alphabet. So that if we do but rightly consider the natural order of those vowels, we shall find, that from this, which is the most open, they diminish gradually down to the U, which is the most shut, and which of all the vowels has the greatest need of the motion of the lips to pronounce it.

II. *Of* E.

There is scarce a letter that admits of more different sounds in all languages than this; particularly in French. We may take notice of three of those sounds which sometimes occur in a single word, as *fermeté, netteté, breveté*, &c. The first is an *e* which I call open, because it is pronounced with the mouth open. The second is generally called *obscure and mute*, because it has a weaker sound than the rest; or *feminine*, because it serves to form the feminine rhimes in French metre. And the third, opposite to this, is called *e* clear, or *masculine*; as also *e shut*: it is frequently marked with a small accent over it to distinguish it from the rest.

Besides this the French language hath another, which is pronounced like an *a*, and therefore ought rather to be called an *a*, since the figure is quite accidental in regard to letters: and perhaps it would be better to write it with an *a*, were it not for pointing out the derivation of words in the original languages. As *Empereur* for *Ampereur*, because it comes from *Imperator*; *en* for *an*, because it comes from *in*; *pendre* for *pandre*, because it comes from *pendere*; *grandement, fortement, difficilement*, &c. *ment* for *mant*, because they come from the Italian.

But as for the other open *e*, which some make use of, as in *bête, fête, tête*, or with an S, *beste, feste, teste*, we ought to look upon it as the same with the first *e* in *breveté, fermeté*, &c. from which it hardly differs, except in some length of quantity or accent. This seems to be well illustrated by the comparison of these two words, *fer*, and *ferre*, where this *e*, which becomes longer in the first syllable of the second word, is nevertheless the same as

that

that of the firſt word. And therefore we may reduce all the French E's to three, or at moſt to four, if we likewiſe include that which is ſounded as an A; and theſe four different ſounds may be obſerved in a ſingle word, as *Déterrement*.

But the latter, which is called the long and open *e*, and appears particularly in theſe words, *bête*, *fête*, *tête*, &c. properly correſponds with the Greek *eta*, whoſe ſound it perfectly repreſents, ſince the aforeſaid *eta* was introduced on purpoſe to diſtinguiſh the long E, ſaying βῆτα, as if it were *béèta*. Which made Euſtathius ſay that βῆ βῆ, *béè béè*, expreſſeth perfectly well the bleating of the ſheep; wherein he is ſupported by the authority of the antient poet Cratinus. So that it is really amazing, there ſhould be people who ſtill pronounce it like an *i*, contrary to the general analogy of the language, ſince Simonides, who invented the two long vowels η and ω, did it with no other intent than to make them correſpond to the two ſhort ones ε and ο; contrary to the unanimous opinion of all the antients, and the teſtimony of the ableſt writers of the latter ages; and contrary, in ſhort, to the ſtanding practice of the beſt ſcholars both in France and other nations; which might be further evinced by a great number of authorities and arguments, drawn from the compariſon of all languages, if it had not been already ſufficiently demonſtrated by thoſe who before us have handled the ſubject.

On the contrary, the *é* ſhut expreſſeth the Greek ἰψιλὸν, like the laſt in *fermeté*. And the other, which is between both, gives a particular grace to the French language, the like of which is not to be found in any other; for it forms the feminine rhimes in verſe, as when they ſay *ferme*, *terme*, &c.

But it is very remarkable that this E, which conſtitutes almoſt one half of the French rhimes, hardly ever occurs twice ſucceſſively in the ſame word, except in a few compounds, as *devenir*, *revenir*, *remenir*, *entretenir*, *contrepeſer*, &c. and even here it is not at the end of the words. For which reaſon in verbs that have an E feminine in the penultima of the infinitive, as *peſer*, *mener*, it is changed into an open *e* in thoſe tenſes which finiſh with this E feminine: ſo that they ſay, *cela ſe péſe*, *il me méne*, as if it were *paiſe*, *maine*, &c. And in the firſt perſons which end with this ſame E feminine, it is changed into an E maſculine in interrogations, becauſe of the pronoun *je* which follows and is joined to it, and which hath alſo an *e* feminine. Thus we ſay, *j'aime*, *je joüe*, *je prie*. But in interrogating we ſay, *joüé-je? aimé-je? prié-je?* And if, to facilitate the pronunciation on thoſe and other occaſions, people would only accuſtom themſelves to put ſome little mark on the *e* feminine, as it is cuſtomary to put under the ç in particular words, it would be diſtinguiſhed from the *é* maſculine, which has its mark over it, and the plain letter *e* might remain for what we call the *e mute* and *obſcure*. And thus we might effectuate, almoſt without any trouble, ſuch a diſtinction in orthography and pronunciation; as may be deemed perhaps of all others the moſt neceſſary in the French language, ſince we ſee daily that not only foreigners, but even thoſe who are verſed in the language, are miſtaken and puzzled in the diſtinction of thoſe two *e*'s. The

The Latins had also their different sounds of this letter. They had their E long and open, which answered to the Greek *Eta*, and for that reason was frequently doubled, as we see in medals and antient inscriptions, *feelix, seedes*, &c.

The second was like the E short and shut of the French, and answered to the Greek ἰψιλὸν. And these two differences of the E are plainly marked in the writings of the antients. *E vocalis*, says Capella, *duaram Græcarum vim possidet. Nam cùm corripitur E Græcum est, ut ab hoste: Cum producitur,* ETA *est, ut ab hac die.*

But beside this, there was a middle sound between the E and the I. Whence Varro observeth that they used to say *veam* for *viam:* and Festus, that they said *me* for *mi* or *mihi:* and Quintilian that they put an E for an I in *Menerva, Leber, Magester,* and that Livy wrote *sebe* and *quase:* and Donatus, that by reason of the affinity of these two letters, the antients made no scruple to say *heri* and *here, mane* and *mani, vespere* and *vesperi,* &c. Hence we still find in antient inscriptions, *navebus, exemet, ornavet, cepet, Deana, mereto, soledas,* and the like. And, as we have elsewhere observed, from thence also ariseth the change of those two vowels in so many nouns, either in the nominative, as *impubes* and *impubis, pulix* and *pulex, cinis* and *ciner,* &c. or in the accusative, as *pelvem* or *pelvim;* or in the ablative, as *nave* or *navi;* and the like nouns of the third declension; and in the second *Dii* for *Dei.* Concerning which see what has been said in the first volume, when treating of the declensions.

The fourth E of the French, which is put for A, was also found among the Latins; whence Quintilian witnesseth that Cato wrote indifferently *dicam* or *dicem, faciam* or *faciem.* And hence, without doubt, it comes that the A of the present tense is so frequently changed into E, either in the preterite, as *facio, feci; ago, egi; jacio, jeci,* &c. or in compounds, as *arceo, coërceo; damno, condemno; spargo, aspergo,* &c. To this also it is owing that they said *balare* for *belare (to bleat)* which is still to be found in Varro 1. de R. R. cap. 2. *Incestus* for *incastus; talentum* for τάλανιον; *damnum* for *demnum,* from *diminuo,* according to Varro. From this same cause it proceeds that we meet with so many words written with E or A in antient authors and in the old glossaries, as *æquiperare* for *æquiparare. Condamnare* for *condemnare,* V. Gloss. *Defetigari* for *defatigari,* Varr. *Effligi* for *affligi,* Charis. *Expars* for *expers,* ἄμοιρος, V. Gloss. *Expertæ* for *expartæ* or *effætæ,* Varr. *Imbarbis* for *imberbis,* V. Gloss. *Inars,* ἄτιχνος, for *iners,* id. *Reperare* for *reparare,* whence comes *recuperare,* and the like.

But it is further observable that the E had likewise some affinity with the O, as we shall shew hereafter; and even with the U. Whence cometh *diu* for *die, lucu* for *luce, allux* for *allex,* the great toe, *dejero* for *dejuro, Neptunus* for *Nuptunus, à nubendo terram, id est operiendo,* according to Cicero, *Brundusium* for βρεντήσιοι, *ulcus* for ἕλκος. And hence it comes that the verbs in EO make UI, *moneo, monui; doceo, docui,* &c.

III.

III. *Of* I.

The I, as we have already observed, was the only vowel over which they did not draw a stroke to mark its being long; which is further proved by the authority of Scaurus. But in order to shew the quantity thereof, they lengthened it in the nature of a capital letter among the rest, pIso, vIvus, ÆdIlis, and the like. Wherefore among all the letters it was called *Long* by Synecdoche.

Hence it is that in the *Aulularia* of Plautus, when Staphilus wants to hang himself, he says that he wanted to make a long letter of himself.

> *ex me unam faciam litteram*
> *Longam, meum quando laqueo collum obstrinxero.*

This is the explication that Lipsius gives of it, which seems far more rational than that of Lambinus, who understands it of all sorts of capital letters; not considering that the Romans had no small ones, and that among the capitals, this alone surpassed the rest.

But if we should be asked whether the I was not also doubled like the other vowels, to signify the long quantity, Lipsius answereth, that, absolutely speaking, it was not. And this is the opinion of the most learned critics, though we meet with some examples to the contrary, perhaps by corruption, as dIvII Augusti, in an inscription in the reign of Augustus.

As therefore the I by its length alone was equivalent to *ii* in quantity, so it has happened frequently to be put for two real *ii*, that is which ought to be expressed in discourse, as dE manIbIs, for *manibiis*. dIs manibus, for *Diis manibus*. And to this are owing those contractions which are looked upon as established in the writings of poets, *Dí* for *Dei*, *otí* for *otii*, *urbem Pataví*, for *Patavii*, Virg. and the like.

But the antients marked likewise the quantity of this letter by the diphthong *ei*, as Victorinus observeth; so that it was the same thing to put dIvI, or dIveI, and the like, the long I and *ei* having the same, or at least a very similar sound. This is so far true, that Priscian thought it was the only way to mark the long I; though what has been abovementioned, sufficiently sheweth there was another.

And this pronunciation of *ei* was become so common among them, that they even gave it to the short words. This shews that it was not perhaps so much a mark of quantity, as of a fuller and more agreeable sound, which sufficiently appears from some verses out of Lucilius which I shall presently produce, and which made this its medium betwixt the two vowels, of which we have taken notice above. Hence it is, that in old copies we still find *omneis*, not only for *omnes* in the plural, but moreover for *omnis* in the singular, and others in the same manner.

And indeed there is no manner of writing, says Victorinus, about which there have been such disputes among the antients, as this. Lucilius and Varro endeavoured to distinguish it, by laying down as a rule to put *i* only in the singular, and *ei* in the plural;

so

so as to say *hujus pueri, amici*, &c. and in the plural, *hi puerei, amicci*, &c. And likewise in the dative *illi* with *i* only, but in the nominative plural *illei* with *ei*. This is proved from the following verses out of Lucilius:

Jam puerei *venere*, E *poſtremum facito atque* I.
Ut plures puerei *fiant*, &c.
Hoc illi *factum* uni, *tenue hoc facies* I,
Hoc illei *fecere, addes* E, UT PINGUIS FIAT.

With the reſt which may be ſeen in Joſeph Scaliger, who extracted them partly from Quintilian, and partly from Victorinus, where it is obſervable, as I have mentioned, that this writing with *ei*, formerly made a fuller ſound; ſince he ſays, *ut pinguius fiat*.

Quintilian nevertheleſs finds fault with this manner of writing, as well becauſe he ſays it is ſuperfluous, as alſo becauſe it is only apt to confound thoſe who begin to learn to read. Whence we may conclude that the pronunciation had changed, and that there was no longer any difference betwixt *ei* and *i*. This made Lipſius ſay, that it is idle now to diſpute, whether we ought to write *omneis* or *omnis, puereis* or *pueris*; ſince according to Quintilian there was not the leaſt difference between thoſe two ſounds in the Latin language. Concerning which ſee what we ſhall further ſay in the 5th chap. n. 3. treating of this diphthong.

CHAPTER IV.
Of the three laſt vowels which are called ſhut.

THE three laſt vowels are O, U, Y. They are called ſhut, becauſe in pronouncing them the mouth is not opened ſo wide as in pronouncing the others.

I. *Of* O.

The O by its two ſounds, long and ſhort, perfectly repreſented the Greek *omega* and *omicron*, the pronunciation of which was very different, ſays Caninius after Terentianus. For the ω was pronounced in the hollow of the mouth with a full and thick ſound, as including two *oo*; and the *omicron* was pronounced on the edge of the lips with a clearer and more ſlender ſound.

The French have theſe two ways of pronouncing, expreſſing the long O by the addition of an S, *coſte, hoſte*, which are different from *cotte, hotte, motte*; or by the diphthong *au, haute, faute*, &c.

The affinity between this vowel *o* and the French diphthong *au*, is not without example among the Greeks, who ſay ἀυλαξ or ἀλαξ, *fulcus*: τραυμα or τρωμα, according to the Dorics, whence it is that the Latins have alſo *caudex* or *codex, caurus* or *corus*, &c. And hence it is perhaps that as this diphthong *au* partook greatly of the A, ſo the O had alſo ſome affinity with A. For the Æolians ſaid ϛρότος for ϛρατός, *exercitus*; ὄνω for ἄνω, *ſupra*. Which the Latins have likewiſe imitated, borrowing *domo* from δαμω, and ſaying *Fabius* for *Fovius*, according to Feſtus; *Farreus* for *forreus*, &c. And in French the A and O are oftentimes joined in the ſame word, *laon, faon, paon*, which are pronounced with a long *A, lân, fân, făn, păn*; though Ramus takes notice that in his time some marked the long O with these two letters AO, which they did perhaps in imitation of the Greeks, who change αο or αω, as well as οα, into ω long in their contractions.

The O hath likewise an affinity with the E; hence it is that of λέγω, *dito*, the Greeks have made λέλογα, *dixi*, and the like; that the Æolians said τρομέω for τρέμω, *tremo*; that the Latins of σπένδω, *libo*, made *spondeo*; of *pendeo*, *pondus*; of *tego*, *toga*; and they say *adversum* or *advorsum*; *vertex* or *vortex*; *accipiter* for *accipitor*, or *accepter*, ἱέραξ, according to Festus, a bird of prey: *hemo* for *homo*; *ambe* and *ambes*, for *ambo* and *ambos*, in Ennius: *exporrectus* for *experrectus*, &c. Hence also it is that there are so many adverbs in E and in O, *vere* and *vero*, *tute* and *tuto*, *nimie* and *nimio*, *cotidie* and *cotidio*, *rare* and *raro*, in Charisius, and such like. And it is by this very analogy, that the nouns in US make, some the genitive in ERIS, as *vulnus*, *vulneris*, and others ORIS, as *pecus*, *pecoris*; *stercus*, *sterceris*, and *stercoris*, &c. And that the verbs have a reduplication in E and O, as *momordi* for *memordi*, *spopondi* for *spepondi*, &c.

But the O had still a much greater affinity with the U. Hence it is that the antients, says Longus, were apt to confound those two letters; and though according to him, they wrote *consol* with an O, yet they pronounced *consul* with an U. And Cassiodorus informs us that they wrote *præstu* for *præsto*; *poblicum* for *publicum*; *colpam* for *culpam*, &c. Pliny in Priscian tells us the same thing, and thence it is that we say *huc*, *illuc*, for *hoc*, *illoc*, which Virgil himself hath made use of.

Hoc tunc ignipotens cœlo descendit ab alto, Æn. 8.

Which is likewise proved by Servius on this passage. And Quintilian observeth that they said, *Hecoba*, *notrix*, with an *o* for an *u*; that of *Odysseus*, the Æolians made *Udysseus*, whence the Latins had borrowed *Ulysseus*. And in short his tutors had wrote *Servom* with an *o*, whereas in his time they wrote it with two *uu*, though neither of those writings did perfectly express the sound which struck the ear.

II. *Of* U.

From what has been said it plainly appeareth that the U had a very full sound, which bordered very much on the O. And Terentianus expressly declared that the U filled the sound of the diphthong OY. In vain does Lipsius, as well as Vossius, pretend that this pronunciation was only for the U long, and that the short one was pronounce like an ὑψιλὸν, that is like a French *u*. For Priscian teacheth the contrary, and doubtless his authority is preferable to theirs on this occasion. And in regard to the argument which they draw from a passage of Varro's, which says that they pronounced *luit* in the present, differently from *luit* in the preterite; we shall shew hereafter in the treatise of accents that this difference was only in the quantity, and not in the sound.

And if any body should still doubt of this truth, we might further produce the authority of antient marbles and inscriptions, which being written according to the simple pronunciation, have frequently *ou* for *u*, not only in long words, as *loumen*, *nountios*,

but

but likewise in the short, as *fouom, fouo*, &c. And *fouis* for *fuit* is in Gellius, lib. 1. c. 12. according as we find it in the edition of H. Stephen, esteemed by all the learned. And it is without foundation that Vossius attempts to correct it.

Besides, we find that Ausonius speaking of the sound of this vowel, does not make this distinction, but says absolutely,

Cecropiis ignota notis, ferale sonans U.

Where mentioning that there is no such sound among the Greeks, he plainly gives to understand that it could not have the sound of ὐψιλὸν; as on the other hand he has sufficiently pointed out the natural sound of this letter by the word *ferale*, whereby he meant the note of the cuckoo, or of the night howl, to which a parasite in Plautus alludeth where he says,

—— Tu tu, *illic inquam, vin' adferri noctuam,*
Quæ tu, tu *usque dicat tibi? nam nos jam nos usque descissi sumus.*

Which perfectly represents the sound of the U like *ou*, according to the note of that wild and well known bird.

And if any body should object that Cicero in his book de Oratore takes notice that heretofore they wrote *Phruges* and *Purrhus* without Greek letters, and therefore that the *u* on those occasions had the sound of ὐψιλὸν; I answer that on the contrary, writing *Purrhus*, they pronounced according to the value of the letters *Pourrhous*; as we see an infinite number of words, which passing from one language to another, assume the sound as well as figure of the language they pass to. And this answer is agreeable to Quintilian, when he says, *Fortasse etiam quemadmodum scribebant, ita & loquebantur.* Though we may likewise say that perhaps sometimes they erroneously pronounced the *u* like an *ipsilon*, and put it in the stead of ὐψιλὸν. But then this was no longer a Latin *u*, but a real Greek Y in power, though not in figure, which is merely accidental to all sorts of letters.

And thus we are to understand the verses of Terentianus, which Vossius endeavoureth to wrest to another meaning, where he says of the three common vowels among the Greeks, namely, α, ι, υ;

Tertiam Romana lingua quam vocant Y non habet,
Hujus in locum videtur U Latina subdita:
Quæ vicem nobis rependit interim vacantis Y,
Quando communem reddit Latino & Græco sonum.

For since he formally declares that this third vowel Y does not belong to the Latin tongue, he plainly sheweth that the Latin U was not sounded like the Greek Y, because otherwise he would have had no reason to say that the Romans were without this letter. And adding that the U was sometimes put instead of this Greek Y, *when*, says he, *it made a sound that was common both to Greeks and Latins*, he lets us know that this U was put there improperly and instead of the Greek Y, which was owing merely to the ambition of the Romans, who made use of Latin characters, that they might seem to borrow nothing of the Greeks. Thus it is that Cassiodorus observes they wrote *Suria* for *Syria*; and Donatus that they put *sura* for *syra*.

Longus mentions the same thing, adding nevertheless that it is better to use the Y in those Greek words. Which shews that they
had

had still retained the sound thereof, even when they made use of the U. For if the U, as a Latin letter, might have been sounded as the Greek Y, that is, like the French U, which is much softer than that of the Latin OU, Quintilian would not have said that in the word *Zephyris*, for instance, *there were two letters*, (the Z and the Y, which he calls *jucundissimas litteras*) *which the Romans had not, but were obliged to borrow of the Greeks whenever they wanted to make use of Greek words, because if they had attempted to write them with Latin letters, this would have produced a rough and barbarous sound*, lib. 12. c. 10.

If after all this there can be any doubt that the real pronunciation of the Latin U was that of the French diphthong *ou*, we need only to observe the manner in which it is pronounced by the modern Italians. And should it be imagined that this U might sometimes have the sound of the Greek Y in Latin; then the Greeks in all probability must have been very much in the wrong, when in making use of Latin words they had recourse to ȣ to express the force of the Latin U, when they needed only to have wrote their ἰνψιλὸν.

To this genuine sound of the Latin U it is owing, as already hath been mentioned, that it was so frequently changed into O, as *volt* for *vult*, &c. because the U being pronounced like the French *ou*, it greatly partook of the nature of O. And for this same reason these two letters are so often changed for one another in analogy. For from *robur* cometh *roboris*, from *dominum* in the singular cometh *dominos* in the plural, and the like.

But it is to be observed that we still retain something of this antient pronunciation of the U in those words where it is followed by an M or an N. *Dominum, dederunt*, &c. This is owing to the natural property of those two consonants, which produce a very particular sound, and are always pronounced broader and fuller, let them be joined with whatever vowel they will: it being the same thing, according to Quintilian, to say *servom*, as *servum*, or *servoum*. Though we have lost this pronunciation in some words where the *n* is followed by a *c*, as *nunc, tunc, hunc, cunctis*, and *defunctis* in the church service.

But if it should be asked whether the U had intirely the same sound as the diphthong ȣ? we may answer it had not, but something very like it; because the diphthongs, as the word implies, were productive of a double sound composed of two vowels, as we see in the French diphthongs, *ciel, beau, mien*, &c. though of one syllable. This was not the case of the U, which had but one, though a full sound. And this is the opinion of Ramus, for otherwise, he says, *it would have passed for a diphthong*. Hence we see that Joseph Scaliger had no right to find fault with Ausonius for saying in this verse,

—Cecropiis ignota notis ferale sonans U.

that the sound of this U, which is *ou*, was unknown to the Greeks, because the sound of the diphthong *ou* was not altogether the same.

But besides this natural pronunciation of the U, there was another, according to Quintilian, that had a middle sound, as it were, between I and U, which was the reason of its being variously written: and thence it is that we still meet with *optimus* or *optumus*, *maximus* or *maxumus*, *monimentum* or *monumentum*, &c. And the antient inscriptions abound with these variations, *stupendium* for *stipendium*, *aurufex* for *aurifex*: and in like manner we say, *capulum ensis*, the hilt, from *capio*: *clipeus* for *clupeus*; *exul* for *exil*, from *exilium*; *facul* for *facile*; *lubet* for *libet*; *manibiæ* for *manubiæ*; *volitare* for *volutare*, Varr. and the like.

III. *Of* Y.

There is hardly any thing further to be said in regard to this sixth vowel, after what has been observed upon this head, when speaking of the U; we are only to take notice that it was always used in Greek nouns, and pronounced very near in the same manner as the French U, which has a middle sound between the Latin *i* and *u*.

The French particularly make use of this letter Y in all words ending in *y*, as *epy*, *fourny*, *garny*, &c. though they have lost its sound, for they always pronounce it as an *i*. And this pronunciation they have even introduced into the Latin tongue, where there is in some measure a necessity for tolerating it because of its being established by custom; but it is by no means to be admitted into the Greek language, where the ἰψιλὸν ought to be pronounced like a French U: which is demonstrated by all the antient and modern grammarians, and may be further corroborated by an invincible argument, borrowed from those words which are formed by the imitation of sound, to signify the cries of animals. For it is beyond doubt that when we say ὑλακτίζειν, *ululare*, μυκᾶζειν, *mugire*, σύζειν, *grunnire*, the original intent was not to convey the sound of an I, but of an U, as the vowel that borders nearest on the cry of those animals.

Therefore it may be observed here in general, that use being the mistress of living languages, and the Latin being now adopted by the church, and in every body's mouth, it would be imprudent to change the pronunciation of it in things universally received. But in regard to the Greek tongue, as it is confined to a small number of literati, it seems to be wronging their abilities to say, either that they are ignorant of the genuine pronunciation of the antients, of which so many learned men have wrote express treatises, or that knowing it, they make a difficulty to conform thereto; since it is now received by the most learned of every nation: and were it not for this (as hath been observed by Mr. Cheek, the king's professor in England, who wrote a learned dissertation on this subject above a hundred years ago) we should be deprived of the whole beauty of the analogy of this language, whether in regard to the numerousness of periods, and the cadence of verse, or to the surprizing relation which the words have to each other in the declensions, conjugations, augments, dialects, and interchanging

changing of letters: which shews a most beautiful proportion in the whole, and greatly facilitates the principles to those who have a mind to learn the Greek tongue.

CHAPTER V.
Of Diphthongs.

WE join the diphthongs to the vowels as the whole to its parts. Lipsius calls them BIVOCALES, double vowels, because they are compounded of two vowels: and it may be observed that there are eight in Latin, Æ, *ætas*, AI, *Maïa*, AU, *audio*, EI, *eïa*, EU, *eurus*, OE, *pœna*, OI, *Troïa*, UI, *harpuïa*. For in this word there is a Greek diphthong, says Servius, though some write it also with a Y only, *harpya*.

These diphthongs used to be pronounced with a double sound, as their name implieth: but the two vowels were not distinguished alike, one being sometimes weaker, and the other stronger.

I. Of the Diphthongs Æ and AI.

Therefore in *æ* and *ai*, the first vowel had its full and complete sound, because the A of itself is stronger than the other vowels, and never loseth the advantage it has over them in pronouncing, as Plutarch witnesseth in his treatise of banquets: on the contrary the latter had a much weaker sound, as may be experienced in *Aiax*. Hence it was that oftentimes they did not distinguish whether it was an E or an I, and for this reason they wrote heretofore with an AI, what afterwards they came to write with an Æ, *musai* for *musæ*; *Kaisar* for *Kæsar*, whence the Germans and Flemings have still preserved the word *Keyser*, to signify *Cæsar*; *Juliai* for *Juliæ*, and the like; as appears by the authority of Quintilian, Longus, Scaurus, and other grammarians. Hence it is that in some words the A hath remained by itself, as AQUA *ab æquando*, says St. Isidorus, so that in the Greek the diphthong *ai* ought always to be more open than the η, and we should lean more upon the A than upon the I. Though we must confess that after the corruption of the language, the Æ was also pronounced like a simple E, for which reason, instead of Æ they frequently put only an E, as *eger* for *æger*, *etas* for *ætas*, *es alienum* for *æs*. And on the contrary the Æ has been sometimes put for a simple E, as *ævocatus* for *evocatus*, and the like, with which the old glossaries abound. And hence it is that Beda in his orthography ranks *æquor* among the words that are written with a simple E. Which he does likewise in regard to *comædia*. Whereby it appears that the corruption which hath been introduced into the pronunciation of the diphthongs, was contested even in his time, that is so early as the seventh century.

II. Of the Diphthongs AU and EU.

The pronunciation still observed in AU and EU, borders nearer upon that of the ancients. For the AU had a great affinity with the O, for which reason they wrote *caurus* and *corus*; *cauda* and *coda*, *lautus* and *lotus*, *plaustrum* and *plostrum*, with a great many others which may be seen in Festus and in Priscian, lib. 1. This the Latins had borrowed from the Dorians, who said, ὦλαξ for αὖλαξ, *sulcus*; τρῶμα for τραῦμα, *vulnus*; where we likewise perceive that the pronunciation of the υ was much fuller than that of the *omicron*, since it bordered upon the *au*, only that they sounded the A somewhat stronger in order to form a diphthong, whence it is that we find *Aorelius* for *Aurelius*. In Veter. Epigram.

The EU was pronounced almost in the same manner as we now pronounce *eudoxia*, *eucharistia*, *euripus*, not joining the two letters all together, but dividing them as little and as nicely as possible, and leaning more upon the U than the E. These two diphthongs had a relation to each other; for from *eurus* comes *aura*, and they have this in particular, that both in Greek, Latin, and French, they have nearly retained the same pronunciation. So that it is quite without reason or foundation that some attempt to pronounce αυ in Greek like *af*, and ευ like *ef*, as if ὐψιλὸ, was an *f*, and not an *u*; or a diphthong could be formed of a vowel and a consonant, instead of two vowels; or in short the *u* ought to have any other effect on both those occasions than the diphthong *u*, which is pronounced *ou* and not *of*, as one would think it ought to be pronounced if those other two sounds were to be admitted.

From this error nevertheless it comes that the French pronounce *un af-tomate*, *un e-vangile*, and not *au-tomate*, nor *eu-angile*, as they say *eu-nuque*, *eu-charistie*. And though it be ill founded, yet it seems to have been introduced a long time ago, since Beda in his poetry takes notice that they said *a-vrum* for *au-rum*, *e-vangelium* for *eu-angelium*. But as to the verses which are quoted out of Tertullian,

Tradit evangelium Paulus sine crimine mundum,

it is not his, no more than the others which are attributed to him, according to what Monf. Rigault hath observed in his notes on this author. And it is contrary to the practice of the antients, who always make *eu* long, as in *eu-ander*, *eu-ans*, and such like.

Namque ut ab Evandro castris ingressus Hetruscis, Virg.

Nec non Evantem Phrigium, Paridisque Mimanta, Id.

Which they would never have done, says Vossius, had the U been separated from the *epsilon*, which is naturally short.

But it is observable that Terentianus declares that these two diphthongs *au* and *eu* were pronounced somewhat shorter than the others.

AU & EU *quas sic habemus cum Græcis communiter,*
Corripi plerumque possunt temporum salvo modo. And lower down.
Ἔυπολις, πευκὴν & ἰυτόυν, *aut poetam* Ἐυριπίδην,
Syllabas primas necesse est ore raptim promere;
Tempus at duplum manebit, nihil obest correptio.

III. *Of the Diphthong* EI.

In the diphthong EI, the E was very weak, so that scarce any other sound was heard but that of the I; hence it is that this E was

was often loft, and there remained only a long I, as in *eo, is, it,* for *eis, eit,* &c. becaufe, as we have already obferved, the long I had almoſt the fame found as this diphthong, as Cicero fufficiently teſtifieth, when he makes an allufion and comparifon betwixt *bini,* and βίνει, and as we likewife fee in the old monumental infcriptions, where they wrote indifferently *dico* or *deico, heic* or *hic, omneis* or *omnis,* &c. Which was owing to a delicacy of the language particularly ufed by well bred people; whereas the vulgar, or illiterate perfons, rather founded the E intire. For which reafon Varro obferves that the peafants faid *vellam* for *villam,* which came from *vehillam* or *veillam.* And in Cicero, Craffius reproves Sulpicius, becaufe by leaning too much on the E in this diphthong, *he did not pronounce like an orator, but like a plowman.* And hence alfo it is that heretofore fome pronounced *leber,* and others *liber,* becaufe it came from *leiber;* and in like manner *Alexandrea* or *Alexandria,* as coming from *Alexandreia:* and the like.

IV. *Of the diphthongs* OE *and* OI.

Terence and Victorinus inform us that thefe two Latin diphthongs had a very great affinity with the Greek diphthong OI. And Ramus in the third book of his fchools, expreffeth the found of the latter by thefe French words *moi, toi, foi.* This has occafioned the changes we fometimes obferve in the antient copies, as *Adelphoe* for *Adelphoi,* in Terence; and in another place *Oinonem* for *Oenonem,* with the like: and ſhews us the reafon why in rendering words from Greek into Latin, they are always changed one for the other, ποινὴ, *pœna,* &c. where we fee that as of AI they made Æ, fo of OI they made OE, only by changing I into E.

Now as among the Latins the O bore a great relation to the U, it happened that OE hath been oftentimes changed into U, as when of *pœna* they made *punire,* that is *pounire,* after their manner of pronouncing the U. And therefore we find in antient infcriptions, *oifum* or *æfum* for *ufum. Coiravit* or *cœravit* for *curavit.* They faid likewife *moerus* for *murus*——*aggeribus moerorum,* Æn. 8. according to Servius, whence alfo cometh *pomœrium* quafi poſt *moerum* five *murum;* we find alfo *moenus* for *moerus* (changing *n* into *r*) and in the plural *mœnia* for *munia,* from *munio.* In like manner *mœnera* for *munera,* &c. Thus it is that the Flemings write *goet,* and pronounce it *goot,* to fignify *good:* and thus we ſtill fay *Puni* for *Pœni; bellum Punicum* for *Pœnicum;* the Carthaginians having been called *Pœni, quafi Phœni,* fays Servius, becaufe they came from Phœnicia, where we may likewife take notice of the change of PH into P. For the Jews and other eaſtern nations, according to St. Jerom, had no P; whence it comes that he always tranflates *Philiſtiim* to fignify the people of *Paleſtine,* though now of one and the fame letter, which is the פ, they make either a P or a PH, putting it with or without a *dagueſh.*

But we are to take notice that this change of the diphthong OI into U, was received only in thofe words where the O was founded ſtronger than the I: whereas in moſt other places, it partook

a great

a great deal more of the sound of the I, as Lipsius sheweth. Which makes us doubt whether Ramus hath sufficiently explained the sound of this diphthong, when he says it was the same as in the French words *moy, toy, soy*; and whether it would not be better represented by these verses out of Virgil, Æn. 11.

Proinde tona eloquio solitum tibi ; meque timoris———*Argue.*
Where *proinde* being only a dissyllable, perfectly expresseth the sound of this diphthong, says Vossius. Hence, as in these words where the O was strongest, it has prevailed, and been afterwards changed into U ; in like manner where I was strongest, it has often remained by itself. For from λοίϚω or λιίϚω comes *libare* ; from *loiber* or *leiber* cometh *liber* ; and thereby we see that it is no wonder that the Athenians did not all understand in the same manner this oracle pronounced at Delphi.

Ἥξει Δωριακὸς πολίμω κὶ λειμὸς ἰν ἀυτῶ.
and that some took λιμὸς for λοιμὸς, *a famine* instead of the plague. Not that those two words had intirely the same sound, says Vossius, but because in reality there was very little difference.

CHAPTER VI.

Of the nature of I and V consonants. Whether there are any triphthongs, or other diphthongs among the Latins, than those above explained.

IN order to explain intirely what relates to the Latin diphthongs, it is necessary for us here to take notice of the I and V consonants.

I. *Whether the I and V were consonants among the antients.*

Scioppius pretends that the I and V were never any thing else but vowels among the Latins, and his principal argument is that in verse we often see them unite into a diphthong, as *fuisset*, of two syllables in Lucilius; *pituita*, of three in Horace ; *suadet, suasit, suetus*, and others, of two in Virgil :

Suadet enim vesana fames———&c.
where the *u* in *sua* is pronounced in the same manner as in *qua*. So that according to him the Latins pronounced *vinum, vale,* just as the Germans pronounce *win, wal,* &c.

Hence he believes that in *navita*, the first syllable was pronounced in the same manner as in *nauta*, because it is only the same word : and the first in *favitor* (which we find in Plautus) in the same manner as in *fautor*, the I being lost in those words, merely because it was scarce distinguished in the pronunciation.

This may be supported by the authority of Tully, when he shews that there was no great difference between *caureas* and *cave ne eas*. For the E of *cave*, being hardly distinguished, no more than in *face, dice,* and the like imperatives, where it is now intirely disused ; they seem to have said *cau-n'eas*, for *cave ne eas*.

II. *Whether*

II. *Whether there are any triphthongs.*

Now according to this opinion of Scioppius, we must also admit not only of more diphthongs than are commonly allowed, but of course of triphthongs, as UÆ in *aquæ*, VEA in *alvearia, laquearia,* &c.

Sea lento fuerint alvearia vimine texta, Virg.

And we find even by Cornutus, that they were admitted by some of the antients; for otherwise they would not give themselves the trouble to refute this opinion. Besides that Charisius expresly declares in the beginning of his first book, that syllables may be long either by a single vowel, as Â; or by three as UÆ.

On the contrary Quintilian says that there are never three vowels in a single syllable, but one of them is changed into a consonant. And Terentianus maintains the same thing.

Syllabam nec invenimus ex tribus vocalibus.

Vossius likewise rejects these triphthongs, insisting that the Romans had at all times the J and V consonants, and founding his opinion on this, that the oriental languages have their *vau* and their *jod*, which answer to these two letters, as we likewise find that they have been adopted by the French and by other vulgar languages.

We read also in Cassiodorus, that according to Cornutus, Varro had taken notice of the V consonant, which he called *va* or *vau*, because of its rough sound. Priscian declares the same thing, and confirms it not only from Varro, but likewise from Didymus. And it does not seem at all probable, that the Latins after following the Æolians in every thing, should not likewise have borrowed their *digamma*, that is the V consonant which supplied its place every where, pursuant to the same Priscian.

This is further corroborated by the figure invented by the emperor Claudius for this V, which was only an inverted *a*. Which doubtless he would never have done, had it not been received in the pronunciation. Whence one might infer that the use of this V consonant was greater than that of the I, for otherwise he would have had no reason to order a new character for one more than for the other: though they are both marked as consonants in the antients, as in Quintilian, Charisius, Diomedes, Terentianus, Priscian, and others.

St. Austin in his book of the principles of logic, observes also as a thing *beyond all sort of doubt*, that in these words *venter, vafer, vinum,* and the like, where V is a consonant, *the sound is strong and full.* For which reason, says he, we drop it in some words, as *amasti, abiit,* for *amavisti, abivit,* &c. in order not to offend the ear. And hence it is, he addeth, that we derive the etymology of the word from *vis,* because *sonus verbi, quasi validus, congruit rei quæ significatur.* Which is consonant to the opinion of Plato in his Cratylus, and to that of the Stoics, who believed there were

were no words, but what could be some way accounted for by the sound of the letters: though Cicero laughs at this opinion, which St. Austin likewise seems to disapprove.

But beside these reasons and authorities, Scioppius's opinion is liable still to three or four difficulties, which it will not be easy to solve.

The first is, that it destroys the position in verse, where one would think that *ad*, for example, in *adjuvat* could not be long, if the I after the D were not a consonant. And it signifies nothing to say with this author, that the *ad* is long by the apposition of the diphthong *iu*, which being hard to pronounce, sustains this first syllable. For if this length of *ad* proceeded only from the difficulty of pronouncing the second syllable, how comes it that this syllable itself was not long, since according to him it lasted longer in pronouncing? And how came it to give to the first syllable a length of time and quantity by sustaining it, when it was neither long, nor sustained itself? But if the length of one syllable might be owing to the fullness of the next, how comes it that the first in *Adauctus*, is not rather long, since the second is so full and so hard to pronounce, as to be long both by nature and position?

The second objection that may be made against him, and which depends on the first, is, that if the j was a vowel in *ab Jove, adjuvat*, and the like, it would be a diphthong with the next vowel, and therefore would lengthen that syllable, whereas it is short. To which it signifies nothing to answer, that all diphthongs are not long by nature, because the first in *queror*, and the second in *aqua, sanguis*, and the like, are not such. For it may be said, I think, that those syllables are not real diphthongs; the nature of the diphthongs, as we have already shewn, being to have a double sound, whereas that of the U was always to become a liquid after these two consonants, Q and G; as in *aqua, sanguis*, &c. and even frequently after S, as in *suavis, suetus, suadet*, and the like, whose genuine pronunciation is to be only of two syllables. And then the U was lost, and slipped away in such a manner, that it had no power or force to lengthen the syllable, unless the following vowel was already long by nature, as in *quæro, suadet*, &c.

The third objection is that if this I and this V had been always vowels, they would have occasioned an elision of the letter *m* or of the vowel in the preceding word, which they do not. As *tollere vento. Incute vim ventis. Interpres divûm Jove missus ab ipso. Audentes fortuna juvat*, Virg. And not *toller, üento, fortun', iuñat*, &c.

The fourth objection is, that even the U and I vowels are frequently changed into consonants, as in *gen-va labant. Ten-vis ubi argilla. Ar-jetat in portas. Par-jetibusque premunt arctis*, according to Probus and Terentianus. Which is much more probable than the opinion of Macrobius, according to whom those verses would begin with a foot of four short syllables.

But whatever may be the result of this question which hath its difficulties on both sides; what we are most to observe is, that in all probability the Latins did not pronounce this I, though a consonant,

sonant, so strong as we do. As may be still seen by the Italians, who always pronouce their I like a vowel, unless they put a G before it, to which they even give something of the D; for though they write *Giacomo*, they pronounce it almost like *Dgiacomo*; but except on this occasion, always *iacomo* or *iacopo*. And in the Latin words where they do not put the *g*, because they cannot alter the orthography, as *jacio, judico, adjuvo*, they pronounce this *j* in such a manner, that we only perceive the sound of the *i* vowel, though they call it *i* consonant. And among the Hebrews the *vau* and the *jod* have a much greater affinity with the sound of our *i* and *u* vowels, than of our consonants.

It is for this reason very likely, that the poets join one of these vowels to others in verse oftener than we imagine. For not to mention *suavis, suetus, suadet*, and others which have this sound of themselves, and not by poetic licence; we find *alveo* of two syllables only, *alvearia* of four, *fuisset* of two in Lucretius, and a great many more, whether this is to be called a diphthong or a triphthong, or a synerefis, that is, when two syllables are contracted into one; examples of which may be seen in the next book, in the section of Latin poetry, chap. 3. n. 5.

III. *Whether the* I *may sometimes pass for a double consonant.*

From the foregoing discourse it is easy to see that the Grammarians had very little foundation to say that the I was sometimes a double consonant, since it appears rather to have been only a semiconsonant. And little does it import to alledge that it makes the syllable which precedes it long by position, as the first in *major*; since it is certain that if the I was a double letter, it might be resolved into two simple ones which is not so much as imagined. And therefore the reason why the first is long, in *major, pejus*, and the like, is not that the *j* is a double consonant in those words, but on the contrary it is because being there a vowel, it makes a diphthong with the first, *mai-or, pei-us*, &c.

And indeed it evidently appears that this *i* cannot form a long position of itself, since in *bĭjugus, trĭjugus, quadrĭjugus*, the *i* is short in the antepenultima before this consonant.

Interea bĭjugis infert se Leucagus albis, Æn. 10.

Which happens not only to the compounds of *jugum*, as some have fancied, but likewise to other words.

Aure rējēctantem mistos cum sanguine dentes, Æn. 5.

as Pierius would have us read it; whereas others put *ejectantem*, which Macrobius, Farnaby and Vossius seem to favour: though this makes nothing at all for the I consonant, the first syllable being long in this word, only because we are to read it with a diphthong *ei-ectantem*, and perhaps they even put two *ii*, as Priscian witnesseth that the antients wrote with a diphthong *eiius, peiius, Pompeiius*, examples whereof are still extant in antient inscriptions; and as we learn from Longus, that Cicero wrote *aiio, Maiiam*, and the like with *ii*.

For

For this very reason the first is long in *Caiius*, and *Caii*, and the like.

Quod peto da Caii, non peto consilium, Mart.

and Lucretius has made it the same in *reii, eii*, as likewise Plautus.

※―――――※―――――※―――――※―――――※―――――※

Chapter VII.
Of Liquids.

THEY generally reckon four liquids, or gliding letters; that is, which run glib and smooth in pronouncing; namely L, R, M, N; though, as we have already taken notice, the two last are not very gliding.

The L and R have so great a relation to each other, that those who want to pronounce an R, and are not able to effect it, because of its great asperity, do naturally fall into the L.

Hence ariseth the mutual change betwixt these two letters. For not only the Attics say κρίβανος for κλίβανος, *clibanus*; and the like; but the Latins have also taken *cantherus* from καυθήλιος, *lilium* from λείριος, *vermis* from ἕλμις, or βίλμις, *a worm*, &c. And by the same analogy of *niger* they have made *nigellus*, of *umbra*, *umbella*, and such like diminutives. They used also to say *conflacuit* for *confracuit*, Varr. *Parilia* for *Palilia*, Festus; just as we say *Alvernia* for *Arvernia*, Auvergne.

But the R was put also for D, as Priscian observeth, *Arvocates* for *advocatos*; *arvena* for *advena*. And in like manner *meridies* for *medidies*, taken from *media dies*, &c. And the R was likewise changed into S, as we shall shew hereafter.

The M with a very obscure sound, and is pronounced on the edge of the lips, whence it was called *mugientem litteram*. It was often dropped in prose, as it is still in verse. *Restitutu'iri*, in the civil law, instead of *restitutum iri*. *Saltæ* for *saltem*, vet. Gloss.

On the contrary the N was called *tinniens*, because it had a clearer and neater sound, the tongue reaching the palate of the mouth, as Nigidius and Terentianus observe. Which sheweth that it was pronounced in *Manlius* the same as in *an*, in *menses* the same as in *en*, &c. Though sometimes it lost great part of its force in particular words, and helped to form a middle sound between it and *g*, as we shall more particularly take notice in the 9th chap. num. 7.

Scaliger in his book de emend. temp. observes that the Chaldeans frequently changed *nun* into *lamed*; *Nabonassar, Nabolassar; Nabonidus, Labonidus.*

It was also customary with the Greeks to change the *n* into *l*, saying for instance, λίτυος for νίτυος, from whence we have *lepus*: πλεύμων for πνεύμων, from whence we have *pulmo*: Μάλλιος for *Manlius*, &c. But sometimes they dropped the *n* intirely, as Ὀρτήσιος, for *Hortensius*: which made Lambinus imagine, that the real name of this Roman orator was *Hortesius*, contrary to the authority of antient copies and inscriptions. Besides, we find by

a mul-a multitude of other examples, that it was usual with the Greeks to drop the *n*, when it happened not to be final, as Γαλλία Ναρ-ϐωνσία, Λυγδυνσία, Ἰσπανία Ταρκωνσία in geographers and historians, for *Gallia Narbonensis, Lugdunensis, Hispania Taraconensis*, Ὀυάλις for *Valens*, &c. Κλήμης, Κρήσκης, Πύδης, for *Clemens, Crescens, Pudens*, in the new testament and elsewhere.

This letter is also sometimes lost in Latin, as when of *abscindo* is formed *abscidi* in the preterite. We likewise meet with *abscidit* for ἀποτέμνει in the present, V. Gloss. Hence they used to write *coss.* to signify *consules*, as Quintilian observeth by cutting off the *n*. But very often this omission of the *n* can be attributed to no other cause but the ignorance of transcribers and sculptors, when we find in the antients, for example, *Clemeti* for *Clementi, cojux* for *conjux, meses* for *menses*, &c. Because as the small strokes that are put over the vowels to mark the long ones ā, ē, ō, have been sometimes taken by the ignorant for titles that made *n* and *m*, as we have already observed; so on other occasions, where they afterwards really signified those same letters, they were omitted by those who believed that they were only marks of quantity. And this is what deceived Lambinus in the word *Hortēsius*, as we have seen but just now.

Quintilian says that the *m* was frequently at the end of words in Latin, but never in Greek, and that the Greeks changed it then into *n*, because the *n* had a more agreeable sound, though it was rare in Latin to see words ending with this letter.

Hereby we see that it is an error to pretend that in Greek the *π* ought to be pronounced like an *m* before β, π, or μ; since at the end of words it would be a barbarism, according to Ramus, to say τὸν βίον, as if it were *tom bion*, τὴν μερίδα, as if *tem merida*, and the like.

But N had also an affinity with R, as *dirus* from δεινός, *furia* from φονία. And from thence comes *Æneus* for *æreus. Cancer* for *carcer*, of which they formed *cancelli. Carmen* for *canimen* from *cano. Germen* for *genimen*, from *geno* for *gigno*, according to Joseph Scaliger upon Varro, and the like. And it was likewise put for S, whence we have *cessores* for *censores* in Varro, as the same Scaliger observeth. *Sanguis* for *sanguen*, &c.

***

Chapter VIII.

Of the mute consonants, and first of those of the first order, P, B, F, V.

WE give the name of mutes to those consonants, which have a more obscure and less distinct sound than the rest. There are six of them in our division, which we disposed according to the relation they bear to each other.

I. Of B and P.

B and P are so near a-kin, that, according to Quintilian, reason required a *b* in the word *obtinsit*, but the ear could distinguish only a *p*, *optinuit*. Hence we find by antient inscriptions, and by the old glossaries, that these two letters were often confounded, *apsens* for *absens*, *optimus* for *obtimus*, *pleps* for *plebs*, *poblicus* for *publicus*, and such like. Hence we have still remaining *suppono* for *subpono*, *oppono* for *obpono*, &c. And several nations frequently pronounce one of these letters for the other, as the Germans, who say, *ponum vinum* for *bonum*, and the like.

The Greeks also used frequently to change these two letters, one for the other; and Plutarch takes notice that it was customary for the inhabitants of Delphi to say, βατεῖν for πατεῖν, βικρὸς for πικρὸς, &c. And hence it comes that whenever an S followeth, we change the *b* into *p*. *Scribo*, *scripsi*, just as the Greeks say, λείβω, λείψω, &c. for the B, according to Priscian, is never suffered to precede the S in any syllable. But this is not so general as this author imagined, since we still meet with *absis* and *absinthium*, for the Greek words ἄψις and ἀψίνθιον.

It is by this same analogy that the Latins have taken *pasco* from βόσκω, *papæ* from βαβαὶ, *buxus* from πύξος, *pedo* from βδέω, *puteus* from βύθος, and the like; as the Greeks have borrowed πύργος, *turris*, from the Phœnician word *Borg*, whence the French word *bourg* seems also to be derived.

These two letters have likewise this in common, that they have crept into several words without any necessity, as *absporto* for *asporto*, see Gloss. *Obstendit* for *ostendit*, see Gloss. *Obstentui* for *ostentui*, ibid. and thence it is that from *urere* they say *comburere*; and hence also, according to Nonius, they say *celebre* for *celere*, &c. And the same in regard to the P. *Dampnum* for *damnum*, see Gloss. *Scampnum* for *scamnum*, Id. *Sumpsi* for *sumsi*, &c. See the preterites, vol. i. rule 51. p. 257.

II. Of the F and the V consonant.

The F was pronounced almost like φ, but not with so strong an aspiration; as Terentianus observes.

F littera à Græca Φ recedit lenis & hebes sonus.

Hence Tully rallies a Greek, who instead of *Fundanius*, said Φundanius, that is a *p* with an aspiration, P. *hundanius*. Nevertheless, upon the decline of the language, these two letters used to be put for one another, as may be seen by the old glossaries, *falanx* for *phalanx*, and in like manner, *filosophia*, *faleræ*, &c.

The V, that is the V consonant, had a fuller sound, but less rough than we now give it, by which we make it border very near upon the F. It had more of the German W, *winum*, *wine*; concerning which see what hath been already said, c. 6. And hence the Greeks frequently changed it into ου *Varus*, Οὔαρος, &c.

III. *Relation between the* V *and the* Digamma.

This V supplied the place of the Æolic Digamma, which was so called because it had the figure of two Γammas, one upon another, thus, F. But we are particularly to observe that the *digamma* was not pronounced so strong as we now pronounce the V consonant, for which reason it produced no position in verse, as we shall shew hereafter. Hence Joseph Scaliger, in his notes on Eusebius, hath extremely well observed this difference between the *digamma* and the V consonant, that after the *digamma* is dropped, the word still subsists, as Φιλίνη, ιλίνη, ὦ Fον, ὦον: whereas the V is necessary to form the word, as *vulgus, volo, vado*, which would be destroyed, were we to say only *ulgus, olo, ado*, &c.

IV. *Other relation between* V *and* B.

This V consonant had likewise a great relation to B, for which reason in words derived from the Greek, one is often taken for the other, as βίω, *vivo*; βία, *vis*; βούλω, *volo*; βαίνω, *venio*; βαδίζω, *vado*; βόσκω, *vescor*; βοὴ, *vox*; βυρὸς, *vorax*; βιϐαίω *voveo*. For we have already taken notice that *e* was frequently changed into *o*, and *ai* into *e*.

Hence it comes that the Greeks sometimes rendered by a β the Latin words that begin with a V, βαλῆρε for *valere*, because, as they no longer used the *digamma*, they had nothing that came nearer to it; especially since the B began already to degenerate from its natural sound, which is that of β. This is a further proof, says Lipsius, that this V was not founded in the present manner, because otherwise the Greeks would as naturally have attempted to express it by φ as by β. Therefore the passage we quoted from St. Austin, chap. 6. n. 2. who calls it *crassum & quasi validum sonum*, ought not, in all probability, to be understood of the roughness, but rather of the fullness of the V, which sounded almost the same as the French diphthong *ou*, and was very near a-kin to the German W. But this does not prove by any means that the Greek B should be pronounced like an V consonant, which we have made appear in the New Method of learning the Greek tongue.

Now what has been here observed in regard to the affinity between the B and the V, greatly favours the pronunciation of the Spaniards and Gascoons. And though this error may seem very gross, yet it is more antient than people imagine. For not only Adamantius hath taken particular notice of it in Cassiodorus, but there are examples of it in old inscriptions, as BASE for VASE, CIBICA for CIVICA, &c. Just as we likewise meet with instances of V for B, VENEFICIUM for BENEFICIUM, SIBE for SIVE; and in the Florentine Pandects, AVEO for ABEO, VOBEM for BOVEM, VESTIAS for BESTIAS, and the like; which is very necessary to observe.

It is likewise in consequence of the affinity and relation betwixt these two letters that of *abfero* is formed *aufero*, whence we have *abstuli*,

abstuli, ablatum. And to this also it is owing that we have *arbilla* for *arvilla*, taken from *arvina*. Likewise *albena* for *alvena*, *advena*, whence cometh *aubain* in French, a foreigner according to Cujas: and also *aubene*, as much as to say *advene: bona caduca sive adventitia*, the *droit d'aubene*, or escheatage, being relative to the estates of foreigners deceased without lawful heirs, and which therefore devolve to the king.

V. *Relation of* B *to* F, *and to* Φ.

But beside this relation of B to V consonant, it had also another to F, and to Φ. For they used to say *bruges* for *fruges*, as Cicero takes notice; of βρέμω they made *fremo*, of βασκάνος *fascinum*, of βένθος *fundum*, &c. And on the contrary they used to say *sifilare* for *sibilare*, whence also comes the French word *siffler*; they said *af vobis* for *ab vobis*; and thence we have still remaining, *suffero* for *subfero*, *sufficit* for *subficit*, *suffusio* for *subfusio*, and others. Whereas the Macedonians, as Plutarch informs us, said Βίλιππον for Φίλιππον, and such like; and according to Festus we say *album* for ἄλφον, a kind of white itch; from ἄμφω cometh *ambo*; and the rest in the like manner.

VI. *Other relations of* B *or* P *to* M, *and of* P *to* F *or* PH.

As the letter M hath a very obscure sound, and is almost as labial as B and P, hence it is often changed into one of these two letters; as *globus*, a globe; *glomus*, a bottom, or clew of thread: *submitto*, *summitto*, μίλλειν, Æol. βίλλειν, παθοῦσα, Æol. μαθοῦσα, *vermis* from ἕρπω, *somnus* from ὕπνος, *polluo* from μιλύνω, μικκύλος, Æol. πικκύλος, whence the Italians have taken *picolo*, little.

Again, as P hath a relation to B, and B to F, so P hath also a relation to F, as *fido* from πειθῶ *persuadeo*, *figo* from πήγω. And it has likewise a relation to PH, either because originally this PH is no more than an aspiration added to the sound of P, or because in process of time this PH was pronounced like an F, which, as we have just now observed, has an affinity with P. Thus *trophæum* comes from τρόπαιον, *romphæa* from ρομφαῖα, *verto* from ῥέπω. In like manner, *caput* from κεφαλὴ, *carpo* from κάρφω, *sapiens* from σοφὸς, &c.

Chapter IX.

Of the second class of mutes, C, Q, G, J.

THERE is an affinity or relation between C and Q, as likewise between G and J consonant. Besides, there is an affinity between C and G; but we must see in what manner.

I. *Re-*

I. *Relation between* C *and* Q.

So great is the relation between C and Q, that several grammarians have attempted to discard the Q as a superfluous letter, pretending that the C and the U are sufficient to express the same sound as Q. And we see that the Greeks have not this letter, which was taken from the *Kophe* or *Koppa* of the Syrians, and in French it has no other force than that of a single K, or that of a C before A, O, U.

Quintilian asserts that the letter K hath nearly the same properties and effect as Q. And Ramus declares, that in the university of Paris the letter Q had always the same sound in Latin as it has now in French, till the foundation of the royal professorships, under Francis I. So that they said *qalis, qantus, qis*, as we see some people pronounce it still. And he observes that at first every body opposed the other pronunciation, introduced by the king's professors, as an innovation by no means to be admitted; though afterwards it made its way.

Nevertheless the letter Q still retains the same sound as K or C before O and U, as we see in *quum*, which is the same thing as *cum*, pursuant to what hath been mentioned in the remarks on the pronouns, chap. 1. num. 4. And in *quo:* hence Cicero, as Quintilian informs us, rallying a cook who was intriguing for some high preferment, made use of these words, *Ego quoque tibi jure favebo*, because they could not tell by the sound whether it was the particle *quoque*, or the vocative of *coquus*, a cook.

But in conjunction with the three first vowels, A, E, I, it has a thicker and fuller sound, which is so particular, that it cannot be expressed by any Greek letters, *Duras & illa syllabas facit*, says Quintilian, *quæ ad conjungendas demum subjectas sibi vocales est utilis, alias super vacua, ut* EQUOS *ac* EQUUM *scribimus, cùm ipsæ etiam hæ vocales duæ efficiant sonum, qualis apud Græcos nullus est, ideóque scribi illorum litteris non potest*. Though this sound proceeds as much from the U as from the Q, because after a G the U has the same effect in *lingua, sanguis,* and others; and heretofore it had the same after S, *suavis, suadet*, &c. which has still continued in verse, as we have already observed.

This shews nevertheless the unreasonableness of some in rejecting the Q, as of Varro according to Censorinus, and of Licinius Calvius according to Victorinus, who never would make use of it; for it is always of service, since its office is to unite the two following vowels into one syllable, where the C denotes they are divided. This makes the difference between the nominative *qui* and the dative *cui*, between the infinitive *sequi*, taken from the verb *sequor*, and the preterite of *seco, secui*, and a great many others. This is further confirmed by Priscian, and by Terentianus Maurus, whom some have placed late in the fifth century, though he must have flourished in the middle of the fourth, since St. Austin quotes him as a dead author in books of his that were written before 390.

And so real is this difference between C and Q, that we find the antient poets have put a C where we always write a Q, when they wanted to divide the words into more syllables than they naturally form. Thus Lucretius useth *cuïret*, a trissyllable, for *quiret*.

———*Confringere ut arcta*
Naturæ primus portarum clauſtra cuïret.

And thus also he made *acua*, a trissyllable, for *aqua*. And in the same manner Plautus wanted to put *relicuüs*, in his Cistell. act. 2. sc. 1.

Quod dedi datum non vellem, quod relicuüm non dabo.
Because if we read it thus, the verse, which is trochaic, will not have its full measure.

II. *Whether Q ought to paſs for a double letter.*

As we have observed that Q supplied the place of C and U, there are grammarians who insist on its being a double letter, and among the rest Capella, Diomedes, and Longus; an opinion which Vossius has also favoured. The ground they go upon is, that the antients wrote QI, QÆ, QID, &c. without a *u*, examples of which are still to be seen in antient inscriptions, whence it follows, say they, that the U was included in Q, and consequently that this is a double letter.

Nevertheless it is beyond all doubt that Q cannot be a double letter, for otherwise the first in *aqua*, *equus*, and the like, would be long, whereas it is short in verse.

To their argument I shall give two answers; the first that it was the custom of the antients frequently to take a single letter for the characters which formed the name of the letter: putting, for instance, a K only for *Ka* or *Ca*, they wrote *Krus* for *Karus*, and yet this did not make the K a double letter. So that they might put likewise a *q* only for *qu*, and *qis* for *quis*, &c.

And thence it appears, to mention it only by the way, that when in Greek writings we meet with ο for υ, this ο stands for the name of the letter, as Quintilian observes; for its name was οὖ, according to Victorinus, just as they said μῦ, νῦ, οὖ; the name of no letter whatever being formed by a simple character. Hence the ε itself was called EI, as we find in Eustathius and Plutarch; so that sometimes, when they wrote only E, they pronounced EI, the single letter standing for the name of the letter itself. And therefore we meet in Athenæus with ΔΙΟΝΥΣΟ for Διονύσου, and in the two Farnesian columns, which were removed from the via Appia, ΤΟ ΤΡΙΤΟ for τῦ τρίτυ, ΗΕΡΟΔΟ for Ηρώδου, and the like.

The second answer I make to their objection is, that when the antients wrote *qis*, perhaps they pronounced it as if it was a K, and the writing changed with the pronunciation. *Fortaſſe etiam ficut ſcribebant, ita & loquebantur*, says Quintilian, And this answer seems the more exact, as in Gruterus's inscriptions we meet not only with *q*, but also with *c* only, for *qu*; *Cintus* for *Quintus*, *ficis* for *fiquis*, As on the contrary we meet with Q only for C. *Qurtius* for *Curtius*, *ſæqulum* for *ſæculum*, *mcqum* for *mecum:* and with *qu* for C, as *liquebit* for *licebit* or *liqebit*; which is proper to be observed in order to correct a multitude of corrupt passages.

III.

III. *Of the* U *which always accompanies the* Q.

But in the present manner of writing the Q is always accompanied of course by a U, which has given occasion to grammarians to start a thousand idle questions; as whether it be a vowel or consonant, whether it forms position with Q for the preceding syllable, or whether it makes a diphthong with the following vowel, &c.

To cut short, I say that this U which always accompanies the Q, is not a consonant, and therefore does not form position; and that it is a vowel, but a liquid vowel, which glides away so nimbly in pronouncing it, *as to be hardly perceptible,* according to Beda; and therefore it does not form a diphthong with the following vowel, because it loseth its whole force as a letter in verse, *amittit vim litteræ in metro,* says Priscian, which made Donatus believe, *that, strictly speaking, it is neither vowel nor consonant.*

Hereby we see that Alvarez, as well as Vossius, had very little foundation to call it a *liquid consonant,* because, if this was the case, it would at least render the first common in *aqua, aquilex, aquilo; eques, equidem,* and the like, which it certainly does not. But a stronger argument that this *u* is only a liquid vowel, is that being used also after G, as in *anguis,* it has been omitted in several words where it formerly took place, as *redigo, extingo,* for *rediguo, extinguo,* &c. And the French use it thus not only after Q and G, as *question, anguille,* &c. but likewise after C, as *cueillir,* &c.

IV. *Relation between* C *and* G.

G is only a diminution of C, according to Quintilian; and therefore there is a very great affinity between them, since of κυβερνήτης we make *gubernator,* of κλέος *gloria,* of *egi actum,* of *nec otium, negotium,* &c. And Quintilian observes, that in *Gaius, Gneius,* they did not distinguish whether it was a C or a G. Hence it is that of *centum* they formed *quadringenta, quingenta, septingenta,* &c. Of *porricere* (which is still used in regard to sacrifices) they made *porrigere,* and the like.

It is supposed that the letter G was not invented till after the first Punic war, because we always find a C instead of G on the column called ROSTRATA, which was raised at that time in honour of Duilius the consul, and is still to be seen in the capitol at Rome, as MACISTRATOS, LECIONES, PUCNANDO, COPIAS CARTACINIENSIS. Which is impossible to account for, unless we take the C in the same sound as K. And it is observable that Suidas, speaking of the crescent which the senators wore upon their shoes, calls it τὸ Ῥωμαϊκὸν κάππα, plainly shewing thereby, that the C and K passed for the same thing; since indeed there was no difference between them in the sound. For whereas at present we greatly soften the C before E and I, pronouncing *Cicero* nearly as if it was *Sisero,* they on the contrary pronounced it in this and in all other words, the same as in *caput* and in *corpus.*

I say the same of G, which always retained the same sound. For whereas we have greatly softened it before *e* and *i*, pronouncing it in *regis* and *rege*, as in the French words *regent* and *regir*; they on the contrary pronounced it every where as in *rego*.

Hence St. Austin saith, *Cùm dico* LEGE, *in his duabus syllabis, aliud Græcus, aliud Latinus intelligit*; giving us to understand, that the Latins pronounced the *g* as strong in *lege*, as the Greeks in λέγε, and that these two words had in his time but one and the same sound.

V. *Relation between* G *and* J *consonant.*

The soft pronunciation which we give to G, is likewise the cause of its having a great relation to the sound with which we pronounce J consonant, when followed by an E or an I. For we sound *regi* like *rejicio*, and *rege* like *pejero*, and so for the rest. But this soft pronunciation of the G is lost, when it happens to be followed by an *a, o,* or *u,* as *regat, rego, regum,* whereas we always preserve it with the J consonant, as *jacio, major* and *majus,* &c.

And if we should be asked whether this J consonant had really this same pronunciation among the antients, we refer to what has been above-mentioned, chap. 6. p. 262.

VI. *Whether the antients pronounced* Gn *in the manner the French do at present.*

Another question may arise, whether the Romans pronounced the G before *n*, in the same manner as the Italians do at present, and as the French pronounce it in these words, *Agnez, magnifique, pagnol,* &c.

In all probability they did not, but pronounced the G in *agnus,* as in *agger,* for this other pronunciation being so particular, and differing so greatly from the usual sound of the G, the antients would not have failed to take notice of it.

It is moreover observable that the G is sounded so very little in these words *Agnez* and the like, that it serves only to denote the liquid N, as the same G in Italian is a sign of the liquid L, *figliola, daughter.* Hence it is that the Spaniards do not use the *g* at all on those occasions, but are satisfied with putting a small tittle over the ñ, to signify its being a liquid, and that it receives this pronunciation, writing *señor,* and pronouncing *segnor.* And for this reason also Ramus, in his French grammar, useth a particular mark for this liquid *n* in French, without putting a *g,* but only a small comma under the *n.*

VII. *That there is still a middle sound between* G *and* N, *which is neither intirely one nor the other, and has given the Greeks occasion to change* N *into* Γ *before* γ, κ, χ, *or* ξ.

Another difficulty may here arise, to know whether the N is changed into Γ on certain occasions among the Greeks, as in ἄγγελος,

Of LETTERS, &c.

ἀγγίλος, ἄγχισα, ἄγκυρα, &c. and whether the Γ be then pronounced as an N. For it seems, says H. Stephen, to be a mistake of the transcribers, who lengthened the ι a little too much in the ligatures of the small letters, and made a γ of it. Hence in MSS. in capitals, such as those he made use of in compiling his Thesaurus, we find those words intire with an N, ΑΝΓΕΛΟΣ, and the like. Besides, Joseph Scaliger, in his notes on Eusebius, quotes, from an antient inscription, ΑΝΚΥΡΑ for ἄγκυρα. And indeed, addeth H. Stephen, it seems ridiculous to say that this N should be changed into Γ, for no other end but that the Γ should at the same time be pronounced like an N.

But in answer to this, we do not say it is pronounced like a Greek N, but as a vulgar *n*; or, to speak more properly, with a middle sound between the N and the G, according to Victorinus, contemporary with Donatus, St. Jerome's master, who acknowledges this change of letters and this pronunciation among the Greeks. Which made Scaliger say, that if we sometimes meet with an N, this must be rather deemed an error of the transcribers, who imagined they should express this sound better by this letter, whereas, according to Vossius, it seems rather to require a new character.

And the Latins had something like it in their language, which Nigidius, as Gellius observeth, used to call *a false N*, as in *anguis, ancora, increpat, ingenuus*, and others: *In his enim non verum N, sed adulterinum ponitur*, these are his words, *Nam si ea littera esset, lingua palatum tangeret*. For which reason Varro, according to Priscian, lib. 1. takes notice that Attius and the antients used to put two *gg* on this occasion, like the Greeks, writing *aggulus, aggens, aggerunt*, and the like.

Chapter X.

Of the third class of mutes, which are D and T.

THE letter D is only a diminution of T, as G is of C, even according to Quintilian. This seems to favour those who in Greek do pronounce the τ like a δ after a ν, saying πάντα as if it were πάνδα; λίοντος as if it were λίονδος; a softening that perhaps may be admitted, though it is not a fault to pronounce it otherwise. But even in Latin it is very certain that there is a great relation between those two letters, in consequence of which they are often changed one for the other, as *at* for *ad*; which made Quintilian laugh at those who scrupled to write them indifferently: *set* for *sed*, *haut* for *haud*, and others in the writings of the antients: *Quit* for *quid*, *adque* for *atque*, &c. in inscriptions, and elsewhere.

The French write *voit* with a *t*, though it comes from *videt* with a *d*. And whenever the *d* is at the end of a word, and the next begin with a vowel or an *h* without being aspirated, they pronounce it like a *t*, and say, for example, *grant esprit, grant homme*, though they write *grand esprit, grand homme*. Which shews that in French we ought always to lean harder upon the final consonants when the next word begins with a vowel, than in any other place.

In every other respect the French have almost intirely preserved the sound of those two letters, except in the T, which is in great measure softened, when joined with an *i*, before another vowel, where it is founded almost like the *s* of the antients, *pronuntio*, as if it were *pronunsio*. Whereas they pronounced it in *litium, vitium*, &c. all the same as in *litis, vitis*; of which no body can entertain the least doubt, because this soft sound is taken notice of by none of the antients, and moreover because it is a constant maxim, that no consonant hath two different sounds, either among the Latins or among the Greeks, this privilege, as Lipsius observes, being reserved for the vowels.

True it is that we have a fragment of one Papirius a grammarian, which mentions that the *ti* before another vowel was pronounced like *tzi, justitia*, like *justitzia*. But besides that this pronunciation does not intirely establish ours, this very author excepts, among others, those words in which an *i* comes immediately after *ti*, as *otii*, &c. Which shews that this pronunciation was introduced only by degrees, and in proportion as the Latin was corrupted by the mixture of foreign languages. Hence also it is, that in the old glossaries we find *eciam* for *etiam*: and in Festus, *Murtia Dea* or *Murcia* (the goddess of sloth) according to the observations of Scaliger.

Chapter XI.
Of the hissing letters.

UNDER the name of hissing letters we include the S, and the double letters which are resolved by S.

I. *Of the letter S.*

S is called a hissing letter, because of its sound. It has been variously received among the antients, some having intirely rejected it, while others affected to introduce it every where. Pindar calls it κίβδηλον, *adulterinam*, and has avoided it in almost all his poems. Quintilian says *it is harsh, and makes a disagreeable sound in the connexion of words*. For which reason it was often intirely rejected, *dignu', omnibu'*, and the like in Plautus, Terence, and elsewhere. In some Latin authors it was also changed into T, in imitation of the Attics, as *mertare, pultare, aggretus*, for *mersare, pulsare, aggressus*, &c.

Others, on the contrary, affected to introduce it every where, *Casmænæ* for *Camænæ*, *dusmosæ* for *dumosæ*, &c. And Quintilian

takes

takes notice that in Cicero's time, and afterwards, they frequently doubled it in the middle of words, *cauſſa, diviſſiones*, &c.

Be that as it may, there is no doubt of its being harſh if it be too hiſſing, or too often repeated; which obliged the French to ſoften it in ſuch a manner, that when it happens to be in the middle of two vowels, they pronounce it like an Z, ſaying *mizere*, and not *miſſere*. And this ſoft ſound they have introduced into Latin words, pronouncing *miſeria*, like the French word *miſere*, though the Romans always ſounded their S in the ſame manner as in *ſeria*, and the like.

This letter had an affinity with R, which is the reaſon of there being ſo many nouns in ER and in IS, as *vomer* and *vomis*, *ciner* and *cinis*, *volucer* and *volucris*, *ſaluber* and *ſalubris*, *pulver* and *pulvis*, and many others, where we muſt alſo ſuppoſe the change of E into I, of which we have taken notice above. Others are in OS and in OR; *labos* and *labor*, *honos* and *honor*, &c.

The Attics were alſo uſed to put the σ for ρ, ἄρσην for ἄρρην, *maſculus*; θάρσαλέος for θαρραλέος, *audax*, &c. Thus from τύρσις comes *turris*; from ἴσω (of which they made ἴσομαι) *ero*; from πράσον, *porrum*; from κίλης, *celer*, and the like. And ſo from *Fuſius*, *Furius*; *Valeſius*, *Valerius*, &c.

But S had likewiſe a relation to D, as appears even by the Z, which includes both theſe letters, as we ſhall demonſtrate in the following numbers; by the increaſe of ſeveral Greek and Latin nouns, *clamis, clamydis*, for *clamis, ys*; *lapis, lapidis*, &c. (whereto we may refer *litis, ditis, militis*, and the like, becauſe of the above-mentioned affinity between D and T) by the compounding particles, *aſſumo* for *adſumo*; by the Greek and Latin verbs, ἅδω, *cano*, ἄσω; *ludo, luſi*, &c. and, in fine, by divers particular words, as from *edit* comes *eſt*, *he eats*, by ſyncope, for *eſit*.

II. *Of the double letters.*

The double letters always include the S, and therefore in great meaſure partake of its hiſſing.

The Greeks have three, Z, Ξ, Ψ; but the Latins have only two, X and Z; which is the caſe of moſt of the vulgar languages.

The X is equivalent to *cs*, as *dux* for *ducs*, for which reaſon it makes *ducis* in the genitive; and likewiſe to *gs*, as *rex* for *regs* (notwithſtanding what Voſſius ſays) for which reaſon it makes *regis* in the genitive. For ſince G and C have ſo great an affinity, as we have already obſerved, and ſince they are ſo frequently changed one for the other, as *negligo* for *nec lego*, there is a very ſtrong probability that the ſame double letter is alſo capable of expreſſing them both.

This X was ſometimes put with a C, as VICXIT, JUNCXIT, and ſometimes with an S, as CAPPADOXS, CONJUXS, &c. S. Iſidore takes notice that it did not obtain before the reign of Auguſtus, and Victorinus informs us that Nigidius would never make uſe of it.

The Z had a ſofter ſound than X, for which reaſon Quintilian calls it *molliſſimum & ſuaviſſimum*. Yet this was not the ſame ſound as we give it at preſent, which is only a moiety of the S. Beſide this it had something of the D, but with a very soft pronunciation; *Mezentius*, as if *Medsentius*; *Zethus*, as if *Dsethus*, &c.

Hence it is that the Dorians changed this letter into SD, whether in the beginning of a word, as σδυγὸς for ζυγὸς; or in the middle, as συρίσδω for συρίζω. Not that the ζ was equivalent to σδ, as Vossius remarks in the first book of his grammar; but by reason of a kind of transposition or metathesis; both Flaccus and Longus observing, that as the X began with a C, in like manner the Z ought to begin with D; so that all the double letters end with S. Yet Erasmus and Ramus pretend the contrary, and Sextus Empiricus endeavours to prove against the torrent of grammarians, that the ζ was as much equivalent to σδ as to δσ.

Be that as it may, the Æolians also changed the δ into ζ, as ζαβάλλιν for δαβάλλιν, *calumniari*; from whence they took ζάβολος for *diabolos*, which we meet with in S. Cyprian and S. Hilary; and which Erasmus renders *delatorem* or *calumniatorem*, and Budeus *adversarium*, and is the usual word by which S. Paulinus distinguishes the evil spirit.

The Latins likewise have frequently changed this ζ into D, and sometimes into S, taking *odor* from ὄζειν; and from μᾶζα, *massa*; from πατρίζω, *patrisso*, &c.

The Z had also the like affinity with G. Hence it is, as Scaliger observeth, that when the modern Greeks would express the month called *Giumadi*, they write ζιυμάδι; and to express a Persian or a foreigner by the word *Agiami*, they write Αζάμι. This was even customary among the antients, as Capella observeth. Z, says this author, *à Græcis venit, licet etiam ipso primo G Græcâ utebantur; nam* ΓΕΤΥΜ *dicebant, nunc* ZETUM *dicimus*. The Latins also of ζυγὸς have made *jugum*, of μείζων, *majus*, and the like, where the *j* consonant had nearly the same sound as *g*. The Italians, to express the J consonant, prefix a G, and pronounce it like *dg*; they write *Giacomo*, but pronounce *Dgiacomo* for *Jacomo*, *James*. And it is observable likewise in French, that they who cannot pronounce the G, or the J consonant before *e* and *i*, (because these letters require to be sounded with a kind of hissing) pronounce exactly a Z, as when they say, *le zibet, du zinzembre, des zettons, ze ne sçai, zirai là*, instead of *gibet, du gingembre, des jettons*, &c.

By all these relations we find it is no wonder that the Z, which in Greek ought to characterize the fourth conjugation, because it is the fourth consonant of their alphabet, is also changed into two σ in the present; that is, that the verbs of this conjugation terminate in ζω or σσω. We find likewise why some take now and then a δ, and others now and then a γ, for the characteristic of their second aorist. This is intirely owing to the affinity betwixt the ζ and those other two letters; which may be observed in a single word; for what the Latins call *viridarium*, the Italians call *verzieri*, and the French *un verger*.

CHAPTER

CHAPTER XII.

Of the aspiration H.

GRammarians are in doubt whether H ought to be ranked among the letters or not, because, say they, it is only an aspiration.

We acknowledge that H is only an aspiration, but we add that it is a real letter nevertheless, because every character instituted by mankind, to apprize us of some change in the pronunciation, ought to be deemed a real letter, especially where it has a place in the alphabet among the rest, as we see that H has. And indeed it is very ridiculous to imagine that H is not a real letter, because of its being only an aspiration, since we see that the oriental languages have three or four letters, which they call gutturals, to express only the different aspirations.

The H supplies in Latin the rough breathings and the aspirate consonants of the Greeks; and thus it has two general uses; the 1. before vowels in the beginning of syllables, as in *honor, hædus, prehendo*; the 2. after consonants, as in *thronus, Rhodus, philosophus, charitas*.

I. Of H before vowels.

With regard to the former use the French have greatly changed the pronunciation of this letter in Latin words, and preserved it only in some French words. For in Latin they hardly pronounce it at all, as in *honor, homo, humor*; and in French it is entirely lost in these very words, *honneur, homme, humeur*; and in most words borrowed from the Latin or the Greek, pronouncing them as if there were no H, but merely *onnæur, umeur, omme*, &c.

Now it is beyond all doubt that this was not the Roman way of pronouncing, but that they sounded the H with as strong an aspiration as it is sounded in words purely French, such as *la hardiesse, la halebarde, la hauteur*, &c. And perhaps they gave it even a stronger aspiration.

This appears by two clear and irrefragable authorities. The 1. of St. Austin, who, complaining to the supreme being that mankind were more diligent observers of the rules of grammar than of his divine laws, mentions that they were so exact in this pronunciation; *Ut qui illa sonorum vetera placita teneat, aut doceat*, says he, *si contra disciplinam Grammaticam, sine aspiratione primæ syllabæ, Ominem dixerit, magis displiceat hominibus, quàm si contra tua præcepta hominem oderit, cum sit homo*. Conf. 1. c. 18.

The second authority is of Catullus, who rallies a person for introducing the letter *h* into every word. For the raillery is not because he pronounced the *h* in a different manner from others, but because, as the *h* had something of a harsh sound, he offended the ear by putting it where it ought not to be.

Chommoda dicebat, si quando commoda vellet
 Dicere, & hinsidias Arrius, insidias :
Et tum mirificè sperabat se esse locutum,
 Cùm quantum poterat dixerat hinsidias.
Credo, sic mater, sic liber avunculus ejus,
 Sic maternus avus dixerat atque avia.
Hoc misso in Syriam, requierant omnibus aures,
 Audibant eadem hæc leniter & leviter.
Nec sibi post illa metuebant talia verba :
 Cùm subito affertur nuntius horribilis,
Ionios fluctus, postquam illuc Arrius isset,
 Jam non Ionios *esse, sed* Hionios. Carm. 85.

Here a person may ask in what manner this H ought to be pronounced, when it is before words beginning with an *i* aspirated in Greek, as *Hieronymus, Hierusalem*, &c. One would think that, since I is never a consonant in the Greek language, and that even the Latins, as already hath been observed, gave it a softer sound than we, this I ought always to pass for a vowel, though with the aspiration, and that we ought to say *Hieronymum, Hierusalem*, &c. just as Arrius said *Hionios*, when he wanted to aspirate the I of *Ionios*; and since even the modern Jews pronounce their *Jod* in this manner.

Yet the practice is various upon this head, some pronouncing it as a vowel, while others give it the whole force of an J consonant, as if it were *Geronimus*, just as the French always say *Gerôme, Gerusalem*, &c. wherein we must conform to the custom of vulgar languages.

II. *Of* H *after consonants.*

In regard to H after consonants, Cicero *de oratore* observes that the antients did not make use of it, and that they only put it after vowels, which made him inclined to say *pulcros, triompos, Cartaginem*, &c. But that at length having reserved the speculation of these things to himself, he had fallen in with the custom of the people in regard to the practical part and to pronunciation; however that they still continued to say *Orcines, Matones, Otones, Cæpiones, sepulcra, coronas, lacrymas*, without H, because this gave no offence to the ear.

Quintilian moreover affirms that the antients used frequently to drop it before vowels, saying *ædos, ircos*, &c. whereas in his time they were fallen into the opposite excess, saying *chorona, præchones*, and the like. But we must consider the language, as it was in its purity.

Therefore as this H after consonants was introduced into the Latin tongue merely to supply the Greek aspirates, it seems as if it ought to be put only after the four consonants C, P, T, R; though this happens (at least in regard to the three last) only in Greek or foreign words.

III. *Of the pronunciation of* CH.

CH is pronounced differently in Latin and in French. For in Latin it is always pronounced like a K, making no difference with the C, except before the vowels E and I, or the diphthong æ, œ, before which the C is pronounced like an antient S, as already hath been observed; whereas the CH always preserves its sound of K; *Achilles* and *Achates* being pronounced in the same manner.

But in French the genuine sound of CH before all vowels, is that which obtains in *char, cher, chiche, chose, chu, chou*. For which reason, though we have retained this *h* with the other consonants in words derived from the Greek, which begin with an aspirate, yet one would imagine it ought to be omitted with the C, as in *caractere, colere, Baccus*, and other such words, to prevent the mistakes of the unlearned, who, being unacquainted with the derivation of those words, might pronounce *cha* instead of *ca, cho* instead of *co*, and *chus* instead of *cus*. And this is the opinion of Monf. de Vaugelas in his remarks on the French tongue, to which we refer the reader.

And indeed there is the greatest probability that both the Greeks and Romans were strangers to this pronunciation, since it is so particular to the French tongue, that the Italians, in order to express it, write *sci*, as *sciolere, sciaractere*, &c. Though it is very certain that the Greek X and the *Ch* of the Latins were pronounced differently from the Greek κάππα and the Latin K or C before any vowel whatever, that is, by giving it a strong aspiration; for otherwise Catullus could not have censured a man for saying *chommoda* instead of *commoda*, as we have seen in the epigram above quoted.

IV. *Of the pronunciation of* PH.

The same may be said in regard to *Ph*: for we pronounce it like F, saying *philosophie*, as if it were *filosofie*. Whereas the antients pronounced it almost like a P with an aspiration, *p-hilosop-hia*, or rather *fhilosofhia*, since it partook, as it still does partake, of the nature of *f* in its aspiration, and yet had not the same sound as it, as appears by the above-quoted testimony of Cicero, who otherwise would not have laughed at a Greek for giving the sound of Φ to F, pronouncing *Fundanius* as if it were Φ*undanius*, that is *Fhundanius*.

V. *Of* TH *and* RH.

In regard to *Th* in *theatrum, thesaurus*, and *Rh* in *Rhodus* and the like, the H is hardly perceived in the modern pronunciation of the Latin, though there is no doubt but it was distinguished by the antients, and in the Greek these aspirations are to be observed.

VI. *From whence the Latins borrowed this aspiration* H.

The Latins borrowed their H from the Greek Ητα, as the Greeks had borrowed it of the Phœnicians, and these of the Syrians, who formerly said *Heta* instead of *Heth*. Which evidently shews that we ought to pronounce *Eta* in Greek, and not *Ita*.

But at first this H was used only as an aspiration; for which reason they wrote ΗΕΡΟΔΟ for ἱερῳδον, ΗΟΔΟΙ for ὁδῷ, ΗΕΚΑΤΟΝ for ἑκατὸν, *centum*; whence it comes that the H formerly signified a hundred, as the first letter of that word, pursuant to the observation of Longus, Scaurus, and Priscian.

They likewise used to put the H with the weak consonants, instead of the aspirates, which were not invented till some time after by Palamedes; so that they wrote ΤΗΕΟΣ for ΘΕΟΣ, and the like.

VII. *Of some relations between the* H *and the Æolic digamma, which at length was changed into* V *consonant, and into* β.

But it is further observable, according to S. Isidorus, whom Chekus and Vossius have followed, that from the H arose the mark of breathings; for splitting it in two, at first they made Ͱ for the rough breathing, and ᚐ for the smooth, which were afterwards rounded, in order to give to the former the following mark ʻ, and to the latter that of a comma. This is further confirmed by antient editions, and among others by Aldus's Hesichius, where the different breathings of the Greek words are marked by these two moieties of the H, namely Ͱ and ᚐ. And if we examine strictly, we shall find that from the former moiety was taken our small *h*, where they only lengthened the second instead of a transverse line. And to this same reason it is owing, that the C in vulgar languages was sometimes no more than a mark of aspiration, or of a stronger sound, as we still see in *Clotaire*, which is the same as *Lotaire*; in *Clovis*, which is the same as *Lovis* or *Louys*, and the like.

But as this mark of aspiration was not rounded in the beginning, perhaps it was owing to this that the *digamma* F, which represented nearly the first half of an H, hath oftentimes passed for a rough breathing, as appears in Fελένη for ἑλένη, Fειρήνη for εἰρήνη, &c. And neither this *digamma* nor the Attic H made any position in verse, as Priscian observeth; which the Romans have followed, their *h* having no power to render a syllable long by position.

The mutual affinity between these two letters is the reason that even in Latin they have been frequently put for one another; *fædum* for *hædum*, *fircum* for *hircum*, *fariolum* for *hariolum*, *fostem* for *hostem*, *heminas* for *feminas*, *hebris* for *febris*, and the like.

But this *digamma* used also, though not so often, to be put for a soft breathing, as Fιλλὸς for ἰλλὸς, *strabus*, *squint-eyed*. It was customary likewise to insert it in the middle of words to prevent the hiatus or concurrence of vowels, as ὅFις for ὅις, from whence
comes

comes *ovis*, ϝοϊ for ὅϊ, from whence *ovum*. Where we see also that the V consonant has ever supplied the place of this *digamma*.

It is owing to all these relations that the rough breathing, the H, the *digamma*, and the V consonant, are oftentimes confounded and interchanged for one another. For example, of Ἐνετοὶ or Ϝενετοὶ the Latins have made *Heneti* or *Veneti*. In the same manner from Ἑςία or Ϝιςία cometh *Vesta*; from ἰσϑὴς or Ϝισϑὴς, *vestis*; from ἰαρ, ἦρ, or Ϝῆρ, *ver*; from ἑσπέρα or Ϝισπέρα, *vespera*; and so for the rest. But sometimes this *digamma*, or this rough breathing, is changed into β, as Passerat sheweth in his treatise of letters; βρήτωρ for ῥήτωρ; βρόδος for ῥόδος. Which particularly obtained among the Cretans, who said βῶον, or ὠβῶον for *ovum*, and the like, always putting a β instead of the *digamma*; whence perhaps ariseth the mistake of pronouncing β like a V consonant.

Now these, as well as most of the preceding variations, are proper to be observed, not only in order to discover the origin and derivation of words, but likewise to understand divers obscure passages, to correct such as have been corrupted, and to decypher the antient manuscripts. Therefore to facilitate the use of them, I have subjoined the following table, where the most considerable of these variations will appear immediately at a single glance; though I did not intend to include them all, but only the most necessary. And here you are to observe, that when I shew that one letter may be put for another, as E for A, *faciem* for *faciam*, this means that we may generally conclude vice versa, as A for E, *inars* for *iners*, *balare* for *belare*; and the same may be said of others which I mentioned above, though I have not inserted them in this table; having been satisfied, for the sake of brevity, with taking notice only of the most usual and most remarkable manner of writing.

TABLE

TABLE

Of the manner of writing of the antients.

THE MANNER OF WRITING OF THE ANTIENTS DIFFERS FROM OURS, EITHER	**In QUANTITY in the diminution of the addition of**	Vowel, as	E. I. O. U.		Eidem *for* idem. Leitem *for* litem, Ubei, &c. Maiia, Caiius, **ēius**, *for* Maia, Caius, &c. Jous *for* jus. Souo, quicuonqu; *for* suo, quicunq; Juus *for* jus. Arbitratuu, luuit *for* arbitratu, luit.
		Consonant, as	C. N. S. P. or B. ST. D.		Vicxit, juncxit, *for* vixit, junxit, &c. Quotiens *for* quoties. Exigunt, exsercere. Amasso *for* amaso, *of* amare. Quips *for* quis. Obstendit *for* ostendit. Stlis *for* lis. Tuad *for* tua. Plebed, marid, estod.
		Both, as			Leibertated *for* libertate.
		A Syllable, as			Postidea *for* postea. Indotestato *for* intestato.
		Vowel, as	O. I.		Fenus *for* fœnus. Popli *for* popoli. Adicito, subice, reice; *for* Adjicito, subjice, rejice.
		Consonant, as	S. R. L.		Osa *for* ossa. Clase, jusit; *for* Classe, jussit. Acera *for* acerra. Felex *for* pellex.
	In QUALITY, in the change of	Vowel, as	E, E, O, O, O, OE and OI, V, V, V, V,	*for* *for* *for* *for* *for* *for* *for* *for* *for* *for*	A. Faciem *for* faciam, &c. I. Leber, Menerva, præsentebos; *for* præsentibus. E. Vorsus, voster; *for* Versus, vester. V. Servos, volnus *for* Servus. Dicont *for* dicunt. AV. Coda *for* cauda; plostrum *for* plaustrum, &c. V. Cœrare, *for* cu are. Oitier, oitile, *for* utier, utile. E. Dicundo, faciundo, ferundo; *for* dicendo, &c. I. Optumus, Maxumus, æstumare. O. Adulescens, epistula; *for* adolescens, &c. Y. Ægurtus, Sulla, Surius; *for* Ægyptus, &c.
		Consonant, as	B, C, D, D, F, L, L, Q, R, S, S, T, V,	*for* *for* *for* *for* *for* *for* *for* *for* *for* *for* *for* *for* *for*	P. Obtimus *for* optimus. G. Cenas, lece, lecio; *for* Genas, lege, legio. L. Fidius, dingua; *for* Filius, lingua. R. Federius for feretrius. B. Af virod *for* ab viro. Sisius *for* sibilus. D. Delicat *for* dedicat. R. Conflacuit *for* confracuit. C. Pequnia *for* pecunia. D. Arlabi, arsinis; *for* Adlabi, adfinis. D. Assum, asversa; *for* Adsum, adversa. R. Asa, casmen, minose; *for* Ara, carmen, minore. D. Alexanter, Casfantra, Set *for* sed. Quit *for* quid. B. Vobem *for* bovem.
					They have also frequently preserved the final letters of prepositions in compound words without changing them, Inlustris, affectus, Conlega, &c.
		Both, as			Aufom *for* aurum. Exfociont *for* effugiunt. Prodigos *for* prodigus.
	In both				Adecito *for* adicito. Addeictos *for* addictus. Continoeis *for* continuis. Deicundo *for* dicendo. Endo *for* in. Fasis *for* farris. Fousiosus *for* furiosus. Maxsumo *for* maximo. Oloi *for* illi. Poplos *for* populus. Poplei *for* populi. Præseted *for* præsente. Proxsumos *for* proximus. Sopera *for* supra. Faxsit *for* fecerit. Rupsit *for* ruperit. Jousit, jousus, *for* jussit, &c.

CHAPTER

Of ORTHOGRAPHY.

CHAPTER XIII.
Of the genuine orthography to be observed at present.

SUCH was the manner of writing that obtained among the antients. But as custom has departed in many things from that antiquity, we must see which is the genuine orthography, to be observed at present in the use of the Latin tongue.

Orthography may be known either by reason, or by authority.

By REASON, when we consider the analogy of the language and the origin of words: thus we have shewn in the preterites, vol. 1. p. 257. that *sumo* makes *sumsi* and not *sumpsi*. Thus we know that *gratia* is written with a T, because it comes from *gratus*; and that *audacia* on the contrary is written with a C, because it comes from *audax, acis*. And we learn that *deliciæ* ought to be writ with a C, because it comes from *delicatus:* that we ought to write *vindico*, and not *vendico*, as it is in most books, because we say *vindiciæ*, and they both come from *vindex*.

To reason also we ought to refer the distinction which we find between certain words, as between *ara* and *hara*, between *abeo* and *habeo*, and the like.

By AUTHORITY, when we follow the manner of writing most usual in good authors, as when we write *caussa, caussæ*, because thus we find it in antient inscriptions, in Cicero, Virgil, and Quintilian.

But as there are many words, concerning which the learned are divided, and others that are written two different ways, for instance, *neglego* or *negligo, heri* or *here*, we shall therefore subjoin an orthographical list of the best authority.

List of some particular words, whose orthography may be depended upon.

AERIUS and ÆTHERIUS ought to be written with an *i* in the penultima, according to Aldus; and the antient copies favour it, as also the Greek analogy ἀέριος, αἰθέριος. Yet we may write them with an E, as well because we find it thus written in some antient copies, as because they are more consonant to the Latin analogy, which says *igneus, malleus,* &c.

ANACHORITA is commonly written with an *i*; and thus we find it in St. Jerom and in Calepine. Yet it would be better with an E, because it does not come from ἀναχωρίζω, *recedere facio*, but from ἀναχωρέω, *recedo*.

APPULEIUS, see lower down, *Sall*.

APSIS or ABSIS, see the heteroclites.

ARCESSO is better than *accerso*, because it comes from *arcio*, compounded of *ar* for *ad*, and of *cio*, to *call*. For the *r* used to be put for *d*, as we shall see presently. This verb hath been already taken notice of in the preterites. There are some who distinguish between these two words, as Charisius, Diomedes, and Agroetius, who pretend that *accerso* is taken for *to bring or to call*; and *arcesso* for *to accuse, to appeal, or to repel*. But Ter. Scaurus and Velius Longus reject this distinction, affirming that which ever way it be written, it preserves the same signification, and is never taken for *arcere, to repel, or keep off*. And therefore it ought to be wrote according to its real derivation.

AATUS

ARTUS occurs in antient manuscripts for ARCTUS, *close, narrow*, though we cannot condemn the latter, which was first introduced for the sake of distinguishing it from *artus*, a joint.

AUCTOR. When it comes from *augeo*, there is no sort of doubt but it ought to take a C, as *auctor patrimonii*; or *auctor*, an auctioneer (see the preterites, vol. I. p. 294.) But when it is taken for the person who begins, or is the author of a thing, then there is some doubt. The antient inscriptions and MSS make use of C even in this sense; which Vossius in his etymologist approves of. And others give also this reason, that it is then, *quasi* ACTOR. But in French we ought always to write it without either C or H. AUTEUR, AUTORITE, &c.

BENIVOLUS occurs in antient writers for BENEVOLUS. And reason seems to confirm it, because the E is frequently changed into I in composition. *Benivolus*, says Beda in his orthography, and *malivolus, malificus*, just as of *pace* is formed *pacificus*.

BUCINA was said for BUCCINA, according to St. Isidorus. And thus we find it in antient MSS and inscriptions.

CÆSTUS and CESTUS, which a great many confound, ought to be distinguished, according to Servius. For the latter is feminine, and signifies the waist of a new married woman, or of Venus, and comes from κεντειν, *pungere*, because it was marked with little points. But the former is masculine, signifying the arms of fencers, and comes from *cædo*.

Sin crudo fidit pugnam committere cæstu, Virg.

CÆTERA, because it is said for ἡ ἕτερα, though we find it with a simple *e* in old MSS and inscriptions.

CECIDI, and not CÆCIDI, with *æ*, though it comes from *cædo*, because the *æ* is what is changed into *i* long, and the first syllable is only an augment. See the preterites, v. 1. p. 172.

COELUM, because it comes from κοιλον, *cavum*.

COEPI, to signify *I have begun*, from the old verb *cœpio*. For *ecpi* cometh from *capio*. See the preterites, rule 28, vol. 1. p. 210.

CONVITIUM ought to be written with a C, and not with a T in the penultima, either because it comes from *vicus*, according to Festus, or because it is said for *convocium*, according to Labeo, by reason it is only a confusion of sounds and reproaches.

CULCITA is better than CULCITRA, according to Vossius, *a mattress, a feather bed.*

DESTRUCTUS and DISTRICTUS, are both good. But Phrigius will have it that the latter ought ever to be wrote, having the authority of antient MSS.

EDEPOL and not *Oedepol*, as some pretend who derive it from *ab æde Pollucis*, but it is compounded of three words, *me, deus, Pollux*, sup. *adjuvet*. Therefore *edepol* is for *medepol*, in the same manner as we still say *ecastos* or *mecastor*, for *me Castor*, sup. *adjuvet*, which are forms of swearing in use among the antients.

EPHEBIUM or EPHEBEUM, is the genuine writing; as in Greek ἐφήβιον or ἐφηβεῖον, and not *Ephæbeum*, or *Ephebæum*, as some will have it.

EPISTULA and ADULESCENS ever occur with a U in antient copies. But *epistola* and *adolescens* are become so familiar at present, that it would seem grating to the ear to pronounce them otherwise.

ETHICA is better than ÆTHICA, says Vossius, because it comes from ηθική. Yet there are many who write it with *æ*, for which reason one may doubt whether we might not comply with this custom; just as we may write *scæna*, in compliance with custom, though it comes from σκηνὴ, as we shall presently see.

FŒCUNDUS, FŒLIX, FŒMINA, FŒNUS, FŒTUS, and their derivatives, are better with a simple E, than with a diphthong, as we find them in antient inscriptions and MSS.

INCHOO or INCOHO, have been always the subject of dispute among grammarians. Yet Verrius and Servius are for the latter.

INCREBESCO, INCREBUI, is the genuine writing, and not *increbresco, increbrui*: just like *rubesco*, and others. Yet we say *nigresco*, which may favour the other way of writing.

INTERNUNDINIUM. Thus we ought to write it, according to Victorinus, and not *internundinum*.

LACHRYMA or LACRYMA: the latter is preferable, because it comes from λα the augmentative particle, and κρυμὸς, *frigus*, tears being only a cold humour that drops from the brain: hence Festus takes notice that the antients wrote *dacryma*, taking it from δάκρυμα,

OF ORTHOGRAPHY.

με, which is the same as θάκρυς, frigus.

LEVIS ought to be written with a simple *e*, whether it signifies *light* or *smooth*, because the latter comes from λεῖος, and the Greek diphthong ει is not changed into the Latin *æ*, but into *i*, or *e* long. Thus the whole difference is that *levis*, smooth, has the first syllable long by nature, and *levis*, light, has the first short. But *lævus*, *left handed*, *unlucky*, is written with an *æ*, because it comes from λαιός.

MARCIUS NARBO, or MARTIUS. Vossius is for the former, because we find that the colony was sent to Narbonne, under the consulate of *Marcius* and *Porcius*: but the latter occurreth in an antient inscription of the town of Narbonne, intending perhaps to allude to the name of Mars, for the greater honour of its founder.

NE ought to be written with a plain *e*, even when it affirmeth, says Vossius, instead of *næ*: though Aldus is for the latter, because it comes from the Greek ναί. But all the antients write it with a simple *e*: concerning which see Faernus, Malaspina, and Lambinus.

NUMUS or NUMMUS. The former appears more natural, for it is derived from νόμος, *lex*, because money was invented to serve as a law in commerce. But the latter is also received, because consonants used frequently to be doubled.

OCIOR and not OCYOR, *readier*, because it comes from the comparative ὠκίων, and not from the positive ὠκύς.

OPPERIOR for *expecto*, and not *operior*.

PARCIMONIA with a C, rather than with an S, as well because it comes from *parco*, like *alimonia* from *alo*, as because it is favoured by antient copies.

PATRICIUS with a C, and not PATRITIUS, because it is derived *à patribus ciendis*, according to Velleius, and others. The same ought to be said of *Ædilicius*, *tribunicius*, *ficticius*, *novicius*, which should be written with a *c*, as Priscian proveth. And this is also the opinion of Aldus and Vossius.

PENTECONTARCHUS, and not PENTACONTARCHUS, because it comes from πεντήκοντα, *quinquaginta*, and the MSS favour it. This observation would be useless, if we did not see a number of fine editions in which it is written with an *a*.

PERLEGO is more usual at present, though the antients said *pellego*, in the same manner as *intellego* or *intelligo*, as appears by the testimony of Terentian, Scaurus, and Vossius.

POENA with *œ* and not *æ*, contrary to the opinion of Marc. Corradus, by reason it comes from ποινή.

POENITET notwithstanding occurs sometimes with *æ*; which may make us put up with the other, though it is always best to write it with *œ*, as we find it in excellent MSS.

POMOERIUM ought to be writ with *œ*, since it comes from *pone* and *moerus*, according to Varro. Yet we find *pomerium* in antient authors.

PORCIUS with a C, and not PORTIUS. For the Porcian family at Rome, of which Cato was descended, took their name from the word *Porcus*.

PRÆDIUM with Æ and not PROEDIUM with *œ*.

PRÆLIUM. Thus it is always writ; and yet Vossius maintains against Frischlinus, that we ought to write it *proelium*: for since Æ cometh from the AI of the antients, as our OE from their OI, it appears that they wrote *proilium*, as well by the authority of Capella, who says, *sed proilium, Oinonem, similiáque planè exoleverunt*, as by the testimony of Muretus, who says that in Plautus it was *proilium* for *prælium*, where the common editions have put *proilio*.

QUATUOR and not QUATTUOR, as Aldus pretendeth; because it is contrary to the antient MSS, as well as to etymology, since it comes from *quater*.

QUICQUID, rather than QUIDQUID, according to Priscian and Victorinus; and it appears by Quintilian that this question had been started so early as his time, and that a great many were for writing it with a C: *ne interrogare bis videretur*, as he says; but he himself pays no great regard to it; *verùm*, these are his words, *hæc jam inter ipsas ineptias evanuerunt*.

RHÆTIA with Æ, because the Greeks call these people ῥαιτοί: though the old inscriptions vary.

RHYTHMUS, thus we ought to write it, and not *rhytmus*, with a single aspiration. For it comes from ῥυθμός.

RIPHÆI, and not RIPHEI, though it comes from φρικός, because the tenuis is changed into an aspirate, says Vossius, and it is confirmed by antient MSS.

S. ÆPII,

SÆPES, SÆPIOS, SÆPIMENTUM, which are commonly wrote with a simple *e*, occur with a diphthong in antient copies, as Pierius, Giffanius, and Vossius have observed. And thus they ought to be wrote.

SALLUSTIUS, and not *Salustius*. APPULEIUS and not *Apuleius*, though it is otherwise in books. But this is contrary to antient inscriptions.

But we must say LUCILIUS and not *Lucillius*, because it is authorised by the antient copies, and likewise by analogy, for it is the same as *Servilius*.

SCENA or SCÆNA, neither of them is bad. The former is more agreeable to analogy, because it comes from σκηνή: and the second has the authority of antient copies and of inscriptions, which seems preferable. Even Varro writes SCÆNA and SCÆPTRUM, though he owns that Actius wrote *scena*, and others *sceptrum*.

SCRIPSI, NUPSI, &c. with *ps*, and not *b*, though it comes from *scribo*, *nubo*, &c. The reason hereof may be seen above, chap. 8. n. 1. p. 268.

SESCUNX and SEXCUNX, which Calepin confounds, ought to be distinguished. For the former, as Budeus observes in the beginning of his book *de Asse*, is *an ounce and a half*; and the latter signifieth *six ounces*, as if it were *sexunx*, the *c* being only a letter added, pursuant to what we have already observed, chap. 11.

And *sexunx* is of the same analogy as *quincunx*, *septunx*, and the rest.

SIDUS, which is often written with a *y*, should never be wrote so, this letter being reserved only for words derived from the Greek, which is not at all the case of *sidus*, whether we take it from *insido*, according to Varro, or from elsewhere.

SILVA ought always to be put with a simple *i*, though it comes from ὕλη, and not from *Sileo*. The same must be said of *Silvanus*, *Æneas Silvius*, *Rhea Silvia*. Which is proved by the authority of antient MSS. and even by the Greeks, who in translating these words write, Σιλυανὸς, Σίλυος, ΣιλβΙα, as may be seen in Strabo, Plutarch, Suidas, and others.

SOLEMNE, rather than *solenne*, as it is written by those who derive it from *solus* and *annus*. For the antient MSS have *solemne*, and Sanctius is strongly for this orthography, because, as Festus observeth, it comes from the old word *solius*, which in the Oscian language signified *totus*, whence also cometh SOLLERS, according to the same author. So that the word *solemne* does not properly signify *what is done every year*, as they pretend, but what is done commonly and usually, or principally and chiefly; with a solemn and extraordinary apparatus, and even with a particular sense of religion, as much as to say ὅλος σεμνὸς; *totus augustus & venerandus*. Hence we find *Nuptiarum solemnia* and *funerum solemnia*, in Tacitus and other writers. Cicero understood it thus, when he said, *Tantum igitur nostrum illud solemne servemus, ut neque isthuc euntem sine literis dimittamus*; our religious, or our usual custom, &c. And Pliny, *Certe novæ nuptæ intrantes, etiam solemne habent postes eo attingere*. Have this religious or usual custom. And Justin, lib. 42. c. 4. *Sed fatum Parthiæ fecit, in qua jam quasi solemne est reges parricidas habere*, where it is a usual thing to see kings that have been parricides: and Horace, *Infanire putas solemnia me*, lib. 1. epist. 1. that is, ΚΑΤΑ *solemnia*, according to the custom of the world. And lib. 4. od. 11. *Qui dies jure solemnis mihi sanctiorque pene natali proprio*. In like manner Virgil in this passage of the 5th book of the Æneid, *Annua vota tamen solemnisque ordine pompas*: for *solemnes* means there only *præcellentes*, which is perfectly expressed by the French word *solemnel*, though several have been led into a mistake by this passage, because of the precedent words, *annua vota*.

SOLLISTIMUM, according to all the antient copies, and not *solistimum*.

SPELÆUM, a den, ought to be written, one would think, with an Æ in the second, because it comes from σπήλαιον. Yet in the old copies it is written with a simple E, which is authority sufficient.

SULFUR, and not *sulphur*, because the φ was never admitted into Latin words, and ought to be used only in those of Greek original.

SUBOLES is better than *sobules*, not only because we find it written thus in antient copies, but because it comes from *subolesco*.

SUBSICIVA, or SUBSECIVA, and not *succisiva*. For which we have the authority of the best MSS and of the antient inscriptions; and it is likewise agreeable to analogy, because it does not come from *succido*, but from *subseco*, according to Vossius.

TÆTER,

TΆΤΕR, and not *teter*, according to the antient copies.

THUS or TUS. See the genders, vol. i. p. 20.

TOPUS, and not TOPHUS, because it is not of Greek original.

TROPÆUM, as we find it in antient MSS and inscriptions: and the analogy favours it, for in Greek we say τρόπαιον, though most moderns now write ΤΡΟΡΗÆUM.

VINEA and TINEA, are always written with an *e* in the penultima, though Ursinus mentions his having seen them somewhere with an *i*.

CHAPTER XIV.

Of some others remarks on orthography.

I. *Of words that ought to begin with capitals.*

THE Romans had no other letters but capitals. But since small letters have been introduced, it is proper to observe, where the capitals ought to be placed.

Words beginning with a capital are therefore;

I. Proper names, as, *Moses, Homerus, Cicero, Roma,* and even adjectives formed of those words, as *Mosaicus, Homericus, Ciceronianus, Romanus,* &c.

Our Saviour's name is likewise wrote often in capitals out of respect, JESUS-CHRISTUS.

II. Nouns that in some measure supply the place of a proper name; as *Dominus* for CHRIST. *Poeta* for Virgil. As also those of arts and dignities, as *Rhetorica, Astrologia, Rex, Dux,* &c. Those of festivals, *Pascha*. In short, all those that are intended to be any way remarkable or to make a figure in discourse. But you must avoid using too many.

III. Words that begin a new period. Yet when the period is very short, you may be satisfied with a small letter, as we shall shew hereafter.

IV. The beginning of every verse ought also to be distinguished by a capital.

II. *Of those words which the Romans expressed by a few letters only.*

The Romans generally expressed their proper names by a few letters only. Some by a single letter, as A for *Aulus*: others by two, as CN for *Cnæus*: others by three, as MAN for *Manlius*, and the like, which may be seen in the preceding book of particular observations, chap. 1. n. 1. p. 227.

The inverted letters signified the proper names of women, as Ɯ for *Marcia*, Ↄ for *Caia*, as already hath been mentioned, p. 229. but Ↄ likewise stood for the syllable *con*, as ↄjux for *conjux*, ↄliberta for *conliberta*, &c.

F by itself made *Filius,* N. *Nepos,* M. F. or M. N. *Marci filius, Marci nepos,* and so for the rest. Q. sometimes stands for *Quintus,* sometimes for *Quæstor,* and sometimes for *Quirites,* according to Diomedes.

VOL. II.　　　　　　　　U　　　　　　　　P. C.

P. C. makes *Patres Conscripti*, R. P. *Respublica*, P. R. *Populus Romănus*, S. P. Q. R. *Senatus, Populusque Romănus*, S. C. *Senatus Consultum*, Cos. *Consul*. Coss. *Consules*, H. *Sestertius*, a small sesterce. See what has been said in the preceding book of observations, chap. 3. p. 235.

When the same letter is repeated, it frequently is a mark of the superlative; thus B. B. is as if it were twice *bene, bene,* and for *optime*, or even for *boni, boni,* that is, *optimi.* In like manner F. F. signifies *fortissimi,* or *felicissimi,* P. P. *piissimi,* L. L. *libentissime;* or *locus laudabilis,* a remarkable passage in a book, says Valerius Probus, as the Greeks used to put a χ to signify χρῆτον or χρήσιμον, and on the contrary a Θ to signify things which they thought worthy of censure or blame. M. M. *meritissimo,* or *malus, malus,* that is *pessimus.*

III. *Of the right manner of putting syllables together.*

I. When a consonant happens to be between two vowels, it must always be put with the last, as *a-mor, le-go,* &c.

II. If the same consonant be doubled, the first shall belong to the former syllable, and the second to the latter, as *an-nus, flam-ma.*

III. Consonants that cannot be joined together at the beginning of a word, generally speaking, are not joined together in the middle, as *ar-duus, por-cus.* Though there are some examples of the contrary in Greek, as ἰχθρὸς, *hostis.*

IV. But consonants that may be joined together in the beginning of a word, ought also to be joined in the middle without parting them. And Ramus pretends that to act otherwise is committing a barbarism. Therefore we ought to join

bd.	he-bdomas,		bdellium.
cm.	Pyra-cmon,		κμίλιθρα, *tabes.*
cn.	te-chna,		Cneus.
ct.	do-ctus,		Ctesiphon.
gn.	a-gnus,		gnatus.
mn.	o-mnis,		Mnemosyne.
phth.	na-phtha,		phthisis.
ps.	scri-psi,		psittacus.
pt.	a-ptus,	*because we say*	Ptolemæus.
sb.	Le-sbia,		σβέσις.
sc.	pi-scis,		scamnum.
sm.	Co-smus,		smaragdus.
sp.	a-sper,		spes.
sq.	te-squa,		squamma.
st.	pa-stor,		sto.
tl.	At-las,		Tlepolemus.
tm.	La-tmius,		Tmolus.
tn.	Æ-tna,		θνήσκω.

Exception to this rule.

Words compounded of prepositions are an exception to this rule, since in these we must ever separate the compounding particle, as *in-ers, ab-esse, abs-trusus, ab-domen, dis-cors,* &c.

And

And the same judgment we ought to form of other compounds, as *jurif-confultus, alter-uter, amphif-bæna, et-enim,* &c.

IV. *Of some other particular marks.*

When a vowel is dropped at the end of a word, we put over it a small comma, called *apoftrophe,* as egon', ain', viden', noftin', &c. for *egone, aifne, videfne, noftine.* And this figure, though rare among the Latins, is very common in French and in Greek.

When we want to separate one vowel from another, we put two points over them, as *aëra,* to shew that they must not be pronounced *æra;* *üi* a diffyllable, to shew that it must not be pronounced *vi* in one syllable, as in Ovid.

Ne temerè in mediis diffolüantur aquis:

where the verse would be good for nothing, were we to read *diffolvantur* in four syllables.

When we want to draw two words into one, we put a small line between them, as in Virgil *ante-malorum.* This is what the antients called ὑφ' ἓν, *unitio.* And its figure is sometimes thus ⁀.

Chapter XV.

Of Punctuation.

THE manner of pointing, that is, of making stops or pauses in discourse, seemeth arbitrary, and to differ in some measure according to the idiom in which a person writes, and even according to the particular turn of stile which he has formed: yet since it has some foundation in reason, we shall mention what is most observable in regard to this subject, according to the practice now established among most of the learned.

I. *Of three sorts of distinctions.*

The distinction observed in discourse, either in speaking or writing, is threefold.

The first is only a light breathing, or a short pause, which seems designed only to sustain the voice, and to avoid obscurity and confusion: this is called κόμμα, in Tully *incifum,* that is, *fragment,* or a part cut off, and is marked by a small *c* inverted thus (,) which we call *comma* or *virgula.* The Greeks give it another name, ὑποστιγμὴ, and the Latins *subdistinctio,* for a reason we shall mention hereafter.

The other is a longer pause, that takes in a greater part of the sentence, but still leaves the mind in suspence, and in expectation of what follows. This is called μίτη, *media,* whence comes the French word *mediation,* or κῶλον, *membrum;* and it is marked with two points, thus (:) But this pause is subdivided, as we shall shew presently, the one which is the complete member, being marked with two points; and the other with a point and a virgula, which some call a *femicolon.*

The third is that which finishes and renders the sentence intirely perfect; it is called *period*, and is marked with a single point at the end of the last word, thus (.) The Latins call it *ambitus*, or *circuitus*; and the Greeks τέλεια ςιγμὴ, *perfect distinction*.

True it is that the antients did not make use of all these different marks. For having but the point only, if they put it at the bottom, they made it their *comma*, which for this reason was called *subdistinctio*; if they put it to the middle of the last word, they made it their *colon*, or *media distinctio*; and if they put it to the top, it was their period or perfect sentence, as may be seen in Diomedes, lib. 2. in Donatus, ed. 1. cap. ult. in St. Isidore, *lib.* 1. *orig. cap.* 19. And it is likewise the opinion of Alstedius, *Encyclop. lib.* 6. *de Grammat. Latinâ, cap.* 19. and of Melanchthon in his grammar. Though Gaza at the end of his grammar says, that if they put the point to the middle, they made it their complete sentence; and if they put it to the top, it was their middle sentence, that is, their *colon* or mediation. This is also the opinion of Vergara, *lib.* 4. *Gramm.* Vossius in his small grammar, p. 272. says, that if they put the point to the middle of the final letter, they made it their *comma:* if they put it to the top, they made it their *colon*; and if they put it to the bottom, their *period*. But as he quotes Donatus and St. Isidore, it is likely he meant something else; the opinion of these authors being clearly expressed in the abovementioned passages.

II. *Of the comma.*

The use of commas is particularly necessary, when we are to make several distinctions, either in nouns, as

Grammaticus, rhetor, geometres, pictor, aliptes, Juven.

In like manner.

Non formosa, sed prudens.

But if there be a copulative conjunction, some are of opinion that it will not admit of a comma, and others will have it here likewise; as *Vir magnus, pius & doctus,* or *Vir magnus, pius, & doctus.* If the conjoined words are synonymous, there is more reason to take away the comma, as *Doctrina & eruditione clarus atque illustris.*

In verbs, as *Hortari, orare, monere non definit.*

Feras, non culpes, quod vitari non potest, Publ. Syr.

In adverbs, as *Serius, ocius, necesse cunctis est mori.*

The comma serves also to distinguish the sense and the members when they happen to be very short, and to have a particular connexion, as when Horace says,

Nos numerus sumus, & fruges consumere nati,

Again,

Quo semel est imbuta recens, servabit odorem
Testa diu, Id.

The comma is likewise necessary to prevent ambiguity, and to render the sense clear and distinct; as *Summa quidem auctoritate philosophi, severè, sanè atque honestè, hæc tria genera confusa, cogitatione distinguunt,* Cic. If there had not been a comma after *confusa,* it would seem to refer to *cogitatione,* which is contrary to sense.

III. *Of*

III. *Of the colon, or two points.*

The two points denote indeed a complete construction and the sense already perfect in itself; but which requires nevertheless something after it to end the sentence. Thus when there are two members in a sentence, each of which has its particular verb, as *Ante omnia necesse est se ipsum æstimare: quia fere plus nobis videmus posse, quàm possimus,* Senec.

Nec verbum verbo curabis reddere, fidus
Interpres: nec desilies imitator in arctum,
Unde pedem referre pudor vetet, aut operis lex, Hor.

But if the period be long, each member is distinguished by two points, as when Cicero speaking of people of property, useth these words, *Quæ primum* (res familiaris) *bene parta sit, nulloque turpi quæstu, neque odioso, tum quamplurimis, modo dignis, se utilem præbeat: deinde augeatur ratione, diligentia, parsimonia: nec libidini potius luxuriæque, quam liberalitati & beneficentiæ pareat.* Offic. 1.

IV. *Of the full point or period.*

The period, as we have already taken notice, ought to conclude with a point, shewing that the sentence is complete. Now we may observe two sorts of periods, the one short, and the other somewhat longer. The short, as

Oderunt peccare boni virtutis amore. Hor.

And then if there are many of them collected in one series, they are distinguished, it is true, by a point; but this point is followed only by a small letter, as in Seneca, *Non est fides nisi in sapiente. apud sapientem sunt ipsa honesta. apud vulgum simulacra rerum honestarum.* And if this happens in verse, as verse must necessarily begin with a capital, you must be satisfied with putting two points, as in the same passage of Horace, whence the above verse was taken.

Tu nihil admittes in te formidine pœnæ:
Sit spes fallendi, miscebis sacra profanis, lib. 1. ep. 16.

Sometimes even in prose, and in long periods, we may put either a capital after two points, or a small letter after a point only, in order to render the sense more distinct, and to increase the pauses, by a greater variety of punctuation.

For an example of the pointing of long periods, we shall give the following, which is no less remarkable for the sense, than for the expression: *Si quis est paulo erectior, quamvis voluptate capiatur occultat, & dissimulat appetitum voluptatis, propter verecundiam. ex quo intelligitur corporis voluptatem non satis esse dignam hominis præstantiâ, eámque contemni & rejici oportere: sin sit quispiam, qui aliquid tribuat voluptati, diligenter ei tenendum esse ejus fruendæ modum. Itaque victûs cultúsque corporis ad valetudinem referantur, & ad vires, non ad voluptatem. Atque etiam si considerare volumus, quæ sit in natura excellentia & dignitas: intelligemus quàm sit turpe diffluere luxuria, & delicatè, ac molliter vivere: quámque honestum parcè, continenter, severè, sobriéque,* Cic. Offic. 1.

V. *Of the semicolon, or point and comma.*

To the three preceding punctuations a fourth is added, namely the point and comma; called a *semicolon*, which denotes a pause somewhat longer than the comma, but less than the two points. As in this example out of Cicero: *Etsi ea perturbatio est omnium rerum, ut suæ quemque fortunæ maximè pœniteat: nemóque sit quin ubi vis, quam ibi, ubi est, esse malit: tamen mihi dubium non est, quin hoc tempore, bono viro Romæ esse, miserrimum sit*, Epist. ad Torq. And in Gellius, *Cogitate cum animis vestris, si quid vos per laborem rectè feceritis: labor ille à vobis citò recedet; benefactum à vobis, dum vivetis, non abscedet. Sed si qua per voluptatem nequiter feceritis, voluptas cito abibit: nequiter factum illud apud vos semper manebit*, Cato apud Gell.

These examples exhibit all sorts of punctuations. But the point and comma particularly takes place in things opposite or contrary; or when we make an enumeration of several parts, as *propria, aliena; publica, privata; sacra, profana*, &c.

VI. *Of the point of interrogation and admiration.*

Interrogations have also the following mark by which they are signified, thus (?) *Parumne igitur, inquies, gloriæ relinquemus?* Cic. *shall we then leave but little glory, you will say?* But the Greeks make use of the point and comma for this purpose, τί ποίεις; *quid facis?*

If the sentence is so far protracted, that the interrogation which appeareth in the beginning, seems to slacken and lose its force, then the mark of interrogation is omitted, as here, *An tu putas esse viros bonos, qui amicitias utilitate sua colunt: nihil ad humanitatem, nihil ad honestum referunt; nec libenter ea curant, quæ ego nisi curarem præter cætera, prorsus me tua benevolentia, in qua magnam felicitatis meæ partem soleo ponere, indignum putarem.*

Some make use also of a point of admiration, which is thus formed (!) as *O me perditum! O me afflictum! O tempora! O mores!* &c.

BOOK X.

OF PROSODY.

SECTION I.

Of the Quantity of Syllables.

THIS treatise of quantity shews the right measure of syllables, in order either to make verses, or to pronounce prose in a proper manner, by preserving the tone and accents.

Quantity is therefore, properly speaking, the measure of each syllable, and the time we ought to keep in pronouncing it, according to which some are called short, others long, and others common.

The short have this mark (˘) and are equivalent only to half a long one.

The long have this other mark (¯) and ought to last as long as two short ones.

The common are those which are sometimes short, and at other times long in verse. We have distinguished them here by this mark (˘) which partakes of the other two.

Now this measure of syllables is known either by rules, or by the authority and reading of poets. The rules are either general or particular, as we are going to explain them.

But we are first to observe that syllables are long or short, either by their nature, or by accident, that is on account of the place where they are put, and the letters that follow them, which is called position. Thus the first in *patris* is short by nature, because it comes from *pater*, whose first is short. But as it is followed by two consonants, it may be also long.

On the contrary *præ* is long by nature, because it is a diphthong; but in compound words, if it precedes a vowel, this sort of position renders it short, as *præire*.

Sometimes a syllable is long, both by nature and position, as *auster*.

But though it may be said that it is by position one vowel is short before another, just as it is long when it precedes two consonants; yet generally speaking we use this word position, only to signify the latter sort of long syllables.

Rules of the Quantity of Syllables.

General Rules.

Rule I.

Every syllable formed by contraction is long.

Examples.

As often as two syllables are joined or contracted into one, this syllable so formed by contraction is long; as *cōgo* for *cŏăgo* or *cŏnăgo*; *cōperuisse* for *cŏŏperuisse*, Lucr. *nīl* for *nĭhil*; *tībīcen* for *tĭbĭīcen*; *īt* for *ĭĭt*; *mī* for *mĭhi*; *vēmens* for *vĕhĕmens*, Hor. and the like. *Sōdes*, for *si audes*; *nōlo*, for *non volo*; *bīgae*, for *bijugae*;

Annotation.

WE place this rule the first, because it is the most general, and may serve for an introduction and inlet to a great many others. For example, a diphthong is properly no more than the union and contraction of two syllables, or of two vowels into one syllable, as *musæ* for *musai*, &c. Thus *Mnæstæūs* a dissyllable, for *Mnesthëus* a trysyllable; *Orpheūs* for *Orpheüs*, and the like, have the last long; because these two syllables are contracted into one by a synæresis, of which we shall have occasion to speak hereafter.

In like manner *alīus* is long, because it comes from *aliīus*; *ambāges*, because it comes from *ambe* and *ago*, from whence was first formed *ambëäges*, and afterwards *ambäges*; *bīgæ*, *trīgæ*, *quadrīgæ*, because they come from *bijŭgæ*, *trijŭgæ*, *quadrijŭgæ*, &c. *bībus* or *būbus*, because it is instead of *bŏvibus*; *jūnior*, because it is instead of *jŭvĕnior*; *nīnus* instead of *nĭvĕnus*; *mālo* instead of *mă* (or *măgis*) *volo*; *stīpendium* instead of *stĭpĭpendium*; *indāgo* because it comes from *indūägo* composed of *indu* for *in* and *ago*. And a multitude of others; which we shall take notice of hereafter.

For we must remember what has been said in the preceding treatise of letters, which ought to be considered as the foundation of this of quantity; that the antients used formerly to write the long syllables with two vowels, as *veenit* for *vēnit* long in the preterite, instead of *vĕnit* short in the present: for which reason the former hath twice the time or measure of the latter.

But we must distinguish between a syllable cut off by syncope and that which is joined to another by synæresis, as for instance *smĭ homo* for *semi homo*; *smĭ animis* for *semi animis*: for whatever is cut off and taken away, can have no manner of influence on the next syllable, which therefore remaineth always in its natural state. This we shall make appear on sundry occasions in the sequel. *scilicet*, for *scire licet*.

Rule

RULE II.
Of diphthongs.

1. *Hence all diphthongs are long.*
2. *Except that* præ *is short, when it precedes a vowel.*

EXAMPLES.

1. Therefore diphthongs are always long; as *foēnum, aūrum, eūrus*; because they are in some measure a contraction or union of two vowels into one syllable.
2. Yet the preposition *præ* is short in composition, when followed by another vowel; as *præest, præustus, præire.*

Jamque novi præeunt *fasces, nova purpura fulget.*

ANNOTATION.

Statius however made it long, having regard to the nature of the diphthong, and not to the subsequent vowel.
—— *Cum vacuus domino* præiret *Arion*, Th. 6.
The first in *Mæotis* is doubtful.
—— *Et* Mocotica *tellus,* Virg.
Longior antiquis visa Mocotis *hyems,* Ovid.
Which is owing to this, that some considered the nature of the diphthong, and others the position or place it held, being before another vowel, pursuant to the next rule. And the same may be said of *rhomphæa,* and *rhomphæalis.*
We find the first of *ænigma, hæresis,* and *sphæra,* short in Prudentius, as that of *hæmorrhois* in Fortunatus. Also the second of *cathæcumenus* in the same Fortunatus, and that of *solæcismus* in Ausonius. Which is by no means to be imitated, since it proceeds only from the corruption of the language, when, as we have observed in the treatise of letters, they wrote the E simple instead of Æ and Œ, because they no longer pronounced the diphthong in those words, but the E only.

RULE III.
Of a vowel before another vowel.

1. *A vowel before another vowel is short.*
2. *But* E *between two* I's *is long.*
3. I *in the tenses of* fīo *without* R, *is short.*
4. Iüs *in the genitive is doubtful;*
5. *But* alīus *is long,*
6. *And* altérīus *short.*

EXAM-

EXAMPLES.

1. A vowel followed by another vowel is short; as *justitĭa, dulcĭa, Deŭs*.

2. But E is long in the genitive and dative of the fifth declension, when it comes between two I's; as *diēi, speciēi*. This happens to all nouns of this declension, except these three, *fĭdĕi, spĕi, rĕi*, which have not the E between two *ii*.

3. I in *fio* is long in those tenses that have not an R, namely *fīo, fīam, fīebam*. Where there is an R, the I is short; as *fĭerem, fĭeri*.

4. I in the genitives in *ius* is doubtful, as *unīus, illīus, ipsīus, totīus, utrīus*.

5. *Alīus* hath I long in the genitive.

6. *Alterĭus* hath I short. Which gave occasion to this verse in Alstedius.

    Corripit alterĭus, *semper producit* alīus.

ANNOTATION.

Solīus, is always long in approved authors. *Alterutrīus* and *Neutrīus*, are always almost long, though *utrĭus* be common.

The penultima is likewise long in *aulāi, terrāi*, and other antient genitives. As also in *Cāi, Pompēi*. And 'tis for this very reason that the nominatives in *ejus*, or *eja* make E long, *Pompēius, Fontēius; Aquilēia, elegēia*: and that the genitive and dative of the fifth have it also long. For they used to say *dieii, specieii*, &c. and this they even did in regard to other nouns of this declension, where the *e* is not between two *i*. We meet with *reii* in Prudentius, *fideii* in St. Paulinus, as well as in Fortunatus and other Christian poets, concerning which, see also the treatise of letters, p. 265.

Fieret hath the first long in Terence, Adelph. a. 1. sc. 2.

    Injurium est, nam si esset, unde id fīeret,
        Faceremus.

Which proceeds undoubtedly from this, that heretofore, as we have observed in the remarks, p. 117. they used to say *feirem, feiri*, as *audeirem, audeiri*, and afterwards they transposed *feirem* into *fierem*. Hence Priscian says that in *fieri*, there is a resolution of one long into two short.

The first is long in *ēheu*, but doubtful in *ŏhe*; as also in *Dīana*, because this word being formed of *Dea Jana* (for *Janus* signifies the sun, and *Jana* the moon, according to Macrobius and Varro) some have considered it as a word formed by syncope of two letters, *Dea-na*, or *D-iana*, where the first is short by nature, as preceding another vowel: while others have considered it as a word which at first only dropped the *a*, so that it remained *Deiana*, of
                                                                                which

Of QUANTITY. 299

which was afterwards formed *Diana*, the diphthong *ei*, as may be seen in the treatise of letters, being frequently changed into *i* long.

Before we go any further, we must say something in regard to Greek words, because they have oftentimes a great many things that seem contrary to the foregoing rule.

OF GREEK WORDS.

Of those which are written with long or short vowels.

In regard to Greek words, the knowledge of their quantity ought to be derived from the language itself. For those which have an η or ω in Greek are long, and such as have an ο or an ε are short.

Thus we see that *arithmētĭca*, *psaltērĭum* must have the antepenultima long, because in Greek we write ἀριθμητικὴ, ψαλτήριον. We see that *Trŏes*, and *Trŏades* have the first long, because in Greek they are written with an ω: we see that *Deïphobus* has the first long and the penultima short, because we write δηίφοϐος.

We see likewise that in *Thermōdontis* the second is long, because in Greek it is an ω, as we find it in Apoll. 2. Argon.

   —— ἐπὶ δὲ ῥόμα Θερμώδοντος.

Hence in Virgil,
  Quales Threiciæ cùm flumina Thermōdontis
  Pulsant, &c.———————— Æn. 11.

It is a mistake to read *Thermŏdontis*; as Pierius hath observed, and Vossius demonstrated, against those, who wanting to avoid the spondaic verse have corrupted the quantity: which has happened also in other places, as we have made appear when speaking of *potestur*, p. 116. And hereby we see likewise that there is no necessity for admitting of what Servius saith, that *Thermodon* is a synerefis instead of *Thermodoon*.

Of those which are variously writ.

When a word is variously written in Greek, the quantity also varies in Latin verse. Thus the first is common in *Eos*, *Eous*, &c. because in Greek we write ἕως, and ἠῶν: ἰῷος and ἠῷος. Which Servius seems not to have sufficiently observed, when he attributes the making of the first short in *Eous* to a pure *licentia poetica*.

The accusative in *ea* coming from nominatives in *eus*, have generally the *e* short, as *Orphĕa*, *Salmonĕa*: but sometimes they have it long, as *Iliōnēa*, *Idomēnea*, which they seem to borrow of the Ionians, who write these words with an η.

Of the three common vowels.

In regard to the three common vowels, α, ι, υ, it would lead us into a long discourse to treat of them with any exactness. The most general remark we can make on this head is that the nouns ending in *aïs*, have generally the penultima long, as *Nāis*, *Lāis*.

The

The terminations *āon*, or *īon*, have also the penultima long; as *Machāon*, *Lycāon*, *Amphīon*, *Pandīon*, &c. as also the compounds of λαὸς, *Menelāus*, *Archelāus*, *Nicolāus*, *Charilāus*.

But these rules are not always certain: for *Phăon*, *Deucalĭon*, and a great many others have the penultima short. The penultima is doubtful in *Orīon*, *Gorīon*, and in *Nereĭdes*.

Of words that have a diphthong in Greek.

Diphthongs must be always long. Hence we see so many Greek nouns that have the *e* or *i* long in Latin, because in Greek they are written with ει, as *Cassiopēa*, *Centaurēa*, *Deiopēa*, *Galacēa*, *Medēa*, &c. Also *Basilius*, *Darīus*, *Clio*, *Elegīa*, *Ephigenīa*, *Antiochīa*, and such like.

Cause of the deviation in Greek words from the foregoing rules.

The Latins nevertheless have frequently deviated from these rules in regard to Greek words, and for three different reasons. The first, because taking these words as if they had intirely lost one vowel of the diphthong, they ceased to consider them as long, but made them pass for short or common. Hence it comes that *chiragra* hath always the first short, according to Vossius, though in Greek we write χειράγρα. And hence Virgil hath:

— *Vos & Cyclópea saxa*, Æn. 1.

though in Greek it is κυκλώπεια. And for the same reason *Chorēa*, *platēa*, and *Mulēa*, a proper name, and some others have the penultima common. To these we may also join *Academīa*, though it is more frequently short, because in Greek it is more frequently written with an ι, than with the diphthong ει.

The second is that they oftener paid more regard (especially in the latter ages, when the Greek was but little known) to the accent, than to the orthography in regulating the quantity. Thus they put *ĕremus*, *pŏĕsis*, *idŏlum*, and such like with the penultima short, though in Greek we write ἔρημος, ποίησις, εἴδωλον, &c. (where the penultima is long) only because the accent is on the antepenultima. This has been particularly the practice of ecclesiastic writers, who neither in this respect, nor in whatever relates to poetry, have been so exact, as to serve for any rule to go by.

Thus in the hymn of the holy Ghost, the word *Paraclĕtus* hath the penultima short, though in Greek it be written with an η, Παράκλητος, *consolator*, which has been owing intirely to the accent on the antepenultima. And thence proceeds the error of those who in the church service have generally wrote *Paraclitus* with an *i*, into which they were also led by the bad pronunciation of those who sound η like a *i*, though to say the truth, this word is neither Greek nor Latin.

The third is that the Romans have sometimes appropriated the Greek words to themselves in such a manner, as to render them intirely conformable to the analogy of their own language. Thus they said *crepĭdas*, the penultima short, as if it came from *crepitum*,

whereas

whereas according to Gellius it comes from ωηπωίδα. And in Ennius we find *Hectorem* long, because he looked upon it in the same manner as *pictorem*, and the like.

But there are still some words whose quantity is disputed, which it will be more proper to throw into a separate list at the end of this treatise, in order to proceed to other rules.

Rule IV.

Of a vowel long by position.

A vowel is long, when followed by two consonants.

Examples.

A vowel is long, whenever it is followed by two consonants, or by a double letter equivalent to two consonants, which is called Position; as *āt pius, Deūm cole. Cārmen, sapiēns*, &c.

Now the double letters are X, Z, as *āxis, Gāza, apēx.*

Annotation.

For a syllable to be long by position, there must be at least one of the consonants in the very syllable lengthened. For if they are both in the next, this does not, generally speaking, make it long; as *frigorĕ frondes; æquorā Xerxes; sæpĭ stilum vertas*, &c. Yet it sometimes happens otherwise, as

Ferte citi ferrum, date tela, scandite muros, Virg.

Which Catullus and Martial seem particularly to have affected, as it is very common in Greek.

Rule V.

Of a mute and liquid.

1. *Whenever a mute is followed by a liquid in the same syllable, the preceding short vowel becomes common in verse;*
2. *But remains short in prose.*

Examples.

1. What has been hitherto said, relates to that sort of position, which they call firm and unchangeable. But there is still another called weak and changeable, which is when after one of these seven letters B, C, D, F, G, P, T, distinguished by the name of mutes, because they have only a kind of obscure sound, there follows one of these two, L or R, which are called liquids or gliding letters. For in that case the
preceding

preceding vowel, which by nature is short, becomes common in verse; that is, it may be put either long or short; as

Et primo similis volŭcri, *mox vera* volūcris, *Ovid.*
Nox tenĕbras *profert, Phœbus fugat inde* tenĕbras, *Id.*
Omne solum forti pătria *est, mibi* pātria *cælum.*

The same may be said of *reflo, repleo, poples, locuples,* and the like.

2. But in prose this position of a mute and liquid, never lengthens a syllable by nature short; therefore it would be wrong to say for example, *locúples, tenébræ,* the accent on the penultima, when it should be on the antepenultima.

ANNOTATION.

These liquids have also the same force in Greek words, as *Cyclops, Pharetra.* But besides L and R, this language hath also the liquids M and N; as *Tecmessa, Cygnus, Progne,* &c.

The position is weakened in Greek, when the vowel is followed by *mn,* or *qd,* or *pt,* whence Martial took the liberty to make the second short in *smaragdus,* lib. 5. epigram. 11.

Sardonychas, smaragdos, *adamantas, iaspidas uno.*

But we are to take particular notice of two conditions necessary for this weak and changeable position. The 1. the mute and liquid must be both in the same syllable. The 2. the syllable we want to make common in verse, namely that immediately preceding these letters, must be short by nature.

Hence the first syllable in *ŏbruo* will be ever long, and not common, because the first condition is wanting, the *br* not being in the same syllable, for it comes from *ob* and *ruo*; the same may be said of *obtueor, quamobrem,* &c.

Again, the first is ever long in *acris, atri, matris, fratris,* for want of the second condition, because they come from *acer, ater, mater, frater,* whose first syllable is long by nature. We must say the same of *ambulácrum, candelábrum, delúbrum, lavácrum, simulácrum, salúbre, volutábrum,* which are long by nature, a circumstance that has not been always attended to by Christian poets.

Vossius further observeth that this kind of position of mute and liquid is so weak, that we ought not easily to make use of it, for the purpose of lengthening a syllable short by nature, without having some antient authority; and he adds for example, that he would not chuse to make the penultima long in *genitrix.*

Now the weakness of this sort of position is owing to the inequality of two consonants, because the liquid gliding away much nimbler than the mute, to which it is joined in the pronunciation, it drags the mute in some measure along with it, or produces an inequality, in consequence whereof the preceding syllable is not sufficiently sustained, as it is when there happen to be two other
conso-

Of QUANTITY.

consonants, for instance *āstra*, or even two liquids, as *tĕrra*; for then there is no inequality in the consonants: or when the liquid is before, as *ars, altus*, for in that case it is sustained by the following mute: or in short when they are in a different syllable, as *ab-luo*, for then the liquid does not draw the mute after it with such force. This the antients must have perceived in the pronunciation, though we are hardly sensible of it at present.

Whether I *be sometimes a double letter, and* V *sometimes a liquid.*

To the double letters by us mentioned, grammarians add likewise the I, when it happens to be between two vowels, because, say they, it then makes the preceding vowel long by position, as *major, rejicio, aio*. But this error hath been sufficiently refuted in the treatise of letters, chap. 6. num. 2. p. 264. where we proved that the first syllable in those words was not long by position, but by nature, and because the antients pronounced it as a diphthong. For otherwise, the vowel before *i* must be ever short, as we see in *semījacens, jurjurando, antĕjacit, bijugus*, and others.

They say likewise that the V after Q is a liquid consonant, because otherwise the first in *aqua* and the like words, would be long. But we have also given an answer to this in the same treaty, chap. 6. n. 2. p. 264.

Hitherto we have been upon the general rules, we must now come to such as are particular, and first of all mention a word concerning derivatives and compounds, because they relate to middle syllables.

OF DERIVATIVE WORDS.

We shall content ourselves with giving an Annotation in regard to derivatives, because it is very difficult to lay down any general rules about the matter. Yet we may observe that in general they follow the nature of their primitive. Thus *ănĭmare* and *ănĭmosus* have the two first short, because they come from *ănĭmus*, whose two first are short also. And on the contrary the two first in *nātūralis* are long, because it comes from *nātūra* where they are long also; and the first syllable of this word is long, because it comes from *nātum*.

Thus the second is short in *virgĭneus* and *sanguĭneus*, because of its being short in *virgĭni* and *sanguĭni*. The penultima is long in *arātrum, ambulācrum, volutābrum*, because it is the same in *arātum, ambulātum, volutātum*: but the first is common in *liquidus*, because sometimes it is derived from *liqueo*, the first short; and at other times from the verb *liquor* which hath its first syllable long, when of the third conjugation. For although we say *liquatur* the first short, we likewise say *liquitur* the first long: but the noun *liquor, oris*, liquour, hath always the first short.

Exceptions

Exceptions to the preceding rule.

There are a great many derivatives short, though their primitive be long; as *dux, dŭcis*, from *dūco*; *dĭcax* from *dico*; *sŏpor* from *sōpio*; *sŭgax* from *sūgio*; *ditio* from *dis, dĭtis*; *fĭdes* from *fīdo*, though Tully derives it from *facio, quia id fit quod dicitur*: but there is more analogy in deriving it from *fido*, just as in Greek πίςις comes from πιίθω, from whence *fido* is also derived according to Vossius. Add to these *mŏlestus* from *mōles*, and several others which may be learnt by use.

There are other derivatives LONG, though they come from short primitives; as *vōx, vōcis*, from *vŏco*; *rēx, rēgis* and *rēgula* from *rĕgo*; *rēgula* from *tĕgo*; *sēdes* from *sĕdeo*; *mācero* from *măcer*; *hūmor* from *hŭmus*; *hūmanus* from *hŏmo*; *sēcius* from *sĕcus*; *maledīcentior*, the third long, from *maledĭcus* short, and others which may be learnt by the use of authors.

But what is most remarkable on this head, is that the derivatives do not follow their primitive, when they drop or add a consonant. For as the first in *rēttulit* is long, because it reduplicates the *t*, though it comes from *rĕfero* the first short: so the following have the first short, though they come from long primitives, because they lose a consonant, as *dĭsertus* from *diſſero*, *fărina* from *fārris*; *cŭrulis* from *curro*, *ŏfella* from *ōffa*; *mămilla* from *mămma*; *tĭgillum* from *tīgnum*; *sĭgillum* from *sīgnum*; and the like.

There are even some that do not follow the analogy of their nearest primitive, but of another more distant, as *fătuus* the first short, which does not follow *fūri* the first long, but φάω, from whence cometh φημὶ, *dico*: as *lŭcerna* the first short, which does not follow the quantity of *lux*, but of τῆς λύκης, whence *lux* itself is derived by contraction instead of *lucis*: as *vădum*, the first short, which does not follow the quantity of *vādo*, the first long, but of βάδω, from whence comes *vado* as well as βαδίζω: as likewise *nŏto*, which does not follow the quantity of the supine *notum*, the first long, but of νόω, from whence comes νοίσκω, νώσκω, γινώσκω, and from thence *gnosco* or *nosco*. And so for the rest.

✢✢✢✢✢✢✢✢✢✢✢✢✢✢✢✢✢✢✢✢✢✢✢

OF COMPOUND WORDS.

The quantity of compound words is frequently known by that of the simple, and the quantity of the simple by that of the compound, which boys will easily discern, provided they are accustomed betimes to the right pronunciation of Latin. For it is the same quantity in *lĕgo* and *perlĕgo*, in *lēgi* and *perlēgi*. As also in *prŏbus* and *imprŏbus*; in *scribo* and *adscribo*; in *vĕnio, advĕnio, advĕna*: and the like.

And this quantity is still preserved, when the vowel comes to change, as in *ĕligo, sĕligo*, taken from *lĕgo*: thus from *cădo* comes *ŏccido*; and from *cædo, occīdo*: from *lædo, allīdo, collīdo*: from *audio, obēdio, obēdis*, &c.

But the following are short, though their primitive be long: the compounds of *dico* ending in *dicus*; as *causĭdicus, verĭdicus,* &c.

&c. *dejŭro* and *pejŭro*, from *jūro*: *cognĭtum* and *agnĭtum*, from *nōtum*, which are shortened by the analogy of simple polysyllables in *ĭtum*; as *tacĭtum*, *bibĭtum*, &c. *nĭhilum*, from *ne* and *hĭlum*; *innūba* and *pronūba*, from *nūbo*; but the antepenultima in *connŭbium* is common. For in Virgil we find *connūbia*, the antepenultima long: and we likewise find it short in *connŭbio*, *connŭbiis*, unless we chuse to make them trisyllables.

Connubio *jungam stabili, propriámque dicabo*, 1: Æn.

The second is long in *imbēcillus*; though *bacŭlus*, hath the first short; and the third is short in *semisŏpitus* taken from *sōpio*, the first long. The participle *ambītus* hath the penultima long, contrary to the nature of the supine *ambĭtum*, as also of these verbal nouns *ambĭtus* and *ambĭtio*. Yet Lucretius makes *ambĭtus* also short in the participle; for which reason Scioppius and Vossius look upon it as common, because this word is compounded of *ambe* and *itus*, even according to Varro; so that when the *i* is long, it comes from the diphthong *ei*, *ambītus* for *ambeītus* (as we say *ambāges* long, from *ăgo* short, because it is said for *ambeāges*:) and when it is short, it conforms to the nature of its supine *ĭtum*, as the others *adĭtus*, *exĭtus*, *inĭtus*, *obĭtus*, *subĭtus*, which are always short, because they are formed without any appearance of contraction.

Now *ambe* comes from ἄμφι, of which was first formed *ambi*, afterwards *ambe*, the φ being changed into *b*, just as in *ambo* taken from ἄμφω; as may be seen in the treatise of letters, p. 270.

RULE VI.
Of divers compounding particles.

1. A, D, E, SE, DI, *are long, when joined to verbs or nouns.*
2. *Yet* DI *is short in* dīsértus *and* dīrémi.
3. Re *is short except in* rēfert *from the noun* res.

EXAMPLES.

1. All those particles are long in composition, *ā-mitto, dēduco, ērumpo, dīripio, sēparo*, and the like.
2. *Di* is short in these, *dĭrimo, dĭrĕmi, dĭrēmptum, dĭsértus, dĭsérti*, &c.

ANNOTATION.

De sometimes preserveth its long quantity before another vowel; as

Dēest *servitio plebes hoc ignis egentis*, Stat.

Which deserves more to be remarked than followed. For in general it is either made short, *Dona dĕhinc auro gravia*, Æn. 3. or it is joined with the following vowel in the same syllable, *Deēst jam terra fugæ*, Æn. 10.

3. *Re* is short in composition, as *rĕdeo*; *rĕfero, rĭ-fers*; *rĕfert, rĕferre*, to tell or relate.

But *rēfert, it behoveth, it concerneth, it is useful*, is long, because it does not come from the particle *rĕ*, but rather from the noun *res*.

Præterea nec jam mutari pabula rēfert, Virg.

ANNOTATION.

The poets, in order to lengthen the particle *re* in composition, do sometimes reduplicate the following consonant, as *relligio, rettulit*. Though we must not imagine that they did it always, as some pretend, not considering that the chief rule of poetry is the ear, which would be sometimes offended with such reduplications. Hence in *revolvo, reverto*, the consonant is never reduplicated, because it is contrary to the nature of this V, which perhaps at that time was not a consonant.

Nor is the consonant repeated in *redeo, redoleo*, and the like, because the D is only a letter that was borrowed already to prevent the hiatus and meeting of vowels. There are also some other occasions, on which it is not practised.

Rule VII.
Of the other prepositions.

1. *The other prepositions are short except* pro.
2. *But* pro *is also short in the following compounds*; prŏfiteor, prŏtervus, prŏficiscor, prŏcella, prŏcus, prŏfanus, prŏfecto, prŏfundus, prŏnepos, prŏfari.
3. *In the following,* pro *is doubtful,* prōpello, prōpulso, prōcurro, prōpago.

Examples.

1. The other prepositions being short by nature, are also short in compound words; as *ădimo, ăbest, ăperio; cŏercuit, cŏmedo, ŏbŭmbrant, ŏmitto, ănhelat, ĭnoffensus, sŭpĕresse, sŭbeunt, pĕragit*.

We must except *pro*, which is long; *prōduco, prōfero, prōveho, prōfugio*, &c.

2. But in the words mentioned in the rule, *pro* is short, as, *prŏtervus, prŏfecto*, &c. and some others which use will shew: as likewise those words where *pro* is the Greek preposition πρὸ, which signifies *ante*,

as *prŏpheta, prŏpontis*, and the like; though sometimes the Greek *pro* is long, conforming to the Latin analogy.

3. In some compounds *pro* is common, as *prŏpello, prŏpulso, prŏpago, as*, a verb; and *prŏpāgŏ, ĭnis*, a noun; *prŏcurro, prŏcumbo, prŏfundo*, &c.

RULE VIII.

Of words compounded without a preposition.

In compound words A, O, are generally long; and E, I, U, are generally short.

But compounds formed by contraction, as also the compounds of dies, ubi, *and* ibi, *have* i *long.*

EXAMPLES.

In compound words two things may be considered, the former and the latter part. As to the latter part there is very little difficulty about it, because it is generally just as it would be out of composition. Thus the second in *dedĕcus* is short, because it comes from *dĕcus*, the first short. *Abūtor* hath the second long, because it comes from *ūtor*, the first long. But it is more difficult to know the quantity of the former part of the compound.

Nevertheless in general it may be said, that these two vowels A, O, are long; and that these other three E, I, U, are commonly short. But we must inquire into this more particularly.

A is long in the former part of the compound, as *quāre, quāpropter, quācunque, quātenus*. Yet there are some short, which may be learnt by use, as *hexămeter, catăpulta*.

E is short, whether in the first syllable, as *nĕfas, nĕfastus, nĕfandus, nĕfarius, trĕdecim, trĕcenti, nĕqueo, ĕquidem, nĕque:* or in the second, as *valĕdico, madĕfacio, tremĕfacio*, according to Virgil (though Lucretius and Catullus make E also long in this sort of words): or in the third, as *hujuscĕmodi,* &c.

The following are excepted, having the first long, *sēdecim, nēquam, nēquitia, nēquaquam, nēquicquam, nēquando,*

quando, memet, mecum, tecum, secum. As also these, which have the second long, *veneficus, videlicet.*

I is short whether in the first syllable, as *biceps, triceps, bicolor, tricolor, bivium, trivium, siquidem*: or in the second, as *agricola, aliger, artifex, causidicus, fatidicus, omnipotens, totidem, unigenitus, universus,* &c.

We must except those where the I changes in declining, as *quidam, quivis, quilibet, qualicumque, quantivis, unicuique, reipublicæ.*

Those also which come from a contraction, as *ilicet, scilicet, bigæ, quadrigæ, pridie, postridie, tibicen* for *tibiicen,* &c.

The compounds of *dies,* as *biduum, triduum, meridies*; but *quotidie* is doubtful.

The following have also I long, *triceni, tricesimus, siquis,* and *idem* masculine. As also *nimirum, ibidem, ubique, utrobique, ubivis*: but *ubicumque* is common the same as *ubi.*

O is generally long, as *alioqui, introduco, quandoque, quandocumque, utrobique,* and others.

We must except however, *hodie, quandoquidem, quoque.*

Also the compounds of two nouns, as *Timotheus, sacrosanctus,* &c.

U is short, whether in the first syllable, as *ducenti, dupondium*; or in the second, as *quadrupes, carnufex, Trojugena.*

But *genuflecto, cornupeta, usuvenit, usucapit,* are still doubtful among grammarians; though the surest way, in my opinion, is to make *u* long on those occasions, because it is an ablative that remains intire in its natural state.

ANNOTATION.

Here we may be asked whether the second is long in *paricida*; *matricida,* because we find them long in Ausonius.

Ut paricidæ *regna adimat Didic.* De Sev. Imp.

Matricida *Nero proprii vim pertulit ensis.*

Though in regard to the latter, there are some who read *matriquecida Nero,* &c.

On the contrary we find that *paricida* is short in Horace.

Telegoni juga paricidæ, Od. 29. lib. 3.

But as *paricida* is a syncope for *parenticida,* being taken not only for one who kills his father, but likewise for a person that violates

Of QUANTITY.

the duty he owes to his parents and to his country, we may say that Horace has made it short, merely by considering the dropping of the syllable, and leaving the others in their natural quantity: whereas Ausonius must have considered this word as formed by contraction, and therefore he made it long.

Of PRETERITES AND SUPINES.

RULE IX.
Of preterites of two syllables.

1. *Preterites of two syllables have the former long,* as ēgit.
2. *But the following are short,* bĭbi, fĭdi, tŭli, dĕdi, stĕti, scĭdi.

EXAMPLES.

1. Preterites of two syllables have the former long, as ēgi, vēni, vīdi, vīci.
2. Yet the preterites of the following verbs are short; *bibo, bĭbi; findo, fĭdi; fero, tŭli; do, dĕdi; sto, stĕti; scindo, scĭdi.*

ANNOTATION.

Some have been for adding *lavi* to the above verbs, because of this verse in Virgil,

Luminis effossi fluidum lāvit *inde cruorem.*

But *lavit* is there the present tense, as well as *lāvimus* in Hor. lib. 1. sat. 5. coming from *lavo, lavis*; hence we meet with *lavēre,* and in the passive *lavi, to be washed,* in Nonius.

ABSCĪDIT is long in Lucan, lib. 6.

Ille comam lævá morienti abscīdit *ephebo.*

And in Martial, lib. 4.

Abscīdit *vultus ensis uterque sacros.*

Which sheweth that this preterite was heretofore doubtful, unless we chuse to say that it comes then from *abscīdo,* compounded of *abs* and *cædo.* But this verb being obsolete, the surest way is to pronounce the above preterite short in prose, *abscĭdit.*

Now this rule of the preterites of two syllables holds also good for the plural; for *flerunt, flarunt, norunt,* and the like, have always the former long.

But we find *juverint* the former short, once in Catullus.

RULE X.
Of preterites with a reduplication.

1. *The two first syllables in preterites that have a reduplication, are short.*

2. But

2. *But the second in* pepēdi, *is long, as also in* cecīdi *from* cædo.

EXAMPLES.

1. Preterites with a reduplication have the two first syllables short, as *dĭdĭci* from *dĭsco*; *cĕcĭni* from *cano*; *tĕtĭgi* from *tango*; *cĕcĭdi* from *cado*.

2. But *pedo* hath the second in *pepēdi* long, as also *cædo* in *cecīdi*.

——— *Qui nullum fortè* cecīdit, Juv.

ANNOTATION.

In regard to the other preterites, if it be a syllable that does not depend on the increase, they follow the quantity of their present, as *cŏlo, cŏlui*, the first short.

Except *p sui*, the first short, from *p no*, whose former is long. And *gĕnui*, which followeth its old verb *gĕno*; as likewise *pŏtui*, which cometh from *pŏtis sum*.

Except also *divīsi, divīsum*, the second long, from *divĭdo*, the second short.

But if it be a syllable that depends on the increase, the rules thereof shall be given hereafter. Yet we may observe at present, that all preterites, either of two or more syllables, ending in *vi*, have ever the penultima long, as *amāvi, flēvi, quīvi, audīvi*, &c.

RULE XI.

Of supines of two syllables.

1. *All supines of two syllables are long.*
2. *Except those of* eo, reor, sino, do, ruo, sero, lino.
3. *The supines of* queo, *and* sto *are short.*
4. *The supine of* cio *is long, and that of* cieo *is short.*

EXAMPLES.

1. Supines of two syllables, as well as preterites, are long; as *nōtum* or *nōtus* from *nosco*; *vīsum*, or *vīsus* from *video*; *mōtum* from *moveo*.

2. But the six following verbs have their supines short; *eo, ĭtum*; *reor, rătus sum*; *sino, sĭtum*; *do, dătum*; *ruo* formerly had *rŭtum*, from whence comes *dirŭtum, erŭtum, obrŭtum*; *sero, sătum*; *lino, lĭtum*.

3. These two have also their supines short, *queo, quĭtum*; *sto, stătum*; but *stāturus*, though derived from thence, hath the former long.

4. *Cio*,

Of QUANTITY.

4. *Cio, cis, civi, cītum, cire,* the former long. *Cieo, cis, civi, cĭtum,* the former short.

Excītum *ruit ad portus, & littora complent,* Virg.
Bacchatur qualis commotis **excīta** *sacris,* Id.

ANNOTATION.

Of the supine STATUM.

It appears that STATUM is short by the substantive *stătus, hujus stătus;* by the adjective *stătus, a, um;* and by the verbal noun *stătio.*

Hic stătus *in cælo multos permansit in annos,* Ovid.
Musa quid à fastis non stăta *sacra petis?* Id.
Campus, & apricis stătio *gratissima mergis,* Virg.

Hence its compounds which change *a* into *i,* make this *i* short in the supine, as *præstĭtum;* hence also the verb *stătuo,* which seems to be derived from this supine, hath the first short.

Urbem quam stătuo *vestra est*——Virg.

Yet the participle *stāturus,* hath the former long.

Tunc res immenso placuit stātura *labore,* Lucan.

As also its compounds.

Constātura *fuit Megalensis purpura centum,* Mart.

And this made Priscian believe that the former in the supine *statum* was also long, though what hath been above mentioned, proves the contrary. Nevertheless we may say, I fancy, that it was heretofore common, since we still see in the compounds, that in those which retain the *a* it is long, though in such as change the *a* into *i,* it is short.

Non præstāta *sibi præstat natura, sed unus,* St. Prosper.

Whence also it comes that *stator* is short in Prudentius, and long in Ovid. And *statim,* which is derived from *stando,* according to Vossius, is long in Avienus and Alcim. Avitus, but short in Catullus, whose authority is preferable in this respect.

Verum si quid ages, stătim *jubebo,* Epigram. 33.

Of CITUM and SCITUM.

CITUM is long when it comes from *cio,* because it follows the fourth conjugation; as it is short when it comes from *cieo,* because it follows the second. But *citus* signifying *quick, lively, active,* is short; whereas for *divisus,* it is long: as *erēctum citum, erēctum non citum.* See Servius on the eighth book of the Æneis.

SCITUM is ever long, whether it comes from *scio,* or *scisco.* *Scitus,* from *scio,* signifies *handsome, pretty, well made, graceful; Scitus puer,* Ter. Coming from *scisco,* it signifies *ordained* and *decreed,* from whence we have *plebiscitum,* a decree of the people. Plautus plays with those two words in his *Pseud. act. 2. sc. 4.*

Ps. *Ecquis is homo* scitus *est?* CH. Plebiscitum *non est* scitius.

Where Lambinus is evidently mistaken, in saying that *scitum* had the first syllable long in *plebiscitum,* but that every where else it was short.

Rule XII.
Of the supines of polysyllables.

1. *The supines of polysyllables in* UTUM *are long.*
2. *As are also those in* ITUM, *when they come from a preterite in* IVI.
3. *But all others in* ITUM *are short.*

Examples.

1. The supines of polysyllables in UTUM are long, as *solūtum* from *solvo, solvi*; *indūtum*, from *induo, indui*; *argūtum* from *arguo, argui*.

2. The supines in ITUM are also long, when they come from a preterite in IVI; as *quæsītum* from *quæro, quæsīvi*; *cupītum* from *cupio, cupīvi*; *petītum* from *peto, petīvi*; *audītum* from *audio, audīvi*.

3. The supines in ITUM are short, if they do not come from a preterite in IVI; as *Tacĭtum* from *taceo, tacui*; *agnĭtum* from *agnosco, agnóvi*; *cognĭtum* from *cognosco, cognóvi*; *monĭtum* from *moneo, monŭi*.

But the penultima in *recensītum* is long, because it cometh from *censio, censivi*, and not from *censeo, censui*.

Of the INCREASE of VERBS.

Rule XIII.
The nature of the increase of verbs.

When the verb hath more syllables in the other tenses than in the second person present, this is called Increase.

Examples.

The increase of verbs is ever regulated by the second person present: so that those tenses which do not exceed this person in syllables, have no increase; as *amas, amant*; *audis, audit*. But those which exceed it by one syllable, are said to have one increase; as *amāmus, audītis*; where the second is called an increase,

crease, because the last is never counted for such. Those which exceed it by two syllables, have two increases; as *amābāmus, docēbāmus.* Those which exceed it by three, have three increases, as *amāvérĭtis,* &c.

Even the increase of the passive is regulated by the second person of the active; as *amāris,* the second is the increase. *Amābāris,* the second and third are increases, measuring them by *amas.*

In regard to verbs common and deponents, we must imagine the second person of the active, and regulate them in the same manner as the rest.

Rule XIV.
Of the increase in A.

1. *The increase in A is long.*
2. *But the verb* do *hath* da *short.*

Examples.

1. A is always long in the increase of verbs, as *exprobrāre, stābam, bibāmus, fuerāmus.*

The verb Do makes the increase DA short throughout; as *dămŭs, dăbunt, dări, dătum,* &c.

Parthe dăbis *pœnas.*

Likewise in its compounds *circúmdămus, circúmdăbunt, circúmdăre, venúndăre.*

But every where else it hath A long like the other verbs; *dābāmus, dābātur.*

——— *Quæ jam fortuna* dābātur, Virg.

Rule XV.
Of the increase in E.

1. *The increase in E is long.*
2. *Except in* beris, eram, ero, erim.
3. *Verbs of the third conjugation have it also short in the first increase of the present and preter imperfect, where there happens to be an* R *after* E.

Examples.

1. E in the increase of verbs, is also long, generally speaking, in all conjugations.

In the first; as *amēmus, amarēmus; amavērunt, amarēris* vel *amarēre, dedissēmus*.

In the second, *docēbam, docērem, docērer, docērēris*.

In the third, *degēbam, legērunt* vel *legēre, legissēmus, legēris* vel *legēre, legētur, legēmur*.

In the fourth, *audiēris* vel *audiēre, audiētur; audivērunt* vel *audivēre*, &c.

2. But it is always short in the following syllables, *beris, eram, ero, erim,* through every person, *amabĕris* vel *amabĕre; docuĕram; potĕro, potuĕro; legĕro, legĕrim, legĕris,* &c.

3. It is moreover short in verbs of the third conjugation, in the first increase of the present and preterimperfect, where there happens to be an R after E; as *legĕris* vel *legĕre,* in the present of the indicative passive; *legĕre* in the imperative passive, and the infinitive active; *legĕrem* and *legĕrer,* in the preterimperfect subjunctive, active and passive.

But it is long even in the third, when one of these conditions is wanting; as if it be in the second increase, *legerēris* vel *legerēre, legerētur,* preterimperfect passive of the subjunctive.

If it be a preterimperfect that has not an R after E; as *legēbam, legēbar,* &c.

Or if it be any other tense than a present or a preterimperfect, were it even then to have an R after E; as *legērunt* vel *legēre* in the preterite; *legēris* vel *legēre, legētur* in the future indicative. In like manner *scribēris,* and *labēris,* &c. because the *b* then belongs to the termination of the present, and not of the future in *bor*.

Scribēris *Vario fortis & hostium*. Hor.
Sic tibi cùm fluctus subterlabēre *Sicanos*. Virg.

And the like. Wherein the third conjugation conforms to the general rule.

ANNOTATION.

It seems that the penultima of the third person of the preterite in ERUNT was heretofore short, or at least common, especially in verbs of the third conjugation, and that one might say *legĕrunt,* as well as *legĕrant, legĕrent, legĕrint, legĕro,* &c. this analogy being particularly founded on the E followed by an R. Which may be further confirmed by the authority of Diomedes, who, lib. 1. hath
these

these words, *Fere in tertio ordine plerumque veteres tertiâ personâ finitivâ temporis perfecti, numeri pluralis, E mediam vocalem corripiunt, quasi legĭrunt, emĕrunt,* &c. And indeed Virgil does not scruple to make it short, not only in those verbs of the third, but likewise in others.

Matri longa decem tulĕrunt fastidia menses. Ecl. 4. 61
Miscuĕrúntque herbas, & non innoxia verba. Georg. 2. 129.
Obstupui, stetĕrúntque comæ, & vox faucibus hæsit. Æn. 2. 774.

For though some would fain read these passages with the third person plural in *erant* or *erint*; yet, as Pierius observes on the second example, the reading in *erunt* has been generally received. Besides, other poets have used it in the same manner.

Nec cithara, intonsæ profuĕrúntve comæ. Tibul.
Abiturus illuc quo priores abiĕrunt. Phædr.
Nec tua defuĕrunt verba Thalasse mihi. Mart.

We might further produce a vast number of authorities, which shew that this is not a *licentia poetica*, as they call it, but the antient analogy of the language, and that we could not condemn a person that would still chuse to follow it, though it be always better to make those words long, were it for no other reason but that the ear, the chief judge of poetry, is more accustomed to it at present.

RULE XVI.
Of the increase in I.

1. *The increase in I is generally short.*
2. *But the first increase in the fourth conjugation is long:*
3. *As also in* velim, sim, malim, nolim.
4. *All the preterites in* IVI *are long; but they make* IMUS *short.*

EXAMPLES.

1. The increase in I, generally speaking, is short, as
In the future of the first and second conjugation, *amabĭtis, docebĭtur.*
In the present of the third, *legĭmus, labĭtur, aggredĭtur.*
Even in the fourth, in the 2, 3, and 4 increase, *audimĭni, audiremĭni, audiebamĭni.*

2. But it is long in the first increase of this last conjugation, which is the most considerable in regard to verse, *audīre, mollītur, scīrent, servītum, scīmus, ībo, abībo.*

3. The following are also long, *sīmus, velīmus, nolīmus, malīmus,* with the other persons, *sītis, velītis,* &c.

4. All

4. All the preterites in IVI are long, *audīvi*. Even in the third, *petīvi, quæsīvi*.

And they all make IMUS short in the plural, *quæsivĭmus*. Even in the fourth, *audivĭmus, venĭmus*.

Observe therefore, that *venīmus* long is the present, *we are a coming*; and *venĭmus* short is the preterite, *we are come*. And so for the rest.

ANNOTATION.

In regard to the terminations of the subjunctive RIMUS and RITIS, concerning which there have been such high debates among grammarians; Diomedes, Probus, and Servius will have it that they are always long in the future, which Vossius seems to favour, though he owns that there are authorities to the contrary, as in Ovid;

——— *Obscurum nisi nox cùm fecerit orbem*;
Viderĭtis, *stellas illic ubi*, &c. 2. Metam.

Again,

Hæc ubi dixĕrĭtis, *servet sua dona rogate.*

In regard to the preterite the thing seems still more uncertain. Diomedes and Agroetius will have it short; on the contrary Probus pretends it is always long.

Hence it plainly appears that those syllables were taken by the poets sometimes one way and sometimes another, and therefore we may hold them common, since Virgil himself says in the preterite,

Namque ut supremam falsa inter gaudia noctem
Egerimus, *nosti*, &c. Æn. 6.

For it is too weak an argument to say with Servius, that he wrote thus through necessity, and by a poetic licence; just as if he who was prince of poets, and perfect master of his native language, could not find another word to make the foot suitable to his verse. And, as a proof of what I say, we find that RIS is rather short than long in the singular, as we shall shew hereafter when treating of the last syllables; which ought to be a presumption for the plural.

RULE XVII.
Of the increase in O.

The increase in O occurs but seldom, and is always long.

EXAMPLES.

The increase in O occurs in the imperative only, and is always long, as *amatōte, facitōte.*

Cúmque loqui poterit; *matrem* facitōte *salutet*. Ovid.

Rule XVIII.
Of the increase in U.

The increase in U is short; but URUS is long, as doctūrus, lectūrus.

Examples.

The increase in U is short, as *sŭmus, volŭmus*.
Nos numerus sŭmus & fruges consumere nati. Hor.
But the participle in RUS, and the future of the infinitive in RUM which is formed from thence, are long, *doctūrus, lectūrus, amatūrus, amatūrum,* &c.

✿✿✿✿✿✿✿✿✿✿✿✿✿✿✿

OF THE INCREASE OF NOUNS.
Rule XIX.
What is meant by the increase of nouns.

1. *The increase of nouns is when the genitive hath more syllables than the nominative.*
2. *The increase of the genitive always regulates the other cases.*

Examples.

1. The increase of nouns is when the other cases have more syllables than the nominative: hence if the genitive does not exceed the nominative in number of syllables, there is no increase, as *musa, musæ; dóminus, dómini:* but in the plural, of *musārum, dominōrum,* the penultima is an increase.

2. The genitive ever regulates the increase of the other cases, as *sermo, sermōnis, sermōni, sermōnem, sermōne, sermōnes, sermōnum,* where the *ō* is always long.

OF THE FIRST DECLENSION.

The first declension has no increase but in the plural, which comes within the rule we shall give lower down, after we have gone through the increases of the singular.

RULE XX.

Increase of the second declension.

1. *The increase of the second in the singular is short.*
2. *Except* Iber *and* Celtiber.

EXAMPLES.

1. Nouns of the second declension have their increase short; *gener, genĕri; puer, puĕri; prosper, prŏspĕri; vir, viri; satur, satŭri.*

2. Yet *Iber*, signifying an inhabitant of Iberia in Asia, or of Spain, makes *Ibēri* long.
As also its compound *Celtiber.*
——*Mistis hic Colchus* Ibēris. Claud.
Gallorum Celtæ, miscentes nomen Ibēris. Lucan.
Vir Celtibēris *non tacende gentibus.* Mart.

ANNOTATION.

We say likewise *Ibēres* of the third declension: but then Priscian thinks it is rather taken for the inhabitants of Iberia towards Colchis: yet from the above example it appears that Claudian did not use it in this sense; and the Greeks say Ἴβηρ, Ἴβηρος, to denote both those nations. One would think that this long increase, which has made its way into the second declension contrary to the analogy thereof, was taken from thence.

INCREASE OF THE THIRD DECLENSION.

RULE XXI.

Of the increase of Nouns in L.

1. ALIS *neuter is long.*
2. ALIS *masculine is short.*
3. ILIS *and* ULIS *are short.*
4. ELIS *and* OLIS *are long.*

EXAMPLES.

1. The neuter nouns in AL make ALIS long in the genitive, *hoc animal, animālis.*

2. The masculines make it short; *hic Asdrubal, Asdrubălis*; *hic Annibal, Annibălis*.

3. The increase of nouns in IL and UL is also short; as *vigil, vigĭlis*; *pugil, pugĭlis*; *consul, consŭlis*; *exul, exŭlis*.

4. Nouns in EL and OL make their increase long, *Daniel, Daniēlis*; *sol, sōlis*.

Rule XXII.

Increase of nouns in N and O.

The increase in 1 ANIS, 2 ENIS, *and* 3 ONIS *is long.*

4. INIS *is short*; 5. *except* IN, INIS.
6. ONIS *either in proper names or gentiles varies.*

Examples.

1. The increase *anis* is long; *Pæan, Pæānis*; *Titan, Titānis*.

2. The increase *enis* is long; *ren, rēnis*; *splen, splēnis*; *siren, sirēnis*.

3. The increase *onis* is long; *Cicero, Cicerōnis*; *sermo, sermōnis*; *Plato, Platōnis*.

4. The increase *inis* is short; *homo, homĭnis*; *virgo, virgĭnis*; *ordo, ordĭnis*; *carmen, carmĭnis*.

5. Except those in IN which make INIS long; as *Delphin, Delphīnis*; *Salamin, īnis*; *Phorcyn*, the name of a man, *Phorcȳnis*.

6. Proper names in *On* sometimes make *ŏnis* short, as *Memnon, Memnŏnis*; and sometimes they make it long, as *Helicon, Helicōnis*, in which respect we must consult the practice of authors.

Gentiles for the most part make *ŏnis* short, as *Macedo, ŏnis*; *Saxo, ŏnis*; Except *Burgundiōnes*, which is rather looked upon as long. Alvarez adds *Eburōnes*, and a few others, in respect to which we must be determined by custom. With regard to proper names, there is very little certainty about them.

Rule XXIII.
Of the increase ARIS.

1. *The increase* ARIS *in masculines is short.*
2. *(Add the neuters,* nectăris, jubăris.*)*
3. *But the neuters in* AR *make* ARIS *long.*

Examples.

1. The increase ARIS is always short, if the noun be masculine, as *Cæsar, Cæsăris; lar, lăris; mas, măris; par, păris; dispar, dispăris; impar, impăris.*

2. These two are also short, though neuters, *nectar, nectăris; jubar, jubăris;* with *bacchar, ăris* also neuter, and the penultima short.

3. The other neuters make ARIS, long, as *calcar, calcāris; laquear, laqueāris; pulvinar, pulvināris; exemplar, exemplāris.*

Rule XXIV.
Of the increase ERIS.

1. *The increase in* ERIS *from* ER *is short.*
2. *Except* Iber, crater, Ser, ver, *and* Recimer.

Examples.

1. Nouns in ER make the increase ERIS short, as *carcer, carcĕris; mulier, muliĕris; æther, æthĕris; aer, aĕris.*

2. Except the following which make it long, *Iber, Ibēris,* a native of Iberia near Colchis. And this noun is also of the second declension. See rule 19.

Crater, ēris; Ser, Sēris; the name of a people who manufactured silk.

Velleraque ut foliis depectant tenui Sēres. *Virg.*
Ver, vēris, the spring. *Recimer, ēris,* in Sidonius, a proper name; and in short all Greek nouns that have an η in the increase, as *poder, ηris; spinter, ηris,* &c.

Rule XXV.
Of the increase of nouns in OR.

1. *All the masculines in* OR *make* ORIS *long.*
2. *Except* Memor

3. *The*

Of QUANTITY.

3. *The neuters in* OR, 4. *as also Greek nouns,* 5. *and* arbor, *make* ORIS *short.*

EXAMPLES.

1. Nouns in OR, when of the masculine gender, make their increase long, as *timor, timōris; lepor, lepōris; vigor, vigōris; decor, decōris.*
——— *Indulget nata* decōri. *Ovid.*

2. Yet *memor* hath *memŏris* short, because it is an adjective, and heretofore they used to say *memŏris* and *hoc memŏre.*

3. If they be neuters, they make ORIS short, *marmor, marmŏris; æquor, æquŏris; hoc ador, adŏris.*

4. Greek nouns in OR have also a short increase, *Hector, Hectŏris; Nestor, Nestŏris; Castor, ŏris; rhetor, rhetŏris.*

5. *Arbor* hath also *arbŏris* short.

RULE XXVI.
Increase of nouns in UR.

1. *The increase of nouns in* UR *is short.*
2. *Except* fur, fūris.

EXAMPLES.

1. Nouns in UR make their increase short; whether in ORIS, as *femur, femŏris; robur, robŏris; jecur, jecŏris; ebur, ebŏris:* or in URIS, as *murmur, murmŭris; turtur, turtŭris; vultur, vultŭris; Ligur, Ligŭris.*

2. Yet *fur* makes *fūris*, long; as also *trifur, trifūris.*

ANNOTATION.

Hereto we must refer the Greek nouns in YR, as *martyr* (or *martur*) *martiris*, or *martŭros*; and the like.

RULE XXVII.
Of the increase of nouns in AS.

1. *The increase* ADIS *from* AS *is short.*
2. *Vāsis from* vas *is long.*
3. *But* măris *from* mas *is short.*

EXAMPLES.

1. Nouns in AS make the increaſe ADIS ſhort; whether they be feminines, as *Pallas, Pallădis,* the goddeſs Minerva; *lampas, ădis,* a lamp; or whether they be maſculines, as *Arcas, Arcădis,* an Arcadian; *vas, vădis,* bail, or ſurety.
2. But *vas, vāſis,* neuter, is long, *a veſſel.*
3. *Mas, măris,* is ſhort.

Rule XXVIII.
Of the increaſe ATIS.

1. *The increaſe* ATIS *from* AS *is long, except* anas, anătis.
2. *But from other nouns* ATIS *is ſhort.*

EXAMPLES.

1. The increaſe ATIS is long, when it comes from a noun in AS, as *ætas, ætātis; pietas, pietātis; dignitas, dignitātis.*
Except *anas,* which hath *anătis* ſhort.
2. The increaſe ATIS is ſhort, when it comes from other nouns than thoſe in AS, for inſtance from nouns in A, *ænigma, ænigmătis; dogma, dogmătis.* As alſo
Hepar, hepătis or *hepătos,* ſhort.

Rule XXIX.
Of the increaſe of nouns in ES.

1. *Nouns in* ES *make their increaſe ſhort.*
2. *Except* merces, quies, lócuples, hæres.
3. *And Greek nouns which make* ETIS.

EXAMPLES.

1. Nouns in ES make their increaſe ſhort, as *miles, milĭtis; Ceres, Cerĕris; pes, pĕdis; interpres, interprĕtis; ſeges, ſegĕtis.* Likewiſe *præſes, præſĭdis,* and the other derivatives of *ſedeo.*
2. Theſe are excepted, *merces, mercēdis; quies, quiētis; locuples, locuplētis; hæres, hærēdis.*

3. And

3. And Greek nouns which make ETIS, as *lebes, lebētis; tapes, tapētis; magnes, magnētis; Dares, Darētis;* and others.

ANNOTATION.

Præs makes alfo *prædīs* long, as likewife *æs, ærīs*; but this is by reafon of the diphthong. And *bes* makes *bāſſis* long by pofition.

Formerly they ufed alfo to fay *manſues, ētis,* long; as likewife *inquies, ētis.* But at prefent we fay rather *manſu̇tus, i, inquiētus, i*; where the penultima ftill remains long, becaufe of their original.

RULE XXX.
Of the increafe of nouns in IS.

1. *The increafe of nouns in* IS *is ſhort.*
2. *Except* Quiris, Samnis, glis, lis, Dis.

EXAMPLES.

1. The increafe of nouns in IS is ſhort, as *pulvis, pulverĭs; ſanguis, ſanguĭnis; Charis, Charĭtis,* uſual in the plural; *Charĭtes,* the graces.
2. In the following it is long. *Quiris, Quirītis; Samnis, Samnītis; glis, glīris; lis, lītis; Dis, Dītis.*

RULE XXXI.
Of the increafe of nouns in OS.

1. *The increafe of nouns in* OS *is long.*
2. *Except* bos, compos, *and* impos.

EXAMPLES.

1. The increafe of nouns in OS is long, as *os, ōris; dos, dōtis; cuſtos, cuſtōdis; nepos, nepōtis.*

Greek nouns in OS have alſo a long increaſe, as *rinoceros, ōtis;* likewife *Tros, Trōis; heros, herōis; Minos, Minōis,* though followed by a vowel, becaufe in Greek they are written with an ω.

2. Theſe are ſhort, *bos, bŏvis; compos, compŏtis; impos, impŏtis.*

RULE XXXII.
Of the increafe of nouns in US.

1. *Nouns in* US *have their increaſe ſhort.*
2. *Except the comparatives in* US.

3. *And nouns that make the genitive in* URIS, UDIS, *and* UTIS.

4. *But* pecus *makes* pecŭdis *short; as* intercus, intercŭtis.

Examples.

1. Nouns ending in US have their increase short, as *munus, munĕris; corpus, corpŏris; lepus, lepŏris; tripus, tripŏdis; decus, ŏris.*

2. The comparatives in US make their increase long, as *melius, meliōris; majus, majōris;* because they borrow it of the masculine, as *major, majōris,* &c.

3. Nouns whose genitive is in URIS, UDIS, or UTIS, make their increase long, as *jus, jūris; tellus, tellūris; incus, incūdis; virtus, virtūtis; salus, salūtis,* &c.

4. These are excepted, *pecus, pecŭdis,* a sheep, a flock; *intercus, intercŭtis,* a dropsy.

Annotation.

This shews, as we have elsewhere observed, that they come rather from *pecudis, hujus pecudis; intercutis, hujus intercutis,* than from *pecus* or *intercus,* which in all likelihood would follow the analogy of the other nouns in *us,* that have *ūtis* long. See vol. i. p. 85, 86. and p. 167. col. 2.

Ligŭris, the name of a people, is also short; which shews that it comes rather from *Ligur,* as Verepeus has given it, than from *Ligus.*

The names of places in US of Greek original make UNTIS, and of course are long by position, as *Opus, Opuntis,* the name of a town, and such like.

Rule XXXIII.

The increase of nouns ending in S with another consonant.

1. *Nouns ending in S with another consonant make their increase short.*

2. *Except* gryps, Cyclops, hydrops, plebs, *and* Cercops.

Examples.

1. The increase of nouns ending in S, with another consonant, is short; as *cælebs, cælĭbis; hyems, hyĕmis, Dolops, Dolŏpis; inops, inŏpis; auceps, aucŭpis;*

2. But

Of QUANTITY.

2. But these have their increase long; *gryps, grȳphis*; *Cyclops, Cyclōpis*; *hydrops, hydrōpis*, whence comes *hydrōpicus*; *plebs, plēbis*; *Cercops, Cercōpis*, the name of a people, who for their malice were metamorphosed into apes, Ovid. Metam.

RULE XXXIV.
Of the noun *caput* and its compounds.

The noun caput *and its compounds, have a short increase.*

EXAMPLES.

Caput, and all its compounds are short in their increase through every case singular and plural, *capĭtis, capĭte, capĭta, capĭtĭbus*; *sinciput, sincĭpĭtis*; *ŏcciput, occĭpĭtis*; *anceps, ancĭpĭtis*; *biceps, bicĭpĭtis.*

RULE XXXV.
Of the nouns in X which form their genitive in GIS.

1. *The increase in* GIS *is short.*
2. *Except* frūgis, lēgis, rēgis.

EXAMPLES.

1. Nouns in X, whose genitive is in GIS, make their increase short, as *Allobrox, Allobrŏgis*; *conjux, conjŭgis*; *remex, remĭgis*; *Phryx, Phrўgis.*

2. The following are excepted, *frux, frūgis*; *rex, rēgis*; as also *lex, lēgis*: but its compounds vary; *aquilex, aquilĕgis*, short; *Lelex, Lelĕgis*, short, the name of a people; *exlex, exlēgis*, an outlaw.

RULE XXXVI.
Of the increase of nouns in AX.

1. *The increase* ACIS *from* AX *is long.*
2. *Except* abax, smilax, climax, storax, fax.

EXAMPLES.

1. Nouns in AX make their increase long, as *pax, pācis*; *ferax, ferācis*; *fornax, fornācis.*

2. These are excepted, *abax, abăcis*; *smilax, smilăcis*, a yew tree; *climax, climăcis*; *storax* or *styrax, styrăcis*; *fax, făcis.*

Add to these *Arctophylax, ăcis,* a heavenly constellation, and a few more Greek names.

RULE XXXVII.
Of the increase of nouns in EX.

1. *The increase of nouns in* EX *is short.*
2. *Except* halex, vervex, *and* fex.

EXAMPLES.

1. All nouns in EX have their increase short, as *nex, něcis; prex, prěcis; frutex, frutĭcis; vertex, vertĭcis.*

2. These three excepted, *halex, halēcis; vervex, vervēcis; fex, fēcis.*

ANNOTATION.

To these some are for adding *vibex*. But we chuse rather to say *vibix, īcis,* according as we have marked it in the genders, vol. i, p. 55. and then it will follow the next rule.

RULE XXXVIII.
Of the increase of nouns in IX.

1. *Nouns in* IX, ICIS, *have their increase long;*
2. *Except* filix, pix, vix, larix, calix, eryx, varix, fornix, salix;
3. *To which add* nix, nĭvis.

EXAMPLES.

1. Nouns in IX make their increase in ICIS long; as *radix, radīcis; felix, felīcis; victrix, victrīcis; vibix, vibīcis.*

2. The following are excepted, *filix, filĭcis; pix, pĭcis; vix, vĭcis,* in the plural *vĭces; larix, larĭcis; calix, calĭcis; erix, erĭcis; varix, varĭcis; fornix, fornĭcis; salix, salĭcis.*

3. *Nix* likewise makes *nĭvis* short.

RULE XXXIX.
Of the increase OCIS.

1. *Nouns in* OX *make the increase* ōcis *long;*
2. *Except* præcox, *and* Cappadox.

EXAMPLES.

1. The increase OCIS from nouns in OX is long; as *vox, vōcis; ferox, ferōcis; velox, velōcis.*

Of QUANTITY.

2. These are excepted; *præcox, præcŏcis*; *Cappadox, Cappadŏcis*.

RULE XL.
Of the increase UCIS.

1. *The increase* UCIS *from* UX *is short.*
2. *Except* lux, *and* Pollux.

EXAMPLES.

1. *Nouns in* UX *make their increase* UCIS *short*; as *dux, dŭcis; redux, redŭcis; crux, crŭcis; nux, nŭcis; trux, trŭcis.*

2. The following are excepted; *lux, lūcis; Pollux, Pollūcis.*

Talis Amiclæi domitus Pollūcis *habenis.* Virg.

ANNOTATION.

In these latter rules, as in a great many others, we have omitted several words, that are not only more difficult to learn, but likewise less useful, since they occur but seldom, and it will be sufficient to observe them in the use of authors.

Such are *atrax, atax, colax, panax,* Pharnax, Syphax, which make their increase ACIS short. Such are also *cilix, coxendix, histrix, natrix, onyx, sardonyx,* which shorten ICIS, &c.

Of the INCREASE of the other DECLENSIONS.

The other two declensions, as well as the first, have no increase, except in the plural. This should be referred to the following rule, which likewise includes the second and third declensions for the increase belonging to this number.

RULE XLI.
Of the increase of the plural.

1. *In the plural increase,* I *and* U *are short;*
2. *But* A, E, O, *are long.*

EXAMPLES.

The plural increase is when the other cases exceed the nominative plural (which always depends on the genitive singular) in number of syllables.

1. And then it makes I and U short; as *sermones, sermonĭbus; vites, vitĭbus; manus, manŭum; portus, portŭum, portŭbus.*

2. But

2. But A, E, O, are long; as *musæ, musārum; res, rērum, rēbus; mēdici, medicōrum; duo, duōrum.*

ANNOTATION.

Here we are to observe that there is a singular increase even in the plural; as in this word *sermonibus*, the second is a singular increase, and is long, because it is ruled by the genitive *sermōnis*. But the penultima is a plural increase, because it has more syllables than this same genitive, and therefore belongs to this rule of plurals.

The former is long in *bŭbus* as well as in *bōbus*, because it is only a syncope for *bovibus*; which happens also to *būcula* for *bovīcula*. True it is that Ausonius has made the former short in *bŭbus*, considering it as in the singular increase of *bos, bŏvis*; but the authority of Horace, Ovid, and Lucretius is preferable to his.

Paterna rura bōbus *exercet suis*, Epod. 2.
Non profecturis littora bōbus *aras.* Ovid.

OF THE LAST SYLLABLE.

Rule XLII.

A final.

1. A *at the end of words is long*;
2. *Except* ită, eiă, quiă, pută;
3. *But it is short at the end of nouns*;
4. *Except the ablative case.*
5. *And the vocative of Greek nouns in* AS.

Examples.

1. A is long at the end of words, as *amā, pugnā, intereā, ultrā, memorā, trigintā*, and the like.

2. There are four adverbs that have the last short; *ită, eiă, quiă, pută*, for *videlicet*.

———— Eiă *per ipsum*;
Scande age.————Val. Flaccus.
Hoc pută *non justum est, illud male, rectius istud.*
Persius, sat. 4.

3. The nouns are short through all their cases ending in A, except the ablative.

The Nomin. Formă *bonum fragile est.* Ovid.
The Accusat. Hectoră *donavit Priamo.* Ovid.
The Vocat. Musă *mihi causas* memorā. Virg.

Of QUANTITY.

The Plural. Déderas promissā *parenti.* Virg.

4. The ablative is long.

Anchora de prorā *jacitur.* Virg.

5. The vocative in A of Greek nouns in AS is also long.

Quid miserum Æneā *laceras?* Virg.

But from the other terminations it is short, as we shall see presently.

ANNOTATION.

Of the vocative ending in A.

The vocative of Greek nouns in ES is short when it ends in A; as *Anchisă, Thyestă, Orestă,* &c. because then this case can be only of the Latin declension. But these same nouns having E in the vocative, make it long, because this is a Greek case and follows the Greek declension which has an *n*.

The Æolians likewise gave the termination A to a great many nouns that were in AS in the common language, as *Mida* for *Midas, Hyla* for *Hylas,* &c. and then their vocative may be short. Hence it is that Virgil in the very same verse has made this last syllable both long and short in the vocative.

Clamassent, ut littus Hylā, Hylă *omne sonaret.* Ecl. 6.

Unless we chuse to attribute the length of one to the cæsura, and the shortness of the other to the position of the next vowel.

Of some adverbs in A.

ANTEA is long in Catullus and Horace:

Petti, nihil me, sicut antea juvat,
Scribere Versiculos. Epod. 11.

CONTRA is long in Virgil.

Contrā *non ulla est oleis cultura: neque illæ.*

We find it short in Ausonius, and in Manilius who was his contemporary. But in regard to the verse, which the Jesuits Alvarez and Ricciolius quote from Valerius Flaccus to authorize this quantity;

Contrāque *Lethæi quassare silentia rami;*

It proves nothing, because the passage is corrupted, and the right reading is this:

Contrā *Tartareis Colchis spumare venenis,*
Cunctāque *Lethæi quassare silentia rami*
Perstat.

POSTEA an adverb is long, according to G. Fabricius in his treatise of poetry, as Vossius observeth. Which appears likewise by this iambic of Plautus.

Si autoritatem posteā *defugeris,* In Pænul. act. 1. sc. 1.

We might also prove it to be short by this verse of Ovid, 1. Fast.

Posteă *mirabar cur non sine litibus esset.*

But it seems we ought to read it in two words, *post ea,* as Vossius says, because being an adverb it is long every where else.

POSTILLA

POSTILLA is also long in Ennius and in Propertius, l. 1. El. 15.
Hyſipile nullos poſtillā *ſenſit amores.*

PUTA for *videlicet*, of which ſome have doubted, is ſhort, as appeareth by Servius on the 2. Æn. where obſerving that the adverbs in A are reckoned long, particularly excepts *pută* and *ită.* This is further confirmed by the above quoted verſe out of Perſius, *Hoc pută,* &c. as Priſcian likewiſe quotes it, lib. 15. and as Caſaubon declares he found it in MSS, though ſome editions read *puto.* With reſpect to the paſſage of Martial which is quoted from lib. 3. epigram. 29. *Eſſe putā ſolum,* &c. it is plain that *puta* is there or *cenſe* or *crede,* and is not then an adverb.

ULTRA is long in Horace :
 Ultrā *quam ſatis eſt virtutem ſi petat ipſam.*
In Virgil.
 Quos alios muros quæ jam ultrā *mænia habetis?*
As likewiſe in Juvenal, Perſius and others,
And in vain does Erythræus quote Serenus to make it ſhort.
 Curāque nil prodeſt, nec ducitur ultrā *cicatrix,*
ſince the beſt copies have *ulla.*

Of the nouns in GINTA.

The nouns in GINTA are eſteemed doubtful by ſome, becauſe they are found ſhort in the old poets, as in Lucilius, and in thoſe of a later date, as Auſonius, Manilius and others: but thoſe of the intermediate time, who flouriſhed during the purity of the language, always made them long.
 Trigintā *capitum fœtus enixa jacebit.* Virg.
And the ſureſt way is to follow this quantity. For as to the paſſages they quote from Martial to prove their being ſhort, Voſſius ſhews that they are corrupted.

RULE XLIII.
E Final.

1. E *at the end of words is ſhort;*
2. *But at the end of Greek nouns it is long;*
3. *And at the end of nouns of the 5th declenſion;*
4. *And of* ohē, fermē, ferē:
5. *And of all adverbs formed of* US.
6. *But* benĕ, malĕ, infernĕ, ſupernĕ, *are ſhort.*
7. *The imperative of the ſecond conjugation is long:*
8. *As are alſo theſe monoſyllables* mē, nē, sē, tē.

EXAMPLES.

1. E is ſhort at the end of words, as *furiosĕ, utilĕ, partĕ, illĕ, frangerĕ, docerĕ, ſinĕ, mentĕ, panĕ, Achillĕ.*
              Haud

Haud equidem finē mentē *reor,* finē numinē *divum Adsumus.* Virg.

2. Greek nouns are long in whatever cafe they happen to be, when they are written with an *n*, according to what hath been already observed, p. 329, as *Lethē, Anchisē, Cetē, Molē, Tempē,* &c.

ANNOTATION.

Achillé and *Herculé* are found fometimes fhort:

Quique tuas præavus fregit Achillē *domos.* Propert.

But then we may fay it is rather according to the Latin declenfion, than the analogy of the Greek. Which frequently happens to nouns that follow the third declenfion in Latin.

3. E is long at the end of words of the fifth declenfion; as, *rē, diē, requiē;* alfo *hodiē, poftridiē,* and the like, taken from *dies.*

Noɛ̃te diēque *fuum geftare in pectore teftem.* Juven.
Famē is alfo long, and ought to be placed here, becaufe it is really an ablative of the fifth declenfion, which came from *fames, famei,* juft like *plebes, plebei,* in Livy and Salluft.

4. Thefe words are long in the laft fyllable, *fermē, ferē, obē.*

Mobilis & varia eft fermē *natura malorum.* Juven.
Jamque ferē *ficco fubductæ littore puppes.* Virg.
Importunus amat laudari, donec ohē *jam.* Hor.

5. Adverbs formed of nouns of the fecond declenfion have alfo E long; as *indignē, præcipuē, placidē, minimē, fummē, valdē* (for *validē*) *fanctē, purē, fanē,* &c.

6. Except *benĕ* and *malĕ,* which are fhort:

Nil benĕ *cum facias, facis attamen omnia belle.* Mart.
Infernĕ and *fupernĕ* ought alfo to be excepted as fhort, unlefs we had authority for the contrary, which is not perhaps to be found. For thus it is in Lucretius:

Terra fupernĕ *tremit, magnis concuffa ruinis.*
Upon which Lambinus fays: *Millies jam dixi ultimam fyllabam adverbii* SUPERNE, *brevem effe: ituque eos errare qui hoc loco & fimilibus legi volunt* SUPERNA. Which neither Defpauter, nor Alvarez, nor Ricciolius have obferved.

7. The

7. The imperatives of the second conjugation have also E long, as *monē, vidē, habē, docē.*

The other imperatives are short. *Vidĕ* and *valĕ* are also sometimes short. And *cavĕ* is but seldom long.

Vadĕ, valĕ, cavĕ ne titubes, mandatāque frangas. Hor.
Idque, quod ignoti faciunt, valĕ dicere saltem. Ovid.

8. Monosyllables make E long, as *mē, nē, sē, tē.*

ANNOTATION.

From this rule of monosyllables we must except the enclitics *que, ne, ve,* and these other particles *ce, te,* or *pte,* as *tuquĕ, biccĕ, tuaptĕ,* &c. because they are joined in such a manner to the other words, that they form but one, and are no longer considered as separate monosyllables.

In regard to imperatives as well of this as of the precedent rule, we may observe with Vossius, that the reason of their being long, is because they are formed by contraction. For *ama,* he says, comes from *amae* ; just as the Greeks say ἄμαι, ἄμα, *mete.* And thus *doceo* should have *docee,* the last short, of which they have formed by contraction *docē,* the last long ; just as in Greek we say δόκεε, δόκει. And though there are some imperatives of the second also short, this is because those verbs were heretofore of the second and third conjugation, as some of them are still ; for we say *fulgeo, es,* and *fulgo, is* ; *tergeo, es,* and *tergo, is,* &c. And hence it is that we find *respondĕ* and *salvĕ* short in Martial.

Si quando veniet ? dicet : respondē*, poeta——Exierat.*
Lector salvĕ*. Taces, dissimulasque ? Vale.* Idem.

Though all these verbs are rather long or short, according to the conjugation in which they have continued.

RULE XLIV.
I Final.

1. I *at the end of words is long.*
2. *But* mihĭ, tibĭ, cuĭ, sibĭ, ubĭ, ibĭ, *are doubtful.*
3. Nisĭ *and* quasĭ, *are short ;*
4. *As are also the neuter nominatives,*
5. *With the Greek datives,*
6. *And Greek vocatives.*

EXAMPLES.

1. I at the end of words is long, as *oculī, Mercurī, classī.*

Dum spectant læsos oculī, *læduntur & ipsī.* Ovid.

2. The

2. The following have I either long or short, *mĭhī*, *tĭbī*, *cŭī*, *sĭbī*, *ŭbī*, *ĭbī*.

3. And these have it short, *nĭsĭ*, *quăsĭ*.

4. As also the neuters in I or Y, *Æpў*, *Molў*, *gummĭ*, *sinapĭ*, *hydromelĭ*, &c. To which we may join these Greek nouns, as *Mesorĭ*, *Paynĭ*, *Phaotĭ*, *Pharmutĭ*, *Tybĭ*, &c.

5. The datives of Greek nouns are also short, as *Mĭnŏĭdĭ*, *Palladĭ*, *Thetĭdĭ*, *Parĭdĭ*, *Tindarĭdĭ*, *Phillĭdĭ*, &c.

6. As also their vocatives, whether in I or Y; as *Adonĭ*, *Alexĭ*, *Amarillĭ*, *Briseĭ*, *Cecropĭ*, *Chelў*, *Daphnĭ*, *Inachĭ*, *Lycaonĭ*, *Parĭ*, *Phyllĭ*, *Thaĭ*, *Tyndarĭ*, whereto we ought likewise to refer all the patronymics in IS, which make IDOS.

ANNOTATION.

Utī is long, as also *velutī*.

> *Namque videbat* utī *bellantes Pergama circum.* Virg.
> *Improvisum aspris* velutī *qui sentibus anguem.* Id.

But *sicutĭ* is short in Lucretius and elsewhere, and perhaps is not to be found of a different quantity, though grammarians mark it as common. *Utique* is short. *Ibīdem, ubīque* and *ubīvis* are long, though they come from *ibi* and *ubi* common. Some have fancied them doubtful because of this verse of Horace.

> *Non* ubĭ *vis coramve quibuslibet. In medio qui;*

But we must pronounce it in two words *ubi vis*, or according to others *ublǐ sis*. *Sicubī*, though common, is generally long.

Nisi and *quasi* which I have marked as short, are reckoned common by some, because there are some authorities for it in the latter poets, and in Lucretius, who says:

> *Et devicta* quasī *cogantur ferre patique.*

But the best authors constantly make them short.

> *Quoque sit armento, veri* quasĭ *nescia quæri.* Ovid.
> *Nihil hic* nisĭ *carmina desunt.* Virg.

As for the Greek nouns, we are to observe that these are sometimes found also long, as *Orestī*, *Pyladī*, and the like datives, because this termination is then intirely Latin, those cases in Greek being Ὀρέστη, Πυλάδη, which are of the first declension of simples. Nor can we even shorten the datives that arise from contraction, as *Demostheni*, Δημοσθένει, *metamorphosi*, μεταμορφώσει, because this would be contrary to the general rule. And if we would also refer *Oresti* to this rule of contraction, we should find more reason to make it long, because it will come from Ὀρέστει, as *Socrati* from Σωκράτει; and so for the rest.

RULE

RULE XLV.
O Final.

1. O *at the end of words is doubtful:*
2. *But the datives and ablatives in* O *are long.*
3. O *in these words is short:* imŏ, duŏ, sciŏ, modŏ, citŏ. 4. *In* eō *it is long;*
5. *As also in monosyllables.*
6. *And in adverbs derived from nouns.*

EXAMPLES.

1. O at the end of words is sometimes long, and sometimes short; as *leŏ, quandŏ, nolŏ.*

2. The datives and ablatives in O are long, *somnō, ventō, odiō.*
    Nutritur ventō, ventō restinguitur ignis. Ovid.

3. O is short in the following words, *imŏ, duŏ, sciŏ,* and its compound *nesciŏ, modŏ,* with its compounds *quomodŏ, dummodŏ,* &c. *citŏ.* To which we may add *egŏ, cedŏ* (for *dic*) *illicŏ*, which are more usually short.

4. *Eō* is long, and so are its compounds, *adeō, ideō.*
    Ibit eō, quô vis, zonam qui perdidit, inquit. Hor.

5. Monosyllables are long, *dō, stō, prō.*
    Jam jam efficaci dō manus scientiæ. Hor.

6. Adverbs derived from nouns are long, because properly speaking they are only ablatives, as *subitō, meritō, multō, falsō, primō, eō, verō. Ergō* is always long, because it comes from ἔργω: but *serŏ* is doubtful.

ANNOTATION.

We find *modō* long in Catullus.
   Hoc quid putemus esse? qui modō scurra.

Serŏ being doubtful follows the general rule. For though it is more frequently short, yet we meet with it also long.
   Heu serō revocatur amor, serōque juventa. Tibul.

Hereto some add *sedulo, crebro,* and *mutuo;* but they are more commonly long.

Profectō is also long, because it is derived from *pro facto,* by changing A into E, according to what has been said, p. 252. Yet we find it also short in Terentianus Maurus.

Now the reason why O is not only sometimes long, and sometimes short, but also generally common of its nature, is because it answers to these two Greek vowels ο and ω, in imitation of which the Latins pronounced several of their words. And thence also
it

it comes that O in Latin is oftener long than short. For in the first place the antients made the verbs almost always long, because in Greek it is an ω. And Corradus excepts from this rule no more than *scio* and *nescio*, which Victorinus asserts to have been made short, to distinguish them from the datives and ablatives; *scio* from *scius*, whence cometh *sciolus*; and *nescio* from *nescius*. Vossius however adds *cedo* for *dic*.

Facti crimen habet. Cedŏ, *fi conata peregit*. Juven.

and he shews that though the most eminent poets make O more usually long in the other verbs, yet those who flourished somewhat later, generally made it short, as Martial.

Nec volŏ *boletos* : *oftrea* nolŏ : *tace*.

Secondly, the datives and ablatives are always long for the same reason; Κύρω, ἔργω, &c.

Thirdly, all the other cases which in Greek end with an ω, are long in Latin, as *Alectō, Echō, Sapphō*, hujus *Androgeō*, hunc *Athō*, &c. But those which end with a ν after ω, are reckoned common in Latin, as Πλάτων, *Plato*; δράκων, *draco*; though Corradus will still have them to be only long, as indeed Victorinus affirms that they were always reckoned by the antients.

Fourthly, the gerunds in Do, according to the same Corradus, and Valerius Probus, ought always to be long. And the reason is because they are only nouns, as we have shewn in the remarks on syntax, book 6. And though they may be sometimes found short in Tibullus, Juvenal, and Ovid; yet they are not so in Virgil, who constantly makes them long.

Fifthly, the interjection O is long by nature, because it is an ω.

O lux Dardaniæ, spes ō fidissima Teucrûm, Virg.

And if it be ever short, it is merely by position, that is because of the vowel that follows it.

Te Coridon ŏ Alexi, Idem.

which we shall account for hereafter, when we come to speak of the manner of scanning verses.

Rule XLVI.
U Final.

Words ending in U *are long, as* vultū.

Examples.

U is long at the end of words, *vultū, cornū, promptū, Panthū*.

*Tantum ne pateas verbis simulator in ipsis
Effice, nec* vultū *destrue dicta tuo*.

Annotation.

Words ending in *u* are long, because this Latin *u* was pronounced with a full sound, like the French diphthong *ou*, as we have shewn in the treatise of letters, book 9. c. 4. n. 2. p. 255. But those which terminate in Y (which was pronounced like the French

French *u*,) are short, *Moly, Tiphy*, &c. Yet *indŭ*, which was used for *in*, and *penŭ* for *non*, are short. They are both still to be seen in Lucretius.

Rule XLVII.
B and C Final.

1. B *at the end of words is short:*
2. C *is long.*
3. *Except* něc *and* doněc, *which are short;*
4. *Except also* făc *and* hĭc *the pronoun, which are doubtful.*

Examples.

1. B at the end of words is short, as *ăb, ŏb, sŭb.*
———*puppi sic fatur* ăb *alta*. Virg.
2. C is long, as *āc, hīc* the adverb, *hōc, dūc, sīc.*
Sīc *oculos*, sīc *ille manus*, sīc *ora ferebat*. Virg.
3. These two are short, *něc, doněc:*
Doněc *eris felix, multos numerabis amicos.* Ovid.
4. The following are doubtful; *făc,* the imperative of *facio,* and *hĭc,* the pronoun.
Hic vir hĭc *est, tibi quem promitti sæpius audis.* Æn. 6.
Hic gladio fidens, hīc *acer & arduus hasta.* Æn. 12.

Annotation.

The adverb *hic* is long, because it was pronounced almost like *ei*, says Vossius, whence it is that in antient marbles, we often find it written thus, HEIC. But as for the pronoun *hic*, Voss. 2. *de arte Gram. c.* 29. says *it is always short by nature,* and that whenever we find it long, it is because the *c* had the full sound of a double letter; for which he has the authority of Victorinus, Probus, and Capella. To understand this, it must be observed, agreeably to what Priscian says, lib. 13. that this pronoun *hic, hæc, hoc,* frequently assumed the particle *ce, hicce, hæcce, hocce,* and that this final *e* being lost by synalepha, there remained only two *cc, hicc, hæcc, hocc,* which is also confirmed by Longus in his orthography. Be that as it may, there is no doubt but this pronoun is much oftener long than short. Horace constantly makes it long; and for twice that we find it short in Virgil, *Solus hic inflexit sensus,* Æn. 4. with the other above quoted of the 6th, it is above fifteen times long, whether he wrote it with two *cc,* or otherwise. The same may be said also of *hoc,* which is always long in the best authors.

But take notice that the verse which Smetius quotes on this occasion, from Æn. 11.

Hic annis gravis, atque animi maturus Aletes,

proves nothing, because *hic* is there an adverb only.

Fac

Fac, the imperative of *facio*, is always long by nature.
    Hoc fac *Armenios* ——— Ovid.
And if we sometimes find it short, it is because they used formerly to write *face*, according to Vossius after Julius Scaliger and Verulen, as in the same poet,
    Jane face *æternos pacem, pacisque ministros,*
though Giffanius is of a contrary opinion.

RULE XLVIII.
D and L final.

1. D *is short at the end of the words;*
2. *As likewise* L,   3. *Except* nil, sol, sal;
4. *And Hebrew words, as* Daniel.

EXAMPLES.

1. D is short at the end of words, as *ăd, sĕd, quidquĭd, istŭd.*

2. Words that terminate in L are also short, as *tribunăl, fĕl, mĕl, semĕl, pervigĭl, pŏl, procŭl.*

3. The following are excepted, *nīl, sōl, sāl.*

4. Hebrew names are also excepted, as *Daniēl, Michaēl, Michēl, Raphaēl,* &c.

ANNOTATION.

Nil is long, because it is a contraction for *nihil*, which is short, according to the general rule;
    De nihilo nihīl, *in nihilum* nīl *posse reverti*. Persius.
The following verse of Ovid is brought against us.
    Morte nihīl *opus est, nihil Icariotide tela.*
But then the reason of the last of *nihil* being long in the second foot, is because of the cæsura.

Of words ending in M.

The Greeks, as we have observed, p. 267. did not end any word at all with this letter, but it was a common termination with the Latins. Yet as it is always cut off in verse before a vowel, there is no necessity for giving any rule about it. However we may observe that the antients let it stand and made it short.
    Vomerĕm *atque locis avertit feminis ictum,* Lucr.
And if we find it sometimes short, this is in virtue of the cæsura, as
    Hæc eadēm *ante illam, impune & Lesbia fecit.* Propert.
In composition it is also short,
    Quo te circŭmagas. Juven.
Concerning which see what is said in the third section of this book, c. 3. n. 1. speaking of the ecthlipsis.

RULE XLIX.
N Final.

1. N *is long at the end of words:*
2. *Except* an, in, *and* dein;
3. *Except also nouns in* EN *making* inis;
4. *As likewise* tamen *and* viden'.

EXAMPLES.

1. N is long at the end of words; as *Dān, liēn, ēn, quīn, sīn.*

Also in Greek words masculine and feminine, as *Titān, Syrēn, Salamīn, Phorcȳn,*

Likewise *Actēōn, Corydōn,* and the like, which have ω.

And Greek accusatives of the first declension, as *Æneān, Anchisēn, Calliopēn.*

As well as the genitives plural, as *Cimmerōn,* because it is also an ω.

2. In the following N is short, *ăn, ĭn*; likewise *forsăn,* and *forsĭtăn,* compounded of *ăn.*

Also *deĭn, proĭn,* for *deinde, proinde.*

3. Nouns in EN, that make INIS, are also short, as *nomĕn, nomĭnis ; pectĕn, pectĭnis ; tibicĕn, tibicĭnis.*

4. As likewise *tamĕn,* and its compound *attamĕn.*

Also *vidĕn',* and such like; as *nostĭn', aĭn', satĭn', egŏn', nemŏn',* which are said by apocope instead of *vidésne, nemóne?* &c.

ANNOTATION.

Hereto we may add the Greek nouns in *on,* which are of the second declension in Latin, as *Ilion,* and the like, which in Greek have an omicron. As also the accusative of nouns whose nominative is short; as *Maiăn, Eginăn, Alexĭn, Thetĭn, Itĭn, Scorpĭn;* and the datives plural in *in,* as *Arcasĭn.*

RULE L.
R Final.

1. R *at the end of words is short:*
2. *But Greek nouns in* ER, *that increase in the genitive, are long;*
3. *Add to these* cūr, fūr, lār, fār, vēr, hīr, nār,
4. *Also* pār, *and its compounds, as* dispār.

EXAM-

Of QUANTITY.

EXAMPLES.

1. R is short at the end of words, as *Cæsăr, calcăr, imbĕr, diffĕr, lintĕr, vĭr, gladiatŏr, robŭr*.

2. Greek nouns in ER are long, when they increase in the genitive; whether this increase be short, as *aēr, æthēr, ĕris*; or whether it be long as *Cratēr, gazēr, podēr, Recimēr, spintēr, ēris*. As also *Ibēr*, though its compound *Celtibĕr* is short, conforming thus to the Latin analogy.

Ducit ad auriferas quòd me Salo Celtibĕr *oras*. Mart. Despauter mentions this noun as doubful, but without authority. Its increase indeed is long, as may be seen above, rule 20. p. 318.

The other Greek nouns that have no increase in the genitive, are short, as *patĕr, matĕr*.

3. The following words are also long, *cūr, fūr, lūr, fūr, bīr, nār*, and *vēr*, which last may be ranked among the Greek nouns, since it comes from ἴαρ, ἴρ, as we have already observed.

4. *Par* and its compounds are also long, *compār, dispār, impār, suppār*, &c.

Ludere pār impār, *equitare in arundine longa*. Hor.

ANNOTATION.

Vir is oftener short. Yet we find it long in this verse of Ovid,
De grege nunc tibi vīr *& de grege natus habendus*. Ovid.
Cor is also doubtful according to Aldus,
Molle cŏr *ad timidas sic habet ille preces*. Ovid.
Molle meum levibus cōr *est violabile telis*. Id.
Unless the passage be corrupted; for every where else it is short.
Greek nouns in OR are always short, though in their own language they have an ω, as *Hectŏr, Nestŏr*, &c. But it is not the same in regard to the termination ON, which continues always long when it comes from ω, as we have shewn in the precedent rule. For which this reason may be given, according to Camerius, that the termination ON is intirely Greek, and therefore retains the analogy and quantity of the Greek, otherwise, to latinize it, we should be obliged to change it into O, as *Plato, Cicero*, &c. whereas the termination OR being also Latin, nouns borrowed from the Greek conform to it intirely without any alteration, and therefore are of the same nature and quantity as the Latin.

Rule LI.
AS final.

1. AS *at the end of words is long.*
2. *But* AS, ADIS, *is short.*
3. *Join thereto the Greek accusative.*
4. *With the nominative* anăs.

Examples.

1. AS at the end of words is long, as *ætās, Thomās, Æneās, fās, nefās*; *Pallās, antis*; *Adamās, antis.*

2. Greek nouns in AS, which make the genitive in ADIS, are short, as *Arcăs, Arcădis*; *lampăs, lampădis*; *Pallăs, Pallădis*; *Iliăs, Iliădos.*

3. The Greek accusatives of nouns, which in Latin follow the third declension, are likewise short, as *Naiadăs, Troăs, Delphinăs, Arcadăs.*

    Palantes Troăs *agebat.* Virg.

4. The noun *anăs* is short, as in Petronius,
    Et pictis anăs *enovata pennis.*
And even the very analogy of the language shews it, having a short increase in the genitive *ănătis.*

Rule LII.
ES final.

1. ES *at the end of words is long.*
2. *Except* Es *from* Sum, *with its compounds.*
3. *And* penĕs.
4. *Greek nouns in* ES *are also short.*
5. *As likewise Latin nouns with short increase.*
6. *Except* pēs, Cerēs, ariēs, abiēs, *and* pariēs.

Examples.

1. Es at the end of words is long, as *nubēs, artēs, Cybelēs, Joannēs, locuplēs, Anchisēs, deciēs, veniēs,* &c.

2. The verb *sum* makes *ĕs* short, with its compounds *potĕs, adĕs,* &c. But *ēs* from *edo* is long, because it is a crasis for *edis,* of which they made *eis, ēs.*   3. The

Of QUANTITY.

3. The preposition *penĕs* is also short.

4. Likewise Greek nouns of the neuter gender, as *hippomanĕs, cacoëthĕs,* &c.

The plural of Greek nouns that follow the third declension of the Latins, makes ES also short in the nominative and vocative, as *Amazonĕs, Arcadĕs, aspidĕs, Delphinĕs, Erinnidĕs, gryphĕs, heroĕs, Lyncĕs, Mimallonĕs, Naïadĕs, Nereïdĕs, Orcadĕs, Phrygĕs, Thracĕs, Tigridĕs, Troadĕs, Troĕs* &c. But the accusative in ES of these very nouns is long, because it is intirely a Latin case, the Greek accusative ending in AS. Thus *bos Arcadēs* is long, and *bos Arcadăs* is short.

5. The Latin nouns in ES, whose increase is short, have *ĕs* also short in the nominative singular, as *milĕs, milĭtis; segĕs, segĕtis; pedĕs, pedĭtis.* But those whose increase is long, are long, as *hærēs, ēdis; locuplēs, ētis.*

6. The following have ES long, notwithstanding that they have a short increase, *Cerēs, Cerĕris; pēs, pĕdis.*

Hic sarta premitur angulo Cerēs *omni.* Mart.

Pēs *etiam & camuris hirtæ sub cornibus aures.* Virg.

ANNOTATION.

Hereto we might join these three, *abiĕs, abietis; ariĕs, arietis; pariĕs, parietis;* though it seems to be rather the cæsura that makes them long; for perhaps they will not be found of this quantity in any other situation.

With regard to what is objected against the compounds of *pes,* that *præpĕs* is short in Virgil,

———— præpĕs *ab Ida.*

And *perpĕs* in S. Prosper,

In Christo quorum gloria perpĕs *erit.*

It is evident that neither of these nouns is compounded of *pes, perpes* being the same as *perpetuus,* and *præpes* coming from προπέτης, *prævolans,* which was first of all in use among the augurs.

We must own that Ausonius shortens *bipĕs* and *tripĕs,* and Probus teacheth that *alipĕs* and *sonipĕs* are likewise short. But the contrary appears in Virgil, Lucan, and Horace. Therefore it is better always to make them long, like their simple.

Poets who flourished towards the decline of the Latin tongue, have taken the liberty to shorten the last in *famĕs, luĕs, prolĕs, plebĕs,* which is not to be imitated. Cicero likewise has made the final short in *alitĕs,* and in *pedĕs* the plural of *pes,* and Ovid in *tygrĕs,* as conformable to the Greek analogy.

Rule LIII.
IS final.
1. IS *at the end of words is short.*
2. *But the plural cases are always long.*
3. *As also the nominative singular of nouns that have a long increase.*
4. *Likewise such verbs as answer in number and tense to* audis.
5. *With* Fis, sis, vis, *and* velis.

EXAMPLES.

1. IS at the end of words is short, as *amatĭs, inquĭs, quĭs*; *ĭs*, pronoun; *cĭs*, preposition; *virginĭs, vultĭs*, &c.

Y has a great relation to I, for which reason it is also short, as *Chelÿs, Capÿs, Libÿs*, &c.

2. The plural cases are always long, as *virīs, armīs, musīs, siccīs, glebīs, nobīs*; *omnīs* for *omneis*, or *omnes*; *urbīs* for *urbeis*, or *urbes*; *queīs* for *quibus*; *vobīs*, &c.

Gratīs and *forīs* are also long, in this respect partaking of the plural cases.

Dat gratīs, ultro, dat mihi Galla, nego. Mart.

Wherein P. Melissus, in a letter to Henry Stephen, acknowledges himself to have been heretofore mistaken.

3. Nouns in IS are long, when their increase happens to be long, as *Simoīs, ēntis*; *Pyroīs, ēntis*; *līs, lītis*; *dīs, dītis*; *Samnīs, ītis*; *Quirīs, ītis*; *Salamīs, īnis*; *glīs, glīris*; *semīs, semīssis*.

But those of a short increase are also short, as *sanguĭs, sanguĭnis*.

4. Verbs make IS long in the second person singular, whenever the second person plural in *itis* is long.

As in the present of the fourth conjugation, *audīs, nescīs, sentīs, venīs*.

5. As *fīs* from *fio*, *sīs* from *sum*, and its compounds, *posīs, prosīs, adsīs*.

As *vīs* from *volo*, and its compounds, *mavīs*; as also *quamvīs, cuivīs*.

Likewise *velīs, malīs, nolīs*.

And

Of QUANTITY. 343

And in fine according to some, as *faxīs, ausīs*, which follow the same analogy.

ANNOTATION.

Some will have *bis, nescis, possis, velis*, and *pulvis* to be common; which is not without authority. But *pulvis* is long in Virgil by a cæsura, and as for the others it is always better to follow the general rules.

Christian poets sometimes make IS short in the fourth, as

——————— ——————— ——————— *non tu*
Pervenīs *ad Christum, sed Christus pervenit ad te.* Sedul.

which is not to be imitated.

Of the termination RIS *in the subjunctive.*

In regard to the termination RIS of the subjunctive, it is so often long and short in verse, that some have been led thereby to believe it was long in the future, and short in the preterite. But this distinction is by no means satisfying; for as we have shewn in the remarks on syntax, book 6. p. 107. the preterite in *rim* is often made to express the future, as well as the past; and therefore we may say in general, that whether in the preterite, or the future, we may always make them short, as sufficiently appeareth from the following examples.

Quas gentes Italûm, aut quas non oraverīs *urbes.* Virg.
Græculus esuriens in cælum jusserīs, *ibit.* Juven.
Dixerīs, *egregie,* &c. Hor.
——————— Dixerīs *æstuo, sudat.* Juven.
——————— *Nam frustra vitium* vitaverīs *illud.* Hor.
Is mihi, dives eris, si causas egerīs, *inquit.* Mart.

And if we should be asked nevertheless, whether it be true, that they are also sometimes long in the future, it is certain there are examples thereof.

Miscuerīs *elixa, simul conchylia turdis.* Hor.

But this may be referred to the cæsura. At least I never met with them long, except on such an occasion. Which shews that we may abide by what Probus says, that this syllable RIS is always short, whether in the preterite, or in the future subjunctive.

Some have also remarked that this last syllable RIS is long only when the antepenultima is short, as we see in *attulerīs, audierīs, biberīs, dederīs, credideris, fuerīs*, and others; so that the penultima being likewise short in all those words, there is a necessity for lengthening the last, in order to admit them into verse. Therefore they will have this to be only a licence, which has nevertheless become a rule; whereas if the antepenultima is long, this last syllable will be ever short according to its nature, as appears in *dixerīs egerīs, fecerīs, junxerīs, quæsiverīs, viderīs,* and others. This remark has some foundation, since it is generally true: but in words where they pretend it is long by poetic licence, there is always a cæsura.

Rule LIV.
OS final.

1. OS *as the end of words is long.*
2. *Except* compŏs, impŏs.
3. *Also Greek nouns written with omicron.*
4. *And* os, offis.

Examples.

1. OS at the end of words is long, as honōs, rōs, ōs, ōris, the mouth; virōs, &c.
2. *Compŏs* and *impŏs*, which Aldus supposeth to be long, are short.
   Insequere, & voti postmodo compŏs *eris.* Ovid.
3. Greek nouns are short, when written in Greek with an *omicron*, as *Arctŏs, melŏs, Chaŏs, Argŏs, Iliŏs*; and the genitives in OS, as *Arcadŏs, Palladŏs, Tethyŏs.* But nouns written in Greek with an *omega* are long, as *Athōs, Herōs, Androgeōs,* &c.
   Viveret Androgeōs *utinam.* Ovid.
4. These nouns are also short, *ŏs, offis,* a bone; *exŏs,* one that has no bones.
   Exŏs *& exanguis tumidos perfluctuat artus.* Lucret.

Rule LV.
US final.

1. US *at the end of words is short.*
2. *But nouns that retain* U *in the genitive are long.*
3. US *is also long in four cases of the fourth declension.*
4. *As likewise in* Tripus.

Examples.

1. US is short at the end of words, as *tuŭs, illiŭs, intŭs, sensibŭs, vulnŭs, impetŭs.*
2. Nouns that retain U in the genitive are always long, whether they make it in UNTIS, URIS, UTIS, UDIS, or UÏS, as *Opūs, Opūntis,* the name of a town; *tellūs, tellūris; rūs, rūris; jūs, jūris; salūs, salūtis; virtūs, virtūtis; palūs, palūdis; grūs, grūis; sūs, sūis.*

ANNOTATION.

Palŭs occurs but once in Horace,

Regis opus, steriliisque diu palŭs, *aptaque remis*.

Which is more to be remarked than imitated, though Palerius followed the example in his poem on the immortality of the soul.

Intercŭs, ŭtis, is also short, because the nominative was *intercŭtis, hujus intercŭtis*, of which they have made *intercŭs* by syncope.

Tellus is likewise short in Martianus Capella,

Interminata marmore tellŭs *erat*.

But this author often takes such liberties, in which his example is by no means to be copied.

3. Nouns of the fourth declension are also short in the nominative and vocative singular, as *hic fructŭs, hæc manŭs*.

Hic Dolopum manŭs, *hic sævus tendebat Achilles*. Virg. But these very nouns are long in the other cases in US, which are four; namely, the genitive singular, the nominative, accusative, and vocative plural; because, as we have observed when treating of the declensions, vol. 1. p. 123. this termination *us* comes from a contraction in all those cases, viz. *uĭs* in the genitive, *manuïs, manûs*; and *uës, ûs*, for the other three, *manuës, manûs*, &c.

4. *Tripŭs, tripodis*, is also long in the last of the nominative. To which we may add *Melampŭs*.

ANNOTATION.

Greek nouns ending in ους make *ûs* long in Latin, because it comes from the diphthong, as *Amathûs*, JESUS. As likewise certain genitives that come from the Greek termination ως, ως, as *Manto, Mantûs; Sappho, Sapphûs*; and the like. There are only the compounds of πους (except *tripŭs* and *Melampûs*) that are short; as *Polipŭs, Oedipŭs*, &c. because they drop the υ of the diphthong according to the Æolians, and only change ος into *us*, as we find by the genitive which makes *odis*, and not *oudis* or *untis*.

Nouns in *eus* are also long by reason of the diphthong, as *Atreûs, Orpheûs, Briareûs*.

The antients used to cut off S at the end of words in verse, just as we do M; hence they said *aliu', dignu', montibu'*; which lasted till Cicero's and Virgil's time.

RULE LVI.
T final.

T *at the end of words is short.*

Examples.

T at the end of words is short, as *audiït, legït, capŭt, fugït, amăt,* &c.

ANNOTATION.

T final was heretofore common, as Capella witnesseth, and as we still see in Ennius; but at present it is looked upon as short. And if we find it sometimes long, this is owing to the cæsura, as in Martial,

Jura trium petiīt *à Cæsare discipulorum.*

And in Ovid

Nox abiīt, *oritúrque Aurora,* Palilia *poscor.*

We are not even allowed, as some pretend, to make it long in the last syllable of the preterites formed by syncope; and if we sometimes find it thus, it is always in consequence of the cæsura, as in Horace,

——— *ut iniquæ mentis Asellus,*
Cum gravius dorso subiīt *onus* ———

However, if beside the syncope of the U, there is also a syneresis of two *ii*, then in virtue of this contraction of two syllables into one, the T, like any other letter, may become long, pursuant to what we observed in the first rule. Thus in Virgil, Æn. lib. 9.

Dum trepidant, it hasta Tago per tempus utramque.

For *ït* is there in the preterite instead of *iit.* Likewise in Ovid, 1 Trist. eleg. 9.

Dardaniámque petit *autoris nomen habentem.*

for *petiit,* and the like; though, generally speaking, they are with a cæsura, as in the last example.

Rule VII.
Of the last syllable of the verse.

The last syllable of the verse is always common.

Examples.

The last syllable of every verse is common, that is, we may look upon it as short or long, just as we will, without being confined to any rule; as in this verse from Virgil:

Gens inimica mihi Tyrrhenum navigat æquōr.

The last of the word *æquŏr* is short by nature, though it passeth here as long.

And in this other verse out of Martial,

Nobis non licet esse tam disertīs.

The

Of QUANTITY. 347

The laſt of *diſertīs* is long by nature, though it is here ſuppoſed to be ſhort.

OBSERVATIONS ON DIVERS SYLLABLES
whoſe quantity is diſputed.

THIS is all we had to mention in regard to the rules of quantity. The ſyllables not included in theſe rules, ought to be learnt by the uſe and authority of the poets, ſuch as moſt of thoſe in the middle of words, and all thoſe which are called NATURE, of which we have given ſome hints in different parts of the annotations.

But as there are many words whoſe quantity is often diſputed, and others where it is perverted by following the authority of corrupt paſſages, or of authors no way deſerving of imitation; I ſhall therefore give here a liſt of ſuch as I thought the moſt neceſſary to be obſerved.

Liſt of words whoſe quantity is diſputed.

ABSTEMIUS, the ſecond long, though Rutilius would fain have it ſhort.

Si forte in medio poſitorum abſtemius *berbis.* Hor.

AFFATIM, the ſecond ſhort in a verſe of Accius's, which is in the 2d Tuſc.

Tum jecore opimo farta & ſatiata affatim.

Some have inſiſted on its being long becauſe of this verſe of Arator,

Suppetit affatim *exemplorum copia, noſque.*

But beſides that we might ſcan it perhaps without making an eliſion of the M, as was frequently practiſed by the antients, and thus make a dactyl of *aſ-fatim*, we muſt further obſerve that this poet (who flouriſhed under Juſtinian at the ſame time with Priſcian and Caſſiodorus) is not ſo exact in his poetry, as to be of any authority with us.

ANATHEMA, when it ſignifies a perſon excommunicated, as in St. Paul, 1 Cor. xvi. 21. is generally written in Greek with an ε, and therefore hath the penultima ſhort. But when it denotes a preſent or an offering hanged up in temples and churches, it is commonly written with an η, as in St. Luke, xxi. 5, and elſewhere; and therefore it hath the penultima long: though ſometimes the orthography of it is altered; being ſtill but one and the ſame word, compounded of τίθημι, *pono*, which takes either the η or the ε in both ſignifications; and then the quantity will be alſo changed.

ANTEA. See p. 329.

ARCHYTAS hath the penultima long, as Voſſius obſerves, and as appeareth by this verſe out of Propertius,

Me creat Archytæ *ſoboles Babylonius beros.*

And by this other of Horace, lib. i. Od. 28.

Te maris & terræ, numeroque carentis arenæ

Menſorem cohibent Archyta.

And therefore it is wrong in Aratus, S. Sidonius, and Fortunatus, to make it long.

AREOPAGUS, the penultima doubtful. Some derive it from *pagus*, the former long, as coming from πηγὰ, *fons*; and S. Auſtin explains it *vicum Martis*; wherein he is followed by Budeus with moſt of the Greek and Latin dictionaries. Others derive it from πάγος, *collis*, the penultima ſhort; which is the opinion of Voſſius, Ricciolius, and others, founded on this, that it appears by Euripides, Pauſanias, Heſychius, Suidas, and the Etymologiſt, that this place was elevated, and appeared as it were on an eminence.

AZYMUS, the ſecond commonly ſhort in Prudentius, and in the hymn of the firſt Sunday after Eaſter.

Sinceritatis

Sinceritatis axyma. Yet by right it should be long, being a word compounded of *a* privative and ζύμη, *fermentum*, whereof the former is long, as appears by ζύμωμα in Nicander, derived from the same root, Μὴ μὲν δὴ ζύμωμα κακὸν χρόνος, &c.

CANDACE, Κανδάκη, the penultima may be pronounced long in prose, by following the accent. But in verse it is short, the same as *Canace*, *Panace*, and the like; which is further confirmed by this verse of Juvenal;

Candacis Æthiopum dicunt arcana, modósque.

CICURARE is to be found no where but in a very corrupt verse of Pacuvius's, quoted by Varro. Yet the two first syllables are supposed to be short, as well as *cicuris*.

CIS, a preposition, is reckoned short by Vossius, though there is no antient authority for it. But the analogy seems to require it. The same may be said of *bis*, which is always short in Ovid, though Arator has made it long. This may be further confirmed by the authority of its derivatives. For though *citraque* is long in Horace, by virtue of the mute and liquid, yet *citro* is short in Sidonius, and *citimus* in Fulgentius, in his Astronomics.

Qua. citimus *limes dispescit nubila purin*.

For which reason Buchanan is censured for having made the first long in *citimus* and *citerior*.

CLEOPATRA has by nature the penultima commen, because of the mute and liquid; for it comes from πάτηρ. So that in prose we ought to place the accent on the antepenultima. But the first and second being already short, the third must needs be long in hexameter and pentameter verses.

CYTHEREA hath the antepenultima short in Homer, writing it with an ε, ἔρεα, as it is derived from ἔρος. But Hesiod writes it with an η, and therefore makes it long. Virgil constantly shortens it. But in Ovid we likewise find it long.

Parce metû Cytherea, manent immota tuorum. Æn. 1.

Annuit atque dolis risit Cytherea repertis. Æn. 4.

Mota Cytheréa est leviter sua tempora myrto. Fast. 4.

CONOPEUM hath the penultima long in Juvenal; but it is short in Horace and Propertius, though it comes from the Greek κωνωπεῖον, because perhaps the Ionians said κωνώπιον.

Sol aspicit conopeum. Lib. Epod.

Fædaque Tarpeio conopea *tendere saxa*. Prop. lib. 3.

CONTRA. See p. 329.

CONTROVERSUS ought, I think, to have the second long, according to the analogy of compound words, by us observed, p. 304. And thus Ausonius has put it, though Sidonius makes it short.

CORBITA has the second long, though it is commonly pronounced short. This is sufficiently ascertained by the authority, not only of Plautus, but of Lucilius.

Tardiores quam corbitæ sunt in tranquillo mari. Lucil.

CREBRE & CREBRO have both the former long, because they are derived from *creber*, which hath it long also. And thus Horace has put it.

Est mibi purgatam crebro *qui personat aurem.*

CROCITO. The second, though commonly made short, is long nevertheless, according to Vossius, because he says it comes from *crocio*, just as *dormito* comes from *dormio*. Yet we find it short in Mapheus 13. Æn.

Dehinc perturbatus, crocitans *exquirit & omnes.*

And in the fable of Philomela:

Et crocitat *corvus; gracculus at frigulos.*

True it is that those authors are not exempt from mistakes; and we have taken notice of several.

Thus

CUCULUS is generally short in the penultima, and every body pronounces it thus, because of this verse of the Philomela:

Et cuculi cuculant, fritinnit rauca cicada.

Yet all classic authors, says Vossius, do make it long.

—— *Magna compellans voce* cuculum. Hor.

Ricciolius, in proof of its being short, quotes the following verse, as he says, from Martial:

Quámvis per plures cuculus *cantaverit annos.*

But it is not to be found among his works.

ELECTRUM has ever the first long, according to Vossius, being written with an η, whether it be taken for amber, or for silver mixed with the third or fourth part gold; though Erytreus,

Erytreus, Ricciolius, and some others, pretend that the *u* being changed into *i*, this syllable may be short: this they endeavour to prove by passages from Virgil, which Vossius shews to be all corrupted, as may be seen in his third book of *Anal.* c. 36.

ERADICO, notwithstanding what the great Latin Thesaurus says, hath the penultima long, as coming from *radix*, *icis*. Nor does it signify to object this verse of Plautus:

Eradicabam *hominum aures quando ac-ceperam*;

because the comic poets are apt to put a spondee for an iambus in the second foot, as appears from this same verse of Terence,

Dii te eradicent, ita me miseram terri-tas.

ERUNT, the termination of the pre-terite, like *tulerunt*, doubtful in the pe-nultima. See rule 15, p. 313.

FORTUITUS hath the penultima common. It is long in Horace,

Nec fortuitum spernere cespitem.

And in this trochaic verse of Plautus:

Si eam senex anus prægnantem fortuitu fecerit.

Which happens also to GRATUITUS. But it is not true, as Duza pretends, that the *i* is never short in those words; for we find the contrary by the follow-ing verse in Statius:

Largis gratuitum cadit rapinis.

FRUSTRA is marked with the last common by Smetius and others. But Vossius assures us it is ever long in an-tient authors, and he will have it that in this verse which is quoted from Juve-nal, to prove it short,

Ærumnæ cumulus quod nudum & frustra rogantem,

we ought to read *frustra rogantem*, ac-cording as Manchinellus says he found it in antient copies. True it is that Ausonius as well as some others have shortened it; yet the safest way is to make it long.

FULICA is found with the first and second long in this verse in Gellius,

Hic fulica levis volitat super æquore classis:

yet every where else they are short;

In sicco ludunt fulicæ, notasque palu-des. Virg.

GÆTULUS, the first and second long, because it comes from Γαιτῦλος.

Destruat, aut captam ducat Gætulus Iarbas. Virg.

Argentum, vestes Gætulo murice tinc-tas. Hor.

Pensabam Pharium Gætulis messibus annum. Claud.

And therefore it is an error in an epi-gram attributed to Martial, to read it as Pierius does,

Tradita est Getulis, nec cepit arcte vocentes. In Spectacul. Centon.

and as it is printed in Plantin's edition by Junius: whereas the old MSS have Tradita Gætulis, &c. And Ricciolius is guilty of the same mistake, when he is for making it short in this verse of Ovid, Hero. Ep. 7.

Quid dubitas vinctam Getulo me tra-dere Hiarbæ.

whereas the best editions have Gætulo tradere Iarbæ.

GESTICULATOR is generally mark-ed long in the second, as coming from *gestire*; but Vossius believes it is rather short, as coming from *gesticulus*. And this is also the opinion of Ricciolius, though there is no authority, one way or other.

GRATUITUS. See FORTUITUS.

HARPAGO, if we believe Calepin, who has been followed by all the com-pilers of dictionaries since his time, hath the penultima long; but they produce no authority for it. Whereas we meet with εἰς ἁρπαγας, the penul-tima short in Automedon's 2d book of epigrams. And it is also the opi-nion of Vossius and Ricciolius, that it hath the penultima short; so that even in prose we ought ever to pronounce it with the accent on the penultima, *hár-pago*.

HORNOTINUS, which comes from *horno*, that is, *hoc anno*, hath the pen-ultima short. See SEROTINUS lower down.

IDOLOTHYTUM, εἰδωλόθυτον, is sometimes pronounced according to the Greek accent. But in regard to quantity the penultima is always long in verse, as it comes from θύω, *sa-crifico*, whence also we have θύμα, *sacri-ficium*, which would not have a circum-flex on the former, unless it was long by nature.

IMBECILLUS, though it comes from *baculus*, hath the second long in Lucre-tius and in Horace.

Imbecillus, iners fen quid vis, adde popino.

And therefore it is wrong in Prudentius to make it short.

INVOLUCRUM hath the penultima long by nature, as well as *lavacrum*, because they come from the supines *lavatum* and *involutum*. Hence it is an error in Prudentius to make it short in this Asclepiad verse:

Contentum involucris atque cubilibus.

But this is further confirmed by the following pentameter of Rutilius:

Investigato fonte, lavacra dedit.

And it would be wrong to use it otherways; though we meet with some instances to the contrary in St. Prosper.

JUDAICUS hath the second short in Juvenal.

Judaicum ediscunt & servant, ac metuunt jus.

Claudian uses it in the same manner; whose authority is preferable to that of the ecclesiastic authors, who make it long.

LATRO, AS, hath the former long in Horace and Virgil.

Nescio quid certe est, & Hylas in limine latrat. Ecl.

True it is that not only ecclesiastic writers, but even Phædrus, have made it short.

Canem objurgabat, qui senex contra latrans, lib. 5.

Though this does not deserve to be imitated, since it is contrary to the practice of those who wrote during the purity of the language.

LOTIUM, which is marked by dictionaries with the first short, ought to have it long, as well as *lotum* from whence they derive it.

Hoc te amplius bibisse prædicet loti. Catul.

MATRICIDA. See p. 308.

MELOS. The penultima short by nature.

Regina longum Calliope melos. Hor.

But they are mistaken who think it is never otherwise (which was the opinion of Politian) as we can prove from Persius.

Cantare credas Pegaseium melos.

Which he undoubtedly designed in imitation of the Greeks, with whom the simple liquids have the power of lengthening a syllable, as well as the double consonants.

Θεὸς δ' ὑπὸ μέλος ὅεισι. Hom.

Which Ricciolius does not seem to have rightly understood, because he attributes it to some dialect, it which perhaps this word was written with an η instead of an ε.

MITHRA hath the former long by nature.

Indignata sequi torquentem cornua mithram. Sta.

For which reason Vossius finds fault with Capella, whom he likewise censures in many other respects, for making it short.

MORUS. See SYCOMORUS lower down.

MOYSES in Christian poets is frequently a trisyllable, the first short, and the second long, contrary to the analogy of the Greek Μωυσῆς.

—— Visit bis Moyses. Prud.

Quid? quod & Eliam, & clarum videre Moysen. Sedul.

NIHILUM. The second short, contrary to the opinion of Gifanius, and some other grammarians.

———— Gigni De nihilo nihil, in nihilum nil posse reverti. Pers.

Nor must it be said that this is done by a contraction or syneresis, because we can produce some other authorities that are irrefragable.

At marite, ita me juvent Cælites, nihilominus Pulcheres. Catul.

NOVICIUS hath the antepenultima long.

Jam sedet in ripa, tetrumque novicius horret. Juven.

Which is so much the more remarkable, as all adjectives in *icius*, derived from a noun, do shorten the penultima. Priscian even insists that this rule is without exception. But of those that come either from participles or verbs, some are long, as *advectitius, commendatitius, suppositius*.

Hermes suppositius *sibi ipsi.* Mart.

OBEDIO hath the second long, because it comes from *audio*. This appears further by the following iambic of Afranius,

Meo obsequar amori, obedio *libens.*

And Plautus,

Futura est dicto obediens, an non patri?

So that it is a mistake in the poet Victor, who lived late in the fifth century, to make it short in the following verse:

Jussit adesse Deos, proprieque obedire tyranno.

OMITTO for *obmitto* hath the first short.

Pleraque differat & præsens in tempus omittat. Hor.

PALAM hath always the former short in antient authors.

Luce palam certum est igni circundare muros. Virg.

Though S. Prosper in his poem makes it long.

PARACLETUS. See p. 301.

PAR-

OF QUANTITY. 351

PARRICIDA. See p. 308.

PATRIMUS & MATRIMUS have the penultima long, which Julius Scaliger, and before him Politianus, believed to be short. This is proved by the authority of Catullus, even as the passage is read by Joseph Scaliger himself.

Quare habe tibi, quicquid hoc libelli est.

Qualecumque, quod ô patrima virgo,
Plus uno maneat perenne seclo.

And analogy requires it thus, because whenever the termination IMUS is added quite intire in the derivation of a word, the *i* is short of course, as *legitimus* from *lex, legis*; *finitimus* from *finis*; *ædiitimus* from *ædes, ædis*; *solitimus* from *solum, soli*, &c. But when there is only MUS added for the derivation, then the *i* before MUS is long, *primus* from *præ* or *pris*, *bimus* from *bis*, *trimus* from *treis* or *tris*. In like manner *patrimus* from *pater, patris*; *matrimus* from *mater, matris*.

POLYMITUS, when it signifies embroidered, or wove with threads of divers colours, hath the penultima short, because it comes from μίτος, *filum*, which is so in Homer. But we are not to confound it with πολύμητις, *learned, one who knows a vast deal*, or πολύμυθος, *a great inventor of fables*, which have the penultima long.

POSTEA. See p. 329.

PRÆSTOLOR is generally pronounced the second long. Thus Valla has made it, upon translating this verse of Herodotus:

Terrenasque acies ne præstolare, sed hosti.

Yet Buchanan has made it short in his psalms:

Vitæ beatæ præstolor.

Which Vossius approveth, so much the more as of *præsto* is formed *præsulus*, or according to the antients, *præsolus*, (who is quite ready) from whence comes *præstolor*.

PROFUTURUS hath the second short, according to the nature of its simple.

Præcipuè infelix pesti devota futuræ.
Virg.

Wherefore Baptista Mantuanus is censured for making it long.

PSALTERIUM, the second long, because in Greek we say ψαλτήριον with an η. Thus we find it in the *Ciris* attributed to Virgil.

Non arguta sonant tenui psalteria corda.

And therefore we must not mind the authority of Aratus, who has made it otherwise.

PUGILLUS is reckoned by some to have the first long, which they prove by its derivative in Juven.

Nec pugillares desert in balnea raucus.

Yet in Ausonius, Prudentius, and Fortunatus, we find it short; which may be further confirmed by the authority of Horace, who shortens *pugil*.

Ut lethargicus hic quum sit pugil,
Et medicum urget.

PULEX hath ever the former long, as appears by Martial:

Pulice, vel si quid pulice, sordidius.

And by Columella.

Parvulus aut pulex irripens dente lacissset.

Yet a great many modern writers make it short, an error into which they have been led by the poem intitled *pulex*, and falsely attributed to Ovid, where we read,

Parve pulex, & amara lues inimica puellis.

But this poem is no more his than the Philomela, in which we find a great number of mistakes.

PUTA. See p. 328.

RESINA hath the penultima long; though some insist on its being common, because of a verse in Martial, L. 3. c. 25. which others think to be a mistake.

RHEA, the former common, because the Greeks write not only ῥίν but ῥείν, (both are to be found in Callimachus. Hence Ovid has made it short.

Sæpe Rhea questa est toties fœcunda, nec unquam.

And Virgil long,

Collis Aventini silvâ quem Rhea sacerdos.

RUDIMENTUM hath the second long, because it comes from the supine *eruditum*. And so Virgil has made it,

——— *Bellique propinqui*
Dura rudimenta ———

And Valerius Flaccus,

Dura rudimenta Herculeo sub nomine pendent.

And Statius,

Cruda rudimenta & teneros formaverit annos.

SALUBER, the second long by nature, as coming from *salus, utis*. Hence it is wrong in Buchanan to make it short:

Nomen, qui salubri temperie modum. Psal. 99.

For we find that Ovid did not use it thus:

Ut faveas cœptis, Phœbe sabuler ades.

SCRU-

SCRUPULUM hath the first long, as coming from *scrupus*;

Quinque parant marathri scrupula, myrrhæ decem. Ovid.

Wherefore in this verse of Fannius in his book of weights and measures, we should read *scriplum,* or rather *scriptlum,* and not *scrupulum.*

Gramma vocant, scriptlum nostri dixere priores.

Since as from γράψειν cometh γράμμα, so from *scribo, scriptum,* cometh *scriptulum,* and by syncope *scriptlum,* even according to Charisius.

SEMPITERNUS, the second long, as Scaliger proveth against Prudentius and modern authors, because it comes from *semper* and *æternus.*

SPADO, the former always short, as we see in Juvenal.

Cum tener uxorem ducat spado, Nævia Thuscum
Figat aprum ———— Sat. 1.
Ut spado vincebat Capitolia nostra Potides. Sat. 14.

In Martial,

Thelim viderat in toga spadonem.

A Phaleucian verse.

Again,

Nec spado, nec mœchus erit te consule quisquam;
At pius, ô mores, & Spado mœchus erat.

So that we must not mind Arator, who, among several other mistakes, hath committed this of making it long.

Australem celerare viam qua spado jugalis
Æthiopum pergebat equis. Lib. 1. Astr.

Which may so much the more impose upon persons not well versed in poetry, as the above verse of Arator is quoted in Smetius with the name of Virgil, through a mistake which has crept into all the editions that ever I saw: though Virgil never so much as once made use of the word *spado.*

SPHÆRA. It is also a mistake in Prudentius to make the former short in this word.

Cujus ad arbitrium sphera mobilis atque rotunda.

For it comes from σφαῖρα. And this may be owing to the corruption which we observed in the treatise of letters, when ceasing to pronounce the diphthongs, they began to put a simple E for Æ and OE.

SYCOMORUS is reckoned to have the penultima common; for being derived from σῦκον (*ficus*) and μόρον (*morum*),

as μόρον in Greek is wrote with an *omicron,* it may be short. But this same penultima may be long, because *morus* in Latin hath the former long, though Calepin makes it short.

Ardea morus erat niveis uberrima pomis. Ovid.

Mutua quin etiam moris commercia ficus. Pallad.

Whereto we may add that this word is differently wrote, some editions having συκομορέα, and others συκαμιναῖα.

TEMETUM hath the penultima long.

Pullos, ova, cadum temeti: sempe modo isto. Hor.

Though Muretus hath made it short.

THYMIAMA, the penultima long by nature, because it comes from θυμίαμα.

TORCULAR, the penultima short, as Despauter and the great Latin Thesaurus observe; which is further confirmed by Vossius and Ricciolius; because it comes from *torqueo,* in the same manner as *specular* or *speculum* from *speculor,* though we find it long in Fortunatus through necessity.

TRIGINTA, and the like. See p. 330.

TRITURO, the penultima long, because it comes from *tritura* or *triturus,* of the same nature as *pictura* or *picturus,* whence also cometh *picturo.* Some nevertheless derive it from *tritero,* as much as to say *tertero,* and pretend therefore that we may make it short.

VIETUS hath the second long.

Nec supra caput ejusdem cecidisse vietam
Vestem ———— Lucret.

Likewise in Prudentius,

———— *Et turbida ab ore vieto*
Nubila discussit.

Nor must we suffer ourselves to be led into an error by this verse of Horace:

Qui sudor vietis & quam malus undique membris.

Because *vietis* is there a dissyllable by syneresis.

VIRULENTUS, the second short, like all nouns of this same termination, as *fraudulentus, luculentus, pulverulentus.*

Ne dictat mibi luculentus *Attis.* Mart.

a Phaleucian verse.

And therefore Baptista Mantuanus is mistaken in saying,

———— *Quem* virulenta *Megæra.*

ULTRA. See p. 330.

UNIVERSI, the second short. But in UNICUIQUE it is long. The reason is

OF QUANTITY.

is because in the latter, *uni* is declined, coming from the nominative *unusquisque*, and therefore retains the quantity it would have uncompounded: whereas in the former it is not declined, as it comes from *universus*, the nature of which is communicated to the other cases. And this analogy ought to take place on all the like occasions, as hath been observed, rule 7, p. 307.

VOMICA, the first long in Sesenus, who lived about the middle of the third century,

Vomica *qualis erit?*————

But it is short in Juvenal, who flourished towards the close of the first,

Et phthisis & vomicæ putres & dimidium crus.

UTRIUS. Vossius in the 2d book *de arte Gramm.* chap. 13. and in his smaller Grammar, p. 285. says that it is never otherwise than long in the second; yet it is more than once short in Horace,

Docte sermones utriusque *linguæ,* lib. 3. Od. 8.

Fastidiret olus qui me notat. Utrius *borum*

Verba probes——Lib. 1. ep. 17. ad Scæv.

And therefore it may be said that *i* in this noun is common, the same as in *unius*, *ullius*, and others of the like termination, of which we have taken notice in the third rule.

Section II.

OF ACCENTS,

And the proper manner of pronouncing Latin.

Chapter I.

I. *Of the nature of accents, and how many sorts there are.*

ACCENTS are nothing else but certain small marks that were invented in order to shew the tone and several inflexions of the voice in pronouncing.

The antients did not mark those tones, because as they were in some measure natural to them in their own language, use alone was sufficient to acquire them; but they were invented in after times, either to fix the pronunciation, or to render it more easy to strangers. This is true not only in regard to Greek and Latin, but also to the Hebrew tongue, which had no points in St. Jerome's time.

Now the inflexions of the voice can be only of three sorts; either that which rises, and the musicians call ἄρσις, *elevation*; or that which sinks, and they call θέσις, *position* or *depression*; or that which, partaking of both, rises and sinks on one and the same syllable. And in this respect the nature of the voice is admirable, says Cicero in his book de Oratore, since of these three inflections it forms all the softness and harmony of speech.

On this account therefore three sorts of accents have been invented, whereof two are simple, namely the acute and the grave; and the other compound, namely the circumflex.

The acute raiseth the syllable somewhat, and is marked by a small line rising from left to right, thus (´).

The grave depresseth the syllable, and is marked on the contrary by a small line descending from left to right, thus (`).

The circumflex is composed of the other two, and therefore is marked thus (ˆ).

As accents were invented for no other purpose than to mark the tone of the voice, they are therefore no sign of the quantity of syllables, whether long or short; which is evidently proved, because a word may have several long syllables, and yet it shall have but one accent; as on the contrary it may be composed intirely of short ones, and yet shall have its accent, as *Asia, dominus,* &c.

II. *Rules*

Of ACCENTS.

II. *Rules of accents and of Latin words.*

The rules of accents may be comprized in three or four words; especially if we content ourselves with the most general remarks, and with what the grammarians have left us upon the subject.

For MONOSYLLABLES.

1. If they are long by nature, they take a circumflex, as *flôs*; *ôs, oris*; *â, ê.*

2. If they be short, or only long by position, they take an acute, as *spés*; *ós, óssis*; *fáx*, &c.

For DISSYLLABLES and POLYSYLLABLES.

1. In words of two or more syllables, if the last be short, and the penultima long by nature, this penultima is marked with a circumflex, as *flôris, Rôma, Românus*, &c.

2. Except the above case, dissyllables have always an acute, on the penultima, as *bómo, péjus, párens*, &c.

Polysyllables have the same, if the penultima be long, as *paréntes, Aráxis, Románo*, &c. otherwise they throw their accent back on the antepenultima, as *máximus, últimus, dóminus*, &c.

III. *Reasons for the above rules.*

Here it is obvious that the rules of accents are founded on the length or shortness of syllables: which has obliged us to defer mentioning them till we had treated of quantity.

Now the reasons of these rules are very clear and easy to comprehend. For accent being no more than an elevation which gives a grace to the pronunciation, and sustains the discourse, it could not be placed further than the antepenultima either in Greek or Latin, because if three or four syllables were to come after the accent (as if we should say *pérficere, pérficeremus*) they would be heaped, as it were, one upon another, and consequently would form no sort of cadence in the ear, which, according to Cicero, can hardly judge of the accent but by the three last syllables, as it can hardly judge of the harmony of a period but by the three last words. Therefore the farthest the accent can be placed is on the antepenultima, as in *dóminus, bómines, amáverant*, &c.

But since the Romans in regulating the accents have had a particular regard to the penultima, as the Greeks to the ultima, if the word in Latin hath the penultima long, this long syllable being equivalent to two short ones, receives the accent, *Rôma, Românus*, producing nearly the same cadence in the ear by reason of their length, as *máximus*.

And as this length may be twofold, one by nature, and the other only by position; and this length by nature was formerly marked by doubling the vowel, as we have already observed in the treatise of letters, book 9. p. 249. so this long penultima may receive two sorts of accents, either the circumflex, that is the accent composed of an acute and a grave, *Românus* for *Romáànus*; or only the acute, that is, which signifieth only the elevation of the syllable, as *Aráxis, párens*.

But if after a penultima long by nature, the last should also be long, as this circumflex accent and the length of the last syllable might render the speech too drawling, they are satisfied then with acuting the penultima, *Románo*, and not *Románo, Rómæ*, and not *Rômæ*, to prevent too slow an utterance.

After this it is easy to form a judgment of the rest. For in regard to the dissyllables, if they are not capable of a circumflex, they must needs have an acute on the penultima, be it what it will, since they cannot throw the accent farther back: and as to monosyllables, the reason why those which are long by nature have a circumflex, is the same as that above mentioned, namely, that this long vowel is equivalent to two, *flôs* instead of *floôs*. And the reason why those that are short, or only long by position, have but an acute, is because they can have no other.

IV. *Some exceptions to these rules of accents.*

Lipsius, and after him Vossius, are of opinion that the rules of accents, which the grammarians have left us, are very defective, and that the antient manner of pronouncing was not confined to those laws of grammar. Yet these rules being so natural, and so well founded in analogy and in the surprizing relation they bear to each other, pursuant to what hath been just now observed, it is not at all probable that the antients departed from them so widely as those critics imagine; and if we meet with some instances to the contrary they ought to be looked upon rather as exceptions, than a total subversion of the general rule, since even these exceptions may be reduced to a small number, and it is easy to shew that they are not without foundation.

The first exception is that compound verbs used sometimes to retain the same accent as their simple, as *calefácio, calefácis, calefácit*, where the accent is on the penultima in the two last words, though it be short, says Priscian, lib. 8. And according to him the same may be said of *calefío, calefís, calefít*, where the accent continues on the last syllable of the second and third person, as it would be in the simple, which is a very natural analogy.

The second exception is that on the contrary compound nouns used sometimes to draw their accent back to the antepenultima, whether the penultima was long or not; as we find in the same

Priscian,

Of ACCENTS. 357

Priscian that they used to say *orbisterræ, virilluſtris, præfectusfabrum, jurisconsultus, intereáloci.*

The third exception is that indeclinable particles also used to draw back their accent sometimes in composition, as *siquando*, which, according to Donatus, had the accent sometimes on the antepenultima; and the same ought to be said of *néquando, aliquando*; as also of *éxinde*, which, according to Servius, has the accent on the antepenultima; and this should serve as a rule for *déinde, périnde, próinde, súbinde* : likewise *exádversum* in Gellius, and *áffatim*, to which may be added *enímvero, dúntaxat*, and perhaps some others, which may be seen in Priscian, or in Lipsius and Vossius, who give a full list of them. Now these two exceptions of drawing back the accent in composition, are only an imitation of the Greeks, who frequently do the same in regard to their compounds. But we must take particular care, says Vossius, that though the accent may be on the antepenultima in *déinde, périnde*, and others, we are not to conclude that it may therefore be on the antepenultima in *déinceps*, and such like, where the last is long; for no word can be accented on the antepenultima, either in Greek or Latin, when the two last syllables are long; especially as each of these long syllables having *two times*, this would throw the accent back too far.

The fourth exception is of the vocatives of nouns in IUS, which are accented on the penultima, though short, as *Virgíli, Mercúri, Æmíli, Valéri*, &c. the reason of which is because heretofore, according to the general analogy, they had their vocative in E, *Virgílie*, like *dómine*. But as this final E was took weak, and scarce perceptible; by degrees it came to be dropped, and the original accent, which was on the antepenultima, continuing still in its place, came to be on the penultima.

The fifth exception may be in regard to Enclitics, which always used to draw the accent to the next syllable, be it what it would, as we shall see in the next chapter.

To these we may add some extraordinary and particular words, as *muliéris*, which, according to Priscian, hath the accent on the short penultima, and perhaps some others, though in too small a number to pretend that this should invalidate the general rules.

Chapter II.
Particular observations on the practice of the antients.

I. *In what place the accents ought to be particularly marked in books.*

THE rules of accents ought to be carefully observed, not only in speaking, but likewise in writing, when we undertake to mark them, as is generally practised in the liturgy of the church of Rome. Only we may observe, that instead of a circumflex, they have been satisfied with an acute, because the circumflex being only a compound of the acute and the grave, what predominates therein, says Quintilian, is particularly the acute, which, as he himself observes after Cicero, ought to be naturally on every word we pronounce.

It is for this very reason that in those books they no longer put any accent on monosyllables, nor even on dissyllables, because having lost this distinction of acute and circumflex, it is sufficient for us in general to know that in dissyllables the former is always raised.

II. *In what manner we ought to mark the accent on words compounded of an enclitic.*

The accent ought also to be marked on words compounded of an enclitic, that is, one of these final particles, *que, ne, ve*; and should be always put on the penultima of these words, whatever it be, as Despauter after Servius and Capella informs us; thus *armáque, terráque, pluítne, altérve*, &c. because it is the nature of these enclitics ever to draw the accent towards it. So that it signifies nothing to say with Melissa and Ricciolius, that if this was the case, we could not distinguish the ablative from the nominative of nouns in A. For considering things originally, it is very certain, as above hath been mentioned, that the antients distinguished extremely well betwixt accent and quantity; and therefore that they raised the last in the nominative without lengthening it, *terráque*, whereas in the ablative they gave it an elevation, and at the same time they made it appear long, as if it were, *terráàque*; whence it follows that they must have also distinguished it by the acute in the nominative, *terráque*, and by the circumflex in the ablative, *terrâque*; and Vossius thinks that some distinction ought to be observed in pronouncing them.

III. *That neither* que *nor* ne *are always enclitics.*

But here we are to observe two things which seem to have escaped the attention of Despauter. The first, that there are certain words ending in *que*, where the *que* is not an enclitic, because they are simple, and not compound words; as *útique, dénique, úndique*, &c. which are therefore accented on the antepenultima.

The second, that *ne* is never an enclitic but when it expresseth doubt, and not when it barely serves to interrogate; and therefore if the syllable before *ne* is short or common, we ought to put the accent on the antepenultima, in interrogations, as *tíbine? hǽccine? síccine? ástrane? égone? Plátone?* &c. whereas in the other sense the particle *ne* draws the accent to the penultima. *Ciceróne, Platóne.*

IV. *That the accent ought to be marked, whenever there is a necessity for distinguishing one word from another.*

We ought also to mark the accent in writing, according to Terent. Scaurus, whenever it is necessary for preventing ambiguity.

ty. For example we should mark *légit* in the present with an acute, *legit* in the preterite with a circumflex. We should mark *óccido*, the accent on the antepenultima, taking it from *cádo*; and *occído* with an acute on the penultima, taking it from *cædo*.

V. *Whether we ought to accent the last syllable, on account of this distinction.*

But if any body should ask whether this rule of distinction ought to be observed for the last syllable; Donatus, Sergius, Priscian, Longus, and most of the antients will have that it ought, and especially in regard to indeclinable words, which they say should be marked with an acute on the last, as *circúm littora*, to distinguish it from the accusative of *circus*. Quintilian, more antient than any of these, observes that even in his time some grammarians were of this opinion, which was practised by several learned men, and that for his part he durst not condemn it.

Victorinus likewise observes the same thing, and says that *poné* an adverb, for example, is acuted on the last, to prevent its being confounded with the imperative of *póno*. So that one might say the same of a great many other verbs, which through an erroneous custom, are marked with a grave accent, at *malè*, *benè*, though we are told at the same time that in pronouncing it ought to have the power of an acute. Which is doubtless owing to a mistake of the Greeks, who frequently commit the same error in regard to those two accents, as if it were quite so consistent to mark the one, when you expressly mean the other.

But the reason why we ought not to put the grave on those final syllables, is evident. Because as the grave denotes only the fall of the voice, there can be no fall where there has not been a rise, as Lipsius and Vossius have judiciously observed: For if the last, for instance, falls in *pond*, an adverb, the first must therefore be comparatively raised, and then this word will no longer be distinguished from *póne*, the imperative of *pono*, which nevertheless is contrary to their intention. Hence Sergius, who lived before Priscian, takes notice that in his time the grave accent was no longer used; *sciendum*, says he, *quod in usu non est hodierno accentus gravis*. Whence it follows either that we ought not to accent the last syllable, or if it must have an accent, then we ought to chuse another, and rather make use of an acute, according to the opinion of some grammarians.

A second mistake some are apt to commit in regard to the last syllable, is when in order to shew that it is long, and to distinguish it from a short one, they put a circumflex, as *musâ* in the ablative, to distinguish it from the nominative *músa*. For the accents were not intended to mark the quantity, but the inflexion of the voice; and as for the quantity, when the custom of doubling the vowels, in order to mark the long syllables, as *musaa*, was altered; they made use of small couchant lines which they called *apices*, thus *musā*, as we have shewn in the treatise of letters, book 9. p. 249.

But since we have lost the use of those little marks, we put up with these accents, which ought rather to be considered as signs of quantity, than of the tone of voice; the circumflex, according to Quintilian, being never put at the end of a word in Latin; though the Greeks do sometimes circumflex the last when it happens to be long.

VI. *In what manner we ought to place the accent in verse.*

If the word of itself be doubtful, we should place the accent on the penultima, when it is looked upon as long in verse, or on the antepenultima, when it is looked upon as short. Thus we should say,

Pecudes pictæque volúcres, *Virg.*

the accent on the penultima, as Quintilian observeth, because the poet makes it long; though in prose we always say, *vólucres*, the accent on the antepenultima.

Hence it may happen that the same word shall have two different accents in the same verse, as in Ovid.

Et primo similis volúcri, *mox vera* volúcris.

Chapter III.

I. *Of the accents of words which the Latins have borrowed of other languages, and particularly those of Greek words.*

IN regard to Greek words, if they remain Greek, either altogether or in part, so as to retain at least some syllable of that language, they are generally pronounced according to the Greek accent. Thus we put an acute on the antepenultima in *elíison*, and *lithóstrotos*, notwithstanding that the penultima is long.

On the contrary we put it on the penultima, though it be short in *paralipoménon*, and the like.

We put the circumflex on the genitives plural in ῶν, periarchῶν, and on the adverbs in ῶς, ironicῶς, and such like, where the *omega* is left standing.

But words entirely latinised, ought generally to be pronounced according to the rules of Latin. And this is the opinion of Quintilian, Capella, and other antient authors; though it is not an error to pronounce them also according to the Greek accent.

Therefore we say with the accent on the antepenultima, *Aristóteles, Ántipas, Bárnabas, Bóreas, Blasphémia, Córidon, Démeas, Ecclésia, Tráseas*, &c. because the penultima is short. And on the contrary we say with the accent on the penultima, *Alexandría, Cythéron, erímus, meteóra, orthodóxus, Paraclétus, pleurésis*, and the like, because it is long.

Greek words that have the penultima common not by figure or licence, but by the use of the best poets, or by reason of some particular dialect, are always better pronounced in prose according to the common or Attic dialect, or according to the use of the best poets, than otherwise. Therefore it is preferable to put the accent on the penultima, in *Chorea, Conopéum, platéa, Oriónis,* and such like, because the best poets make it long.

But if these words have the penultima sometimes long and sometimes short in those same poets, we may pronounce as we please in prose, as *Busiris, Eriphylus.* But in verse, we must follow the measure and cadence of the feet, pursuant to what has been already observed.

These are, I think, the most general rules that can be given upon this subject. Nevertheless we are oftentimes obliged to comply with custom, and to accommodate ourselves to the manner of pronouncing in use among the learned, according to the country one lives in. Thus we pronounce *Aristóbulus, Basilius, idólium,* with the accent on the antepenultima, notwithstanding that the penultima is long; only because it is the custom.

And on the contrary we pronounce *Andréas, idéa, María,* &c. the accent on the penultima though short, because it is the custom even among the most learned.

The Italians also pronounce with the accent on the penultima, *Autonomasia, harmonía, philosophía, theología,* and the like, pursuant to the Greek accent, because it is the practice of their country, as Ricciolius observeth. Besides Alvarez and Gretser are of opinion that we ought always to pronounce it thus, though the custom not only of Germany and Spain, but likewise of all France, is against it: and Nebrissensis approves of the latter pronunciation, where he says that it is better to accent those words on the antepenultima. Which shews that when once the antient rules have been broke through, there is very little certainty, even in practice, which is different in different countries.

II. *Of the accents of Hebrew words.*

Hebrew words that borrow a Latin termination and declension, follow the Latin rules in regard to accent: and therefore we put it on the penultima in *Adámus, Joséphus, Jacóbus,* &c. because it is long.

But if these words continue to have the Hebrew termination, and are indeclinable, they may be pronounced either according to the rules of Latin words, or according to the Greek accent, if they have passed through the Greek language before they were received by the Latins; or in short according to the Hebrew accent.

But should these three circumstances concur, then one would think there is no reason for pronouncing otherwise than according to the received use and custom of the public, to which we are often obliged to conform.

And therefore, pursuant to this rule, we should say with the accent on the penultima, *Aggéus, Bethsúra, Cethúra, Delóra, Eleázar, Eliséus, Rebécca, Salóme, Sephóra, Susánna;* because the penultima of these is not only long by nature, but it is likewise accented both in Greek and Hebrew.

If these words are intirely Hebrew, it is better to pronounce them according to the Hebrew accent; and therefore we should raise the last in *eloí, ephetá, sabaóth,* and such like.

In respect to which we are however to take notice, that as most of these words are received in the liturgy of the church of Rome, there is a necessity for pronouncing them according to established custom, so much the more as they are in every body's mouth all over the world. Hence it is that, contrary to the last rule, we generally put the accent on the antepenultima in *Elísabeth, Gólgotha, Melchísedech, Móyses, Sámuel, Sólomon, Samária, Síloë,* and some others.

Hereby it appears to be a mistake, which great numbers have fallen into, to think with a certain person called Alexander the dogmatist, that not only Hebrew words, but all that are barbarous and exotic, ought to be pronounced with the accent on the last. Which has been learnedly refuted by Nebrissensis, and after him by Despauter, though this has been the custom of several churches, in regard to some tones of the psalms, because of the Hebrew accent therein predominant.

Chapter IV.

Further observations on the pronunciation of the antients.

I. *That they distinguished between accent and quantity, and made several differences even in quantity.*

WHAT we have been hitherto saying relates to the rules and practice of accents, to which we ought now to conform. But the pronunciation of the antients was even in this respect greatly different from ours; for they not only observed the difference between quantity and accent, according to what hath been said in the treatise of letters, book 9; but likewise in quantity they had several sorts of long and short syllables, which at present we do not distinguish. Even the common people were so exact, and so well accustomed to this pronunciation, that Cicero, in his book de Oratore, observes, *that a comedian could not lengthen or shorten a syllable a little more than he ought, but the people would be offended with this mis-pronouncing, without any other rule than the discernment of the ear, which was accustomed to judge of long and short syllables, as well as of the rising and sinking of the voice.*

Now as the long syllables had two times, and the short ones only one; on the contrary, the common or doubtful were properly those that had only a time and a half: which was the case of the weak position, where the vowel was followed by a syllable beginning with a mute and a liquid, as in *pätris.* For the liquid being the last, glided away too nimbly, and was too weak in comparison

rison to the mute with which it was joined; and therefore it was owing to this inequality that the foregoing vowel was not so firmly sustained as if there had been two mutes, as in *jacto*; or two liquids, as in *ille*; or as if the mute had been in the last syllable, as *martyr*; or, in short, as if the mute had been at the end of a syllable, and the liquid at the beginning of the next, as in *ābludit*, *āblatus*. In all which cases the syllable would have been long by a firm position, and would have had *two times*: whereas in the other, having only one time and a half, for the reasons above-mentioned, this half measure was sometimes altogether neglected, and then the syllable was reckoned short; and at other times it was somewhat sustained and lengthened to an intire measure; and then the syllable was looked upon as long in verse. And hence it appears for what reason when the syllable was long by nature, as in *mātris*, the mute and liquid did not render it common, because as it came from *māter*, whereof the former is long of itself, it had its *two times* already.

But even when a syllable is long by a firm and intire position, still we are to observe that there is a great difference between being thus long by position, and long by nature.

The syllable long by nature was somewhat firmer and fuller, being a reduplication of the same vowel, pursuant to what hath been observed in the treatise of letters, as *maalus*, an apple-tree, *poopulus*, a poplar-tree, *seedes*, &c. Whereas the syllable long by position only, had no other length than its being sustained by the two following consonants; just as in Greek there is a great difference between an *eta* and an *epsilon* long by position.

But as there was a difference in the pronunciation between a syllable long by nature and a syllable barely long by position, so there was a difference also betwixt a syllable short by nature and a syllable short by position only, that is from its being placed before another vowel. For the latter always preserved somewhat of its natural quantity, and doubtless had more time in verse than the syllable short by nature. Thus it is that in Greek the long vowels, or even the diphthongs, were reckoned short, whenever the following word began with another vowel or a diphthong, without there being any necessity for cutting them off by *synalœpha*. Thus it is likewise that in Latin *præ* is short in composition before a vowel, as *praēiret*, *praēesse*, &c. And thus it is that the Latins have often used those syllables, as

Et longum formose valē, vălĕ, inquit *Iola*. Virg. Ecl. 3.
Insulaē Ionio *in magno quas dira Celæno*. Æn. 3.
Victor apud rapidum Simoenta sub Ilio alto. Æn. 5.
Te Corydon ō Alexi ———— Ecl. 2.

And an evident proof that these syllables still preserved at that time something of their nature, is their being sometimes long on those occasions:

——— *Cum vacuus Domino praēiret Arion.* Stat.
ō ego *quantum egi! quam vasta potentia nostra est!* Ovid.

II. *Difficult*

II. *Difficult passages of the antients, which may be solved by those principles.*

This affords us some light towards clearing up several passages of the antients, which appear unintelligible, unless they be referred to the above principles. As when Festus says, INLEX *productâ sequenti syllaba significat, qui legi non paret: Correptâ sequenti, inductorem ab illiciendo.* For it is beyond all doubt that the last in *inlex* or *illex* is always long in quantity, since the *e* precedes the *x* which is a double letter; but one was pronounced with *n*, as if it were ἴλληξ; and the other with an *ι*, as if it were ἴλλιξ. One like the long *e* in the French words *fête*, *bête*, *tête*; and the other like the short *e* in *Prophète*, *nette*, *navette*, &c. Hence the one made *illegis* in the genitive, preserving its *e* long as coming from *lex*; and the other *illicis*, changing its *e* into *i* short, which it resumes from the verb *illicio* whence it is derived.

Thus when Victorinus says that IN and CON are sometimes short in composition, as *inconstans, imprudens*; and that they are long in words where they are followed by an S or an F, as *instare, infidus*; this means that in the latter the *i* was long in quantity, and short in the former, though it was always long by position; so that this I, thus long in quantity, partook of the nature of EI, *infidus*, nearly as if it were *einfidus*, &c. And this helps to illustrate a difficult passage of Cicero de Oratore, whence the above author seems to have extracted this rule; *Inclitus*, says he, *dicimus primâ brevi litterâ, insanus productâ: inhumanus brevi; infelix longâ. Et ne multis: in quibus verbis eæ primæ sunt litteræ quæ in* SAPIENTE & FELICE, *productè dicuntur, in cæteris breviter. Itemque composuit, concrepuit, consuevit, confecit,* &c. Where by *sapiens* and *felix*, he marks the words beginning with an S or an F, as Gellius, lib. 2. c. 17. explains him; and where by the word *long*, he does not mean to speak of the accent, but of quantity, it being manifest that the accent of *infelix* ought to be upon the second, and not upon the first; which is still more clear in *inhumánus*, where it is altogether impossible that the accent should be upon the first.

Thus likewise are we to understand Aulus Gellius, when he says that *ob* and *sub* have not the power of lengthening syllables, no more than *con*, except when it is followed by the same letters, as in *con-Stituit* and *con-Fecit*: or (as he continues) when the *n* is intirely dropped, as in *coöpertus*; so that they pronounced *coöpertus, coönexus*, and *coögo*, as he repeats it himself, lib. 11. c. 17: when he says in the same book that this rule of the following of S and F, was not observed in respect to *pro*, which was short in *proficisci, profundere*, &c. and long in *proferre, profligare*, &c. that is, they pronounced *prooferre, prooftigare*: when he says, lib. 11. c. 3. that they pronounced one way *pro rostris*, another way *pro tribunali*, another *pro concione*, another *pro potestate intercedere*: when he says that in *objices* and *objicibus* the *o* was short by nature, and that it could not be lengthened but by writing those words with two *ji*, the same as in *objicio*: when he says that in *composuit, conjecit, concrepuit,*

crepuit, *o* was likewise short, that is, that it had only the sound of an *omicron*: when he says that in *ago* the first was short; whereas in *actito* and *actitavi* it was long: and when he says that in *quiescit* the second was short, *perpetua linguæ Latinæ consuetudine*, though it comes from *quies* where *e* is long.

Thus it is that Donatus and Servius distinguish between the persons of *sum* and *edo*, as *es, est; esset, essemus*; in this that the first *e* is short when it comes from *sum*, and long when it comes from *edo*.

In fine, thus it is that Julius Scaliger proves against Erasmus, who found fault with some feet and numbers in Cicero, that *sunt* is short, because it comes from *sumus*. And the whole we have been saying is very necessary to observe, in order to comprehend what Cicero, Quintilian, and others have wrote concerning the numbers and feet of a period: and to shew that when the nouns, and even the prepositions, had different significations they were frequently known by the pronunciation.

III. *Whether from the difference they made in the pronunciation of short and long vowels, we may conclude that* U *was sounded like the French diphthong* OU *in long syllables only.*

From what we have been now observing in regard to the different pronunciation of the long and short vowels, Lipsius and Vossius were induced to believe that the pronunciation of the Latin U, which sounded full, like the French diphthong OU, regarded only the long U; and that the short was sounded in the same manner as the Greek *upsilon*, that is like a French U. But this opinion we have sufficiently refuted in the same treatise, c. 4. n. 2. and from what we have been mentioning it plainly appears, that when two different pronunciations are observed in a vowel, one longer or fuller, the other shorter or closer, as in *āgo* and *āctito*, in ἄλλη and ἄλλιξ, this does not mean that we are to take a sound of so different a nature as *lustrum* and *loustrum*, *lumen* and *loumen*.

Therefore when Festus says that *lustrum*, with the former short, signified *ditches full of mud*; and with the former long, implied the space of five years; he meant it only in regard to quantity, and not to a pronunciation intirely different: and all that we are to understand by it is, that one was longer than the other by nature, as would be the case of *lŭstrum* and *lūūstrum* or *lūstrum*, though they are both long by position.

And this helps to explain a passage of Varro, which Lipsius and Vossius have misunderstood. When he says that *luit* hath the former short in the present, and long in the preterite. But he means nothing more than that in the present tense U was short by nature, and in the preterite it was long, so that they pronounced *lūit*, according to the common rule of preterites of two syllables, which generally have the former long: this did not hinder however the first of *lŭit*, even in the preterite, from being short by position;

as the diphthong *æ*, though long of itself, is short by position in *præit* according to what we have already observed. And therefore, all things considered, notwithstanding that this passage of Varro is the strongest argument that Lipsius and Vossius make use of, yet it does not prove that the Romans formerly pronounced their U any otherwise than nearly as the French diphthong *ou*, or as it is pronounced by the modern Italians.

But an invincible argument, in my opinion, (to mention it here only by the way) that U short and U long had but one and the same sound, is that the word *cuculus*, which hath the former short and the second long, as we have shewn, p. 348. was certainly pronounced in the same manner as the French would pronounce *coucoulous*, since in French we still say *un coucou*, and in both languages these words were formed by an Onomatopeia, or imitation of the sound, in order to express the note of this bird.

SECTION III.

Of LATIN POETRY,

And the different species of metre; as also of the feet, the figures, and beauties to be observed in versifying; and of the manner of intermixing them in divers sorts of composition.

Divided in the clearest order and method.

AFTER having laid down the rules to know the measure of syllables, whether long, short, or common, in the treatise of quantity; and the manner of pronouncing them properly in prose, in the discourse upon accents; we must now treat of Latin poetry, and the different species of verse, though this subject is less relative to grammar than the precedent.

Verses are composed of feet, and feet of syllables.

CHAPTER I.
Of Feet.

I. *Of the nature of feet in verse.*

FEET are nothing more than a certain measure and number of syllables, according to which the verse seems to move with cadence, and in which we are principally to consider the rising ἄρσις and the sinking θέσις, of which we took notice when treating of the accents. These feet are of two sorts, one simple, and the other compound. The simple are formed of two or three syllables, as we are now going to explain.

II. *Of feet of two syllables.*

The feet of two syllables are four.

1. The SPONDEE, *Spondæus*, consists of two long ones, as *Mūsāē*; and is so called from the word σπονδὴ, *libatio, sacrificium*, from its being particularly made use of in sacrifices, on account of its majestic gravity.

2. The PYRRHIC, *Pyrrhicus*, consists of two short ones; as *Dĕŭs*; and is so called, says Hesychius, from the noun πυρρίχη,

signifying

signifying a kind of dance of armed men, in which this foot was predominant; and which is supposed to have been invented by Pyrrhus, son of Achilles; though others will have it to be the invention of Pyrrhicus the Cydonian.

3. The TROCHEE, *Trochæus*, consists of a long and a short, as *Mūsă*; and takes its name from the word τρέχω, *currere*, because it moves quickly. But Cicero, Quintilian, and Terentianus, call it *Choreus*, from the word *chorus*, because it was well adapted to dancing and music.

4. The IAMBUS, *Iambus*, the reverse of the Trochee, consists of a short and a long, as *Dĕō*; and is so denominated, not from the verb ἰαμβίζω, *maledictis*, *incesso*, which is rather a derivative itself from the foot Iambus, but from a young woman named *Iambé*, who is said to have been the author of it; or rather from ἰάπτω, *maledico*, because this foot was at first made use of in invectives and satyrical pieces, as we are informed by Horace,

Archilochum proprio rabies armavit Iambo.

III. *Of feet of three syllables.*

We reckon eight feet of three syllables, of which no more than three are used in verse, viz. those immediately following the Molossus.

1. The MOLOSSUS, *Molossus*, consists of three long ones, *audīrī*, and takes its name from a certain people of Epirus, called *Molossi*, who particularly affected to make use of it.

2. The Tribrac, *Tribrachys*, consists of three short ones, *Prĭămŭs*; whence its name is derived, being composed of τρεῖς, *three*, and βραχύς, *short*. But Quintilian generally calls it TROCHEE.

3. The DACTYL, *Dactylus*, consists of one long and two short, *Carmĭnă*, and derives its name from δάκτυλος, *digitus*, because the finger is composed of three joints, the first of which is longer than any of the rest. Cicero calls it *Heroüs*, from its being particularly made use of in relating the exploits of great men and heroes.

4. The ANAPÆST, *Anapæstus*, consists of two short and one long, *Dŏmĭnī*, and is thus denominated from the verb ἀναπαίω, *repercutio*, because those who danced according to the cadence of this foot, used to beat the ground in quite a different manner from that which was observed in the Dactyl.

5. The BACCHIC, *Bacchius*, consists of one short and two long, *ĕgĭstās*, and is so called from its having been frequently used in the hymns of Bacchus.

6. The ANTIBACCHIC, *Antibacchius*, consists of two long and one short, *cāntătĕ*, and takes its name from its opposition to the precedent. But Victorinus says that the *Antibacchic* is composed of one short and two long, as *lăcūnās*, where it is plain that he gives the name of *Antibacchius* to what the others call *Bacchius*. Hephestio calls it *Palimbacchius*.

7. The AMPHIMACER or CRETIC, *Amphimacer sive Creticus*, is composed of one short between two long, *cāstĭtās*. Both these names are mentioned in Quintilian. The former comes from

ἀμφὶ, *utrinque*, and μακρός, *longus*; and the latter is owing to the particular liking which the people of Crete had for this foot. Which shews that it is a mistake in Hephestion to read Κριτικός, instead of Κρητικός, Cretan.

8. The AMPHIBRAC, *Amphibrachys, short on both sides*, consists of one long between two short, *ămārĭ*; which plainly shews its name. Diomedes takes notice that it was also called *scolius*, from a kind of harp, to which it was particularly adapted.

These are the twelve simple feet, of which no more than six are used in verse; three of two measures, namely the *Spondee*, the *Dactyl*, and the *Anapæst*; and three of a measure and a half, *viz.* the *Iambus*, the *Trochee*, and the *Tribrac*.

And the reason is, because a foot, in order to have its proper cadence, ought to have two parts or half feet, by which the antients frequently measured their verses. Now every half foot can have no more than one measure, which is the space in pronouncing one long syllable or two short ones; for more would make an intire foot, as a Trochee (⁻⁻) or an Iambus (⁻⁻).

Thus the Pyrrich, having in all but one measure, which is the value of two short syllables, is rather half a foot than a foot. The Molossus having three long ones, which make three measures; and the Bacchic, Antibacchic, and Amphimacer, having two long and one short, which make two measures and a half, one half foot of each of those four feet would have two measures, or a measure and a half, which is too much.

And it is the same in regard to the Amphibrac, though it contains in the whole but two measures, because its long syllable being between two short, and one of the half feet being obliged to be of two successive syllables, it must necessarily be composed of a long and a short, consequently it will have a measure and a half.

There remain therefore only the six above-mentioned, three of which have half feet equal, and answering to the unison, *viz.* the Spondee, the Dactyl, and the Anapæst. The others have them as one to two, which answers to the octave; *viz.* the Trochee, the Iambus and the Tribrac.

Therefore we must not fancy that the Amphimacer or the Cretic (⁻⁻⁻) ever enters into the composition of a comic verse, as no such thing hath been mentioned by any of the antients that have treated of this sort of metre. But if there are verses that seem to be incapable of being measured without having recourse to this foot, as this of Terence,

Student facere, in apparando consumunt diem.

it is to be supposed that in such a case they rather made use of a synerefis, by contracting *apparando* into three syllables, *apprando*, according to the opinion of Vossius in his grammar, and of Camerarius in his problems.

Thus we may take it for certain that there are but six feet necessary for composing all sorts of verse, which may be comprized in the following rule.

RULE OF THE SIX NECESSARY FEET.

All verse whatever is composed but of six sorts of feet; the Spondee ⁻ ⁻, the Trochee ⁻ ᵛ, the Iambus ᵛ ⁻, the Tribrac ᵛ ᵛ ᵛ, the Dactyl ⁻ ᵛ ᵛ, and the Anapest ᵛ ᵛ ⁻.

IV. *Of compound feet.*

Compound feet are formed of two of the preceding joined together; and therefore are rather a collection of feet, according to the observation of Cicero and Quintilian.

They are generally reckoned sixteen, the name of which it is proper to take notice of, not only by reason there are some sorts of verse which are denominated from thence, but because otherwise we shall not be able to understand the remark of Cicero and Quintilian in regard to the numerosity and cadence of periods.

1. The double Spondee, *Dispondeus*, is composed of four long ones, *concludentes*, that is, of two Spondees put together.

2. The Proceleusmatic, *Proceleusmaticus*, consists of four short, *hominibus*; and therefore it is formed of two Pyrrhics. It seems to have taken its name from κέλευσμα, *hortatus nauticus*, because the captain of the ship generally made use of it to hearten the crew, being very well adapted by its celerity to sudden and unexpected occasions.

3. The double Iambus, *Diiambus*, two Iambus's, one after another, *severitas*.

4. The double Trochee, or double Choree; *Ditrocheus*, or *Dichoreus*; two Trochees, one after another, *comprobare*.

5. The great Ionic, two long and two short, that is, a Spondee and a Pyrrhic, *cantabimus*.

6. The small Ionic, two short, and two long that is, a Pyrrhic and a Spondee, *venerantes*.

These two feet are called Ionic, from their having been used chiefly by the Ionians. One is called Great, *Ionicus major*, five *à majore*, because it begins with the greatest quantity, that is, with two long ones; and the other small, *Ionicus minor*, or *à minore*, because *à minore quantitate incipit*, that is, with two short.

7. The Choriambus, *Choriambus*, two short between two long, *historiæ*. That is a Choree or Trochee, and an Iambus.

8. The Antispast, *Antispastus*, two long betwixt two short, *secundare*. And therefore it is composed of an Iambus and a Trochee. It derives its name from ἀντισπᾶσθαι, *in contrarium trahi*, because it passes from a short to a long, and then the reverse from a long to a short.

9. The first Epitrit, *Epitritus primus*, one short and three long, *salutantes*; and therefore is composed of an Iambus and a Spondee.

10. The

10. The second Epitrit, *Epitritus secundus*, a long and a short, and then two long, *cŏncĭtātī*; and therefore consists of a Trochee and a Spondee.

11. The third Epitrit, *Epitritus tertius*, two long, then a short and a long, *cōmmūnĭcānt*; and therefore is composed of a Spondee and an Iambus.

12. The fourth Epitrit, *Epitritus quartus*, three long and one short, *īncāntārĕ*. And therefore it is composed of a Spondee and a Trochee.

These four last feet derive their name from ἐπὶ, *supra*, and τρίτος, *tertius*, because they have three measures, and something more, namely a short syllable. But the first, second, third, and fourth, are so called from the situation of the short syllable. The second was also called Κάρικος, the third Ρόδιος, and the fourth μονογενὴς, as Hephestion observeth.

13. The first Pæon, one long and three short, *cōnfĭcĕrĕ*; and therefore it consists of a Trochee and a Pyrrhic.

14. The second Pæon, a short and a long, with two short, *rĕsŏlvĕrĕ*; and therefore it consists of an Iambus and a Pyrrhic.

15. The third Pæon, two short, a long and a short, *sŏcĭārĕ*; and therefore is composed of a Pyrrhic and a Trochee.

16. The fourth Pæon, three short, and one long, *cĕlĕrĭtās*; and therefore consists of a Pyrrhic and an Iambus.

The Pæon may be also called Pæan, these words differing only in dialect. And it was so denominated from its having been used particularly in the hymns to Apollo, whom they called *Pæana*.

The Pæon is opposite to the Epitrit. For whereas in the Epitrit there is one short with three long; on the contrary, in the Pæon you have one long with three short; where each of the four is named according to the order in which this long syllable is placed. The first and last Pæon compose the verse called *Pæonic*.

These are all the simple and compound feet. But, to the end that they may be the better retained, I shall exhibit them in the following table, in the order above described.

A REGULAR TABLE
Of all the FEET.

THEY RECKON IN ALL EIGHT AND TWENTY FEET, viz.	XII. SIMPLE, of which no more than six are used in verse, which we have marked in capitals with a particular cypher.	Of two syllables, 4.	Quantity.	1. SPONDÆUS, Pyrrichius, 2. TROCHÆUS, five Chorcus,	Lēgī, Pret. Lĕgĭt, Pref. Lēgĭt, Pret.	
			Difpofition.			
		Of three syllables, 2.	Quantity.	3. ÏAMBUS, Molossus, 4. TRIBRACHYS, 5. DACTYLUS, 6. ANAPÆSTUS, Bacchius, Antibacchius, Amphimacer, Amphibrachys,	Lĕgūnt. Lēgērūnt. Lĕgĕrĕt. Lēgĕrăt. Lĕgĕrēnt. Lēgēbānt. Lēgĭffĕ. Lēgĕrānt. Lĕgĕbăt.	
			Difpofition.			
			Difpofition.			
			Quantity.			
	XVI. COMPOUNDS of two feet of two syllables. Of the two first, one has four long, and the other has four short. The following six have two long and two short. The four next have three long and one short. And the four last, three short and one long.	I. Of the same foot repeated, 4.	Two Spondees, Two Pyrrichs, Two ïambus's, Two Trochees or Chorees.	Difpondæus, Proceleufmaticus, Dïiambus, Dichoreus,	Mācēnātēs. Tĕnŭĭbŭs. ămǣnĭtās. Pērmănērĕ.	
		II. Of two contrary feet, 4.	Spondee & Pyrrich, Pyrrich & Spondee, Choree & ïambus, ïambus & Choree,	Major ïonicus, Minor ïonicus, Choriambus, Antifpaftus,	Pūlcbērrĭmŭs. Dĭōmēdēă. Hĭftŏrĭās. Sĕcūndārĕ.	
		III. Of two feet not contrary, where the long predominate, 4.	ïambus & Spondee, Trochee & Spondee, Spondee & ïambus, Spondee & Trochee,	Epitritus, three long and one short,	1. Vŏlūptātēs. 2. Cōncĭtārī. 3. Cōmmūnĭcānt. 4. ēxpēctārĕ.	
		IV. Of two feet not contrary, where the short predominate, 4.	Trochee & Pyrrich, ïambus & Pyrrich, Pyrrich & Trochee, Pyrrich & ïambus,	Peon vel Pean; three short and one long,	1. Cōncĭpĕrĕ. 2. Rĕſōlvĕrĕ. 3. ălĭĕnŭs. 4. Tĕmĕrĭtās.	

Chapter II.
Of verse in general.

VERSE is nothing more than a certain number of feet disposed in a regular order and cadence. The Latins call it *versus*, from the verb *vertere*, to turn, because verses being set in lines, when you come to the end of one, you must turn your eye to the beginning of the other, in order to read or write it.

The Greeks call it ςίχος, *order*, or *rank*, because of the same disposition of lines. And from this word joined with ἥμισυς, *dimidius*, comes *hemistichium*, an hemistich or half verse.

Verse is called also κῶλον, *membrum*, with regard to the intire stanzas it composes, and to which they gave the name of *metrum*. And from thence come the words δίκωλοι, stanzas composed of two sorts of verse; τρίκωλοι, of three sorts, &c.

In the general notion of verse, there are three things to consider: the cæsura, *cæsura*; the final cadence which they call *depositio*, or *clausula*: and the manner of scanning or measuring.

I. Of the cæsura and its different species.

The word *cæsura* comes from *cædere*, to cut; and this name is given in verse to the syllable that remains after a foot, at the end of a foot, from which it seems to be cut off, to serve for a beginning to the next word.

The Greeks for the same reason call it τομή or κόμμα, and Cicero, as also Victorinus, *incisio* or *incisum*.

The cæsura is commonly divided into four different species, which take their name from the order wherein they are placed in verse, which the antients, as hath been observed already, used to measure by half feet. Therefore calling them all by the word ἥμισυς, *dimidius*, and μερίς, *pars*, they specified them by the numeral nouns according to their order, thus,

1. *Triemimeris*, from the word τρεῖς, *three*; that which is made after the third half foot; that is, in the syllable immediately next to the first foot.

2. *Penthemimeris*, from the word πέντε, *quinque*; that which is made in the fifth half foot; viz. in the syllable which follows the two first feet.

3. *Hephthemimeris*, from the word ἑπτά, *septem*, that which is made in the seventh half foot, viz. in the syllable which follows next to the three first feet.

4. *Ennebemimeris*, from the word ἐννέα, *novem*, that which is made in the ninth half foot, viz. in the syllable next to the fourth foot.

The three first cæsuras are in this verse of Virgil.

Silvestrem tenui musam meditaris avenâ.

All four in this:

Ille latus niveum molli fultus hyacintho.

To those four we may add a fifth species of cæsura called,

5. *Hendechemimeris*, from the word ἑνδεκα, *undecim*, because it is formed in the eleventh half foot, that is in the syllable next to the fifth foot, as in Virgil,

Vertitur interea cælum, & ruit oceano nox.
Sternitur, examinísque tremens procumbit humi bos.

But it is very rare, and ought to be used with great discretion, as Virgil has done in these two verses, and a few others.

II. *In what place the cæsura is most graceful; and of the beauty it gives to verse.*

In heroic verse or hexameter, the cæsura is most graceful after the second foot; as

Arma virúmque cano, &c.

Otherwise we should endeavour to place it after the first and third foot; as

Ille meas errare boves, &c.

But a verse that has no cæsura, especially if it be an hexameter, is very disagreeable to the ear; as

Urbem fortem nuper cepit fortior hostis.

Though in Catullus's epithalamium we meet with one that is esteemed.

Tertia pars data patri, pars data tertia matri.

And when the cæsura is not till after the third foot, the verse is not much more agreeable; as in Lucretius.

Et jam cætera, mortales quæ suadet adire.

III. *That the cæsura has the power of lengthening short syllables.*

Now it is observable that the cæsura hath such a power, as to lengthen a syllable that was short by nature, even when it is followed by a vowel; whether after the first foot, as

Pectoribūs inbians spirantia consulit exta.

Or after the second;

Omnia vincit amōr, & nos cedamus amori.

Or after the third;

Dona debinc auro gravīā sellóque elephanto.

Or after the fourth;

Graius homo infectos linquens profugūs Hymenæos.

And the reason is extremely natural, because as the antients pronounced their verse according to the cadence of the feet; and the syllable which thus remaineth at the end of a word, was predominant in the next foot, whose beginning it formed; it ought to receive such a force in the pronunciation, as thereby to sustain all the syllables of that very foot. Hence the cæsura produces this same effect likewise in smaller verses, as in the following Sapphic of Ausonius.

Tertius hōrūm mĭhĭ nōn măgĭstĕr.

And in this Phaleucian of Statius,

Quō nōn dĭgnĭŏr hās sŭbīt hăbēnăs.

And 'tis also by virtue of this same figure that the enclitic Quᴇ is long in Virgil and other poets;

Limi-

Limin**aque**, laurúsque Dei, totúsque moveri, Æn. 3.
Sid**eraque** ventique nocent; avidæque volucres, Ovid.
Without pretending that the *que* is common by nature, as Servius would have it: or that those passages should be read in another manner, since they are not the only ones, as some imagined, that are to be found in antient authors.

It is also by this figure that Virgil seems to have made the latter long in the nominative *fagōs*, in the following passage Georg. 2. which has puzzled all the commentators.

Et steriles platani malos gessere valentes:
Castaneæ fagōs, ornúsque incanuit albo
Flore pyri ⸺

For the meaning seems to be this, *fagos* (A Greek nominative for *fagus*) *incanuit flore castaneæ, & ornus flore pyri*. And this is the explication Vossius gives it, which seems to be much clearer and more natural than any other I have seen hitherto.

IV. *Of the final cadence called* DEPOSITIO, *and of the four names it gives to verse*.

The Latins give the name of *Depositio* to the final cadence, which terminates as it were the measure of the verse. The Greeks called it ἀπόθεσιν; but they likewise termed it καλάληξιν, that is, *terminationem, clausulam*; for καλαλήγειν, signifies *desinere*.

And thence ariseth the distinction of verse into four species, ACATALECTIC, CATALECTIC, BRACHYCATALECTIC, and HYPERCATALECTIC, which are terms more difficult to retain than the thing itself, and which we are obliged nevertheless to explain, in order to render those intelligible, who make use of them, when treating of poetry.

1. The Acatalectic or *Acatalect*, ἀκαλάληκλ⊙, *non desinens*, is that which does not stop short, but has its full measure, having neither too much, nor too little. Hence it is by the Latins called *perfectus:* as the following iambic verse of four feet.

Musæ Jovis sunt filiæ.

2. The Catalectic or *Catalect*, καλάληκλ⊙, is that which seems to halt by the way, having a syllable too little to arrive at its journey's end: hence it is that Trapezont calls it *pendulus*, and others *semimutilus*, by reason it does not want an intire foot, but only half a one. As the following.

Musæ Jovem canebant.

3. The Brachycatalectic, or *Brachycatalect*, βραχυκαλάληκλ⊙, is that which is still more mutilated and deficient than the former, because it wants an intire foot; for which reason the Latins called it *mutilus:* such is this other of three feet instead of four.

Musæ Jovis gnatæ.

4. On the contrary, the Hypercatalectic, or *Hypercatalect*, ὑπερκαλάληκλ⊙, is that which has something more than its just measure, or the end where it ought to terminate. Whether this surplus be a syllable, as in the following verse:

Musæ sorores sunt Minervæ:

Or whether this be an intire foot, as in the following:

    Musæ sorores Palladis lugent.

Which is also called ὑπέρμετρον, *excedens metrum,* because the Greeks dividing their iambics and trochaics into dimeters and trimeters, that is into verses of four or six feet, and allowing two feet to each metre, that which hath five of them, exceeding this first sort of metres, has more than is necessary to make a full measure. But the whole of this will be further illustrated by what is to follow presently, where we shall shew that without amusing ourselves too long about these terms, we ought to consider the defect of a syllable sometimes in the beginning, and sometimes at the end of a verse.

Chapter III.

Of the measure or manner of scanning verse, and of the figures used therein.

THE manner of measuring and scanning verse consists in dividing it into the several feet of which it is composed.

The Latins call it *scansio,* because it seems as if the verse climbed up by means of those feet. The Greeks term it ἄρσιν, *elevationem,* and θέσιν, *positionem,* which hath been observed already. Attilius calls it *motum & ingressionem carminis.*

A verse is scanned either by the measure of distinct feet, as hexameters and pentameters; or by the measure of two feet according to what we mentioned in the preceding chapter. But in order to scan verse, there are four principal figures to observe, *Ecthlipsis, Synalæpha, Synæresis,* and *Diæresis:* to which we may add *Systole* and *Diastole.*

I. *Of Ecthlipsis.*

The word *Ecthlipsis* comes from ἐκθλίζειν, *extundere, elidere,* to break and to bruise. It is formed by cutting off the *m* final of a word together with its vowel, when the following word begins with another vowel; as

    *Mul*tum *ille &* terris *jactatus, & alto.* Virg.

    O *curas homin*um, ô quan*tum* est *in rebus inane.* Pers.

Formerly by this figure they used also to cut off the *s* final, either the *s* only, in order to hinder the length of the position, when it was followed by another consonant; or the *s* and the preceding vowel, when the next word began with a vowel, just as they used to do with the *m:* as

    Doctu' *fidelis, suavis homo* facundu' *suoque*

    Content' ātquĕ *beātus, scitus, facunda loquens in*

    Tempore, commod' *& verborum vir paucorum.* Ennius.

    Delphinus jacet haud nimio lustratu' *decore.* Cic. in Arat.

    Longè erit à primo, quisqui' *secundus erit.* Alcin.

And this is still more usual in Terence and other comic writers, as *eju'* for *ejus, omnibu'* for *omnibus, dignu'* for *dignus,* &c. In other

                                                      pure

pure writers this is rare, though some think that Virgil did not scruple to make use of it in divers places, as in the following.

Limina tectorum, & medii' in penetralibus hostem.

As Pierius says it was wrote in antient MSS, as Farnaby still reads it, and as Erythræus thinks it ought to be read; which he endeavours to defend not only by the authority of Lucretius, but moreover by several other passages in Virgil. Though others read *medium* instead of *mediis*.

Now as the letter *s* was sometimes cut off before a consonant in order to prevent the position, the same was practised also on the *m* by antient writers, as

Lanigeræ pecudes & equōrŭ' dŭellica proles. Lucret.

Sometimes it was left standing, as we now leave the *s*, and then it was made short, as already we have observed, when treating of quantity.

Cōrpŏrŭm officiu' est quoniam premere omnia deorsum. Lucr.

II. *Of Synalæpha.*

The synalæpha is in regard to vowels and diphthongs, the same as the Ecthlipsis in respect to *m*. For it is formed by cutting off a vowel or a diphthong at the end of a word, because of another vowel or diphthong with which the next word begins, as

Conticuer' omnes intentiqu' ora tenebant. Virg.

The Latins for this reason give it the name of *collisio*. But the word Συναλοιφὴ properly signifies *counctio*, coming from ἀλείφω, *ungo*. So that the metaphor seems to be taken from fat or unctuous things, the last lay of which makes the other disappear.

III. *Directions in regard to the use of those two figures, Ecthlipsis and Synalæpha.*

These two figures are smoother, when the vowel subsequent to that which was cut off, happens to be long, than when it is short: as appears from this verse of Catullus.

Troja, nefas, commune sepulchrum Europæ, Asiæque.

This is owing to the nature of the voice, which having thus lost a syllable at the end of a word, ought in return to be sustained at the beginning of the next, to prevent too great a bending and precipitancy in the cadence. And it is observable particularly in regard to the ecthlipsis, that Virgil generally makes it fall on a syllable long by position; as

Postquam introgressi, & coram data copia fandi.

Illum expirantem transfixo pectore flammas. And the like.

The synalæpha on the other hand seems to have a particular smoothness, when the following word begins with the vowel that was cut off at the end of the precedent, because then it does not depart so much from the natural sound which we are accustomed to hear in those words: the remaining vowel having nearly its own value, and that of the vowel suppressed in the foregoing word, as

Ille

Ille ego qui quondam gracili modulatus avena. Virg.
Ergo omnis longo solvit se Teucria luctu. Id.

Be that as it may, we must always take care that the pronunciation arising from these figures be not too harsh, or disagreeable to the ear, which is the judge of these matters. Nor should they be too often repeated, especially in elegiac verse, which requireth a particular softness; whereas in heroics they may sometimes occasion a more extraordinary gravity, according to particular occasions; as in this verse of Virgil:

Phillida amo ante alias.

Which he has designedly strewed with soft figures, extremely well adapted to the subject. As on the contrary he intended to represent something hideous, when he described Polyphemus,

Monstrum horrendum, informe, ingens, &c.

Again:

Tela inter media, atque horrentes Marte Latinos.

Except in such cases, these figures should not be seen above twice in the same verse. Nor should they readily be put in the beginning of a verse, though Virgil has sometimes done it with elegance, as when he says:

Si ad vitulam spectes; nihil est quod pocula laudes.

These figures are also harsh at the beginning of the sixth foot, as in Juvenal.

Loripedem rectus derideat, Æthiopem albus.

Though we meet with them in Virgil:

Frigida Daphni boves ad flumina: nulla neque amnem.

And even in the middle of a pentameter, as in Propertius,

Hercules, Antæique, Hesperidumque comes.

We may likewise observe that they are not the most graceful at the end of the fifth foot in heroic verse, as in this of Catullus.

Difficile est longum subito deponere amorem.

Though there are several instances of them in Virgil, who seems even to have affected them on some occasions, as

Juturnamque parat fratris dimittere ab armis.

Where he might have said, *demittere fratris ab armis.*
Again,

———— findit se sanguine ab uno,

Where he might have said, *se sanguine findit ab uno.*

Thus in the 4th Georg. he expresseth Orpheus's concern in this beautiful verse:

Ille cava solans ægrum testudine amorem.

Now these figures produce very near the same effect in the last dactyl of the pentameter, if they are used with great discretion, as

Quadrijugo cernes sæpe resistere equo.

The ecthlipsis and synalæpha are also sometimes at the end of a verse, whose last syllable is cut off by the first word of the next verse, which begins with another vowel; as

Aut dulcis musti Vulcano decoquit humorem,
*Aut foliis undam————*Virg.
Omnia Mercurio similis, vocemque, coloremque.
*Et crines flavos————*Virg.

Et

*Et magnos membrorum artus, magna offa, lacertofque
Exuit——————— ———— Idem.*

Which led some into a mistake that an hexameter might sometimes end with a dactyl. But this opinion we shall refute more amply, chap. 4. n. 5.

IV. *The synalæpha omitted.*

The synalæpha is sometimes omitted either regularly, or by licence. Regularly, as in *o, heu, ah, pro, væ, vah, hei,* and the like interjections, which sustain the voice, and retard the pronunciation, because of the passion they express, which vents itself outwardly, and thereby hinders those words from being cut off. As

O pater: ô hominum, divûmque æterna potestas. Virg.
Heu ubi pacta fides, ubi quæ jurare solebas. Ovid.
Ah ego ne possim tanta videre mala? Tibul.

The same may be said of *io,* since we find in Ovid,

Et bis io Arethusa, io Arethusa vocavit.

The synalæpha is omitted by licence: first when it is considered as a consonant, as the French do with their asperated H, saying not *l'honte,* but *la honte.*

Posthabitâ coluisse Samo: hîc illius arma. Virg.

Whence, I think, we might infer that the H may sometimes produce a position in verse; though it is difficult to prove it, the authorities that are brought on that account, being generally joined with a cæsura, as when Virgil says:

Ille latus niveum molli fultus hyacintho.

Secondly the synalæpha is omitted without any other reason than the will and pleasure of the poet, who takes this liberty in imitation of the Greeks, as

Et succus pecorī et lac subducitur agnis. Virg.

We meet likewise with examples of this figure both before H and before another vowel in the same verse.

Stant & juniperī & castaneæ hirsutæ. Virg.
Clamassent, & littus Hilā, Hilā omne sonaret. Id.

But be that as it may, this figure ought to be very rarely used, because it produceth what we call an *hiatus* in verse, which we should endeavour to avoid; especially when the syllable is short, though there are instances of some in Virgil, as *Hilā* in the fourth foot of the abovementioned verse. Again,

Et vera incessu patuit Deā. Ille ubi matrem, &c.

Where the poet thought he might stop at *Dea,* because the sense ends there; and then begins another sentence.

The long vowel, or the diphthong that is not cut off by synalæpha, becomes common in verse. Therefore it is short by position, that is because of the next vowel, in these here:

Nomen & arma locum servant: tē amice nequivi. Virg.
Credimus? an qui amant ipsi sibi somnia fingunt? Id.
Tē Coridōn ō Alexi! Trahit sua quemque voluptas. Id.
Implerunt montes; flerunt Rhodopeiæ arces. Id.

On

On the contrary it is long in these.

  Lamentis gemitúque & fœmineō ululatu. Id.
  Ante tibi Eoæ Atlantides abscondantur. Id.

There are even instances of its being long and short in the same verse, as

  Ter sunt conatī imponere Peliō *Ossaū.* Id. 1. Georg.

And in the same book,

  Glaucō & Pănŏpeæ & *Inoŏ Melicertæ.*

For *o* in *Glaucō*, not being cut off, remaineth long: and *æ* in *Panopeæ* (the first and second of which are short) not being cut off, is made short by position.

But it is proper to observe that as the most antient authors did not allow themselves this liberty, but generally put a *d* to remove this hiatus, as in the following verse of Ennius quoted by Tully.

  Nam videbar somniare med' *ego esse mortuum.*

Where to make it a complete trochaic, we must necessarily read it with this *d*. And there is something like it in the French language, where to avoid the same kind of gaping, they frequently insert a *t*, as *a-t-il fait, fera-t-il*, &c.

V. *Of the contraction of syllables, which includes the* SYNÆRESIS *and the* SYNECPHONESIS.

We have just now shewn in what manner syllables are cut off by synalæpha, when they meet together, one at the end of a word, and the other at the beginning of another. But as this meeting may likewise happen in the middle of the same word, we are oftentimes obliged to contract them into one syllable. And this is what some grammarians have called *episynalæpha*, as much as to say, a second species of *synalæpha*: others *synesis*, from the verb ἰζάνω, *subsido*: others *synæresis*, from the verb συναιρέω, *una complector, in unum contraho*: and others *sinecphonesis*, from the verb ἐκφωνέω, *pronuncio, effero*. Though some make this distinction between *synæresis* and *synecphonesis*, that in the former the two vowels remain intire, and are only united in a diphthong; whereas in the latter, one of the two is cut off and intirely lost in pronouncing; as *alvearia* of four syllables, *ariete* of three; *omnia* of two. But since it is very difficult, as we have observed in the treatise of letters, to determine on many occasions, whether in this contraction of syllables they formed a diphthong or not; and besides this diversity of names and figures is puzzling to the learner; we have therefore comprehended all these figures under the word *contraction of syllables*, after the example of Quintilian, who includes them all under the word COMPLEXIO: for which reason we have mentioned in the title the words SYNÆRESIS and SYNECPHONESIS, leaving it to every body's option to apply which of these terms he pleases, and to what passages he pleases, if thereby he thinks he shall render himself better understood.

Now this contraction is particularly formed by drawing E or I into one syllable with the following vowel.

OF LATIN POETRY.

E and A; *anxietate, eadem*, diffyllables; *anteambulo, usqueadeo, alvearea*, of four syllables.

Seu lento fuerint alvearia *vimine texta.* Virg.
Anteambulones *& togatulos inter.* Mart.

Two *ee*, *deeſt* of one ſyllable; *deerit, deerant, deeſſem, deero, prebendo*, of two.

E and I; *dein, dehinc* of one ſyllable; *deinceps, deinde, proinde, ærei, aureis, anteit*, of two ſyllables; *anteire* of three ſyllables.

E and O; *eodem, alveo, ſeorſum, deorſum*, of two ſyllables; *graveolens*, of three.

E and U; *eum, meus*, monoſyllables in comic writers; and ſuch like.

In like manner is formed the contraction of I and A; *omnia* of two ſyllables; *vindemiator, ſemianimis*, of four.

Of I and E; *ſemiermis* of three ſyllables.

Of two *ii*; *Dii, diis, ii*, of one ſyllable; *iidem, iiſdem*, of two; *denarius* of three.

Of *i* and *o*; *ſemihomo* of three ſyllables.

Of *i* and *u*; *huic, cui*, in one ſyllable; *ſemiuſtus, denarium, promontorium*, of four.

Examples of all theſe may be eaſily found among the poets; for which reaſon I ſhall be ſatisfied with giving only a few.

Atria, dependent lychni laquearibus āureīs. Virg.
Bis patriæ cecidere manus, quin protinus ōmniā. Id.
Aſſuetæ ripis volucres & fluminis ālveō. Id.
Seu lento fuerint ālveāriā *vimine texta.* Id.
Præcipuè ſanus, niſi cūm pituītā moleſta eſt. Hor.

And this figure is particularly applied to nouns in *eus* and their genitive in *ei*, as *Mneſteus, Orpheus, Pantheus*, diffyllables; as alſo *Mneſtei, Theſei*, diffyllables; *Ulyſſei, Achillei*, triſſyllables. Likewiſe in the vocative, *Pantheu*, a diffyllable, and others of the ſame ſort.

But we are further to obſerve, that *u* being of its nature a liquid vowel after *s*, as well as after *q* and *g*, according to what we have obſerved in the treatiſe of letters, it ſlides away and is dropped in *ſuadeo, ſueſco*, and *ſuavis*, with their derivatives, as *ſuada, ſuade, ſuaſit, ſuaſor, ſuave, ſuetus*, diffyllables; *ſuadela, ſuavibus*, triſſyllables, and the like; without there being any neceſſity to call this a licence; for if at any time it occurs otherwiſe, this is rather by licence, being contrary to the nature of this *u*, which is a liquid vowel in thoſe words, as well as in *qua*, and the like.

Tum celerare fugam patriaque excedere ſuadet. Virg.
Suadet *enim veſana fames, manditque, trahitque.* Virg.
*Et metus & male*ſuada *fames, & turpis egeſtas.* Id.
Suetus *hiat tantum, ceu pullus hirundinis ad quem.* Juv.
Suave *locus voci reſonat concluſus, inanes.* Hor.
Tum caſia atque aliis intexens ſuavibus *herbis.* Virg.
Neſciaque humanis precibus manſueſcere *corda.* Id.
——— *Adeo in teneris* conſueſcere *multum eſt.* Id.
*Non in*ſueta *graves tentabunt pabula fœtas.* Id.
Arcadas inſuetos *acies inferre pedeſtres.* Id.

Candidus

Candidus infuetum *miratur limen Olympi.* Id.
Nec tibi tam prudens quifquam perfuadeat *autor.* Id.
At patiens operum, parvoque affueta *juventus.* Id.

ANNOTATION.

Sometimes a Synalæpha meets with a Synerefis, as
  Uno eodemque *tulit partu, paribufque junxit*
   Serpentum *fpiris.* ——— ——— Virg.
where we fee a Synalæpha of the *o*, which is cut off in *uno*; and then a *fynerefis* in *eodem*, which is a diffyllable; fo that we muft fcan the verfe thus,
  Un' ōdemque, *tulit*, &c. in like manner,
  Uno eodemque *igni, noftro fic Daphnis amore.* Virg.
  Unā eādemque *via fanguifque, animufque fequuntur.* Id.

VI. *Of* DIÆRESIS.

DIÆRESIS is contrary to the preceding figure, and is properly when two fyllables are made of one, as *aulaï* for *aulæ*, *vitaï* for *vitæ*, *diffoluenda* for *diffolvenda* in Tibullus.

VII. *Of* SYSTOLE *and* DIASTOLE.

SYSTOLE is the fhortening of a long fyllable, and derives its name from συςίλλειν, *contrahere*. Quintilian gives the following example hereof in his firft book, chap. 5.
  Unīus *ob noxam & furias*, &c.
Which perhaps fheweth that in his time the fecond of *unius* was generally long, though now we look upon it as common; and Catullus, who lived before Virgil, made it alfo fhort.
  Rumorēfque *fenum feveriorum*
  Omnes *un*īus *æftimemus affis.* Carm. 5.
Others for an example of Syftole give *stetĕrunt*, and the like preterites, when we find them fhort in the penultima. But we have fhewn, when treating of quantity, rule 15. p. 314. that heretofore this fyllable was common. So that we fhall find but very few examples of this licence in pure authors. And in regard to the others, as in the following verfe attributed to Tertullian, where we find the firft fhort in *Ecclefia.*
  Sin *& Apoftolico decurrit* ēcclefia *verbo.*
We have more than once obferved that the writers of the latter ages can be no authority.

DIASTOLE, on the contrary, is when we lengthen a fyllable fhort by nature. This figure takes its name from διαςίλλειν, *diducere, diftendere*; and perhaps occurs more frequently than the other; becaufe it feems lefs exceptionable to add to than to take away from a fyllable. Though, to tell the truth, thofe licences were feldom permitted except in proper names, or extraordinary words, as *Āsiācŭs, Prīămĭdēs*, &c.
  Atque hic Prīamidem *laniatum corpore toto.* Virg.
  Et quas Prīamides *inaquofæ vallibus Idæ.* Ovid.
  Ecquid ibi Āsĭacus *cafuras afpicit arces?* Id.

Of LATIN POETRY.

For with regard to the other examples which Ricciolius produceth in his book, intitled *Prosodia Bononiensis*, there is very little stress to be laid upon them, since they are either corrupted or misunderstood, or taken from inaccurate writers whose example is no rule to us. As when he says that it is by this licence *recido* taken from *cado* hath the first syllable long, and in his table he refers to this verse of Horace,

Transverso calamo signum: ambitiosa rĕcīdet
Ornamenta. In arte.

Where it is obvious that *recīdet* hath the former short by nature; besides that it comes from *cædo*, and not from *cado*, having the second long, and being put for *amputabit, he will cut off*. When he says the same thing of *quatuor*; whereas this word is so far long by nature, that neither Horace nor Virgil ever used it otherwise. Also when he mentions *malitia*, as having the first long, and strives to prove it by a pentameter out of Ovid, where all the editions that ever I saw have *militiam*, and where indeed it is nonsense to read *malitia*. As the intire distich will demonstrate,

Tempora jure colunt Latiæ fecunda parentes:
Quarum militiam votáque partus habet. Fast. 3.

Quintilian likewise mentions *Italiam*, as an example of this figure, when Virgil says,

Ităliam fato profugus, &c.

Which is not perhaps exempt from difficulty, since Catullus, who was prior to Virgil, made the first long in *Italus*.

Jam tum cum ausus es unus Italorum. Carm. 1.

So that there is reason to doubt whether it be not as much a licence in Virgil to make the first short in *Italus*, as to lengthen it in *Italia*.

VIII. *Of the caution with which we ought to make use of those licences.*

But here it is to be observed that we are not allowed to use those figures and licences on every occasion, especially now that the Latin is no longer a living language. *In licentia magis inventis quàm inveniendis utimur*, says Servius. And it is easy to see that the antients were very cautious in this respect, since Ovid, writing to *Tuticanus*, makes an apology for not having said any thing in his praise, because the word *Tuticanus*, which hath the second short between two long, cannot have a place in verse.

Quod minus in nostris ponaris, amice! libellis,
Nominis efficitur conditione tui.
Lex pedis officio, fortunáque nominis obstat,
Quaque meos adeas est via nulla modos.
Nam pudet in geminos ita nomen scindere versus,
Desinat ut prior hoc, incipiatque minor:
Et pudeat si te qua syllaba parte moretur,
Arctius appellem, Tuticanumque vocem.
Nec potes in versum Tuticani more venire,
Fiat ut è longa syllaba prima brevis:

Aut ut ducatur, quæ nunc correptius exit,
Et fit porrectâ longa secunda morâ.
His ego si vitiis ausim corrumpere nomen.
Ridear, & merito pectus habere neger. Lib. 4. de Pont.
Eleg. 12.

I thought it right to give this whole passage at length, in order to prove that even in proper names, where Servius pretends we may do what we list, they were so cautious as to admit nothing that might offend the ear, which is the judge of these as well as all other words.

And this appears further from Martial, who makes an excuse for not having inserted the name *Earinus* in verse, because it consists of four short.

Nomen nobile, molle, delicatum,
Versu dicere non rudi volebam;
Sed tu syllaba contumax! repugnas:
Dicunt Ἐάρινον, *tamen Poëtæ,*
Sed Græci, quibus est nihil negatum,
Et quos Ἄρες, Ἄρες, *decet sonare:*
Nobis non licet esse tam disertis,
Qui musas colimus severiores. lib. 9. Epigram. 12.

Whereby he shews the difficulty of Latin poetry beyond the Greek, because Homer, in the fifth Iliad, has made the first of this word Ἄρες both long and short in the same verse. The same he has also done by ἀνὴρ, Theocritus by κάλος, and others in the like manner.

Chapter IV.
Of the chief species of verse.
And first
Of Hexameters, and such as are relative thereto.

LATIN verses may be divided into three principal species, viz.

Hexameters, and such as are relative thereto, as Pentameter, which is generally joined with it, or makes part thereof; as the Archilochian, and others, of which we shall speak hereafter.

Iambics, which are of three sorts of measure, namely Dimeter, that have four feet; Trimeter, that have six feet; and Tetrameter, that have eight feet; not to mention those which are either defective or redundant.

Lyrics, the name we may give in general to all such as cannot be referred to the two first species, because the most elegant are used in writing odes, as Asclepiads, Sapphics, and others.

I. *Of Hexameter verse.*

Hexameter verse is so denominated from the word ἓξ, *sex*, and μέτρον, *mensura*, because it consists of six feet, the first four of which
may

Of LATIN POETRY.

may be indiscriminately either Spondees or Dactyls; the fifth must be a Dactyl, and the sixth necessarily a Spondee.

1 | 2 | 3 | 4 | 5 | 6
Ab Jŏvĕ princĭpĭ-ūm Mū-sæ, Jŏvĭs ōmnĭă plēnā.

The intermixing of Spondees and Dactyls contributes greatly to the beauty of this verse.

1 | 2 | 3 | 4 | 5 | 6
Īlle ĕtĭ-am extīn-cto mĭsĕ-rātūs Cæsărĕ Rōmām,

1 | 2 | 3 | 4 | 5 | 6
Cūm căpŭt ōbscū-rā nītĭ-dūm fĕr-rūgĭnĕ tēxĭt,

1 | 2 | 3 | 4 | 5 | 6
Īmpĭă-que ætēr-nām tĭmŭ-ērunt sæcŭlă nōctēm. Id.
1 Georg.

Otherwise those which have most Dactyls, are generally more agreeable than those which have most Spondees: as

Dīscĭtĕ jūstĭtĭ-ām mŏnĭ-ti, ēt nōn tēmnĕrĕ dīvōs.
Æn. Virg. 6.

But the great art is in making use of Spondees (which are flow) and of dactyls (which are rapid) according as they are best adapted to the things we want to express. Thus Virgil has represented the great labour of blacksmiths in lifting up their heavy hammers, in the following verse which abounds with Spondees,

Illi inter sese magnā vi brachia tollunt. Georg. 4.

and the gravity of an old man in the following, which is preparatory to a speech of king Latinus.

Olli sedato respondit corde Latinus. Æn. 12.

and the slowness of Fabius, whereby he saved the commonwealth, in this other:

Vnus qui nobis cunctando restituit rem. Æn. 6.

On the contrary, he expresseth the rapid motion of a horse by the following verse abounding with Dactyls:

Quadrupedante putrem sonitu quatit ungula campum. Æn. 8.

and the swift flight of a pigeon by the following,

——————————— *Mox aëre lapsa quieto*
Radit iter liquidum, celeres neque commovet alas. Æn. 5.

and the fury of the wind and tempest by these, where he has put two Dactyls in the beginning:

Qua data porta ruunt, & terras turbine perflant,
Incubuere mari, totumque à sedibus imis.

and by this other;

Intonuere poli, & crebris micat ignibus æther. Æn. 1.

The fifth foot of this verse is sometimes a Spondee, and then it is called a Spondaic verse; which, to make up for the slowness of two Spondees at the close, has generally the fourth foot a Dactyl:

Cara deum soboles, magnum Jovis incrementum. Ecl. 4.
Constitit, atque oculis Phrygia agmina circumspexit. Æn. 2.

And this verse seems more agreeable, when it concludes thus with a word of four syllables; though they reckon about ten or twelve in Virgil, that end with a trisyllable, such as these:

Pro molli viola, pro purpureo narcisso. Ecl. 5.
Stant & juniperi, & castaneæ hirjutæ. Ecl. 7.

There are even two in this poet that have not the fourth foot a Dactyl:

Aut leves ocreas lento ducunt argento. Æn. 7.
Saxa per & scopulos, & depressas convalles. Georg. 3.

II. *Whether an Hexameter verse may sometimes end with a Dactyl.*

Here a question may arise whether an Hexameter verse may not sometimes have the sixth foot a Dactyl, as the fifth may be a Spondee: but it is certain it cannot, though some authors have believed the contrary. And the reason may be this, at least if we can give credit to Erythreus, that those verses having been heretofore made intirely of Spondees, as indeed there are some of that sort in Ennius,

Olli respondit Rex Albaï-Longaï.

they have ever preserved their Spondee at the latter end; just as the Iambic having consisted at first intirely of Iambuses, the last foot has always remained an Iambus.

And when we find some of those verses that seem to finish otherwise, it is either by reason of a Synalæpha, the end of the verse being considered as joined to the beginning of the next, according to what we have observed in the precedent chapter, or by reason of a Synerefis or contraction of two syllables into one, of which we have also taken notice in the same chapter, n. 5. as in Virgil:

Inseritur vero ex fœtu nucis arbutus hōrrī-da
Et steriles platani ——— ——— Georg. 2.
Bis patriæ cecidere manus, quin protinus ōmniā. Æn. 6.

So that we must conclude the first verse at *horri,* and keep *da* for the next, pronouncing it thus, *ărbŭtŭs hŏrrī-d' Et steriles platani,* &c. And as to the third verse, we must make *omnia* a dissyllable.

III. *Division of Hexameters into Heroic and Satyric, and cautions to be observed in order to render them elegant.*

Hexameters may be divided into Heroic, which ought to be grave and majestic; and Satyric, which may be more neglected.

In regard to the former, we may make a few remarks here for rendering them elegant, over and above what has been said of the intermixture of their feet.

1. These verses, except the Spondaïc, ought not to conclude with a word that has more than three syllables, except it be a proper name; as

Amphion Dircæus in Actæo Aracyntho. Ecl. 2.
Hirtacida ante omnes exit locus Hippocoontis. Æn. 5.

Quarum

Quarum quæ forma pulcherrima Deiopeiam. Æn. 1.

Or some other uncommon word, or to express some passion.
Per connubia nostra, per incœptos Hymenæos. Æn. 4.

2. Neither ought they to conclude with a monosyllable, except it be the word *est*, or some other that begins with a vowel, and forms an elision of the precedent word, whereby it seems to be connected and incorporated with it.

Semiputata tibi frondosa vitis in ulmo est. Ecl. 2.
Quem circum glomerati hostes hinc cominus atque hinc. Æn. 9.
Una dolo divum si fœmina victa duorum est. Æn. 4.

Or when there are two monosyllables one after another, which produce nearly the same effect as a word of two syllables;

——————— *Tuus ô regina! quid optes*
Explorare labor, mihi jussa capessere fas est. Æn. 1.
Ne qua meis esto dictis mora: Jupiter hac stat. Æn. 12.

Or in fine there be some particular reason which shall render this uncommon ending more graceful; as in Virgil.

Sternitur, exanimisque tremens procumbit humi bos. Æn. 5.
Vertitur interea cælum & ruit oceano nox. Æn. 2.
Dat latus, insequitur cumulo præruptus aquæ mons. Æn. 1.
Prima vel autumni sub frigora, cum rapidus sol. Georg. 2.
Tum pietate gravem ac meritis si forte virum quem
Conspexere, silent——— Æn. 1.

And several others in the same poet, but most of which have their particular grace and beauty, as when he says again,

Ipse ruit, dentésque Sabellicus exacuit sus. Georg. 3.
——————— *sæpe exiguus mus.* Georg. 1.

In regard to which, Quintilian. lib. 8. c. 3. observeth; *At Virgilii miramur illud; nam Epitheton* exiguus *aptum & proprium efficit, & casus singularis magis decuit, & clausula ipsa unius syllabæ addit gratiam. Imitatus est itaque Horatius,*

Parturiunt montes, nascetur ridiculus mus. In arte.

But Horace has likewise expressed the usual avarice of mankind most admirably in these two verses, which terminate in the same monosyllable,

Isne tibi melius suadet, qui ut rem facias, rem
Si possis recte: si non quocumque modo rem? Lib. 1. Epist. 1.

Except on such particular occasions, it is certain we ought to endeavour to avoid putting monosyllables at the end of hexameters, and that Erythreus had not much reason for blaming the judgment of Servius and Quintilian on this article; since excepting the two particular cases abovementioned of the elision and the two monosyllables, and of those other peculiar beauties, we shall find very few in Virgil, considering the length of his work. As for the enclitics they ought not to be considered as monosyllables, because they are incorporated with the word to which they join; for which reason they do not so much as follow the rule of monosyllables in regard to quantity. Whereto we may add, that Servius himself excepts the names of animals, as *mus, sus*, &c. So that there remains but very few of those which Erythreus has thought fit to mark, whereby we can be induced to believe that in so delicate a point as cadence he had a more exquisite ear than either Servius or Quintilian, who without all manner of doubt must have been better judges than we of their native language.

3. Hexameters are also, generally speaking, somewhat displeasing, when they conclude with several words of two syllables, as the following of Tibullus.

Semper ut inducar blandos offert mibi vultus. Lib. 1. Eleg. 6.

4. The want of cæsura likewise takes off a great part of their beauty: though Virgil made one without a cæsura till after the fourth foot, the better to express the transports of a violent passion by those broken and unconnected feet.

Per connubia nostra, per incæptos Hymenæos. Æn. 4.

And Horace to express the pains and trouble he had in writing verse amidst the hurry and noise of the town, has done it by this verse without a cæsura, which has scarce the appearance of verse;

Præter cætera, Romæ méne poëmata censes
Scribere posse, inter tot curas, tótque labores. Ep. 2. l. 2.

5. On the contrary the varying of the cæsura gives them a particular grace, as we have already observed, c. 2. n. 2. And especially that which is made in the fifth half foot. But this same cæsura is remarkably beautiful, when it finishes the sense; as

Arma virúmque cano, &c. Æn. 1.

especially if this sense includes some remarkable sentence; as

Omnia vincit amor, & *nos cedamus amori.* Ecl. 10.

Stat sua cuique dies: breve & irreparabile tempus. Æn. 10.

Or at least, when the verse containing two distinct sentences, the cæsura includeth one; as in Virgil,

Nos patriæ fines, & dulcia linquimus arva. Ecl. 1.

Fluminibus salices, crassísque paludibus alni. Georg. 2.

The cæsura is also beautiful, when it is formed on the last syllable of a word relative to that which ends the verse; as in the same poet;

Tityre tu patulæ *recubans sub tegmine* fagi,
Silvestrem tenui *musam meditaris* avena. Ecl. 1.
Nec tam præsentes *alibi cognoscere* divos. Ibid.
Julius à magno *demissum nomen* Iülo. Æn. 1.

6. But we must take care that this same cæsura does not rhime fully with the end of the verse, that is, it must not include the vowel that precedes the last syllable: which are called LEONIAN verses, from Leonius, a monk of the abby of St. Victor at Paris, who brought them into vogue towards the middle of the twelfth century, for he lived till the year 1160. And yet some of these are to be found even among the antient poets, as

Ora citatorum dextra contorsit equorum. Virg.
I nunc, & verbis virtutem illude superbis. Id.
Si Trojæ fatis aliquid restare putatis. Ovid.

But these rhimes are not so much observed, when some word immediately follows that hinders us from resting upon them; as

Tum caput orantis nequicquam, & multa parantis. Virg.
Illum indignanti similem, similémque minanti. Id.

And

And they are still less taken notice of, where there is an elision with them, as,

 Æneam fundantem arces, & tecta novantem. Id.
 Cornua velatarum obvertimus antennarum. Id.
 Ad terram misere, aut ignibus ægra dedere. Id.

by reason that pronouncing those verses, as they did, with an elision, they did not sound them like rhime; *fundant' arces, velatar' obvertimus: miser' aut ignibus,* &c.

IV. *Of neglected hexameters.*

Excellence of those of Horace.

Neglected hexameters are such as Horace made use of in his satyres and epistles, which we undervalue through ignorance, because they have not the majesty and cadence of heroics, like those of Virgil: not knowing that Horace wrote so on purpose, to render his versification more like to prose, and that it is a studied negligence, which he has varied with such beauties, and such purity of stile, as to be no less deserving of admiration in its way, than the gravity of Virgil. This is what he has declared himself so elegantly in the following lines, *Serm. lib.* 1. *sat.* 4.

 Primum ego me illorum dederim quibus esse poetas
 Excerpam numero. Neque enim concludere versum
 Dixeris esse satis: neque si quis scribat uti nos.
 Sermoni propiora; putes hunc esse poetam.

But this simple, and in appearance, humble manner, is almost beyond the reach of imitation: and they who prefer Juvenal's satyres to those of Horace, seem to have but a very indifferent notion of the fine taste in writing, and to be incapable of distinguishing between real eloquence and declamation. One single fable of Horace's has more beauties than the most elaborate passages of Juvenal. As in the 3. *sat. lib.* 2.

 Absentis ranæ pullis vituli pede pressit,
 Unus ubi effugit, matri denarrat, ut ingens
 Bellua cognatos eliserit. Illa rogare
 Quantane? num tandem, se inflans, sic magna fuisset?
 Major dimidio. Num tanto? cùm magis atque
 Se magis inflaret: non si te ruperis, inquit,
 - Par eris. Hæc à te non multùm abludit imago.

There is nothing so pretty as those little dialogues, which he inserts in his discourse without *inquam* or *inquit*, as if it were a comedy. In this manner he writes to Mecænas, lib. 1. ep. 7.

 Non quo more pyris vesci Calaber jubet hospes.
 Tu me fecisti locupletem. Vescere sodes.
 Jam satis est. At tu quantum vis tolle. Benigne.
 Non invisa feres pueris munuscula parvis.
 Tam teneor dono, quam si dimittar onustus.
 Ut libet: hæc porcis hodie comedenda relinques.

But the most admirable of all, is the picture he every where draws of the humour, paſſions, and follies of mankind, not even ſparing himſelf, as when he writes to his ſteward, lib. 1. ep. 14.

> *Rure ego viventem, tu dicis in urbe beatum:*
> *Cui placet alterius, ſua nimirum eſt odio ſors.*
> *Stultus uterque locum immeritum cauſatur inique,*
> *In culpa eſt animus, qui ſe non effugit unquam.*

See alſo his deſcription of a miſer, lib. 2. ſat. 3. beginning with this verſe, *Pauper Opimius*, &c. And the ſtory of Philip and Menas, lib. 1. epiſt. 7. which is far beyond all that we can ſay of it.

I hope I ſhall be indulged this ſhort digreſſion in favour of a poet, whoſe excellence in hexameters is not ſufficiently known to a great many; and who ought to be read conſtantly in ſchools, in order to acquire the purity of the Latin tongue, leaving out whatever may be prejudicial to the purity of morals.

V. *Of Pentameter verſe.*

A pentameter is denominated from the word πέντε, *quinque*, becauſe it conſiſts of five feet, of which the two firſt may be either ſpondees, or dactyls; the third always a ſpondee; and the two laſt, anapæſts; as

$$\overset{1}{\mid} \quad \overset{2}{\mid} \quad \overset{3}{\mid} \quad \overset{4}{\mid} \quad \overset{5}{\mid}$$
Nōn sŏlĕt īngĕnĭ īs sūm-mă nŏcē-rĕ dĭēs. Ovid.

Others meaſure it by leaving a cæſura after the two firſt feet, then two dactyls and another ſyllable.

$$\overset{1}{\mid} \quad \overset{2}{\mid}\mid \quad \overset{3}{\mid} \quad \overset{4}{\mid}$$
Nōn sŏlĕt īngĕnĭ īs sūmmā nŏ-cērĕ dĭ-ēs.

Now becauſe this middle ſyllable ought to make part of a ſpondee in the firſt manner of meaſuring the verſe, ſome have queſtioned whether this ſyllable could be ſhort; yet there is no doubt but it may, becauſe the cæſura has the ſame force here as any where elſe, of lengthening a ſyllable; and we find ſufficient authority for it among the antients.

> *Perſpecta eſt igitur, unica amicitia.* Catul.
> *Lacteus, & miſtus obriguiſſe liquor.* Tibul.
> *Vinceris aut vincis, hæc in amore rota eſt.* Propert.
> *Qui dederit primus oſcula, victor erit.* Ovid.
> *Theſſalicamque adiit hoſpes Achillis humum.* Id.

VI. *Obſervations for making elegant Pentameters.*

In order to make this verſe agreeable and elegant, we are to obſerve,

1. That there be a cæſura after the ſecond foot. Hence this verſe is intolerable, which happens to be at the end of the 50th pſalm of the vulgate tranſlation.

> *Imponent ſuper altare tuum vitulos.*

2. That the cæſura be not followed by an eliſion, as in theſe verſes of Catullus.

> *Troja virûm, & virtutum omnium acerba cinis.* Carm. 69.
> *Illam affligit odore, ille perit podagra.* Carm. 72.

3. That

Of LATIN POETRY.

3. That the most graceful pentameters end with a diffyllable, as generally in Ovid.

Mœnia finitimis invidiosa locis.
Non bene cœlestes impia dextra colit.
Tempora si fuerint nubila, solus eris.

Sometimes they end with a word of four syllables, as in the same poet,

Non duris lachrymas vultibus aspiciant.

And of five, as in the same also,

Arguor obscœni doctor adulterii.

But they are very seldom agreeable, if they end with a triffyllable, though there are a great many such in Tibullus, as

Sera tamen tacitis pœna venit pedibus.

Or with a monosyllable, as in Catullus.

Aut facere, hæc à te dictaque, factaque sunt,

unless there is an elision of the monosyllable, because it is then no longer considered as a monosyllable, according to what we have observed in regard to hexameters, as

Invitis oculis littera lecta tua est. Ovid.

4. We ought also to avoid perfect rhimes, such as this in Ovid.

Quærebant flavos per nemus omne favos.

But when the rhime goes no farther than the last vowel, so far is it from being a fault, that it is rather a great elegance, as

Huc ades & nitidas casside solve comas. Ovid.
Fulmineo celeres dissipat ore canes. Id.
Jordanis refugas in caput egit aquas. Buchan.

VII. *Six lesser verses which make part of an Hexameter.*

And 1. *Of three which form the beginning.*

Of the verses relative to an hexameter, there are three which form the beginning of it.

The 1. is called *versus Archilochius*, because of its author Archilochus, who gave his name to several sorts of verse; but particularly to this, which is composed of two dactyls and a cæsura; whence it is called *dactylica penthemimeris* by the scholiast of Aristophanes.

     1 | 2 |
Pŭlvĭs ĕt ūmbră sŭ-mus. Hor. lib. 4. Od. 7.

The 2. consists of three dactyls with a cæsura, and is called *Alcmanius*, or dactylica *bephthemimeris*. To which we may refer these half verses in Virgil

     1 | 2 | 3 |
Mūnĕră lætĭtĭ-āmquĕ Dĕ-i. Æn. 1.
Infabricata, fugæ studio, &c. Æn. 4.

The 3. contains the first four feet of an hexameter; the last of which is always a dactyl.

    1 | 2 | 3 | 4
Lūmĭnĭ-būsquĕ prĭ-ōr rĕdĭ-ĭt vĭgŏr. Boet.

VIII. *Of the other three lesser verses, which form the end of an hexameter.*

The first contains the four last feet, and is called heroic, or dactylic-tetrameter. Horace makes use of it in three odes.

    1 | 2 | 3 | 4
O fŏr-tēs pē-iōrăquĕ pāssī.

The second is formed of the three last, the first of which is always a spondee. And it is called *Pherecratius*, from Pherecrates, an Athenian poet, who was the inventor thereof, and acquired a reputation by his comedies. Horace makes use of it in 7 odes.

    1 | 2 | 3
Quāmvīs Pōntĭcă Pīnūs.

But instead of the first spondee, Catullus frequently useth a trochee, as

    1 | 2 | 3
Prŏdĕ-ās nŏvă nūptā.

And Boetius now and then puts an anapæst, as

    1 | 2 | 3
Sĭmĭlĭ sūrgĭt ăb ōrtū.

The third hath only the two last feet of an hexameter, and is called Adonic, from Adon son of a King of Cyprus. Boetius has put several of them successively in his first book *de Consol.*

    Gaudia pelle,
    Pelle timorem;
    Spemque fugato,
    Nec dolor adsit.
    Nubila mens est,
    Vinctaque frenis,
    Hæc ubi regnant.

Chapter V.

Of Iambic verses.

And first

Of the different species of Iambics, according to the different feet of which they are composed.

IAMBIC verse is so called, because of the foot iambus that predominates therein.

It may be considered either according to the difference of the feet it receives, or according to the number of its feet, namely four, six, or eight. At first it consisted entirely of iambuses; some

Of LATIN POETRY.

some of that sort are still remaining, and known by the name of pure iambics: as in Catullus the praise of a ship.

   1 | 2 | 3 | 4 | 5 | 6
  Phăsē-lŭs īl-lĕ quēm vĭdē-tĭs hō-spĭtēs,
   1 | 2 | 3 | 4 | 5 | 6
  Ăit fŭĭs-sĕ nā-vĭŭm cĕlēr-rĭmŭs, &c. Carm. 4.

And in Horace, the iambics which he has joined to the hexameters in his epodes, od. 16.

   1 | 2 | 3 | 4 | 5 | 6
  Sŭīs ĕt īp-să Rō-mă vī-rĭbŭs rŭīt.

Afterwards, as well to remove this constraint, as to render the verse more grave, they put spondees in the odd places; as

   1 | 2 | 3 | 4 | 5 | 6
  Pārs sā-nĭtā-tĭs vēl-lĕ sā-nārī fŭīt. Senec. Hipp.

Therefore joining the spondee and iambus together, the antients measured them by third epitrits, as St. Austin observeth. Hence those of six feet were called trimeters, as being composed of three epitrits only; and those of four, dimeters, as consisting only of two. Which seems to prove that the odd feet were also obliged to be spondees, and the even ones iambuses.

But in process of time they took more liberty. For

1. In the odd places they put indifferently either an iambus or a spondee, except in tragic verses in the fifth foot, where Seneca made it a rule never to put an iambus, because two iambuses successively at the end of the verse render it less majestic.

   1 | 2 | 3 | 4 | 5 | 6
  Ămŏr tĭmē-rĕ nē-mĭnēm vērŭs pŏtēst. Sen. Med.

2. The tribrac having the same time as an iambus, because its two short syllables are equivalent to one long; it has been put instead thereof, except in the sixth foot, where they have indispensably preserved an iambus.

   1 | 2 | 3 | 4 | 5 | 6
  Prŏhĭbē-rĕ rătĭ ō nŭl lă pĕrĭ-tūrŭm pŏtēst. S. Hipp.

3. The dactyl and anapæst having also the same time as the spondee, they have been put instead thereof, wherever they can be put, that is in all odd places.

   1 | 2 | 3 | 4 | 5 | 6
  Quī ..ătŭ ĭt ălĭ-quīd, pār-te ĭnāu-dītă āl-tĕra,
   1 | 2 | 3 | 4 | 5 | 6
  Æquūm lĭcēt stătŭē-rĭt, haud æquŭs fŭīt. Sen. Med.
   1 | 2 | 3 | 4 | 5 | 6
  Dŏmĭnā-rĕ tŭmĭ-dŭs, spī-rĭtŭs āllōs gĕrē:
   1 | 2 | 3 | 4 | 5 | 6
  Sĕquĭtŭr sŭpĕr-bōs ūl-tŏr ā tērgō Dĕūs. Id. Her. Fur.

4. The comic poets have gone further, and satisfied with ending the verse with an iambus, they have inserted every where else those feet which are allowed to be put in odd places; namely the Iambus, the Tribrac, the Spondee, the Dactyl, and the Anapæst.

  1 | 2 | 3 | 4 | 5 | 6
Virtū-te āmbī-re ŏpōr-tēt nōn făvĭtō-rĭbŭs
  1 | 2 | 3 | 4 | 5 | 6
Săt băbēt făvĭtō-rŭm sēm-pēr quī rēctē făcĭt.
  1 | 2 | 3 | 4 | 5 | 6
Hŏmō sum, hūmā-nī nĭhĭl ā me ălī-ēnŭm pŭtō. Ter.

Almost all Phædrus's fables are written in this sort of verse.

  1 | 2 | 3 | 4 | 5 | 6
Āmīt-tĭt mĕrĭtō prŏprĭ-ŭm quī ălī-ēnum ăp-pĕtit. l. 1. f. 4.
  1 | 2 | 3 | 4 | 5 | 6
Făcĭt părēn-tēs bŏnĭ-tās, nōn nĕcēs-sĭtās. l. 1. f. 13.
  1 | 2 | 3 | 4 | 5 | 6
Ĭnōps pŏtēn-tĕm dŭm vult ĭmĭ-tārī pĕrīt. l. 1. f. 23.
  1 | 2 | 3 | 4 | 5 | 6
Sŭccēs-sŭs īm-prŏbō-rŭm plŭ-rēs āl-lĭcit. l. 2. f. 3.

II. *Of a Scazon or Claudicant Iambic.*

Another difference in the feet of an iambic hath produced a kind of verse called Scazon, from the word σκάζων, *lame*; because having begun with spondees in the odd places, and with iambuses in the even, they change the cadence of the verse, which particularly depends on the two last feet, taking for the fifth indispensably an iambus, and for the sixth a spondee.

  1 | 2 | 3 | 4 | 5 | 6
Nīmī-rum īdem ōm-nēs fāl-lĭmŭr, nĕque ēst quīsquām.
  1 | 2 | 3 | 4 | 5 | 6
Quĕm nōn ĭn ălĭ-quā-rē vĭdē-rē Sūf-fēnŭm
  1 | 2 | 3 | 4 | 5 | 6
Pōssīs. Sŭus cŭique āt-trĭbŭ tŭs ēst ērrōr.
  1 | 2 | 3 | 4 | 5 | 6
Sed non vĭdē-mus măn-tĭcæ quŏd īn tērgo ēst. Catul.

III. *Of Iambics according to the number of their feet.*

Of these there are three sorts; of four feet, called Dimeters, because the Greeks used to measure them two feet to two feet, for the reason above given; of six feet, called Trimeters; and of eight feet, called Tetrameters.

1. Of Dimeters, or four feet.

Most of the hymns of the Latin church are in this sort of verse. But when the quantity is not observed, as in that of the Ascension, so beautiful in regard to the sentiments;

    1 | 2 | 3 | 4
Jēsū nōſtrā rĕdēm-tĭǒ,
Amor & deſiderium, &c.

It is a certain proof that they are falsely attributed to St. Ambrose, who had a very good knack at writing these verses, and generally ended them with a trisyllable, which is their best cadence, as

    1 | 2 | 3 | 4
Jēsū cŏrō-nă vīr-gĭnūm,
Quem mater illa concipit,
Quæ ſola virgo parturit!
Hæc vota clemens accipe.

The antients seldom or ever used this sort of verse by itself, but they generally joined it to trimeters, or hexameters.

2. Of Trimeters, or Iambics of six feet.

These are the most agreeable Iambics, being the verse in which tragedies are written. They are most graceful, when they terminate with a word of two syllables,

    1 | 2 | 3 | 4 | 5 | 6
Quīcūm-quĕ rē-gnō fĭ-dĭt, ĕt māgnā pŏtēns
Dominatur aula, nec leves metuit Deos,
Animumque rebus credulum lætis dedit. Sen.

Or with a trisyllable, beginning with a vowel, that makes an elision of the last syllable of the precedent word.

Juvenile vitium eſt regere non poſſe impetum. Sen.

Generally speaking there ought to be a cæsura after the two first feet; yet there is sometimes a peculiar beauty in sentences that have not the cæsura till after the third foot.

Qui nihil poteſt ſperare, deſperet nihil. Sen. Med.
Qui non vetat peccare, cùm poſſit, jubet. Sen. Troad.
Minimum decet licere cui multum licet. Sen. Ibid.
Quod non poteſt vult poſſe qui nimium poteſt. Sen. Hipp.
Curæ leves loquuntur, ingentes ſtupens. Sen. Hipp.

But it is likewise to be observed that in all the above verses we are not to pause till after the cæsura, which follows the third foot.

3. Of Tetrameters, or Iambics of eight feet.

We meet with this kind of verse no where but in comic poets; as in Terence.

    1 | 2 | 3 | 4 | 5 | 6 | 7
Pĕcū-nĭam īn lŏcō nēglĭgĕ-rĕ, mā-xĭmum īn-tērdum eſt
    8
lŭcrŭm. Ter.

```
     1    | 2 .|    3    | 4 | 5    | 6  |  7
    Ōmnēs quĭbŭ' rēs sŭnt mĭnŭ' sĕcŭn-dǣ măgĭ' sŭnt nĕscĭŏ
       | 8
    quō-mŏdō
     1  | 2 | 3  | 4 | 5   | 6  | 7  |  8
    Sūspĭcĭ-ōsī, ăd cōn-tŭmē-lĭam ōm-nĭa ăc-cĭpĭŭnt măgis:
      1 |   | 2 | 3 | 4 | 5   | 6  | 7  | 8
    Prōptēr sŭam īm-pŏtēn-tĭam sē sēm-pēr crēdŭnt nĕglĭgī.
                                                     Ter.
```

IV. *Of Iambics either defective or redundant, whereto we must refer those which are commonly called* TROCHAICS.

Besides these three sorts of Iambics, which have exactly the syllables of their four, six, or eight feet: there are some that have more or less than one or two syllables. And grammarians not considering this redundancy or defect till the end of the verse, have called them, as already hath been observed, p. 375. Κατάληκτοι, βραχυκατάληκτοι, ὑπερκατάληκτοι. But here we may make two observations.

The first is, that the syllable may be wanting as well in the first foot, as in the last. So that what they call trochaic verses, that is which have Trochees or Chorees in odd places, are nothing more than Iambics, that want a syllable in the first foot. Thus this verse of Horace,

```
              1   | 2 |   3    |  4
    ———— Nōn ĕbŭr, nĕque āu-rĕŭm,
```

is a dimeter that wants a syllable in the beginning.

And the long verses of fifteen half feet, which we more particularly distinguish by the name of Trochaics, are nothing more than tetrameter iambics or of eight feet, the first of which wants a syllable; as there are others where it is wanting at the end.

```
        1   | 2 | 3 |  4   |   5 | 6 | 7 |
    ———— Prō pēccā-tō mā-gnō, pau-lŭm sūp-plĭcĭī sătĭs ēst
        8
        Pătrī. Ter.
    ———— Pallidi fauces Averni, vōsque Tænarei specus. Sen.
```

And this is what grammarians do partly acknowledge, when they say that these verses are only Trimeters, to which a Cretic or Amphimacer (-υ-) was added in the beginning. For this Cretic making an iambus (υ-) of those two last syllables, no more is wanting than one with the first to make the two first feet of the Tetrameter.

Hence it follows that if you take away this Amphimacer or Cretic from one of those verses which they call Trochaic, you make an Iambic of six feet; as in the second above quoted, beginning

ning to scan it from the word *fauces*; and, on the contrary, adding this foot to an Iambic Trimeter, you make a Trochaic of it. As if in this,

Suis & ipsa Roma viribus ruit. Hor.

you were to put *præpotens* in the beginning.

The second observation is that Iambics, which are a syllable short at the latter end, have always an Iambus before the syllable that remains alone, though this be an odd foot: and therefore they may pass for defective Scazons, as well as for Iambics.

|1|2|3|
Hăbĕt ōm-nĭs hōc vŏlūp-tas. Boët.

|1|2|3|4|5|
Nŏvæ-quĕ pēr-gūnt īn-tĕrī-rĕ lūnæ. Hor.

|1|2|3|4|5|6|7|
Nām sī rĕmīt-tēnt quīp-pĭām Phĭlū-mĕnām dŏlō-rēs.
Ter.

1. Of Imperfect Dimeters.

Imperfect Dimeters are either defective or redundant. Defectives either want a whole foot at the latter end;

|1|2|3|
Mūsæ Jŏvīs nātæ ———

or a syllable, which may be wanting either in the beginning, and these in Horace consist intirely of Iambuses,

|1|2|3|4|
——— *Trū-dĭtūr dĭēs dĭē.*

or at the end, so that before the last syllable there is always an Iambus; and then the verse is called *Anacreonteus*, as

|1|2|3|
Adēs Pătēr sŭprē-me,
Quem nemo vidit unquam. Prud.
Habet omnis hoc voluptas,
Stimulis agit fruentes. Boët.

Dimeters in which a syllable is redundant at the latter end, are like those which form the third verse of an Alcaic ode, which Horace most frequently useth, as *Motum ex Metello,* &c. lib. 2. Od. 1.

|1|2|3|4|
Et cūn-ctă tēr-rārūm sŭbā-ctă.

2. Of Imperfect Trimeters.

There is but one sort, namely such as want a syllable at the latter end, which have always an Iambus before the last syllable. Horace has made use of them, lib. 2. Od. 18. where he joins them to the first sort of defective Dimeters:

Non ebur neque aureum
1 | 2 | 3 | 4 | 5 | 6
Mĕā rĕnī-dĕt īn dŏmō lăcū-nar——
But we shall take notice of the defective Arcilochian hereafter.

3. *Of Imperfect Tetrameters.*

Of these there are two sorts of defectives. One such as want a syllable in the beginning, and which we have observed to be erroneously called Trochaics. The hymn on our Saviour's passion, *Pange lingua,* is of this kind, each verse of which is divided, as it were, into two; so that the stanzas which appear to be of six verses, are in reality no more than three.
1 | 2 | 3 | 4 | 5 | 6 | 7 | 8
--Pān-gĕ līn gŭā glō-rĭō-sĭ prǣ-lĭūm cērtā-mĭnīs :
--Et super Crucis trophæum dic triumphum nobilem:
--Qualiter Redemptor orbis immolatus vicerit.

The other sort of defectives are those that want a syllable at the latter end, where the foot preceding the last syllable, though in the odd place, is ever an Iambus. There are some in Catullus that are pure Iambics,
1 | 2 | 3 | 4 | 5 | 6 | 7 |
Rĕmīt-tĕ pāl-lĭūm mĭhī mĕūm quŏd īn-vŏlā-stī--

✱✱

Chapter VI.

Of Lyric verses, and those any way relative to Lyrics.

UNDER the word Lyrics I comprehend all verses that cannot be referred to the two species above-mentioned; because the chief of them are made use of in odes and in tragic choruses, though we meet with some that are not used in those pieces, as the Phaleucian; and others that are used there, though belonging to the two first species.

We may therefore divide them into three sorts: 1. Choriambics: 2. Verses of eleven syllables: 3. Anapæstics, and a few others less usual.

I. *Of four sorts of Choriambics.*

The antients gave the name of Choriambics to verses which they measured by a Choriambus, that is, by a foot composed of a Choree and an Iambus (¯ ˘ ˘ ¯) though they may be measured likewise by simple feet. There are four sorts.

The

Of LATIN POETRY.

The first and smallest is called a Glyconic, which consists of a Spondee, a Choriambus, and an Iambus. Or more simply of a Spondee and two Dactyls. There are two intire Choruses of this verse in Seneca.

$$\overset{1}{\textit{Illī}} \,\, \overset{}{\textit{mōrs}} \mid \overset{2}{\textit{grăvĭs}} \,\, \overset{}{\textit{ĭncŭbăt,}} \mid \overset{3}{\textit{}}$$
Quī notus nimis omnibus,
Ignotus moritur sibi.

But Horace never uses them without the Asclepiad verse.

The second is the Asclepiad, consisting of a Spondee, two Choriambuses, and an Iambus; or of a Spondee, a Dactyl, a Cæsura, and two Dactyls.

$$\overset{1}{\textit{Mæcē-nās}} \mid \overset{2}{\textit{ătă-vīs}} \mid \overset{3}{\textit{ēdĭtĕ}} \mid \overset{4}{\textit{rēgĭbŭs.}} \,\, \text{Hor.}$$

The third is longer than an Asclepiad by a Choriambus, or by a Dactyl and a long syllable, as lib. 1. Od. 11.

$$\overset{1}{\textit{Seū plū-rēs}} \mid \overset{2}{\textit{byĕ-mēs}} \mid \overset{3}{\textit{seū}} \mid \overset{4}{\textit{trĭbŭ-ĭt}} \mid \overset{5}{\textit{Jūpĭtĕr ūltĭmam.}}$$

The fourth is like the first, except that it finishes with a Spondee.

Heū quām præcĭpĭ-ĭī mērsă prō fūndō. Boët.

$$\overset{1}{\textit{Ō quām}} \mid \overset{2}{\textit{glōrĭfĭ-cā}} \mid \overset{3}{\textit{lūcĕ}} \mid \overset{4}{\textit{cŏ-rūscās.}}$$

Therefore we must not read at the latter end of this hymn to the Virgin,

Qui tecum nitido vivit in æthere.

a sm would fain alter it: but

Qui tecum nitidâ vivit in æthrâ.

as it is in the antient editions, and as George Cassander reads it in his collection of hymns: the word *æthra*, which is necessary for the measure of the verse, being not only in Virgil more than once, as we have elsewhere observed, but likewise in Cicero, *Aërem complexa summa pars cæli, quæ æthra dicitur.* 2. de Nat.

II. *Of verses of eleven syllables, Sapphic, Phaleucian, and Alcaic.*

I join these three sorts of verses together, because (except the fourth sort of Choriambics, which are very little used) none but these are always and indispensably composed of eleven syllables. Yet the name of HENDECASYLLABIC is particularly appropriated to the Phaleucian.

I. *Of Phaleucian verse.*

The Phaleucian verse is so called from a poet of the name of Φάλαικος. They consist of five feet; a Spondee, a Dactyl, and three Chorees or Trochees. Catullus makes likewise the first foot an Iambus or a Trochee. They may be extremely elegant

gant without a cæsura. There is hardly a Latin verse that sounds more agreeably in Epigram than this, if it be well wrote. Catullus excells in it, but it is pity that he has mixed such a number of things offensive to chaste ears. We shall give here an example of this verse from the 14th epigram of the first book to Licinius Calvus.

    1 | 2 | 3 | 4 | 5
Ni tē plūs ŏcŭ-līs mĕ-īs ă-mārĕm,
Jucundissime Calve! munere isto,
Odissem te odio Vatiniano.
Nam, quid feci ego, quidve sum locutus,
Cur me tot male perderes Poëtis?
Dii magni, horribilem & sacrum libellum,
Quem tu scilicet ad tuum Catullum
Misti, continuo ut die periret,
Saturnalibus, optimo dierum.
Non, non hoc tibi, salce, sic abibit.
Nam si luxerit, ad librariorum
Curram scrinia, Cæsios, Aquinos,
Suffenum, omnia colligam venena,
Ac te his suppliciis remunerabor.
Vos hinc interea valete, abite
Illuc, unde malum pedem tulistis,
Sæcli incommoda, pessimi Poëtæ.

2. *Of Sapphic verse.*

Sapphic verse was invented by Sappho, from whom it derives its name. It has the same feet as the Phaleucian, but differently disposed, viz. a Choree, a Spondee, a Dactyl, and two Chorees.

    1 | 2 | 3 | 4 | 5
Crēscĭt īndūl-gēns sĭbĭ dīrŭs hȳdrŏps. Hor.

After three Sapphics they generally put an Adonic. Yet there are choruses where you find a longer series of Sapphics.

They are harsh to the ear, unless they have a cæsura after the two first feet; though there are several in Horace that have it not.

Quam Jocus circumvolat & Cupido. lib. 1. Od. 2.
Phœbe Silvarumque potens Diana. In Carm. secul.
Lenis Ilithya tuere matres:
Sive tu Lucina probas vocari,
    Seu Genitalis.

Sapphics and Phaleucians may be easily changed into one another; thus this Sapphic verse in Horace,
    Non eget Mauri jaculis nec arcu,
may be changed into a Phaleucian only by transposing the words:
    Non Mauri jaculis eget, nec arcu.

And

And this Phaleucian in Martial

Nympharum pater, amniumque Rhene,

becomes a Sapphic, by transposing it thus:

Rhene nympharum pater, amniumque.

3. *Of Alcaic verse.*

Alcaic verse derives its name from the poet Alcæus. It hath two feet and a half of an Iambic (which they call *Penthemimerim Iambicam*) and two Dactyls. Hence in the first foot it may have an Iambus.

   1 | 2 | 3 | 4

Vĭdēs ŭt āl-tā stet nĭvĕ cāndĭdŭm. Hor.

Though generally it has a Spondee.

   1 | 2 | 3 | 4

Aūdī-rĕ mā-gnōs jām vĭdĕ-ōr dūcĕs.

   1 | 2 | 3 | 4

Nōn īn-dĕcō-rō pūlvĕrĕ sōrdĭdŏs. Lib. 2. Od. 1.

This verse is never put by itself, but after two of them it is customary to subjoin, as a third, an Iambic of four feet, with a long syllable redundant.

Et cuncta terrarum subacta. Hor.

4. *Of the lesser Alcaic.*

The lesser Alcaic consists of two Dactyls and two Trochees. I have placed it here, though it consists but of ten syllables, because it has a relation to the great Alcaic.

   1 | 2 | 3 | 4

Prætĕr ă trōcem ānĭ-mŭm Că-tōnĭs. Hor.

III. *Of Anapæstic verse.*

All verses of the third species have the number of their syllables determined, except these. The Anapæstic is so called, because it was originally composed of four Anapæsts. But as they afterwards took the liberty to put, instead of the Anapæst, a Spondee or Dactyl which have the same quantity, namely four *times*; thence it comes that this verse, though called Anapæstic, has not sometimes so much as one Anapæst. The chorus of tragedies is frequently composed of this sort of verse; which requires no cæsura.

   1 | 2 | 3 | 4

Quāntī cāsūs hūmā-nă rŏtānt,
Mĭnùs in parvis fortuna furit,
Leviúsque ferit leviora Deus. Sen. in Hor.

Of this sort of verse there are some that have only two feet, and which

which now and then are joined to the others, though Seneca on the death of Claudius has put them by themselves.

Deflete virum
Que non alius
Potuit citiùs
Discere causas,
Una tantùm
Parte audita,
Sæpè & neutra.

IV. *Of Archilochian verse, and others less frequently used.*

We have already made mention of the Archilochian verse, called *Dactylica Penthemimeris*, p. 391. where we observed that there were several sorts of this name. We shall here take notice of two more.

The first are called *Heptameter Archilochian*, which have the four first feet of an Hexameter, whereof the last is always a dactyl; and three Chorees or Trochees, as

| 1 | 2 | 3 | 4 | 5 | 6 | 7 |

Sŏlvĭtŭr ācrĭs hў-ēms grā-tā vĭcĕ vērĭs ĕt Fă-vōnī.

The second are *Iambic-Archilochian*, as they are called by Diomedes, comprehending the Iambic Penthemimeris, as well as the above-mentioned Alcaic, and then three Chorees, as

| 1 | 2 | 3 | 4 | 5 |

Trăhūnt-quĕ sīc-cās māchĭ-næ că-rīnăs.

Horace has joined these two verses together, and formed thereof the fourth ode of his first book. But the latter may be measured another way, by leaving a syllable at the end.

| 1 | 2 | 3 | 4 | 5 |

Trăhūnt-quĕ sīc-cās mā-chĭnă cărī-năs--.

So that these verses are nothing more than Iambics that want a syllable, but always require their third foot to be a Spondee; whereas the others, of which we have made mention above, p. 397, suffer it to be an Iambus. Thus they may be changed into perfect Trimeters, only by adding a syllable; for instance, if we were to put in the precedent verse *carinulas* for *carinas*.

I shall take no notice of other sorts of verse that are very seldom used, but proceed to say a word or two concerning compositions in verse, and the mixture that is made of different sorts of metre.

Chapter VII.

Of compositions in verse, and the mixture of different sorts of metre.

AFTER having explained the nature of verse and its various species, it now remains that we treat of compositions in verse, which the Latins comprehended under the word CARMEN, whether it be an epigram, an ode, an epistle, a poem, or other work. Hence it is that Catullus's epigrams are called *Carmen* 1, *Carmen* 2, &c. that the odes of Horace are intitled, *Carminum libri*; and that Lucretius stiles his first book *Carmen*.

Quod in primo quoque carmine claret.

Hence a single verse cannot be called *Carmen*, unless it be perhaps an intire epigram or inscription, comprized in one verse; as Virgil calls the following verse *Carmen*.

Æneas hæc de Danaïs victoribus arma.

I. *Compositions of one sort of metre only.*

Compositions in verse may be considered, either according to the matter, or to the versification.

According to the matter they are divided into epic poem, satyr, tragedy, comedy, ode, epigram, &c.

According to the versification, which is the only point we consider here, they are divided into verse of one sort only, or into verse of different sorts. The former is called *carmen*, μονόκωλον; and the other *carmen*, πολύκωλον.

The verses most frequently used in composing intire pieces are Hexameter, Iambic-Trimeter, Scazon, what they call Trochaic, Asclepiad, Phaleucian, and Anapæstic.

Those less frequently used in single pieces are Iambic Dimeter, Glyconic, Sapphic, and Archilochian in Prudentius.

Those used very rarely are Pentameter, in Ausonius; and Adonic, in Boëtius.

II. *Compositions of different metre, and their division into stanzas, called* STROPHES.

Compositions of different metre are, generally speaking, but two or three sorts. But these are again divided according to the number of verses contained in the stanza, (by the Greeks called ϛροφὴ) which being finished, they return to the first sort of verse with which they began. With this difference from the French, that the latter generally conclude the sense in one stanza; whereas the antients seldom observed this rule except in elegiac verse,

verse, where the distich ought to end with a full point, or at least a colon: for Horace does not scruple to complete a sense, begun in one stanza, with the two first words of the next, especially in stanzas of two verses; as

   Eradenda cupidinis
 Pravi sunt elementa : & teneræ nimis
  Mentes asperioribus
 Formandæ studiis. Nescit equo rudis
  Hærere ingenuus puer, &c. lib. 3. od. 24.

And even in stanzas of four verses, where it does not sound so well,

 Districtus ensis cui super impia
  Cervice pendet ; non Siculæ dapes
   Dulcem elaborabunt soporem ;
    Non avium citharæque cantus
 Somnum reducent. lib. 3. od. 1.

III. *Compositions of two sorts of metre. And first of those in which the stanza has but two verses, and which are called δίκωλον δίστροφον.*

 The Latin stanzas consist only of two, three, or four sorts of verse; Catullus alone having made one of five. And as to compositions of two sorts of verse, there are none regular except stanzas of two or of four verses, but not of three. The former is called *Dicolon-distrophon,* and the latter *Dicolon-tetrastrophon.*

 There are a vast number of the former sort. I shall take notice only of nine that are most frequent, and of which (except the elegiac) there are examples in Horace. It will be easy to judge of the rest which are to be found in Boëtius, Prudentius, or Ausonius, by what we have said concerning the different species of verse.

1.

 The first sort is the Elegiac consisting of Hexameter and Pentameter. It is so called, because it was made use of in funerals, from the Greek word ἴλιγος, weeping, ἀπὸ τῦ ἴ ἴ λίγιιν, as those do that weep. Which made Ovid say,

 Flebilis indignos elegeia solve capillos,
 Heu nimis ex vero nunc tibi nomen erit.

2.

 The second an Hexameter, and a lesser Archilochian. Horace,

 Diffugere nives : redeunt jam gramina campis
  Arboribusque comæ.
 Quis scit an adjiciant hodiernæ crastina summæ
  Tempora Di superi?

3.

 The third an Hexameter, and the verse which contains the four last feet of an Hexameter. Horace,

Dant

Of LATIN POETRY.

Dant alios furiæ torvo spectacula Marti:
Exitio est avidis mare nautis:
Mista senum ac juvenum densantur funera: nullum
Sæva caput Proserpina fugit.

4.

The fourth, an Hexameter and an Iambic Dimeter. Horace.

Nox erat, & cœlo fulgebat Luna sereno
Inter minora sidera.

5.

The fifth, an Hexameter, and a Trimeter of pure Iambics. Horace.

Altera jam teritur bellis civilibus ætas,
Suis & ipsa Roma viribus ruit.

6.

The sixth, an Iambic Trimeter followed by a Dimeter. Horace.

Beatus ille, qui procul negotiis,
Ut prisca gens mortalium,
Paterna rura bobus exercet suis,
Solutus omni fœnore.

7.

The seventh, is an Iambic Dimeter that wants a syllable of the first foot, and a Trimeter that wants a syllable at the latter end. Horace, lib. 2. Od. 18.

Truditur dies die,
Novæque pergunt interire Lunæ:
Tu secanda marmora
Locas sub ipsum funus, & sepulchri
Immemor, struis domos, &c.

8.

The eighth, a Glaconic and an Asclepiad. Horace.

O quisquis volet impias
Cædes, & rabiem tollere civicam,
Si quærat pater urbium
Subscribi statuis; indomitam audeat
Refrænare licentiam,
Clarus postgenitis: quatenus, heu nefas,
Virtutem incolumem odimus,
Sublatam ex oculis quærimus invidi.

9.

The ninth is composed of an Heptameter, and an Archilochian Trimeter, of which we have made mention above, p. 402. Horace has wrote the 4th ode of the 1st book in this metre.

Pallida mors æquo pulsat pede pauperum tabernas,
Regumque turres, ô beate Sexti! Lib. 1. od. 4.

IV. *Compositions of two sorts of metre in stanzas of four verses. Which are called* δίκωλον τέτράςροφον.

Of these there are two species in Horace.

1.

Three Asclepiads and a Glyconic.
*Lucem redde tuæ, dux bone, patriæ ;
Instar veris enim vultus ubi tuus
Affulsit populo, gratior it dies,
Et soles melius nitent.*

2.

Three Sapphics and an Adonic.
*Auream quisquis mediocritatem
Diligit, tutus caret obsoleti
Sordibus tecti: caret invidenda
Sobrius aula.*

V. *Compositions of three sorts of metre, in stanzas of three verses. Which are called* τρίκωλον τρίςροφον.

There is but one species of these in Horace, consisting of a Trimeter, an Archilochian, and a Dimeter; and some of the antients believed that the two last made only one great Archilochian.
*Petti ! nihil me sicut antea juvat
Scribere versiculos
Amore perculsum gravi.*

Prudentius also made the preface to his book of Hymns, of the three first species of Choriambics, beginning with the smallest, and ascending to the greatest,
*Dicendum mihi, quisquis es,
Mundum quem coluit mens tua perdidit,
Non sunt illa Dei quæ studet, cujus habeberis ?*

VI. *Compositions of three sorts of metre, and stanzas of four verses. Which are called* τρίκωλον τέτράςροφον.

Of these there are also but two species in Horace.

1.

The first consists of two Asclepiads, a Pherecratian, and a Glyconic.
*O navis referent in mare te novi
Fluctus. O quid agis ? fortiter occupa
Portum, nonne vides ut
Nudum remigio latus ?* Lib. 1. od. 14.

2.

The second is the most agreeable and the most common of all Horace's odes, among which there are no less than thirty-seven of this sort.

We have already taken notice of the three species of verse that are used in these odes, chap. 6. n. 3. p. 401.

> *Damnosa quid non imminuit dies?*
> *Ætas parentum pejor avis, tulit*
> *Nos nequiores, mox daturos*
> *Progeniem vitiosiorem.* Hor. l. 3. od. 6.

The above are the principal species of metre, and compositions in verse. But as it will be of use to be able to consider them at one view, I have thought proper to exhibit them in the two following tables; which suppose a person to be acquainted with the six necessary feet, of which I shall at the same time give a small table, to the end they may be known in the large one by the initial letter of their name. Where it must be observed that I call the foot containing a long and a short (-v) a Choree rather than Trochee, to give it the C, and to let the Tribrac have T. The long cæsuras I have distinguished by the same mark as the quantity (¯).

THE FIRST TABLE.

OF DIFFERENT SPECIES OF V[ERSES]
reduced to three.

FEET.	
1. Spondée	S.
2. Iambus	I.
3. Choree	C.
4. Tribrac	T.
5. Dactyl	D.
6. Anapæst	A.

ALL VERSES MAY BE REDUCED TO THREE SORTS, viz.

I. Hexameters and Pentameters.
- Intire.
  - Hexameters.
    - Ordinary. 4. S. or D. | the 5. D. | the 6. S.
    - Spondaics. Ending with two S. . . . .
  - Pentameters.
    - . . . . . . 2. S. or D. | the 3. S. | the 5. and
- Parts.
  - Beginning.
    - 1. Archilochian. 2. D. and a syllable. . . .
    - 2. Alcmanian. 3. D. and a syllable. . . .
    - 3. . . . . 3. S. or D. | the 4. D. .
  - End.
    - 1. Dact Tetram. The four last feet. . . . .
    - 2. Pherecratian. S. | D. | S. . . . .
    - 3. Adonic. D. | S. . . . . .

II. Iambics, according to
- The quality of their feet.
  - Pure Iambics. That is, all Iambuses. . . . .
  - Mixed with I. or T. with S. or D. and A.
    - Ordinary, ending with an I.
      - More exact, having in the even feet. viz. { 2. and 4. I. or In the uneven S. or D. or A.
      - Neglected, having in even what the exact ones have only the uneven.
    - Scazon. . . . Ending with an S. after an I. .
- The number of their feet.
  - Of 4 feet called Dimeters.
    - Perfect. . . . .
    - Defective
      - Of a foot. . . . .
      - Of a syllable. { In the begin At the end. . tics.
    - Redundant Of a syllable at the end. . . . .
  - Of 6 feet Trimeters.
    - Perfect. . . . . . .
    - Defective Of a syllable. . . . .
  - Of 8 feet Tetrameters.
    - Perfect. . . . . . .
    - Defective of a syllable. { In the beginning called Trochai At the end. . . . .

III. Lyrics.
- Choriambics.
  - 1. Glyconic. . . . . 1. S. | 2. D. . . . . . .
  - 2. Asclepiad. . . . . S. | D. | - | D. | D. . .
  - 3. Alcaics. . . . . S. | D. | - | D. | - | D.
  - 4. Alcmanian. . . . . . . S. | D. | - | D. | S. . .
- Of eleven syllables.
  - 1. Phaleucian. . . . . . . S. | D. | C. | C. | C. .
  - 2. Sapphic. . . . . C. | S. | D. | C. | C. . .
  - 3. Alcaic. . . . . . . S. or I. | I. | - | D. | D
  - * Small Alcaic. . . . . D. | D. | C. | C. . . .
- Anapæstics, and others.
  - Anapæstic. . . . . 4. A. or D. or S. . . . . . .
  - Heptameter Archilochian. 4. feet, one Hexameter and
  - Trimeter defect. Archiloc. I. or S. | I. | - | 3. C. . .

E

EXAMPLES

OF THE

DIFFERENT SPECIES OF VERSE

Contained in the foregoing Table according to the correspondent figures.

1. Ab Jove principium, Musæ! Jovis omnia plena. *Virg.*
2. Cara Deûm soboles, magnum Jovis incrementum. *Id.*

3. Non solet ingeniis summa nocere dies. *Ovid.*

4. Pulvis & umbra sumus. *Hor.*
5. Munera lætitiamque Dei. *Virg.*
6. Luminibusque prior rediit vigor. *Boëth.*
7. O fortes pejoraque passi. *Hor.*
8. Quamvis Pontica pinus. *Id.*
9. Gaudia pelle. *Boëth.*

10. Phaselus ille quem videtis hospites. *Catul.*

11. Pars sanitatis velle sanari fuit. *Sen.*

12. Homo sum, humani nihil à me alienum puto. *Ter.*

13. Sed non videmus manticæ quod in tergo est. *Catul.*
14. Fortuna non mutat genus. *Hor.*
15. Musæ Jovis natæ.
16. Truditur dies die. *Hor.*
17. Ades Pater supreme. *Prud.*
18. Et cuncta terrarum subacta. *Hor.*
*. Pars sanitatis velle sanari fuit. *Sen.*
19. Novæque pergunt interire Lunæ. *Hor.*
20. Pecuniam in loco negligere, maximum interdum est lucrum. *Ter.*

21. Vos precor vulgus silentum, vosque ferales Deos. *Sen.*
22. Nam si remittent quippiam Philumenam dolores. *Ter.*

23. Ignotus moritur sibi. *Sen.*
24. Mæcenas atavis edite regibus. *Hor.*
25. Seu plures hyemes, seu tribuit Jupiter ultimam. *Hor.*
26. O quàm glorifica luce coruscas!
27. Ni te plus oculis meis amarem. *Catul.*
28. Crescit indulgens sibi dirus hydrops. *Hor.*
29. Audire magnos jam videor duces. *Hor.*
30. Præter atrocem animum Catonis. *Hor.*

31. Quanti casus humana rotant. *Sen.*
32. Pallida mors æquo pulsat pede pauperum tabernas,
33.   Regumque turres; ô beate Sexti. *Hor.*

THE SECOND TABLE

OF THE

MIXTURE OF LATIN VERSE in Composition.

With the figures referring to the precedent table, to point out the examples.

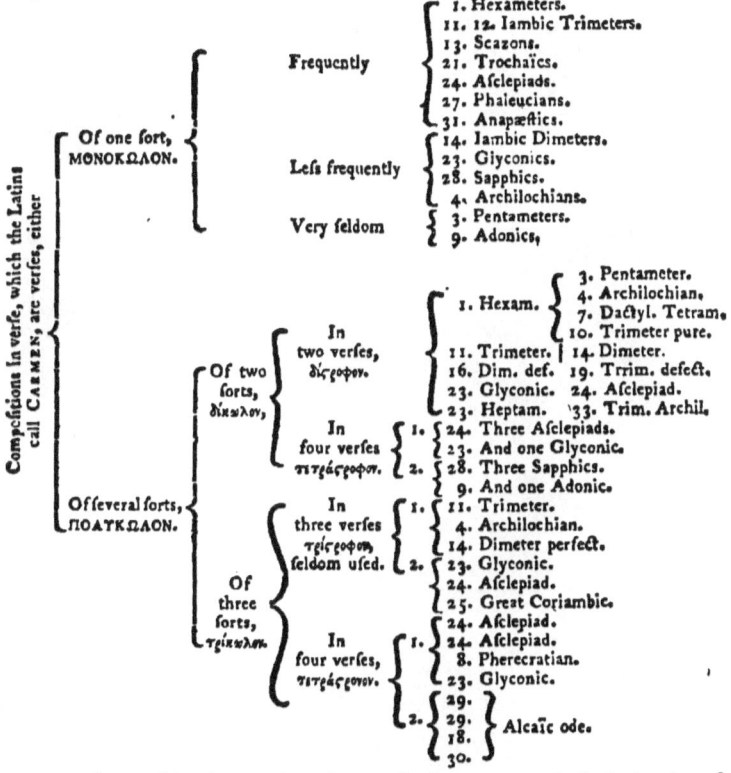

Compositions in verse, which the Latins call CARMEN, are verses, either

- Of one sort, ΜΟΝΟΚΩΛΟΝ.
  - Frequently
    - 1. Hexameters.
    - 11, 12. Iambic Trimeters.
    - 13. Scazons.
    - 21. Trochaïcs.
    - 24. Asclepiads.
    - 27. Phaleucians.
    - 31. Anapæstics.
  - Less frequently
    - 14. Iambic Dimeters.
    - 23. Glyconics.
    - 28. Sapphics.
    - 4. Archilochians.
  - Very seldom
    - 3. Pentameters.
    - 9. Adonics.
- Of several sorts, ΠΟΛΥΚΩΛΟΝ.
  - Of two sorts, δίστροφον,
    - In two verses, δίστροφον.
      - 1. Hexam. { 3. Pentameter. 4. Archilochian. 7. Dactyl. Tetram. 10. Trimeter pure.
      - 11. Trimeter. | 14. Dimeter.
      - 16. Dim. def. 19. Trim. defect.
      - 23. Glyconic. 24. Asclepiad.
      - 23. Heptam. 33. Trim. Archil.
    - In four verses, τετράστροφον.
      - 1. { 24. Three Asclepiads. 23. And one Glyconic.
      - 2. { 28. Three Sapphics. 9. And one Adonic.
  - Of three sorts, τρίκωλον.
    - In three verses, τρίστροφον, seldom used.
      - 1. { 11. Trimeter. 4. Archilochian. 14. Dimeter perfect.
      - 2. { 23. Glyconic. 24. Asclepiad. 25. Great Coriambic.
    - In four verses, τετράστροφον.
      - 1. { 24. Asclepiad. 24. Asclepiad. 8. Pherecratian. 23. Glyconic.
      - 2. { 29. 29. 18. 30. } Alcaïc ode.

Examples of this mixture of verses may be seen more particularly in the 7th chapter, art. 3, 4, 5, and 6.

FINIS.

www.ingramcontent.com/pod-product-compliance
Lightning Source LLC
Chambersburg PA
CBHW022112290426
44112CB00008B/652